Prisoners of a L
The South African ...

Prisoners of a Dream:
The South African Mirage

Historical essay on the Denton Hearings on "The Role of the Soviet Union, Cuba and East Germany in Fomenting Terrorism in Southern Africa" before the Subcommittee on Security and Terrorism of the Committee on the Judiciary, United States Senate, March 22, 24, 25, 29 and 31, 1982, Washington, D.C.

Leo Raditsa

Prince George Street Press
Annapolis, Maryland

Library of Congress Cataloging-in-Publication Data

RADITSA, LEO.
  Prisoners of a dream: the South African mirage / by Leo Raditsa.
  "Historical essay on the Denton hearings before the Subcommittee on Security and Terrorism of the Committee of the Judiciary, United States Senate, 'The role of the Soviet Union, Cuba, and East Germany in fomenting terrorism in southern Africa,' March 22, 24, 25, 29 and 31, 1982."
  Includes bibliographies.
  1. Communism—Africa, Southern. 2. Revolutions—Africa, Southern. 3. Terrorism—Africa, Southern. 4. Africa, Southern—Politics and government—1975–. 5. Communist strategy. 6. United States—national security. 7. United States. Congress. Senate. Committee of the Judiciary. Subcommittee on Security and Terrorism.
  I. Title.
  HX450.A6R34   1989
  322.4'2'096—dc19

© 1989 by Leo Raditsa

All rights reserved. No part of this book may be reproduced, in any form or by any means, without permission in writing from the publisher.

Printed in the United States of America

ISBN: 0-927104-00-8

Prince George Street Press
P. O. Box 252
Annapolis, Maryland 21404

*This essay is for the Denton witnesses,
who taught me more than any book,
and made it possible for me to understand
the books I did read,
and for Senator Jeremiah Denton and
Joel Lisker, Chief Counsel of the Committee,
who brought them to Washington,
and showed them the respect they deserved.*

Contents

List of Acronyms ix

Acknowledgments xi

Introduction 1

Chapter 1 The Measure of Change: The Past   11
1. The Unification of South Africa in 1910 11
2. The Conquest of the Bantu in the Nineteenth Century Before Unification 17
3. What it Meant to Live Among the Bantu 29
4. The Ambiguity of British Policy 32
5. The Conflict in Character Between Boers and British 35
6. The Breakdown of British Vacillation: The Anglo-Boer War 38
7. The Way They Thought About the Africans—Merriman, Smuts and Selborne 42
8. South Africa on Its Own 50

Chapter 2 Violence Against Change   65
1. No to Reform 65
2. The Campaign Abroad—And the Words that Didn't Make It 76
3. The New Constitution 80
4. The Fronts 85
5. Harsh Times for a Man Against Murder: Buthelezi 91
6. Before the New Constitution 102
7. The Cannon Fodder of the Revolution 113
8. The 1987 Election 122
9. Undoing the "NO"; its Persistence 133

Chapter 3 Room with a Mirror Blocking the View: American Policy in South Africa and Southern Africa   157
1. Repeal of the Clark Amendment: Moderate Republicans Waver; "Constructive Engagement" 157

viii   Contents

    2 America's Heart of Protest 172
    3 Who Knows What's Going On? 210

Chapter 4   The War for Southern Africa   225

    1 The Start and Spread of War 229
    2 The Unseen War: Infiltration, Terror—and Words 231
    3 The Fall of Portugal and Rhodesia 236
    4 Vorster's "Outward Reach" Policy 238
    5 Banda's Importance 244
    6 Rhodesia: The End Begins 247
    7 Angola Catastrophe 253
    8 Spinola's Book—Lev Davidovich Bronstein's "Dustbin of History," Savimbi's Lesson 259
    9 Portugal Joins the Warring Club that Calls War Peace 271
  10 The Triumph of the West and Mugabe over Rhodesia—a Model that Counts 275
  11 South West Africa: A Largely Untold Tale of Dangerous Progress 287
  12 The Fighters: Savimbi's UNITA and RENAMO 307
  13 A World Uncovered: The Death of Machel 338
  14 Malawi, the Cost of Another Way 342
  15 The Captive Mind in Africa: The Planned Coup Against Banda 344
  16 The "Winged Words" of Vladimir Ilyich Ulanov and Yosif Djugashvili ("Soso"): The Third International and the United States' and Europe's War in Africa 345
  17 Bear Hug, Grand Maneuvers: South Africa Strives for Credibility at the Risk of Abandoning South West Africa, Savimbi—and Itself 357

Chapter 5   Gulags for Southern Africa: The Denton Hearings   373

Notes 447

Index 466

List of Acronyms

ACOA	American Committee on Africa
ADA	Americans for Democratic Action
AFM	Armed Forces Movement (Portugal)
AFSC	American Friends Service Committee
AI	Amnesty International
AID	Agency for International Development (United States)
ANC	African National Congress (South Africa)
AWB	Afrikaner Weerstandsbeweging
AZAPO	Azanian People's Organization (South Africa)
BSAC	British South Africa Company
CAA Act	Comprehensive Anti-Apartheid Act (United States)
CALC	Clergy and Laity Concerned (United States)
CBTU	Coalition for Black Trade Unionists (United States)
COD	Congress of Democrats (South Africa)
COSAS	Congress of South African Students
COSATU	Congress of South African Trade Unions
CP	Conservative Party (South Africa)
CPC	Colored People's Congress (South Africa)
DPSC	Detainees' Parents Support Committee (South Africa)
DTA	Democratic Turnhalle Alliance (South West Africa)
FIDA	Federal Independent Democratic Alliance (South Africa)
FNLA	National Front for the Liberation of Angola
FOSATU	Federation of South African Trade Unions
FRELIMO	Front for the Liberation of Mozambique
FSAM	Free South Africa Movement (United States)
HNP	Herstigte Nasionale Party (South Africa)
ICCR	Interfaith Center on Corporate Responsibility (United States)
ICRC	International Committee of the Red Cross
IDASA	Institute for a Democratic Alternative in South Africa
IGFM	Internationale Gesellschaft für Menschen Rechte
IPS	Institute for Policy Studies (United States)
ISA	Internal Security Act (South Africa)
ISL	Industrial Socialist League (South Africa)
JMC	Joint Management Center (South Africa)
LP	Colored Labor Party (South Africa)
MPC	Multi-Party Conference (South West Africa)
MPLA	Popular Movement for the Liberation of Angola
NAACP	National Association for the Advancement of Colored Peoples (United States)
NCC	Nambian Council of Churches
NCDP	Namibia Christian Democratic Party
NEC	National Executive Committee (of the ANC)
NECC	National Educational Crisis Committee (South Africa)

List of Acronyms

NGK	Dutch Reformed Church (South Africa)
NPC	Nambian Parents' Committee
NSC	National Statutory Council (South Africa)
NUM	National Union of Mines (South Africa)
NUSAS	National Union of South African Students
OAU	Organization for African Unity
OCC	Operations Co-ordinating Committee (Rhodesia)
PAC	Pan African Congress
PCP	Communist Party (Portugal)
PDM	Popular Democratic Movement (Portugal)
PF	Patriotic Front (Rhodesia)
PFP	Progressive Federal Party (South Africa)
PPD	Social Democratic Party (Portugal)
RF	Rhodesian Front
RICA	Reformed Independent Churches (South Africa)
SABC	South African Broadcasting Corporation
SACC	South African Council of Churches
SACP	South African Communist Party
SACTU	South African Congress of Trade Unions
SADCC	Southern African Development Coordination Conference
SADF	South African Defense Force
SAIC	South African Indian Congress
SAMCOR	South African Motor Corporation
SARHWU	South African Railways and Harbour Workers' Union
SASOL	South African Coal, Oil and Gas Corporation
SASP	South Africa Support Project (United States)
SATS	South African Transport Services
SAWG	South Africa Working Group (United States)
SDS	Students for a Democratic Society (United States)
SPCC	Soweto Parents' Crisis Committee
SWANU	South West African National Union
SWAPO	South West African People's Organization
SWAPOLCOIN	South West African Police Counterinsurgency Force
SWATF	South West African Territorial Force
TGNU	Transitional Government of National Unity (South West Africa)
TVBC	Transkei, Bophuthatswana, Venda and Ciskei
UCASA	Urban Councils Association of South Africa
UCCP	United Christian Conciliation Party (South Africa)
UDF	United Democratic Front (South Africa)
UFP	United Federal Party (Rhodesia)
UNHCR	UN High Commissioner for Refugees
UNITA	National Union for the Total Independence of Angola
WOA	Washington Office on Africa (United States)
ZANU	Zimbabwe African National Union
ZAPU	Zimbabwe African People's Union

Acknowledgments

I have made new friends, and learned the depths of old friendships, writing this essay. Some helped me with doubts and criticisms, sometimes with fierce opposition, others told me all they knew, and kept sending me documents and clippings from all over the world, and introduced me to people I needed to meet. They did what they could, and they knew what they could not do. They knew I was the writer, not they. The work, needless to say, is my own. From some of my students I received support and help I hardly expected for this project that had nothing to do with what I teach and they study. That was quite a lesson. On principle I used no researchers and did the work on my own time and at my own expense. The list: Joel Carmichael, Lev Navrozov, Musa Navrozov, John Rees, Sheila Rees, Martha Powers, Bruce Rickerson, Meg Hunt, Jason Bockman, Alex Kornfeld, J. Walter Sterling, James Carey, David Bolotin, Erich Isaac, Rael Isaac, Herbert London, Peter Shaw, Carl Iannone, Ernst Badian, Istvan Fehervary, Giuliano Bonfante, Vittoria Bonfante, Eva Jaunzems, Martin Hitchcock, Lewis Gann, Vice Admiral James Bond Stockdale, Rev. J. Winfree Smith, Carole Cunningham, Janet Orlin, James O'Gara, Candace de Russy, Peter Witonski, Virginia Armat, Brian Crozier, Ronald Baxter, Margaret Calhoun, C.W. Van Melle Kamp, Somerset Morkel, Abe S. Hoppenstein, Alayne Reesberg, Sol Singer, Robert Lowenberg, Joel Lisker, Linda di Paola, J.A. Parker, Michael Harkavy, Emile Capouya, Sean Cleary, Christine Krupa, Fran Wermuth, Bogdan Raditsa, Mburumba Kerina, and lastly, my wife, Larissa Bonfante, who said the right things at the right moment not too often, including *alea jacta est*, the other day.

February 22, 1989
Annapolis, Maryland

Messieurs, je ne viens pas prêcher la tolérance. La Liberté la plus illimitée de religion est à mes yeux un droit si sacré, que le mot tolérance, qui voudrait l'exprimer, me parait en quelque sorte tyrannique lui-même; puisque l'existence de l'autorité, qui a le pouvoir de tolérer, attente à la liberté de penser, par cela même qu'elle tolère, et qu'ainsi elle pourrait ne pas tolérer.

Mirabeau

I wonder whether, in this play *Rhinoceros*, I haven't put my finger on an open wound of our times. I have often been very much struck by the power of what one might call a current of opinion, by its swift evolution and contagiousness. People allow themselves to be seized by a religion, a new doctrine, a fanaticism. One then witnesses a real mental mutation. And when people no longer share your opinion you have the feeling you're facing monsters. They would kill you with the best conscience in the world if they realized you didn't think like them. In the past quarter-century, history has proven to us that people so transformed not only resemble rhinoceroses: They really become such!

Ionesco

Democracy in Europe cannot be democracy in Africa. Any politician, any statesman who interprets democracy in Africa in terms of the British Constitution, the American Constitution, the Swiss Constitution . . . does not know what he is doing. Because we are not here living under the British conditions, the American conditions . . .

There was a time in Britain when they did worse things than we are going to do to these people now . . . Britain is tolerant today because the Government has been established for centuries . . . The people in Britain today take everything for granted—trade unionism, free assembly, and freedom of the press—but I can quote instances after instances to prove that it was not so in Britain at one time . . . Therefore we have to do things here which in Britain and America, [at] the stage they have arrived at in their own history, [are] repugnant to their idea of freedom and justice, but [to us], [at] our stage of development are the normal thing to do.

Kamuzu Banda

Introduction

"I saw the inconceivable mystery of a soul that knew no restraint, no faith, and no fear, yet struggling blindly with itself."
CONRAD

For five days in March 1982, Senator Jeremiah Denton, Chairman of the Subcommittee on Security and Terrorism of the Committee of the Judiciary of the United States Senate, held hearings on "The Role of the Soviet Union, Cuba and East Germany in Fomenting Terrorism in Southern Africa." The hearings were packed: Television, the newspapers, all were there.

But the hearings went unreported, and they are practically unknown in the United States and, worse still, in Washington, in the Senate and even in the State Department. None of the three people I talked to on the State Department's South Africa desk had read them—one had not heard of them. The printed record, one thousand copies, sold out quickly. There will be French, German and Afrikaans translations.

The Committee heard nine witnesses, all black Africans, most of them former members of the African National Congress (ANC) or of the South West African People's Organization (SWAPO), six of them in their twenties; one, a mature man, had been at the top of the South African Communist Party (SACP) in the early sixties. In addition to about 150 pages of direct testimony, the printed record contains about 1,800 pages of texts and photographs and documents captured by the South African Defense Force in Angola: orders for the murder of tribal chiefs in South West Africa (from New York!) and most startling of all, facsimile reproductions of the notebooks of young blacks in terrorist training camps in Angola.

The testimony and these documents show that the ANC, SWAPO, the SACP, the other terrorist organizations and the Soviet and eastern European agents active in southern Africa dread most of all rebellious and defiant but politically innocent blacks caught in their organizations who want change and transformation but not the destruction of the South African government. They show that these terrorist organizations will do anything to break these blacks who love their country and their parents.

I came upon these hearings more or less by accident: I heard John Rees, the editor of *Early Warning*, at an Accuracy in Media conference toward the end of November 1985 refer to them as an example of the newspapers' and television's suppression of important information. For five days I resisted the temptation to look them up in the library. I was at work on a book on the wars of the Roman Republic seen through the eyes of Rome's enemies, I feared distraction. When I began to read the hearings, I could not believe the world that met my eyes. I was not unread in the writings about prisons and camps. But the testimony of the Denton witnesses was different from anything I had read in the European and oriental accounts of totalitarianism. It was much more innocent, and more simply defiant than the defiance in the free West that almost asks to be exploited and manipulated. More nakedly than in any testimony I knew, even Nadzheda Mandelstam's *Hope Against Hope*, the Denton witnesses showed totalitarianism's naked attacks on life not only in murder, but most of all in its unerring sense for anything defiant and constructive, for the best in human beings. This purity came because these young men and women were innocent but not gullible. They had no idea what they were getting into. They seemed to show me the whole history of our times, not only in Africa or in totalitarian countries.

I told myself I would give myself three months, essentially to restate the hearings and pull them, and the accompanying documents, together. I met the deadline with an article finished at the end of February 1986. No magazine in the United States would publish it. *Commentary* the magazine that commissioned the article did not even bother to state its reasons for its rejection, and mislaid the typescript for six months. In some cases, editors would not look at the article; in others, after agreeing to read it, they did not acknowledge its receipt. Here was sworn testimony before a congressional committee, and no one outside the government would pay attention to it. Congressional testimony is a crucial source of unvarnished information in the United States because on Capitol Hill you can speak your mind without qualification, the name of political freedom.

After the rejection of the first article that simply restated the evidence in the documents and the testimony, I started work on a longer article, placing the hearings into the general southern African and South African context: the first version of this book. The article, much longer, also met with no response. One major publisher told me that he did not think the South African government would last long enough to give him the time to bring the book out.

I learned that if you wanted to write anything about South Africa in the United States, you had first of all to heap abuse on the South African government. Nobody, of course, told me that. They did tell me that before I did anything else I had to get on my knees and curse apartheid, not, of course, in those words. I could tell the difference between prayer and ideological mouthing. I was not willing to say these things: I did not feel them, and I did not believe many of the writers who said they felt them. There was a hollow ring to their words. It seemed to me the South African government was doing a great deal, and running real risks, risks any schoolboy could tell. As for cursing apartheid, it made me uncomfortable, like cursing the holocaust with which it is often compared. It made me uncomfortable especially because the more I read and interviewed people, the more I became convinced that the South African government was undoing apartheid, and that the majority of the South African people had rejected it, no easy decision for the Europeans and Afrikaners who are outnumbered more or less five to one, who remember their past and their ancestors.

I began to read South African sources with nausea. That disgust, that physical nausea, is the measure of the cold-blooded mechanical propaganda against South Africa that we take so much for granted that we do not even hear it. You do not feel its intimidating force, its presence in your own body, until you attempt to deny it, to point to the obvious, or even merely to argue with it. Somehow, I had always known it was orchestrated. But I had not really understood what this orchestration meant until I saw how it worked, how news releases by the Cubans and other totalitarian countries at the UN in New York went directly into the "Third World" press, to be picked up a few days later or a few weeks later by some of the major newspapers of the West. In some sense we all know this, most of us. But when you see how it works, how routinely and mechanically the distortion is disseminated, and how thousands and thousands, and finally millions of people die or are enslaved because of it, then it is another matter. This enslavement now threatens the last remaining free countries in southern Africa, Malawi, Botswana, South Africa and South West Africa, a catastrophe that would also seal the fate of the countries that have shown so much fight in them, Angola and Mozambique.

The nausea I felt *before* reading South African sources left me after I actually began to read. I found little in them that was disgusting. I found a tough people living in extraordinary circumstances whose politics involved much uproar, much straightforwardness and courage, and some violence that the government had almost always stood up against. I also found much freedom. Even early in the century there were Bantu newspapers. There was an innocence about much of this writing—the innocence that comes of acknowledging truth and tragedy. Obnoxious laws were unhypocritical—which meant their harshness had limits. It also meant they could be changed, and that changing them would mean something. One way or another the worst often came out, often through the courts and the newspapers. Above all the courts impressed me.[1]

As I read, I kept asking myself why this indignation and hate had broken out just at a time when the South African government, and the South African people, European, African, Colored, Indian and the other minorities,—they are all minorities,—were taken up with fundamental change.

Were we simply seeing the outburst of pent-up hatred that had been held back for generations at last breaking out because loosening-up was mistaken for weakness? But why then was this hatred and disgust so virulent abroad? You would expect that free countries would welcome such change and understand its risks, understand that the South African government needed support at this time, perhaps its most vulnerable since the fashioning of the Union in 1910.

The campaign against South Africa has intensified the more the country has changed. In other words the campaign, both within South Africa and outside, is reactionary. It is against change in the name of change. To justify itself it has to deny that any change is taking place. In fact the changes that had taken place were only recognized in the United States after the May 1987 elections gave the Conservative Party the place of official opposition, instead of the Progressives, because then the people who had before ignored reform could complain of its cessation. To justify itself, the campaign has to deny that any change is taking place. Because it wants to deny the obvious, it increases in intensity as the changes increase. In the face of this barrage, it took me two years to understand the South Africans mean it about change. About that I am now sure. The South African government means it when it says it wants to negotiate a new constitution.

In a 1976 essay recently published, Aleksandr Solzhenitsyn remembers that similar distortions and misinformation made, and still makes, it impossible for the West to understand the changes that were taking place in Russia before the Bolsheviks seized power. This misinformation about Russia that prevailed in the West before 1914 because of "the emotional bitterness, the intolerance and lack of objectivity of [Russian expatriates] temporarily frustrated in their aims of subversion and revolution" is the first of the defamatory campaigns that have now become routine against one country after another:

And so, at the very moment of her most reassuring economic and social development on the eve of the First World War, Russia's image in the West was fashioned by men who rejected and hated Russia, her way of life and spiritual values, and by force of inertia this image has persisted to this day.[2]

I now fear the South Africans are moving too fast, not to please the West, but because they respect the West, deeply. Any country these days that respects the West is in trouble because the West does not respect itself enough to keep realities before its eyes. Israel is another example of a small country in trouble because it respects the West.

South Africa's defiance of the West, until 1988, especially her readiness to strike at the countries supporting the terrorists operating in South Africa and South West Africa, also showed her respect for the West. For she could not bring herself to believe that the West would not only not take her changes seriously, but also that it would not understand the necessity of retaliation against terrorists. She could not bring herself to realize that in some ways, especially in her readiness to openly acknowledge her errors, she was more Western than Western countries, in closer touch with the toughness and straightforwardness that had made the West the most daring and constructive of the peoples the world has ever known since the Romans and the Greeks. And perhaps as ready, as the Greeks and the Romans, to acknowledge its faults and mistakes, its outrages, to recognize that men and women are mighty strange.

The West could not even remember that South Africa was in Africa, that it had kept the ideals of Europe, and suffered its tragedies, in a land, a continent, stranger to Europe than any other because it was more distant from it in time, and therefore, paradoxically, its deepest mirror. It could not remember that the South African government could not easily reintroduce juries because it had to worry about witnesses who might be witch doctors controlling African juries. Europeans, even Afrikaners, are not good at recognizing witch doctors.

The feelings in the United States about South Africa go deep, but they are not spontaneous. They are the feelings of people who cannot keep their eyes on the feasible because of the blinding light of principles no one could object to. The campaign against South Africa is the most deep-going since the campaign against the Indochina War that brought millions of people into a condition worse than slavery—because slavery had juridical definition that allowed for manumission, and also repeal. In some ways it goes deeper than the campaign against Indochina because the United States is less straightforwardly involved and because American soldiers are not fighting and dying in southern Africa and South Africa and because we do not deal straightforwardly with our own blacks. Finally, it goes deeper because we have not faced up to terrorism, in part because terrorism has not attacked us, directly, or has only just begun to attack us, with the wiping out of Pan Am flight 103 on December 21, 1988, a few days after the United States recognized the PLO. Paradoxically it goes deeper because there are fewer immediate realities than in the Indochina War to bring us to our senses about the consequences of the destruction of South Africa, not only for South Africa and southern Africa, but for us and the rest of the West.

The campaign seeks to disarm South Africa in the same way the United States was disarmed in the Indochina War: by undoing its will. Strong countries have come to make us uncomfortable, even if they are little and isolated. They show us some of the niggardliness of soul that vents itself in indignation, of the narrowness of soul that has come to possess us especially since the fall of Saigon because we will not recognize we brought that defeat upon ourselves.

It seemed to me, as I wrote, that this narrowness went to the heart of Western lack of self-confidence. Western governments did not have the courage to insist on the possibility of change without violence, through reform. Like it or not, they subscribed to Mao's dictum that power grows out of the barrel of a gun,—but somebody else's gun. We too showed, it seemed to me, not only in our words, but in our actions, that we did not believe in rational change without destruction. In the name, and with the excuse, of a cause no one could argue against until it hits one's daily life, we were fascinated by totalitarian violence. It paralyzed us. That seemed to me the dirty little secret that ran its smell through everything. We did not believe in ourselves. We respected the people who killed with equanimity, no, who murdered the weakest and the most vulnerable. For as the reader will see, the war for southern Africa with the exception of Angola has gone on almost always without open battles between soldiers. Finally, open-faced fighting that respects its enemies is the only kind of war sovereign legitimate governments are equipped to fight, although now they fear it more than totalitarian violence. For we have grown comfortable with totalitarian murder, and the blackmail it serves. Strangely, the more the murder in the present increases, the more we cry out against the past's murder, especially the murder of the Jews which seems to obsess people more now than twenty years ago.

This essay is almost as much about the United States as it is about South Africa and southern Africa, and behind it all, it is about Europe. Europe is still at the center of things, like it or not. And the War that now goes on throughout the whole world is not only for Europe but about which Europe will prevail, for Europe is divided. There is no other alternative. For it was the Europeans who discovered and opened up the world, and it is only the Europeans who can close it up again at the cost of their, and the rest of the world's, destruction. Even the notion that there is an alternative to Europe is a European notion.

These judgments have led me to defend the past, the only guide to distinguishing the illusions of the present. Respect for the past when it is genuine also means regard for the future, for what the future will think of us, not a thought that comes much to people's minds these days. But a thought much on the minds of the ancients, like Julius Caesar and Cicero, who knew they would never be forgotten. We all live, almost all of us, as if we were the last men, the most pitiless narcissism. This narcissism keeps us from realizing we may be the last of men, for there can be no men without governments, not parodies of governments. But like it or not the future will judge us, will take our measure, perhaps only in private. It is because we fear that judgment that we are so merciless toward the past.

The enormity of the things going on now in the world increases the evasiveness, and the rationalization. It breaks minds in a way simple genuine rebellion or revolt would not, for simple rebellion in a far-off land is not a matter that usually concerns other nations: The violence of Sikhs in India is barely noticed. But rebellion that is forced on people to serve other countries does. We call it "revolution" in unwitting recognition of the difference. "Revolution" now is simply another word for conquest but a conquest that makes it impossible to identify the conqueror.

What we are now witnessing is the slow turning of the free countries to totalitarian ways of thinking, and acting, especially in their passivity, and in the readiness of many governments to cooperate with, to become willing or unwilling accomplices, of totalitarianism. Solzhenitsyn calls this slow turning "the wind of the epoch" that compels a man "to turn his gaze away from the shards of truth." He meant historians but the remark applies just as much to governments, and even more to television and the newspapers. The way to totalitarianism is long. A jet will not get you there, or defeat in battle because battle means respect for your enemies. You have to walk it.

The totalitarians, especially the Soviets, are good at urging this complicity, at manipulating the West. They are good at it because of our dishonesty, our willingness to ignore the obvious, our resentments, our confusion. A little firmness, a little resilience, a simple "No," would dispel a good deal of this complicity.

Two years ago Mario Cervi and Alberto Pasolini Zanelli, two remarkable journalists of *Il Giornale* in Milan, after remarking that it was the first responsibility of governments to keep order, pointed out that Western positions in regard to South Africa were indistinguishable from Soviet positions. In 1987 and 1988 the Soviets appeared to reverse themselves: They adopted the positions the West should have taken when the reforms that had been slowly building since at least 1978 began to take hold in 1984. They said they were against violent revolution because the South Africans were undoing apartheid themselves. These words that appear to endorse reform actually meant that the process that had started could take care of itself, that the soft approach would have more effect now than open brutality, soft words that is,—for the terrorism of the ANC continued.

An article in a Soviet magazine in August 1988 showed something of the calculations behind these apparent assurances. The writer, an official in the Soviet Ministry of Foreign Affairs, wrote of the "white tribe rapidly losing its will and readiness to fight for the ideals of yesterday . . . searching for new ideals" it is unable to find. "A situation of powerless equilibrium . . . not only in the political and ideological but also economic fields" showed "the slide towards revolution has already begun." He meant that the South Africans were caught in a trap because no matter what they did they could not devise constitutional arrangements that the world outside South Africa, or what passes for the world, would accept. There were too many contradictions for outsiders to understand, especially outsiders not interested in the feasible. But the destruction would take time. He went on with a fairly accurate description of the course of the present undeclared war against South Africa he assumed would go on in the future:

In the South African context, a revolution can take place only over a relatively long period of revolutionary struggle, international pressure, complicated diplomatic and political maneuvers and . . . delaying counter-revolutionary traps by the ruling state system.[3]

The time of confusion had begun, a time that would test South Africans more deeply than the previous years of open hostility, for it took on their good faith and straightforwardness, the other side of their toughness. This confusion won its first notable successes in foreign affairs. In the agreement mediated by the United States signed with the Cubans and the MPLA regime in Angola on December 22, 1988, the South African government agreed to withdraw almost all its troops from Namibia four months before any major Cuban withdrawal from Angola, and one month before the Cubans pulled their forces back from the border with South West Africa. For more than a decade until March 1986, South Africa had insisted on the withdrawal of all Cuban troops from Angola before its departure from South West Africa in order to ensure that Namibia's independence would not simply be a cover for a Communist takeover. The agreement also meant the immediate cessation of South African supplies and arms to Savimbi who became entirely dependent on the United States whose State Department had not wanted to aid him. The South Africans appeared to have abandoned South West Africa, the way they had abandoned Rhodesia in 1975–1980, also under American pressure. The apparent collaboration between the Soviet Union and the United States had left the South Africans with the choice of defying both "superpowers" or of submitting. "What other alternative did we have?" a South African diplomat asked me, not a question I had expected. They might at least have held out for adequate verification of Cuban withdrawal that the Brazilian officer responsible for UN verification said, a few days later, would depend on "trust" and the Cubans: "The two countries [the MPLA regime in Angola and the Cubans] are allies—there is no reason for us to mistrust them . . . When they tell us there are no more troops we will tell the United Nations that they have all gone."[4]

But diplomacy and the propaganda I have been describing is abstract and full of beguiling words. Always it appeals to your best intentions. It seeks to paralyze you, to make you feel guilty for suspecting the worst, and especially saying it. Because they are abstract, these mechanisms are difficult to grasp until you see what the organizations they are promoting do to individuals in the flesh, how they take advantage of the hopes and energy and honesty, especially of the young, to seek to crush them, just as the propaganda takes advantage of the yearnings of those it bombards. It is this process of exploitation that the Denton Hearings showed. Without these witnesses, I would not have had the confidence to attempt to see the whole situation in southern Africa and in the international campaign against South Africa. These witnesses showed me that the terrorist organizations and the Soviets, the mainland Chinese and all the other totalitarian countries that support, supply and instruct terrorism, fear above all defiance, real defiance that knows the breath of honesty. They envy it with an envy almost as powerful as the envy people feel when they see real love. It overpowers them. They will do anything to stop it. But with these witnesses they failed.

The Denton witnesses showed me this cold rage with a confidence and precision, a clarity and depth, that few other things in life have. Their words had the effect of great art upon me, of the deepest religious thought, but they were plain and unassuming the way art almost never is. They had the plainness and unassumingness art suggests but does not itself possess. And I could not understand, rather I could understand all too well, why nobody listened. It was all too plain and simple, but it had taken such brutality to get it that simple, such suffering.

In the light and words and experiences of these witnesses, the indignation and anger, the outcries, that surround us almost everywhere, seemed not only like cowardly hatred, but something worse, dirtier, a hatred of simplicity, of life itself. They meant to make people hard because they feared softness and love. And always they used people by telling them they could be, and could have, anything they wanted. We are simpler than we take ourselves for, and than our demands, especially our political demands, lead us to think, these demands that fear most of all that simplicity. Some of these witnesses were even joyous, at least they suggested the possibility of joy, of a joy that had little to do with the euphoria and urgency that accompanies so much of the indignation they had learned coolly to see through.

Above all, at least first of all, it was the testimony of Nokonono Delphine Kave that struck me deepest,—a highly intelligent, courageous, well-born South African whose defiance had drawn her down into the empty center of the twentieth century maelstrom. Her words had the ring of truth like few I have ever heard. They were without recrimination or hate, and so pure, so simple, that they made me understand James Stockdale's baffling advice, not to let yourself hate your captors. Stockdale tells of an American flyer, his first cellmate after two years and three months of solitary in Hanoi:

Doe's personal political line was all the way to the right—right up against the wall. From what he said, it appeared to me that just sullen, nasty hatefulness was his main weapon in the torture room . . . there was no doubt that he hated the North Vietnamese. "But hate," I told him one day, "is a hell of a debilitating emotion. You're a big Las Vegas gambler—when you go up to that crap table, do you set about to *hate* the croupier? No, you've got to mousetrap him, and keep your mind clear, free of hate, if you're to win. Same thing here with Communists. Think of ways to skin those sons of bitches alive, but don't hobble yourself emotionally by going around all choked up in a seething ideological rage all the time."[5]

Kave's words so took the measure of the men who had tortured and bullied her in Zambia and in the Soviet Union that you felt only pity and contempt for them. Her words gave themselves no airs and, thereby, made the attack on life as plain as the light of day. They made it plain that only the inner strength of men could resist and dispel this attack, only the magic of the simply living.

At first I did not understand the importance of the testimony of Bartholomew Hlapane, in a different way as important as Kave's because it dealt with the relations of the South African Communist Party (SACP) with the ANC in a past that seemed further away than the Anglo-Boer War, the fifties and the early sixties. But a past essential to understanding South Africa's present. Like, as far as I can tell, almost everybody now writing about South Africa, I knew next to nothing about the SACP despite the information available in South African sources. These sources taught me the importance of Hlapane's testimony.

Throughout, from the first chapter that gets at some of the essential facts of earlier South African history, I have applied the lessons the Denton witnesses taught me. But the reader who does not feel ready to read a whole book in order to read its last chapter on the Denton Hearings may begin with Chapter V and then return to Chapter I.

Every line in this essay means to show the pattern of the attack on the living and the feasible, the not perfect but better, in South Africa, in southern Africa and in the great world, as it used to be called, of international diplomacy,—the same attack the Denton Hearings show against individuals. Without the Denton testimony, I would not have written a word. Because of it, I had to write all the words I have written. Nobody who reads and studies this testimony and these documents will ever look upon our world with the same eyes.

1

The Measure of Change: the Past

Thou trustest upon the staff of this bruised reed, this Egypt, on which if a man lean, it will go into his hand and pierce it.
2 Kings xviii. 21., quoted by John X. Merriman in a letter to Jan Smuts in 1907.

Alle menschliche Gebrechen sühnet reine Menschlichkeit.
Simple humanness expiates all our ills.
Goethe, quoted by Jan Smuts in a letter in 1948 following the sentence, "The deeper human feeling is the only clue to knowledge."

1 The Unification of South Africa in 1910

"Reform should be a continuing process in any society but it is common that from time to time specific societies experience times during which more intensive reform is needed," runs a routine National Party statement issued to the Johannesburg *Star* on May 4, 1987. These words, to sum up the two-and-a-half years of uproar, violence and change that followed the introduction of the new constitution with the election of Indian and Colored representatives to their own legislative chambers in 1984, reminded South Africans, and the world, that meaningful change means change within continuity, not repudiation of the past.

They meant that P.W. Botha's reforms need to be measured against the situation he inherited, not only apartheid, but the policies that preceded it. For the South African government works within a tradition, especially within a juridical and constitutional tradition, far and away the oldest in sub-Saharan Africa. A tradition more than three hundred years old in the Cape Province; more than a hundred and fifty years old in the Orange Free State and the Transvaal; less developed in Natal, a self-governing colony only in 1893, still "British to the core" in aspiration in 1910, the time of a unification that did not stir its enthusiasm.[1]

This long history has withstood many wars and disruptions without a decisive break in its continuity. Wars in fact renewed it, they lent it a variety and depth that baffles the contemporary world. Like all the few living constitutions that the world knows, it is unique, it must be understood in its own terms before it can be judged in the terms of self-evident truths that now often are made to serve the ignorance of facts, the past's facts.

This tradition, and its tragedies, has also produced a people, or peoples, that vividly remember their own past,—in contrast to the United States,— something that James Bryce already noticed in a book, *Impressions of South Africa*, that rewards careful reading, published in 1897, just before the Anglo-Boer War. "South Africa has had a great deal of history, especially in the present century, and there are few places in which recollection of the past are more powerful factors in the troubles of the present."[2] Before his trip to South Africa, Lord Bryce had served as Great Britain's ambassador to Washington, and he had written a book on the United States, *The American Commonwealth*, often mentioned after Tocqueville.

Of all Great Britain's dominions South Africa was the only region, Bryce also stressed, not peopled by a majority of Europeans, and not in the temperate zone but with a temperate climate except for Natal, that enjoyed self-government. He called it the "gift of self-government," with the Cape Colony and Natal, not the two Boer republics, primarily on his mind. Except for unimportant Malta and the Falkland Islands, all the other colonies were Crown Colonies, "peopled chiefly by Colored races,—Negroes, Indians, Malays, Polynesians, or Chinese—with a small minority of whites," under the direct administration of the Colonial Office in London:

The one exception to this broad division, the one case of self-governing communities in which the majority of the inhabitants are not of European stock, is to be found in South Africa. The general difficulty of adjusting the relations of a higher and a lower race, serious under every kind of government, here presents itself in the special form of the construction of a political system which, while democratic as regards one of the races, cannot safely be made democratic as regards the other.[3]

Because our day's conventions allow little reference to specific past events, in unwitting deference to totalitarians, for nothing dissolves ideology as quickly as recall of the past's facts, it is difficult to measure meaningful change and appreciate it. Almost all leaders, including South African leaders but less so, nowadays speak as if their countries had no past any one cared to recall,—

as if they would flinch at the memory of their ancestors, because they fear the disappointment of their illusions about the future,—a most telling contrast with the period of the Anglo-Boer War and the unification of South Africa (1899–1910). The letters and speeches of those days, both of South African and British statesmen, teem with the recall of specific events in the past for guidance in the present. They make for more embarrassing and upsetting reading than the Denton Hearings themselves. The Denton Hearings, alas, betray a world we know only too well, *in the back of our minds*, a world we ignore because it is more familiar than ourselves.

The late Alan Paton, alone as usual, recently argued strongly against depriving change of the background that could give it meaning, making it easy for press and pundits to dismiss any change as "cosmetic." A big change for Paton. Until the present turmoil, he rarely recalled South Africa's past in anything but almost anecdotal fashion. He made little sense of its foreign affairs, even in his biography of the South African statesman, Jan Hofmeyr, a masterpiece because of its capacity to admit doubt: "There's a word that I have decided to cut out of my vocabulary and that's 'cosmetic'."

Paton went on to argue P.W. Botha's difference from the prime ministers who preceded him, all of them: "P.W. [Botha] has said things no prime minister had said before—not one, not even Louis Botha or Smuts. He said that he wanted a future for every child in this country, white, black or brown [the last a reference to the Coloreds]. He said that if these people are good enough to go and fight on our border, they are good enough to have a place at home."[4]

But despite his authority, Paton's words carried little weight. Most of the men who wrote and spoke about South Africa, including almost every member of Congress in the United States, had never heard of P.W. Botha's predecessors, and they were not about to find out.

Journalists and present day officials dread nothing more than the past. They dread it much more than their conscience, or the ideology that they take for their conscience, for it would teach them to distinguish between the two. "That was a long time ago," I was told by a blandly arrogant State Department official. I had asked whether he knew what Nelson Mandela was in for. By "long ago," his way of saying he did not know, he meant twenty-five years—but I doubt he even knew that.

Before the outpouring of indignation and contempt, not only from the totalitarians, but from the free West, especially the United States, that grew louder with every change, the South African government merely noted its disappointment with some dignity. It did not remind the West of what South Africa had meant to it, and means to it. It did not speak of the 231,209 (84,694 nonwhite) volunteers who fought in the First World War, of the 406,133 (125,670 nonwhite) volunteers who fought in the Second World War, or of the volunteers in the Korean War. (Stretcher-men and laborers, the nonwhites did not bear arms and sometimes protested against it.) To recall deeds, especially your country's deeds that everyone should know, embarrasses to the quick. The government did not remember that one of its greatest leaders, Jan Smuts, and not the only one, had understood the Western crisis, not only during the

Second World War and immediately after, but also during the First World War and at Versailles, that he had seen it whole, with more clarity and downrightness than European, let alone American statesmen.

Instead of referring to the past, South African officials spoke quietly of the present. They said they had expected "the left and Communist world would redouble its efforts to stop and frustrate reform," the more it unfolded, but that they had not expected an increase in condemnation from the West: "What we did not realize—where we have been wrong—where South Africans are bitterly disappointed and disillusioned—is that rising reform has brought rising condemnation, not rising recognition. This has and continues to erode the credibility of the reform movement in South Africa,"—words of Kent Durr, Deputy Minister of Finance, Trade and Development, in London in November 1986, just a few weeks after the passage of sanctions against his country in Washington.

The African National Congress (ANC) and the United Democratic Front (UDF), groups that sought to make the townships and all of South Africa "ungovernable" after the introduction of the new constitution, indulged no such reticence about the past. On the day after the May 6 election in 1987, the UDF made it clear it wanted to undo all of South African history, everything, unification, the nineteenth century, to turn it to dust and ashes: "[Parliament had been illegitimate] since the very first whites-only Union government of 1910 gave political shape to and confirmed the process of colonial conquest and land dispossession that had taken place over the three previous centuries."[5]

"Illegitimate," Talleyrand's word for Napoleon's usurpation, a word only the Communists now use because they know the taste of its absence.

I could barely believe my eyes when I read these words. The only thing they left out, the return of the lions, who could take care of themselves. These words also strangely echoed Louis Botha's and Jan Smuts' words in the dark harsh years immediately after the Anglo-Boer War when the horror of what they had been through came back to them with an admonitory force their courage had stilled during fighting: "Do you not see that South Africa is dying? . . . Dying not only to the British Empire, but in herself—dying of wasted blood and treasure, of a broken spirit, of crushed ideals, of an ineradicable hatred and social disruption. Another generation of this sort of thing, and South Africa will revert—and rightly revert—to the Bantu," Smuts wrote the Attorney General in Cape Town in a plea for release of Boers still in jail, barely two months after peace in 1902.

The Boers felt that conquest had reduced them to the level of the Natives—in the Natives' eyes. The Natives squatting on the farms "refuse to work [because] they look upon the Boers as a humbled and subordinate race, put on the same level as themselves under the heel of the conqueror," ran a memorandum written to the Labor Commission Smuts wrote and Louis Botha signed, a few years later.

But in contrast to the UDF and the ANC, Smuts and Botha did not want this chaos. They realized that the capacity for self-government defined the difference, the rational difference between Europeans and Natives. Two generations before, in 1830, the Scottish superintendent of the London Missionary Society in South Africa, John Philip, had also observed that the Europeans counted not so much because of individual differences, but because of their capacity to make something of themselves as a whole, to rule themselves:

Individually, savages may be as rational (as far as their observation goes) as Europeans, but it is in union and government that they lack the justice and lawfulness of civilized nations. The power of the chief . . . tends to express force rather than justice. But without a religious basis for their civilization they use their knowledge only to rob their neighbors and then lose all again in marauding expeditions.[6]

In contrast to the UDF and the ANC that want the destruction of government in the name of equality and "participatory democracy," Smuts knew internecine "racial or racialist strife,"—"race" then meant the differences between Boers and British and English-speaking newcomers, not the difference between Europeans and Natives,—would destroy even the rudiments of government in South Africa. It would turn the land back to the Natives, he did not add, although he probably meant, in much worse shape than before. The return to the state of nature is much crueler than the original untouched state.

Some writers take these fears for exaggerated expressions of inherited prejudice, a word Smuts hardly knew. For instance, the most recent biographer of Smuts calls them, "a reiteration of the old instinctive fears of the African enemy, based not on observable evidence but upon prejudice fed by memories of former battles, by more recent Darwinian theory and by an inner sensation which was irrepressible."[7]

Smuts was afraid, not of the Bantu, but of the British and the Boers, for he understood that their failures to rule themselves would be disastrous not only for the Europeans, but for the Natives too. Besides, the war had been real not only between the Boers and British, but between the Boers, British and the various Bantu tribes. Recovery did not mean forgetting.

At stake after the Anglo-Boer War was the love of country, and the authority born of it that made self-government possible, not hatred and fear of the Bantu, whose repossession of the country in event of European failure would be "well-deserved": "These people [investors] have never loved their country or felt a passion for it in any shape or form. South Africa they regard with unconcealed contempt—a black man's country, good enough to make money or a name in; but not good enough to be born or die in. What is there in common between such people and the Boers the fibres of whose very soul are made of this despised soil?," Smuts wrote against the mining companies' insistence on importing Chinese labor, instead of hiring the poor whites of South Africa in 1904.[8]

Above all men like Smuts and Louis Botha, and their English counterparts, the high commissioners for South Africa, Lord Milner, and his successor Lord Selborne, and their highly informed, often brilliant advisers, during the Anglo-Boer War and the decade after, understood that without the rule of law, no change was possible. They knew it, they did not have to say it, it was the air they breathed. Call it confidence.

This tradition and understanding still persists in the present South African government, the child of the Anglo-Boer War, and among South Africans today, both black and white and Indians and Coloreds. Their common bonds today are stronger than their differences,—differences that show more distinctly because of their closeness, not because of their distance.

The child of this confidence in Boers and British, which took the rule of law for the air it breathed, was the constitution and unification of South Africa in 1910, barely eight years after the Anglo-Boer War. The constitution of 1910 preserved continuity, the juridical traditions of the four provinces and their self-government, at the same time that it transformed them into a unified central state. A liberal state but liberal in the sense of Hobbes, not of Montesquieu. The new constitution did not subordinate the sovereignty of Parliament to Montesquieu's division of powers between legislative, executive and judiciary that became the checks and balances of the *Federalist*.[9]

The designers wanted a state capable of decisive action in danger they assumed as a matter of course, and also capable of swift change whose necessity they foresaw. They had no illusions of deciding matters once and for all, quite a contrast with the American constitution, especially after the Civil War. They rejected federalism as incapable of swift decisive action and change. They judged it the cause of Civil War in the United States,—a disaster much before the eyes of the South Africans, and their British advisors, in the years after the Anglo-Boer War.

They also did not think of themselves as a model for other nations, another refreshing contrast with the United States. Their inclusion in the British Empire that Smuts called the British Commonwealth of Nations for the first time in 1917 and their own defeats taught them the modesty of not insisting too much. They were interested in the world's acceptance, not in changing it.

The capacity of this constitution to distinguish sovereignty from despotism has shown itself now for almost three generations in its preservation of freedom of speech, independence of the judiciary, contract, property, political opposition and in its readiness to allow economic and intellectual growth, no small achievement anywhere, especially in a continent that knows no other such country.

There is a modesty at the core of this tradition that has allowed the government to countenance those who doubted it at the same time that it insisted on its sovereignty. This modesty comes from the South Africans' readiness to assume responsibility for themselves, and, what amounts to the same thing, not to hide their thinking or their acts from the world,—the real significance of the unification and the adoption of the constitution in 1910.

The measure of the changes in the South African constitution in 1983–1984 can only show against this background of unification, and the transformation of the four provinces into a central government in 1910. They were changes made against that background of continuity that had survived a disastrous war, they presume that suffering and that success.

The frequent reminders of Paton, Chief Mangosuthu Buthelezi, Jonas

Savimbi, and other men of their stature, that the South African Government is not to be swept away, confirmed in the May 6, 1987 election, acknowledge that continuity and its confidence. This confidence allows much self-doubt and open admission of errors among South Africans and among South African statesmen, dangerous and foolhardy admissions in anything but a strong state that knows limits. Admissions some of the West, especially the United States and some of its journalists, have learned from the totalitarians, good teachers of things one should not learn, to hold in scorn and contempt. But how can people change who do not admit they were wrong?

Paton himself, who in the late fifties and sixties unremittingly called the government of South Africa "domination" and "white supremacy," gave the sovereignty Smuts and the other men of 1910 meant,—the preservation of law and order,—its greatest tribute, almost inadvertently, when he remarked in 1968: "If a situation seems unchangeable there is no reason to believe violence will change it"—imperishable words.

Even earlier, in 1958, Paton betrayed the confidence that comes of that sovereignty that allowed him in his last years, in contrast to other younger South African liberals, to come to the whole-hearted support of his government in the hour of its need' and courage and vulnerability: "I believe there are sound objective reasons why South Africa, though it will undoubtedly experience great and painful change, will not experience irreconcilable conflict."[10]

2 The Conquest of the Bantu in the Nineteenth Century before Unification

But the changes at work today, "irreversible," in the judgment of the managing director of a major company, go deeper than the unification of 1910.[11] They seek gradually to undo or, at least to mitigate, the consequences of the British and Boer conquest of the Bantu in the nineteenth century that set the Native policy, later turned into apartheid.

Again, Paton in an astonishing reference to South Africa's past before the unification of 1910,—I know no other passage of his that admits the word "conquest,"—tried to explain these facts of life to New York readers not about to understand "conquest" anywhere, let alone South Africa: ". . . It is one of the great ironies of my political life that just as the Afrikaner nationalist is at last beginning to realize that the day of conquest has gone, and just as he is taking the first tottering step toward the undoing, he is confronted by the violent manifestation of black hatred of his apartheid laws . . ."[12]

Paton also added, in a remark that betrays his innocence of history, that nothing is easier to accomplish and harder to undo than conquest. They are at least equally as difficult,—as the present division of Europe shows.

Paton meant the South African government intends to undo conquest but preserve the rule of law. This is the same conquest Smuts and other South African statesmen knew the Anglo-Boer War had almost undone at the cost of the destruction of all government, the conquest the UDF and the ANC now want to use as a pretext to overthrow the South African government.

"Never again will the Zulus be crushed by might," Mangosuthu Buthelezi, Paton's close friend, one of the most intelligent and courageous leaders in South Africa, recently remarked in private conversation. He meant the opposite his words seemed to say. He meant not that he was about to rebel in the classical sense, to start the tribal wars again, but that he could tell feelers of peace when he saw them. He went on to remember the Zulus' warlike past that had led Bryce to say of both the Zulus and the Xhosa that "The British army has encountered no more daring or formidable enemies."

Buthelezi meant his recall of the Zulus' proud past to justify his trust in reconciliation in the present, to remind his people and the other blacks they had enough of a past for confidence. "The Zulus are a warrior people. Some say I am trying to dominate with a Zulu imperium because they fear our past reputation. But we are not a tribe. The Zulus were the mightiest *nation* here in the nineteenth century."[13]

He went on to list his royal ancestors, genealogy that embarrasses the West, because it implies continuity with the past,—ancestors is not a word that comes readily to our lips,—in its way the same continuity that the South African government insists upon,—the continuity that alone can make for change without destruction.

Conquest meant two things that, incidentally, show the respect between victors and conquered Buthelezi meant to recall,—and that the twentieth century does not know: the Bantu never became slaves and they were never massacred wholesale.

Both because they never became slaves, and because the Natives' cruelty in war had come home to English public opinion, the Bantu did not excite much attention in London: "The frontal attack on the wickedness of slave-owners had aroused such popular emotions as were much less easily moved to show concern for the land rights of African tribes, led possibly, by a savage murderer like Dingaan [the Zulu chief, defeated at the Blood River in Natal on December 16, 1838, a South African national holiday, "the day of the vow"]. They were at any rate already 'free'."

British policy did not treat the Bantu, usually referred to by the names of their many chiefs, like the American blacks, but like the American Indians. It modeled the reserves, later to form the core of the homelands, in part on British policy in the thirteen colonies toward Indians before the war for independence.

The second truth, that neither Boers nor British ever murdered peoples, is much darker. It tells more about us and our times than about the South Africans:

There is one vital difference [with the Indians in the United States]. To the credit of all South African races, white and black, the long struggle never degenerated into indiscriminate slaughter. It is the crux of the whole matter that the Bantu survive, in massive numbers if in less favorable conditions than might have been, as a social factor in all the country's affairs.[14]

The words are of the great English historian, W.M. Macmillan, deeply sympathetic to the tribes, who elsewhere emphasized, almost to his surprise, that the Boers and the British only resorted to force for the sake of law and order: "To the credit of all concerned, including the colonists, the resort to force was always regarded only as a means to a higher end, *law and order* . . ."[15]

In a kind of desperation with a past whose bluntness in words and in war unnerves us, most of all because it explains its fundamental restraint, we praise the men of the past for not doing something they never even thought of. Nowhere in the documents I have read does even the thought of the murder of peoples ever cross the minds of these men. Neither the governments and the societies of Europe of that time knew the undercurrents of murderousness. Murderous thoughts, 'Exterminate all the brutes,' kept their torment in those days for lonely individuals like Kurtz who could not cope with their greatness in worlds that could neither live with or without it—as Conrad, and probably Marlow, knew in *Heart of Darkness*: "No eloquence could have been so withering to one's belief in mankind as his final burst of sincerity." It is we, not the past, who have turned the words, "Take care of them," into an expression that can mean what it says, or its opposite.

These days it falls to the South African *Jewish Herald* to remember these truths. "The government of P.W. Botha has not drawn up any plans for the final extermination of the black population," it wrote in June 1985 in answer to Desmond Tutu's calling apartheid Nazism, standard Soviet propaganda except that the Soviets would have put "fascism" in the place of "Nazism." No rabbi in Germany, the newspaper went on, had known the freespokenness "the bishop enjoyed in South Africa," brave words because obvious.[16]

Men who become willing terrorists like Oliver Tambo, the president of the ANC,—in contrast to youths like the Denton witnesses, trapped into terrorism,—probably could not, and cannot stand this straightforward toughness, not murderous because tough, that characterized the Boers and the British in the nineteenth century, and that still lives in the South African government. They desire to reduce it to their own level. Around 1941, before apartheid, Tambo on a full scholarship, was expelled from Fort Hare, the legendary black university, because of his refusal to subscribe to a pledge on conduct, spiritual life and religious duties the warden requested,—an expulsion that did not destroy his career. Tambo took care of his career himself.[17]

The conquest in the nineteenth century occurred largely in piecemeal fashion, more because of tensions between the Boers and their British rulers than because of the Natives. There was no set plan, only a chain of events that finally showed the raw face of their significance in the Anglo-Boer War at the end of the century, tragic because not inevitable.

Nobody foresaw the conquest or the strong state that followed upon it, not the Dutch, not the British,—not the Boers themselves. It surprised everybody, because the land had a way with its peoples, and its peoples knew how to yield to it without surrendering.

South Africa has always been an unwanted, at least an unexpected child, who knew how to surprise itself as well as its guardians and how to thrive under desultory tutelage. The settlers had, as Bryce profoundly understood, from the beginning broken their ties with Europe and developed a distinctive character. The humble origins of the Dutch precluded strong ties to the mother country. France had expelled the French Huguenots. In contrast, the Americans, the educated New Englanders and the Virginians of good social position, kept up close ties with England.

Neither the Dutch in the seventeenth century nor the British in the nineteenth century meant to establish a full-fledged colony in the Cape. The British had not thought of the Cape, in Bryce's phrase, as a place for "supporting a great civilized community and furnishing a new market for British goods":

The Dutch took it that they might plant a cabbage garden; the English took it that they might have a naval station and a halfway house to India.[18]

Britain had "never cared to bend her energies to the development of South Africa,"—and, above all, to spend any more money on it "than she could help." For money was too precious to give away in those days, and belief still strong enough not to fancy it for appeasing guilt. British statesmen did not know what to do with South Africa, and they only needed its ports at Cape Town and in Natal, the English people cared less. Haphazard but unremitting in its expansion, the colony had meant no end of trouble. There was no way of either leaving it alone or controlling it:

English statesmen have for more than fifty years been accustomed to say that of all the Colonies of Great Britain none has given to the mother country so much disquiet and anxiety as South Africa has done.[19]

Almost from the beginning, long before they met the Bantu, the settlers had known they were alone in the world,—long before the British took the colony and drew the Boers into big-time history, at least five Native wars in a century. On top of that, the Anglo-Boer War, that gave South Africa a place among the nations of the world, a place nobody sought, although it was to become the conscious object of Smuts' policy after unification, in a time in contrast to the present world, not promiscuous in the recognition of the appearance of sovereignty: ". . . The old Cape settlers had a language of their own, and a sense of blood-kinship to hold them together that has enabled the Dutch element to remain cohesive, and given them an Afrikander patriotism of their own—a patriotism which is not Dutch, for they care nothing for the traditions of Holland, but purely Afrikander." So Bryce described the Boers before the coming of the British and the expansion beyond the Cape Colony. "Autocthonous" Lord Milner called the Boers in tribute, and exasperation, upon the eve of his departure from South Africa in 1905.

Besides the absence of slavery and wholesale massacres, the relative lateness of contacts between the Boers and the Bantu, then called Kaffirs, now blacks or Africans, needs emphasis. A word on the changing names. They tell a good deal about change, and the underlying intractability of the situation, despite men's thoughts and wishes, but also of contact, sometimes brutal contact, but continuous contact nevertheless. One generation's name becomes a term of abuse in the next. In the nineteenth century the term Kaffirs or Caffres meant a dreaded respected enemy from the Islamic word for unbelievers Islamic Africans still use, but that now can cause an uproar in South Africa. The change from Natives (the capital came in the twenties) or Bantu (Zulu for 'the people," a name also of the twenties) to Africans in the late fifties in the South African press made a difference despite the similarity of meaning of all three terms: people born of the country,—the "aborigines" of the Aborigines Protection Society in London in the first half of the nineteenth century. Changes difficult to comprehend but that tell of much more than fashion: they show each generations' eyes.

Extensive contact between the South Africans and the Bantu began on the remote frontiers of the eastern Cape, just at the time slavery became a political issue in the United States. Before 1820, the year the Missouri Compromise showed Jefferson that slavery could divide the states between north and south, the Cape settlers had had little to do with the Bantu for more than one hundred fifty years. They lived beyond the frontiers of the colony. An ordinance of 1828 in the Cape allowed field cornets, and, it turned out later, traders and missionaries, to grant "passes" to Africans from across the frontier to work in the Cape Colony. The prohibition of slavery in the territories newly annexed to the Cape, which foreshadowed the general abolition of slavery throughout the British Empire in 1834, made for this demand for labor. By the eighteen forties, the use of African labor had become common in the far-off eastern Cape. But even late in the nineteenth century, Bantu rarely appeared in Cape Town because of local Colored laborers. By the time of the Anglo-Boer War and unification, the blacks in the United States had been in contact with the whites for at least three times as long as the South Africans with the Bantu.

The real drama of contact with the Bantu took place beyond the frontiers of the British Empire, not in the Cape Colony and Natal annexed in 1845. It made South Africa, and uncovered a whole new world, again a succession of events nobody foresaw, or planned.

Under the impact of a ferocious Native war that broke out in the eastern Cape in 1835 and because of dissatisfaction with British reforms in the Cape, some of the Boers left the Cape for the territories beyond the Orange River, and between the Great Fish and the Kei Rivers in the eastern Cape. Within the space of less than a generation they had spread out through much of the territory of modern South Africa. They formed two republics: the Orange Free State and the South African Republic (the Transvaal), which Britain recognized in 1852 and 1854. It did not entirely renounce suzerainty, a vague claim of authority over them.

The British fought, and tried to make peace, with the many tribes like full-fledged nations until John Philip persuaded them of the senselessness of such policy. The Boers lived among the Natives with skirmishes and raids but without attempting a military settlement. This apparent indecisiveness baffled British officers who at the same time admitted the Boers understood more about bush warfare: "If we could obtain the cooperation of men trained in and accustomed to bush warfare [the Boers], the Caffres would no longer appear such dangerous enemies," wrote a British commander in 1852.

At the same time the Boer style of unceasing but intermittent fighting, "an incessant desultory war with the Natives," Bryce called it, repelled the British. It promised Boers squatting "here and there over the country" in no order or political settlement.

This movement of small groups of men and women and children with servants, the total number by 1837 probably not more than six thousand, this readiness to face wilderness with only rifles, courage, and faith, without the protection of British troops and the terror of their wars, bears the name of the Great Trek. It astonished the men like John Philip who saw it, and probably also the Trekkers, because of its suddenness of decision and determination. It took more than ten years before its consequences came home to the British and the rest of the world.

On the spot, Philip who saw it first had immediately sensed its difference from the previous moves of the Boers with their flocks and herds away from Cape Town that had extended the Cape Colony's frontiers five hundred miles, and even from the previous departures of some Boers across the Orange River who had continued to pay their taxes in the Colony. In contrast to these movements, the Trek unmistakably signified a break, not a revolt, but a decision to leave, to say good-bye, and take one's chances on one's own.

Philip, who did not speak Afrikaans, looked in wry bafflement, he a priest, at the faith of the Trekkers: "Compensation money [for the emancipated slaves] has turned their heads, and they turn it into powder and shot to expel the Canaanite from the Land of Promise [Natal that the Boers soon left because of their inability to come to any agreement with either Zulus or British]. . . . The only part I am taking is that of a spectator, and my only resource is prayer," he wrote in 1838 in wonderment at the continued exodus of the Boers that he had first witnessed four years before.

"Where on my tour in 1832 there were not fifteen Boers, there are now 1,100," Philip had written of the northern frontier beyond the Orange River in 1834, proof, he thought, that African cattle thieving was not as bad as the Boers complained. In the eastern Cape he seems to have seen the Boers in the same year actually cross the frontier:

A fortnight ago a Proclamation appeared prohibiting Boers from crossing the boundaries of the Colony under a penalty of ten pounds. In face of that, twelve Boers have passed through this Settlement, in front of the chain of posts, into Caffreland. Another party crossed last week behind the Winterberg, refusing to obey the Field Cornet who ordered them to return.[20]

The Boers preferred loneliness to the protection of British arms and the Empire. That was what baffled, even threatened, Philip. For the tribes, especially the Xhosa, could have more than once overrun the Colony, had they but realized their strength, and the Colony's vulnerability, the vulnerability of all civilized settlements to the irresistibility of barbarian hordes that Thucydides had remarked on long ago in a passage whose importance Adam Smith underlined in *The Wealth of Nations*. John Philip knew those words and probably also did some of the governors and men in the colonial office in London.

"The question is not what to do with the Kaffirs, but what will the Kaffirs do with us?," Philip wrote in May 1846 in uncharacteristically wry acknowledgment of danger in the face, after Xhosa tribes had attacked and burnt scattered farm houses, raided cattle and driven their farmers into towns and villages in the Colony itself, not merely in the disputed land between the Fish and the Kei rivers in the eastern Cape. But the Boers understood just what Philip could not conceive: They might be safer on their own in constant danger beyond the protection of British arms. British might precipitated furor in the Natives.

The sudden full-scale Xhosa insurrection in 1835 had helped to precipitate the Great Trek because it seemed to show the futility of British policy. The insurrection turned to empty words the instructions the new governor, Benjamin D'Urban, a name the most important city in Natal remembers, had come out with from London in January 1834, "not [to] propose or assent to any Ordinance whatever" that imposed "any disabilities or restrictions" on non-Europeans apart from Europeans. Barely a year later, in December 1835 after the fighting's end, despite his previous determination upon Philip's advice to substitute a civil for military administration that would secure the Xhosa in their lands and stop Boer reprisal raids for cattle-thieving, D'Urban determined to expel the tribes and annex the whole territory between the Fish and Kei rivers, a decision London rejected over the objections of the King:

Our losses were under 1,000, theirs over 4,000 of their warriors. There have been taken from them also—besides the conquest and alienation of their country—about 60,000 head of cattle, and almost all their goats; their habitations are everywhere destroyed and their gardens and cornfields laid waste. They have been, therefore, chastised—not extremely but perhaps sufficiently, and will, I think, have such a salutary recollection of what they have suffered as to prevent a recurrence.[21]

In contrast to D'Urban's attempt to call his actions a full-scale war, one of his bravest commanders, later a governor, called the fighting, "Smithfield Market cattle driving:" "You gallop in and half by force, half by stratagem, pounce upon [the Kaffirs] wherever you find them, frighten their wives, burn their homes, lift their cattle, and then return home in triumph."[22]

He meant there had been only hit-and-run attacks, sometimes in the night, bush guerrilla warfare. Not at all like today's guerrilla warfare because it was without a strategy, let alone a political program, but like it in its avoidance of open battles. The nineteenth century saw only two or three open battles in all the Xhosa wars, not the case with the Zulus.

He also meant more profoundly that the war could have no political consequences, because the Xhosa did not understand war as an instrument of policy: they did not understand threats meant to bring future stability. "There must be no more *threatening*. The Caffres *never threaten* when they *really intend* to do anything. Expulsion must never be thought of—far less threatened," runs a missionary's extraordinary explanation of the ineffectiveness of British policy in 1846.[23]

Already in 1837 men in London realized that dealing with the tribes as if they were full-fledged nations that understood the difference between war and peace only led to the classical chain of wars. "Compacts between parties negotiating on terms of such disparity" made agreements "rather the preparatives and the apology for dispute than securities for peace" stated the parliamentary Aborigines report Philip helped to draft that year.

Philip meant that outright domination and annexation without expulsion of the tribes, in short reserves, the reserves later to turn into the homelands, served better to prevent further fighting than treaties, unenforceable because between such unequals. But London, always reluctant to take on the responsibilities of annexation that had no strategic importance, vacillated.

Despite the terror of the wars, and because of this vacillation, the Boers took off on their own,—terror whose memory lived on in South Africa in the twentieth century: "The emotional storm raised by that unhappy war [D'Urban's in 1835] and its immediate sequel has, it is not too much to say, been a dominant force in the country's history ever since," Macmillan wrote in the nineteen sixties in unwitting reconfirmation of Bryce's observation of the past's persistence in South Africa two generations before.[24]

The decision of some Boers to leave eventually drew Britain after them into the country that was to become South Africa, an initiative the government would probably never have taken on its own. The two republics away from the sea drew Britain in because of their importance, which rivaled the strategic importance of the Cape, an importance that the discovery of diamonds in 1867 in the Orange Free State and gold in 1886 in the Transvaal underlined but did not create. It was the capacity of the Boers to found states that drew Britain on, almost in envy of their authority and confidence. The conflict between the two races, as they called themselves, between the British and the Boers, went much deeper than interest. It went to the heart of modernism.

"Stubborn conservatism," the refusal to accept change, above all equality between races, often are made to explain the individual decisions of the Boers to leave. The Boers could not stand the various laws that brought their personal relations with their Hottentot and Colored servants and laborers under public control: "The original cause of this great dispersal of the strength and energy of young South Africa was horror at equality between black and white so many saw implied in the legislation of 1828 and 1833."[25] These laws culminated in the emancipation of slaves in 1834 and in the qualified franchise for all people regardless of race in the Cape Colony in 1854.

But matters were not quite so simple Macmillan knew. The Boers did not object in principle to these reforms. They thought they would not work, they knew the government in the Cape could not keep order for them on their far-flung farms. Caught between ideals nobody could object to but that the government could not enforce, the Boers accepted the abolition of slavery in their two republics, but insisted on their authority. "It is our determination to maintain such regulations as may suppress crime, and preserve proper relations between master and servant," wrote Piet Retief, murdered treacherously in the course of negotiations with the Zulus in 1837 for land in Natal. He added:

We are resolved, wherever we go, that we will uphold the just principles of liberty . . . and will take care that no one shall be held in the state of slavery . . . .[26]

Even Philip, no friend of the Boers who baffled his heart, admitted in 1828 they would have obeyed a forceful coherent government. This admission later made him see that the repeated decisions of small groups of Boers to leave amounted, not to a rebellion, but to a criticism of British ineptness and inconsistency. The Cape state attorney confirmed Philip's judgment in repeated opinions that the "emigration" of the Boers broke no laws:

The Boers, like all ignorant people, just take as much as is given them. They acknowledge no other limit. When Government assumes a commanding aspect, no people on earth are more submissive. And it is lamentable to observe how for so many years their ruinous encroachments have been winked at, and even encouraged by the Frontier authorities.[27]

The Boers in other words were not about to put up with a government desultory in its reforms because they threatened disorder rather than change. Besides they knew, as the qualification of the franchise in the Cape itself showed, that nobody thought complete equality either desirable or possible. They preferred the insecurity of life on their own to reforms without bite. "The Hottentot legislation was bitterly resented—possibly all the more because weak administration may have made these measures fully more irritating than they were effective,"—Macmillan's judgment.[28]

The refusal to introduce slavery in the two Boer republics showed the Boers objected to the means of emancipation not the principle. The few Boer slave holders had suffered losses upon emancipation because compensation for them had been set at considerably less than their value, in Bryce's judgment: three million pounds for thirty thousand. Also, the provision for payment in London forced some of the settlers to sell their claims to middlemen for less than their value. The pamphlet Smuts wrote in 1899 to explain the Anglo-Boer War, *A Century of Injustice*, addressed incidentally to the Queen, recalled these grievances:

The discontent, so often, and to his detriment, ascribed to the Boer was exaggerated and misrepresented, as for instance, in the matter of the freeing of the slaves, when he was described as being inhumanly against their liberation. No! Your majesty, it was not the Christian Boers' repugnance to the emancipation, but his opposition to the means employed in effecting same under blessed British rule.[29]

In 1906 the English born prime minister of the Cape, J.X. Merriman, testified to the persistence of this calumny against the Boers, διαβολή he might have called it, in a letter to Smuts: "The Native question will be made a rod to beat the Dutch with by those very brutes who are now burning Native churches in Natal because they are Native . . . The 'loyal' Press is always ready to hold up the Dutch as slave-drivers and oppressors while they claim for themselves a perfect immunity from criticism whatever they may please to do." These words, uncannily, might describe the prestige media today in the United States.[30]

By the end of the century the ideals that had angered the Boers two generations before because of their impracticality, appeared to Smuts more sinisterly as simply a cover for a conquest that made the Boers' straightforward insistence on inequality innocent in comparison. Like Merriman he recognized the spiritual exhaustion of the twentieth century, its exploitation of ideals, before it showed its full face: "Our future is dark. God alone knows how dark. *Perhaps it is the fate of our little race to be sacrificed on the altar of the world's ideals*; perhaps we are destined to be the martyr race which must redeem our sordid money age from the charge of absolute worldliness and selfishness," Smuts wrote to his wife, in the depths of the Boer War on June 2, 1901, the first words she received from her husband after the death of their eighteen-month old son, almost a year before, and after the death of Smut's mother.[31] More than two generations later, the youths before the Denton Committee learned something of this sacrifice to the world's ideals, the cost of defiance in a world that knows its exploitation.

Inequality in the Boer republics knew its limits in the spread of the Gospel. In the constitution of the South African Republic (the Transvaal), the *Grondwet*, six years after the British recognized its independence in the Sand River Convention of 1852, the clause expressing the people's will that there be "no equality between Colored and white inhabitants either in Church or State," followed later by the specification that "no Colored persons nor half-castes [the Coloreds of today] are admitted to meetings of Volksraad, nor to any civic privileges," is immediately preceded by a profession of faith that ends: "The people permit the spread of the Gospel among the heathen, subject to definite safeguards against fault and deception."

By "fault and deception" the citizens probably meant "the dogma of equality of the black man and the white" that Bryce remarked at the end of the century "was wholesome to inculcate so far as equality of protection was concerned, but its wider application led the early philanthropists [he meant men like John Philip] of South Africa as it led their excellent contemporaries, the Abolitionists of America, to some strange conclusions."

The Boer republics denied the Bantu citizenship, they did not deny the Bantu were men, the reason of their restraint. A generation later, Bryce noted, the missionaries too had learned not to ignore differences. The dogma of equality, that often roused the wrath of the Boers, has "now been silently dropped": ". . . Perceiving that other influences ought to go hand in hand with religion in helping the Natives forward, the missionaries now devote themselves more than formerly to secular instruction, and endeavor to train the people to habits of industry."[32]

The *Grondwet* of 1858 also acknowledged perpetual potential danger, not only for the Europeans but also for the Bantu, that the Boers accepted as their way of life to the bafflement of British officers: "To the Assistant Field-Cornets, and Field-Cornets is entrusted the preservation of order, to the Commandants, the commandos [traditional Boer militia], in case of internal insurrection of the Colored population" it ran after stating that the army comprised, "if necessary" to keep each other in order, "all the Colored people in this country whose chiefs are subject to it." In other words Africans would serve to keep the peace among the tribes and clans.

The discussions after the Anglo-Boer War, especially between Smuts and the Cape prime minister, Merriman, before the constitutional convention of 1908, continued to recognize danger. They characterized the future state as an *imperium in imperio*, almost an echo of the *bellum in pace* of a colonial governor's description of the situation in the eastern Cape, two generations before.

Imperium in imperio meant the newly unified South Africa would live both in a state of peace and in a state of readiness for war within its own territory, a consequence of the Boers' decision neither to expel or massacre the Natives or put them in reserves. In contrast to the states of Europe, with frontiers to separate peace and war, South Africa's sovereignty would always have to show its raw face within its territory. Its frontiers would not separate it from the Bantu. At the constitutional convention in 1908, the sense of danger moved one delegate to argue against Britain's immediate cession to South Africa of their protectorates, Basutoland (now Lesotho) and Bechuanaland (now Botswana) and against the surrender of the independence of Swaziland that Britain guaranteed. The departure of British troops would leave the South Africans to face Native uprisings alone.

Uprisings meant, not cold-blooded revolution, but sudden outbreaks of passion, *furor*, a term the Romans used for the unpredictable violence of tribes that they distinguished sharply from the wars of republics and monarchies,— in contrast to contemporary foreign policy that assumes any group capable of making a state. Even when Smuts wrote in his student days at Cambridge in 1892 of "a race struggle . . . destined to assume a magnitude such as the world has never seen and imagination shrinks from contemplating," he meant irresistible outbreaks of passion and envy, the *furor* of the Romans, not the theses of the Third International in 1919–1920 he can nowadays be so easily mistook to foresee.

The men who made South Africa were not obsessed with revolution. They knew the dangers of liberal ideas applied to inappropriate situations, they also knew the hypocrisy that increasingly infested their apparent innocence that had shown itself in Cecil Rhodes' surreptitious attempt to overthrow the South African Republic in 1895, an attempt that shook Smuts. But they barely suspected their degradation to serve totalitarian purposes: ". . . The only reward to which I can look forward, is to hand on the love of civil liberty—that before these dark days we used to associate with the name of English—to young men like yourself and others, who may perhaps live to see South Africa an oasis in the wilderness of democratic socialism which seems overrunning the world and which is used by plutocracy for its own ends," Merriman wrote Smuts in 1905 with the warm authority of the time, exactly a generation that separated them, a measure they both respected enough not to mention,—an older man's blessing, full of foreboding.[33] His last words above practically describe the character of Kurtz in *Heart of Darkness* for they describe the same emptiness as Marlow sensed in Kurtz: "[The wilderness] echoed loudly within him because he was hollow at the core . . ."

Anxious to give the past the benefit of our enlightened views, we forget its accomplishments. Whatever else the Boers did they went among the Bantu. "The immense widening of the area of contact and conflict with the Bantu tribes is indeed the outstanding consequence of the Great Trek, and the aspect most consistently ignored," Macmillan had to remind himself almost in an afterthought, because he was so intent on reimagining such contact without tragedy.[34]

Two generations later, the consequences of the Boers' plunge into the wilderness with their flocks and herds met Bryce's startled eyes almost everywhere:

Everywhere in South Africa, except in the Witwatersrand and Cape Town, the black people greatly outnumber the whites.[35]

In the Cape Colony and the Transvaal, they numbered more than three times the whites, in the Orange Free State nearly twice, in Natal ten times,— not to speak of the rest of southern Africa below the Zambezi where the disproportion ran to something like 750,000 Europeans to somewhere between 6 to 8 million blacks.

Even Philip, the man who led Macmillan to think it could have been otherwise, knew in his heart that the harshness, and the bloodshed, could at best be limited, but not altogether avoided—especially since life was cheap among the Bantu, as the first missionary of the London Missionary Society to South Africa had already pointed out in 1816: "They [two chiefs] do not see the wrong of committing murder when a person is accused, for example of withholding rain . . . In fact life is of little value. One human life is reckoned as equal to three beasts." He had also known the power of witch doctors he called prophets: "They think nothing of murder if the prophetess ascribes any calamity to the poison of a particular individual." The preamble of a new law code in Natal in 1850 tells something of the struggle to give the word murder meaning: "Know ye, therefore, all Chiefs, Petty Chieftains, Heads of Kraals and Common People, *a man's life has no price; no cattle can pay for it.*"[36]

In an astonishing letter of 1835, arguing for annexation and reserves as the only way to save "the Caffres . . . from annihilation," Philip wrote:

. . . No Tribes will be allowed time to rise into civilization and independence on our borders, if they are in immediate contact with our colonists . . . Contiguous nations never can be independent of each other without a balance of power, and there can be no such balance betwixt this Colony and the uncivilized tribes upon our borders . . . Barbarous nations may rise to civilization and independence situated in the midst of nations in similar circumstances with themselves, and even in that case it must require long periods of time, and they must work their way to those points through great difficulties and much bloodshed; but in immediate contact with civilized nations— never! It may do very well to produce a momentary excitement on an English platform to talk of raising up civil governments in Africa, as a man would light one candle by the gleam of another; but woe to the cause of missions and humanity in Africa if our missionaries beyond a certain point have no better light to guide them in their labours.[37]

3   What it Meant to Live Among the Bantu

Philip explained the Africans' outbreak of *furor* largely in terms of expulsion from the land, still a very deep question in South Africa as polls unexpectedly showed German researchers in 1977:[38] "The Caffres can understand what it is to be punished for *stealing* and *murder*—but no argument will ever convince them that it is either *just* or *reasonable* to take their *land* from them," a missionary wrote Philip in 1846.[39]

But Bryce was probably closer to the truth though more distant from events, maybe closer to the truth because more distant from events, when he argued that the tribes also fought with such sudden unpredictable ferocity because of the challenges to their customs: ". . . It was probably as much the unwillingness to have their customs disturbed as the apprehension for their lands that made many of the tribes oppose to the advance of the Europeans so obstinate a resistance."[40]

Philip, in contrast, hardly ever mentioned the European threat to traditional life, probably because he could not conceive the Gospel as an upsetting teaching to anybody. But conversions among the tribal Bantu were few, and at the cost of contempt, ostracism and even in some cases deprivation of tribal rights. For conversion meant the birth of an individual.

The missionaries, and sometimes the governors, attacked the bride-price, the *lobola*, long called "the sin of buying wives," to protect Christian converts,—provisions, especially in treaties, that the tribesmen took for an attack on custom. Some governors insisted on the use of English in schools "to the total exclusion of the Kaffir dialect."

Dress caused endless questions for administrators, soldiers and especially missionaries. "The necessity of wearing clothes," the phrase of a governor, was often on their minds, but in a way, especially among the missionaries, that showed they regarded nakedness as nudity, as another sort of dress with its own conventions, not a vestige of the earthly paradise. The governors and commanders instead just bluntly wanted the Natives to cover themselves.

"Usually naked," the men have "their points of delicacy," Philip remarked of his first tour beyond the Cape in 1831. As for the chiefs: "They do not all adopt European dress entirely, because all their people could not afford to do so, and they would alienate their sympathy. It is customary for them to dress when they dine with British officers or people. Then they are immaculate. At interviews they wear skins." One missionary went "amongst the Caffres wearing their clothes and eating their food"—a "great good" Philip called it but went on to tell of another missionary who "made a fool of himself by wearing skins when the chiefs themselves would have worn black coats."[41]

The Chiefs living to some extent in two worlds dressed for both. Mandela on the day of his final speech at his trial in 1963, wore the skin of a wild animal over his European clothes,—a sight that left its mark on the Afrikaner youths who saw it.

Philip read Adam Smith but not enough to prevent his surprise at the discovery in 1833 that technical change counted as much as preaching. Such was his concentration on the Gospel and conversion. "In a country like this the mechanic may do as much for the Kingdom of God as the missionary, and the man who subscribes money to purchase a pump to raise the water of a river at a missionary station does a service as truly acceptable to God as the man who lays out his money sending missionaries and Bibles to the heathen."[42] The colonial governors, not the missionaries, insisted on teaching the Natives to plough.

The silence about equality Bryce noted also brought the recognition of Native custom that did not violate "general principles of humanity recognized throughout the civilized world"—but relatively very late: in the Transvaal in 1885, and in the Union in 1927 with the Native Administration Act. Measures that looked like progress then, because they testified to flexibility that had cost almost a century to learn, now look like hardbound reaction. States can never be entirely right in such matters,—and neither can they leave them alone. So it was also with the decision to use Native languages in the first years of school.

Problems of custom,—who knows whether to call them African, black, Bantu or Native,—persist, it should go without saying, in the present right now in South Africa, for customs, the unspoken languages of life, like languages, have lives of their own no matter what people or governments say or do to deny them.

At present, the *lobola* discourages women from educating their daughters, because they assume they will not work after marriage—an assumption experience begins to deny. Because married women are minors according to custom and have to get permission from their husband to travel and work,— and *ninety-nine percent of women* are married under tribal, or civil law that endorses this custom,—they cannot in theory buy property in the townships, permitted since June 1983. In fact administrators have allowed them to purchase. But as legal minors they cannot get loans.

Legislation in Parliament meant to straighten out loans, mortgage and property rights of women carries a provision that seeks to mediate between the old and the new: "A woman who enters into a customary union becomes subject to customary law with regard to her status and her capacity to engage in, for example, lease-hold transactions, and might be affected by her being subject to customary law."[43] The law's apparent equivocation annoys South African middle-class black women who blithely ignore the explosive confusion that abrupt changes, and the exploitation of vulnerability, especially in relations between men and women, can bring. More superficial similar changes have shaken the United States and a good deal of the West close to its core.

At the core of differences in the nineteenth century was polygamy, and on polygamy the missionaries would not yield somewhat to the bafflement of aristocratic Bryce who knew the importance of religion for building character but also the Old Testament: "A visitor from Europe is at first surprised to find how seriously [the missionaries] regard [polygamy] and asks whether the example of the worthies of the Old Testament does not make it hard for them to refuse baptism to the Native who seeks it, though he has more than one wife." Bryce went on to add, hastily in the afterthought of a footnote: "After listening to [the missionaries'] argument, I did not venture to doubt they were right."[44]

About polygamy nowadays, it is hard to get information, except that it persists. In New York, I was told "We too practice polygamy," when I tried to bring up these matters and others: the serious violence between the Pondos and the Zulus in 1985, the accounts that occasionally appear of murder of witches in townships in the Johannesburg *Star*. I think the men I was talking to, some of them prominent journalists and professors, meant the endless catalogues of adulteries in novels and so on. They did not distinguish between infidelity and polygamy. Alas, they did not have the class to mention Abraham—in New York!

Besides their exiguous numbers and their inner strength, the plain distaste of the Boers for the blacks impressed Bryce, especially because they treated them, as far as he could tell, fairly. "Deep and widespread as is the sentiment of aversion to the Colored people which I am describing, it must not be supposed that the latter are generally ill-treated. There is indeed a complete social separation. Intermarriage, though permitted by law in the British Colonies, is extremely rare, and illicit unions are uncommon. Sometimes the usual relations of employer and employed are reversed, and a white man enters the service of a prosperous Kaffir. This makes no difference as respects their social intercourse . . . But apart from this social disparagement, the Native does not suffer much actual wrong . . . there are no lynchings, as in America, and the white judges and magistrates, if not always the juries, administer the law with impartiality."[45]

The "social disparagement" that unsettled Bryce had hit John Philip to the quick, two generations earlier. Philip understood that the superiority of a civilization's achievements did not justify the arrogance of individuals who often did not understand the achievements that benefited them. Without saying it outright, he meant the whole, the body politic, was different in kind from the sum of its parts, in part because it allowed the best individuals to count for more than they would in a crowd, practically a definition of civil government. "The Caffres," he wrote in 1830, "acknowledge the white man's superiority in science and the arts, but do not individually feel inferior to those they meet; though they despise the contempt of the colonists, yet it rankles in their minds and *degrades them in their own estimation.*[46]

However real and ugly the contempt, the sense of inferiority may also have been real. Steve Biko in testimony before a South African court in 1976 also spoke powerfully of the sense of inferiority that overcame black students face to face with Western culture in the universities, in front of words and thoughts they could not entirely grasp. He did not, however, blame humiliation entirely on white contempt, a measure both of the increase in confidence of blacks and whites in South Africa, and of Biko's greatness.

The contempt, aversion is probably the better word, that hit both Bryce and Philip, two generations apart, did not represent the mere psychological indulgence we call "race prejudice." In some sense rational, it was the other side of the toughness that kept order in an extraordinary situation. Authority had to overcome numbers and their implicit force, the task of all governments, but extreme in South Africa. The Boers shocked Bryce, but they held his respect, and surprised him.

The most important change in South Africa since Bryce's visit in 1895, before the recent reforms, has been the conversion of most of the Africans to Christianity. Bryce foresaw this conversion despite the few converts of his day, especially "among the wild or tribal Kaffirs," the Africans on the reserves or lost in the fastness of the country: "Notwithstanding the slowness of the progress [of the Gospel] hitherto made, the extinction of heathenism in South Africa may be deemed certain, and certain at not a distant date."[47] Bryce took conversion only for the end of heathenism, he did not know what would take its place, what would become of Christian Africans.

Seventy-seven percent of South Africans are nominally Christian according to a study in 1985,—in contrast to the 1911 census' estimates of 26 percent Christians among Africans (with a stunning 48.5 percent in the Orange Free State); Christians among Coloreds and Asiatics already numbered 68 percent in 1911.

Merriman may have meant these conversions and the future, nobody could tell, they might bring as well as the "inevitable and creditable" economic rise of the Native in a stunning sentence he wrote Smuts in 1906. "It is the large, silent movement of the foundation of society that really matters, and it is in that quarter that the danger lies."[48]

The National Government that the Anglican priest, Trevor Huddleston, described in 1955 as "more indignant in public over any challenge on [its claims to be a Christian state] than previous governments" never enforced segregation of worship.[49] In 1957, Hendrik Verwoerd, then minister of Native Education, tried to end "mixed" worship but, taken aback at resistance from worshippers, he retreated, the only time he ever retreated. Later Parliament passed a law against "mixed worship" the government never enforced.[50]

4 The Ambiguity of British Policy

The vacillation of the British, the changes of policy following upon the fall of governments, continued after the Great Trek they had provoked, but on a grander scale. The British neither annexed the territory beyond the Orange and Vaal rivers the Boers occupied nor renounced control. In 1880 they granted independence to the South African Republic (the Transvaal), after annexing it in 1878. But they insisted on the vague concept of suzerainty instead of sovereignty. Suzerainty meant control of all foreign affairs, of treaties with all other states and tribes, except the Orange Free State.

These provisions left the republics to rule themselves, but not to deal with others. This past of isolation made Smuts and Louis Botha urgent in their pursuit of unification after the Anglo-Boer War: They feared the two Boer republics otherwise might continue to isolate themselves, not, today's contrast, that the world might isolate them.

The Boer republics did not learn rebellion and defiance, except for the revolt of the South African Republic in 1880, from British vacillation. They only sought to look after themselves, they had learned nobody else would take care of them. This self-reliance knew indignation and bafflement, the διαβολή Athens first named, that swept even then over the two republics, and later the South African government. A small outnumbered people's quiet assumption of responsibility for itself strikes the world, and some of its leaders, more to the quick than the inverted dependence of servile rebellion.

Even in the daring last minute negotiations before the Anglo-Boer War that Smuts undertook on his own, apparently without the knowledge of the president of the South African Republic, Paul Kruger, the South African Republic showed flexibility. It acquiesced to Milner's original demand of more or less immediate enfranchisement of the immigrants to the Transvaal after the discovery of gold in 1886 in exchange for Britain's tacit renunciation of suzerainty—despite the startled Cape Prime Minister Merriman's opposition.

This self-reliance cost the two Boer republics, and all South Africans after 1910, contempt and disasters. But they have survived, increased and prospered because they could tell self-reliance from rebellion.

Britain saved the Boers of the South African Republic from the consequences of their only important rebellion in 1880. It acquiesced to Boers' defiance that its defeat of the Zulus in 1878 unwittingly facilitated. British readiness to grant limited independence divided opinion in England. Three years before, barely anybody had noticed the annexation of a territory almost as big as the United Kingdom.

Fifteen years later, almost on the eve of the Anglo-Boer War, Bryce still had to defend British acquiescence to rebellion. He blamed the war on the ineptness of the British administrator of the newly-annexed territory. Boer character had gotten to him. He had been incapable "of making allowances for the homely manners of the Boers and of adapting himself to the social equality which prevailed among them," a tactful description of men who did not stand on ceremonies or mince words, straightforwardness an officer might take for defiance.[51] Bryce argued that acquiescence "seemed a light evil in comparison" with war with the Afrikaners who had gone off on the Great Trek that might provoke a civil war among the Afrikaners who had remained behind in the Cape Colony. Bryce's description of the past disaster that British acquiescence had prevented reads like a picture of the war about to come. He did not sense its imminence:

Among the Africander Dutch of the Cape Colony and Natal the feeling for the Transvaal might probably light up a civil war through the two Colonies. The power of Great Britain would of course have prevailed, even against the whole Dutch-speaking population of South Africa; but it would have prevailed only after much bloodshed, and at the cost of an intense embitterment of feeling, which would have destroyed the prospects of peace and welfare of the two Colonies for many years to come. The loss of the Transvaal seemed a slight evil in comparison.[52]

The war that broke out a few years after these words did divide, not only British and Afrikaners, but Afrikaners against themselves, in a conflict that British might from outside South Africa could end but not settle—as Bryce had foreseen: "You know as well as I that thousands of burghers of the late Republics [the two Boer republics beyond the Orange River] fought along with you just as thousands of Colonials [from the two British self-governing colonies] joined us. The Cape rebels are at least no worse than the National Scouts [Boers who had left the republics to fight on the side of the British]," Smuts wrote the Cape attorney general soon after peace in 1902.[53] *La guerra non si leva si differisce a vantaggio di altri.*

Contrasts between commanders and missionaries in the field and London also prompted British vacillation, not only the fall of governments in London. The commanders in the field wanted a firm policy only the Empire then could pursue,—and that the South African government would pursue after unification. Instead of Boer ways of dealing with the Natives and living among them, they wanted to face the Natives with a clear choice of labor on farms or life on the reserves, as the Cape governor Harry Smith wrote the secretary of state Earl Grey in London in 1849. They thought that the Boer way of going in among the Natives and dealing with them on a day-to-day basis in accepted danger, meant continual instability, and worse, sudden eruptions that might threaten the two British colonies.

The readiness of the Boers to live among the Natives made British sovereignty necessary: "They [the Bantu] understood that *intermixed* as the Boers were with them, it had been found impracticable to operate a perfect separation, whence flowed the necessity of bringing black and white under the general protection and supervision of His Majesty," wrote a missionary, an intimate advisor of the great Basuto chief, Moshesh, to John Philip in 1849 to explain the British governor's imminent annexation of territory beyond the Orange River. But London would not have the annexation.[54] Four years later, 1854, it recognized the Orange Free State under British suzerainty.

Earl Grey feared for "the destruction of the less civilized races." The governor responsible for the annexation warned him that London's rescindment "would be regarded by every man of colour as an unprecedented and unlooked for victory to his race, and be the signal for revolt and continued resistance to British authority." But Grey decided in 1852 only to hold the Cape for strategic reasons, the minimal policy. He was not about to renew the "failed . . . attempt" to civilize the Natives:

. . . Apart from the very limited extent of the territory required for the security of the Cape of Good Hope as a naval station, the British Crown and nation have no interest whatsoever in maintaining any territorial dominion.[55]

It took two generations, and the Anglo-Boer War, to bring the strong central state capable of swift decisive action that British commanders in the field and missionaries thought the Great Trek's intermixture of Europeans among vast numbers of Africans required. Both the British and the South Africans recognized there was no ready way to turn the Bantu into citizens within the space of several generations,—acknowledgment of realities that strikes some contemporary writers as merely the misapprehension of narrow men who did not enjoy the largeness of our views.

5 The Conflict in Character Between Boers and British

Before the Anglo-Boer War, Bryce sensed deeply the force of the contrast between the Boers and the English, the capacity of the Boers to make the English feel their own weaknesses that was to drive Milner to set England to war. "Firmness of character," which also explained the readiness to take off beyond the frontiers more or less alone, "has given [the Boers] a power disproportionate to their numbers," Bryce wrote.[56] They made him feel the costs of the industrial revolution to England, its grinding up of character and the past, of the taste and intimacy of life. The South Africans, he wrote, "are exempt from some of the dangers which threaten the industrial communities of Europe and North America."

In contrast to Bryce's description of Boer character as something actual he had experienced in his own eyes, Milner's was programmatic, "satanic" Smuts called it. Boer character made Milner fear the disintegration of the "British race," a preoccupation with disintegration common throughout Europe at the time: "The racial bond . . . deeper, stronger, more primordial than material ties is the tie of common blood, a common language, common history and traditions."[57]

Something of this inner strength of character and matter-of-fact courage came to Bryce in individual encounters that visibly unnerved him, for instance, with Paul Kruger, the president of the South African Republic. One of the last survivors of the Great Trek, Kruger had "followed his father's cattle across the prairie," then a boy of ten:

He is one of the most interesting figures of our time; this old President, shrewd, cool, dogged, wary, courageous; typifying the qualities of his people, and strong because he is in sympathy with them; adding to his trust in Providence no small measure of worldly craft; uneducated, but able to fool the statesmen of Europe at their own weapons, and perhaps all the more capable because his training has been wholly that of an eventful life and not that of books.[58]

Bryce also felt this unassuming dignity in ordinary encounters:

The general equality of conditions has produced a freedom from assumption on the one hand, and from servility on the other, and, indeed, a general absence of snobbishness, which is quite refreshing to the European visitor. Manners are simple, and being simple, they are good. If there is less polish than in some countries, there is an unaffected heartiness and kindliness. The Dutch have a sense of personal dignity which respects the dignity of their fellows, and which expresses itself in direct and natural forms of address. An experienced observer dilated to me on the high level of decorum maintained in the Cape Parliament, where scenes of disorder are, I believe, unknown, and violent language is rare."[59]

The forging of a new language, the child of Dutch but unlike Dutch "almost incapable of abstract thought or [of] being a vehicle for any *ideas beyond those of daily life*" because of its adoption of many "Kaffir or Hottentot words," also came to Bryce as another expression of Boer character and its rootedness in the land. He saw that the Boers knew their country and lived in it in a way he could no longer imagine in England,—something that worked outright jealousy in Milner.

This language held its ground against English to the bafflement of "an Englishman or American who knows how rapidly his language has become the language of commerce over the world" because it fitted the country and came from the country. Biko was to say much the same of Afrikaans in court in 1976, almost three generations later. Buthelezi at about the same time called it an "indigenous" language. The concreteness of the language told of life in Africa: "They are people who live in the concrete," Bryce remarked.

This concreteness, with its matter-of-factness, made Bryce feel that the "baggage of metaphysical and abstract terms," empiricism's armory, which the British carried about as a matter of course, encumbered their perception of events. "This [unwillingness to express abstract thought] might give English a great advantage if the Boers wished to express abstract ideas. But they have no such wish, for they have no abstract ideas to express."[60]

He meant that Afrikaners called England's empirical bluff, for the Boers were empirical without a philosophy of empiricism. They did not have to tell themselves how they thought in order to think—that took his breath away.

This concrete matter-of-factness also showed itself in South African statesmen in the years before unification, and even reached the group of brilliant young British advisors who had come to administer the conquered republics after the end of the Anglo-Boer War, and quietly foster unification, the famous "kindergarten," quite a contrast with today's South Africa experts: "Duty number two [after the collection of information] would be what you described as writing a *Federalist*. Only I suggest that what we want is something which is less a disquisition on federal government in general and more a discussion of the hard concrete problems which have to be met in South Africa," one of these advisors, Lionel Curtis, wrote Smuts in 1907, after casual mention of the final goal, "National Union extending from Tanganyika to the Cape of Good Hope."[61]

The readiness to stick to actualities made it possible for South African statesmen to sense the stubbornness and coldness, the imperviousness to argument of men of the best intentions, before they had shown their paralysis before totalitarianism: "Progressivism has been tried in the balance and found wanting. See that you never give its professors a chance in your country . . ." Merriman wrote Smuts from the Cape in 1906 after remarking that the "moderates," in contrast, will "at any rate give a hearing to their opponents." And again: "It is the great fault of these doctrinaire folk that they make no allowance for the natural man who is not to be governed by formulae." And, "What an age this is for worship of shibboleths! And what devout worshippers the Liberals are of that cult!"

But the sensitivity of South Africans to world opinion already worried Merriman,—sensitivity that shows South African insistence on realities of life in Africa, like all real defiance, did not come easily: "I never recollect a Commission that came to South Africa that did no more harm than good. We are such good easy people, so ready to swallow anything that comes from outside whether it is a political nostrum or anything else," Merriman wrote Smuts again in 1906.[62]

The language like the Boer character it bespoke survived the Anglo-Boer War. At the center of everybody's foreboding, together with the extension of the qualified Cape franchise without regard to race in the years immediately after the Anglo-Boer War, "the language question" was unexpectedly quickly settled at the constitutional convention in 1908, because of the resilience of the president of the former Orange Free State,—and because of the wisdom of English public men whom the war had taught the meaning of Smuts' words in the letter published in *The Times* in 1903 under Louis Botha's signature: "Do you think the Boers will love and admire their conquerors for openly trying to Anglicize their children and for putting their language on the same footing practically as Zulu, Sesuto or any other foreign language. It sometimes seems to me that the Government has forgotten every lesson of Transvaal history."[63] Instead of the more or less forced Anglicization of Milner and the colonial governors of the nineteenth century, who had even published their decrees against emigration beyond the Orange River in English the Boers could not read, both Afrikaans and English would serve as the legal languages of the new country.

Despite his sense of the contrast between the character of the Boers and British, Bryce tried to argue that the conflict sprang from "far more than the jealousy of two races," it came of "a collision of two types of civilization, one belonging to the nineteenth century, the other to the seventeenth," not from two sides of one civilization or from one civilization facing itself:

His [the Boer's] isolation, not only in a distant corner of the southern hemisphere, but in the great wide, bare veldt over which his flocks and herds roam, has kept the Boer fast bound in ideas and habits of a past age, and he shrinks from the contact of the keen restless modern man, with the new arts of gain and new forms of pleasure, just as a Puritan farmer of Cromwell's day might shrink were he brought to life and forced to plunge into the current of modern London.[64]

Bryce meant the Boers brought him up face to face with a world uncannily familiar whose language he could instantly recognize but no longer understand or speak,—a bit like Kipling's recognition, upon his return to India after school in England, of the sounds of a language he had spoken as a child. He meant the world of Hobbes and Milton, a world that knew how to return from terrorism and repent,—in contrast to the world after the Congress of Vienna that knew restoration without repentance. He meant a world that knew certain things were irremediable, that, above all, knew the necessary compatibility of freedom with harshness and limits,—and that an outpouring of energy and life was not enough.

But Bryce knew better. He knew that war, like death, makes all times each others equal. He knew that men do not fight and die against overwhelming numbers because of their loyalty to a past time, but because they sense that the enemy who threatens their lives fights from weakness, weakness that no might or victory can dispel.

6 The Breakdown of British Vacillation: the Anglo-Boer War

Perhaps twenty percent of the Afrikaners of the two republics, most of them women and children, died in the Anglo-Boer War. The war ended with 110,000 men, women and children in camps, 31,000 Boers prisoners of war, 24,000 of them in Ceylon. About 21,000 men, women and children, about 1,200 men, 4,000 women, 16,000 children, died in the camps because of starvation and disease that had started before their imprisonment, and because of incompetent British administration.

In the two Boer republics, farms had been burnt to the ground, crops destroyed, cattle killed, to keep the Boers from living off their lands as they fought. These were the consequences of the Boers' turn to guerrilla warfare after the British had captured Bloemfontein and Pretoria in the spring of 1900 and formally annexed the two republics, barely eight months after the start of the fighting. The British commander had not anticipated the capture of the capitals would not end the war. For the first time the twentieth century knew the word refugee.

The Anglo-Boer War shook not only South Africa but the world, especially Britain. "We are still living in the aftermath of the Boer War," a former editor of an important Afrikaans newspaper, Piet Cillier, recently remarked. He meant that the continuity with the past, the memory of sufferings, made it impossible for Afrikaners to turn to simple oppression: "It is simply not true and it is not fair to say that the Afrikaner freedom fighter of eighty years ago has abandoned his principles. We're just having a devil of a time trying to figure out how to extend that freedom to others."[65]

He might have been quoting Smuts who wrote the Cape attorney general immediately after the war in 1902: "I was not fighting for 'Dutch' supremacy or predominance over English Africanders, but for a United South Africa in which there would be the greatest possible freedom, but from which the disturbing influence of Downing Street would have been finally eliminated," except that Smuts like everybody else, including the two British high commissioners for South Africa, held the undoing of conquest unfeasible.[66] Piet Cillier means what Louis Botha had said at Versailles, when he and Smuts had been against making Germany pay for the war, against a march of triumph into Berlin: "My soul has felt the harrow. I know what it means."[67]

Botha meant,—Cillier means,—that the sufferings of the Afrikaners had taught them to see both sides, to know that no one was absolutely right, the opposite of the lesson of the two world wars to much of the rest of the world. The capacity to see both sides made it possible for South African statesmen, above all, but not only Jan Smuts, to see the war had not ended, both at Versailles and after the Second World War whose consequences are now unfolding in southern Africa itself, especially among the blacks. "We shall get no peace now and Europe will know no peace hereafter. And in the coming storms these new states will be themselves the first to founder," Smuts wrote Lloyd George in 1919.[68] And after seeing Budapest, Prague and Vienna, still in 1919: "Nothing so burns up every particle of self as the sights I have passed through during the past week."[69] In September 1948, in a letter to Winston Churchill, Smuts still saw beyond words to the actual situation on the ground,—the lesson the Anglo-Boer War had taught him: ". . . The real danger before us [is] . . . the peaceful infiltration which Russia is pursuing through her fifth column in all parts of the world . . . Russia has abused our joint victory to fasten her ideology on much of Europe and to open the way to complete conquest of the West. And our present policy of continuing the German vacuum is helping her in the sinister game."[70]

The capacity for such analysis as well as the readiness of South Africans to fight and die in both world wars and the Korean War shows perhaps more than anything else that the Anglo-Boer War had turned South Africa into a European nation in Africa, not an inevitable outcome, but an outcome that tells of the responsibility and greatness of the men, British and South African, who saw to it.

"The Anglo-Boer War brought a pastoral unsophisticated, and very private people into contact with the outside world in the most bitter way." This recent sentence of John Chettle of the South Africa Foundation forgets that the Boers had struggled with that world since the French Revolution first brought the British to the Cape in 1795, a struggle that made South Africa, and will probably see to its survival—with honor. For the South Africans know how to respect and defy,—and how to admit they were wrong. Chettle's misapprehension shows how hard it is to remember one's own history, not quite the same thing as knowing it in one's own flesh.[71] For the decision to leave, the Great Trek, was never a complete break, resilience and modesty that accounts for its success, its lack of self-destructiveness, its endurance, its capacity to survive its mistakes.

The suffering in the camps shook England already in 1901 because of a report by a woman, Emily Hobhouse, that "created a situation in which C.B.'s native worth could not choose but commit itself."⁷² The Liberal leader, Campbell-Bannerman, the C.B. of the letter, called the camps, "the methods of barbarism," in the House of Commons in 1901, a phrase that stuck enough to contribute to the Liberal victory in 1906 which reversed English policy towards South Africa, renounced outright force, and made self-government the precondition of unification:

You think it is bad to be an Afrikander at this moment—believe me; its *far* worse to be an English person. Your defeat may be bad but it is material; *ours* is moral. Your country is in its youth and will overcome all difficulties—ours is, we greatly fear, undergoing decadence—at any rate for the time—if not permanently.⁷³

Emily Hobhouse wrote Smuts in 1904 these words that the man most responsible for the war, Lord Milner, came close to acknowledging when he left Johannesburg a year later. It was a world that could still suffer its mistakes, and recognize them in its suffering.

The real cause of this devastation had been Milner's decision, independently of London, that retention of British control of South Africa required crushing the Boer republics. "An imperialist out and out," he had called himself in 1904. But command was not Milner's only passion, he had more programmatic visions that made him liable to self-deception: He wanted to preserve British character. But the war showed Emily Hobhouse and a good deal of English public opinion the very disintegration of the British race Milner had wanted to prevent.

Smuts had caught all the hidden smoldering torment of this man often described as "logical and lucid to a fault."⁷⁴ "There s something in his very intelligent eyes that tells me he is a very dangerous man," Smuts had written his wife during negotiations to prevent war in 1899.⁷⁵

Smuts had grasped the wild look in Milner's eyes, he had sensed the insides in a man who struck others as without insides because he had rid himself of similar wildness without losing its energy. At Cambridge, five years before, partly through his reading of Whitman, he had rid himself of his sense of sin's hold on life, an experience he compared to St. Paul's of grace, with enough concreteness to make me believe him—and that turned him into a statesman rather than a divine.

Years of astonishing growth followed, growth that showed itself in swift changes, in resilience in decision whose abruptness some took for arbitrariness, even opportunism: A year after graduation from Cambridge with first class honors in law, he left the Cape, the world of his childhood and youth, for the Transvaal because of his disillusionment with Rhodes' betrayal of his South Africa policy. His daring break with the world of his childhood and youth as well as with England that he knew better than most Afrikaners, a private version of the Great Trek, exactly two generations after, brought him maturity, and swift acceptance among the much older leaders of the South African Republic.

In the following harsh years, Smuts' growth showed itself in yielding to events without surrendering to them, to master them: after the failure of his last minute negotiations in 1899, he devised a bold strategy, the capture of Durban in the first months of the war before the arrival of British troops from all over the world in numbers, to bring Britain to negotiate, a strategy that might have worked had the Boer generals pursued it, boldly, after their first victories. After defeat and the fall of the capitals, he played a major part in the turn to guerrilla warfare, and again in the turn to negotiations. He could distinguish between defiance and self-destruction.

Like the First and Second World War that followed it, the South African War destroyed governments. But in contrast to the European wars that would follow, it led to the formation of a stronger, more legitimate government—because, unlike the European wars it foreshadowed in its brutality, victors and defeated respected each other enough not to insist on unconditional surrender.

These men could tell the difference between tragedy and the euphoria that evades the experience of tragedy, to make settlement impossible. Milner had been clumsy in his imitation of Rhodes who, in 1895, had sought to steal the country Milner conquered. But Milner, whatever else he was, was big enough to dread the memory of the war he had largely caused: "I engaged in [the great struggle to keep this country within the limits of the British Empire] with all my might, because I was from head to foot one mass of glowing conviction of the rightness of our cause [striking language, almost of a lover]. But a frightfully destructive conflict of that kind is at best a sad business to look back on,"[76] he said in his speech in Johannesburg in 1905. On the point of leaving South Africa a few days later, he answered Smuts' letter of farewell: "I feel that I have always been able at least to understand the point of view of my opponents."

The day after his reply to Smuts' farewell, Milner showed his old harshness, shot through with realism, and undeniable flashes of greatness, in his private advice to his successor Lord Selborne: Only "years of strong patient policy" would decide South Africa's permanence in the Empire that conquest had made possible. He warned Selborne not to trust any Afrikaner leader, for they all strove with "duplicity and deceit" for "a separate Afrikander Nation and State, comprising no doubt men of other races [men of European descent, as the constitution of the Union was to put it five years later], who are ready to be 'Afrikanderized,' but essentially autochthonous, isolated and un-British."[77]

But his letter to Smuts, the day before, shows he sensed his successor would not follow him in his "Milnerism," now largely the *sfogo* of man who had come to know events bigger than his will, because he, and his government, respected their enemies. They respected them because they both had fought "for causes and principles, not for any personal gain": "And no doubt, as you say, something will ultimately be evolved out of all this, which will be different from either of the policies which have contended in the past."[78]

Unification in self-government five years later showed the truth of Milner's intuitions that his victory would bring a success that betrayed his expectations: the expectations that had precipitated the war. He had grown big enough to know that real success would always disappoint the men who sought to mastermind it. Smuts knew that, too.

7 The Way They Thought About the Africans— Merriman, Smuts and Selborne

In retrospect much has been made of the differences between the British and South Africans, between the Boers of the Cape and the Boers of the two republics, on the "Native Question" in the years after the war and before unification. The truth is more nearly the opposite. British and Boers, Cape Colony and Transvaal, Merriman and Smuts, Milner and Selborne all finally agreed that politics could only exacerbate the Natives.

Partly because of Smut's assurance, and Selborne's wisdom, Merriman's foreboding in 1904 that "the crux of any union in South Africa will be Native policy" proved empty. ". . . I fear that recent events may set up the sort of division that there used to be between the North and South in America, which indeed still operates," he had gone on in explanation.

He feared the Native question also because it might occasion interference, "the benevolent and wholly ignorant interference of England [that] does infinite harm . . . to the four millions of South Africans with black skins . . . as to us." And again: ". . . I feel that, little as we may like it [Native representation] is the only door to escape the meddlesome and ignorant philanthropy of Downing Street [a recall of the nineteenth-century missionaries' influence on London] so prompt to find out motes in their brother's eye and so very oblivious of the beam in their own." And still again later in 1906: ". . . The alternative [to the extension of the Cape qualified franchise without distinction of race or color throughout South Africa] undoubtedly is friction and interference on the part of the Imperial power which cannot abdicate its functions . . . interference . . . often, perhaps generally, ill-judged, ill-timed and ill-considered."[79]

In this astonishing exchange of letters in 1906 with Merriman, a man of the Cape like Smuts had been, who had come to South Africa from England at the age of six, Smuts readily acknowledged the dispossession of the Africans: "I sympathize profoundly with the Native races of South Africa whose land it was long before we came here to force a policy of dispossession on them."

But Smuts did not believe politics and the qualified franchise Merriman proposed, for both black and white as in the Cape, would undo the injustice: "But I don't believe in politics for them. Perhaps at bottom I do not believe in politics at all as a means for attainment of the highest ends," an admission of limitations characteristic of South African politics, of the readiness to think concretely Bryce had identified a few years before. "But certainly so far as the Natives are concerned politics will to my mind only have an unsettling influence," and in any case the franchise was unrealistic, as Merriman himself acknowledged, since it "would not affect more than a negligible number [of Natives]."[80]

Smuts was not interested in the appearance of solutions to still indignation abroad, one of Merriman's uncharacteristic reasons for arguing for the qualified franchise. Merriman had argued for partial accommodation to the spirit of the times in Europe, "[The Natives] are the workers and history tells us the future is to the workers," in the same months that he had unblushingly declared South Africa ". . . is and I hope will remain a society on an aristocratic basis."[81]

Smuts' incapacity to see a political solution did not mean resignation, only an acknowledgment of limitations, of the possible: "When I consider the political future of Natives in South Africa I must say that I look into shadows and darkness; and then I feel inclined to shift the *intolerable* burden of solving that sphinx problem to the ampler shoulders and stronger brains of the future. Sufficient unto the day etc. . . ." The last words meant to suggest, without direct mention, the sufferings of the war, too deep and alive to bear, or to need, more than suggestion. He went on to presage the changes now at work: "My feeling is that strong forces are at work which will transform the Africander attitude to the Natives . . ."

Faced with this blunt fundamental statement, Merriman left off the debonair confidence of a man like Smuts at ease in both worlds that allowed him to see through hypocrisy, at the same time that he argued partial accommodation to it, with sparks in his eyes and energy in his words,—a gaiety of confidence that might have made London feel cumbersome and awkward in its perceptions. Against Smuts' essentially Christian sense of the limits of politics, almost a recall of the *Grondwet* of 1865, against his sense of a world elsewhere that in its silence could deal with realities beyond politics, Merriman argued the supremacy of politics in words startling enough today to invite misreading as an apology for totalitarianism:

Allow me to say that for an ardent young liberal who reproved my Toryism your frank expression of disbelief in politics as 'a means for the attainment of the highest ends' does somewhat surprise me! Surely to all men 'politics' are not the means, they are themselves the highest ends; not politics which center themselves on the dreary wrangles of the ins and the outs but the politics which aim at making a small city great, and at raising the whole life and character of *every class* in the community. There can be no higher ambition nor any more worthy object. Otherwise let materialism have full swing.[82]

Merriman who earlier in his letter had written, "God forbid I should advocate the political enfranchisement of the Native barbarian" (he used "barbarian" in the classical sense of foreigner or alien with no experience of self-government under law) meant the supremacy of politics in the classical sense of Plato and above all Aristotle. But Aristotle's affirmation, his resilience, had grown of Plato's doubt. Merriman meant that political life, the life of communities under law, could alone complete man, not transform him. Smuts instead believed in the transformation of man—but not through politics.

The disagreement was plain enough to show each man the insufficiency of his thinking. It went deep enough to allow for a compromise that made way for unification and the new constitution without overturning the status quo anywhere in South Africa, perhaps the compelling reason for the agreement: The qualified franchise with no distinction of color or race would remain in the Cape without extending to the rest of South Africa.

Characteristically, Merriman, whose intelligence, charm and recall of events are so strong in his letters and speeches you can almost hear his voice, had been so taken up in the intricacies of the Cape Parliament that he came to the constitutional convention in Durban in 1908 largely unprepared. In contrast the Transvaal delegation under Smuts came formidably prepared, and fresh with the battlefields of the war upon their eyes after the train ride down from Johannesburg.

Smuts' capacity to see the limits of politics, with an assurance that did not possess Merriman, came because in the midst of action he had always lived his own life—besides politics. Even during military operations, and his hazardous incursion through the Orange River Colony and into the Cape, roughly five months with 340 men in 1901, he read and studied, the Bible, St. Augustine, Kant and books captured from the British,—not so much "an astonishing achievement," his most recent biographer's words, but the rare mark of a man who grows through books instead of devouring them in distraction.

Smuts did not live action because he wanted flight or evasion: he was not a runner. The absence of flight struck some as unearthly serenity, even resignation, even arrogance, diabolical but never mean, Paton called the Smuts he knew in the thirties, in part because he disappointed the easier expectations of his pen: "What innocence, what confidence looked out of those blue eyes!"[83]

His unpredictability, his apparent unpredictability, that struck some as close to opportunism, grew from this depth of experience. He could reach this depth in his countrymen because he was not driven.

He had an appetite, not a hunger, for life, that allowed him to see dangers and to face them, those that he sensed could be faced,—an appetite for life like Tolstoy's, but more modest, without Tolstoy's terror before disillusion. He knew a soft sense of limits that freed him also, remarkably, of guilt, and allowed him to acknowledge obvious facts guilt might make others deny.

Terrible events excited his awe, not his dread, because he knew man's place in the world. Africa taught him that, more than Europe could teach it to its sons. There was no mistaking his voice for the voice of a European statesman even when he spoke the language of European statesmen, most of all when he spoke that language. His was the voice of a European who had never come back, not the voice of a colonial who knew he could go back, nor of a colonial who had won independence only to be drawn deeper into Europe's clutches the more he thought he did without it.

I concentrate on Smuts because his greatness is easier to understand because he spoke, and wrote, in English: "The fact is that the Boers are a silent people and would rather suffer in silence than make a parade of their grievances," he had written in the letter published in *The Times* in London 1903. But his greatness also tells of the greatness of the much older men around him who trusted him with major responsibilities before he was thirty, of his and their intelligence and courage, and seriousness.

Of the death in 1904 of Paul Kruger, who had impressed Bryce, Smuts wrote: "He typified the Boer character *both in its brighter and darker aspects* and was no doubt the greatest man—both morally and intellectually—which the Boer race has so far produced" (Italics mine).[84] "The greatest, cleanest, sweetest soul of all the land—of all my days," Smuts called Louis Botha upon his death a month after the peace of Versailles.[85] You cannot tell the actions of these men without recalling their character and their capacity for doubt, the other side of their confidence. This is their and their time's uncomfortable legacy to us.

But without Selborne's good sense, his steadfastness in the face of illusions, Smuts and Merriman might never have agreed. Selborne, a bluff fairminded man, who could distinguish between policy and public opinion; who deserves the immortality, in contrast to Milner, he did not seek; who lent authority something of innocence, the innocence that now embarrasses us almost to the core because we cannot distinguish it from gullibility; who could say of the famous qualified Cape franchise with its writing requirement that the African "might just as profitably be taught to write his name and address in hieroglyphics" for all it proved of the difference between "a civilized, as opposed to a barbarous Native;" who knew in his way the eloquence of silence the Boers had taught Bryce, and even in the end Milner; and who, therefore, also knew how to speak when it counted, and say, in a passage that means more now than at its writing that he would speak of England, ". . . as that is my own country, and therefore that one I know best, and as that in which parliamentary institutions had their first birth,"—Selborne disappointed Merriman's forebodings.

Selborne agreed with both Merriman and Smuts to deny them both—the best definition, I can think of, of aristocratic confidence. Selborne wanted the Native policy out of politics entirely: "It is suggested on one side that the Colored people and Natives have the same right to the franchise under the same conditions as white people, that is, that if, in the Cape Colony, for instance, they can fulfill the same conditions as to education and ownership of property as the white people, they should have the same votes, or in the Transvaal, that, if they are of full age, they should have the same vote."

Both propositions were "absurd." The requirements of the Cape, possession of property worth seventy-five pounds and the capacity to write name and address, amounted to no proof of civilization. As for the Transvaal "nobody who has been a week in the country could possibly honestly say that every Native of full age was entitled to, or competent to receive, the vote," Selborne wrote in extraordinary notes he sent to Smuts and Botha eight months before the convention of 1908. He did not intend to press for the extension of the qualified franchise while in attendance, with the colonial governors, in Durban, but not a direct participant.[86]

Selborne was not about to take either the accomplishments or the qualities of Europe for granted. Gradual change counted: ". . . The progress of the mass of people towards civilization . . . quite unmistakable . . . no doubt is slow, but it is all the surer because it is slow." To think in terms of a political solution amounted to a flight from responsibility. The Natives wanted strong chiefs.

The Natives wanted consistency and bite in rule. The continual changes in European government bewildered them. "The complete absence of the two principles of government which the Native most thoroughly understands, that is that government should be personal and that it should be consistent and continuous," characterized European institutions, "the embodiment of impersonality." The bitterness of a Zulu who had told the Natal Native Affairs Commission, he preferred the cruelty of chief Shaka, who had organized the Zulus militarily, "to the days of parliamentary government" had struck Selborne to the quick. In contrast to the abrupt changes in British policy that looked like vacillation, consistency marked Boer conduct enough to make Merriman's remark that "a 'poor white' . . . can manage Native labour in a way that no English miner will ever be able to do," the common opinion of the time.

Selborne did not flinch the consequences, so evident today, of the assumption of responsibility for the Native, of "trusteeship," as Merriman also called it. The Natives had blamed the chiefs, they blamed the whites for all their troubles, readiness to blame that showed they already accepted the "Government as trustee for the Natives in special degree": ". . . Every evil under which they suffer is put down by the Natives to the Government . . . in three cases out of four, the evil has not been caused by the actions of the Government; yet it is always put down to the Government, just exactly as the Natives, in the old days, would have attributed every good or evil to their Chief."

Assumption of responsibility meant that the government "cannot afford to exclude from its purview any detail of Native life" including the measures of town governments: "It must try and look at every little thing from the Native point of view as well as from the white point of view, and it should use the whole of its authority to prevent the Natives being irritated by what I may call a policy of pin-pricks." Selborne foresaw the dangers of his recommendations that sought to allow change and at the same time recognize realities. South African government policy after 1948 paid attention to the "Native point of view,"—at the expense of more than "pin-pricks," especially for the Africans who lived between two worlds with homes in neither.

For Selborne the "average level of the civilization" counted. He distinguished sharply between the Coloreds, the people of mixed white and indigenous ancestry born in the Cape (long before extensive contacts with the Bantu) and the Natives. This judgment, his most important, shows realities moved him more than prejudice.

He was fierce against "the sheer folly of [classifying the Coloreds] with Natives." The identification of Coloreds, customary and somewhat arbitrary, depended merely on skin color that came in all hues. There were many Coloreds "who have reached the level of civilization of the white man"—in contrast to the "few Natives." Also, "reversion from civilization is much commoner with [the Natives]": "There are many Colored people who are quite white inside, though they may be colored outside, there are some indeed, who are quite white outside also."

For the few Natives in the "locations" near the towns, "a class necessary to the convenience of the white settlers," Selborne insisted on "fixity of tenure" with "full power to eject any objectionable character . . . with sufficient reason." For the Native agricultural workers, he argued against elaborate pass systems, for the "free circulation of labor."

He was fierce also against any restrictions to protect the whites from the competition of Native labor. They meant slavery different only in degree "no doubt from what we generally regard as slavery": "Any artificial impediments in the way of development of such character and such capacity as Providence has given to the black man . . . is, let us not deceive ourselves, . . . simply slavery."

Selborne went *sans ambages* to the core of whites' fears that the numbers of Natives might obliterate their identity. These fears intensified in war and defeat's humiliation also testified to the progress of the Africans, to the beginnings of prejudice in the contemporary sense that obscured realities: "The great danger to the white man in this country is lest he should lose those characteristics which have made him what he is by being pampered and coddled and insured against competition in the struggle for life, and by being allowed always to regard the black man as the hewer of wood and the drawer of water . . ." He added in reassurance: "The black man is absolutely incapable of rivalling the white man. If the white man is ever out-rivalled by the black man, it will be entirely the fault of the white man."

To apply Adam Smith to grotesquely rudimentary conditions Smith had never even imagined, Selborne sensed he had to go deeper than Smith. Restrictions on black labor betrayed the whites' fear that they were no better than the blacks. This fear was the other side of the contempt Philip had noticed. More profoundly still, Selborne sensed the whites feared to experience their actual superiority, the oscillation at the core of Christianity that knows confidence only lives in the face of deeper doubt.

Selborne also argued strongly for the other side of British policy for more than two generations, the reserves, that he noted were unpopular with the whites of the Transvaal. "A safety valve, an insurance of orderly progress," he called them, that "sort out automatically the less from the more progressive part of the Native population." In 1903 Louis Botha, at the same time that he wrote of "the black population with its insoluble problems," had criticized postwar British government for its plans for new reserves, the nucleus of the later homelands, "breeding places for all those evils which exist in Basutoland and Zululand [and Swaziland]" instead of "gradually [fostering] the desire for work and the increase in economic value of the Natives."[87] In 1908 in contrast, Selborne mentioned Basutoland as an example of progress he had seen.

At the heart of these notes that summed up, for the future, distinctions a century of wars and policy had produced in a situation always in movement was Selborne's sense of the intangibility of civilization. Economic progress, property or technical achievements like writing, even education and extraordinary individuals, very rare and liable to appear anywhere, did not define civilization. In the face of ". . . vast and unknown forces, such as the evolution of millions of human beings from barbarism to civilization," Selborne knew he could only draw direction from the past,—the slowness of meaningful change, its main lesson:

Now, parliamentary institutions in England are 550 years old, and yet the great bulk of the population, white working men, have not yet had a vote for 50 years! If, in the case of a country which came into contact with Roman civilization nearly 2,000 years ago, and which has actually had parliamentary institutions for 550 years, the great bulk of the population has only been considered fit for the exercise of the franchise for less than 50 years, how absolutely absurd it is to suppose that the Natives of South Africa, the great majority of whom have not been in contact with any civilization for 100 years, should be fit to exercise the franchise on the same basis as the white man of the country, by extraction either British, or Dutch, or French, all three nations whose first contact with civilization dates back to Roman times before the Christian era! No, if the Natives of South Africa are to receive the franchise at all, they must be led up to it in exactly the same gradual way in which the white men were, and, in my opinion, no system can be wisely devised which will apply equally and similarly to Natives as to white men.

Such plain words these days make everybody, including myself, uncomfortable. But they are not very different from the recent conclusions of an open-minded journalist after covering Africa in the fifteen crucial years after "independence":

. . . The concept of loyal opposition, presupposing some basic national consensus usually absent in Africa, is considered by most ordinary Africans to be crazy; neither that consensus nor any form of liberal individualist tradition exists. People's attitudes are fiercely determined by ties of family and clan. At its gentlest, politics means that a nascent opposition will be absorbed by traditional African palaver into the single party; if not, it is silenced, perhaps violently. The secret ballot thus becomes unnecessary. When, last year, I discussed with a group of Zimbabwean secondary school teachers the danger that people who hold minority views would be afraid to vote, the teachers proved to be unanimously hostile to the secret ballot, for the simple reason that it is "un-African."[88]

Botswana is about the only country in southern Africa that allows a little opposition because of its special circumstances: no deep tribal differences; the stability that nearness to South Africa provides; and because its first president, a hereditary chief knew,—like Kamuzu Banda of Malawi,—the difference between defiance and revolution, independence and the transformation of man.

In South Africa none of the homelands, with their legislatures made up of appointed chiefs as well as elected representatives, has an opposition. Even

Buthelezi does not tolerate opposition in KwaZulu. Not because he does not love freedom, his every word shows the contrary, but because he knows you do not grow away from centuries of strong personal authority by ignoring them. At best decisions are taken by consent, and sometimes harshly. The personal authority, short and straight, Selborne recognized, shows through the dress of parliamentary forms, Selborne's "embodiment of impersonality." The president of Bophuthatswana, Chief Lucas Mangope, an able man who knows stability requires swift words and action, recently told students at the homeland's university to go to South Africa to demonstrate. Their university was for study.

For Selborne the only test of civilization that really counted was its transmission over at least three generations in ordinary people. For civilization showed its depth not in the apparent conduct of one individual but in the capacity of parents to hand it down to their children,—just the bond the terrorists and their attendant front organizations try to break, reverse or confound in the townships today in South Africa. For three generations the franchise granted to few individual Natives, on grounds Selborne sketched vaguely, should not descend by inheritance—with polygamy a crucial criterion. Bryce too, a few years before, in words I barely dare quote, had also feared reversion.

It is in this instability of his will, and his proneness to yield to drink, or some other temptation, rather than in his intellect, that the weakness of the savage lies. And a man with hundreds of generations of savagery behind him is still, and must be in many respects a savage, even though he reads and writes, and wears European clothes, and possibly even a white neck tie.[89]

These words appear outrageous today because the risk now is not the relatively innocent reversion to savagery of individuals Bryce identified. The cruelty that counts today, which does not even know itself as cruelty, and that is the alternative to gradual reform for all of South Africa, comes also from us, from totalitarianism's parody of free institutions. This parody has been skillfully adapted to South Africa in the so-called Freedom Charter, with its ambiguous recall of the remnants of tribal traditions like communal ownership of the land, the programmatic document of the ANC and most of the other terrorist and front organizations that reject reform.

The cruelty in some of the townships in South Africa amounts to a reversion to savagery that, however, serves Western political purposes: the institutions of rudimentary totalitarianism *through terror*, complete with "people's courts" and "street committees." In its bare-faced cruelty, the "necklace" recalls the cruelty of tribal wars. But it also has unmistakable Western totalitarian features: The victim is sometimes made to light the tire that will burn and choke him to death. This murder shows the vulnerability, the docility of blacks to Western manipulation. In the West, there were outcries in 1985 because the South African police helped the blacks to resist, the so-called "vigilantes"!

Our governments and media, have been so ambivalent and weak in the face of this cruelty, because they sense it is as much our child as Africa's. I say the West, not the other Europe, because in Africa, especially southern Africa, the West's unwitting abetment of totalitarianism makes it barely distinguishable from its enemies: "White Europeans and Americans decide what is a 'Third-World viewpoint' . . . They want to use Third World people to export their own kind of revolution. I admit this infuriates me . . . I sometimes wonder if they're interested in South Africa or in the blacks of South Africa. They speak so casually about the need for people to die. Maybe they are caught up in some grander designs,"—Buthelezi's recent description of this complicity.[90]

The West's complicity with totalitarianism goes deep. It comes of a sense that the West's wars, especially the World Wars, the Korean War, and more recently the war for Indochina, make it no better than its enemies because nothing could justify such violence. But the test of civilization has never been anything else than the capacity to face itself, to distinguish its own faults from the outrages of others, and to fight limited wars to prevent them.

In their specific African version the fallacies at the core of this complicity now make up a fog of opinion, and inform State Department policy in South Africa. They first began to show themselves about twenty years ago in books that wore academic dress but with as little relation to inquiry as astrology to astronomy. For instance, one widespread book in 1969, an American academic equivalent to the South African Freedom Charter stated:

If we look back behind the horizon of civilization, we find a condition of life among our Neolithic and Paleolithic ancestors which, while materially impoverished in comparison to the absurd affluence of middle-class America, was nevertheless plentiful enough to support the vital needs of tribes and villages, and to allow a good deal of time for communal culture. It is not at all clear . . . that these simple folk spent their lives drudging away under the whiplash of near starvation. In fact, we have reason to believe that many of them (especially during the Neolithic period) lived a decently comfortable life in wise symbiotic relationship with their environment. Most important, the evidence is that they lived mainly in egalitarian communities where domination . . . did not take its toll . . . Repressive class-based regimentation—the social form we call 'civilization'—only *follows* upon the destruction of primitive tribal and village democracy.[91]

This scribbler,—and good speller, for he knows how to spell decadence without understanding it,—wants his ancestors anonymous, because he senses he cannot call Adams or Hamilton on a first name basis,—let alone Abraham. For the past can tell the difference between intimacy and familiarity that comes of the dread of intimacy. Selborne instead remembered his own ancestors by name, because he still lived in a world that did not have to argue the importance of the Romans' prohibition of human sacrifice among primitive peoples, not the case today.

8 South Africa on Its Own

Unification meant the end of wars within South Africa, of the tribal wars, and war between the British Empire and the Boers—with the Cape in-between. In fact future war was not much on anybody's mind at the constitutional convention—except for the reminder of the Imperial Government's cruiser squadron in the harbor of Durban. Those ships that meant to show South Africa's dependence on Britain for defense actually turned out to presage Britain's on South Africa. From then on South Africa would fight for Britain and for Europe, even in Korea. Now the European war threatens its own territory directly.

Unification made one government responsible for Native policy, for a situation that a century of wars, of the individual initiatives of Boers and missionaries—and the *furor* of the tribes—had created. Assumption of responsibility slowly blurred the distinction between administration and politics Selborne had insisted upon. Because crucial matters, like the first important legislation of the new country, the Natives Land Act of 1913, had to be decided in Parliament in public, they turned into political matters that Africans also discussed. They were political matters about which there was fundamental agreement, especially among whites, until perhaps the 1987 election showed differences, mainly of pace, that should not be exaggerated.

The Natives Land Act of 1913, supported by missionaries and Africans, meant to keep the Natives from losing their lands to white purchase, the original purpose of the British reserve policy. Once freed of British direction, the new government adopted the policy of the reserves, the later homelands, the British had urged on the South African Republic (the Transvaal) after they relinquished annexation in 1880.

The Act also extended the prohibition that had existed in the Boer Republics against Native purchase or rent of land to all of South Africa, provisions that the Courts later ruled could not be applied in the Cape because of the "entrenchment" of the Cape franchise in the constitution. The prohibitions of purchase of land outside the reserves discouraged Native ownership of land, for the law's permission of purchase of land within the reserves conflicted with Native traditions of communal ownership of land under the chief. In some sense the prohibition of land ownership was not a prohibition, but a continuation of the alien status of the conquered Africans, whom the British also had held could not legally own land unless naturalized by the Crown.[92]

The Act also provided for the eviction of squatters from European-owned lands that during the Anglo-Boer War had so frightened the Boers and moved Louis Botha in 1903 to argue for ". . . a large influx of white labouring population": "The still precarious position of the white race in South Africa *in the midst of such numbers of prolific Native races* [not simply "blacks"] will be greatly strengthened thereby; and the prospect of making this country really great and winning for it an honourable place among the nations of the world will be greatly improved"[93] (Italics mine).

The eviction of squatters without ninety-day contracts of labor for a year made for uncertainty in Native life. It drove many Natives back to the reserves where only about half of them had anything approaching a home, according to a government study of 1916.

Evictions had their most immediate effect on the Transvaal, with about forty percent of the Africans, proverbially, the province of squatters and wanderers. Of the roughly 1,400,000 Natives in the Transvaal in 1916: about 230,000 squatters lived on the unoccupied European farms; 390,000 as laborers and "labor-tenants"; 270,000 in the mines, mostly from outside South Africa; about 500,000 on the newly "scheduled areas," the reserves, areas often accessible only through difficult bush track.

In the center of the Transvaal, south of the core of industrial South Africa today, from Bloemhof in the west to Ermelo in the east, a distance of three hundred miles, the dispersion of Africans left barely thirty-five square miles Native enough for "scheduling." "In 1927 [in Natal] I found one sugar-belt magistrate tearing his hair to make provision for a 'good little *tribe*' whose huts had been reduced by eviction from European farms from more than one hundred to barely ten,"—an incident Macmillan witnessed in 1927 that betrays the uncertainty of Native life.[94]

The reserves amounted to about seven percent of the land of South Africa; in Natal and Zululand that Natal had annexed in 1896, to somewhere between a third and a quarter. By 1936, after the Native Trust and Land Bill planned the purchase of fifteen million acres in addition to the already scheduled twenty-two million, the reserves amounted to thirteen percent of all South Africa's land, some of it, in the Transkei and Natal, the most fertile in the country. This figure of thirteen percent is now often quoted in derision, and out of historical context. For in the territory considered South Africa before Union, that included Bechuanaland (now Botswana), Basutoland (now Lesotho) and Swaziland, territories whose eventual incorporation in the Union the British and everybody else assumed, once the new government showed it respected reserves, the reserve territory would have amounted to about forty-six percent of all of South Africa.

Besides protecting African land, the legislation reinforced regulation of Africans outside the reserves, later called "white areas," that Selborne had argued against, and segregation, which the African National Congress accepted, fair segregation: "We make no protest against the principle of segregation insofar as it can be fairly and practically carried out," John Dube, the president of the ANC, wrote Louis Botha in 1914, an often-quoted statement.

Subsequent legislation reinforced and at the same time went against some of Selborne's recommendations. The Urban Areas Bill of 1923 turned into law conditions Selborne had taken for granted, African residence in "locations," separately administered and financed outside of the towns, conceived of as European creations with some justification, for political liberty is inextricably connected with towns. It defined African presence purely economically, to minister to European needs, almost Selborne's words—with hints at insecurity of tenure against Selborne's recommendations.

There were also moves to limit the employment of Africans, to "reserve," the later word, certain occupations for whites, against one of Selborne's strongest recommendations. For Selborne had realized that legal restrictions on economic competition excited racial prejudice, "slavery" he had called it. They were indefensible because they openly meant to impede progress. They betrayed white fears that ought not to be indulged.

In 1922 the tightening of qualifications for apprenticeships limited them to Europeans; in 1924 the Industrial Conciliation Act limited labor arbitration to Europeans. In 1926 Color Bar Legislation, twice rejected in the Senate, finally passed in joint session of Parliament that undid the Senate's veto. It was strongly opposed by Smuts because it would provoke African hostility, and by some important divines, including the Archbishop of Cape Town, for moral reasons. It excluded Africans from certain occupations. In part in reaction to demands by agitators in India for demands for equal political rights for Indians and Europeans in East and South Africa, a way to embarrass the British government of India without risk, Smuts introduced legislation in 1924 to segregate Indians in towns, not passed before his government lost office. This bill was significant because it first showed the government's readiness to treat other peoples like the Africans. Selborne had foreboded such rashness.

The year 1936 brought crucial constitutional changes, first elaborated ten years before in 1926 after Smuts lost office, but passed only after the National Party had fused with Smuts' party to form the United Party in 1933. The new law first introduced the concept of group representation, now often called "power sharing," a term the Progressive Federal Party (PFP) introduced in the late sixties, that is at the core of the 1984 constitution. At first meant to abolish the qualified Cape franchise for all men regardless of race, already implicitly undermined by the introduction of the unqualified franchise for women in 1933 throughout the Union, the law passed in compromise form. It listed the Cape enfranchised Natives on a separate electoral roll, for the election of three white representatives of natives to the House of Assembly, in addition to four white representatives elected in four constituencies throughout the nation.

Only eleven men voted against the bill, among them Smuts' most able minister, Jan Hofmeyr, opposition that "very much disturbed" Smuts, Hofmeyr wrote a friend in those days. Hofmeyr opposed the law on constitutional grounds, because it meant to take away "a vested right which has been in existence and which has not been abused for more than eighty years." These words were not an entirely correct recall of the past, for the Cape had passed the unqualified franchise in 1853 before the presence of Bantu in the Cape in number.[95]

In any case time had proved Smuts right in his intuition, in the exchange of letters with Merriman in 1906, that the Cape franchise would prove of negligible importance. From 1903 to 1927 the Africans on the Cape common-roll had risen from 8,117 to 14,912, from seven to nine percent of the total, to drop to 11,000 in 1936. Against the extension of the qualified franchise to the whole country, Hofmeyr had also argued in committee for its restriction to ten percent of the electorate.

Hofmeyr proved right in his prediction that the bill despite its entrenchment in the constitution would not last. For the exclusion of Natives from the common-roll in the Cape was followed by the repeal of the Representation of Natives Bill in 1960. In 1956 the Coloreds too were put on a separate roll to elect four white members to represent them, representation later abolished to exclude them also entirely from Parliament until the reforms of 1983.

In arguing for the passage of the bill in 1936 the Afrikaner prime minister had said, in Paton's characterization, that the South Africans fear most "the intermingling of blood and black domination," unabashed words as usual that reflected actual realities, not fantasies: "Rather withdrawal from South Africa, rather death and racial extinction than [assimilation]" a leading liberal, R.F.A. Hoernlé described the attitude in his country three years later.[96] Today South Africans still fear black domination but not the intermingling of blood, and more importantly the government no longer looks for final settlement.

The debate and the passage of the law in 1936 had a huge effect in South Africa: Hofmeyr received many messages of support and congratulations for a symbolic, he recognized, opposition. He knew very well he had no other constitutional alternative except the status quo.

But the government, the South Africans, both British and Afrikaners, mistook their decision for a repudiation of British liberal policy. They forgot that the qualified franchise had been the work of the Cape, not of London's imposition. They took their repudiation of the franchise for defiance of the British—in part because they were defying their own consciences, defiance beyond politics' coping. They were saying without really knowing it, as developments in the next two generations with all their contradictions were to show, that the qualified franchise and education were not enough to test civilization. It was Selborne's wisdom without his elegance. But it also went beyond Selborne. "Group Representation" that at first simply took the Africans off the common-roll with Europeans turned out in the years to mean that *the Africans and other peoples had to rule themselves, before they could be trusted in responsibility for ruling others.*

The South Africans were also signifying that they knew they had to live in moral ambiguity, like any free state, despite their denials. Moral ambiguity was the real cost of Selborne's wisdom to an independent people governing itself and others within one territory, a cost an empire could ignore or fob off with demands for unrealistic reforms: "I am going to see to it that you get time to speak whenever you want to," the speaker of the House told Helen Suzman at the start of every session for the thirteen years she was the only PFP member in Parliament, beginning in 1952.[97] These words came of the readiness to cope with moral ambiguity.

Only the readiness to stand such moral ambiguity can explain the paradox that later, after 1948, after winning "office on an uncompromising programme of apartheid, the Nationalists —ironically enough—did infinitely more than all their predecessors combined [including the Africans] to improve conditions in urban areas," as Lewis Gann and Peter Duignan remarked in a good book that like all good books about South Africa raises more questions than it answers.[98]

Smuts went along with the compromise that passed the Representative of Natives Bill in 1936 because in some sense he knew it was right, and because he wanted to preserve the United Party, the union with some of the Afrikaners that the prime minister, Hertzog, had initiated. This union alone would make it possible to bring South Africa into the war.

For above all Smuts and Hofmeyr had Hitler on their minds. They sensed the life-and-death challenge Europe barely comprehended,—a challenge that also represented a deep but distorted criticism of liberal democracy and its capacity to cope with peace and war, and distinguish between them.

Smuts' concentration on Europe and world danger was not an evasion of his responsibilities at home as Paton, and other more small-minded historians, take for granted. It was a recognition of priorities that subsequent events have proved correct. The Native problem was trivial in contrast to the destruction of Europe. Smuts knew that South Africa might not be able to deal with its home situation if Europe's and the United States' confidence weakened enough to serve their enemies, weakening he had recognized at the start in 1917 and at Versailles.

Already in the twenties, but especially in the period after the Representation of Natives Act of 1936, the mirage of separation began to draw people. Leading liberals, like Hoernlé made logical arguments for separation, even though Hofmeyr, in the debate in 1936 and then again in 1947, just before the National Party unexpectedly won office, had argued its impossibility. The impossibility of separation had led Hofmeyr already in 1931 to write, once "differentiation" proved no longer practicable, "then difficult, indeed, will be the path which South Africa must tread, between a policy of repression and subjection on the one hand and a policy of identity and equality on the other. It will have great need of vision and of faith, if it is to find the road," a statement that foreshadows P.W. Botha's policy away from apartheid in the late seventies.[99]

The mirage that drew people towards separation they knew impossible did not amount to a consensus except in the incapacity to conceive of another way: "Separation had become a magic word, and had put ministers of religion and professors under its spell, but they did not understand that it was impossible," Paton's description of the mood in South Africa just before the National Party's unexpected victory.[100]

But even after the election in 1948 some seven years of argument and discussion on every level passed before South Africans took the slogans they had at first dismissed as electioneering in earnest. Already in 1948, however, the unease underneath apparent unanimity showed itself in bitter criticism without reading of the Fagan Commission Report Smuts had commissioned. Released after the election, the report argued for recognition of a "permanent Native population in the urban areas." The movement to the cities might be "regulated" but not "reversed" because of a "natural economic phenomenon engendered by necessity." It held "total segregation" completely impracticable.

By economic necessity the report meant the industrialization that had begun in earnest during, and in part because of, the Second World War just at the time leading South African economists argued against the possibility of major advances. In 1945 manufacturing accounted for more than any other pursuit; by 1965 it exceeded the total of agriculture, forestry, fishing and mining and quarrying.[101] By 1960 the proportion of African town to country population had reached 38 to 62 percent, roughly the proportion in Russia at the beginning of the century. Now it approaches 50 percent—with 57 percent of all South Africans, and 83.6 percent of Afrikaans-speakers, in towns and cities, according to the 1980 census. In contrast, in 1921, people in towns numbered 12.5 percent. The country had a life of its own, besides politics. "This is the tragedy of Afrikaner politics that the most able men devote their lives to drawing blueprints for the impossible," was Paton's judgment of the policies denying the consequences of this expansion they could impede but not check.[102] In part, but only in part, Botha's reforms, especially the inclusion of black trade unions in collective bargaining in 1979, meant to face this urbanization and industrialization. These have probably already passed their harshest phase—an industrial revolution enough in itself to shake a society to its foundations, even one without deep differences in its population, as the transformation of Italy since 1945 shows.[103]

Despite his lack of alternatives, Hofmeyr sensed in 1936 that the very movement he opposed, "reaction" he called it, that passed the Representation of Natives Bill, would eventually turn against itself: "The tide of reaction is still flowing forward. I know that those of us who are opposing that tide cannot hope to check it. The puny breastworks that we put up must be swept away, but I do believe that the mere putting up of those breastworks is going to accelerate the day when the tide will turn, as turn, I believe it some day will . . ."[104] The start of the turn can be fixed symbolically with the foundation of the Institute for Race Relations by a few dedicated liberal-minded South Africans outside of politics in the following year.

The contrast between political unanimity,—the absence of any but symbolic opposition that argued agreement about realities—and inner unease broke out, not in a political but in a spiritual crisis that Hofmeyr had also sensed. It showed itself in individuals in worship, the first ground of Europe's approach to the Africans. In 1944, before apartheid, Alan Paton first experienced his country in his soul, not in political argument:

The emancipation of a white person from color prejudice is very seldom a sudden conversion. It is rather the result of a number of experiences. Yet there is one experience that lives in my memory. Through it I knew that I was no longer primarily a white person. I had never been militantly white, but now I became militantly non-racial. I saw a vision, there is no other word for it.[105]

Belief accounts for Paton's ferocity, and his restraint many years later, in the late fifties and early sixties, in his attacks on the government that never turned to abuse and only rarely into contempt. It also accounts for his readiness to criticize without a political program of his own: He only wanted government not to make things worse, the purpose of Botha's reforms. Botha like Paton knows that crucial things must also be allowed to take care of themselves.

Whatever else South Africa is, it is a believing country. There is no making sense of what goes on in South Africa today without understanding this belief, for faith and the economy are the two things that unite the country, and provide the sufficient confidence for change without destruction.

Just this faith allows a highly intelligent Colored leader, Franklin Sonn, principal of an important technical school for Coloreds, to insist on the possibilities of accomplishment "despite the system." He gave the American Lutheran priest, Richard Neuhaus, a vivid sense of the confidence in dealing with government that comes of this common reference to a world besides the immediate. Neuhaus had asked him what difference pious oppressors made: "It makes a very big difference! It is a help to know that the Afrikaner knows the meaning of righteousness. It makes it possible to challenge him on the level of his sense of decency and moral and religious feelings. When you quote the Bible and he knows you are not using the Bible just to make a political point, then you have his attention. Believe me, I have seen it happen, often."

Sonn went on to show the resilience, the resistance to resentment's ideological bait, that comes of the faith Hofmeyr mentioned when he spoke of "the difficult way," faith that after all also provided confidence for the first contacts with the Bantu,—and was the gun's other side as it is today: "It is realistic to recognize that things are not so simple as oppressor versus oppressed. It is realistic to recognize that the powerful are not completely in control of their situation. They are human beings too, with sin, and limits and not always knowing what is right . . . You cannot overlook the quality of persons. I have learned to place a great deal of faith in people who I know twice a day have their quiet periods of thought, their quiet period with God, who read their Bible and pray earnestly about what they are doing. I have no doubt that P.W. Botha is such a man."[106]

From this confidence comes the capacity to distinguish the immediately possible from the world men live outside of politics, to accept limits in politics in spite of injustices or mere inequalities or differences that have to be lived with but cannot be denied: "Now the government may feel forced to set up certain restrictions, certain requirements for citizenship. Every government in the world does that. But the ethics of the government are not the ethics of the church," a Dutch Reformed theologian, David Bosch, recently remarked.

He went on to insist on theology's independence of politics, the other side of the difference: "I have a great worry that we may end up doing the right thing for the wrong reason. In politics people like Botha are pragmatic, and that is good. But in the church there should be more than pragmatism . . ." He means he dreads yielding to change, simply out of guilt and fear that he knows can only lead to ruin.

The distinction between belief and politics also gives Bosch the strength to go his own way. He will listen, he will not live to please: "I confess that my chief concern is not that we be more respectable in the eyes of the secular world. I am not contemptuous of that, but that is not the main thing. The main thing, ultimately the only thing that counts is that we become more fully the church of Jesus Christ."[107] Such a readiness to deal with critics face to face, not defiantly, but with a readiness to speak their minds without apology, characterizes much of South African diplomacy. It earns South African diplomats private trust, and public contempt. More importantly it shows the mean between alternating totalitarian flattery and abuse of Western ideals to manipulate them that so paralyzes the West.

Apartheid culminated the reaction that Hofmeyr sensed in 1936 would eventually turn upon itself. It turned the Native Question into racial prejudice that came home to individuals despite their denials. In part this was because of the killings at Sharpeville in 1960, one burst of a panicky machine gun that led to the first declaration of a State of Emergency: "For a brief time in the nineteen fifties people thought the rationale [for apartheid] was firmly in place, but then there was Sharpeville and everything that has happened since then, and fewer and fewer people really believed what we were saying," W. Esterhuyse, a professor of philosophy at Stellenbosch, recently told Neuhaus. But Sharpeville had such an effect for deeper reasons.

Apartheid came home to individuals not so much by turning the reserves into permanent homelands that could one day achieve independence (contrary to Selborne's expectation of their dissolution in a undefined future), a decision that reflected the intractable reality of tribal languages and tribes; not by severely increasing the control of movements between townships and from the homelands into the townships that Selborne had argued against; not by introducing all manner of regulations that separated Europeans from other peoples, whites from nonwhites "wherever possible, in offices, entrances, exits, cinemas, halls, restaurants, hotels, schools, universities, churches," offensive regulations undone in the last ten years except in the public schools and on some beaches. Apartheid made itself indefensible, indefensibility Hofmeyr had sensed in his phrase "tide of reaction" in 1936 long before it actually showed itself, when it treated the Coloreds and the Indians like the Africans— against Selborne's strongest advice a little more than a generation earlier.

In its treatment of the Coloreds and the Indians apartheid was reactionary. Especially in the instance of the Coloreds it tried to undo a way of life that among the Cape Coloreds had developed over three centuries. It did not simply elaborate and strictly control a situation it inherited from both Boers and British, the case with the Africans. By treating the Coloreds and the Indians as if they were no different from the Africans, apartheid undermined its only justification, the recognition of actual differences. It made separate development difficult to distinguish from racial discrimination, a confusion Stellenbosch professors who put together separate development now blame on the government.

It was apartheid's treatment of the Coloreds that moved the South African journalist, Al J. Venter, to write his remarkable inquiry on the Coloreds, published in 1972, a book that cleared his eyes to write his first-hand accounts of terrorism and guerrilla war in Rhodesia, Angola and Mozambique. The new situation of the Coloreds taught him to distinguish a threat South Africa had to fight, from one it might do something about, at least not make it worse. Sharpeville had prepared him to appreciate the significance of the first spontaneous defiant riot, with no deaths, of the Coloreds in Glendale, a township near Port Elizabeth, two years later, a riot often called the Sharpeville of the Coloreds.

Venter chose the Coloreds because they were closer to him than the blacks, all around him all his days. He had not chosen to see them until he started on his inquiry, dumb-bunny inquiry that trusted to his eyes and ears, with few academic flourishes, and was all the more moving because of it. The shocks of recognition that moved Venter take the measure of the roars of indignation against South Africa that now inhabit the world. He also chose the Coloreds because the worsening of their condition was entirely the responsibility of the Nationalist government. P.W. Botha's insistence on a constitution that included the Coloreds, and the Indians, a few years later, acknowledged that responsibility.

In contrast to the Africans, the Coloreds had a long past of living more or less among Europeans. They had no tribes and no tribal languages. (About 2,200,000 of almost 3,000,000 Coloreds speak Afrikaans only, the rest English.) They never fought the Europeans. Because they come from no identifiable territory, the years of discussions of a homeland for them did not come to anything. They could only convince men who thought history could be undone.

The core of the category was made up of the Cape Coloreds, the recognized descendants of legitimate and illegitimate unions of whites with the original inhabitants of the Cape, the aborigines, long before contact with the Bantu. But in time the category came to include all individuals clearly neither Bantu nor European. In 1858, the *Grondwet* called the Coloreds who had followed the Boers north, "half-castes," to distinguish them from the Bantu. In 1908, an act defined a Colored person as "any Native or Asiatic or any other person who is manifestly a Colored person," almost the words of Selborne's description in the same year.

The vagueness betrays customary distinction that, before the Registration of Population Act of 1950 introduced rigid government classification, made it possible for Coloreds who could to pass for whites. A study in 1936 estimated that between 1911 and 1921 somewhere between 40,000 to 80,000 had passed as whites, of a population of 515,000, 480,000 in the Cape, in the middle twenties. The study guessed that more than 700,000 of 1.6 million Europeans in the thirties had Colored blood.[108]

Apartheid's attempt to define Coloreds legally, on the basis of custom and reputation, exposed the category's incoherence. It rigidified racial discrimination that merely customary definition had mitigated despite its humiliations.

The courts did not flinch this incoherence. In 1967 the Supreme Court of Cape Town ruled void because of vagueness, a government proclamation of 1959 as amended in 1961 that defined the Coloreds as the Cape Coloreds, Cape Malay, Griqua, Chinese, Indian and "other Asiatic" and "other Colored,"—the last a catch-all category that betrayed the basic confusion.[109] It included men of lighter complexion than recent immigrants from Portugal and elsewhere in southern Europe who themselves did not know who they were. Especially the border-line Coloreds were not easy to identify,—in contrast to the Africans: "Even a highly qualified medical man would hesitate on deciding the race of a small baby. In many cases, such as with Indians and Africans the race is obvious, but it is highly irresponsible to choose between Colored and white," a South African doctor told Venter. It tells something about the level of discussion in the United States that the Coloreds, who are much more like American Blacks than the Africans, are almost never mentioned.

Indians, Coloreds and Africans who had bought land in the roughly three hundred "black-spots" in Natal and the Cape Province before the Land Act of 1913 all suffered because of the forced removals under the Group Areas Act that numbered 834,000 people since 1960 according to a study in 1983.[110] But the Coloreds and the Indians suffered most from these expulsions that invalidated title deeds and forced the sale of property at less than market value.[111] They suffered most because they had lived in small and large towns close to whites, sometimes for as much as a century. The older Coloreds still spoke to Venter of the times when they had grown up and played with white children. The Africans in contrast had no such times to remember.

The fear of removal, "rescheduling," introduced uncertainty for years. Some Coloreds were moved more than once. In some instances, removals took people out of districts they could have never left on their own like Sophiatown, an African slum in Johannesburg, and Cape Town's District Six, a Colored area that outsiders found "colorful" but that Venter, after living there a year, called a "vicious slum": sixty thousand people, an illegitimate birthrate of thirty percent for the thirty years before 1974 and much alcoholism.[112] In others, they broke up small old communities and forced Coloreds, who mostly worship in the four Afrikaner denominations, to leave the graves of their dead behind and their churches empty: thirty-five in the Cape built before the century. "On the one hand you have people without churches, on the other churches without people," remarked a sensitive observer. Their ancestors' graves meant much more to Coloreds than to whites, usually the case with people simple enough to know dread. There was little Colored or Indian resistance or protest. Paton, and a decade later, Venter, who wrote fiercely against this painful uprooting and the persistent insecurity it brought, both realized many South Africans did not imagine the day-to-day consequences of laws plausible in Parliament and the newspapers.

The Population Registration Act humiliated straightforwardly, without scientific pretensions: Reputation decided on the testimony of friends, appearance, later descent, were the criteria for classification. South African doctors resisted the least public attempt to justify the laws as anything more that the rigidification of custom.

The Afrikaner national student organization, the Afrikaanse Studentebond, at a congress in Pretoria in 1971 passed a resolution, with nine abstentions, that held there was no white blood among the Coloreds, that they were not the "cousins" of whites. Prominent professionals in Cape Town reacted with remarks that such matters "cannot be decided by resolutions and political announcements": "There is historical as well as human genetic evidence for a major white contribution to the genesis of the Colored people." Another doctor dismissed the students' assertion that the Colored people descended only from Bushmen, Hottentots and Asiatics: ". . . There is ample evidence to show that [the Coloreds] have a considerable amount of Caucasian, that is white blood." Another published a study, statistical, not strictly scientific, of blood types that showed blood group patterns thirty-four percent Western European among Coloreds. A former Dutch Reformed archivist, after a study of records in old family Bibles, church registers and archives estimated something like seven percent Colored blood in whites.[113]

After Colored soldiers returned from the War in 1945, before removals and segregation of Coloreds, South African public men recalled the past, not race:

We Europeans must never forget that we, as a race, are responsible for their existence. It can never be as if there were no White father in the background . . . They have no tribal life. They speak no native language as a general rule. Economically and culturally they represent a lower stratum of European civilization—not a totally different nationality. We can never segregate them.[114]

The Coloreds were, and are, a mirror, not only of the whites, but also of the Africans. In 1985, after the repeal of the Immorality Act and Mixed Marriages Act, the deputy minister of constitutional development and planning said, not only that children of mixed marriages would be classified Cape Colored, the historical core of Coloreds, but also that couples with one white parent could apply to live in white areas and for their children to attend white schools.[115]

The laws now publicly recognize a process that has gone on for centuries, and in spite of the laws since 1949, the year of the laws against mixed marriages and love affairs between the races—with what *gradual* consequences nobody can tell.

The very blatancy of South African social laws after 1948 should serve to show the South African government means it when it repeals them. Whatever else it did, the South African government never hid, it never did things for show abroad. This straightforwardness not only allowed restraint, it made for the preservation of the judiciary, as Buthelezi implies in recent remarks before the secretary general of the International Commission of Jurists: "[Although the South African courts] administer obnoxious laws, the judicial process to a very large extent, remains untainted and uncorrupted."[116]

In the constitution introduced in 1983 and 1984, P.W. Botha, following plans hinted already under John Vorster, distinguished Coloreds and Indians from Africans at the same time that he continued their distinction from whites. He compromised between Selborne's fiercest advice against blurring the distinction between Coloreds (who then included Indians) and Natives and the conception of "group representation" that had first shown itself in 1936. Botha realized South Africa could not deal with the actual differences among blacks without exploiting them, without distinguishing the Coloreds from them. He wanted to rid apartheid of its irrational distortions that exploited differences to deal with, and recognize, the differences themselves—without paralyzing the sovereignty that made reform possible.

In the new constitution with its provision for separate houses for Coloreds and Indians, the new appeared in the dress of the old, the pretext for journalists and activist groups to call the changes "cosmetic," apartheid in new dress, but not entirely, as Paton's rejection of the spoiling adjective meant to show. They gave the Coloreds and Indians citizenship, a voice and role in national decisions, the franchise and responsibility for their own affairs. Besides, who could tell the future?

At about the time of the introduction of the Colored Representative Council in 1964, the first outline of "group representation's" self-government, Prime Minister Verwoerd had hinted in private at the possibility that self-government for the Coloreds would lead in time to equality with Europeans.[117] The very sight of Colored representatives settling their affairs in public changed Venter's view of the Coloreds after the first Colored election in 1968: 293,348 voters, out of 570,000 registered, fifty-three percent for parties in favor of apartheid, forty-seven percent for the opposition Labor Party:

> The level of debate, the wealth of repartee, formal courtesy and occasional punctilio, the rancour and manifest frustration which emerges daily from a long succession of speeches—some good, others lamentable—leave a vivid, if somewhat frightening impression in the minds of those to whom this is new ground . . . [It provides] an insight to the passions and aspirations of a society which many White people wrongly believe they know. The real surprise follows when the Colored is seen in action within the confines of his own corridors of power where freedom of speech is guaranteed and the niceties of life are, for the time being, set aside until the session is over. It is only when one sees this other side of the complex and multifaceted Colored character, angry and demonstrative—the Currys, the Leons, the Jakobus Rabies, the Arendses and the Swartzes (and the quiet, almost Westminsterian dignity of chairman Mr. Phillip Sanders, a Freestater who would do justice to the British House of Commons given a different enunciation a little more precise)—that one realises how little we really know of these people classified Colored.[118]

Venter's surprise at the capacity of public life to make men, almost a recall of Merriman's side in the exchange with Smuts in 1906, shows how the new constitution and Botha's introduction of elections for community rule in the black townships often dismissed as "imperfect," as mere arrangements for "stooges," may work on all South Africans.

But neither was the Union of 1910 itself "perfect." Its only perfection was the recognition of its limitations, of the government's capacity to act swiftly to effect limited change, powers that proved crucial in 1960 and in the several years of violence that followed upon reform. Besides, the Union itself was to a certain extent introduced from the top. But nobody ever called the South Africans "stooges," in part because of the tact of British public men, tact the war had taught them.

All these reforms under Botha, these "imperfect" changes, even the change of constitution, no small matter in a country with a living constitution, were taken for weakness that boded collapse, both within South Africa by groups the ANC led that rejected any change, and even more so abroad.

From the time the whites accepted the constitution in 1983, and especially after the elections for the Colored and Indian Houses at the end of 1984, unrest seized South Africa, real defiance and at the same time violence that by March 1985 turned more and more against blacks who did not reject the system, who wanted to make the best of reforms or who simply did not want to take sides,—violence of blacks against blacks. Some stability, but not normality, came to South Africa from the declaration of the State of Emergency nationwide on June 12, 1986. Abroad the anticipated elections on May 6, 1987 provided some respite from clamor, an unanticipated consequence.

The New York Times dismissed the election as a charade, *before it knew the results it did not bother to report*, because it feared the South African whites would not vote to its satisfaction: "If there were any chance that Mr. Botha's National Party might lose, there'd be no election." But the election's undisturbed exercise of sovereignty, under heavy security, calmed the West.[119] People finally sensed the Republic of South Africa was not about to succumb to servile shows of violence. The government had kept the confidence of its voters.

This acknowledgment was made reluctantly after cries of bitter disappointment. For the first time in New York, I heard muttered descriptions of P.W. Botha as the man who had "after all started the reform process," an admission unthinkable before the elections. South African blacks in New York, one after the other, spoke of having been "suckered into" fantasies of immediate change, an implicit rebuke of the illusions men outside South Africa had helped foster that did not miss its mark.

The disappointment went deep, not only because it broke illusions. It showed these illusions grounded in an irresponsible and childish misreading of a vast living country, a country with eyes, ears, tongues, brains, loyalty and courage the West badly needs. The real struggle in South Africa has been between the men and the government who wanted limited but fundamental change and those who wanted to stop change because no change was swift enough. These men wanted to consume the entire system in violence, they could not cope with swift change as the situation in the schools showed. The Denton Hearings show this struggle within individuals the ANC and other terrorist groups recruited.

2

Violence Against Change

1 "No" to Reform

Many blacks said, 'Who called on him to speak for us?' Imagine him telling business to withdraw. What will happen to the people who lose their jobs? His only alternative is a war and a revolution he will not have to fight . . . we are angry . . . when outsiders tell us that violence is the only way to achieve change. It will be my children's blood that will be shed. We don't want to destroy what we have built.

. . . With our boxes of matches and our necklaces, we shall liberate this country . . .

Lucy Mvubelo, the legendary leader from Soweto who had led a successful bus boycott in Johannesburg in 1944 and a strike of the garment workers in 1947 against the passage of the Job Reservations Act made the first statement in 1979: She meant Jesse Jackson, who had kept her waiting three hours without ever even showing up, and other foreign radicals who incited South African blacks. The Job Reservations Act, suspended in 1979, prohibited employment of blacks in slightly more skilled occupations.

The second speaker (whose statement finally won some attention in the European press) needs no introduction. Teddy Kennedy had himself photographed with her in double profile on his visit to South Africa in early 1985; she had won the Robert F. Kennedy Award about six months earlier: She is Winnie Mandela, a heroine for our times.[1]

The contrast between Mandela's words, as usual the straight ANC line, uttered on April 12, 1986 and Mvubelo's, now an almost forgotten figure, seven years before, measured the cost of the risks P.W. Botha had run: an insurrection that sought the appearance of the full-fledged "revolution" expected abroad since Sharpeville in 1960. The violence, however, was directed not at whites but at blacks who would not go along with rejection of reforms and the "system."

Mandela meant the favorite method of murder in the black townships of South Africa:

The victim's hands are tied behind his or her back with picture framing wire and a tire filled with gasoline placed over the neck and then lighted. A slow agonizing death is often accompanied by stoning and sometimes eating of the burnt flesh, even before the victim has died. The intimidation impact of such atrocities on frightened black moderates is tremendous, especially since many black Africans believe in reincarnation and that if their body is burned, they will return later in life as an animal or insect.[2]

Bryce would have grasped the significance of the last detail.

The violence Mvubelo foresaw, and Mandela exulted in, broke out in earnest in late September 1984, at the time of Indian and Colored elections for the three-house Parliament in South Africa's new constitution. It lasted twenty-two months until the declaration of South Africa's second State of Emergency on June 12, 1986 brought it partly under control.

In July 1984, a few months before it broke out unremittingly, Mvubelo had a first-hand taste of this violence. A terrorist organization that aptly named itself the South African Suicide Squad almost killed her and one of her children and burnt her home in Soweto to the ground. A few days before a leader of the largest "anti-apartheid" coalition, the United Democratic Front, had said publicly at a meeting in Soweto that he hated Mvubelo—the public targeting of a victim. "They claim that I am a stooge. But I have done so much to better the lives of black South Africans," Mvubelo said in tears before the ruins of her house.[3]

The violence of Mvubelo's dread and Mandela's exultation was directed by blacks against blacks, by extremist blacks against blacks who wanted to work "within the system." These blacks wanted to take advantage of the reforms of the South African government, especially of the elections in the townships instituted in 1979 that meant to substitute local black self-rule for white civil service administration. The cry of the ANC and the United Democratic Front (UDF) was "Make the townships ungovernable." Blacks attacked, sometimes murdered, blacks they called "collaborators." Around three hundred town councillors had been murdered in the twenty-two months before the second State of Emergency.

The State of Emergency markedly reduced deaths, and police killings. In all, between September 1984 and April 1987, something like 2,387 people died. In 1985 police keeping order caused half the deaths, violence between blacks about a third. In 1986 the situation reversed, blacks caused half the deaths, the police a third. In the period from January to April 1986, blacks murdered 175 blacks and destroyed or badly damaged 720 homes and 228 businesses, while 143 blacks died in police actions meant to protect lives and property. In the entire period from September 1984 to June 1986, 1,503 men were killed, 836 in police actions (including 40 policemen), 667 by black extremists. Just before the declaration of the State of Emergency on June 12, 1986, deaths reached 221 in May to drop to 33 by December. Between March 1986 and August 1986 there were 955 deaths, between September 1986 and February 1987, 187, roughly one death a day in the latter six months, in contrast to five a day during the six months before. Fifty-eight percent of the deaths occurred in the Transvaal with its five homelands, twenty percent in the Eastern Cape, eight percent in Natal including KwaZulu.[4]

The State of Emergency showed an instance of its effect in the Eastern Cape, an economically impoverished area that had seen some of the worst violence since late 1984. This country is still in some sense a frontier because of the nearness of the two homelands born of the British-Xhosa wars, and their alternation of conquest and negotiation in the nineteenth century: the Ciskei and Transkei. The Ciskei now numbers about eight hundred thousand, the Transkei almost three million, the most populated homeland besides KwaZulu with almost four million.

By April 1987, the rudiments of the UDF seizure of power were disappearing in the Eastern Cape: no negotiations by white wholesalers and bus company owners for safe passage; no tributes of one hundred and fifty rand a month and "donations" of chickens, goats and turkeys from black store-owners to make up for profits from white-store boycotts, complete with quotation of the Freedom Charter's command: ". . . The people shall share in the country's wealth"; the street committees the UDF had organized in classic totalitarian fashion, to stem the violence it had encouraged, mostly undone; UDF leaders, except one, detained, the regional president on trial for a necklacing murder; the boycotts fading.

People had the confidence to talk freely to reporters of the two years now past: "The comrades took one lady who had bought goods in town and tore up her new shoes and tore her clothes and painted her." A friend of a black store owner who had suffered exactions admitted he had joined a mob of four hundred "willingly": "I was woken up around four in the morning by a number of people carrying sticks who said we must chase the comrades."

The government's rough methods meant to force people not to yield to intimidation, to stand up to violence with police support: Townships were sealed-off with razor sharp wire, with checkpoints at the few access roads, manned sometimes by the "comrades" of a few months before. In Langa vigilante groups murdered four UDF activists and beat up others who had escaped the police, after the South African government had bulldozed the settlement, about half shacks. The township of forty-thousand had seen many necklacings and "peoples' courts" "sentencing" suspected informers and consumer boycott breakers to whippings with *sjamboks* and "strokes with a cane," in a deadly pantomime of the South African judiciary's language. The bulldozing left four churches, a stark acknowledgment of limits that baffled Western reporters. "But surprisingly few tears were shed for the Langa comrades,"—

remarked a reporter who had seen the Eastern Cape townships in the days of "liberation" and after.[5]

Unable to overwhelm the State of Emergency through violence, the ANC and the UDF sought to overwhelm it with broad-based "mass" campaigns against the detention of children, and through politicization of the unions through a new organization, the Congress of South African Trade Unions (COSATU), formed in November 1985. Their immediate object in 1987: to discredit the May elections.

On the whole, until a slight but marked changed occurred in early 1986, the international press paid more attention to deaths from police actions than to blacks murdering blacks. It took up events like the uproars and further killing at banned funerals with their vivid anger and public grief. The blurred reporting, the emphasis on "police brutality," a phantom phrase from the sixties, made it difficult for the public to realize two things: Only the South African government and its modest security forces had the authority and strength to keep the blacks from tearing each other apart. And a much darker truth: The South African government had succumbed to the largely orchestrated indignation about brutality enough to inhibit its police for a time. In some townships, perhaps eleven, South African police, rather than kill more blacks and provoke more indignation, appeared simply to allow the riots to burn themselves out, to abandon the moderate blacks to violence and murder. The South African police were waiting for things to get bad enough to blunt indignation at their intervention.

The "brutally repressive," "whites-only" "oligarchic regime" "police state" in South Africa has a very small police force, forty percent black,—another paradox the media in the United States generally choose to ignore. It numbers about 21,500 blacks and 23,200 whites according to a 1984 report of the Commissioner of the South African Police. The figure for blacks includes Indians and Coloreds who numbered 4 percent and 6.4 percent, respectively, of the total force. Soldiers who served in the townships in 1985, the first full year of troop use, numbered a *total* of 35,372 deployed, often mixed-in with police in ninety-six African townships; in 1986 troops with the police never numbered more than 10,000 to 15,000.[6]

The number of South African police averages 1.4 men per thousand against a Western European average of 6 per thousand. New York alone numbers a police force of nearly 28,000 for a population of 7,000,000 in the five boroughs, not including about 4,000 transit police and unnumbered private security men that patrol neighborhoods and guard entrances to private apartment buildings, universities and office buildings—numbers that show their effectiveness in almost empty streets after dark. The South African police wants to raise its ratio to a modest three per thousand by 1995.

Such small numbers of police presuppose respect for laws and swiftness of action—like other South African institutions. For instance, banning, an institution as idiosyncratic as Athenian ostracism, isolates an individual in his home on his own compliance. These institutions and the reliance on small numbers of police assume acquiescence to authority not enforced at the point of a gun. Such confidence is incomprehensible to some Americans, like the priest Neuhaus who calls banning "infantile." But it comes from more than a century of living closely among alien peoples, defeated enemies neither slave nor citizen, the *imperium in imperio.*

The shock in South Africa at the deployment of army troops in the townships beginning in late 1984 testifies to this confidence. There were demands for immediate withdrawal not only from the End Conscription Campaign but also from the respected women's civil rights organization, the Black Sash. They called the use of troops a symptom of militarization of society and "of the abuse of power." The Progressive Federal Party objected in principle to the use of troops to quell domestic civil unrest.

In answer to the South African civil-rights protest, the minister of law and order said that withdrawal of troops would drive men in the townships "to murder one another on an unknown scale." The army opened up twenty-eight complaint centers that got little business, probably because of intimidation.

These protests lent unwitting support to Communist strategy and propaganda that the ANC and the UDF spread abroad. The 1981 SACP Central Committee meeting minutes captured in an ANC house in Gaborone in 1985 concentrated on infiltrating the army and the police: "One of the important features of the present situation is that it is becoming increasingly clear that the whites alone could not carry the burden of defending a racist state. Blacks are increasingly being mobilized at all levels to collaborate in their own oppression . . . As never before work in the army and amongst the black police is vital."

The minutes resort to the same word, "militarized," as the Black Sash and the End Conscription Campaign: "Our economy and society is militarized." Elsewhere they read: "We must single out vicious policemen. We should find ways of dealing with the white police."[7]

Police Brutality

Accusations of police brutality and torture are also part of this strategy to parody and discredit the government. The South African courts have been unequivocal in their condemnation of "assaults" (beatings) and extreme deprivations in prison. At the same time they have acknowledged, as one magistrate said, that "the purpose and express terms of Section 17 . . . do not appear to me to reveal any intention on the part of the legislature to alleviate the lot of a detainee during his detention." In other words pressure, severity, harsh conditions but no physical abuse or torture. That the appellate court in this 1964 case faced a request for a court order to provide a detained prisoner with the same "reading materials" allowed a trial prisoner shows something of the South African courts' readiness to deal with niceties.

In 1985 the South African press reported seventeen court actions, involving eighty-three detainees, to restrain the police from beating and torture of men held under the Internal Security Act (ISA) or the partial State of Emergency. The provincial supreme courts in Natal and Port Elizabeth granted the most important temporary edicts to restrain the police. In Natal in his order to the police not to assault or unlawfully interrogate, the judge president said in full bench session that the state had to ensure the release of prisoners "with [their] physical and mental health unimpaired": "If it is true that detainees are being assaulted in the custody of police, it is a state of affairs which no civilized nation . . . can tolerate for one moment." In Port Elizabeth, the court ordered its interdict forbidding assaults upon detainees held under emergency regulations read to all present and future detainees in the Port Elizabeth and Uitenhage judicial district. This was the first interdict protecting the unnamed as well as the named.[8]

A brave district surgeon, Dr. Wendy Orr, and forty-three others, had sought this interdict. In December ninety-three more affidavits alleging assaults were filed in Port Elizabeth in support of Dr. Orr's September application. Of 170 detainees arrested on August 15, about half claimed beatings, most with injuries to show: weals, bruises, blisters, lacerated lips, split cheekbone skin, a few perforated ear drums. These charges won wide attention in the international press and prompted demands in the South African Parliament for a judicial inquiry.

In September the release of the report, financed by the Ford Foundation in the United States, *Detention and Torture,* by a professor of psychology and others at the University of Cape Town led to several months of debate in the South African newspapers with many letters from readers. Of the 158 former detainees these professors questioned, 23 had been held in 1974–1976, 71 in 1977–1980, 78 in 1981–1983, 4 in 1984, none in the partial State of Emergency in 1985 or in the national emergency in 1986.[9]

Throughout the study insists on the definition of torture of the United Nations' Declaration Against Torture in 1975: both physical and mental suffering and pain. By psychological torture, the South African report means, not totalitarian psychological torture like the imprisonment of men who think otherwise in insane asylums in the Soviet Union or the repeated written confessions and "struggles" in China, but threats, insults, alternating good-and-bad guy interrogation, false accusations. These are questioning techniques used by the police in many countries. Physical torture in the report means beatings, forced standing, abnormal body positions like squatting, kneeling, forced gym exercises like push-ups, bright lights, overheated or cold rooms, cold water thrown on prisoners, bags over the head with the threat of suffocation. Electric shock, cigarette and chemical burns, and the "helicopter treatment" (victim suspended between two tables from a piece of wood passing under his knees, with his hands handcuffed in front of his shins) were the most serious. In contrast to Wendy Orr's figure of fifty percent, eighty-three percent of the detainees questioned for the report claimed "some form or other of physical torture," seven percent cigarette and chemical burns, twenty-five percent electric shocks. About eighty percent claimed psychological abuse, with no former detainee reporting "an entire lack of psychological abuse." That means nobody claimed there was no pressure at all.

The few direct quotations from former prisoners in the report led me to suspect that the questions asked them, not reprinted in the report, prompted desired answers: ". . . Everything's taken away from you, your cigarettes, your matches, your belt, you are almost stripped naked except for the basic clothes you've got on. I think one should spend a bit of time on just the effect of being locked up for the first time in your life . . ."; "I was sort of getting mental disorders, because I remember one day I just jumped up and screamed. I just wanted to get out of the cell, at least to the outside, even in the yard"; "They interrogated almost without any breaks because they would tell me to do some exercises such as push-ups, sit-ups and the rest of the exercises"; ". . . I had to encounter a lot of threats from the police. I would get so nervous whenever the doors [of the cell] were opened"; "I was fairly exhausted, it was fairly strenuous being interrogated constantly, and fairly stressful."

These answers betray markedly milder treatment than in the appearance elaborate statistical tables,—mild treatment especially in contrast to the truths hinted at now and then that the South African police suspected: "He [the police interrogator] told me that I had received military [the ANC phrase for terrorist] training, and myself and a friend had been recruited to leave the country."

On December 12, three months after publication, the minister of law and order criticized the anonymity of the men who had complained to the psychologist and his associates. Why had they had no recourse to authorities for their alleged maltreatment? At the same time the government said that of a total of 1,007 men held under the ISA between 1982 and 1985, 137 had made charges of police beatings, mostly not prosecuted. In April and May 1986, the minister with some justification called the "Torture Report" "thoroughly subjective and politically biased" and meant to "bring into disrepute and under suspicion the government and the system of security legislation." But there had been brutality, probably without the minister's knowledge: In October 1985, a judge in Natal and Helen Suzman and an other PFP MP had severely criticized the minister for "losing control of his staff."

Nowhere does the report acknowledge the actual danger the government and South Africa faces except to dismiss it as "paranoia"—and blame it on the government: "[Conspiratorial and terrorist organizations] are created and produced in the first place by the repressive forces of the regime."

Written in highly-qualified language, language that often takes back in one sentence the words it has asserted in another, language only men with the long habit of reading academic studies can penetrate, the study only shows its bias nakedly in its conclusion. It calls the distinction fundamental in South African security legislation between psychological pressure—plain fear—and beatings and torture "rather arbitrary." It complains against the "systematic" destruction of an "independent judiciary" by detention but it dismisses with contempt the judiciary's insistence on facts and individuals: ". . . The courts are unlikely to forgo traditional rules, most notably the piecemeal or particularistic approaches to the merits of each individual case . . ." It dismisses "the purportedly reformist policies of P.W. Botha" as "neo-apartheid forms of domination." It does not distinguish between defiance and terrorism, riots and burning murder: ". . . Detention is unquestionably a political strategy, designed to quell, contain and eradicate democratic political opposition which could threaten the white minority South African regime." Nothing will do: "In conclusion, it may be noted that justice is hardly to be expected in a fundamentally unjust society."

The report's proposals for reform, not only no physical abuse, but no threatening questioning, no detention, would make any police force, let alone one facing an insurrection, powerless.

There is nothing in the report or in the available court evidence that betrays systematic torture and justifies the routine statements in American publications that the security crackdown in South Africa is "more severe than those in the Communist East bloc" or David Rockefeller's equation of South Africa and the Soviet Union in 1985.[10] To anyone who has read the writings of totalitarian prisons and concentration camps, (the writers of the report have not), who has read Bruno Bettelheim, Andrei Sinyafsky, Vladimir Bukovsky, James Stockdale, Aleksandr Solzhenitsyn, Varlam Shalamov, Nien Cheng, Nadzehda Mandelstam, Haing Trong, Armando Valladares, the actions of the South African police, even their brutalities appear relatively innocent.

They show a very tough police in a difficult situation, sometimes maladroit, sometimes cruel, trying to panic prisoners into talking. They want the truth, not false confessions. They do not want to break their prisoners' souls, to turn them into the living dead. The only book they allow detainees is the Bible. That tells a good deal. It also tells a good deal that they are mocked and laughed at as well as respected and feared, the lot of all imperfect authority. I don't know of any jokes against the totalitarian police.

The will of the government and the courts to control the police shows in their actions. In 1986 the government forbade police—and army—membership in the Afrikaner Weerstandsbeweging (AWB), a right-wing extremist group. In March 1988 a South African court sentenced two white policemen from an elite squad to death pending appeal for the murder of two blacks and the attempted murder of a third.[11] They received an unexpected reprieve along with two other white policemen convicted of murder and six blacks complicit in murder, the "Sharpeville six," in November.

One more important thing tells of the constraints upon the South African Police, even when cruel. None of the detainees say their suffering made them better men—in contrast to the accounts of those who have lived through totalitarian prisons. In our time most of the men able to talk of the soul seriously have been through totalitarian universities. There are pages in Solzhenitsyn's *Gulag Archipelago* with the depth and knowledge of Plato's *Republic*. Those who have not been to these men's universities, like the professors at Cape Town who wrote the "Torture Report," ought to respect their experience and knowledge. They have turned a serious matter into an occasion for whining that undermines the self-respect of South African blacks, as a South African writer in England said recently of the entire anti-apartheid movement:

While Jews and Japanese obey the stern inner voice of their own culture, black people are inclined to heed the indulgent outer voice of contemporary social theory. That outer voice, coming from fashions in political philosophy and from bodies such as the United Nations Organisation and the anti-apartheid movement, tells black men that they are not to blame for their own misfortunes, that they must rely on others to help them, and that, like animals, they are incapable of sin. In adversity the inner voice tells Jews to work harder, the outer voice tells blacks to whine louder. The anti-apartheid movement thus helps to bring about the profound demoralisation of black people which I believe is responsible, more than anything else, for their plight in Africa and abroad.[12]

These words sound all too familiar to my American ears. They mean getting things through "political" demands undermines self-respect—in contrast to hard work.

The small number of police means that they must act without a moment's hesitation or doubt in crowds that heavily outnumber them. The police allow themselves ten seconds to abandon their trucks before they go up in flames after arrival at disturbances. An American reporter, a Vietnam veteran, out to investigate South African "police brutality" saw six policemen armed with shotguns full of bird-shot and side arms disperse a crowd of over three hundred "within minutes."[13]

The small number also betrays neglect of the townships. South African police, however, say that more men would not bring down the murders, mostly not the work of organized crime. Soweto had 1,391 murders in 1984, almost fifteen percent of the national total—a high rate but no rival to Lagos in Nigeria or other black African cities.

Long before apartheid, the *Rand Daily Mail* ran a daily "crime list." Biko wrote that it was "a miracle for anyone to live up to adulthood" in a township—a sentence he explained to a South African court in 1976: "When you are in a township it is dangerous to cross often from one street to the next . . . [Kids on errands] meet up with these problems; rape and murder are very, very common aspects of our life in townships . . . You see an old man being assaulted by a number of young men for apparently no reason whatsoever except that of course possibly it is the end of the month and possibly he might have some money around him."[14] A poll in Durban in 1975 showed forty-nine percent feared crime above all; against twenty-five percent, the police, among blacks with primary education. The figures for blacks with some secondary education were forty-six percent and thirty-seven percent, respectively. Only two percent in the first group, one in the second feared authority.[15]

In 1985 some of the town councils began to organize their own municipal police. In 1986, the South African Defense Force, the South African Police and the Railways Police were training 8,000 men and women for these police forces, 4,846 for town and village councils, 3,500 to guard the homes of community councillors in ten different centers. Helen Suzman insisted on effective training for these policemen to exercise "good judgment in unrest situations, which call for experience and self-control." The government had recently granted the new police more powers, including arrest, and there had been abuses: In the

Vaal triangle, the supreme court ordered the municipal police to stop arresting and assaulting the chairman of the Vaal parents' crisis committee.[16]

The international uproar against the proclamation of the State of Emergency on June 12, 1986, showed, however, that despite the media's belated coverage of blacks murdering blacks, no Western government was about to reaffirm the first duty of government, to keep order.[17] Men independent of the South African government had confirmed evidence of ANC plans for widespread violence on June 12, the tenth anniversary of the upheaval in Soweto. We, who live in a country whose natives have feared to walk the streets of their cities at night for twenty years, are too far gone for such common sense. Even President Reagan in his crucial speech of July 22, 1986, called for revocation.

Recently, a South African couple got something of the fear even England lives with across to an English reporter who had questioned the responsibility of their return home after three hard years of escape to London:

If you are talking about fear, about physical safety, then I have never known anything like the sheer terror you experience on a London tube train late at night.[18]

(A poll, a little after the State of Emergency, that included country homeland blacks, showed the blacks of South Africa wanted it both ways. Almost two thirds thought changing apartheid did not justify violence, fifty percent expected the peaceful settlement of present conflicts. At the same time, fifty-nine percent, ninety percent in the townships, "hated" the State of Emergency, and fifty-one percent thought it wrong to work within the system. This apparent ambivalence showed UDF-ANC intimidatory propaganda against "collaboration" and against the State of Emergency was still working somewhat.)[19]

Despite the decline in murder, the United States government continued to say the State of Emergency had no justification even after the 1987 elections showed acceptance of its necessity in South Africa. The United States' refusal to accept the State of Emergency came because it did not want to admit the reforms it barely acknowledged could precipitate violence.

Nobody abroad, and few within South Africa, accused Botha of recklessness—of taking risks that even a cursory reader of history knows usually bring disaster. The Conservative Party (CP) argued that the promise of power-sharing had brought increasing social and political instability and declared it would reverse "constitutional reform" and bring back "strict Verwoerdian apartheid" at its congress in 1986. But despite these declarations, the conservatives seemed responsible or realistic enough to realize the process could be slowed, controlled, but not reversed, especially because most South Africans accepted it. Earlier, more than four years ago, they had argued that any concession would undermine the government, a judgment that led the *Economist* in a moment of truth to remark: "In the long run they may be right."[20]

In the midst of the start of this violence that the State of Emergency was to bring under some control, the new Parliament had assumed office in January 1985. With its Indian and Colored representatives under the threat of not merely verbal attack for "collaboration," it took significant measures: repeal of the law that prohibited marriage and liaisons between the races, which had occasioned the prosecution of something like eighteen thousand South Africans; repeal of the Political Interference Act that made illegal parties not racially exclusive; amendments to the Black Urban Areas Act to allow black workers to achieve permanent residency after ten years instead of fifteen that dropped the requirement that they remain with one employer, modifications the courts reinforced but still required they find "approved accommodation," difficult because of the housing shortage, before bringing their families.

The repeal of the Mixed Marriages and Immorality Acts, had caused an uproar upon Botha's first suggestion of it in 1979. Its repeal brought awed appreciation from men of the stature of Alan Paton and Mangosuthu Buthelezi—but not from an international press that would not appreciate its attack on the irrational underpinnings of "apartheid" or "separate development," as the South African government calls it.

The government continued its reforms. In a major speech before a conference of the National Party on September 30, 1985, a few months after the close of the new Parliament, Botha committed himself to treat *all* South Africa—except the four independent homelands—as one political whole and to move towards a universal franchise. He meant that the rights of the blacks in the townships would no longer depend on the homelands: "I thus finally confirm that my party and I are committed to the principle of a united South Africa, one citizenship and universal franchise." "Universal franchise" did not mean "one-man, one-vote" but "geographical and ethnic units" that "should have autonomy on matters that affect only that unit, while units on the central level should jointly manage matters of mutual concern"—in short some kind of federal system in everything but name. He made it clear that the government was ready to negotiate with black leaders, not only tribal chiefs and the elected leaders of the non-independent homelands, but "church leaders" and perhaps the leaders of the ANC and UDF, presumably on condition that they renounce violence. At least, so the *Economist*, alone in its recognition of the speech's importance, read the phrase "political leaders."[21]

Botha reiterated many of these intentions and announced a plan to abolish the "pass laws" in the next few months, a promise inconceivable only two years before, in his speech to open the second new Parliament on January 31, 1986. He also proposed a National Council to give Africans a voice in the executive with a view to negotiating a new constitution. He spoke of autonomy and self-rule for the African townships in the large cities. These measures meant to help identify and create the credible black leaders essential for reform.

At the same time the minister of constitutional development and planning Chris Heunis bluntly made it clear reform did not mean a non-racial society blind to tribal, language and racial differences, the slogan of the ANC and the UDF: "If we think we can have a people's democracy as in western Europe, there will be no democracy left." Curiously Heunis did not mention historical differences, the ones that count the most. Abolition of the Influx Control Act (the "pass laws") passed in June meant the partial or total repeal of thirty-four laws and the amendment of three more. A witty South African law journal remarked the act might have been better named "The Prevention of Illegal Squatting Amendment Act": fifteen of its nineteen sections dealt with squatting. These provisions showed the government's expectation of a flood of Africans from the countryside, and its determination to cope with them responsibly. There was to be controlled squatting on designated lands with a provision for services and some sort of local government that could eventually turn into a township. By 1988 visitors could see these new agglomerations near some of the large cities.

Helen Suzman called the abolition of the "pass laws," barely noticed in the United States, the most important reform ever, the director of the South African Institute of Race Relations, said that "along with the statutory recognition of black trade Unions in 1979" the change was the "most important reform in South Africa since World War II"—despite the unacceptably wide control of illegal squatting. Suzman also was quick to point out an increase in trespass arrests, 35,635 in the first five months of 1986, in contrast to about 20,000 for all of 1985, that might amount to "influx control" by another name.

Also passed in June 1986, the Restoration of South African Citizenship Act granted citizenship to men living in South Africa before their homelands achieved independence or who had lived in South Africa for five years, about 1,750,000. In response to criticism that the government had done nothing for the seven-and-a-half million souls still in the four independent homelands, Botha said: ". . . The South African government does not grant citizenship unilaterally to the citizens of her independent states." He meant he took the independence of Transkei, Bophuthatswana, Venda and the Ciskei (the TBVC) seriously—in contrast to the rest of the world, except for a few Israeli and Japanese businessmen who invest in them.[22]

Just at the moment when the United States, Great Britain, and the Common Market were blocking new investment that might capitalize jobs for the men from the countryside, who would bring down the cost of labor, South Africa was opening her doors to them—despite the two hundred thousand township youths who come on the job-market every year.

2 The Campaign Abroad— And the Words that Didn't Make It

Oliver Tambo, president of the ANC, dismissed Botha's promises three weeks before he made them, good proof of Botha's seriousness:

We are convinced that the Botha regime has no intention whatsoever to accede to the demands of the majority of the people . . . We must not be misled by the enemy's promise to abolish influx control [the 'pass laws'] . . . nor must we be taken in by the promises of a so-called common citizenship.

At the same time Tambo, "a quiet Christian gentleman" the *Economist* called him, speaking at celebrations on January 8, 1986 for the seventy-fourth anniversary of the ANC,—and the twenty-fifth anniversary of its terrorist arm (Umkhonto we Sizwe, usually translated, "Spear of the Nation")—declared the ANC's intention to escalate violence in South Africa in the black townships, and to "bring the war home to the whites."

Tambo and a good deal of the audience laughed when a South African reporter asked whether the ANC intended to punish the lower cadres responsible for the murder of five women and children at a beach resort in Natal on Christmas Eve. These murders, along with the killing of seven other whites in land mine explosions near the Botswana and Zimbabwe borders, had made a deep impression on South Africa.[23]

The ANC's open declaration of war, Tambo's words, came because there had been too much change—not too little—because there had been enough change to make the ANC fear that without terror in townships and a tidal wave of propaganda in Western media and international organizations, especially the UN and its many agencies, the Organization for African Unity (OAU), and most lately the Commonwealth, the South African government might win the confidence of the the blacks, even the black youths.

Though not reported directly in the press, Tambo's astonishing words from Lusaka, the capital of Zambia, rejecting Botha's reforms and calling up violence, were immediately relayed to the American public by Desmond Tutu and to the world elite by the *Economist*, of course without direct mention of the reforms or Tambo and the ANC: "We can't keep on having people tinkering with peripheral issues when the basic problem is political power." Tutu, who spoke at celebrations for Martin Luther King's birthday—celebrations exaggerated enough to betray more nakedly than usual the undercurrent of unease that has pervaded a good deal of American political life since the fall of Saigon in 1975—knows propaganda works best in the United States when you appear to make it up out of your own head in a folksy way. Like the ANC, Tutu has an unmistakable courtier's ear for American idiom, television idiom: incitement to murder, in short, with the personal touch, and in total innocence.

The *Economist* did it differently with innocent freshness of intelligence, double-first at Oxford and the rest of the palaver that in the business, newspaper, government and executive bureaucracies works more wonders than the beauty of young women. It said it baldly like a schoolboy with a love poem, his first, in his hand. Mandela was to be released, the ANC recognized. The consequences would be unstoppable, but that was no matter (especially if you didn't live in South Africa). In such words, without saying so openly, it endorsed the terrorism of the ANC and of Mandela, who had helped found the "Spear of the Nation." It argued the South African government should yield to it without bothering to explain why it should back down on making renouncement of violence the condition of Mandela's release. Most astonishing of all, the *Economist* uncritically accepted Mandela as the unquestioned leader of the blacks when everybody knows that Mandela has sat in jail for twenty-five years.[24] In fact Mandela is useful to the ANC as a mythical "leader" because he is out of touch with the situation in South Africa and helps to justify the ANC's own distance from events within South Africa, the usual distance of exiles and the imprisoned, and its determination to deny their possibilities.

Both Mandela and the ANC agree on his expendability, on his absolute obedience to the organization: "I would only leave home if the ANC leadership ordered me to do so," Mandela told Nicholas Bethell in 1985. At the same time he declared he would not obey "any restriction" of the South African government upon release. "The revolution is bigger than I am, it is something you give yourself to. Mandela, for example, is important but he is not critically important. He would be offered the leadership after the revolution, but I know he would decline it, and that's because he believes in collective decisions," remarked an ANC leader, Johnny Makatini, in New York at about the same time.[25]

Recognition "before the revolution" that "there is no alternative to armed struggle," is the chief requirement for a part in ANC collective decisions "after the revolution," Makatini also said. In other words, no renunciation of violence, as Mandela had again said at about the same time, despite strict prison regulations against interviews: "[There is] no room for peaceful struggle in South Africa."

These statements came after Botha had formally informed Mandela and fourteen other prisoners who had served fifteen to twenty years of the possibility of release on condition of renunciation of violence. "All that is required of him now is that he should unconditionally reject violence as a political instrument . . . that he will not make himself guilty of planning, instigating or committing acts of violence for the furtherance of political objectives, but will conduct himself in such a way that he will not again have to be arrested," Botha had said a few days before the offer in debate in Parliament.[26] Rearrest, Botha knew, would not be easy.

Mandela and nine others were arrested in 1963, on a farm near Johannesburg that yielded documents in Mandela's handwriting, 106 plans for attacks on police stations, power houses, homes of black policemen, communications centers, thousands of hand grenades and land mines, fifty tons of explosives, enough to kill a quarter of a million people. The documents showed that Algeria, still on the ANC's mind as a model for South Africa, was training hundreds of South African terrorists. The court refused to condemn Mandela to death despite his plea of guilty on three of four counts, because he had been charged under laws that did not distinguish as sharply as the common law of High Treason between intentions and acts.[27]

At the same time that Tambo's call for an increase in violence in South Africa was immediately transmitted to the West without attribution, the secretary general of the ANC, Alfred Nzo, broadcasting in Zulu, made it clear that violence within South Africa and the mobilization of international "opinion" were complimentary sides of one strategy meant to divide the whites of

South Africa against themselves: "It has become abundantly clear that with increasing pressure from the international community, the apartheid regime will become divided against itself and this will spell its demise." Documents later published showed this analysis reflected straight South African Communist Party strategy. I have also heard this analysis more than once from State Department officials in the United States.

In broadcasts of congratulations, also in Zulu, to South Africa, for the ANC anniversary, the Soviet Union described the "apartheid regime" as surrounded by a "wall of resistance." These words betrayed knowledge and support of the ANC's and the UDF's strategy of total refusal of all the reforms of the South African government and of threats to the lives of all black "collaborators." The Soviet Union also openly admitted its "active support" of the ANC, including the training of terrorists in the Soviet Union and in eastern Europe, and called on "all progressive forces worldwide" to stand behind it with "comprehensive support" until "victory": "It is obvious to anyone that the regime is doomed. The revolution of the oppressed grows in intensity daily and shows no signs of abating."[28]

A few days later the ANC, the self-described leader "of all the oppressed peoples of South Africa," responded to the Soviets' call for the unity of "all progressive forces" with a call for "a grand alliance of all anti-government groups": the UDF, the South African Council of Churches (headed by Desmond Tutu) and so on. In response, the UDF blamed the ANC's escalation of violence on Botha's inflexibility and endorsed the ANC's demands:

Our peoples' demands are very clear: Apartheid must be dismantled. Nelson Mandela and all other political prisoners must be released unconditionally; the ANC and other banned organizations must be unbanned to take their rightful place in the creation of a new and better future for all South Africans; all detainees must be freed; the state of emergency must be lifted and all troops taken out of the townships.

These bland words meant, actually, to show up the South African government as intransigent and rigid—and to spread "the wall of resistance," named in the Soviets' congratulations, and blame it all on the government. The UDF announced the ANC's increase in violence, it took up its demands. But it knew the South African government would never concede them without the ANC's renunciation of violence. These contradictions, like the final disingenuousness of the "Torture Report," these demands for things beyond granting, meant to demoralize the blacks, to paralyze and to trap them into violence. They produced young blacks who mouthed words like these:

We have numbers and youth on our side; after all, there will be 45 million people in South Africa at the turn of the century and only 5.5 million whites. We can only grow stronger. Secondly, we have the world on our side and that is relevant. Finally it is the world that tells us we have morality and democracy on our side. Hence the whole pie is there for the taking . . . We accept [war]. But with South Africa completely isolated, the economy will eventually wind down, and you cannot fight a war with a shattered economy. War will be an easy jive.[29]

And even this was not enough twistedness to satisfy the twentieth century's muse of history who must be going stir crazy: Six months later these UDF demands showed their pale faces in President Reagan's crucial speech on July 22, 1986 against sanctions! Even those who wanted to defend the South African government, or more importantly, keep the West from pursuing suicide, found themselves unwittingly with the weapons of her enemies in their hands. A fitting plot for a new Greek myth—except that it has already been written: *The Seven Against Thebes.*

3 The New Constitution

Strengthened by the violence that broke out among blacks in September 1984, the "wall of defiance" had taken shape in the two years before, after Botha decided to move on the political level: enfranchisement of the 2,800,000 Coloreds and the 800,000 Indians who were to have their own representatives in separate houses of Parliament with authority to decide their "own affairs" and to vote on "general affairs" along with the white Parliament. For the first time, after four-and-a-half years of fairly successful social and economic reform, Botha ran into the determined opposition of all colors, but especially from organizations that claimed to represent the blacks.

In 1983 Botha's main task was to convince the white electorate to vote the constitution that he said embodied plans announced in 1977 to distinguish "joint decision-making on matters of common interest and separate decision-making on own affairs." The constitution meant to distinguish the Indians and the Coloreds sharply from the Africans in order to promote "national unity" with the whites without "throwing overboard separation, differentiation, [Hofmeyr's word in 1934] or self-determination." It would not bring mixed schools and residential areas because it respected local governments. There would be no forced integration from the top: "No one is being asked to accept integration."

Botha called CP and PFP alternatives "mirages in the desert" and accused the PFP of fostering an "exclusive psychosis" among Africans. In contrast to the "totally voteless" Indians and Coloreds, the constitutionally more advanced Africans had self-government they had accepted "of their own accord," blunt words, in this instance, of the minister of constitutional development and planning Chris Heunis. They helped make fierce attacks against the homelands a stock theme of activist groups outside Parliament.

South Africa was not about to "walk the path of Africa" with all groups in the same Parliament, Heunis also said. He did not need to apologize for a constitution that saw to maintaining white security. He meant sovereignty. A First World and a Third World nation, South Africa needed different constitutional arrangements, allowing for difference, unity and change. The West had to understand. Only consultation and negotiation could bring change. The inclusion of the Indians and the Coloreds had been carefully prepared for years, not "foisted" upon them, the PFP's charge.

Another minister, Piet Koornhof, now ambassador in Washington said that a "fourth chamber would destroy the process of self-government for blacks" in the homelands that had evolved since 1910: "You will have to create a chamber for each of the ten black nations in South Africa and then one for each of the four independent states."[30] South African public men are not given to prevarication, and when they are evasive they let you know it—the only way to hold white confidence in change—and everybody else's. At the same time the government appointed a cabinet committee for blacks outside the homelands in the townships that ring South Africa's major cities.

The debate on the new constitution reached the whole country, an astonishing change. Nobody was about to let Botha forget he had attempted the possible in a world where many governments regularly promise the impossible. He had presented a constitution, easy to criticize, that, however, might work—in contrast to the constitutions in many countries of the world, perfect on paper, that have little to do with their country.

The struggle for the constitution turned into a struggle against it, not directed primarily at the white electorate but against the government and at the world outside, a struggle against change because the proposed change was not enough. It also made it pitilessly clear that blacks in the townships had no grassroots political organizations, only organizations that spoke for them, sometimes from outside the country like the ANC, without representing them. The homelands had their governments, the townships nothing except their newly elected town-councils that the activists attacked constantly. Biko had been against organizations because they undermined self-responsibility and too often betrayed their followers, profound objections. The one exception was Inkatha, primarily Zulu, that Buthelezi had founded in 1973, because he sensed the vacuum, on principles not too different from Biko's: self-help instead of demonstrations.

During the campaign, black leaders, especially Buthelezi, and the organizations that presumed to represent the blacks attacked the constitution. For the first time, the whites heard their voices, even though the Africans had no vote—a paradox of South African politics, unheard of before, taken for granted abroad.

The white voters' decision to adopt the new constitution by a two-to-three vote in November 1983 was widely viewed in South Africa as the most important decision since the whites had chosen independence and broken with the Commonwealth in 1960. The decision of the Coloreds and the Indians to take part in the elections, which meant breaking nonwhite solidarity, did not come easily: Only about thirty-one percent of registered voters voted in the first elections almost a year after the referendum, in contrast to a Colored vote of nearly fifty percent in the elections for the Colored Representatives Council in 1968, and the forty-eight percent that a poll in early 1987 expected in the next elections of 1989.[31]

Both Coloreds and Indians thought it better to fight within the system than outside it. The Colored Labor Party (LP), the opposition in the Representative Council, with a plurality of popular votes, voted overwhelmingly, only nine of three hundred against, to support the constitution.

The substance of LP leader Allan Hendrickse's repeated words: The Coloreds, a conglomeration, not a race, a constituent part of the black community, would not be "intimidated or browbeaten" by radical, irrational, and irresponsible elements in the black community or by the government. They had to look out for themselves before they could help others. The readiness of Botha to split his ranks, the break in 1982 that led to the formation of the CP, proved his sincerity. The Coloreds who suffered from both whites and blacks, because in-between, had a "calling" to overcome the threatening polarization between blacks and whites—a translation, into practical politics in the real world, of the fancy in the thirties that saw a bridge between blacks and whites in Colored miscegenation.

The LP rejected protest for negotiation from its new place within the system, a system that depended on consensus to some extent, because negotiation was better than the rigid outright "no" of impotence, Hendrickse remembered a few years later: "Our people have been working at protest politics for decades, and now it's time to go beyond that . . . We live in a massively unjust society, and we'll never live in a perfect society, and as long as it's not perfect there will always be a market for people who have nothing to say but no, no, no. But I'm not one of those people," —politics that can teach you something about day-to-day living.[32]

But the LP leaders did not have an easy time of it. In something like thirty meetings throughout the country they faced angry, sometimes violent, followers of Allan Boesak, the Colored leader who called himself a "black" who passes for a "white," chaplain of the Colored University of the Western Cape, a patron of the UDF, in his total rejection of "the system." By April 1983, six months before the referendum, the LP called off all further public meetings.

Indian leaders made the same rough decision to work within an imperfect system, to "face reality" as another LP leader had put it. "The voice of protest would be better heard in a chamber than outside," said one Indian leader, at the same time he criticized the new constitution for its continuation of racial classifications.

The whites too voted for the constitution, not because they approved of it entirely but because it meant movement—and the possibility of further change. Even the government made it plain that the constitution was a "patchwork" arrangement, the best possible in actual circumstances, only a start. The constitution had shortcomings, but the country "cannot come up with anything better right now," Koornhof said.

Black spokesmen, and the PFP, did not accept these explanations: A major change was underway and they, who outnumbered everybody else, were left out—an argument, in appearance irrefutable, not the same thing as self-evident, that only knowledge of actual circumstances could refute. It made little impression on the white electorate in South Africa but great headway abroad.

The government faced this indignation in two somewhat contradictory ways. It further excited black aspirations, but tried to postpone them for the future with assurances, as Koornhof put it, "that all races would receive full political rights within fifty years"—assurances echoed by the President of the Ciskei, Lennox Sebe, one of the few homeland leaders to support the constitution: He said it was only a matter of time before all Africans would receive "some form" of political rights.

The government reiterated that the blacks did not figure in the new constitution because they had "a separate constitutional path to follow because of multinationalism," as Chris Heunis put it. By "multinationalism" Heunis meant that the differences among South Africa's blacks, centuries of tribal stratification into at least six major groups, made it impossible to treat them as if they were all the same because of the color of their skin. He meant the government was not about to drop the homelands policy overnight. But he also pointed to the give in the situation that showed in the institution of elections in the townships since 1979—"an exciting new development."

Buthelezi rejected outrightly this suggestion that community elected councils were, not merely local bodies, but "part of the substitute for excluding Africans from Parliament." The government would drive his people "to take up arms if it tries to foist on us a status of independence which we reject"—a reference to KwaZulu's rejection of independence in a referendum in 1978. In other words, no combination of town councils and homelands would do for inclusion in the nation.

In response the government announced its readiness to negotiate with "any leaders willing to cooperate in finding answers," and, a crucial step, it recognized the permanence of large numbers of Africans outside the homelands. These offers meant to show a possible way out of the contradiction of exciting aspirations and insistence on the homelands—in time.

The white right wing and the white liberals, the PFP, rejected this two-sided, disarmingly open, stance of the government, often called two-faced abroad, for the same reason from opposite perspectives: the right wing because the least concession meant the ruin of the entire system, the liberals because nothing would do except everything—the same all-or-nothing stance of some blacks, at least some black organizations. The white middle instead wanted to move along, slowly, with Botha: They knew they had to take risks, but they could tell the difference between risks and recklessness.

Right-wingers and liberals agreed on one thing: The new constitution subverted Parliament and threatened constitutional rule, a danger the CP called greater than communism. The conservatives argued for preservation of separate development and its extension with homelands for the Indians and Coloreds, an "impractical and immoral" and retrogressive proposal, Heunis said. The liberals concentrated on the new constitution's "exclusion" of blacks, proof of its "reentrenchment of apartheid," a central issue in the last weeks before the referendum. Helen Suzman came out for one-man, one-vote, because the blacks would not stand for less—and "which was exactly what they should get," an unrealistic position, she admitted *in private* in 1987.[33]

Both right-wingers and liberals held, rightly, that the power of the president and the President's Council limited the previously absolute powers of Parliament. The president had the absolute power not subject to appeal of the courts to distinguish between "general affairs" legislation for all three houses and "own affairs" that each house alone decided. Upon request of the president, the President's Council could make a final decision on a "general affairs" bill not passed by all three houses,—a provision both liberals and conservatives sensed substituted consensus negotiation for a simple vote in Parliament. Over time such arrangements might transform the government. They were right.

The liberals' decision to oppose the constitution because of its "exclusion" of blacks led them to hold public meetings of opposition with Buthelezi and Inkatha,—a daring move the government took for intimidation of white voters for the sake of blacks. This move also began the undoing of the act that forbade mixed parties. The outright repeal of this act showed the truth of Hendrickse's remark that the new constitution made it "politically" impossible for South Africa to remain static.

The rigidity of the liberals' opposition to the constitution, their insistence on policies they knew impossible, did not even convince their own voters. Their near fixation on the "exclusion of blacks," a historical distortion, for inclusion is the question, promoted the appearance of polarization between black and white that the PFP claimed a "yes" vote would bring.

But, especially in the long run, their readiness to make Buthelezi's voice count in the white campaign underlined the defenselessness of the majority of Africans. They were against violence according to the polls—any sensible man's expectation. After the campaign, Buthelezi turned on his hints during the campaign that a "no" vote would mean violence and that he might undertake a "marriage of convenience" with the ANC and PAC; he said of the PFP: "People like yourselves will remind us all to do everything in our power to moderate the harsh black political forces which will emerge after a 'yes' vote." The UDF, instead, called the PFP's acceptance of the constitution after the referendum, a loss of integrity.

The PFP's campaign swayed the government to adopt some of its demands, for instance, the end of inequities in education, it reached Buthelezi, the most important black leader, it made it easier for the press abroad to dismiss important changes. But it did not reach its own. Only an estimated ten percent of PFP members voted "no," more than half, five out of seven, voted "yes," in contrast to 600,000 CP voters out of 700,000 "no's." These defections persisted in the election of 1987.[34]

The risks of the PFP's stance so nearly rejecting the entire system showed themselves in two breakdowns: the visit of its leader Frederik van Zyl Slabbert and three other PFP MP's to the ANC in Lusaka in 1985, a few months before Botha called for action against violence, not debate; and Slabbert's flight from his party into "extra-parliamentary" activities in the next year,—just at the time Buthelezi grew outspoken against violence, the ANC, the UDF and the Congress of South African Trade Unions (COSATU).

Such flights and lapses told of the depth of the change underway, that led Paton, two years later, to write of undoing "conquest." The new constitution transformed the constitution of 1910 that had allowed South Africa to become the only industrial nation in Africa. It undid one of apartheid's major distortions, the equation of the Indian and Colored peoples with Africans. The black voices the liberals sponsored made their opposition heard in the world. The conservative opposition, nowhere near as emphatic and addressed only to whites, had little impact abroad, also because it was predictable. The liberal opposition obscured actual change and the government's determination. In the name of impeccable principles, the liberals, without a practical alternative, set themselves against change. No one, especially abroad, that did not distinguish between one country and another, Africa from Europe, could object to these principles. Paton, a leading liberal of a generation before, supported the government quietly but firmly. His support made a real difference to individuals within South Africa and abroad, but it did not count much in the propaganda battle, especially abroad: Paton had no organization behind him, he was not about to allow himself to be used.

4 The Fronts

The opposition to the constitution throughout 1983 and 1984 unleashed a struggle among blacks in the following years that broke down into violence between relatively few extremists, "comrades," outright thugs, the ANC and other trained terrorists and the majority of defenseless blacks with only local organizations, and few of them. By the end of 1986 with the violence in the townships more or less quelled, the attack concentrated on Buthelezi and his Inkatha, the only grassroots black organization, despite its concentration largely in Natal, capable to some extent of bridging the homelands and the townships. In 1983 Inkatha had two thousand branches and 750,000 members.

The propaganda of powerful front organizations heard throughout the world as well as in the townships masked the violence with ideology that made it look like spontaneous defiance. But it was not all forced: There was actual spontaneous defiance and anger. But the fronts twisted it to their own purposes to reject the entire system, not only the constitution, an all-or-nothing posture to precipitate violence by excluding all other alternatives. Their strikes and boycotts excited the young's resentment, they put the young on the streets with no way out but "confrontation." The ANC openly called for violence.

But the loyalty of the blacks to their country showed itself as well as the whites'. In local organizations and in Inkatha, they rejected the constitution, not the South African government. In Biko's tradition, and against Selborne's prediction, they also blamed themselves, not only the government. They wanted to resist half from within the system, half from without. Later, these moderates took to their defense,—the so-called vigilante groups. Their loyalty to their country showed in their readiness to give information to *stop* the terror to the South African Police at the risk of their lives. The South African Police's deep infiltration of the fronts and of the ANC, apparently even abroad, showed itself again recently in the tracking down and killing of Cassius Make, a member of the ANC National Executive Committee (NEC), in Swaziland on July 9, 1987: A middle-ranking ANC cadre actually a police agent had betrayed him. But the extent, momentum and organization of the ideological "onslaught" it had often predicted to unbelieving journalists took the government aback—despite its information. The government had been taken up with the constitution, and in the years before, with the loosening of apartheid. Just this readiness to let-up had prompted black protest and the organization of the fronts. The "onslaught" that surprised the government was the fruit of its years of reforms, the very proof of its loosening up.

The most important of the fronts, the UDF, was a huge coalition of all sorts of organizations from church associations to garden clubs, five hundred in 1983, the year of its founding, more that seven hundred recently. In the preceding years of reform many of these groups had organized locally to seek better schools and housing and so on. Some had overlapping membership, others few members at all. The UDF gradually turned these local groups away from the feasible to the national and international attack on apartheid. With remarkable geographical distribution, in appearance decentralized and pluralistic, the UDF is actually manipulated from the top—the antithesis of a grassroots organization.

From the beginning it made it clear it would have nothing to do with the "system," with reform and the new constitution. It declared itself open to all, blacks and whites, *except those willing to work within the system.* "The politics of refusal needed a united front," said Allan Boesak, one of its patrons. It wanted no part of "a government that had silenced the peoples' leaders and driven others into exile,"—an obvious reference to the ANC with its headquarters abroad and other terrorist organizations. Its first constituent meeting in August 1983 voted resolutions against "American and British imperialism."

With a program indistinguishable from the ANC's except for its apparent renunciation of violence, the UDF wanted to replace the South African government. One of its leaders said in 1983: ". . .The UDF is not simply an organization of the people—it is the people,"—an outline for a one-party state.

The UDF wanted the immediate overthrow of the system and the surrender of the government: The release of Nelson Mandela without renunciation of violence would mark the first step in the recognition of the UDF and ANC who themselves hold no elections as equals of the present South African government. These demands were to make more headway abroad, especially in Washington, than within South Africa.

In the beginning public evidence about the ANC's role in determining UDF propaganda and policy on crucial matters like cooperation with the government or other black leaders was hard to come by. The South African government did not publicly contest the UDF's claimed independence of the ANC. You had to rely on the similarity of their programs to show their interdependence,—and on trusted sources in Washington and South Africa. But the names of the co-chairmen, Albertina Sisulu and Archie Gumede, were suggestive: Sisulu was the wife of Walter Sisulu, a former ANC secretary-general sentenced with Mandela in 1964. Gumede was, and may still be though he denies it, an ANC leader. In March 1986 he showed up at the funeral in Maputo of Moses Mabhida late president of the SACP and longtime member of the ANC's National Executive Committee (NEC). In the winter of 1985–1986, two treason trials of UDF leaders promised public evidence of ANC manipulation of the UDF. One was thrown out of court for lack of evidence,—an action that told of the independence of South African judges. The other ended in December 1988 with the conviction of eleven defendants almost all active in the UDF for treason or terrorism, five with sentences of up to twelve years, six with suspended sentences with restrictions on political activity. The judge found that the UDF was the internal wing of the ANC amid outcries in South Africa and in the United States whose newspapers had not followed the trial. In October 1986 the government had declared the UDF "an affected organization,"—a prohibition of foreign funding. Over half of the UDF's funds came from abroad, from ANC supporters in Scandinavia, western Europe, and the United States, according to the UDF's treasurer.

For two or three years until the necklacings in the townships really took hold, the UDF passed itself off as a loose coalition of an irresistible popular movement of "democratic peace-loving people" against a government that wanted to divide people and "entrench apartheid." Like the pedigrees of its leaders, its noticeable Marxist undertones were ignored, for instance, the remark of a union leader at a rally of ten thousand after the first UDF national congress in 1983 on the need for a "powerful mass-based political organization capable of waging a political struggle on behalf of all oppressed and exploited."

These words recall the minutes of the SACP Central Committee meeting, dated 1981 on internal evidence, the South African Defense Forces captured in an ANC house in Gaborone in 1985: "[The meeting concentrated] . . . on the search for more effective ways of strengthening the Party's role as an independent vanguard of the proletariat and as part of the liberation alliance . . . The key question which dominated the discussion on almost every item was that of internal organization and leadership and the strengthening of the Party's presence amongst the masses, particularly the working class."

By 1985, however, the UDF's 1983 call for unity, except with those who worked "within the system," began to show its consequences: "[Unless] we begin to address ourselves to the redistribution of wealth and the creation of conditions of equality in all spheres of life, power sharing [a phrase the South African government had by then taken over from the PFP after rejecting it in 1983] will remain hollow and will continue to be rejected by the UDF." These words of a UDF spokesman recall the Freedom Charter that UDF speakers in 1983 had said would not be the basis of UDF unity.

The UDF spokesman went on to call for a climate favorable to "mass participation" to turn negotiation into a democratic process. This strategy meant to smash and/or co-opt local associations that have a surprising resilience in South Africa in order to facilitate the UDF's, and finally the ANC's and SACP's, control from the top. Tocqueville believed these local associations more important for democracy in America than the constitutional arrangements that came long after.

The UDF, in its publication *Isizwe* with Cuba as the example also called for the transformation of "apartheid capitalism" into "work [that] is not seen as an unpleasant duty . . . is not slave labor for a boss. In a socialist country, work is a way of developing yourself as a full human being learning skills and working together with others."[35] In April 1985, the UDF leaders, in their words "the real leaders of the people," called for the government "to transfer power to the people." They wanted the army and police disbanded; the three houses of Parliament and the elected town councils, the two most significant constitutional changes, undone; all security laws scrapped.

Buthelezi repeatedly pointed to the violent consequences of the UDF's insistence on excluding anybody "within the system": "The UDF attacks anybody who, in its judgment, it terms collaborators, or anybody it regards as working within the system," upon ANC instigation; "They [the ANC and the UDF] actually desire to attack blacks who do not agree with them. That is their official policy." He openly repeatedly accused the ANC of "actually telling ordinary black South Africans to kill other black South Africans," for instance, in September 1985.[36]

Buthelezi might have been quoting the 1981 Central Committee minutes which almost defined the front it called for in terms of attacks on collaborators: "Perhaps time is right for a new national body to tie together all the expressions of opposition which emerged during that [unidentified] campaign. On the question of attacking black collaborators, it is necessary that the attacks be accompanied by propaganda explaining why."

For its part, the ANC no longer denied its connection with the UDF: "Allow me to single out the creation of the UDF as a historic achievement in our peoples' efforts to unite in the broadest possible front,"—said ANC president Oliver Tambo.[37] His description strikingly resembles "the new national body to tie together all expressions of opposition" that the SACP wanted.

The technique of cooperation: The UDF called the school demonstrations, the consumer boycotts, the strikes and the rest of "the civil disobedience" that the world took for total black support of the ANC, and more importantly, for rejection of the government; the "necklace" and other violence the ANC encourages saw to attendance and compliance.

The strategy aimed to use the energy and defiance against actual grievances in particular situations to form "mass organizations" that have little or nothing to do with those grievances. It set the mood, especially abroad, for ridicule and contempt for the government's reforms. In New York in those days, 1985–1986, you could not mention reforms in South Africa in academic circles without provoking visible expressions of dumbfounded contempt I had never seen so nakedly before.

The minutes of the 1981 SACP Central Committee betray acute awareness that terror alone without "political confrontation" could not achieve anything but the appearance of random brutality. Terror needed a cover entirely unconnected with it: "The highly impressive armed actions which had raised the reputation of the whole movement could become counterproductive if the level of political confrontation and political work lags behind." The terror of violence had to get words: "Our propaganda is weak . . . We must cultivate propaganda inside the country"; "People are ready for a broad-based mass movement demanding peace and opposing the regime's aggressive policies" linked to "the international situation"; "We must issue strong propaganda in language the people understand," almost Lenin's words; "It is clear that we cannot win by spectacular armed actions alone"; "Our military underground is still way ahead of the political underground in public activity."

The last two sentences, incidentally, show that the SACP takes its control of the ANC terrorist wing for granted, for the ANC, not the SACP, had carried out the armed actions they mention. The SACP has no terrorists of its own.

The UDF provided the SACP and the ANC with the cover they wanted. The UDF gave credibility to ANC and SACP propaganda within South Africa. In the world outside the UDF gave terrorism a human face. It made it appear as if there was widespread *spontaneous* support for the goals of the terrorists among Africans. Abroad, the UDF made it possible to acquiesce to terrorism without knowing it because the UDF appeared to repudiate murder. Within South Africa among the blacks it turned actual defiance and anger into an ideological shield that made people helpless before violence and complicit with it. This technique of winning acquiescence to violence with its denial is the double-speak technique of totalitarianism everywhere. It works abroad because we will not know our fear. The increase in indignation against South Africa abroad best measures this unacknowledged fear. Its apparent irresistibility shows the extent of the underlying panic.

This renewed demonstration of the ANC's capacity to operate through legal fronts may be the ANC's most important achievement after the organization of its terrorist wing in 1961.[38] In 1981 the SACP knew it could not take the initiative for "a new national body to tie together all expressions of opposition": "The fraternal organizations [the ANC] should be guided on this question. It is not appropriate for the Party to initiate the call. We must work out the mechanics."

"Mechanics" means a department in the ANC to control and coordinate legal fronts within South Africa. Mac Maharaj a member of both the ANC's NEC and of the SACP is in charge of fronts. Maharaj is also responsible for "discipline," for internal intelligence and counter-intelligence and the prevention of infiltration within the ANC—a department named in grim innocence Internal Reconstruction and Development. Maharaj knows both terrorism,— he received "military" training in the Soviet Union,—and organization: Once a leading member of the British Communist Party, he played a crucial role in setting up the ANC's "mission" in London in 1950, still its most active center for propaganda and diplomacy. "Not taking the initiative" means more flexibility than common Communist practice usually allows: "It is sometimes the individual cell and occasionally the individual cadre who must carry the burden of translating the Party's broad directives into action in the specific circumstances in which he finds himself." But the flexibility means only that SACP and ANC cadres must adapt rigid indoctrination to local circumstances. The notebooks of black youths in terrorist training camps of the ANC's sister organization, SWAPO, published with the transcripts of the Denton Hearings, show routine continued instruction in organizing and manipulating fronts and coalitions. The words sound eerily familiar, they could apply to any country in the world, the United States as well as South Africa. To the youths who hear them they at first ring with the authority of Western science, one young South West African in flight from SWAPO told me. He had heard words like these:

Unity of all democratic forces in struggle against imperialism

Different democratic forces actively participate in anti-imperialist struggle:

1. Workers movement in Capitalist Countries
2. Peasants movements
3. Movements of intellectuals
4. Youth movements and women movements
5. Movement for peace antifacist antiracist movement
6. Student movement
7. Movement for human rights
8. Movement for former war-prisoners

The political platform for rallying the democratic forces advanced by Communist-parties:

1. Peaceful Capitalist existence of states with different social systems
2. Solidarity with peoples and countries which are the objectives of aggressive claims of imperialism
3. Struggle against war-danger for peace in the world
4. Non-proliferation of nuclear weapons complete ban of its usage in military purposes
5. Struggle of social economic transformation[39]

The day after the elections in 1987, the UDF publicity secretary, in words perhaps meant for the universities, wanted to substitute the "participatory democracy" he thought had prevailed in some townships in the last years for parliamentary democracy: "We are talking about direct as opposed to indirect political representation, mass participation rather than passive docility and ignorance, a momentum where people feel that they can do the job themselves, rather than waiting for their local MP to intercede on their behalf."

The means to bring this world to the South African townships, "the rudimentary organs of people's power": student organizations, parent organizations. The basic unit: the street committee elected by all of a street's residents.

The UDF publicity secretary talked almost longingly of the world before the State of Emergency. No mention of intimidation and murder: at least eleven UDF activists or officials missing or killed at the hands of unknown assailants in 1985:

Never have our townships seen such debate, such mass participation, such direct representation—and not just on the part of political activists, but on the part of ordinary South Africans who throughout their whole lives have been pushed around like logs of wood.[40]

"Sacrifice now and live in Utopia tomorrow" runs a 1985 UDF flyer, from the eastern Cape, addressed "To the Head of the House" demanding a "levy" of fifty rand a month from each household in addition to ten rand a month for each child: "You as head of the house are to give the STRUGGLE as follows . . . *People refusing will be dealt with in the usual way.*" (Italics mine).

The sense of inebriation, of utopian expectations this ideology with and without its intimidation had produced was strong enough for Botha to meet it head on in his speech opening Parliament to announce elections in 1987: "The point of view that a paradise on earth can be achieved by violent revolution is nothing but a dangerous and totally naive dream." He had to say these words in part because newspapers like the Johannesburg *Star*, their black reporters at risk especially after the increase in by-lines since 1984 exposed their names, would not print stories critical of the UDF.

In July 1987, the president of the UDF said he would urge black support of Indians and Coloreds in the elections for the three house Parliament in 1989, a reversal of the UDF's rejection of the system that the government welcomed, and the UDF, at first, quickly rejected. But by early 1988 there were signs that some UDF members might stand in the October town council elections—just the offices that had brought lynching and the threat of lynching in 1984 from UDF followers. Town-councillors had not been the only victims: In May 1986 in Cape Town, for instance, crowds murdered a veteran of the South African Defense Force thrown-out of a UDF rally.[41]

5 Harsh Times for a Man Against Murder: Buthelezi

I realize that there are people who hate my guts for daring even to grope for a peaceful solution after the violence that has been unleashed against blacks in the past ten months.
BUTHELEZI *in 1977*

These were the hardest times, and the best of times, for Chief Mangosuthu Buthelezi, leader of 6 million Zulus and elected minister of the Zulu homeland, the home of almost 3.75 million Zulus. Both within the system, and outside it, practically he alone spoke out against the violence and exposed it with a voice that carried. Buthelezi was against self-destructiveness, not against self-defense. He knows the difference between a fight and a riot, a thug and a soldier, between tough limited change and negotiation and the magical resort to words that promise everything: "The churches make moral pronouncements and the others [the ANC and other terrorist organizations] talk about revolution, and *they both think that if you say something is so, then it is so*"[42] (Italics mine).

Buthelezi conceded there might have to be "violent revolution" but not in the present because of the overwhelming strength of the South African government. He repeatedly referred to its restraint with awe, he criticized the police for ineptness in crowd control: "[The ANC's attempt to overthrow the government for twenty years] cannot succeed because it has no supply lines and an armed struggle of the magnitude which could lead to the defeat of the government would require logistical support, communications infrastructures and the transport of goods and people which go far beyond its ability to develop and maintain."[43] These words came before the elections of 1987 made the government's strength self-evident, when almost nobody either within South Africa or especially abroad spoke of the strength of the government,—unwitting testimony to its restraint.

Buthelezi was not against fighting, but only as a last resort, upon decision of the people, if ". . . the people at any time are forced to take the option of violence, I am not afraid to lead them as the peoples' options are my options." He would "start by recruiting his own sons before recruiting other peoples' children," he added, speaking like the ruler he is.[44]

He recalled courage to exorcise violence. This courage alone could distinguish between a terrorist and a soldier, between a revolutionary organization that tries to impose the violent seizure of power on a people through violence, and from outside the country, and the actual rebellion of a people when there is no other resort—almost the thinking of Locke. This distinction the witnesses before the Denton Committee learned in the harshness of terrorist training.

Because he can tell violence from the courage of a soldier, Buthelezi knows the power of straightforwardness to undo slander. This sensitivity appears "thin-skinned," "embarrassingly excessive," to Neuhaus who also calls him a "model of self-effacement." But Buthelezi does not fear this sensitivity because he can think on his feet. Our times demand this informality, it judges men on how they act when caught by surprise. In the United States this requirement, paradoxically, leads to evasiveness and duplicity. "What criticisms should I not answer? . . . You cannot know which criticisms are important. *Something very small, said by somebody very small, can become very big . . .*"[45] (Italics mine).

His freespokenness also makes it possible for Buthelezi to speak against bloodshed, especially since September 1984, and mean it, to distinguish it from its exploitation for indignation: "[Those who criticize us from abroad] speak so casually about the need for people to die . . ." And to remind people, for instance in 1987, of actual change more or less ignored abroad: "We are reaching a stage where the economy is dependent on black people, we are reaching a stage where the whites and blacks are interdependent."[46] During the summer miners' strike in 1987, the National Party newspaper said outright that the whites could no longer fill the mines' increasing need for skilled labor.

Buthelezi's words, incidentally, show the wisdom of his consistent support of economic growth and foreign investment ten years before, in 1977: "However grudgingly, one has to admit that even through exploitation there was some progress even for victims of that exploitation. Today South Africa is the economic giant of Africa. It has always seemed to me that change which destroys the base of future development of southern Africa would be self-defeating." Then as now Buthelezi's capacity to think on his feet kept him from saying one truth to deny another: "At the same time, I am only too aware of the fact that black people have been abused beyond the point of human endurance."[47]

Buthelezi believes deeply enough not to sport his faith, and he readily distinguishes between martyrdom and self-destructiveness, a distinction that makes Communist manipulation of the ANC obvious and Desmond Tutu's ambivalence in the face of violence pathetic. "I do not say that the ANC is a Communist organization. That is too simple. But if you ask me whether in fact the people who are really calling the plays in the ANC are puppets of Moscow, then the answer is yes. I do not hesitate to say that. I am convinced it is true. I know these people and there is no other way of explaining their behavior," he said about a year before the number of Communists in the ANC became a futile journalistic puzzle in the newspapers of the world.[48] For it is not the number of Communists in the ANC that counts. For sixty years the ANC has been infiltrated by Communists who in the fifties turned it into a Marxist-Leninist organization.

Buthelezi's unassuming trust in the Church showed itself in 1978 after Desmond Tutu had asked him to leave the funeral of Robert Sobukwe: "I am most astonished that a cleric who holds the position of Bishop Tutu should ask me to leave merely to give political credibility to a bunch of political thugs who abused, instead of honored, the memory of Sobukwe."[49] Sobukwe had led the black nationalists out of the ANC in 1959 after it took up the ideology and the tactics of the SACP, to found the Pan African Congress (PAC).

Buthelezi had left Sobukwe's funeral after stone-throwing and a close attempt on his life that Tutu responsible for order did not condemn outright. Tutu later explained that he wanted to frighten Buthelezi into resigning from office in the homelands. Tutu wanted Buthelezi to deprive himself of office to show he was a protest leader, and to get himself arrested to prove he was not a "collaborator." Buthelezi would not count without his office, he did not flee responsibility. He knows the provocative shows of defiance Tutu so wanted betray ingrained servility, not independence, as Mommsen wrote of Pompey.

Buthelezi's readiness to fight within the "system" goes to the heart of the struggle in South Africa, and in the West since 1917. I mean the struggle between opposition that comes of strength, necessarily limited, and opposition of weakness that knows itself in violence, that wants simply to destroy.

It is a life-and-death struggle between living men, and within them, between men and the self who can stand change, necessarily imperfect and incomplete, and those who cannot—who cannot stand the stirring of the living present because of the "torment of the ideal," Nadine Gordimer's phrase.[50]

Those who are able to take imperfection do not fear the necessarily slow gradual changes for the better. They face basic realities, for instance, the responsibility of blacks in South Africa also for their own condition, they can take disappointment as well as relief.

Buthelezi's readiness to live and fight within the "system" showed in KwaZulu's rejection of independence in a referendum in 1978, perhaps his most important act. KwaZulu's rejection of independence challenged the policy of separate development on its own terms, for the stated policy of the South African government foresaw eventual independence for all ten homelands but only upon their freely given consent: "I am criticized for accepting the leadership of a so-called homeland under the apartheid system, but if I were not here and some other leader accepted independence for KwaZulu, then the struggle would be lost, there would be no hope for a national convention, for a negotiated future for South Africa, and the whites could do whatever they wished forever . . . We single-handedly have made certain South Africa will remain a black nation."[51]

Buthelezi's decision to stay helped bring the government's grant of citizenship to blacks from the independent homelands living in South Africa. It recognized the permanence of the black population in South Africa outside the other unindependent homelands in 1985 at the same time that it insisted on the autonomy of the homelands—a declaration inconceivable a few years before. "There is no question of forcing together peoples who do not wish to be joined, or of keeping people apart who wish to come together," Botha said against a background of three "non-negotiables": one-man, one-vote nationwide, a fourth Parliament for blacks, abdication of the whites. The minister of cooperation and development, Gerrit Viljoen, made plain the eventual consequences of the modification of separate development: "The question is not whether black people will urbanize, but where and how."[52]

Buthelezi not only rejects violence, he rejects demonstrations, an attitude all but incomprehensible in the West today. He understands, like Biko, that actions that come of self-respect count, that the symbolic defiance of civil disobedience, for instance in school boycotts, betrays fear of responsibility: "We know that we have a lot of steam to let off. We have every reason to be angry about a million wrongs in South Africa. But this is not an occasion just for letting off steam. The millions of people who support us expect direction from us."[53]

Buthelezi rejects demonstrations for the same reason the ANC, SACP, the UDF and other terrorist and front organizations excite them: because they are terrorism's other face, because they do not bring change but serve to prevent it. They isolate children from their parents, and turn both against the "system," they make individuals say "no" when a "yes" might really count, and take courage.

In the wake of the disturbances in Soweto in 1976 that reached the western Cape but never Natal, and that doubled Inkatha membership within six months, Inkatha rank and file members called demonstrations ineffective and undignified; more importantly, they criticized them for setting children against parents and, thereby, against their entire past—just the aim of the

UDF, the ANC and other "radical" deracinated organizations: "We feel like members of a family, in acknowledging and respecting our elders, and we want to keep it that way. We know that our grandparents themselves fought for freedom, and we respect what our parents have done. This creates great solidarity, consciously or unconsciously. This applies even to migrant workers [in the townships],"—bland and commonplace language for truths.[54]

But Inkatha members betrayed something like defensiveness in their dismissal of demonstrations. Probably because in their beginnings, in the month before June 16, 1976, in contrast to the demonstrations after September 1984, the outbreaks of defiance against introduction in African schools of both Afrikaans and English as teaching languages had been spontaneous: "Gatsha [Buthelezi] can precipitate demonstrations such as Sharpeville or Soweto whenever he wants to. And if anything like that happened in Natal the rest would seem like child's play . . . But at present we don't think such demonstrations would be useful." And another Inkatha member: "We reject the apartheid system as totally as anyone else . . . We doubt that much can be achieved by the constant excitement of student protest."[55]

Buthelezi's dislike of demonstrations has profound roots, not only among the Zulus, who know the difference between war and riot, but also in the thirties before total Communist infiltration in the then Zulu-dominated ANC. In the thirties hostility against Communists brought the resignation of the president-general of the ANC. His successor, Pixley Seme, the founder of the ANC in 1912 who was married to Buthelezi's mother's sister, refused to let the ANC strike, demonstrate and burn passes—despite the SACP's instigation of confrontations that the police swiftly dispersed after they broke out in Durban. In a context that clearly shows they understand they need demonstrations to make terrorism effective,—"Our military underground is still way ahead of the political underground,"—the 1981 SACP Central Committee meeting minutes still recalled the quickly repressed pass-burning campaign in Durban: "We must speak to the people and lead them as for example we led the great anti-pass campaign in Natal in 1930."

Buthelezi's rejection of violence and demonstrations, his freedom from resentment, his freespokenness, especially his repeated attacks on the UDF and the ANC for prompting "black-on-black violence," stir hate: The danger to his life that showed itself at Sobukwe's funeral is real.

In its almost weekly attacks on Buthelezi, the ANC radio has called Buthelezi, not Botha, "the major political foe of the ANC inside South Africa." It has called him again and again, a "collaborator," a "stooge," a "tribalist" in phrases like "treacherous faces of the Buthelezi type" and "his [Botha's] salaried puppets . . . like Gatsha Buthelezi": "The puppet Buthelezi is being groomed by the West and the South African racists to become a Savimbi . . . The onus is on the people to neutralize this snake which is poisoning the people . . ." In 1987, the comparison of Buthelezi with Savimbi found its way into a major article on Buthelezi in the *New York Review of Books*.

These phrases meant imminent necklacing when used of other less visible individuals in the townships, especially town councillors. They also mean to prepare for Buthelezi's murder, Inkatha leaders said outright.[56] "In general the top collaborators must be dealt with physically but the bulk of those below them should be dealt with politically," remarked "comrade G" in the 1981 SACP Central Committee meeting minutes.

Buthelezi does not seem to have understood the damage a front organization, like the UDF, that represented everybody and nobody, could do. He knows that the paralysis ideology brings makes people helpless before slaughter—the real object behind the agenda of many organizations in our time. But he did not really believe it. Buthelezi probably cannot understand people who do not want to act in the actual world but want to undo it in the name of another.

Like all men of action who distinguish between the possible and the impossible,—and like Savimbi of Angola he has more than a touch of greatness about him,—Buthelezi is fundamentally innocent despite occasional obvious cunning in tactics. He is immersed in the feasible. The day-to-day responsibilities of office, prosaic details of life and death take him up. "I am at this time deeply concerned about our producing enough food to eat," he had to remind even his own legislature in 1977. He assumed the good sense of blacks. Most polls bear him out. He assumed their respect for authority, their respect for the government. He probably did not conceive the UDF could win the confidence of foreign journalists.

At first he attempted to dismiss the UDF as in "real danger of becoming only a paper organization" and as "two or three steps away from the people," in contrast to his own organization that he described, rightly, as "the largest black political constituency ever created in the history of this country." He jeered at the UDF for "forming committees and getting the audience to clap."[57] All accurate characterizations but beside the point: The UDF was interested in stopping change, not in getting things done. It promised the impossible, the immediate transformation of the world.

He thought words would also tell against the ANC. In a rally in Soweto in 1983, he distinguished between black grassroots organizations, like Inkatha, and the ANC today which was out of touch with the actual situation within South Africa, and should not try "to dictate to us from the capitals of the world." All ANC leaders have lived outside South Africa since 1977, many since they fled in the nineteen sixties. He also stated repeatedly that the ANC had chosen the path of violence and terrorism in 1961 without consulting the blacks in South Africa. His movement was dedicated to the traditional ideals of the ANC, the ideals that had inspired the ANC before total Communist infiltration and before it turned to terrorism in 1961. Inkatha uses ANC songs and colors.

He did not sense the drawing power of organizations like the ANC and the UDF,—understandably, for even today there is little evidence of willing adherence. He did not sense the threat of these organizations to change, and the fascination their rejection of everything, their insistence on immediate transformation, and the ANC's open incitement of violence, might exercise abroad and among township blacks, especially on black adolescents and children.

Buthelezi's innocence, the innocence that allows him to think on his feet, also lends his words intelligence strong enough to let you imagine his tone of voice from the transcripts of his remarks. In the United States, he shocks his audiences, who do not expect good sense from political leaders, let alone black leaders, with his "conservatism." Like Savimbi, and like Moynihan at the UN, he provides an accurate measure of the influence a first-rank figure can achieve without the backing of the make-believe world of the UN, the Organization of African Unity (OAU), and the Commonwealth that live off words and the media, a world he sees clearly. For he knows how the other world, the real one, is put together. He turns up frequently at the right spot at the right time throughout the free world: in San Francisco, in New York, at the House of Lords, at an important Christian Democratic congress in Rome in May 1986. The exception: the fall of 1986, when he arrived in the United States after the passage of the CAA Act. The press treated him like a dull exotic curiosity. He had been outwitted, apparently, by the indirect advice of a State Department that dreads strong voices and likes to test leaders and countries for their readiness to do themselves in. But even then his intelligence got through: More than once I have heard his comments through word of mouth.

Buthelezi's rejection of demonstrations for their betrayal of servile disposition that does not bring self-respect or the respect of others, his understanding that the present can only lead into the future if it recalls the past,—let alone his references to his ancestors and Zulu victories and defeats,—and above all his confidence, his spontaneous anger at violence, make him a man, who whether he wants to or not, challenges basic assumptions in the West, unspoken assumptions, the ones that count most because they come of the unfaced past.

For the prestige media,—not for all newspapers,—Buthelezi is not merely incomprehensible, he excites something like disgust. You can actually feel their guts wince at his words. In 1987, an American reporter criticized Buthelezi's Inkatha for "rarely attempting to challenge the system" and for undermining "consumer boycotts and other kinds of popular protest" that often lead to violence: "[Inkatha] spent more energy teaching women how to sew and teenagers how to grow crops than how to organize serious protest."[58] These words are the way you say, "Let them eat cake," in Manhattan.

The reasons for this instinctive distaste before Buthelezi are not pretty. It is not American innocence and good faith that impels the unquestioning acceptance of demonstrations, but the unacknowledged humiliation of having yielded to mobs, mobs of the well-to-do, of the student sons of the rich and the mighty, of their own children, the only mobs the European world knows, but mobs nevertheless. For the war for Indochina was not lost on the battlefield, but on the streets of American cities and above all on American university campuses, and not by accident, but as a result of a deliberate Communist strategy. It used those crowds, like in South Africa. They were terrorism's other side, its children, essential for breaking minds and will. Vien, the organizer of the demonstrations in France against the Indochina war in 1952–53, told James Stockdale, in between torture sessions in Hanoi in the summer of 1966, before the "anti-war" demonstrations had started in earnest in the United States:

Our country has no capability to defeat you on the battlefield. But war is not decided by weapons so much as by national will. Once the American people understand this war, they will have no interest in pursuing it. They will be made to understand this. We will win the war on the streets of New York.[59]

Throughout slander's violence, Buthelezi has managed to keep open the possibility of dialogue with the South African government in spite of, and in a sense because of, his refusal to talk to P.W. Botha for years. Because he is half in the system, he can put off negotiating without rejecting negotiation.

He knows you cannot change people overnight,—and that the ruin of the South African government would bring ruin to whites and blacks, blacks especially. He knows the roots of the blacks in the country and the homelands. Half the blacks still live in the homelands. More importantly, until the recent introduction of elections in the townships, and the even more recent acceptance of the permanency of blacks there, the only self-government blacks exercised, whatever its defects, was in the homelands.

Also Buthelezi knows how to wait, because he knows where he is going: "The future of South Africa is a black and white future"—unless the UDF and the ANC seize power.

The roughest test of Buthelezi's carefully articulated position against violence started in August 1985 when serious fighting broke out in Natal after the murder of a UDF "civil rights" leader or "activist": Seventy died—the first serious violence to involve Natal, in itself a testimony to Buthelezi's leadership and confidence.

After the murder of Victoria Mxenge, outside her house in the Durban township of Umlazi on August 2, national student associations, including the Congress of South African Students (COSAS), called a week-long school boycott, the first in Natal that year. On Tuesday, August 6, the second day of the boycott, pupils demonstrating on the main road in north Durban, attacked an Indian shop. Toughs joined them and there was widespread looting and arson. Clashes also occurred, especially at schools not out on boycott in Umlazi: attacks on policemen, school principals and shops, one student shot dead. Well-prepared, for instance, with all the school telephone numbers, the student organizers had gone from school to school to get principals, who sometimes called the police, to close.

On August 7, at the memorial service for Mxenge in a movie house in Umlazi, violence continued between the mourners, UDF members and sympathizers, and Zulus who allegedly started the attack: sixteen dead, one hundred injured. On August 9, Indians, and then African shack-dwellers, looted and burnt down the Phoenix Gandhi settlement. Inkatha called out all its branches, some of them leading groups a thousand strong, to "restore law and order." There were house-to-house searches for loot and UDF activists. By the weekend Inkatha announced relative calm in the townships: Thirty-seven of the dead perished in police actions, twenty-three in fighting between vigilantes and others.

On August 7, Buthelezi said that the men responsible for the violence came from outside the townships. There were continuing clashes between UDF and Inkatha supporters throughout September. In October the regional court in Durban found seven Inkatha members guilty of attacks on UDF supporters' homes. In August alone, property damage ran to two million rand, according to Buthelezi.

Tension between the UDF and Inkatha had been evident long before the August and September outbreaks Mxenge's murder precipitated. Already in 1983, just after its founding, the UDF sought to organize protests around issues like housing, forced removals and transportation in the Durban townships. It even tried to keep Inkatha officials, "collaborators" it called them, out of some areas. In 1984 the UDF sought an injunction to keep Buthelezi from holding a rally in a Durban township. In May 1985, two months before Mxenge's murder, an Inkatha Central Committee member Winnington Sabelo warned UDF members to leave the townships around Durban or "face action," a threat the secretary general of Inkatha, Oscar Dhlomo, told the UDF to ignore. Because of mounting requests, Buthelezi had asked the South African government, again in May, to allow him to issue licenses for firearms to citizens to "defend themselves from attack." Sabelo's wife was murdered and their three children badly injured by men with AK–47s, a weapon used practically only by the ANC.

Despite Buthelezi's repeated statements that non-violence did not amount to defenselessness, the resort to force in August and September 1985 did not come easily to Inkatha leaders. A year and a half later they were still visibly shaken by the decision to fight back against provocations they knew meant to compromise Inkatha. But they were determined not to lose control of the townships around Durban, and, above all the schools: "They killed my wife, and for one reason: I refuse to let the townships be disrupted," Winnington Sabelo told the American reporter baffled by Inkatha's rejection of demonstrations, as he pointed to buses bringing children home from school. It was 1986, a time of boycotts elsewhere in South Africa. "We are *not* responsible [for the violence]. When we say we are committed to non-violence, we mean it. But there's no way we're going to be sitting ducks. We reserve the right to retaliate," Buthelezi told the same reporter.[60]

The latter half of 1986, and especially 1987, tested Buthelezi's loyal opposition. They also brought more violence to Natal *after* the declaration of the State of Emergency in June 1986 began to bring relative quiet to the townships in the Eastern Cape and the Transvaal. After the murder of Mrs. Sabelo in August, Buthelezi had foreseen this violence that had spared Natal in the previous two years, the beginning of civil war, he had called it.

Throughout 1986 Buthelezi blamed the killings which had brought the

State of Emergency on the new constitution. He said he would not serve on the National Council unless it meant to replace the 1983 constitution.

He continued his attempts at patchwork reconciliation with the ANC, PAC and the UDF that had failed with his attempt at "a marriage of convenience" in 1983. In July in written evidence before a committee of the House of Commons, and also in South Africa, he called for the unconditional release of Mandela, an important shift that showed the effect of tidal waves of propaganda. But he added: "As much warmth as I feel for [Mandela], I would reject him being imposed on us."

Buthelezi's overtures to Mandela, who refused to see him until his release, made the ANC in Lusaka shifty: They preferred Mandela in jail, Buthelezi said. At the same time, he repeatedly made it plain that the ANC's violence could not bring democracy to South Africa but only provoke a white-black "backlash." He rejected the insistence of important Inkatha members that "we too should be trotting off to Lusaka making subservient noises,"—a reference to the visit of leading South African businessmen and newspaper editors, including the chairman of Anglo-American, to ANC headquarters in Lusaka on September 13, 1985.

But he also supported some government positions. He spoke out against divestment. The crumbling of apartheid, he said, made the education of black youths an absolute priority—the judgment of the government also.

For eight months in 1986 against a background of continuing violence between Inkatha and the UDF, Buthelezi played a leading role in the so-called Natal Indaba, negotiations that won wide attention abroad, in the United States especially among conservatives who yearned for a quick solution in South Africa that would not force them to distinguish South African realities from American illusions.

The government's acceptance, against vehement right wing opposition, of a joint executive council to administer both KwaZulu and Natal, inaugurated the Natal local initiative: "It is time we stopped looking over our shoulder for nods and winks from government. We are going to come up with suggestions that suit the people of Natal," said Oscar Dhlomo, secretary general of Inkatha in 1985, after the government's acceptance, in principle, of the joint executive.

The government stressed that the acceptance of a joint KwaZulu and Natal administration had nothing to do with the Indaba, without directly opposing the local negotiations it knew "held deep political implications." Probably it expected that the thirty-five negotiating groups, including two Afrikaner organizations, would not come to an agreement.

The National Party in Natal sent observers but refused to participate because such participation would amount to endorsement. The CP, the UDF, the ANC, the PAC, the Herstigte Nasionale Party, COSATU and the Azanian People's Organization (AZAPO) refused to participate.

But the negotiating groups did agree except for the two Afrikaner groups who refused to sign, one saying that the negotiations ended "before the real issues had been discussed." The agreement proposed a two-house legislature: the first with one hundred members, sixty-six directly elected, in constituencies with all parties competing, thirty-four by proportional representation; the other, with fifty members, ten each from five ethnically defined groups with Afrikaners divided from English-speakers and a South African group for those who did not want to accept ethnic classification. There was also a bill of rights, its most striking provision: the right to "lawfully own and occupy property anywhere in the province." In all areas of the local legislature's competence like housing, education, economics and social planning, the Natal parliament could repeal or amend any act of the South African Parliament. Provision was made for the local authority of chiefs outside the provincial parliament.

Such a design means Inkatha would easily dominate the first chamber, alone responsible for the election of the prime minister, with about seventy percent of the seats. Buthelezi would be prime minister, an election the whites and Indians could accept because of Buthelezi's extraordinary virtues. But a constitution cannot be accepted, or work, because of confidence in one man.

The National Party leader, in Natal, not the government, immediately rejected the proposal because it did not secure the political rights of minorities: "It was clear a majority party would effectively exercise sole power in the legislative and executive authority, as was the case in a typical Westminster system." The government said it would consider the proposals Natal had not yet submitted.

The Natal-KwaZulu initiative posed a problem for the government, not so much because "the end result would be a one-man, one-vote system," the objection of the NP representative in Natal, but because it implied more autonomy for Natal than any other province. On the one hand Botha had said that "South Africa must find solutions in the devolution of power"; on the other, the government had just substituted central-government appointed Regional Service Councils for elected provincial councils everywhere except in Natal, a change the PFP rightly attacks as centralizing, but without regard to the government's appointment of men of all races to these new councils.

With some irony, the autonomy the central government had granted KwaZulu in expectation of its independence had had its effect on the Natal design. Buthelezi was not about to surrender any of KwaZulu's powers. He had made the already existing powers of the self-governing homeland the starting point of Inkatha's negotiations with the other thirty-four groups, a situation that led one of the Afrikaner groups that refused to sign to call the design, "a constitution where the jurisdiction of the KwaZulu government had been extended over the whole of Natal."[61]

In addition the government faced hints of separatist tendencies. The right wing parties were calling for "their land in South Africa . . . the old Boer republics of the Transvaal, the Orange Free State, and northern Natal," a historically accurate description of the land the Boers who had left the Cape had opened up. A Cape Colored Labor Party representative called for a Western Cape Indaba: "The crucial point is that the [provinces] should get together themselves—as in Natal—and not have their boundaries and composition forced upon them by the central government." These moves toward regional autonomy with their hints of the old differences between the two republics and the two self-governing colonies might challenge the strong central government that the constitution of 1910 had made, not only the constitution of 1983. And all at a time when the government faced war abroad.

The violence in Natal after the State of Emergency intensified during the Indaba negotiations. Zulus, youths, and Inkatha against the UDF. Ideological differences set off cycles of vengeance which resembled tribal feuds that in the past lasted sometimes ten years and more, and reached even the Zulu migrant workers around Johannesburg.

In 1986 there were about eighty-six deaths; in 1987, fifty deaths between January and August; another eighty in September in clashes near Pietermaritzburg after an Inkatha youth congress lured away youths from the UDF. (Youths in Inkatha in 1986 numbered over four hundred thousand, the largest single group, a result of vigorous recruitment in the previous three years.) In December another seventy-seven people died, a total for 1987 of over three hundred. These murders occurred not in KwaZulu, but in townships in Natal around Pietermaritzburg, almost a no man's land. Buthelezi's tough KwaZulu police had no jurisdiction there. The South African Police was waiting, as it did in the townships two years before, for the situation to become bad enough to make its intervention indisputably necessary. The killings centered on the townships around Pietermaritzburg because the South African government had allowed the KwaZulu police to impose order in townships around Durban after the 1985 killings.

The ANC/UDF violence was meant to discredit Buthelezi and Inkatha. It was meant to bring Buthelezi down to their level. Especially abroad, Inkatha was called the aggressor. But in the north, the murder in Natal sobered some blacks:

If this is the type of retribution that will become common when blacks rule blacks, then perhaps we need a great deal more oppression to make us humble, responsible and dignified in our anger against oppression. Come the day of liberation I will take my kids and make a beeline for Beirut. Perhaps it is tough there, but not so primitively savage.[62]

6 Before the New Constitution

For more than four years, before the struggle for and against the constitution took up South Africa in 1983 and broke into open violence in 1984, since his assumption of the prime ministership in September 1978, P.W. Botha had pursued reform. In 1983 Botha called the new constitution a continuation of the changes that had started in 1977.

But the introduction of the new constitution also forced a break with the preceding years, both because of the resort to the States of Emergency, a necessity that shocked South Africa, first the partial one from July 1985 to March 1986, and the national one from June 12, 1986, the first State of

Emergency since Sharpeville in 1960. And more importantly, because thinking and action had a life of their own: By 1985, the government had made decisive moves toward the evolution of black political rights, moves inconceivable a few years before.

Six years after the assumption of office Botha faced an apparent full-scale insurrection against change that in 1987 he called a revolution incited from abroad. Could he have avoided it? Did he move too fast?

Already before Botha South Africa knew expectancy. A few years before Botha took office in May 1976, in Vorster's South Africa, a then unknown black student leader, Stephen Biko, had remarked in extraordinary five-day public testimony at a trial that at times reached the level of dialogue with the court on the difference between defiance and "revolution,"—in itself a remarkable tribute to the South African judiciary,—that the air was "vibrant with change": "In my view this government is not necessarily set on a Hitlerized [course]. I think it is biding its time. I believe that inevitably the government will listen to Black opinion"; "What I mean here is that both sides—that is now Black and White—see the need for a solution in a sense. Both sides reject the present situation."[63] Biko's words,—perhaps more than anything else could,—show that Botha was on to realities, not fancies.

Three years later Mvubelo spoke as if a good deal of the change had already occurred: "A never ending list of laws was passed to keep the black man down. But all of these efforts are crumbling or have already crumbled. South Africa has a new prime minister, and a definite new direction is being taken . . . Clearly, there is only one solution, and that is by way of evolution, by negotiations, and utilization of opportunities which arise, by cooperation when necessary and resistance when necessary."

Mvubelo was partly right. There had been rapid economic change in the previous ten years. Economic growth, with changes in proportions of income,—the policy that Kent Durr, the able deputy minister of finance and of trade and industry called in 1986 a policy of "*inclusion* rather than *exclusion*, economically, constitutionally,"—had started before Botha's reforms and before the unrest in Soweto in 1976. From 1970–1975, African incomes doubled, and Asian and Indian incomes increased, while white earnings remained steady, with a yearly expansion of the Gross Domestic Product from 1971–1977 of 15.7 percent. Disparities were still acute. In the period 1980–1985, the reduction in disparity between white and nonwhite incomes continued, despite little growth, in part because of the inclusion of black trade unions in collective bargaining since 1979,—the most important of Botha's changes before repeal of the "Pass Laws" in 1986. From 1981 to 1985 real earnings for nonwhites outside of agriculture grew at 2.6 percent compounded yearly, for whites at 1 percent. From 1970 to 1982 the ratio of white to nonwhite earnings in mining fell from 19.8 to 5.6, "a spectacular drop" as Durr called it, in manufacturing, from 5.8 to 4.1.[64] A study made by the Bureau of Market Research of the University of South Africa in October and November 1985 of 6,400 individuals in Pretoria and ten other city areas showed that individual incomes in Soweto averaged seventy-four percent of the white average, an average of R 1,756 against white monthly income of R 2,374 average. The lowest individual monthly earnings averaged R 1,030 in Kimberley. Household yearly earnings ran R 9,624 in Soweto, R 9,359 in Pretoria, R 8,828 in the East and West Rand, R 5,611 in Bloemfontein, the lowest.[65] Companies in Johannesburg now direct much advertising primarily toward the black market, as Buthelezi was quick to note.

The disturbances in 1976, and the mood Biko sensed a few weeks earlier came in the wake of improvement, changes, expansion, not of desperation. Botha sensed this buoyancy and disregarded the dangers, especially in his words—in part because he was confident of South Africa's strength, confidence that also showed itself in his foreign policy, in the offer of a common market for all of southern Africa in 1979.

A party man all his life, Botha became prime minister unexpectedly because of his capacity to maneuver and win support within his party, to talk to individuals and persuade, after a deep-going scandal put Vorster's expected successor, Cornelius Mulder, out of the running. Mulder, later a founder of the CP, would not have undertaken the gradual dismantling of segregation and the recognition of the permanency of blacks in South Africa outside the homelands. Until his death in 1988, Mulder, CP representative in the President's Council, argued with force that Botha's changes had to lead to one-man, one-vote.[66] Botha, in contrast, was ready to undertake the enormous risk of limited imperfect change. These are the contingencies that sometimes decide the life of nations, free nations.

Expected to be tough, hard-line, Botha argued for a new generation's right to take a fresh look at its country because things change constantly. Botha was not moving alone; and he knew it. He had the confidence to say what many white South Africans thought but would not admit they thought—and not only white South Africans. "We are moving along in a changing world; we must adapt or die" (August 1979). In Soweto a few days later: "This is not just a courtesy call. Our presence here is proof that we are prepared to open our hearts to you." Again, in the same August 1979 speech: "There are higher things in life than to stare at the color of a man's skin. We are prepared to allow Black people into our kitchens to prepare our food, but the moment a Black appears next to us in the post office, we say, 'Go away.' What kind of nonsense is that?" He did not shrink from raising aspirations: "I believe in reforming and improving policies, if this is out of conviction and realistic idealism. We must be prepared to eliminate worn-out practices and restrictions . . . South Africa dare not follow the path of oppressing other races" (January 1979).[67]

Especially in his visit to Soweto, Botha seemed almost to return to the advice of the Anglican priest, Trevor Huddleston, in 1955, before apartheid, but not at the expense of bluntness that showed his spontaneity's good faith: "If I had to choose a motto expressing just one truth that has served me well in South Africa I would say, '*Always* act on impulse.' And after twelve years' experience I would say the same. You will make mistakes, of course. But as Chesterton said somewhere, 'the man that never made a mistake never made anything.' "[68]

Botha's ministers spoke the same blunt language. Gerrit Viljoen, minister of national education: "The core of South Africa's problem is that answers to the problems of the past are not full answers to the problems of the present . . . Let us be honest with each other: Things have not worked out as we wanted. We will have to adapt policy and reform it in accordance with the existing reality of our situation."[69] Another minister, answering charges of betrayal at a heated provincial congress of Botha's party in Natal in 1979: "Those who say I am selling out the Whites can go to hell. If you don't love your children, I love mine, and I want to give them a future. That future includes White identity—but it certainly does not include White privilege."[70] These words stung, they were not meant for the general public but mostly for Botha's own party, which holds a majority so indisputable in Parliament, a changing majority the elections of 1987 showed, that the PFP sometimes said it took itself for the state.

Botha and his ministers' confidence moved not only Mvubelo, but Paton, Buthelezi and others: "When I first met him [Botha] on January 22, 1978, I found that unlike his predecessor, at least this man was a human being," Buthelezi said. Lennox Sebe, soon to become president of the independent homeland, the Ciskei,—independence recognized only by South Africa: "We are entering a new era. This is the first time we have got a leader who is prepared to stretch his hand of friendship to the Blacks. It is also refreshing to meet a man who has a philosophy, and not an ideology." The last crucial distinction explains Botha's resilience.[71]

It took more than words to show the whites he meant it. In August 1980, a stunning cabinet reshuffle convinced sceptical journalists in South Africa: He put in sixteen ministers who either matched or outdid him on reform. In 1982 Botha's struggle with his own party showed its earnestness. Sixteen MP's broke with him to found the Conservative Party, the most important change in South African politics since the National Party took office in 1948 according to many in South Africa. But a country's responsibility for itself magnifies domestic politics. The close referendum in 1960 (a majority of 74,580 votes out of 1,629,336) that brought a republic and an immediate break with the Commonwealth in 1960 meant more.

Botha concentrated on social and economic reform to facilitate the economic and social transformation of the country, reform that he expected would lessen the pressure for political change and make it easier. He knew most things had to take care of themselves. But coping with actual opportunity puts more of a strain on individuals than political agitation.

Botha's emphasis on economic and social change before major political change, which the 1983 constitution disrupted, had, like everything he did, deep roots in South Africa's past, not only in Lord Selborne's advice and in Smuts' exchange with Merriman in 1906, but also in Hofmeyr's thinking in the thirties: ". . . [Hofmeyr's] view was that the 'Native problem' had acquired an entirely false emphasis, and should be regarded as subordinate to the question of economic adjustment," Paton's characterization.[72] Not a new idea. In 1906 a friend at Cambridge had written Smuts: "The U.S.A. committed an act of great folly in giving the franchise at first, and indiscriminately to all negroes, but they are committing something worse than folly in the way in which by various crooked methods, by social intolerance and injustice, they are now trying to deny to the considerable numbers of negroes who are showing full capacity for progress in education, culture and efficiency as civilized citizens, all opportunity for industrial, commercial, civic and social progress."[73] About five percent of slaves could read upon emancipation in 1863 in the United States,—the conventional guess, probably too high.

Botha moved immediately in three areas: in the public area of so-called "petty apartheid" (desegregation of beaches, theaters, restaurants, business areas); in the economic area with the grant of property rights in the townships, first through freehold lease and then through outright ownership, and with the registration of black unions. Never illegal, and with the right to strike since 1973, unions had not been allowed, since 1924, to join the Industrial Councils that reach most industry-wide collective bargaining agreements. In 1979 Botha improved technical and vocational training for blacks,—including 200 percent tax concessions for companies with training programs,—he appointed a committee to plan for the "equality of education for all population groups."

All these changes were far-reaching and have continued gradually on local initiative. In 1986 Pretoria desegregated, the last remaining major city hold-out. Elevators, post offices and public buildings had been desegregated by 1979, before Botha, almost overnight and without incident. By 1987 no laws forbade owners of theaters and hotels in central business districts throughout the country from doing business with all races. Coloreds no longer had to worry about driving far enough to reach the few hotels previously open to them between Cape Town and Johannesburg. Beaches desegregated more slowly—against the CP's warning during the election of 1987 that those who "swim together, rule together." In Durban in 1986, for instance, there were three white beaches, seven open to all, two African, one Indian—the white beaches near the waterfront hotels. Also in 1986, the Port Elizabeth City Council reaffirmed its decision to open all beaches despite a referendum, with seventeen percent participation of 6,104 against, 4,957 for. The railroads that had already bothered Selborne in 1908 still held out with indecisive optional measures—in contrast to public transport in central cities. City central business districts opened up to businessmen and customers of all races, upon local initiative, at least forty-four in 1985, sixty in 1988 with forty-five more scheduled. Blacks fill city parks, once only for whites. Of 43,000 students at the English-language universities 17 percent were nonwhite, 6.3 percent African, 4 percent colored, 7 percent Indian in 1985. With every fifth student black in 1987, the University of Witwatersrand reckons half or more students may be black by 1995. After the defiance in Soweto in 1976, Cape Town and Witwatersrand had asked the government to allow them to readmit blacks who since 1959 had needed special permits that kept black enrollment at about 2.5 percent. There is increasing integration of nursing staffs and admission of patients of all races to hospitals, at least to special units, with segregated wards, especially at private hospitals, 250 out of 672. After attempting to apply the "own affairs" distinction to medicine that the PFP called "a scandalous waste of resources," the government turned over health administration to the multi-racial Regional Service Councils, the new provincial governments. In 1986 community and health organizations voiced the "strongest opposition to any attempts to replicate the tricameral system in health care," after the Transvaal provincial government instructed a hospital in Johannesburg to admit only coloreds to ease overcrowding. The threat of some doctors not to comply brought the unacknowledged suspension of the directive. The new Transvaal ambulance service is color blind.[74] The changes took aback travelers who had known South Africa five and ten years before—especially the little racial hostility among individuals. ". . .The battle over apartheid is over," the Canadian journalist, Peter Worthington, recently remarked.[75]

There were also limits. There was no talk of desegregation of schools, separation that the readiness to admit blacks to universities on tough standards shows has strong practical reasons. But private schools, first allowed to admit blacks with special permits in 1976, now admit blacks freely and also receive public subsidies—after a few Catholic schools in the Transvaal unable to get permits admitted blacks anyway despite a government threat to cut subsidies.

Three important apartheid laws still exist: the Population Registration Act, the Group Areas Act, the Separate Amenities Act. The National Party has never listed repeal of the Population Registration Act that classifies population according to race in its reforms. As for the Group Areas Act that segregates urban residential areas, a poll in 1986 showed only about twenty-six percent of whites against residential desegregation, telling evidence of change in thinking and growth in confidence in the whites in the last ten years. Also in August 1986, a full congress of the National Party approved desegregation of residential areas where segregation was impractical. In September 1986 the government announced the end of criminal enforcement of the Group Areas Act except at the request of local communities. By 1987 some in government spoke openly of repeal, they thought it wrong to tell people where to live. The statement in March 1987 of twenty-eight Afrikaner academics, roughly half the senior faculty of Stellenbosch, called for swift "scrapping" of the act "in its entirety," they doubted, rather cynically, "any significant effect on established residential areas,"—the American experience.[76]

Actually, for six or seven years the government has allowed the "greying" of white suburbs, especially in Johannesburg but, more recently, also in Cape Town, Durban and Port Elizabeth. By 1988 the three white suburbs of Johannesburg, Hillbrow, Berea and Joubert, numbered up to a third black tenants. It took until 1987 for the North American media to discover these changes that the South African government did not advertise, and even then they paid them little more than passing notice. Actual change was too much for them. In October 1987 Botha proposed to legalize the already desegregated areas upon "a request from the ranks of the community,"—the white legal residents—and provide for the establishment of new areas open to all. He did not call for repeal of the entire Group Areas Act, he wanted to follow change, not force it: ". . . No group should force its own values and way of life upon others." In April, 1988 legislation for these desegregated areas and for new ones was expected within weeks despite strong CP attacks against loosening the Group Areas Act that won them three parliamentary by-elections in the previous weeks. In November the President's Council rejected an amendment to the Group Areas Act that would have allowed the eviction of illegal residents from white areas despite a National Party majority in the Council. The refusal to vote on it of the Indian and Colored Houses of Parliament had forced the amendment into the President's Council—the new constitution at work. In his October 1987 speech, Botha also rejected outright repeal of the Separate Amenities Act that segregated public facilities, he was uncertain how the courts would "apply the common law in modern times" after thirty years of disuse. Again, he showed he wanted to let things take care of themselves, especially since the last ten years had brought much more local desegregation of public areas upon local initiative than residential desegregation.

On a deeper level, beyond everyday humiliations, registration of black unions probably counted the most. In the beginning the numbers of workers in unions were small, but they covered many factories and have continued to increase (from 150,000 to 1,000,000 in 1987). After first insisting on racial exclusivity in defiance of its commission's recommendation of full freedom of association, the government left the unions to decide: Some are racially exclusive, others are not. Instead of collective bargaining, some black trade unions preferred plant by plant bargaining, especially with foreign companies whose operation under the Common Market rules or the Sullivan Guidelines that favored black advancement and wage increases set an example for South African companies.

Also, in striking confirmation of the expectation of the commission which recommended registration that free association would mean more effective use of manpower, the unions on the whole stayed out of politics—until the organization of the Congress of South African Trade Unions (COSATU) in late 1985. In 1983 several unions and the major non-racial union group, Federation of South African Trade Unions (FOSATU), turned down UDF overtures: Joining would provoke divisions among their members because they did not all think alike,—the best criticism of the UDF I know. Union leaders suspected the ANC would take over the unions like the men who seized power in Angola, Mozambique and Zimbabwe,—not their kind of future.[77] In unionized companies senior management now spends a good deal of time negotiating wages and work conditions,—in contrast to the swift black wage settlements in the seventies.

From the beginning Botha made the limits of reform clear: One-man, one-vote was out of the question because one-man, one-vote on a national scale presumed homogeneity of population. Any future political "dispensation" had to begin with the recognition of groups. In 1985, the time of the greatest modification in the government's stance since 1983, he insisted in January on the differences between South African peoples that the new constitution recognized in the distinction between "own affairs" and "general affairs": "It remains the government's point of departure that, because of the diversity of

South African society, it is neither desirable nor praticable to accommodate all communities in the same way." In March: "The question is no longer whether African communities shall be given political rights, but how it shall be done without one population group being placed in a position to dominate permanently the other."[78]

Full political rights for individuals in South Africa were only possible within their own groups. But groups for blacks no longer meant only the homelands, for in 1985 the government recognized that "links" to the homelands could not provide blacks in the townships with political expression beyond the local level. At the same time, again in March, Botha reiterated his commitment to economic and political change: "I am committed to a programme of reform designed to broaden democracy and to improve living conditions of all South Africans regardless of race, color or creed,"—with maintenance of law and order. Magnus Malan, the minister of defense, was more blunt. "The surest way to chaos and anarchy" was nationwide one-man, one-vote: "I can, however tell you [the new political arrangements] won't be a one-person, one-vote system in a unitary state, nor will it be black or white domination."[79] Botha also said he was ready to consider reorganizing the President's Council to include Africans.

Behind all these remarks lay sovereignty. The South African government's thinking betrayed its presence, its actions defended it, especially the insistence on order. But it never mentioned it. The word was too embarrassing, and too important, the necessity of plain-speaking did not allow such depth. To continue and to countenance such diversity, and such danger abroad, sovereignty would have to remain clearly somewhere—in white hands but dependent to some extent on consensus, the consensus the violence of the ANC, the UDF sought desperately to destroy. "We live in dangerous times . . . We live at a time in which South Africa has, as a result of outside interference, been made a crisis point." These are Botha's words for sovereignty in his October 5, 1987 speech on the Group Areas Act.

Besides sovereignty, the realization that reform meant "decentralization," that local democracy and local everyday changes in the townships counted most, worked at the heart of the government's thinking,—Tocqueville's deepest wisdom. But it did not say it often, a mark of the success of the ANC and UDF violence against "collaborators," especially the elected town councillors. But Botha did repeatedly call the credibility of black local governments vital.

Botha wanted to work within the context of actual differences in the population but to strip them of their irrational underpinnings. For instance, the refusal to recognize change, and the desire to prevent it, had nourished the insistence on a link between the townships and the homelands. The repeal of the pass laws, in contrast, means that blacks can now freely choose between the dangers and the identity-threatening but relatively prosperous life in the townships and the hardships, narrowness, poverty and assurances of tribal country life—a freedom of choice that can only increase tension because it increases responsibility. Even in the homelands self-government means the blacks have to live in two worlds. Biko foresaw these conflicts in 1976, he said often that white reform would mean little unless blacks managed first to assume responsibility for their own lives instead of blaming whites.

These differences are real. Apartheid and separate development may have exaggerated them, but I doubt it. For without the experience of European sovereignty and the missionaries, the various tribes would not have even thought of calling themselves black or Bantu or native or African instead of Xhosa and so on. The British and the Boers did not have to divide them to subdue them piecemeal, they never even thought of uniting. "Tragedy is imminent since the tribes have no common bond of union," John Philip remarked in a letter of 1842. In 1918, Pixley Seme, Buthelezi's uncle, a graduate of Columbia, called the feuding between the tribes "racialism," not the relations between Europeans and Bantu: "The demon of racialism, the aberrations of the Xhosa-Fingo feud, the animosity that exists between the Zulus and Tongas, between the Basuto and every other Native must be buried . . . We are one people. These divisions, these jealousies, are the causes of all our woes and of all our backwardness and ignorance today."[80]

In any case, apartheid and separate development did not create these differences. More importantly nobody knows what can take their place and how they disappear.

Most superficially these differences show themselves in language. There are at least six major native languages and twenty-seven dialects. The blacks in Soweto read their newspapers in English but they talk native languages among themselves with a modification of Zulu or English as *lingua franca*. The blacks, the most talented of them at least, are remarkable in mastery of language, but the difficulties of common life that requires some fluency in two or even three languages, one *totally* unrelated to the other two, are formidable—as any American ought to be able to imagine. We are not talking of the differences in Indo-European dialects the natives of Europe speak—except the Hungarians, Finns and Turks.

Then there are differences between the blacks of the townships, the places of most of the murder, and the blacks in rural homelands. The established Zulus in Soweto do not get along with Zulu migrant workers from Natal—let alone with the Zulus in the KwaZulu.

And behind them all the tribal differences that go so deep they are not taken *for* nature, an abstract concept, but to be *in* nature, with a specificity that conceives of a magnolia tree or an elm tree but not tree itself—for the good reason that there is no such thing as simply a tree.

There are six million Xhosa and Zulu, four million Sotho, three million Tswana, one million Shangaan, six hundred thousand Venda and the same number of Ndebele. The Zulus and Xhosa singly number much more or equal the population of each of the nine southern African countries except Mozambique and Tanzania. Xhosa are not about to allow themselves to be ruled by Zulus—and so on. We are not talking about the differences between the Sicilians and the Piedmontese, let alone the Croatians and Serbians, in themselves no jokes:

Tswana, Zulu, Sotho and other Bantu-speaking peoples were neither Anglicised nor Afrikanised. They remain distinct ethnic groups, even in cities where English has become a *lingua franca*, and where African writers have developed a vigorous branch of English literature. South Africa, in other words, is not a melting pot; it is an ethnic and racial mosaic, comparable in certain aspects to such multi-ethnic communities as the old Austro-Hungarian Empire, but with the added difference that nearly half the population remains in tribal societies.[81]

Differences so deep are beyond comprehension for Americans. They dread them. For if the South Africans, pioneers like the Americans, who also made a country that broke with Britain, have exaggerated differences, the Americans have so ignored or hidden them lately that they try to live as if they had neither past nor parents—who would dare say ancestors! Another kind of blindness that tells of irremediable longing and leads to extraordinary parochiality that passes for cosmopolitanism. A lady writer in *The New York Times* recently declared she could not read Hawthorne and John Adams with confidence because she is not descended from them.[82] The real appeal of communism and totalitarianism, among the few blacks really convinced,—in contrast to those trapped in chaos, ideology and fear,—may come because of the promise swiftly to wipe out these layers and layers of centuries of stratification,—a promise bespeaking murder.

Botha also took risks abroad, for there is no separating South Africa's domestic situation from her role in a region that numbers 61 million souls, besides the 32 million in South Africa and 30 million just north in Zaire, the land crucial to domination of all of Africa. In 1979 and 1980 Botha announced a plan for a confederation or common market of the southern nine nations that won the enthusiastic adherence of leading South African businessmen, a notable breakthrough for the National Party. At first he approached Zimbabwe, Malawi (the only country with diplomatic relations with South Africa—since 1967) and Botswana, Lesotho, and Swaziland, already part of a South African customs union,—not Tanzania, Mozambique, Angola and Zambia, all more or less drifting into war with South Africa, in words.

He meant these countries to give some political acknowledgment to South Africa's overwhelming predominance in the region (85% of its GNP, 90% of its energy, 58% of cereals grown, 71% of meat, 94% of wheat, 20% of maize, 75% of total exports, 68% of imports, 97% of coal mined, 98% of iron ore mined—with 36% of the total population in 24% of the surface area) and to their dependence on its ports and railways and its know-how and international commercial connections. He offered to work with them. But the election of Mugabe in early 1980 brought all this to nothing. To counter Botha's offer Mugabe founded the South African Development Coordination Conference (SADCC), allegedly to reduce the southern African countries' dependence on South African ports and transportation for overseas trading, an organization useful for the war of words against South Africa, and in extracting money from abroad, especially after September 1986. It meant begging, in blue suits at green tables, to do for work and trade.

But the South Africans keep trying to make economic sense prevail over guerrilla war—and fighting. In early 1988 the chief executive of the South African government electric company, Escom, proposed a regional power-grid to the nine SADCC nations: "The sub-continent has a simple choice—economic stagnation caused by political division with growing unemployment and worsening poverty, or economic dynamism stemming from co-operation in the non-political sphere."[83]

Botha's confidence at home and abroad comes from strength, a dreaded word today in the West that ignores fighting on the ground to lose itself in calculations of future nuclear wars. He offers the olive branch because he has a sword. His officers are serious about force, they know it can only help politics decide their future. Their rule, twenty percent force, eighty percent politics, acknowledges they are not entirely right. Botha's readiness to fight on the ground abroad and to keep order at home, to draw limits, proves his good faith in negotiations. In contrast, the CP talks of bringing southern Africa to its knees in a week, the PFP proposes isolationist policies that would weaken and eventually undo South Africa, both at home and abroad.

In 1985–1986 estimates of the army numbered 106,400, (64,000 conscripts on two-year service); 42,400 professionals; 150,000 reserves, capable of long periods of active service and subject to yearly refresher training; 130,000 local militia. Total mobilization in a crisis, with severe slowing of the economy: 400,000.[84]

The strength of South Africa that gives Botha the confidence to run such risks, the risks of fundamental but limited change at home that even schoolboys know frequently brings disaster and negotiated peace abroad, has been a good deal of his own doing. Minister of defense from 1966 to 1980, Botha understood that South Africa's independence, and break with the Commonwealth, required readiness to face trouble on her own, especially after the non-mandatory Security Council arms embargo of 1963 that won the adherence of forty-four countries but not of France, and the mandatory embargo in 1977.

Botha instituted conscription for whites and voluntary service for Coloreds (in the crack Cape Corps), African and Indians. His readiness, for the first time, to allow *all* South Africans to bear arms was the most important change before the registration of unions. In his first ten years the military budget went from one million rand to almost two billion. To face up to the arms embargoes of 1977, he organized an arms industry that now supplies about eighty percent of South Africa's needs and exports arms even to NATO and Israel. He saw to the invention of weapons specifically designed for South Africa's fighting, mine-proof troop carriers and surface-to-air missiles. He instituted counter-insurgency training and founded the South African Defense College in 1973. He played an important part in the decision to intervene in Angola in 1975.

Botha did not invent his policy of change with order both at home and abroad in policy papers. It comes of his life and character, a combination of military and political experience uncommon today in the West, except in Israel, a nation that has good reason to understand South Africa, and to stand by her. In 1917 a friend of Chaim Weizmann, with Arthur Balfour and Lloyd George, moved the British government to announce it would do its best to make Palestine a Jewish national home, the Balfour Declaration. His name was Smuts.

7 The Cannon Fodder of the "Revolution"

The violence that has overtaken some of the townships has occurred against a background of greater economic opportunity, and since 1976, of precipitate expansion in education. It has come in reaction to progress, not because of the lack of it. It has come with the government's increasing involvement with the blacks, for instance, in providing low-cost housing and medical services. It has come with the relaxation of apartheid, with improvement, not because of the lack of it. Improvement made humiliations and hardships more unbearable. The chance for change, and the incapacity of some to stand it, explains the violence, the passivity in the face of it and its instigation.

The violence has received something like support from the blacks who have most benefited from the system, who have had the guts, and the luck, to take advantage of its opportunities, a South African version of "radical chic" that betrays the strains of withstanding change. A majority of the spokesmen for blacks, middle-class intellectuals, students and clergy in urban areas, support disinvestment and sanctions—in contrast to about twenty-five percent of everyday blacks in the townships, and less in the country, a study of eleven major polls since the new constitution showed in January 1987.[85] In November 1987 the Institute of Race Relations said the number of blacks ready to risk their jobs for sanctions had shrunk from one-to-four to one-to-seven in the previous two years.

The young are at the center of the disturbances and violence, sometimes the very young. Schools have been the way into the streets of murder—and the way out of them. The anxiety before the loosening of apartheid, the defiance and aspirations, first showed themselves in 1976 in the schools. The extremists, often school drop-outs, sought to exploit these fears of the unknown, especially after the new constitution.

At the core of the tension between parents and children, teachers and students, that these disturbances show, and which radical organizations seek to exploit to obliterate all distinctions of tribe, age, sex and so on,—obliteration that undoes life as well as tension,—are numbers—numbers the South African officials I have met keep before their eyes.

More than fifty percent of the twenty-five million blacks of South Africa (including the six million in the independent homelands) are under fifteen. In the total population of South Africa half are dependents in contrast to a third in the United States and Japan. In eleven years, the year 2000, the year Buthelezi expects a majority of black managers in factories, the black population is expected almost to double, to at least forty million, maybe fifty million; the Coloreds and Indians to reach six million, roughly equal to the whites.

For the ANC, the SACP and the many front organizations these numbers mean the young are the "cannon fodder" for the "seizure of power" as the training books of SWAPO terrorists, published along with the Denton Hearings, show,—standard indoctrination throughout the world: "The youth is the main force in all sectors of the movement. It is the main power in any society . . . *Its main task is to implement policies set by the elders*"; "Political ideological education is the life blood in the war . . . *secondary school students are the best of all*" (Italics mine). The 1981 SACP Central Committee meeting minutes: "Amongst the student organizations, there is not enough national unity"; "Guidance must be given to the churches, youth organizations, etc." Papers captured in the same raid on the ANC house in Gaborone, Botswana, on June 14, 1985 that yielded the 1981 Central Committee minutes also outlined a strategy of school boycotts for political purposes.

The boycotts mean to turn the children against adults, to intimidate the adults, and more importantly to make children completely submissive to organizations,—in the name of freedom,—the core of totalitarianism. The use of children to intimidate moderate adults had become a regular practice in the townships of the eastern Cape, Buthelezi observed already in April, 1985. About six months later, the South African police declared: ". . . A large number of mobs responsible for all kinds of violence and other unrest-related lawless acts consisted of children."[86]

The school-children's boycotts made an impression on all South Africa, even on well-informed South African observers, and outside South Africa. They gave the impression of irresistible and uncontrollable defiance: ". . . The intensity and duration of school and student boycotts over the past two years has far outstripped that of worker protests in political stay away strikes," wrote Lawrence Schlemmer, a sociologist whose self-evident goodwill earned him the repeated fire bombing of his house and research institute in 1986.[87]

But the disruptions that made such an impression reached relatively few areas at least in 1986, as a report to Parliament in early 1987 showed: Unrest in 1986 disrupted 260 black schools, out of 7,300, 3.5 percent at any one time, with seventy-three schools closed, 1 percent.[88]

In the face of this unrest and its exploitation, the South African authorities have sought to distinguish actual grievances from their political exploitation—and to maintain examination standards, usually including deadlines. In 1983–84 the able minister of education Barend du Plessis (since minister of finance) admitted student grievances but made it plain he would not allow their exploitation by student organizations, especially the Congress of South African Students (COSAS), a UDF affiliate (banned in 1985), to gain control of the educational system. In the schools also, the UDF and the ANC wanted to use the government's readiness to admit mistakes in order to take control.

Anybody who has ever taught knows what such a policy, easier to state than to follow, means in the classroom, especially in a system that allows corporal punishment, only abolished in England in 1986. It means alternation between strictness and laxness that turns teachers into "the target for abuse from both parents and students" as Es'kia Mphahlele from the University of Witwatersrand recently put it. It also means vacillation overcomes the weaker teachers and principals.

The policy also shows the tenacious commitment to education barely a generation old. Not more than a third of African children attended school in 1954, the year the government took over African education. Ten years before, there had been only 230 government schools, four-fifths built in the previous twenty years, against 4,360 mission schools.[89]

The government recognizes the schools are crucial in the battle for change against violence. It stresses "its commitment to equal educational opportunities for all" at the same time that it insists on the "exclusion of education from politics," as Botha put it in his address opening Parliament that announced anticipated elections in 1987. Botha also mentioned the involvement of parents "as partners in the education of their children,"—a remark meant to distinguish actual parents from organizations that pretend to represent them like the Soweto Parents' Crisis Committee (SPCC) and the National Education Crisis Committee (NECC), "the radical groups [who abuse] education for political purposes" and who make attendance at school dependent on political demands.

The recognition of education also means rapid money. In early 1986 the government budgeted ten billion rand for ten years for black education. In a budget of almost 40.5 billion rand for 1986, a little more than 6 billion went to education, the top item in the budget, a 19.3 percent increase over the previous year, with an allocation 27.3 percent higher for black primary and secondary education,—1.15 billion rand, an eight-fold increase in eight years.

These figures still show a six-to-one discrepancy with white education, the media often quickly point out without mentioning that black teachers earn less because they are less qualified. (Salaries represent about eighty percent of the budget.) A 1982 study found that seventy percent of black teachers were "underqualified," the standard: completion of secondary school and the teacher training diploma.

The ratio of teacher to pupils in black schools in 1983 was about forty-three-to-one, in white eighteen-to-one. To reduce that ratio to thirty-to-one by the year 2000 would mean an increase to 239,943 from 95,500 teachers active in 1980.[90] The roughly 250,000 new African pupils each year also slow the diminution of the students to teacher ratio. They require eight thousand new teachers and the construction of three hundred large schools each year just to stay even. There has been continuing substantial reduction in "double sessions," one teacher for two classes each day, and in the "platoon system," two teachers in the same room for two classes.

Also, as any teacher knows, money, especially large sudden increases, does not necessarily mean improvement, especially in situations like those in the townships where little improvements count most. The qualities and the resilience that count in teaching cannot be called up in a moment. They take years and much resource to learn. South Africans know that: "Even huge and dramatic increases in expenditure by the government cannot restore quality in the short to medium term, because the real bottleneck is qualified and motivated teachers."[91]

The money for black education largely comes from whites. Despite the introduction of a general sales tax, about eleven percent of the population, mostly non-African, those that earn over 1,400 rand a month, pay eighty percent of taxes according to a 1986 private study.

The drop in the pass rate for matriculation exams, exams classroom teachers neither correct nor design, tells a great deal about the consequences of sudden expansion. In 1984 50 percent of 75,000 African candidates passed, 11.5 percent at university admission level, results that "provoked anger and despair among pupils, parents, teachers and community leaders,"—as an Institute of Race Relations report said of the comparable results in 1983.

On top of that, not all registered pupils take examinations. For instance, in 1985 seventy-four percent of 91,000 eligible students wrote examinations, only ten percent in Soweto, five percent in the eastern Cape, the centers of disturbances.[92] In Soweto the Parents Crisis Committee (SPCC) had called for a boycott of matriculation examinations until the end of the State of Emergency and the removal of soldiers from Soweto. There was much intimidation, students took their examinations under armed guard in some areas in 1985. In contrast in 1984, 91.5 percent of whites passed their exams, 45 percent at university level. But the contrast that tells is with previous black results.

In contrast, from roughly 1963 to 1976 the pass-rate averaged sixty percent, and the university admission rate around thirty percent. The drop in the general pass-rate to fifty percent, and in university admission to often under ten percent, occurred from 1980 on, the years the number of candidates increased at a rate of between ten and twenty thousand a year, from 14,574 in 1979 to 91,000 in 1985. The rapid increase in enrollment in secondary school, 147,000 in 1974 to 918,000 in 1986, brought increasing failure, especially at the top, at the university admission level.[93]

Somebody had to be blamed for the failure. There were charges of bias against Africans; the Soweto newspaper, *The Sowetan* did not help: It charged too easy grading in certain subjects instead of bias, after checking three years of examinations in 1984. South Africa is a country where nobody ever gets away with doing anything entirely right, one of freedom's many names, a place that looks fear in the face—another more important name.

The schools had expanded too rapidly for the teachers to cope with borderline students, students with ability but without confidence, the hardest challenge in any school. Maybe no teachers could cope with those students.

But the UDF, the SPCC and the NECC had the answers: first, close the schools; then in 1986, and especially in 1987, return to the schools to transform them, to take them over. Not the lack of opportunity but rather the rapid expansion of opportunity, with the will to make harsh judgments between students able to cope and not, led to political agitation and boycotts meant to control the schools, not reform them.

But the parents did not take this coerced "no." Their anger made "their" organizations flinch from the total "no" of the year before already in April 1986 after it caught the attention of journalists.[94] In 1987 the NECC's substitution of the slogan "People's education for people's power" for "Liberation before education" betrayed its new tactic: attendance at schools instead of boycotts— a change the South African government greeted with relief. But this change probably signifies, not the cessation of the struggle, but its continuation on home-territory, within schools instead of outside them. At the same time the new labor federation, COSATU, started on "political" manipulation of unions.

About six months before the NECC changed tactics the South African educational authorities granted students the representatives their organizations had demanded in 1985.[95] Recognition of the representatives depended on: secret ballot elections, concentration on educational matters within their own school, no affiliation with organizations outside, and no attempt to take over the responsibilities of principal, teacher or parent organizations. The South Africans recognized student representatives despite the exploitation of particular grievances in school boycotts in 1984 and 1985 for support of political demands, the same everywhere, also abroad, that had nothing to do with particular schools: the end of the first partial State of Emergency, the removal of the police and army from the townships, and an "alternative curriculum of people's education."

In contrast, in the very same days that the South African government allowed African pupil organizations in their schools, the Colored minister of education Carter Ebrahim banned student organizations in Colored schools and colleges and empowered principals to suspend students and teachers who were "guilty of any action detrimental to the administration or discipline of the educational institution" or who undermined "lawful authority."[96] In other words, the Coloreds whose children only boycotted in earnest in 1985 handled their own more severely than the South African government dealt with African students,—and this under a Colored minister who does not believe each racial group should handle its own education separately as the new constitution provides for all but Africans in the townships. Upon petition of Franklin Sonn, an important principal, and two parents for revocation of Ebrahim's regulations, the Cape Supreme Court only invalidated the suspension of students and teachers.[97] Rational and resilient, the South African policy to allow African pupils a voice that does not serve other peoples' purposes may in time bring change that counts, habits of self-rule that show among Coloreds in their toughness against themselves.

The decision to form the NECC, taken at a two-day conference of 160 education organizations that the Soweto Parents Crisis Committee (SPCC) called in Johannesburg on December 28 and 29, 1985, tells a familiar story. As usual, there was little way of knowing whom the SPCC representatives represented and with what mandate—the question the UDF, COSATU and the ANC also raise. The conference repeatedly called for the unbanning of the South African Students' Organization and made the unbanning of COSAS a precondition for continuing school attendance in 1986,—organizations banned because they had meant to use grievances to control the schools.

On a first and hasty reading, harmless and boring, the resolutions of the

Johannesburg Conference look different in the context of UDF and ANC and SACP directives. Their primary purpose is organization and "mobilization," a word used repeatedly. They want to coordinate student organizations with trade unions and the community organizations that the UDF coalition claims to represent: "To forge close links between students, workers and community organizations and to coordinate action in these different areas."

The resolutions want face-to-face agitation and a national organization to control it, they want to use the schools and the children to get to the parents, they want "to take the struggle for a non-racial, democratic South Africa into every school and hence into every home."

Within the schools, they want to obliterate all distinctions between teachers, parents and students and their organizations, "so that parents, teachers, and students can come to understand each other's demands and problems." The obliteration of the distinctions between parents', teachers' and students' organizations means to facilitate "fusion," a word Lenin liked, of all parents, teachers and students throughout the nation so that "interaction can take place between different schools to develop the education struggle to higher levels." (The deadbeat hint of Hegel, "higher levels," betrays the resolutions as the work of trained, indoctrinated men, no mere protesters or educators, let alone parents). The SPCC and the NECC want a few individuals, close to the ANC, UDF, and COSATU, at the top of a supposedly representative organization, to speak for every parent, teacher and student in the townships. The design is simply a school version of the UDF's strategy for the entire country—and a part of it.

About learning, the resolutions say nothing except for a bland remark, here and there, on the elimination of illiteracy and ignorance followed by the demand for the elimination of "exploitation of any person by any other."

Education means indoctrination: "[People's education] equips and trains all sectors of our people to participate actively and creatively [the voice of Manhattan!] in the struggle to attain people's power in order to establish a non-racial democratic South Africa and allow students, parents, teachers and workers to be mobilized into appropriate organizational structures which enable them to enhance the struggle for people's power and to participate actively in the initiation and management of people's education in all its forms."

"In all its forms" means any conceivable activism, for instance, impelling "the workers to resist exploitation and oppression at their workplace." A remark in the 1981 SACP Central Committee minutes best glosses this phrase: "The strength of the enemy lies at the point of production." A recent ANC broadcast also helps: "Let us sabotage everything that belongs to our places of employment: delivery vans, machines, even office equipment."[98]

At the same time that it wants to "eliminate capitalist norms of competition," and abolish "individualism," in other words no failures in school, people's education stimulates "critical thinking and analysis"—contradictory aims that promise everything to everybody, with the last phrase meant to reassure Washington and American foundations and their coffers.[99] The South African police's sobriety before this nonsense avoided even understatement: "Adults should refrain from manipulating children in the name of the so-called cause."[100]

Outside of the schools, on the streets, there was murder, the other side of the boycotts, paralysis, and the arrest of children, the detentions. These detentions met strong criticism in South Africa in 1985 *before* the international campaign of 1986 and again in 1987. The latter at about the time the children returned to school.

The detained under age sixteen numbered more than two thousand, Helen Suzman charged in Parliament in 1985: "There were certainly many hair-raising stories of children being subjected to violent treatment in police cells by the security police and many were held in solitary confinement." In October 1985 a conference in Johannesburg of law, pediatric, medical, psychiatric, psychology and education professionals and church and welfare organizations called for an end to the detention of children.[101] In response the police facilitated visits to children,—and continued the "unavoidable" arrests. In the first partial State of Emergency from July 21, 1985 to March 7, 1986, 3,681 men under twenty-one had been detained, in the first days, largely members of COSAS and other youth groups, many of them under fifteen.

Just short of a year after the start of the second State of Emergency, in April 1987, there were 1,424 youths in detention. Among them: 2 twelve years old; 19 thirteen years old; 75 fourteen years old; 110 fifteen years old, 316 sixteen years old, 461 seventeen years old; 455 eighteen years old. Of the eighteen year olds, 26 were held for murder, 9 for attempted murder, 36 for assault and intimidation, 79 for arson. Of the sixteen year olds, 22 for murder, 3 for attempted murder, 24 for assault and intimidation, 76 for arson. By October 1987 youths in detention numbered 69 in all: 16 sixteen years old, 52 seventeen years old.[102]

In face of the attempt at the end of 1986 and in 1987 to make detention an international issue, the new minister of law and order Adriaan Vlok, a man who did not take the detention of children easily and could say it, spoke in a statement on June 2, 1987 of adults "used to incite children to . . . violence" and quoted the ANC's instructions " 'children should be present at the executions and should rejoice in the death of the enemies of the proletariat'": "After careful study . . . I reached the conclusion that blame for the detention of children rested on the shoulders of revolutionary minded radicals, who *calculatedly singled out children and forced them to commit horrendous deeds against the community*"[103] (Italics mine). The Vietcong in the sixties, the PLO with its contacts with the ANC, also used children to provoke atrocities,—the PLO in the West Bank in 1987 and 1988.

Men like Desmond Tutu meant to use children in the press abroad like the ANC used them in the street, to discredit the coming "whites-only" elections and the State of Emergency then bringing some order and reassurance to the townships. They meant the detention of children to hit the West in the guts. It cannot deny but will not acknowledge its own unreadiness to face its children, especially in the United States, where children, among the well-off, often influence the political positions of their parents, without discussion.

The South African Police did not underestimate the forces at work. The exploitation of emotional issues such as detention, especially of children, largely determined the intensity of radicalism, the South African Commissioner of Police testified before the Supreme Court in Cape Town. He meant propaganda like an advertisement printed just before the 1987 election in the South African *Weekly Mail* and elsewhere:

The victimization of a country's most precious resource, its children, is beyond the pale of civilized norms. What threat can a thirteen year old be to Africa's most powerful military and economic machine? How can an eleven year old child endanger the security of the state?[104]

Children between sixteen and eighteen were responsible for the violence and atrocities in the country, the officer of the South African Police in charge of detainees testified before the same court. Somehow, in part because of the government's deft response, and in part because the public in the United States and Europe now sensed manipulation, the campaign did damage without taking off.

In response to decisions of the courts, the South African government again drew the necessary distinctions. It apologized for the ineptness of its ban on demonstrations against detention of children. It had not distinguished between "campaigns,"—it did not use the words it meant: "civil disobedience,"—and criticism voiced, it did not add, by individuals. And it chose the toughest policy—as in education: to punish resolutely and at the same time to handle each case individually, and to restore family ties when possible. Vlok had parents traced, not always possible because of false names, "to determine if they were prepared and able to accept responsibility for their children."

Vlok took this decision despite his knowledge of the incapacity of many parents to control their offspring,—parents caught like the school teachers between rebelling youths and organizations that exploited them. A thankless decision, like the decision to encourage the return of youths that had fled South Africa in the wake of the disturbances of 1976. But a necessary decision meant to preserve the authority of the government, to show the government's toughness did not serve mere repression.

The parents Vlok meant to strengthen spoke openly of their and their children's powerlessness before violence that meant to force them both to rebel: "We tried to keep him at home, but the comrades came and told him he must fight for the cause, so he went with them. We wished to tell him not to go, but the comrades told us that if we interfered, they would burn down our house. For us parents, it is very difficult," a mother of a fourteen year old in Gugeletu, a township near Cape Town, told a reporter from an American newspaper in late 1986, with docility that betrays defenselessness.[105] Their children's defiance and recklessness had taken aback parents. Children in 1976 had been more innocent of coercion: "They [the children] won't take anything we say because they think we have neglected them. We have failed to help them in their struggle for change in schools. They are now angry and prepared to fight and we are afraid the situation may become chaotic," a town councillor said on June 14, 1976 just before the demonstrations that broke down in violence at nightfall in Soweto on June 16.[106]

Still earlier, in the forties and fifties, before apartheid and slum reconstruction, parents spoke in softness that betrays a world innocent of the political exploitation of children: " 'Father, I've come to give you my child, you must take care of him. Father he is naughty, very, very naughty. I can do nothing with him. He dodges school. He is a loafer. He stays out at night. . .' How often have I heard these words? . . . and [the child] is out of control. I know the chances are that he is already with a gang . . . When I look down at him I see a hardness already forming around his mouth, in his eyes. . ."[107]

The campaign against detentions did not take off because people had come to sense the difference between manipulated violence and defiance,—a difference the UDF and the ANC sought to obscure. People believed the police even when its unfortunate language betrayed the jargon of terrorists. The South African commissioner of police spoke blandly in language he had learned from informers and captured documents of ". . . the current psychological climate aimed at mobilizing the masses for a people's revolt . . . to provoke a general attitude of hostility towards the government and to isolate and estrange it from the masses."

In the United States too something of the truth began to get through—*but only after passage of sanctions.* In testimony on the eve of Tambo's visit to Washington on January 19, 1987, before an informal committee of the House of Representatives,—testimony carried on cable television several times and, in excerpts, on the radio, but not on major networks or newspapers,—John Gogotya, a black Soweto leader, said the State of Emergency had meant sleep for the first time in years. The cry "Tambo, Tambo" chanted and danced through the streets of Soweto, had always meant somebody would burn that night. He added a rendition that betrayed terror, not merely dread,—and the matching resilience that had brought him to speak in Washington unreceptive in the full blush of righteous unease after the passage of the CAA Act on October 2, 1986. Also, the evidence about crimes of children that began to come out in South African courts counted, for newspapers trusted it more than police reports, unwitting acknowledgment of the South African judiciary's independence. South African law holds children fourteen and over responsible, in the Roman-Dutch juridical tradition.

The youths tried before the Port Elizabeth Supreme Court for the murder of Benjamin Kinikini, a town councillor cut to pieces along with two sons, a nephew and a friend, in March 1985 after the police shot twenty at a banned funeral in Langa, near Uitenhange, were fifteen, seventeen and twenty-one. "I was told to commit murder by leaders of the 'comrades' in Kwanobuhle [the township that includes Langa]," the twenty-one year old told the court, words that startled South African journalists. These youths had set fire again to a mutilated corpse for a television crew to film: "While the camera rolled, they danced around the flaming body, chanting and grinning and poking it with sticks."[108]

The affidavit of the official monitoring detentions before the Supreme Court in Cape Town in 1987 includes teenage testimony. A seventeen year old confessed to necklacing a UDF member—with other youths, of course. A fourteen year old told of burning buses, a township car, and a policeman's home—again with other youths he called "comrades," an appellation used in ANC membership forms, which begin with a request for *all* false names. A fifteen year old told of stopping taxis, destroying groceries and pouring bleach detergent on the head of a woman—the intimidation behind the "irresistible" shopping boycotts. A sixteen year old boy: "Our group burnt three houses . . . I hurled the first [gasoline] bomb and it hit the door. The others also threw their bombs. The house was completely burnt out. The man's house was burnt, because he owed Stoki money. We burnt the house upon instruction of Impi . . . The third house did not burn completely. My bomb fell in the garden . . ."

An eleven year old girl: "I participated when the man was burnt behind the Indian's store . . . We all [never alone, always on orders and in groups] stabbed the man with knives . . . I stabbed the man twice with an Okapi knife between the shoulders. Impi stabbed the man with a garden fork in his side. The man was chased behind the Indian's shop where he fell. He lay on his back. Impi placed the tire on his chest and poured petrol over him . . . He managed to set him alight with the third match. Impi was almost burnt himself when he set the man alight."[109]

8 The 1987 Election

The election of May 6 surprised nobody because it disappointed nearly everybody. It reminded everyday people, within South Africa and abroad, that there was a real country out there that could exercise its will calmly in a state of near insurrection. Not Botha's reforms or his speeches, not the toughness and fundamental restraint of the police, but the vote showed a country that could decide for itself despite abuse and insult it took with equanimity: The campaign did not concentrate on resentment at sanctions.

The elections showed that authority, especially in Africa, comes not from words but from sovereignty—the exercise of the general will. This confidence surprised South Africans themselves; they had almost forgotten that constitutions distinguish people from a crowd. "They understand we're not about to embark on policies that could result in our own destruction," Botha remarked almost a year after the elections.[110] He meant the Soviets, he could as well have meant his own country, or even himself. After the elections people believed what they had only known before: There was going to be no "revolution."

In the rest of 1987 and the first six months of 1988, there were repeated attempts abroad to ignite the passions of previous years. But it would not work: People had heard it before. Instead the press scorned Botha for slowing the very reforms it had ignored before the elections,—a belated and oblique admission that it took the South African government seriously.[111]

In his decision to turn to the electorate in an anticipated election at the end of January 1987, barely six months after the State of Emergency, Botha again showed his sense of timing. It was three months or so after the United States had turned its back on his government in anticipation of a black seizure of power, and a few days after the secretary of state in the United States had received Oliver Tambo. Botha could not have transformed the government of the country in the midst of concerted insurrection without repeated choice of the apt moment—the severest test for a lifetime party man who must deal from the inside with men he knows best, enough to know he hardly knows them. Perhaps he had not foreseen the insurrection at home and the uproar abroad his readiness to change would occasion. But he knew how to keep his head in the face of insurrection.

The decision, taken after consultation with the ministers' councils of the three houses, to dissolve only the white House of Assembly was as important as the timing, and little noticed. Botha took this decision in spite of polls that predicted much greater participation of Coloreds in future elections, or because of them. He wanted to face the white voters who had approved the constitution in 1983 and new voters, "mostly young people who have the right to participate in decisions about the future," for perhaps the last time in a separate election. He wanted to face them before the crucial elections of 1989 for all three houses of Parliament, elections that Botha announced he wanted to postpone in August 1987. This change that requires a constitutional amendment betrayed a government harboring few illusions about the seriousness of the situation despite its victory.

Amendments have to pass all three houses of Parliament. The Colored leader Allan Hendrickse, who supported the new constitution in 1983–84 because he knew it would have a life of its own, made repeal of the Group Areas Act a condition for Colored approval of the amendment. He was opposed by one of his ministers whom he cannot dismiss. Hendrickse prevailed. Botha will have to risk the loss of more votes in 1989 to the right wing that won about half of the Afrikaner vote in 1987, the new constitution at work.[112]

Botha's turn to the whites in 1987 underlined white responsibility for the entire country, despite the changes, a rude reminder of realities that count more for blacks, Coloreds and Indians than whites. For blacks, Coloreds and Indians would suffer more from the destruction of the South African government. After eight years of reforms, the last two-and-a-half of near insurrection in the black townships, Botha turned to voters to get his bearings. He wanted approval of his past acts, of his two-sided policy of negotiation and fighting abroad and reform and enforcing order at home. The election slogan, "Reform—Yes, Surrender—No," succinctly expressed this policy that distinguishes between actual change and seizure of power in the name of change.

In the campaign Botha concentrated on the Progressives because he feared the right wing. He meant to make it clear to the politically decisive Afrikaners that he understood the real risks of reform. National Party advertisements ran a photograph of Helen Suzman embracing Winnie Mandela (courtesy of Time magazine) with the question: "Isn't it time the PFP leadership decided whose side it is on?" following Lenin's remark that a demoralized country can be taken without a shot.

The Progressives merely irritated Botha, especially in their contempt for reforms. Their criticism in Parliament was important, but they had no real alternative that anybody could take seriously. He attacked them because he wanted to face men who clearly knew the risks and would measure the courage these risks required of him and his followers. He knew the Afrikaners he lost to the right wing would not come back easily. Right wing taunts that he had lost white confidence may have gotten to him.

Five parties, and a record 480 candidates competed in the long, expensive campaign punctuated by terrorist attacks, rent boycotts, strikes and demonstrations at universities and in white areas. The NP alone campaigned in all constituencies. Nearly one-third of the electorate did not vote.

The right wing said the NP had "methodically and recklessly" rejected the principles of the old NP and could not define its present policy. It rightly rejected negotiation with the ANC "even if it renounced violence." It was "not prepared under any circumstances to negotiate the future of whites with any other nation, of whatever color." It wanted to stop "multiracial" provincial and local government, to reinstitute the pass laws, and the prohibition of marriage between races and to undo the new constitution. The right wing was asking Botha whether he really meant it, and whether he saw the dangers, a double question that matched Botha's two-sided policy.

The Progressives in contrast asked no questions, they did not even cry, "not enough." For that would have meant admitting Botha had done something. They called for removal of troops from the townships and from South West Africa. These demands were close enough to the UDF position to dismay voters who have to make rough-and-ready judgments that go to the heart of the matter. The PFP demands appeared to question self-defense.

In contrast to the other four parties, the Progressive Federal Party showed its ambivalence about self-defense in its refusal either to praise or condemn the South African Defense Force commando raid to stop the infiltration of 150 terrorists into South Africa. The commandos blew up an ANC terrorist transit facility and weapons cache in Livingstone in southern Zambia, just before the elections, on April 25. The Natal *Sunday Tribune*, a newspaper close to the Progressives, betrayed the ugliness behind the party's reticence: "[The raid] looks altogether too much like an election ploy,"—an accusation immediately in the press in the United States. The attacks resulted from the constant watch on a "terrorist infiltration route from Zambia through Botswana" for terrorists flown from Zambia "with the full knowledge of the Zambian authorities." The Denton witnesses and much other evidence corroborates this South African army statement that, however, did not still immediate British and American condemnation of the raid.[113]

These condemnations did not spring from nations' individual judgments of actual circumstances. Almost automatic they show the effects of the UN's undermining of traditional international law (*jus gentium*) which countenances cross-border raids in self-defense. The UN Security Council's adoption of a mandatory arms embargo in 1977, reinforced in 1986, transformed apartheid from a matter "essentially within . . . domestic jurisdiction," into a "threat to the peace." For the UN Charter (Chapter VII, 39–51, especially 39 and 41) provides for mandatory embargoes and sanctions only in situations that justify "armed force."

The right wing won almost thirty percent of the vote; the Conservative Party (CP) 26 percent and 22 seats, instead of 18 in contrast to the National Party's 52 percent and 123 seats, instead of 117, out of a total of 166; the PFP won 20 seats, a loss of 6, and 17 percent of the vote. Because the CP, a new party, had never faced a general election before, and besides concentrated on undoing the rival right wing Herstigte Nasionale Party (HNP) in preparation for the elections of 1989, its successes amount, not to an increase but to a measure of reform's seriousness. The right wing's 600,000 votes came largely from former NP Afrikaners who not only doubted reform but who knew danger first-hand, from the 250,000 farmers, practical not ideological men. Right wing votes also came from the 50,000 or 60,000 white miners and blue-collar workers who face economic insecurity and black competition for jobs. All CP victories were in constituencies in the northern Transvaal—some along the borders that already know the land mine war that Angola, Mozambique and Rhodesia knew and South West Africa knows. The CP also won one-third of the votes in the Orange Free State.

In something like twenty-five constituencies the right wing came within a thousand votes of winning, in eight the combined CP and HNP vote outdid the National Party vote. Besides its suggestion of a possible doubling of CP seats in the next election, the right wing's successes won the CP the important title of "Official Opposition" from the Progressives, a role that allows it to set the questions of debate and to call for votes of confidence.

Botha will now have to face the men from the National Party who would not go along with him in 1982. Both Botha's gains and the CP's rise to official opposition show that the South Africans take him seriously. The vote shows a strengthening of a middle of tougher liberals and resilient conservatives, and deep-going change within the National Party. For the National Party won more seats from moderates, including English speakers, who want change without ruin, than it lost to its former party members, the founders of the CP. 400,000 of the NP's one million votes came from English-speaking whites, the NP guesses. "In a way South Africans voted for more reform but also for more security."[114]

The CP shares a similarity and a difference with the PFP. Like the PFP, it does not have a viable alternative. For events and, more importantly, men's minds have outdone the CP's policy of return to something like twelve independent homelands, including homelands for Indians and Coloreds. But unlike the PFP, the CP does not have the backing of the press, neither the Afrikaans or the English press.

CP opposition will serve to set crucial limits, especially in the rejection of one-man, one-vote, limits Botha himself has never denied, and the Progressives pretended publicly they did not see,—limits defined by the readiness to fight to the finish: "If a black majority ruled, South Africa would not be a Western democratic country. If South Africa were a unitary state, there would have to be a common citizenship and universal suffrage . . . No matter what checks and balances were imposed, there would be majority rule."[115]

The CP will also test the depth of Botha's commitment to reform, a commitment not to be measured by the government's announcement of a coherent plan that Buthelezi and the twenty-eight signers of the Stellenbosch statement want. For Botha understands meaningful change, the change of heart Buthelezi, and Smuts, a generation before, called for, is in fact occurring today. Such a change cannot come from a plan from the top, as Botha said in perhaps the deepest sentence of his speech announcing elections: "A constitution merely reflects a community's political and social culture and all the underlying values, norms and principles. They cannot be created by a constitution."

Polls showed that attitudes corresponded to the election results, even among non-voting blacks. Of 1,500 whites questioned in November and December 1986, three out of four supported fundamental reform and "power-sharing," Botha's vague phrase, with blacks; more than fifty percent because they believed no effective settlement possible without negotiation. Thirty-seven percent thought the pace of reform right; twenty-eight percent too slow; seventeen percent too fast. More than half supported mixed residential areas open to all races on condition that communities decide on integration, not the central government.

The poll also showed that hard-headedness about foreign affairs matched the readiness for domestic change, toughness that vouches for the capacity to distinguish change from appeasement: Two-thirds believed that South Africa should defend South West Africa regardless of consequences and forty-two percent that sanctions against South Africa would increase, even under a PFP government. Less than twenty-seven percent accepted government negotiations with the ANC.[116] This toughness that reflects the two sides of Botha's policy shows South Africans take change in earnest.

A nation-wide poll of blacks a few months later showed less than eight percent supported violence. Only about one percent thought demonstrations and boycotts would bring change,—striking evidence that Buthelezi's and Inkatha's stand against demonstrations is not merely eccentric. About fifty-seven percent, eighty-six percent of blacks over fifteen, believe in a negotiated solution. Forty-nine percent thought majority rule bad, twenty-eight percent good, eighty-six percent wanted arrangements that prevented any group dominating another. Over forty percent thought Botha and the government, along with the South African people, most capable of dealing with the situation. No other group or individual, except the government and Botha who was also thought twice as likely to succeed as Nelson Mandela, received more than ten percent endorsement.[117]

A poll in April 1978 of 150 "radically minded" black men in Soweto showed similar results: Fifty-seven percent wanted a negotiated solution between groups; thirty-five percent black majority rule; four percent partition; two percent independent homelands with more land and towns.[118]

These polls show what any man capable of common sense with a bit of experience of history would guess, but our time needs numbers to confirm the plainness of the day, like the man in Molière who had to be told he spoke prose. Besides, polls would not much matter without a government strong enough to hold elections. What counts is the readiness to resist intimidation, not in the anonymity of polls, but openly. "It is necessary for moderate Whites and Blacks,—no matter how difficult and dangerous it sometimes is for the latter,—to state unequivocally that we shall not be intimidated by and certainly shall not be governed by barbarians. Even if those barbarians have the support of the USA and the Soviet Union," wrote *Die Vaderland* on May 4, 1987, bluntly admitting that the blacks were in greater danger, and had already tasted a bit of totalitarianism.

Botha was not speaking against the wind to men who would not understand, when he said in his address announcing elections that "South Africa must stand against the spirit of revolution incited against us from abroad,"—words that make the West uneasy. These words shock me also, but they are nevertheless true. Only a man who can distinguish actual defiance from its exploitation could state them with equanimity.

"Abroad" means both the Soviet Union and the other totalitarian states, their trainers of killers, agitators and organizers, and the West's haphazard but deadly cooperation with them. This complicity means the best of times are also the worst of times. It means that a country moved, and moving in its depths, must also face the possibility of its ruin from the outside, the return of Europe but of Europe at its most degraded, of totalitarian Europe,—and under American patronage!

A few days before the election, Helen Suzman saw some of the possible consequences of the PFP's ambivalence, of its rejection of reform without an alternative of its own, when she was kept from speaking at the University of Witwatersrand, a campus "radical students" held "virtually to ransom," she said.

In disarmingly mild words to a *New Yorker* reporter a few weeks before, Suzman had declared she would not put up with the danger she recognized for perhaps the first time, as if danger were simply a matter of taste: ". . . If blacks did take over altogether and there was no rule of law and no bill of rights, I don't think I'd stay in South Africa . . . I've stayed so far under a government I don't like, but at least there have been elections—for those who vote—and a fairly good legal system, and, until recently, a relatively free press. It wouldn't bother me in the slightest to live under a black president or a black prime minister, provided he wasn't socialist or Marxist or bureaucratic."[119]

Leaving is the alternative for Helen Suzman, the alternative to her party's lack of alternatives—to its unwillingness to state outright the impossibility of national "unqualified franchise." But it is not an alternative for South Africans, black, Colored, Indian and white. For them, South Africa is their country, part of their name, not a rented private house you leave at will. In the fall of 1986 in New York Paton said in quiet ferocity, which unnerved his reporter because it admitted no doubt, that his children were staying, the best proof of all his words, all his days. In 1988, the Managing Director of BMW (South Africa) wrote: "With the exception of those whites who are relative newcomers to South Africa, I have come across none who comfortably or confidently contemplate living in Europe or America should whites be forced out of South Africa . . . White South Africans have become 'Africans'."[120]

The casual sobriety that overtook Suzman did not reach liberals and her party before or after the elections. Before, they expected to double their seats to fifty and form a "new force," with academics, business leaders, the three independent candidates and about the same number of National Party MPs. After, they continued to abuse reform in barrenness of soul. ". . .The question . . . is not whether any reform might be better than Nationalist, but whether anything could be much worse," remarked Kenneth Owen, a prominent journalist, once editor of the *Rand Daily Mail*, now editor of *Business Week*, words that were prefaced with the remark that ". . . Only the Marxists have put forward answers which integrate means and ends, revolutionary method leading to socialist dictatorship."[121]

Owen means he can not get along without the answers, at the same time that he has none, impatience that makes it impossible for him to accept imperfect change, Nadine Gordimer's "torment of the ideal." Half a generation ago this rigidity that runs the risk of serving totalitarian dogma had startled Venter: "Speaking generally, and there were exceptions, of course, I found that the more liberal a person's image was regarded (by the Establishment such as it is in South Africa) the less inclined he or she was to assist in a *project which can only in the long run result in an improvement in the Colored status quo*"[122] (Italics mine).

The Colored leader, Franklin Sonn, knows the name of this congenital lack of bite in the liberals' opposition: "The black African and Afrikaner are alike in being spiritual creatures. They will not trust anyone who does not speak to the soul."[123]

Sonn means that because liberals are irremediably secular, they shrink from the feasible. In contrast, Paton came to his opposition in the fifties and sixties because of his worship. His voice, consequently, could not be denied, even in its outlandish dismissal of the commonplace realities of foreign affairs, the only fault he shared with today's liberals. You had to listen to Paton because of his confidence that truth was bigger than himself.

The election was held under tight security, for the UDF, the ANC, and above all, the newly formed labor federation, COSATU, meant to show that despite the relative quiet in the townships the State of Emergency had not worked. They sought to precipitate labor confrontations to further the politicization of the unions and to challenge the system head-on, the new ANC strategy to replace the violence in the townships the State of Emergency had brought under some control. The chairman of the commission that recommended the registration of black unions in 1979 in the confidence that statutory regulation would prevent their politicization, Nic Wiehahn, immediately recognized this strategy in a measured article: ". . . Labor relations will be applied in the ANC's struggle against the present dispensation."[124]

The confrontations sought to make a mockery of the elections. They tried to show insurrection had spread outside the townships to the unions. Despite some disruptions and the participation of 1.5 million people in the May Day demonstration, largely organized by COSATU, they did not succeed.

Unions that claim to represent five hundred thousand of the more than a million black union members are affiliated with COSATU,—affiliation that does not mean they all share COSATU's politicization of labor. Almost immediately after COSATU's organization, Buthelezi called it a new ANC front because of its call for disinvestment: "Those who have supported sanctions so far from inside have done so as surrogates of the ANC."[125]

In February 1986 the COSATU Central Committee, its eyes on its ten thousand worker-elected practical-minded shop stewards, declared against affiliation with any political organization within or outside South Africa. A few weeks later, on March 5–6, 1986, it met with the ANC in Lusaka. The joint communiqué read: "There is a common understanding that . . . lasting solutions can only emerge from the national liberation movement, headed by the ANC and the entire democratic forces of our country, of which COSATU is an important and *integral* part"[126] (Italics mine). An ANC document the government released in 1986, "ANC Planning for 1987," shows the ANC means to coordinate its successes abroad with a "mass movement" within South Africa centered on the UDF, COSATU and the churches—despite "the sporadic nature of contact between ourselves and the leadership of the broad democratic movement."[127]

In 1987 a member of the ANC National Executive Committee emphasized in almost the same words as the ANC-COSATU statement of 1986, that, "Our liberation struggle, as it stands now, is led by the ANC." The ANC wanted only one federation of unions—COSATU: ". . . Because if we allow the situation wherein [another] federation is formed, another one may emerge and another one and another one. That divides the forces who are not acting in unison. Our main objective is that, because of its importance, the working class ought to be united. That is why our own concentration and focus is on one federation, one country. We would like to see workers organized in one powerful federation in our country."[128]

In contrast leaders of unions in COSATU, who unlike COSATU's leadership and the ANC are in direct contact with workers, have insisted on independence: "The unbanning of the ANC is a long way away. In any event, close links with these organizations [the UDF, ANC] can mean the unions becoming just another typical government-controlled [in the event of an ANC regime] labor movement."[129] In response COSATU's leadership has temporized, and affiliated with the UDF, and spoken against free enterprise. At the same time that he denied COSATU was an ANC front, "We are not their puppets and they are not ours," Sidney Mafumadi, assistant general secretary of COSATU, admitted agreement with the ANC: "It is clear there can be no solution to South Africa's problems without the ANC. We do not want to ignore coincidence of many of the perspectives of ourselves and the ANC."

The adoption of the Freedom Charter, "as a guiding document in the struggle against national oppression and economic exploitation," in March 1987 by the National Union of Mines (NUM),—with about 110,000 members, about a third of the non-foreign African workers on the mines, the largest group in COSATU,—betrayed COSATU's link with the ANC. For the Freedom Charter is one of the ANC's and SACP's most important tools for forming and manipulating fronts. "The workers' struggle in the mines cannot be separated from the struggle in the community . . . Apartheid and capitalism are two inseparable evils that must be smashed," read the preamble of the NUM resolution.[130] At its first congress, the president of COSATU had announced a political attack on apartheid: pass-burning campaigns (before repeal of the pass laws in July 1986), rent and tax boycotts.

COSATU's pursuit of political aims through South Africa's strict and sophisticated labor legislation—procedures for settling disputes, an industrial court, prohibition of strike treasuries—showed itself in the NUM's strike on August 9, 1987, the first legal African strike to last more than a few days: three weeks. The small difference between NUM's demand for a 30 percent wage increase, down from an original 40 to 55 percent, and the mining companies' offer of staged increases of between 16 to 24.5 percent, a final offer, up from 12.5 percent to 17.9 percent, was small enough to make it clear that wage demands were only a pretext again to get on the media nightly, and possibly to precipitate a national and illegal solidarity strike, to renew the insurrectionary atmosphere that had prevailed before the State of Emergency.

None of this came off despite media attention, because the strike was legal. The companies enforced the law's limits enough to make the serious violence against workers who wanted to work plain to the world, and the press reported it. The companies controlled the violence without the direct intervention of the South African police, they were not able to control the intimidation.

The companies hit hardest were the most progressive, especially Anglo-American which had argued for the recognition of black unions in the late seventies and allowed the NUM's recruiters into its hostels for migrant workers with the result that it employs eighty-six percent of the NUM's members. Encouragement earned Anglo-American the epithets treacherous, cowardly and ruthless from the NUM during the strike. In contrast the strike barely touched the other huge mining company, Gold Fields, that had allowed the NUM only telephone access to its hostels. On August 9 two non-striking workers were necklaced. On August 10, the day Parliament repealed the last restrictions on the advancement of blacks to mine manager positions and above, a worker who had refused to strike was strangled with a wire coat hanger. On August 12 the attorney-general of the Transvaal charged seventy-eight officials and members of the NUM with conspiracy to murder and subversion, arrests the NUM called "clearly an attempt to break the strike and undermine the union's right to conduct legitimate trade union activities." A total of eighteen workers were killed, three in confrontations with mine security, fifteen in fights between strikers and non-strikers, twelve were workers who had refused to strike.

In negotiations during the strike, and later in 1987 with the Chamber of Mines, the mining companies' organization, the NUM refused unambiguously to renounce violence because it had deep roots the NUM could not control. It blamed the violence on the security police and called for a "demobilization of mine security" and for a commitment not to call in the South African Police.

All these demands and explanations that make the system responsible for violence resembled the UDF's and the ANC's propaganda in the townships in 1984–86: The NUM wants complete control of workers in just the way the UDF and the ANC wanted control of the townships. This intimidation threatens all the accomplishments of trade unions since 1978.

A few months after the strike, the industrial relations advisor to the Chamber of Mines, blamed the NUM's ruthlessness on too-rapid organization that some of the mines had encouraged. He did not minimize the situation: ". . . The intolerance of dissent is becoming part of our trade union make up . . . Can we have a relationship, agreements, procedures and mutual trust with organizations whose stated objectives, if realized, will lead to the annihilation of our enterprises?"[131]

But the general secretary of the NUM, Cyril Ramaphosa, hardly needed the encouragement of Anglo-American to radicalize. In March 1987 Ramaphosa blamed the politicization of the NUM and COSATU on the detention of black leaders, especially union leaders, an analysis the *Economist* accepted without attribution.[132]

Two years before in a speech in May 1985, Ramaphosa had, however, not blamed detentions for his determination to turn the unions to "revolution"—to "[raise] the consciousness of the working class by clarifying issues and *building cadres*" (Italics mine). He had seen no other way but revolution. He publicly rejected "organizing workers in South Africa as the art of the impossible" in favor of politicization that government registration of the unions in 1979 had sought to prevent: "[Organizing the mine-workers] has been the art of the impossible because it has been the art of trying to make a fundamental change in a system by using structures and instruments that were designed to perpetuate that system. It has been the art of the impossible because it has been the art of trying to make a revolution with moderate tools that were invented to prevent a revolution . . . The black miner has been condemned to seek radical ends within a framework which was designed to prevent sudden and radical change."[133]

The application of the strategy, because of the indignation at the State of Emergency abroad and its unnoticed partial success, is new, not the intention to exploit labor for political purposes. Unions had been on the minds of the SACP Central Committee in 1981, less on their minds than infiltration of the police, the army, the attack on the "Bantustans" and terrorism, but on their minds: "It is also of great importance for our future strategy and tactics to examine the strike weapon as an instrument of *political* struggle . . . it is vital that our whole movement becomes clear on the role of the general strike *in the context of revolutionary struggle*" (Italics mine).

The main action to overshadow the election culminated in COSATU's call for National Days of Protest on May 5 and 6, a call that came also from the UDF, the newly founded South African Youth Congress and other black student groups.

In response, both the Universities of Cape Town and of Witwatersrand closed to protest the election and the recent arrests and roughing-up of stone-throwing students—despite statements by students, black and white, at the University of Witwatersrand that they were "fed-up" with unrest.[134] In the weeks before student demonstrators had kept Dennis Worrall, the former ambassador to Great Britain who had broken with the NP to run independently, Conor Cruise O'Brien and Buthelezi from speaking—in addition to Helen Suzman. Like the NUM several months later they attacked men who accepted some of their goals but who rejected their methods, especially intimidation. Little crucial differences hurt the most.

Right or left wing extremists number about three to five percent of students according to officials in the government's Bureau of Information in Johannesburg and Pretoria—not negligible numbers because their violence and intimidation captures events and prompts exaggeration in the media abroad. Justification for the unrest had been provided by a booklet published in the middle of 1986, "Perceptions of Wits," that recommended "reverse discrimination" in teaching appointments, "community organization" pressure on "liberal" teachers and so on,—the university equivalent of the SPCC resolutions in late 1985, drafted after consultations with SACP and ANC members abroad.[135]

In October 1987 the government announced it would cut its subsidies, which cover seventy to eighty percent of costs, to universities that did not protect freedom of speech,—a measure *The Washington Post* could barely comprehend.[136] It also prohibited the use of university bulletin boards and stationery to promote banned organizations and unlawful strikes. The numbers of "revolutionary" posters in universities, in fact, startled visitors to South African universities who had known them a few years before.

A six-week strike against the South African Transport Services (SATS) set the stage for the National Days of Protest. The strike provoked two confrontations with the police, on April 22, the strike's last day, and, in the strike's aftermath, on April 29: six deaths and thirteen injured, including seven policemen. The police entered COSATU House on the twenty-second in pursuit of two hundred workers and terrorists informers had told them were hidden there. On the twenty-ninth the police returned to COSATU House to arrest eleven men after the necklacing of five workers who had returned to work.

The COSATU violence sought to prevent rehiring. The SATS management had started to rehire because it estimated seventy-five percent of the sixteen thousand workers dismissed because they had not worked had been intimidated—threats to their families and their houses. Only a thousand workers had showed up for rehiring on the twenty-second.

Intimidation also helped the union that called the strike, the South African Railways and Harbour Workers' Union (SARHWU), to beguile its sixteen thousand workers with assurances that SATS would pay them despite its denials,—bad faith or misjudgment that cost the workers sixteen million Rand. "Questions then arise concerning the motives of the trade union leaders. Do they really care about the fate of the worker who is now unemployed? Or is it simply another way of blocking the existing and tested bargaining mechanism to bypass the 'system'?" wrote the Afrikaans newspaper, *Beeld*, with 76,000 circulation, the largest in the Transvaal, on April 27, before the murder of five men who had returned to work. In contrast to the ten registered unions that represent eighty percent of the two hundred thousand SATS workers, SARHWU, with its headquarters in COSATU House, was unregistered.[137]

Towards the end of the election campaign, on April 15, the minister of defense, General Magnus Malan, made it clear the State of Emergency would continue. Effective locally-elected town councils; security for individuals and groups in the townships; a normal situation in the schools; fundamental resolution of union labor problems, including unemployment; improvement in housing were the criteria for "willingly [thinking] about lifting the State of Emergency."[138] The government meant to finish what it had started, a statement that dismayed newspapers hoping for a swift end to the emergency.

Malan meant the reforms made in the last years could not take effect without continued protection. He also meant to break the rudimentary peoples'-street-committee regimes, radical-front organizations in the schools and in labor, and the ANC, a process that would take time, because despite detentions, it calls for trials.

He was also asking the electorate to endorse this policy—they did. He meant the government was serious about stopping violence, something the radical fronts wanted to prove impossible. These were the costs of freedom in Africa.

9 Undoing the "NO"; its Persistence

In the year following the elections, the government concentrated on overcoming the intimidation and the ideological "No" to discussion, negotiation or change that had spread, especially in the churches and in the unions, after the curtailment of violence in the townships. It sought to reach Tutu and the South African Council of Churches (SACC) and to keep the UDF, the NECC and COSATU and the so-called alternative press from spreading the "No," a difficult task that tells something of the South African government's confidence. Probably the challenge in the churches is the most serious, more serious than the attempt to politicize the unions and to spread propaganda through the "alternative press" because it aims directly at the heart of the country, its deepest confidence and strength. An ANC document the South Africans seized in a raid on ANC command-posts hidden in houses in residential neighborhoods in Maseru, the capital of Lesotho, in 1982, outlines infiltration of churches, trade unions and student organizations.[139]

In the short range, the government's eyes were on the October 1988 local elections throughout all of South Africa, both black and white, except the homelands. For these elections would show the government's success in overcoming intimidation on the local level. As it turned out, 27.3 percent voted according to official estimates.

In the long range, the government sought to find credible black leaders beyond the local level, the central problem both blacks and whites have faced since the loosening of apartheid. "The body [the National Statutory Council (NSC)] will be as credible as the leaders who participate in it," said the junior minister in charge of renewed public negotiations with blacks for the NSC, Stoffel van der Merwe, in September 1987, at the same time that he acknowledged the absence/lack of "defined leadership" among Africans: "It is most important that people must be part of the process of creation otherwise they do not understand why it has to be done this way and not that way."[140]

In measured words Van der Merwe also made it clear the government might talk to blacks detained in the present or past not convicted of violence. The readiness to negotiate meant standing the imperfect and compromise, the test of good faith: "We are not busy with a public relations exercise. What we have to create is essentially a compromise. People will have to step down from their ideals to reach the compromise. That compromise will eventually have to be sold at the grassroots level, so there is no sense in reaching such an agreement with a person who is not in a position to sell it to his own constituents at the grassroots level."

Van der Merwe focused on the Africans' unwillingness to believe the government would allow change, another name for intimidation: "The one thing that is lacking in this situation is the conviction among people that government actually wants to enter into a negotiation process with a view to creating a democratic future."

To overcome this paralysis Van der Merwe called for a change of heart: ". . . The best way to guarantee rights is to have a situation in the hearts of people and not only in the constitution. That might sound a bit wishy-washy, but is it not a fact? What does that mean? It means that there must be a realization among people that they need each other, that it is in their own interests to respect the rights of others and of other groups at every level. If that can become a living realization, then you have got the real guarantees. What you want is a situation in which people do not want to hurt each other, in which one group does not want to destroy another."

These are improbable words from a government minister. But South

Africa like the United States is an improbable country—but with this difference: It knows it is improbable.

In his call for a "change of heart," Van der Merwe implied the creation of a new confidence in Africans, an almost impossible task. Especially since Van der Merwe said nothing of the past that despite its harshness was also strict and unhypocritical enough to allow the changes now taking place. His silence betrayed the unwitting effects of "armed propaganda" on him.

In broadcast after broadcast the ANC attacks this past, every bit of it— broadcasts Van der Merwe, in charge also of accurate information for the press from the police and the army, knows well in contrast to most whites:

Gone are the days when one policeman on a bicycle could come and collect a dozen men in the township and herd them like cattle to the police station . . .

Calls for outright murder follow the mockery of the old authority:

Police and soldiers must be killed even when they are in their homes, in or out of uniform. These angels of death must be made to pay for their crimes. Let us show no mercy, because they themselves have none.[141]

Blacks repeatedly told a sensitive American priest of "the powerful appeal to hate and kill [these broadcasts] generate in one's heart." These broadcasts come, not only in English and Afrikaans, but in Venda, Sotho, Zulu, South Sotho, Tsonga, and Xhosa and in many dialects, they come not only from ANC stations in Zambia, Angola, Mozambique, Dar es Salaam, Tanzania and Addis Ababa, but also from Communist nations, East Germany, mainland China, Ethiopia, Rumania, Vietnam, Cuba, Czechoslovakia, North Korea, Bulgaria, Albania that broadcast from Botswana and Lesotho. The use of indigenous languages explains the wildness of these broadcasts that in English baffle comprehension.[142]

Within South Africa, the ANC and the Communist regimes recognize the differences they deny abroad in their demands for one-man, one-vote for one South Africa. They seek to move the Africans not in the languages that unite them but in the mother tongues hardest for them to dismiss, stunning tacit confirmation of the South African government's insistence on South Africa's peoples' differences that Western newspapers ignore or ridicule in contempt.

The viciousness the broadcasts invite persists even two years after the introduction of the State of Emergency. In May 1988, the minister of law and order explained delays in bringing youths sixteen and seventeen years old in custody to trial because the police could not protect witnesses: "A witnesses' life in most of these cases means absolutely nothing and the necklace murders have become so easy to commit by ruthless murderers that witnesses do anything to avoid giving evidence against an offender for fear of being burnt alive."[143]

The naked show of force, barbed wire, armored cars, and soldiers startles visitors who had known South Africa twenty years before as much as the changes, the loosening of apartheid, that they do not entirely realize necessitated it. By "change of heart" Van der Merwe means the stuff to overcome the fear after the curtailment of violence. But this fear does not come from past humiliation and harshness, but from present murder. It does not fear Afrikaners, it fears black extremists.

Long before the State of Emergency the government, especially the army, had realized that the curtailment of violence and a police presence would not restore confidence, let alone allow it to expand, among Africans who already reckoned on the eventual inevitability of a black government they did not necessarily welcome. But what black could say the last, even to his friends, except in the privacy of polls? Propaganda serves to keep even the South African government from mentioning the obvious.

Already in April 1986, the minister of defense, Malan, in Parliament had revealed an extensive network to serve as a "warning system" for threats to the state and to prevent disturbances: twelve Joint Management Centers (JMCs) connected with sixty smaller JMCs and 345 "mini-JMCs" staffed entirely with civil servants but under the direction of the State Security Council that directs the military and political war both at home and abroad. Meant to deal with the obstacles, besides outright violence, to the growth in confidence, the JMCs do not take the initiative.

Both the South African government and the many active private organizations have a healthy sense they can only help those willing to help themselves in coping with change real enough to provoke an ANC member long out of the country to defect upon his return,—and to turn in the three other white terrorists, among them a former *Rand Daily Mail* reporter, trained in Angola, Cuba and the Soviet Union. The four were armed with Soviet heat-seeking ground-to-air Soviet Sam–7 missiles, the first confirmed in South Africa, and radio equipment that put them in direct contact with ANC headquarters in Lusaka.[144]

The JMCs see to the establishment of local governments, a daunting task, not only because of fear, but because of the inexperience of civil life, probably the main reason for the relatively low turn-out in the 1988 local elections,— the other side of fear. In 1986 a Potchefstroom University commission report on the disturbances that broke out in the Vaal Triangle, the area of Pretoria, Johannesburg and Vereeniging, on September 3, 1984 criticized the government for its failure to bring home the realities of local self-government to large numbers of Africans in the townships: Many had not even heard of the elections. The commission also warned blacks that did not vote in local elections: "If [the Africans] refrain from participating in elections, they should not be too quick to complain about the quality of councillors eventually placed in power by the handful who did exercise their franchise."[145]

But even before the State of Emergency, the successes considerably outnumbered the failures, testimony to black courage. Of 192 community councils, 23 town councils and 19 village councils, constituted as of April 1986, 4 town councils, all in the eastern Cape, and 37 community councils had collapsed by July 1986 according to the Sowetan. The administrator of the Cape said in June 1986 that "intimidation and victimization" had brought the collapse of forty percent of African local governments in the eastern Cape, only 17 of 45 community councils survived. In the whole country about twenty percent of the councillors, 245 out of 1,277, had received permission to bear arms.[146]

With disingenuous gullibility that typifies some South African liberals, a PFP MP remarked that the collapses might force the government to negotiate with the true leaders of the African community, presumably the "comrades" and the "street-committees," of the eastern Cape especially. He meant violence, the readiness to kill, rather than the guts to face it down, brought out natural leaders,—an uncannily accurate reflection of constant ANC propaganda especially in broadcasts. These broadcasts compared spontaneous anonymous local "governments" to vegetation—as if weeds were free,—botanical blood lust, the opposite of the formality of government:

The seeds of people's power are beginning to germinate and spread their roots. People's committees, street committees and comrade committees are emerging as popular organs in the face of the collapse of the racist stooge administration. Already in many areas there are developing free zones . . .

The accompanying call for blood to water this vegetation, "people's power" feeds on complicity, betrays the effectiveness of the JMCs' and the army's support of local African governments, a day-to-day face-to-face struggle against the faceless. For in classic Communist practice that requires the surrender of one's name, "people's power," to make everybody and nobody responsible, names only its enemies, not itself:

Those collaborators who are serving in the community councils must be dealt with. Informers, policemen, secret police and Army personnel working against our people must be eliminated. The puppets in the tricameral parliament and the Bantustans [the homelands] must be disposed of.[147]

The English-language press' contempt for the government's and the Africans' struggle to overcome mob rule in the townships, like violence's fascination of the PFP MP, betrays the effect of violence's "No" in the townships on the whites. It took not the government that acts more effectively than it speaks, but the leader of the black Urban Councils Association of South Africa (UCASA) to remind the English newspapers that Africans democratically elected town governments: "[The English language press] would like to see the councils go down the drain, and I am not afraid to say that."[148]

Despite these difficulties in local government in 1986 that argued against entrusting blacks with national responsibilities at least until the October 1988 local elections measured success in overcoming mob intimidation, the government resumed public discussion of a national role for blacks with Van der Merwe's interview in September 1987. It accepted in principle the argument of UCASA,—the same position Buthelezi had taken upon the first introduction of local government in 1984,—that local responsibility could not be made to substitute for a national role: "Blacks want full participation in the decision-making organ—Parliament—and are not interested in making decisions at the black local authority level."

Is this foolhardiness or courage? "Courage seems a constant concern of South Africans—especially Afrikaners, who possess it in such quantities that it could be mistaken for bullheadedness . . . and [for] almost a failing," wrote the sensitive Canadian journalist, Peter Worthington, after his visit in early 1987.[149]

Behind this courage there is the intelligence of experience, the only quality that distinguishes courage from recklessness. The South Africans still know what every statesman used to know: only governments, not international organizations that protest good intentions but take no responsibility, and account to no one, can express the confidence necessary, not merely to curtail, but to overcome violence. They know men can construct governments to save themselves from themselves, the lesson in 1910, and before in the Boer republics, the lesson of Smuts and Merriman even in their differences. Only an expression of the general will of the Africans could gradually overcome their intimidation of each other in renewed confidence that they could obey themselves despite local and tribal differences in national institutions that would in part treat them as one people. This was probably the deepest thinking of the South African government.

Also in September 1987, the minister of constitutional development, Heunis, repeated his description of the National Statutory Council (NSC) upon its first introduction in January 1986 as "one of the most fundamental reform steps that this government, or any other government, has yet taken in the history of our country." He again described the NSC as an interim body to "plan and prepare for a dispensation which provides for participation by all South African citizens in the processes of government." He also emphasized its mandate to "investigate and consider any matter which, in its opinion, is of national interest, including existing or proposed legislation and steps taken or contemplated by the government."[150]

Quite a view: The government meant the NSC to negotiate an entirely new constitution at the same time that it granted it a somewhat undefined role in the present. The nine black representatives from the ten million blacks outside the homelands were to be elected on a geographic basis without regard to tribes, a significant modification of the original plan that had provided for their appointment by the state president. Another six Africans were to come from the homelands, either the chief ministers or men they appointed. In addition the majority party leaders in the three-house Parliament, cabinet members and ten other men the state president nominated were to make up the NSC.

The government had been meticulous in its vagueness about the design of a settlement in order to exorcise the accusations of "collaborator" and "stooge" that mark blacks who dare show a public face, another effect of "armed propaganda." It has repeatedly stated it wants a system with no one group dominating another—without explicitly repudiating the past. But it cannot answer any sensible man's question, who will be in charge, another way of asking where is the sovereignty,—and this in a country used to strong forthright government. "Our future is very bleak," Van der Merwe said, if a system without one group dominating another proves impossible.

Van der Merwe went further: In order to show the government's good faith he renounced the past more explicitly than in his call for a "change of heart." In order to make the limits for the future clear, he dared not say the past governments of South Africa were better than a future tyranny or totalitarian regime: "We do not want to exchange one form of domination for another, to move from white minority domination to black majority domination . . . we have to take the principle of one-man, one-vote and apply it in such a way as to enable us to build a lasting democracy, not a democracy that will deteriorate into a one-party system or one-man dictatorship in five or six years or in five or six months." This vagueness about the future the government thinks necessary to win the consent of blacks, disoriented whites and weakened support for the NP, Van der Merwe acknowledged in April 1988, after the three CP by-election victories followed upon the temporary failure of the government's re-opening of discussion for the NSC in the fall of 1987: "The troubles of the NP have stemmed from a lack of clarity or lack of blueprint for reform . . . When people become uncertain they are vulnerable to the siren song of the right wing."

But despite its admission of the costs of delay the government continued to wait, a daring and dangerous policy it well knew: "Democracy, like a butterfly, is most vulnerable when it is in an emergent stage." It waited because it did not have the answers, in contrast to the "revolutionaries" as Botha said in Parliament in his April 21, 1988 speech. This waiting amounted to continuing its stance since 1978: "Reform consists, by its nature, of an almost interminable series of small steps, and not of a few spectacular leaps. It is easy to discount each of these small steps as being inherently of no significance—it takes one forward only a minute little part of the awesome distance that needs to be covered."[151]

What is one to make of this daring and this vagueness that looks so much like foolhardiness—and that tries people who do not know the hendiadys, patience and courage, the motto of the Orange Free State before the Union of 1910? The South African government is not hypocritical, it is not disingenuous, it is not about to repudiate the tradition of strong sovereignty of 1910 and earlier in the Boer republics.

This sovereignty has been strong because it grew out of consent, it never imposed itself. The Afrikaners have never really wanted to rule anybody but themselves. They defeated the Africans and held them in check, but they have never really been outright conquerors despite Paton's affirmation I quoted at the beginning of this essay. They have always been fearful of ruling others. They ruled the Africans in haphazard fashion, because they had no choice, mixed up as they were with them, especially in the Transvaal, because they could not leave them entirely alone. Now that they, and the Africans, are assuming responsibilities they both sought to avoid, and much greater risks, they have to bear scorn and isolation. Call it irony.

The South African government seems to want to win the consent of the blacks to an imperfect system capable of gradual political change,—in a situation of too swift economic and social change,—that would give Africans a meaningful but not a decisive voice in national affairs as well as all the authority those who obey themselves in their "own affairs" enjoy. It could probably win this consent without constant outside interference from abroad.

Imperfect is the word to keep in mind, the word Van der Merwe perhaps forgot in his unwitting renunciation of South Africa's past. He forgot it because like almost all public men these days, he dared not say things could get worse, the mark of a time that tries to live on promises because it fears hope, a word incomprehensible without theology, and that uses facts to deny the evidence of its eyes.

Too much insistence on the refusal of blacks to show their faces in public belies the political courage, not only of the many blacks in private discussions with the government, but also of the blacks who have openly stated their readiness to talk—of men like John Gogotya, a man of silences and discretion as deep as his forthrightness who had the guts to testify against the ANC in Washington in January 1987. These men have been more or less ignored because they made it harder to belittle the government.

In July 1987 Gogotya's new organization, the Federal Independent Democratic Alliance (FIDA) announced its readiness to deal with the government at a gathering of four thousand delegates in Johannesburg. They would negotiate as long as the NSC was not "just a talking shop" and negotiations were open-ended with no political group dominating another, a reference to other black organizations: Gogotya attacked the violence of the ANC and the PAC.

FIDA grew out of a group, Operation Advance and Upgrade, that Gogotya had organized "on the lines of Inkatha,"—a comparison that means Gogotya, like Buthelezi and Biko, understands blacks must first of all take responsibility for themselves despite the temptation of blaming others the world wishes upon them. A few weeks later in September, Gogotya in Soweto accused the UDF and Azanian People's Organization (AZAPO) of provoking, with media help, atrocities in the townships that black journalists feared to report. He also pointed out that Soweto residents had not elected Dr. Nthato Motlana's Soweto Committee of Ten.[152] This civil courage, the prerequisite of self-government, earned him the label of "collaborator" in American State Department cables.

Almost a year before, in October, 1986, Bishop Isaac Mokoena and Thamsanqa Linda, chairman of a town council in the eastern Cape, home and business fire-bombed in 1985, had announced they might sit on the NSC. They had just founded the United Christian Conciliation Party (UCCP) on a program of Christian values, multi-party democracy and free enterprise. The UCCP rejected "all forms of violence, whether individual or collective, regardless of political motives," Mokoena said.

In London a few days later, Mokoena welcomed the news that the government had *finally* cut off the UDF's foreign funding: "It is encouraging that they [UDF] have been cut off from the outside world because they have been carrying a lot of outside influence which has resulted in incalculable damage to the cause of Africans. I think the government took too long to take this action." In November, he called on foreign churches to stop funds to

Desmond Tutu's SACC because it distributed them to "faceless radicals" who wanted to "eliminate all opposition and create chaos," a call Buthelezi reiterated in July 1987 in an appeal to West German churches.[153]

Mokoena's Reformed Independent Churches' Association (RICA) numbers four and a half million in contrast to the nine hundred thousand African Anglicans the SACC and Desmond Tutu claim to represent. A report in 1986 estimated that the independent African denominations numbered 3,720 churches and forty percent of the blacks in all South Africa including the independent homelands.[154] The disruptions, the demonstrations and the violence mean to keep the government from reaching these blacks, and the world from hearing them,—to force them to say "No" by preventing them from saying "Yes."

A few weeks after its introduction of the NSC Bill on November 5, 1987, the government released a close collaborator of Mandela, condemned to life imprisonment along with him and six others in 1964, Govan Mbeki. Mbeki's son heads the information and propaganda department of the ANC in Lusaka. The government made it clear to the press that gave the news prominence that Mbeki's amnesty meant to foreshadow Mandela's unconditional release which Buthelezi had made a condition for his participation in the NSC.

The day after he walked free Mbeki rehearsed all his positions at his trial twenty-three years before with the addition of the label "dummy institution" for the NSC: "I support Umkhonto we Sizwe (the terrorist wing of the ANC) for as long as the ANC deem it necessary. I am still a Communist Party member and I still embrace the Marxist view."[155] In 1964 Mbeki had ignored about a hundred prosecution questions to insist he was "morally without blame" after confession of the facts of the indictment: membership in the SACP and in the command of Umkhonto we Sizwe, accession to acts of sabotage. Mbeki had resisted the strong arguments of a black American, Max Yergan who had turned him and other Africans at Fort Hare to Marxism before 1937. Yergan had returned to South Africa in 1952 during the "Defiance Campaign" to speak publicly against Marxism-Leninism.[156] A month later, the government accused Mbeki of taking orders from the outlawed ANC, a charge his interview in *The New York Times* on November 25, 1987 substantiated, and called his release a mistake.

The release of Mbeki, despite a past that gave no hint he could come back, showed the extent the government would go to show its good faith at a moment, in contrast to 1985–1986, when it was "under no immediate pressure at home or from abroad," as South African newspapers noted. The government must also have calculated that failure might bring the South Africans weary of "thirty years subjection to warnings and information about a 'total onslaught'" to their senses about present dangers.[157]

In fact a few days after Mbeki's release, the editor of *Business Day*, Ken Owen, wrote as if he had never heard of SACP infiltration of the ANC and no longer could recall the trial of 1964: "Mbeki's overt declaration that he is a Communist throws some clear light, at last, on the implications of dealing with the African National Congress under its present leadership . . . To negotiate with any delegation that includes Mbeki is to negotiate the future with the South African Communist Party..."[158]

After the failure of this experiment the government on February 21, 1988 curbed the organizations, among them the UDF, COSATU, National Education Crisis Committee (NECC) and the Detainees' Parents Support Committee (DPSC), that kept alive the "No" of the previous years of violence,—amid uproar in the media especially in the United States and Britain. Tutu openly threatened violence: ". . . We are heading for war," blamed it on the government, and precipitated his brief arrest with twenty-five other "church leaders," not simply priests, with a deliberate violation of a statutory prohibition of protests near Parliament.

The decision to limit "only the activities of the organizations which endanger the safety of the public" that some of the press in South Africa called "banning" meant to substitute restrictions on organizations for detention. The DPSC's listing even of youths held for a few hours as detainees, had brought it home to the police that organizations have no living relatives. Allegations in a World Council of Churches newsletter of police torture and brutality to children had mostly come from children the DPSC had plainly instructed and intimidated, the minister of law and order had warned on August 16, 1987. The curbs, on the UDF and COSATU especially, meant to prevent ideological disruption and intimidation of the October 1988 local elections. The limitations on COSATU forbidding its political campaigns, not its union activities, read like a catalogue of American newspaper headlines on South Africa: no campaigns against local township government; against the NSC; against the new constitution; for the legalization of banned organizations (the ANC); for release of detainees; for active boycotts; for the commemoration of riot anniversaries or to honor prisoners dead or alive.

The newspapers abroad, in the United States especially, described the seventeen limited organizations simply as "leading anti-apartheid" groups without a reminder of the repeal of most apartheid laws, an unwitting confirmation of these organizations', especially the ANC's, insistence on the absence of any change at all.[159] They called COSATU simply "the country's largest trade union federation," without mention of its ties with the ANC or the SACP, without quotation of its resolution in 1987 "to forge links with worker organizations in Africa, Nicaragua, El Salvador, the Philippines, Angola and Mozambique," or of the words of its general-secretary, also in 1987: "Workers throughout the world are victims of US-government-sponsored terrorism . . . In this country we are also victims of that kind of imperialism."[160] They did not mention the NECC's exploitation of the schools for indoctrination. Above all the word "front" did not show its face, in the United States the media hardly know its meaning, despite P.W. Botha's and other South African officials' careful explanations: "As for the so-called crackdown, we didn't interfere with the normal activities of these opposition groups, only with the subversive aspects of their operations . . . Church matters, labor union activities are absolutely free. So are cultural and educational organizations. But we are interfering when organizations are used as fronts to commit subversive acts."[161]

There was no way a fairly innocent or ignorant or disingenuous reader, difficult distinctions these days in the United States, could understand the curbed organizations were not simply civil rights groups, but groups that used civil rights to prevent change as Van der Merwe had warned several months earlier: ". . . It is part of the known and accepted doctrine of revolutionaries to use and to abuse the instruments of democracy, such as freedom of speech and due process of law in order to undermine and eventually overthrow the existing system."[162]

A few days after the restrictions on organizations, the minister of law and order introduced a bill to prohibit foreign funding of parties and organizations with political goals. The millions of public dollars pouring into South Africa precipitated the bill's attack on a long-standing anomaly. In Parliament a few months earlier Botha had said that the "quarter million dollars at least" to fund the meeting of some sixty whites, mostly Afrikaners, with the ANC in July 1987 had come "mainly from various Western governments and institutions." In 1982, a government commission established that only one percent, not enough to pay Tutu's salary, of the twenty million rand the SACC spent in the years 1975–1981 came from within South Africa. The money came first of all from the Lutheran Church in West Germany that receives more than it knows what to do with from a federal tax, then from Denmark and the Netherlands—with about three percent from church groups in Great Britain and the United States.

In his remarks attacking the "safari" to the ANC, Botha had gone on to hint more directly at American public funding of the former PFP leader Slabbert's extra-parliamentary Institute for a Democratic Alternative in South Africa (IDASA) that had sponsored the meeting: ". . . The interference of foreign governments and their embassy personnel in the furtherance of extra-parliamentary politics . . . their support for such organizations as IDASA . . . [is] making use of South Africans to do their 'dirty work' for them while at the same time they are undermining the sovereignty of the Republic of South Africa . . . No self-respecting Government will allow its hospitality to be abused in this way." The last words sound quaint because most Western governments regularly put up with Soviet and eastern European use of their embassies for subversion and spying—except for desultory expulsions and remonstrances.

Trusted sources in Washington went further than Botha. They told me that the entire "civil rights" challenge, in the unions, in the schools, in the churches, was fed on American public funds that Congress had appropriated in the 1986 CAA Act but could not control: Congressmen had no idea where the money they had voted went.

About a month later the government suspended for three months the weekly, *New Nation*, owned by the Catholic Church, and reiterated the warnings it had made in early January to four other newspapers, including *The Weekly Mail*, for among other things their coverage of Mbeki's release and for generally promoting a "revolutionary climate." The renewable suspension of the *New Nation*, a newspaper addressed to blacks, with a larger readership than its fifty thousand run, came because of its defiance of previous warnings not to "promote the image" of the outlawed ANC and "hatred or hostility" against the security forces with advertisements that "implied police torture," as a senior official put it: "[*New Nation*] did not change its editorial policy at all after being given initial warnings."

Its editor, Zwelakhe Sisulu, a Harvard Nieman Fellow in 1984, the son of a man condemned to life imprisonment with Mandela and of a UDF leader, a committed Marxist trained in journalism in the United States, a combination that spells camouflage, had been detained for more than a year for speeches exciting school children on behalf of the NECC and other "security reasons," unconnected with journalism, that a provincial supreme court upheld in November 1987.[163]

Two things should be said about these warnings and this suspension, the first since the government closed *The World*, the predecessor of *The Sowetan*, in 1977 for printing instructions for Molotov cocktails and the like: they aimed, with the exception of *The Sowetan*, only at newspapers started in the last few years, the so-called "alternative press," in themselves the children of violence and wearing its masks; secondly, they were measured, no outright closures or direct control. This restraint earned the government more abuse throughout the world at each warning than outright suppression once and for all,—the rewards of restraint.

This restraint aims to stop the spread of propaganda that enforces the "No" to any dealings with the government, no small matter especially among a population of Africans seventy percent literate but often at third-grade level— and not only among them.[164] When I first read *The Weekly Mail*, which received still another warning in late April, again amid uproar in the press in the United States and Britain that probably boosted the circulation it seeks abroad,—it is one of two newspapers the School of International Affairs at Columbia University gets from South Africa,—I could not believe my eyes: It wrote as if there had already been a revolution in the country, as if the government no longer existed, a replica of the ANC's blindness to alternatives, but presented as actual news, as reality decked-out with some major corporation advertisements. Despite the crudeness I felt the strong undertow of temptation that the vivid promises of a sweet future, especially in rough tense times, exercise,—the political equivalent of drugs. A paper in Mandela's hand found in 1963 among detailed plans for explosives, sabotage and terrorism throughout South Africa promised that "South Africa will become a land of milk and honey under Communist rule."[165] I asked myself what does the government censor if it does not censor this?

The editor of *Business Day*, Ken Owen, called this newspaper's jumble of sweet nightmares in days that need to distinguish toughness from cruelty, "radical chic." But the assumption that the South African police tortures routinely that these papers pass off as almost fact means to dismiss the credibility of the government. The government investigates particular abuses to maintain this credibility in the face of indifference to ANC and other terrorism outside South Africa.[166]

In its admonitions to the "alternative press" the government sought to hold strictly to its distinction between the dissemination of propaganda that sought to undermine the government, and above all the respect that marks sovereignty, and criticism that strengthened it, with the American example, fifteen years ago, before its eyes, as Van der Merwe said with pitiless clarity that testified to the earnestness of the rest of his September 1987 interview: "If you permit dissemination of all information, then you must allow [banned organizations like the ANC] to put out their propaganda. This has never been allowed in other countries where power [an unfortunate word for sovereignty] is at stake. The exception was when the Americans, while engaged in the Vietnam war, allowed Communist propaganda right into every home in the United States. It was a disaster."

The dissemination of such propaganda in the United States had two lasting consequences: the refusal, especially among the relatively affluent and the "educated," despite their unwillingness to inform themselves enough, to give the government the benefit of the doubt in foreign affairs and the consequent disappearance of much common sense in political discourse—practically a description of Lenin's demoralization.

Finally, the sovereignty of Parliament guarantees the truth will come out in South Africa: There is no way the government can suppress words or inquiries in Parliament or keep the press from quoting them. Both the tough sobriety of some of the South African mainstream press, and Slabbert's announcement in April 1988 that he might again seek a seat in Parliament, after his impulsive abandonment of PFP opposition leadership in 1986, testify to Parliament's capacity to preserve the distinction between free-spokenness and license, the core of republican liberty.

The uproar about the government's restrictions on COSATU, the UDF and other organizations and its warnings to the "alternative press" allowed Desmond Tutu to regain a fleeting prominence in the international media he had not enjoyed for perhaps three years. "One of the few credible black leaders still able to voice anti-apartheid outrage at increasing repression," *The New York Times* called him in a sentence stinking of Manhattan rewrite.[167] More importantly, it led to a crucial exchange between Botha and Tutu.

In two letters, one to Tutu released for publication on March 17, 1988, and one sent to the general secretary of the South African Council of Churches, Frank Chikane, a week later, March 24, 1988, P.W. Botha tried to reach Tutu and the rest of the SACC. Tutu tried to call the exchange a Church-State confrontation, in some sense rightly, but with the important difference that Botha spoke for worshippers against Tutu's disregard. He sought to distinguish between the holy and the secular, Tutu to confound them,—quite a reversal. And a reversal that allowed Botha to make the historically correct, and these days breathtaking, statement that political freedom depends on freedom in worship: "Religious freedom is the cornerstone of proper human rights."

Botha's words belied, Tutu's confirmed, the routine SACP assumption of the frailty of belief, already evident in widely-distributed SACP pamphlets during the Second World War that shook some MPs: "We declare that we do not believe in God and we know very well that the priest and the bourgeoisie speak in the name of God only for the purpose of promoting their own interests."[168]

Botha's clarity about civil life's dependence on belief in the face of an archbishop who cannot address the spirit allowed Botha clearly to distinguish between the "persecution" Tutu admitted more than once he wanted to provoke, a "frenzy of rumor and expectation regarding possible action by the Government," Botha called it, and subversion: There would be no "action by the Government against certain members of the clergy . . . unless they take part in subversive and revolutionary activities."

Could Tutu really claim after the readiness of Botha to receive clergymen and union leaders, publicly and secretly, that the so-called march on Parliament, "an illegal action was necessary, and worthy of the cause and message of Christ and the Churches" because "you have virtually no other effective and peaceful means of witnessing effectively,"—and not "to a large degree planned as a calculated public relations exercise," especially since the priests knew their "actions were illegal"?

In the very days when a special emissary arrived in South Africa to show the archbishop of Canterbury's support, amid letters of criticism from priests and worshippers in the English press, Botha called Tutu's and other Anglican bishops' faith, my word, violence: "You do not hesitate to spread malicious untruths about South Africa here and abroad. You should be fully aware of the numerous misleading statements concerning local support for sanctions and for the ANC, alleged atrocities by the security forces, the treatment of youths, and the fabrication of false testimony for especially the overseas media. You love and praise the ANC/SACP with its Marxists and atheistic ideology, landmines, bombs and necklaces perpetrating the most horrendous atrocities imaginable; and you embrace and participate in their call for violence, hatred, sanctions, insurrection and revolution."[169]

This expense of spirit in a waste of hatred amounted almost to self-excommunication: ". . . Individual members of the clergy who claim to be messengers of God, are in reality messengers of enmity and hatred while parading in the cloth, and hiding behind the structures of the church . . ."

Not a new story: in 1961 two Anglican priests in a mission school in Swaziland sent black youths to Communist countries for terrorist training; in 1964, a South African court sentenced a seventy-two year old Anglican priest, Arthur Blaxall, to two years and four months, quickly remitted, for using money from London for fostering the goals of several subversive groups.[170]

Botha also spoke on behalf of the other clergymen Tutu's and the SACC's embrace of violence intimidated, a sign of fear's grip outside the townships, not only in the civil life of the country, in the unions, schools, press, but at the quick of its confidence: "At the same time responsible church leaders who proclaim the true gospel of Christ, lament the fact they are at times intimidated into a conspiracy of silence by those who have chosen the radical path."

A public man, a statesman had to defend belief, and worshippers, before an archbishop whose most important audience, not a living one, was the "media" abroad, fitting punishment for an unbeliever:

I request you urgently not to abuse the freedom of religion and worship, and the goodwill of the people and the Government of South Africa for the pursuance of secular and revolutionary objectives . . . Can you quote one single instance from the Word of God in which it appears that Christ advocated violence against the State; or led a demonstration against the State; or broke a law of the State?

The ANC Radio Freedom broadcast Botha quoted provides a good description of Tutu's purposes: to give "the democratic movement a voice in all the churches"; to make the churches sacrifice their worshippers to undermine the government,—and of the bitter hollowness of Tutu's soul:

The Church must now be developed into a fierce battleground against the regime . . . we must organize our forces for a physical confrontation with the hordes of the apartheid regime . . . In the name of justice we must take up the fight; we must participate in such means of struggle; the democratic movement must be given a voice in all churches; church service must be services that further the democratic call; the church must be for liberation.

In answer to his appeal Botha got a routine denial of Tutu's ANC/SACP service that showed there was no way of reaching Tutu, as almost any observer might have surmised: "I want to state the obvious: that I am a Christian religious leader. By definition that surely means I reject communism and Marxism as atheistic and materialistic. I try to work for the extension of the kingdom of God."

To show the priority of his faith over his frenzy, Tutu, on the edge of farce, as often, told the age of the Church, as if a heap of centuries indicated more than faith's possibility: ". . . The Bible and the church predate Marxism and the ANC by several centuries."

Tutu's disingenuous reliance on his foreign audiences' ignorance, and his desperation, a desperation in consonance with the spiritual famine in the United States, showed not only in his refurbishment of tiresome canards: the discrepancies in funding in black and white education; the "many pro-Nazi Afrikaners" during the Second World War, but most of all in his readiness to talk as if the Dutch Reformed Church (NGK) had not repudiated apartheid: ". . . It is for these and other reasons that our church and other churches have declared apartheid a heresy. I am quite ready to debate this issue with a theologian from your church [NGK], whom you might care to nominate."[171]

This refusal to recognize changes in the NGK, the political equivalent of "cutting," betrays the rigidity the ANC/SACP want, to justify violence,— blindness less excusable in Tutu who knows South African life first-hand in contrast to the ANC largely abroad, and who also knows the SACC and the NGK held discussions in October 1986, the first since the late nineteen sixties.

At a general synod in October 1986, the majority of 379 NGK ministers and elders revised their testimony of 1974; revision decided upon at the general synod of 1982, in a document, *Kerk en Sammelewing*, quickly translated into English as *Church and Society*, not a common occurrence: "The application of apartheid as a political and social system . . . cannot be accepted on

Christian ethical grounds, since it conflicts with the principles of neighbourly love and righteousness, and because it inevitably impairs the human dignity of *all* involved in it."

The "enforced separation and division of peoples" cannot be derived from the Bible, a reversal of the testimony of 1974 that held God had established separate nations as the context of religious, social and political life. About racial discrimination it was unequivocal, even adopting the uncontrollable word "racism" instead of the definable phrase, "racial discrimination,": "Racism is a grievous sin which no person or church may defend or practice. Anyone who defends it in theory or by attitude or action in practice alleges that one race, people, or group of people is inherently superior, and another race, people, or group of people is inherently inferior, is guilty of racism. Racism is a sin which tends to assume collective and structural forms. As a moral aberration it despoils a human being of his dignity, his obligations, and his rights. Because it leads to suppression and exploitation, it must be rejected and opposed in all its manifestations."

In a remark so obvious that the necessity of stating it betrays intimidation, the NGK stated that apartheid had not caused all human suffering, before it confessed its responsibility: "To the extent that the church and its members have been party to [apartheid's impairment of human dignity], we confess it humbly and penitently."

The NGK's synod lent the Federal Council's distinction between reform and violence five months earlier more bite. The Federal Council of all the Dutch Reformed Churches, African, Indian and Colored as well as white, had made all responsible for the tension, hostility, and polarization in South Africa. It had urged swifter reform but in an orderly Christian way without bloodshed and violence. The NGK accepted civil disobedience "in theory" as "the very last possibility of resistance to injustice (i.e., when every other potential solution has persistently and repeatedly come to nothing)," but it rejected it in South Africa: "Inasmuch as in practice [non-violent resistance and civil disobedience] still issue in violence, with leaders unable to control their followers, and instigators of violence frequently misusing such actions for their own purposes, neither can the Dutch Reformed Church lend its support to these methods."[172]

Most South Africans of all races probably support this stance, for they are still proud enough and ready enough to face tragedy to tell the servility of most demonstrations, even Tutu's—perhaps most of all Tutu's:

The Archbishop, who lives in the style of the oppressors rather than of the oppressed, has employed every device of rhetoric, and every trick of moral blackmail, to ensure that sanctions are imposed. He accuses the Germans of opposing sanctions because, he says, they still bear the taint of Nazism. The Japanese he accuses of being still bound by their Nazi alliance. He accuses Mrs. Thatcher and Mr. Helmut Kohl of having decided that black people are expendable. He accuses black people who oppose sanctions of being like the Jews who collaborated with the Germans "to line their pockets." Coming from anybody else, such intemperate and far-fetched nonsense would be dismissed as mere ravings; coming from the winner of the Nobel Peace Prize, a Christian Archbishop, his rhetoric will shape public attitudes. The cunning with which he has baited his traps is (if one dare apply the word to a holy man) diabolic. Any black South African who now complains that he has had enough of deprivation will be dismissed as the equivalent of a Jewish collaborator with the Nazis. Any trade unionist who, in a shrinking labour market, begins to doubt that workers can thrive in a shrinking economy, will find that he has been so smeared in advance by the Archbishop that he will get no hearing. Any German or Japanese who doubts that the way to liberation passes through the empty bellies of children will find that the Archbishop has employed the European holocaust to brand him as a Nazi. There is one thing, and only one thing, left for the victims of sanctions to do. They can insist that Archbishop Tutu and his highly privileged, prosperous family share the suffering which he has called down on the heads of his people. He should earn no more than the least of his parishioners, and eat no more than any of them. He should travel no farther, dress no better, be no warmer or drier than the least of them.[173]

Again, Tutu's exploitation of the past to smear present critics that this *Business Day* editorial brilliantly describes differs only from standard Soviet technique in its use of "Nazi" instead of "fascism." In South Africa also, Tutu's litany is not new, as Bruno Mtolo, the repentant terrorist who testified against Mandela in 1963, makes clear of his indoctrination in the fifties: "In all our Marxist classes the Nationalist Government was compared to the Nazis in Germany, during the wartime, and when the thought came to me of the six million Jews and Communist Party members who were exterminated, I was convinced beyond doubt that I would be killed by the police."

This testimony of the Dutch Reformed Church cannot be rescinded simply, in contrast to laws or political measures based on the possible. Its repudiation for mere political reasons, because of a right-reaction would destroy belief, and the church's self-respect, Tutu's probable object, that also shows in his contemptuous hint that Botha bosses the NGK. After about eight months of discussion, twenty-five hundred members left the NGK because of the synod's resolution that opened services to all racial groups, to form their own church.[174]

Has the "armed propaganda," not only terrorized the Africans but begun to polarize the whites? The break-up of white confidence is the final purpose of the spread of intimidation in the institutions, especially in the press and the Church, but also in the unions and the schools, the battleground of one of the government's greatest efforts that may decide the future. There are now seven million black children in school in all South Africa, including the independent homelands, a figure that awes the South African officials most in a position to grasp its consequences.

The "armed propaganda's" most notable successes, the first signs of unequivocal division, not merely disagreement between the men responsible for the political destiny of the country and the financial elite, and among the Afrikaners, were the pilgrimages, in defiance of the government, of prominent men to the ANC in September 1985 and July 1987.

In the instance of the July 1987 visit, the gullibility and the ignorance, and the naiveté of the sixty or so Afrikaners, professors, businessmen, newspapermen, clerics, astonished even the ANC members, carefully "selected revolutionary propagandists, cunning diplomats and several prominent SACP members" with terrorist "leaders deliberately excluded," who met them, as Botha put it in Parliament in words that betray the resources of South African intelligence: ". . . The ANC delegation was astonished they were not seriously confronted on fundamental matters, such as their Communist links and the second phase of revolution . . . at [the white delegation's] resigned acceptance of the 'historic reality' of the armed struggle and the ANC's explanation that nationalization would not take place immediately after so-called 'liberalization.'" Right after the talks on July 30, 1987 a car-bomb explosion in Johannesburg injured, at least, sixty-eight.

In September 1985 the business leaders who visited with Oliver Tambo and six other ANC members in Lusaka did no better. Despite Tambo's clear statement that the ANC would nationalize "monopoly capital," the chairman of one of the three corporations Tambo claimed controlled the South African economy, in his jottings after the meeting remarked on "the absence of traditional Marxist-Leninist jargon and dogma" among their "hosts": "It was difficult to view the group as hard-line Marxists, blood-thirsty terrorists interested in reducing South Africa to anarchy and seizing power, with a hatred for whites . . . A more attractive and congenial group would be hard to imagine. There was a total lack of aggression, animosity or hostility. It was almost like a reunion. In fact, sometimes I worry that we got on a little bit too well!"[175]

But their clothes betrayed their condescension, the other side of their gullibility, qualities combined that blocked the obvious from their eyes: the ambassadors of the rand wore safari suits and leather boots—in contrast to the Western business suits and regimental ties of the ANC—as if boutiques could exorcise murder.

Besides these divisions that the ANC/SACP would like to turn to polarization, there have been breakdowns among the elite: on March 17, 1988 the police put a price of R50,000 on the head of Hein Grosskopf, elected junior mayor of Johannesburg in 1981. The police suspected him of an explosion outside a court house (besides a university professor for a father, Grosskopf has an appeals-court judge for an uncle) in Krugersdorp: three black men dead, twenty injured, mostly women and a fifteen month old baby, a PLO-type car-bomb of at least twenty-five kilos that but for the failure of two Soviet tiny limpet mines in a toilet in the court house would have killed many more.

Along with demoralization of the police the intimidation of the judiciary is part of usual terrorist tactics to undermine a people's will, for instance, in Italy and Germany as the minister of law and order showed in words perhaps better left unsaid: "We as the executive will continue to protect our courts against such criminal acts."

Such betrayals are not new occurrences: Abraham Fischer, son of a judge-president, grandson of a prime minister of the Orange Free State and a delegate to the convention that forged the Union of South Africa, a Rhodes Scholar in 1932, who returned to South Africa in 1937 at the age of thirty "a changed man" after Oxford, the London School of Economics, and a "study tour" of eastern Europe and a visit to Moscow, to marry a niece of Smuts' wife, was convicted for life in 1966 for among other counts, training terrorists. In its restatement of the indictment, the prosecution said Fischer, "a member of the South African Communist Party, together with others, conspired with the ANC and Umkhonto we Sizwe to further recruitment of persons for instruction and training in the preparation, manufacture and use of explosives to commit acts of violence and destruction in South Africa . . . He trained and instructed them in the art of warfare and military training generally, for purposes of causing a violent revolution in the Republic." His condemnation won Fischer the 1966 Lenin Peace Prize in 1967.

Both in his organization of legal fronts in the fifties, a consequence to some extent of the the South African government's suppression of the SACP in 1950, and in his organization of protests against detention in the early sixties, Fischer devised many of the techniques the ANC and other groups have used since 1984. "Rabid" against a new 90–day detention law that was undoing the SACP,—Mandela and his collaborators were arrested six days before,—Fischer, in early July 1963, ordered the use of relatives, especially children, in demonstrations with signs: "I want my daddy"; "I want my mummy back"; "Free my son." He also wanted the coordination of these protests with the Liberal Party, the Progressive Party, the Black Sash, the Christian Institute, the United Christian Movement, the National Union of South African Students (NUSAS). The newspapers were to be penetrated. ". . . Get one story a day into the newspapers advertising the plight of the 90–day detainees," ran his order, especially aimed at the *Sunday Times* and the *Rand Daily Mail*. A secret directive of the SACP dated July 10, 1963 the South African Police seized ran:

The police want to smash the resistance of those they have detained by keeping them in solitary confinement. We must defeat this move:

a. By getting relations of detainees to pester the police and with demands to see them to take them clothes and food.
b. By organizing meetings of the wives to go to the Chief Magistrate demanding the release of the men and women.
c. By holding protest meetings.
d. By using all means [newspapers] to keep the minds of the public thinking about those unjust arrests. This will strengthen those inside.[176]

Lenin had outlined the essentials of the techniques Fischer brilliantly elaborated in his twenty-one points for admission to the Third International in 1920 that called a "combination of lawful and illegal work . . . absolutely necessary" in countries "where in consequence of martial law or other exceptional laws Communists are unable to carry on their work lawfully." Upon threat of exclusion from the Party of "any members who reject these conditions," these points required propaganda in the army, "newspaper columns, popular meetings, labor unions or cooperatives," and infiltration in "all responsible posts and in the labor movement (party organization, editors, labor unions, parliamentary faction, cooperatives, municipalities, etc.)" Appended to the SACP's constitution at its founding conference in 1921, these conditions, especially the directive that allowed only one party from each country membership in the Third International, had played a crucial role in the organization of a single controlled disciplined Communist movement in South Africa.[177]

Fischer was no mere apparatchik or hypocrite: He was a driven tormented man who until he went underground in January 1965 had enough in him to keep something like contact with the world he was forsaking. He constantly groped for its soft-underbelly until its strengths drove him to his own destruction. During the Second World War and its aftermath he was active, with other Communists like Joe Slovo, in the South African Friends of the Soviet Union, an organization that put out pamphlets on the Soviet Union with titles like: "Where Women Enjoy Freedom!" During the Korean War in 1953 he reserved his germ-warfare attacks for the United States, like the Soviets, but accused both the American and South African air force of taking the lives of forty-eight thousand women and children in an incendiary bomb attack on a North Korean town. In 1956, he led the defense of 156 men, among them at least twenty-five members of the outlawed CP, and many other well-known Communists, including Joe Slovo: charges dropped against sixty-one, the rest acquitted because of insufficient evidence.

No mere deception could have allowed Fischer to enjoy the trust of the top of society,—and the suspicions of the police. "I have absolute faith in his integrity and shall accept his word without hesitation," a Johannnesburg lawyer testified at his first trial. In the same days, the police who had tricked him into admitting he was a Communist, secretly requested three-months leave on bail for Fischer from the court to argue a case before the Privy Council in London because they wanted to follow his movements,—but also because they trusted his promise to return. A promise he kept, to flee, a few months later. In London, the English press greeted him as a "dedicated liberal" and a "fighter for human rights." A few months after his flight, the *Times* in Ghana, on March 3, 1965, headlined a full-page article from Fischer underground: "In the Land of Legalized Torture Lip-service is Paid to Democracy," with the legend under his photograph, "Bram Fischer, South African Freedom Fighter,"—unchanged propaganda themes today. The cause of his flight: his total exposure in court. His purpose underground: to reconstitute the almost destroyed SACP.

And Fischer, with his fronts and demonstrations, was in his way "a fighter for human rights,"—but he was also an instigator of terrorism, a divided man but with something like one soul until he went underground to suffer the mutilations of plastic surgery for a disguise. He pretended not to understand his mother tongue, Afrikaans, upon his final arrest.

Besides a remarkable counter-intelligence agent, the two men who gave the crucial evidence at Fischer's two trials had also been at the top of SACP: Petrus Beyleveld, an Afrikaner, and Bartholomew Hlapane, the man who almost seventeen years later also testified before the Denton Committee in Washington. In 1941 Beyleveld had helped found a veterans' organization, the Springbok Legion, to take advantage, especially after 1944, of the enthusiasm of soldiers returning from the war. He had been chairman of the Congress of

Democrats (COD), a front founded after the suppression of the SACP in 1950, in 1953.

In rough defense cross-examination Beyleveld showed some of the stuff it took to come back, the one thing Fischer could not do. With head bowed, almost as if he were speaking to his cell, he admitted he had "failed as a Communist": "You can call me what you like . . . I don't care. I was faced with a decision to make. I took it and I shall be able to live with my conscience after this . . ."[178]

The ANC/SACP's constant calls throughout the world for the release of Nelson Mandela, a release Govan Mbeki's conduct after amnesty in November 1987 shows they do not want, serves to subordinate all subsequent events, especially since 1984, to the strategy of terror and demonstrations and propaganda to discredit the government the SACP/ANC devised, and the courts exposed, in the early sixties. On July 17, 1988, the evening news program of the first channel of Italian State Television, in a long report, took the suppression of a concert in Johannesburg for Mandela's birthday, quite matter-of-factly, for evidence that the South African government could not control the crowds that wanted to bring it down,—the legacy of Fischer, and of Lenin's twenty-one points.

These calls also serve to mask this subordination. For the people, organizations, governments and most of all the demonstrators that respond to the ANC/SACP calls for the release of Mandela take him for a popular "civil rights" leader unjustly condemned. They do not recall, probably they never knew, the strategy whose realization in the present they unwittingly justify, that Mandela and others like Joe Slovo who still control the ANC/SACP devised in the early sixties. The prosecution outlined it at Mandela's trial:

The accused deliberately and maliciously plotted and engineered the commission of acts of violence and destruction throughout the country . . . The planned purpose was to bring about in the Republic of South Africa chaos, disorder and turmoil which would be aggravated, according to their plan, by the operation of thousands of trained guerrilla warfare units deployed throughout the country at various vantage points. These would be joined in the various areas by local inhabitants as well as specially selected men posted to such areas. Their combined operations were planned to lead to confusion, violent insurrection and rebellion, followed, at the appropriate juncture, by an armed invasion of the country by military units of foreign powers.[179]

Already in 1977, an escaped KGB counter-intelligence agent who also said as many as four hundred KGB agents might be active in South Africa, identified the Soviet-Cuban war in Mozambique and Angola as the "military units of foreign powers" of Mandela's prosecutor: "All the Soviet Union is doing in Angola and Mozambique is geared towards getting to South Africa."[180]

The prosecutions' outline of ANC/SACP strategy leaves out one essential, the campaigns abroad, in Europe, in the UN and especially in the United States, a startling omission. Nobody in the nineteen sixties could foresee the astonishing success in mobilizing "public opinion" abroad,—even in 1984 the vehemence of protest probably surprised the ANC/SACP,—before the propaganda against the Indochina War forced the acquiescence of the United States government and distanced the rest of the world, especially Western Europe, from the United States, and the United States from its government.

The government's readiness to reform and relax previous severity, and the majority of whites' support of gradual change, is new in South Africa, not terror, old and hackneyed, but effective enough to impede change, and to turn a good deal of the world's eyes against it. Especially since chaos in Mozambique, war in Angola, the steady deterioration in Zimbabwe seem to point to the future in South West Africa and South Africa. In the first six months of 1988 terror killings increased in South Africa: ten attacks in February, nineteen in March, fifteen in May, twenty-one in June. July started with a limpet-mine explosion in a restaurant in East London and a car-bomb explosion outside a stadium in Johannesburg, two white rugby spectators dead, more than thirty injured. Both "soft" targets.

The life of Bram Fischer and the flights of other Afrikaners into terrorism show one thing: The exploitation of self-respecting non-violent African defiance and demands for social and economic reforms for the destruction of the South African government would not have been possible without the breakdown of European, and also Indian and Colored men, who became Communists and who formed the SACP to follow orders from abroad.

The first members of the SACP, a few hundred, were nearly all European, many of them Jewish emigrants from eastern Europe to South Africa after the Anglo-Boer War.[181] The Soviets imposed concentration on the Africans, first of all with orders for mixed meetings to the Young Communist League founded in 1921, an unheard of demand that bewildered and seriously divided the white SACP members who had not taken their hatred of "capitalism" for a native rebellion. The Soviets pursued this policy, not because they were interested in the Africans, but because they did not think they could overthrow the government without them. "A victorious revolution is unthinkable without the awakening of the native masses," Trotsky wrote in 1935. Despite Comintern orders in 1927 that the SACP break the color bar, to recruit Africans for the eventual foundation of a "Black Republic," and that it put blacks in all top leadership positions in the Party, apparently an order from Stalin, the whites retained control even after the blacks numbered nearly 1,600 out of 1,750 members in 1928. In 1929, an order of the Comintern, to limit the party to selected trained "revolutionaries who were to work through the "masses," reinforced this control,—and kept hundreds of ignorant blacks from joining the party.[182]

This exploitation of Africans is an old story in South Africa: The infiltration of white Communists, largely from Europe, into the first African trade union, the Industrial and Commercial Workers Union, founded in 1919, discredited its attractive high-spirited leader, Clements Kadalie, "a pawn in the pay of Moscow," the *Cape Times* called him in 1924, inaccurately. A police report Smuts ordered after the miners' strike in 1946,—50,000 strikers; poor, illiterate Africans who wanted to work beaten seriously; nine dead,—showed SACP members with European names active throughout the country in the unions.

The Africans were meant to do the dirty work and suffer the consequences, as many SACP directives the police captured showed:

It is our duty to pick out workers who show promise who are loyal to the Union, to give them the necessary education. We must try to recruit every Trade Union official who is a member of the Party to organize regular classes in economics and political theory among the members of his union . . . to recruit the best of them into the Party.[183]

In response to this report, made public only in 1952, the newly-elected government of the National Party sought to isolate the instigators through banning and suppression of their organizations, first of all the SACP in 1950,— the policy it still pursues today to control disturbances, and to prevent "the encouragement of hostility between Europeans and non-Europeans and non-European races of the Union," as the Suppression of Communism Act put it in 1950. In accordance with this conception, the numbers isolated were small, six hundred "named" Communists in the first years. The removal of Communists from the unions,—fifty-three union leaders "named"; forty-eight forced to resign by 1953,—led the underground Communists to put the Africans directly into the streets to paralyze the police with overwhelming numbers: the pass-burning "Defiance Campaign" in 1952. Undistracted by the numbers, the police brought the campaign swiftly to an end with the arrest of about sixty agitators.

The policy of the South African government assumes that the spontaneous irresistible movements of large numbers of people, even in the dramatic conditions of South African blacks caught between two worlds, are not a common occurrence. In fact, they have occurred largely against the totalitarian regimes that claim they seized power because of them, among peoples who know tragedy, for instance, in Poland. This readiness to assume the manipulation of crowds is old-fashioned, Merriman's "society on an aristocratic basis,"— but also an attitude that Biko, profoundly suspicious of leaders, shared. I guess he was old-fashioned too.

Soviet penetration of South Africa through the SACP would not have been possible without Europeans, and Coloreds and Indians. After the outlawing of the SACP, they turned the ANC, finally in the fifties after a decade at least of infiltration, from a democratic, loosely organized, voluntary organization of Africans into a tightly organized undemocratic organization, largely controlled by nonblacks. The more the ANC appeared as a militant "nationalist movement" for the advancement of blacks against "brutal government oppression," the more the Communists tightened their control.[184] The ANC's turn to terrorism that brought it completely under the control of the SACP would not have been possible without these Europeans. The KGB worked through them.

The insistence on ignoring racial differences, the Soviet mark on the SACP almost from its beginning, that drove Bram Fischer to adopt a child of one of his African servants, an experiment that failed, has actually worked to maintain nonwhite predominance in the SACP and to establish it in the ANC. Before the ANC's adoption of a "multi-racial" stance in 1969 that allowed whites in key positions, the SACP coopted only ANC Africans, above all those in the ANC's National Executive Committee, into its Central Committee. After 1969, the threat of the charge of "racism" protected the mostly white, Colored and Indian SACP members in top positions in the ANC.[185] The realization that the SACP used color-blindness to gain control of the ANC and exploit Africans for its own purposes helped prompt Bartholomew Hlapane to expose Fischer—and turn his back on the SACP/ANC Central Committee.

To say that the present situation in South Africa turns on these breakdowns of nonwhites, especially of men at the top of society, says little more than that a society, capable of intelligence, movement and decision,—words for the respect of liberty,—must first of all face itself in its sons and daughters, and its parents, the lesson of the *Oedipus Rex*. Smuts knew what he meant when he called the future of the natives, a "Sphinx problem," in his correspondence with Merriman in 1906. But the South Africans, especially Afrikaners, are used to these life-or-death differences, they can see them in their past, for as Smuts also pointed out, the Anglo-Boer War was also a civil war between the Afrikaners,—but a clean one without masks.

The young South Africans I know have been to Botha's school. They back his reforms but are ready to fight. They have served in the army. Some have fought in Angola—sometimes, they discovered to their horror, in hand-to-hand combat against little more than children kidnapped into SWAPO. They do not want the bloody future that the failure of negotiations at home and abroad would bring—but they will face it. They listen to outsiders, but they have an admirable awareness that they are responsible for what will become of them. "We remain open to comment and advice from others provided that such comment and advice do not constitute interference in South Africa's internal affairs . . . We shall weigh such advice carefully, but in the final analysis we shall act as our conscience dictates, because we, not they, will be answerable to history for the consequences of our actions," Botha said upon taking the oath for the new office of state president in the new constitution in September 1984. He meant history is tragic. The twentieth century instead likes killing it can ignore, without the fuss of tragedy.

3

Room with a Mirror Blocking the View: American Policy in South Africa and Southern Africa

Es gibt einen Punkt von krankhafter Vermürbung und Verzärtlichung in der Geschichte der Gesellschaft, wo sie selbst für ihren Schädiger, den Verbrecher Partei nimmt, und zwar ernsthaft und ehrlich.
NIETZSCHE

There comes a point in a world's sick self-indulgence and rot when it takes sides honestly and in good faith with criminals who want to undo it.

1 Repeal of the Clark Amendment; Moderate Republicans Waver; "Constructive Engagement"

... South Africa's racial policies are only one aspect of the dynamic situation on the African continent. There is a great struggle for freedom ongoing in Angola and Mozambique ... why is it then that a double standard is being applied to Africa on human rights? Is discrimination against blacks in South Africa more deplorable than the Ethiopian policy of starving enemies of the state? Is apartheid more appalling than the Mozambique concentration camps and the Mozambique government's selling of young slave laborers to labor in East German factories?

Senator Steve Symms of Idaho said these words on May 14, 1985, a few months before the threat of passage of sanctions in the Senate against South Africa already passed in the House, led Reagan to co-opt those sanctions, lightly modified, in an executive order on September 9. Reagan's order reversed his policy of "constructive engagement," adopted at the beginning of his first administration against conservative opposition: Senator Jesse Helms had delayed the confirmation of Reagan's appointment of Chester Crocker as assistant secretary of state for African affairs for six months. Symms' words introduced a motion to repeal the Clark Amendment of 1975 that forbade covert aid to Angola—a sudden unexpected motion that passed with breathtaking ease, in the Senate in June 1985 (63–34), in the House in July (236–185).

In the indignation against South Africa heating up Washington in those days, Symms' plea for consistency, his reminder of the sufferings of Africans in the grim never-ending wars north of South Africa, told somewhat. The war had cost one million estimated dead in Angola alone since 1974, largely "civilians," Africans, most of them: illiterate, simple, ignorant, religious, subsistence tillers of the soil, tribesmen, whom the hammer of war has done more to turn into Europeans, Europeans of the kind that counted, than centuries of Portuguese dominion.

Symms, who was in touch with Jonas Savimbi, sensed that Congress was high on a moral fix in South Africa in part because it did not want to face the war in southern Africa, especially the extensive Soviet-Cuban involvement that came as a result of the withdrawal Congress had imposed on the United States. The United States could not pursue a rational policy in South Africa until it faced up to its past decisions in southern Africa and, more importantly, remembered South Africa's crucial role in southern Africa,—a role Chester Crocker also recognized.

The repeal of the Clark Amendment put Congress in contradiction with itself. It gave Reagan's policy in southern Africa the possibility of real bite, but at the same time Congress threatened to undermine Reagan in South Africa with sanctions.

The contradiction lived not in Congressmen's minds, but at the expense of their minds because of their ambitions. Symms' words persuaded on the floor of the Senate because Angola was not alive in the media,—and because the vote was not on aid to Savimbi, but on a restriction against aid that had almost been repealed in 1981. In contrast South Africa was the target of the media,—of "beltway hype" and domestic civil rights groups,—lobbying the Congress mistook, well before the outbreak of demonstrations, for an irresistible "grassroots movement" like the movement that had in appearance swept the country during the years of the war for Indochina. The absence of popular pressure on Angola, its apparent presence against South Africa, and dread of the past, of crowds in the streets, made the difference. Besides, defense of South Africa could only cost votes,—an attitude that betrayed contempt for voters',—especially black voters',—readiness to listen to argument and facts.

It took the resignation in 1987 of an assistant secretary of state, Alan Keyes, long after the destruction of "constructive engagement," finally to get at this contempt publicly: "It is my sincere conviction, contrary to all stereotypes that even some blacks, liberals and others like to portray, that black people in this country are thinking human beings, and if I have a case to make based upon facts and reason, they are going to judge it on its merits." TransAfrica, the organization primarily responsible for coordinating protests and lobbying against South Africa, immediately called these words, words that betrayed the condescension that had held Washington by its throat for three long years, "a black face on an anti-black policy," the American equivalent of the cry "stooge" and "collaborator" in the townships of South Africa.[1]

The disciplined *daily* protest against the South African Embassy in Washington, before South African consulates in a dozen other American cities and before American companies active in South Africa broke out a few weeks after the outbreak of violence against the new constitution in South Africa and against the elected black administrations in the townships,—on Thanksgiving Day, November 21, 1984, just after Reagan's crushing victory in his second presidential campaign.

The timing was not coincidental: The groups organizing the demonstrations in the United States were in touch with activists in South Africa. By early 1986 the demonstrations in the United States had led to three thousand arrests, largely painless and symbolic, and without charges.

These demonstrations had immediate effect, especially a sit-in on November 21 in the office of the Ambassador from South Africa by four black "activists"—Randall Robinson, Mary Frances Berry, a Carter appointee to the United States Civil Rights Commission, and the Reverend Walter Fauntroy, a non-voting delegate to the House of Representatives from Washington, D.C. The President received Desmond Tutu in the White House, and Republican representatives in the House wrote an extraordinary letter to the South African ambassador to mark the occasion. Reagan made remarks that appeared to downplay "constructive engagement," reform in South Africa, and South Africa's economic and political role in southern Africa.

The letter, signed by thirty-five members of the Conservative Opportunity Society,—some of whom were reported not to have read it,—went further. Almost mesmerized by media showing the South African police beating blacks, throwing tear gas, and even shooting, without any explanation of the circumstances or reasons, the writers took the violence that had broken out in South Africa at the end of September not as a result of reform but as proof of the refusal to change:

Events of recent weeks in South Africa have raised serious questions about your willingness to move more progressively and aggressively toward real human rights reforms . . . We view the violence in your country and the questions raised by it with alarm.

The letter held that continued support for "constructive engagement" required "real steps toward complete equality for all South Africans . . . ,"—in other words, "one-man, one-vote" in countrywide elections.

Mindful that the Republicans had enjoyed a majority in Congress in only four of the last fifty-two years, and not since 1954, the signers of the letter thought they could moderate left wing Democrats, the Black Caucus, and the lobbying groups by appearing to lend them "bipartisan support,"—and also win the votes of blacks, who rarely vote Republican. The letter stunned other Republicans, who did not argue against it publicly, into private remonstrance.

Two weeks after the publication of the letter on December 4, P.W. Botha spoke out against the new assumptions on the widely-viewed television program *Sixty Minutes*:

A system of one-man, one-vote in a unitary state, in the Republic of South Africa, will simply not work. It simply will not work. I am not prepared to overthrow orderly government. This is the minimum requirement for me, orderly government.

But his words prompted no defense of "constructive engagement" in Congress.

The reporter who interviewed Botha, Morley Safer, described South Africa without using the word "black":

Race or ethnicity in South Africa is the inescapable Topic A. Being Afrikaner or English, Italian or Portuguese, Jewish or Indian or Zulu or Tswana or Xhosa or Sotho is stated almost immediately to a visitor.

But that too made no impression on Congress or the media. The illusion that South Africa was an issue with only one side had begun to work its paralysis of mind and heart.[2]

In contrast to the demonstrations and sit-ins, the campaign for divestment, disinvestment, and sanctions had started at the beginning of Reagan's first term, in 1981. Divestment, disinvestment and sanctions had been the goal of the American Committee on Africa (ACOA), and the ANC's counterpart abroad to terrorism at home, for almost a generation. Divestment means the selling of stock in companies in business in South Africa. Disinvestment means companies sell out in South Africa, mostly to South Africans, but also to foreigners. (The divestment lobbying groups targeted state and city pension funds because they are exempt from the 1974 Employees Retirement Income Security Act that brought pension funds, whose assets in the United States exceed a trillion dollars, a staggering sum, strictly within the compass of traditional trust-investment law that countenances only prudent investment for profit.)

By October 1986 New Jersey and Massachusetts had totally divested state funds, including pensions. Fifteen other states had partially divested. In August 1986 the State of California announced the gradual sale of its investments through pension funds etc. in companies doing business in South Africa, except for non-discriminatory loans for health, housing and education. There were proposals for divestment in nearly all other state legislatures. At least five major cities,—Boston, Cincinnati, Philadelphia, Jersey City, Washington, D.C.,— had totally divested, fifty-five others had taken partial measures. The refusal of thirty American cities, including Los Angeles, and the state of Maryland to grant contracts to companies that also did business in South Africa,—"selective contracting"—also began to tell. At least six billion dollars had been withdrawn from South Africa. Between 1977 and March 1986 eighty-four universities and colleges had divested about a half billion dollars, not including the huge and wealthy University of California that later announced the gradual sale of its holdings of over more than three billion dollars. *The Economist*, in October 1986, reported that pension funds, universities, and public investors had committed themselves to divestment sales that exceeded twenty billion dollars, probably too low, since the commitment of the State of California alone amounted to ten billion dollars. By June 1987, almost a year later, twenty-one state legislatures, seventy-two cities and fourteen counties had taken some economic measures against South Africa.[3]

Also by June 1987 something like 140 American companies, over a third of the total of somewhere between 350–400—the most dramatic flight—had left: seven in 1984; thirty-nine in 1985; forty in 1986 with another eleven announcing their withdrawal. Among the names once taken for confidence: Eastman Kodak, Coca-Cola, Exxon, General Motors, IBM, followed, in 1987, by Ford Motor Company, Citicorp and ITT. In contrast two percent of British companies, five out of twenty-one Canadian, and Alfa Romeo of Italy and Renault of France, a total of about forty foreign companies, left in the same period. Only Swedish companies equalled American withdrawals, seven out of eighteen.

Some of these companies, especially in the automobile industry, left because of low profits, others because of fears of "selective contracting" in the United States. Some left for both reasons because they thought "South Africa was no longer worth it." The leading commodity broker, Phibro-Salomon, left after the loss of fifty million dollars worth of municipal bond underwriting from the City of San Francisco at the cost of "a sizeable exporting business in commodities from South Africa: steel, chrome alloy, gold, coke and coal," as its chairman put it. The fear of local and state government boycotts also got Bell and Howell in early 1986 to leave, about 13 million dollars worth of business in South Africa against total revenues of 759 million in 1985. Sperry Computers put the general disproportion between profits in South Africa and the risks of embargoes by local and state governments in the United States bluntly: the total installed computer base in South Africa did not equal Chicago's. At AT&T it was some employees who pressured the company into cutting most of its ties with South Africa. The threat of a boycott by Harvard and Yale law students, those *arbitri elegantiarum*, all political these days, was enough for the largest law firm in Washington, D.C., Covington and Burling, to drop South African Airways.

Among the companies outspoken against racial discrimination that left, IBM, GM and Ford, along with Mobil that did not leave, had called for tightening the Sullivan Code that asked for training programs and amenities for black workers as well as contributions to black housing, education and community projects. These contributions had cost American companies about two hundred million dollars between 1977, the code's first year, and 1986.

IBM and GM sent funds, before The Comprehensive Anti-Apartheid Act

(CAA Act) restrictions, to help its local managers and associates buy them out. In contrast to GM that proposed paying lawyers for its black employees challenging beach segregation in Port Elizabeth, IBM had avoided political entanglements. "We are in business to conduct business, not to conduct moral crusades or to carry out political activities," said its chairman.

Sales to local South African management by almost twenty percent of the departing companies, often like GM's and IBM's, with "buy-back" provisions, meant to keep the businesses from the big mining and insurance companies that bought almost half of the departing companies: In 1987 four leading companies controlled eighty-three percent of the Johannesburg stock market, in contrast to seventy percent in 1983. Of a hundred American companies gone by 1987, fewer than twenty closed down their operations, the goal of the activist lobbies in the United States.

The Ford story is instructive. In addition to divesting itself of its forty-two percent ownership, twenty-four percent to an employee-owned trust fund, eighteen percent sold for one dollar to a local company, Ford in 1986 granted its subsidiary South African Motor Corporation (SAMCOR) sixty-one million dollars, for plant and equipment, to help the company to survive. The mainly black sixteen thousand workers, who had struck against Ford's divestment,— they took it for bankruptcy,—and their national union, voted approval of this grant. In December 1986, Representatives Howard Wolpe and William Gray, informed almost a year before of the transfer that the United States Treasury had also approved, and seven other representatives suddenly accused Ford of violating the CAA Act's prohibition against new investment with "massive new financing for a rich and powerful South African firm" as they called struggling SAMCOR. All along SAMCOR was paying its detained workers fifty to seventy-five percent of their wages, not a fact the DPSC advertised.[4]

IBM did little better against the anti-apartheid lobbies and protestors, manipulated finally by the ANC, because it had not closed down its operations entirely. It had promised a "full range of IBM products and services will continue to be available in South Africa" and to meet "all our commitments to our customers dealers, agents, employees and suppliers." In 1988 six IBM employees, including an IBM electronics engineer, and twenty-five religious organizations that owned no more than twenty-five thousand shares of stock put a motion before IBM's roughly one million stockholders to "stop all sales and services to South Africa, including all direct or indirect shipments of IBM computers, equipment, software, parts, supplies and materials, until apartheid ends." On *The New York Times* op-ed page they cited the call in January 1987 of the State Department's Advisory Committee, co-chaired by the IBM chairman, for a "comprehensive multilateral trade embargo" against South Africa in the event of its continued "intransigence." Their demand accorded entirely with the new guidelines, also of January 1987, of the American Committee on Africa (ACOA), American Friends Service Committee, Interfaith Center on Corporate Responsibility, TransAfrica and Washington Office on Africa that call for "an end to all corporate involvement in or with South Africa and Namibia," both "direct investments" and "franchising, licensing or management agreements with or for any entity in those countries." These guidelines in turn followed ANC instructions, reiterated at a conference in Tanzania in December 1987, and distributed widely by the UN Center Against Apartheid: "Action should be taken against those companies that engage in bogus disinvestment."[5]

American cities' threats not to buy books for their schools and libraries from publishers who would not sign affidavits not to sell to South Africa impeded the sale even of professional scientific writings to South African universities and hospitals, for instance, the University of Cape Town Medical School with eighty percent black patients. In Houston, Texas a city ordinance that required such affidavits prevented the director of public libraries from subscribing to the *Wall Street Journal*, the *Readers' Guide to Periodical Literature*, the films of the Encyclopedia Britannica and two South African newspapers for four months until he persuaded the city council to except "publications, where the public official responsible for the procurement certifies in writing that such procurements are necessary to provide adequate levels of service to the public."

The American Library Association in the Spring of 1987 defeated a resolution for libraries' freedom of purchase, called "racist" in debate. The open standing vote saw its supporters, including the director of the ALA's Office for Intellectual Freedom, hissed. To its honor, the American Institute of Archaeology refused to endorse the boycott of South African scholars at the International Archaeological Congress in Great Britain in 1986.

Amateurish well-intentioned totalitarianism, and all the more effective because of it, the boycott on publications and professional relations with South African scholars that the ANC called "a natural consequence of the development of the mass democratic movement and the emergence of an alternative democratic power" anticipated the ANC's control of all intellectual life in a future South Africa. "But it's a good cause," remarked Nat Hentoff, catching his breath in days that knew little irony.[6]

Another "good cause," a campaign against Royal Dutch Shell, was launched in the United States by the United Mine Workers in January 1986 upon the prompting of the Free South Africa Movement (FSAM): public meetings, demonstrations, shareholder resolutions. At the same time that it called Shell Oil "a strategic pillar supporting the apartheid regime" the mining union admitted "unashamedly acting" in self-interest in endorsing the FSAM's campaign. Through its exports of coal from South Africa, "mined under slave conditions," Royal Dutch Shell hoped "to undermine coal mined in North America and to lower the standard of living of coal miners in this country . . . Through our action here today we are simultaneously helping our black brothers and sisters throw off the yoke of oppression and helping ourselves do the same right here at home." Again, all in accordance with ANC instructions that foresee the spread of the campaign abroad: "The Shell campaign should be intensified internationally."

The campaign started in the United States not only because of the mine union's hostility but also because of Shell's vulnerability: More than half of its 3 billion dollar profits in 1985, 1.7 billion, came from the United States, in contrast to one percent from South Africa. With these results: threats to life and attacks on service stations in the Netherlands, the city of Oslo's refusal to buy, and full-page Shell advertisements in the *Weekly Mail* in Johannesburg for a free press and against detentions.

The flight of banks in the middle of 1985 also shows that the turning away from South Africa started long before the CAA Act prohibited investment and loans. Federal government action followed, it did not initiate, wide-spread "selective contracting," especially on the local and state level in the United States, and the "banker's sanctions," the name for the flight of American banks in financial circles. The flight of capital, more than ten billion rand, started with Chase Manhattan Bank's decision in July 1985 to freeze unused credit and not renew loans. Its quick spread to other American banks, and finally some foreign banks, made it impossible for reserves and trade surplus to cover South Africa's fourteen billion dollars of short term loans (out of a total foreign debt of twenty-four billion).

The start of capital flight in the United States shows that "activist" organizations, and especially "selective contracting," touched off the panic. The telling economic grounds: the worst drought in memory, a drop in the price of gold from 850 dollars an ounce in 1980 to 400 dollars in 1984, a foreign debt almost two-thirds in short-term loans, were not enough to frighten banks in other countries, even in England, the only other country to suffer, in the ANC's phrase, sustained "grassroots action involving the people." The New York City Council's decision in 1985, not to deal with banks that lent to the South African government probably led Citicorp and other leading banks to prohibit lending. In all, by 1986, 60 out of 105 important banks, and among them the biggest 9, had prohibited lending, with 37 also prohibiting private loans. It was worries about its business in the United States, seventeen billion dollars in assets, and to a lesser extent its declining profits in South Africa, that determined Barclays' decision to leave in November 1986, and not its loss of business on account of boycotts in Great Britain, for instance, a drop from thirty to fifteen percent in the total of student accounts. First in 1985, and then in 1986, the federal government, especially the executive, faced what was, in appearance, again to use the ANC's phrase, "a concerted people's sanctions campaign" to "compel even the most intransigent opponents of sanctions to reverse their position." Because it chose not to face it down, it ended up yielding. The panic of 1985 reinforced the belief of Western governments, first of all the United States Congress and the State Department, that the South African government and system would fall. A fall the CAA Act sought to hasten, a year later, just at the time that the South African government showed renewed toughness.

Reagan apparently signed his executive order in September 1985 because he feared Congress might vote its legislation against South Africa in defiance of a presidential veto,—legislation sponsored by the leading Republican Senator, Richard Lugar, who argued that it was "not a disinvestment bill" because a clause that prohibited new investment and bank loans in South Africa had not survived negotiations with the Senate. But Reagan had not threatened a veto before he signed. In the middle of the summer the White House told a group of conservative lobbyists and senatorial aides, who said they could find votes to prevent an override after the President announced a veto, that they should find the votes first. Lugar,—and perhaps also Reagan,—thought they could make the issue go away for good by co-opting it with meaningless measures—instead of fighting.

Reagan's yielding had unremitting consequences, whatever the niceties of his refinement of Congress' legislation—of which the omission of a deadline for mandatory sanctions was the most important. His yielding made public defense of South Africa and serious attention to its reforms, more difficult. The most immediate consequence: the disregard of Botha's important speech on unitary citizenship and abolition of the pass laws a few days after Reagan's executive order. Reagan's yielding also gave the impression he was sacrificing his known convictions to a popular ground swell, just the ANC's goal. Even "conservative" Republicans supported the proposed legislation. Reagan's sickness and his preventive surgery for cancer were probably decisive in his loss of control of South Africa policy.

In the wake of Reagan's wavering, the Foreign Office decided sanctions were inevitable, whatever Margaret Thatcher's convictions, and despite the absence of strong public sentiment in Britain. In Europe, where the governments had shown quiet interest in Botha's reforms and where South Africa was even less at the center of peoples' minds than in Britain and the United States, the machinery of the Common Market also began to move.

The summer of 1985 was the best time to fight in the United States, even if it meant losing—and winning by losing. It was the best time for making the case against sanctions and, even more importantly, for making available hard information about South Africa and southern Africa. Even a year later Reagan's July 22 speech made discussion of Communist domination of the ANC immediately *hoffähig* in much of the serious press in the world. In contrast, the silence in Congress, and of the President in 1985, made it look like no case could be made for the Republic of South Africa.

By the spring and summer of 1986, the infernal machine of international organizations had begun to move, it seemed, almost everywhere at once: at the OAU in Addis Ababa, in the Commonwealth, in the Common Market, and in the Scandinavian Regional Association, and of course in the UN which, at a meeting in Paris not even attended by the major European nations, with France, Holland, Portugal, and Sweden present only as observers, timed exactly for the anniversary of the Soweto upheavals on June 16, singled out the United States for attack. The president of the ANC, Oliver Tambo, spoke on French television, and there was a mass against apartheid in Notre Dame.

This major institutional onslaught, probably taken by many as an expression of irresistible popular will, *but other people's will*, had the quite extraordinary effect of isolating major leaders and making them appear helpless in their own countries, almost caged in them, despite the known popular support they enjoyed: Reagan, Thatcher, and not least the new prime minister of Sweden who had to rush back from vacation in tennis shoes to tell the Social

Democratic Party that he was not about to make policy that was in violation of the international accords on free trade on the spur of newspaper headlines,— the successor to Olaf Palme, but not of the same stuff. There was more activity than anybody could keep track of or make sense of, but it took up space in the newspapers and on television, for international organizations get headlines. Kaunda and Mugabe bellowing threats and insults that uttered in Zambia or Zimbabwe would get little attention, were heard throughout the world because they were at a small Commonwealth meeting in London.

International organizations do not meet on the spur of the moment: The UN meeting in Paris was especially meant to give an international face to the planned demonstrations and upheavals approaching insurrection in South Africa for the tenth anniversary of Soweto, upheavals that Botha's State of Emergency prevented—at the price of the UN Security Council's unanimous condemnation.

Extraordinarily neither in 1985 in the United States nor in Britain in the first half of 1986 did anybody bother to spell out what specifically they wanted to achieve with sanctions, what they meant by satisfactory progress toward "ending apartheid," a nebulous phrase that in Soviet and ANC propaganda was a transparent code-word for the ruin of the South African government.

This vagueness that betrayed definiteness only in its scorn for anything the South African government did came because the men in politics and in the media most fanatic about sanctions wanted the downfall of the South African government and its replacement by the UDF/ANC—but would not say so openly. In contrast, the demands finally made in the second half of 1986, first in the Commonwealth Group Report, then in President Reagan's speech on July 22, and finally in the CAA Act, clearly spelled the ruin of the South African government—to anyone not historically illiterate. But again, they did not openly say they wanted "revolution."

At the end of the Commonwealth conference in August 1986, there was cynical depression: Sanctions, their unintended effects unconsidered, would not sway the South African government. But the West had somehow to prove to the world it cared about "apartheid." The same mood inhabited the House after surprise passage on June 18 of a bill upon a motion of Ronald Dellums, a prominent member of the Black Caucus. The bill stopped all trade with South Africa except in strategic minerals, and ordered American companies to leave within ninety days—complete disinvestment, in short. "Sanctions are a statement of where we stand as a nation, not an attempt to bring a government down," said William Gray, a representative from Pennsylvania who protests too much.

But sanctions and disinvestment are a hostile act, close to an act of war, which puts the West in a position indistinguishable from the Soviets, who openly stated they wanted to destroy the Republic of South Africa.

Incidentally, the passage of Dellums' extreme amendment on a voice vote, which Washington took for the unanimous will of the House, occurred only because the few Republicans in the chamber that torrid late afternoon,— all of them signers of the letter to the South African ambassador a year and a half before,—did not call for a reported vote. They calculated the measure's extremity would shock the political world to its senses instead of stampeding it,—another example of substituting cleverness for forthright opposition.

Julian Amery, a Tory elder statesman, and one of Britain's best heads for foreign affairs, asked the crucial question in Parliament in June, 1986, the question that nobody asked publicly in the United States: Would Britain and the United States be able to keep the call for the dismantlement of apartheid from turning into the demand for one-man, one-vote that, he said, would divide Britain and his party? He received a chilling reply from a foreign office minister, Lynda Chalker, who was soon to receive Oliver Tambo: "With regard to majority rule, we cannot support a society that does not give a democratic vote to each and every one of its people."

President Johnson had said much the same thing, a very long time ago measured in the swift pace of contemporary events, in 1966: "The foreign policy of the United States is rooted in its life at home . . . We will not support policies abroad which are based on the rule of minorities or the discredited notion that men are not equal before the law." In a crucial speech on his first trip to Africa in 1976, Kissinger portrayed himself as bringing in a new era of "self-determination, majority rule, equal rights, and human dignity for all the people of southern Africa."

Johnson's statement was at least honest—but foolish. Kissinger's was as foolish and as evasive as it was in appearance irresistible. Johnson's came at a time when one of America's greatest statesmen, Dean Acheson, was arguing strongly for a reversal of American policy against Rhodesia. In the name of high-sounding principles no one could object to, Kissinger meant to distract from the American failure, a few months before, to support those fighting the Communist take-over in Angola. The United States had failed both those inside the country—the resistance movements, the National Front for the Liberation of Angola (FNLA) and Savimbi's UNITA and South Africa,—and those outside, especially Kenneth Kaunda, the president of Zambia. The price of Kissinger's evasiveness was new targets, the spread of the war to other countries, the war of words, the deadliest. The urgency that came from not acknowledging betrayal impelled Kissinger to substitute negotiation, a word for "accommodation," for concentrating on the situation on the ground. He warned South Africa. He wanted deadlines: two years for majority rule in Rhodesia on his ten-point plan, a timetable for the independence of South West Africa.

Kissinger succeeded in distracting the West, but not the best African leaders who, whatever they said, recognized realities. "The West's levity of approach constantly amazed" Felix Houphouet-Boigny, president of the Ivory Coast: "You didn't stop [the Soviet advance]; you didn't even think of it. Do you still exist? Are you not now fascinated and paralyzed by the Soviet Union? The Soviets advance when they have nothing before them. In Angola, believe me, they took their precautions. They hesitated for months."[7]

Kissinger's excitement of aspirations to mask American betrayal also betrayed the American past, the past that counts. For South Africa the immediate, or even the eventual, introduction of one-man, one-vote would mean the destruction of the rule of law—the real name of "revolution." The deepest utterances of the history of the United States, the words men died to fulfill, tell that the destruction of the rule of law in the name of freedom means ruin. Lincoln hated slavery but he faced a civil war for a constitution whose destruction he understood would undo the rule of law—and ruin everybody. He understood that constitutions that work are living constitutions, not mere pieces of paper, as idiosyncratic as men: They grow, they are not fashioned overnight. Besides, the president of the United States is not elected by one-man, one-vote.

By 1985 this yearning for a moral fix, regardless of the consequences, that Kissinger took up in 1976 was again drawing the United States, and the West after it, blindly towards war on the wrong side. In a bizarre article, not without occasional depth, Conor Cruise O'Brien actually proposed a joint US-Soviet intervention in South Africa under UN auspices,—a clear violation of the UN Charter, chapter 7, that the mandatory sanctions against Rhodesia in 1966 had also violated.

Like many outlandish remedies for South Africa, O'Brien's had a pedigree: In 1964 the Carnegie Endowment calculated that a blockade of South Africa required fifty warships and three hundred airplanes, at about twenty-eight million dollars a month. The Carnegie study anticipated a call for the UN Security Council to consider plans for sanctions, published in a report in the same year that the Security Council had unanimously commissioned upon a resolution Norway sponsored.[8]

It was just this yearning for a moral fix that drew Symms to bring Congress to its senses by making it look at the actual war overcoming southern Africa: "It is just tragic in my view that the United States of America, the bastion of hope and liberty in the world, cannot help and support those brave people [the resistance in Angola and Mozambique] who are really fighting our war in Africa."

South Africa's support for this resistance should not keep the United States from helping: "We can encourage internal reform of South Africa's racial policies and still be true to our principles and act to defend our interests."

In the following years, financial circles especially held that only sanctions against South Africa could win the acquiescence of African states to American "cold-war" policies in southern Africa, a reversal that substituted public relations for Symms' common sense.[9] This reversal also betrayed contempt for Africans' capacity to grasp realities: At least some African states approved the American help in Angola they would not support publicly. Symms, in contrast, sensed that an unequivocal policy in southern Africa would also lend bite to America's support of reform within South Africa, no matter what people said, because it showed the United States capable of distinguishing realities from appearances. The insistence on meaningful independence for Angola and Mozambique also meant the United States would muster the toughness in the face of South Africa that respect for government required,—this was probably Symms' deepest intuition.

Symms thought facing the courage, the fighting and dying in Angola and

Mozambique that went on despite State Department mediation, and after years of American paralysis, might bring the United States to distinguish between the feasible in South Africa and moralistic pantomime. His efforts to reinforce Reagan's original policy that aimed at all of southern Africa, not only at South Africa, amounted also to severe criticism, especially of its tendency to want to settle at any cost in spite of the fighting, instead of recognizing that the little progress in negotiations had occurred because of the fighting: ". . . The present U.S. policy is premised on victory through negotiations, a concept which has badly served U.S. interests."

Symms, in fact, had sought repeal of the Clark Amendment because he had just heard that the State Department seemed about to move to implement UN Security Council Resolution 435 of 1978 on South West Africa, a "paper settlement." No one could impose this settlement on South Africa, except in all-out war, Symms argued, because it meant the surrender of the huge underpopulated territory, barely a million people in a territory greater than Great Britain and France, to the Soviet-controlled terrorists of SWAPO. The General Assembly had recognized SWAPO as the "sole and legitimate representative of the Namibian [SWAPO's name for South West Africa] people" in 1976, a non-binding resolution, like all General Assembly resolutions, the United States rejects.

Already before, in early 1984, Chester Crocker had alarmed Symms with his positive response to the Angola regime's offer,—the first after three years of "shuttle diplomacy," a bureaucratic euphemism for begging,—of *partial* Cuban withdrawal from Angola in exchange for South Africa cutting off *all* help to the resistance in Angola, to Savimbi's UNITA.

Symms could only make these criticisms after calling for the repeal of the Clark Amendment. His call for repeal amounted to an admission of some Congressional responsibility for the distortions and imbalances in administration policy.

Crocker, however, had been too comfortable with these distortions. In fact, he had done them one better. In addition to not seeking repeal of the Clark Amendment, an item on the Republican Platform in 1980, he had wished Savimbi away. Savimbi, despite CIA assurances to Crocker that he could not last, had survived—and, as Simon Jenkins in an article of journalistic genius in the *Economist* remarked, had come to haunt his nights.[10] In a crucial article in 1980, a few months before he took office, Crocker had not mentioned the Clark Amendment or Savimbi. He wrote as if he did not see the constraints on American policy. Drawn on by the mirage of the Rhodesian settlement that put Mugabe in power in early 1980, he spoke of the war for southern Africa as almost over: "Conflicts in Namibia and Angola seem tantalizingly close to some resolution, an eventuality that would further erode a Soviet position already weakened by Robert Mugabe's current line in Zimbabwe." Crocker did not mention the fighting in Mozambique.

In appearance modest and restrained, the words "some resolution" are crucial: They could be made to mean settlements—"accommodation," the State Department later called it,—at the expense of liberty, a word that stayed off peoples' lips. In 1988, in rounds of negotiations in exotic places, Brazzaville, Cairo, Governor's Island off Manhattan, Crocker still pursued the same language, the language of the mirage.

Alexander Haig's demand in January 1981, relayed to the South Africans in June, for the total withdrawal of the Cubans from Angola before settlement in South West Africa and recognition of the MPLA regime in Angola led the South Africans to go along with Crocker's negotiations, especially in the first four years of the Reagan administration. Haig's readiness to stand up to Kissinger's 1976 deadlines and UN Resolution 435 that had followed them in 1978 in the Carter administration came in part because South Africa had decided to prevent a SWAPO seizure of power in the name of independence for South West Africa. In 1980 the South African Defense Force (SADF) had killed 1,300 SWAPO guerrillas, out of an estimated seven or eight thousand, against seventy-two South African dead. "Our object is to break the *military* force of SWAPO," said the South African general in command in South West Africa, in February 1981, a few weeks after the breakdown of the UN talks on South West Africa in Geneva and Haig's first statement in Washington of his conditions. The general's qualification *"military,"* my emphasis, meant he distinguished between SWAPO's political role within South West Africa, a role that South Africa recognized, and its violence from abroad. But his precision, usual in South African statements, did not keep him from perhaps inadvertently conceding SWAPO the status of soldiers instead of terrorists.

At the time relief at the United States' readiness again to face the war in Angola kept almost everybody, especially diplomats, from facing the blunt fact obvious to military men that there was no real reason to suppose the Americans, who had let the Cubans in, could now get them out. Haig's promise of a little realism because of its contrast with UN fantasies, brought the South Africans to join Crocker in the pursuit of a mirage. Their acceptance of negotiations meant they conceded their defense of South West Africa for more than two generations did not importantly differ from the six year old Cuban invasion of Angola.

On top of that Crocker would not understand that Haig's condition of Cuban withdrawal meant negotiations had to follow Savimbi's successes on the battlefield, not ignore them. In another article he argued the primacy of the war in Angola,—in the name of conservatives and moderates at home and abroad, not really in his own. He feared open support of Savimbi might harden the MPLA against negotiation. In a confidential memorandum *The New York Times* leaked he worried more about acceptance of the new policy than success on the ground which would bring acceptance as a matter of course: "African leaders would have no basis for resisting the Namibia-Angola linkage once they are made to realize they can only get a Namibia settlement through us, and that we are serious about getting such a settlement."

The change that counted for Crocker was that negotiations would depend on him and the United States, not the UN. On top of that, as if to betray the idleness of American promises, he wrote as if he could do it all with words: "Our credibility in Moscow and Havana depends on adopting a strong line against the principle of introducing external combat forces into the region—a message best communicated by greater reliability in U.S. performance worldwide." But the problem was getting the combat forces out,—not their introduction.

Like almost everybody else, Crocker also underestimated South African strength both abroad and at home, especially at home. With Botha at the bare beginning of reform, Crocker wrote as if South Africa was weak and vulnerable, with sympathy that bordered on condescension—as if the government of South Africa had no fight in it, no energy, no confidence. But it was the United States that had little confidence and, therefore, ran the continual risk of succumbing to its substitute, paralyzing ideological rigidity.

Crocker did not argue strongly for the U.S. support of a South Africa about to take risks, but simply foresaw in resignation the violence reform might occasion: "South Africa's political climate is in a fragile transition phase, and it may prove to be easier to destroy and destabilize its potential than to build on it."

He paid faint lip-service to the things that counted: "South Africans are at the beginning of a potentially long process." South Africa was a sovereign country—with a long constitutional, juridical, and cultural history, a real past—in contrast to every other African country below the Sahara. He did not call it a "republic" or use the word "free." Few professors do. But he knew it was not the United States' business to tell it how and when to change.[11]

The inherent imbalance in Crocker's conception explains how the United States came to concentrate on South Africa because the South Africans, in contrast to the Communist regimes in Angola and Mozambique, would listen. In southern Africa, in contrast, only negotiations that paid attention to the situation on the ground,—to the ongoing war,—and therefore recognized the importance of Savimbi and South Africa could be effective.

You could not negotiate without taking sides, and taking sides meant facing the international dimension of the war,—the Soviets and Cubans. "Who knows if the crude Realpolitik of southern Africa might not have resolved some of this mess, had America not chosen to raise expectations but simply stayed away," Simon Jenkins wrote after giving Crocker's policy the benefit of every doubt.

But Jenkins did not argue the South Africans should have dealt with the Cuban and Soviet presence without the United States, whose reluctance to face up to the Soviets was one of the main reasons for the prolongation of the war for southern Africa. Probably the South Africans were too patient with the United States, which twice flew South African Defense Force officers to Washington to tell them not to worry about a Soviet "total onslaught" on southern and South Africa.

But imbalance of conception, especially Crocker's evasiveness, despite Haig, about the consequences of the Clark Amendment, cannot explain the reversal of Reagan's policy. It cannot explain the crushing vote for sanctions, 84 to 14, in the Senate on August 15, 1986, against South Africa. It cannot explain why the United States turned its back on South Africa just at the moment when the National Party took the risk of further reforms, including the loosening of residential segregation (the "Group Areas Act") in areas where it was impractical,—reforms the the United States had urged on it repeatedly. It cannot explain how the United States under Reagan, who had wanted to support South Africa, did more against South Africa than Carter, who had limited himself to righteousness—and the loss of Rhodesia in part upon Kissinger's instigation. It cannot explain how Reagan lost control of his foreign policy.

2 America's Heart of Protest

I was taken aback by the demonstrations against South Africa when they broke. I took them for an irresistible expression of people's sentiment. I dared not impugn their motives. For who dares be too suspicious in a society that hangs on to good faith for dear life? They genuinely feel it, I told myself, with unnervingly familiar impatience. But I did not believe myself.

I remembered that almost out of thin air in 1977–78 demonstrations for divestment had broken out simultaneously on about six campuses and then as suddenly vanished without a trace, except for the unnerving sense they could break out again any time. I knew first hand that *some* of the students taking the initiative on my campus were disturbed, incapable of studying and getting anything right, unable to face their own insecurity—students straightforward teachers would either have brought to their senses or expelled long ago.

Besides, I did not like the intimidatory atmosphere,—the air thick with self-righteousness that brooked no argument and wanted no information. There was a cold hardness to it all. Friends cautioned me when I returned to teach, right after Reagan signed his executive order on September 9, 1985, not to say a word about South Africa.

Old teachers at major universities also spoke of intimidation. But this did not bother me as much as it should have. I had come to take it for granted. American universities are easy to intimidate,—and the atmosphere has been latently intimidatory in most of them since the sixties, an intolerance that exists more on the faculties (who, however, tend to blame it on the students) than among the students who are hungry for information but on the whole not daring enough to get it on their own.

It was only when I began to look into the demonstrations that I discovered I barely knew the world I lived in. I had taken them for spontaneous. I discovered that they had been organized by interlacing networks of organizations, much like the networks, and *sometimes* including the same organizations Erich and Rael Isaac had untangled in *The Coercive Utopians*. These organizations had been preparing for years, in some instances for more than a generation. They were in close touch with the ANC and SWAPO and the international organizations that shield them, the UN, the UN Committee on Apartheid, the OAU, and the Commonwealth (through Zambia, Zimbabwe and Tanzania). Since 1981 they had also been lobbying state legislators and city officials for disinvestment.

John Rees, the editor of *Information Digest* and *Early Warning*, had sketched out the entire strategy of the South African lobbying groups in the same year the lobbying started, 1981. But few had listened, and nobody in the major media, as usual. A man with an uncanny sense for deception, Rees had learned, first hand and from the inside, how demonstrations and lobbying worked. For about five years, at the end of the sixties and in the early seventies, he had joined Students for a Democratic Society (SDS), the National Lawyers' Guild and other radical groups. In the seventies with the FBI forbidden from even reading the writings of organizations that had not committed a crime, Rees may have been the only man in the United Stated keeping track of these groups.[12]

I was stunned: There had been no such thing as a spontaneous grassroots movement breaking out all over the country more or less on its own. The Reagan administration,—and Congress too,—had been subjected to a concerted but hidden campaign that might have outdone a tougher, more courageous, more clear-headed man than Crocker unless exposed. Instead the major media had promoted the campaign,—media that had betrayed their bad faith when they ignored Senator Denton's hearings in 1982.

I am saying that real feeling on this matter does not run as deep as people assume. Dread yes, and paralysis before the "race issue," but not real feeling. For real feeling leads to individual action, to speaking and writing, to the assumption of responsibility, not to flight from it. It does not have to be called forth and instigated. For the mark of feeling is that it moves itself and, thereby, takes responsibility for itself.

The capacity of race to paralyze the perception of differences goes very deep. Hitler meant just such questions when he said that men will only die for something they do not understand. But this kind of paralysis, this kind of not knowing what one thinks, is the opposite of real feeling. It seeks relief from its incoherence in flight into political action, but always at the instigation of somebody else. Its mark is that someone else calls the tune.

The Soviets know this distinction between paralysis that takes itself for feeling, but only when instigated, and actual feeling that shows itself in effective words instead of demonstrations. They dread real feeling because they are helpless before it. They counterfeit real feeling in order to defend themselves from it.

In the sea of pages of Kissinger's memoirs there is an instructive incident: the breakdown of the North Communist negotiators when they realized that the Americans were not about to betray Nguyen van Thieu—one of the real moments in those "negotiations."[13] A Russian friend of mine in exile from the Soviet Union told me another story that tells the same lesson differently: He saw a Soviet journalist he knew break into tears when she heard an atrocity story she had manufactured for *Pravda* on the radio. She wept even though she knew her lies—because she knew they were lies.

Also, why are demonstrations taken so for granted and feared? Most governments in Western history have had a healthy distaste for crowds in the streets, admittedly relatively unorganized, but not leaderless crowds, because they represented a breakdown in order. They knew the point was to get them off the street quickly. During the Indochina War, the American government instead continually encouraged demonstrations. It did all it could to make them respectable—"expressions of dissent," it called them.

But demonstrations do not use words, they do not attempt to persuade. They represent a breakdown in communication, a refusal to speak, which means a refusal to recognize there might be two sides to an issue. There is always something of an underlying threat in them. They show contempt, not the respect for opponents that makes debate and decision possible.

That the government of the United States could not distinguish speech from the refusal to speak came from its own tongue-tiedness, the most bizarre feature of the years of the war for Indochina. During those years the government rarely defended or explained its policies. President Johnson did not attempt to refute the media's now acknowledged misinterpretation of the Tet victory as a defeat in 1968. This silence still marks public life in the United States, which knows the noise of slogans and ideological catchwords but little of coherent informed argument that might remind us of actual dangers.

The weary tone of the voices of people I interviewed in Washington about the demonstrations told me more than their few words, which amounted mainly to the name *TransAfrica*. The tone said they had seen it all before.

A Harvard Law School graduate who had never pursued a career—the secular equivalent of a priest without a vocation—Randall Robinson had founded TransAfrica in 1978 to support the ANC and SWAPO in southern Africa and the Marxists in the Caribbean. A former executive director of the Congressional Black Caucus, Robinson knew how to pressure Congress backwards and forwards.

In 1979 TransAfrica, together with the Washington Office on Africa (WOA), the recently founded lobbying arm of the American Committee on Africa (ACOA), itself founded in 1951 with the help of the ANC, brought together a constellation of organizations in the South Africa Working Group (SAWG) which were in turn to form the core of the Free South Africa Movement (FSAM), launched by the sit-in in the South African Ambassador's office in Washington on November 21, 1984.

FSAM was made up of thirty well-known national organizations not directly concerned or connected with South Africa. Among them: The American Friends Service Committee (AFSC), Americans for Democratic Action (ADA), Amnesty International (AI), Clergy and Laity Concerned (CALC), founded by the National Council of Churches to oppose U.S. support for South Vietnam, the Coalition of Black Trade Unionists (CBTU), and the notorious Institute for Policy Studies (IPS).

Of these organizations, IPS is the most influential in Washington, because of its close connections with men in government and Congress since it started in 1963. It enjoys the confidence of a "think tank" dedicated to disinterested research even though "action," it has often said, is as important to it as "research." It concentrates on defense,—and weakening the tie with NATO,—intelligence, and the economy. Democratic congressmen ask it for proposals and even sketches of legislation. Once it gave them a plan that would have cut American defense spending in half in ten years—at the expense of its allies.

Not openly pro-Soviet (almost nobody is, not even the Soviets), not even anti-American, it wears a grimly liberal mask within the United States that pretends to protect the American values it seeks to undermine. But abroad in its Transnational Institute it shows its face in its magazine *Race and Class* that openly supports Soviet- and Chinese-backed insurgencies throughout the world. In 1979 IPS started the Campaign to Oppose Bank Loans to South Africa that soon came under the UN Center on Transnationals—which seeks to organize "third-world pressure against countries doing business with South Africa." The ANC, SWAPO, and the Zimbabwe African People's Union (ZAPU), Robert Mugabe's organization, attended an IPS meeting in Amsterdam in 1979 meant to minister to their "research needs": The ANC wanted details on backing from the "private sector and foreign multinationals" for South Africa's synthetic oil production.

To get things done, Robinson understood, moving important organizations deeply involved in Washington political life like the IPS was better than moving directly,—the technique of the UDF in South Africa,—because it made it look to Congress like South Africa had everybody by the gut, not just American blacks. The WOA openly stated that "its considerable clout comes from the support of influential domestic allies who are not usually identified as African lobbyists or registered as such."

TransAfrica openly announced it intended to undermine the foreign policy of the Reagan administration at a conference, of still another "activist" organization, the South Africa Support Project (SASP), sponsored at Howard University in Washington on June 8, 1981, "Building Forces Against United States Support for South Africa." "We realize . . . that in order to create change in our government's foreign policy, we must create change here at home . . . The U.S. government is not synonymous with the American people . . ." ran the national declaration, called a "black statement," despite the attendance of white "activists." It went on to threaten: "When a government is not representative of its populous [they have better things to do at Harvard than learning to spell and write], the people must find ways to act directly; in such situations, the tactic of petitioning the government for redress is futile." And to hint at violence and sabotage: "Because of who we are [blacks] and where we are within the American system, we as a people have an immediate direct hands-on capability." It called for propaganda, "an effective massive education drive." To change the government's policy it went on, ". . . We must create change here at home."

Robinson wanted to celebrate the street agitation of the Vietnam years: Harvard reunions were not enough.

Members of the ANC and SWAPO were prominent at the conference. The president of the ANC,—the man who gave the press conference in Lusaka at the beginning of 1986,—Oliver Tambo, gave a major address. Afterwards the terrorists toured the United States to spread the word and press the flesh,— and to call for the murder of men who stood up to them back home.

The initiation of a "legislative campaign in the United States against public investment in South Africa," was the subject of another conference supported by the UN Special Committee Against Apartheid at the United Nations in New York a few days later, June 12–13. About two dozen state and municipal representatives were brought together with "trade union, civil rights, church, and community organizations who form the backbone of local coalitions pressing divestment action." Robinson had draft divestment legislation ready for the state and local politicians probably cowed by the UN surroundings.

The sponsors amounted to a round-up of the usual suspects: TransAfrica, American Committee on Africa (ACOA), Washington Office on Africa (WOA), Clergy and Laity Concerned (CALC), Interfaith Center on Corporate Responsibility (ICCR), the Connecticut Anti-Apartheid Committee, United Methodist Church Office for the United Nations, and the American Friends Service Committee (AFSC) that holds, like many of these organizations,—and the UDF in South Africa,—that "the inherent violence of the status quo" justifies terrorism.

A note from Grenada's ambassador to the United States, captured by the American rescue mission in October 1983, betrays Robinson's and his associates' in the House of Representatives readiness to exploit the unease, in the face of race, of white politicians with a rawness beyond novelists because so obvious: ". . . In my opinion both Randall Robinson, but more so members of the Black Caucus such as Judge [Congressman] George Crockett, want to step up their participation in national politics, and especially in foreign policy. Maurice Bishop [invited to Washington a few months before the American rescue put a stop to TransAfrica's activities in the Caribbean] and the Grenada Revolution represent a very controversial but 'meaty' political issue. As national black politicians they want to 'score one' both with the black community but particularly with the white establishment with which they maintain love-hate relations. Therefore, this one is a big one for them in the racial struggle for recognition of 'credible black leadership,' and it is also a big one in anti-Reagan political warfare."[14]

Robinson's cynicism outdid his idealism: He was interested in power in the United States, but not particularly in the plight of blacks in South Africa or the Caribbean. "Although it has no mandate to do so, TransAfrica continues to present itself as the representative of the views of black Americans," wrote The Lincoln Institute, a research group that presents black middle class views, in an important pamphlet about TransAfrica. This observation goes also for all the predominantly white organizations lobbying Congress and local and state legislatures in the name of whites.

A poll that caused something of a sensation,—a sensation that tells of the distance from common sense realities,—a poll of blacks and their leadership, taken in 1985, before the partial July 1985 State of Emergency, but after unremitting media coverage of violence in South Africa and demonstrations in the United States, bore out the Lincoln Institute's sense of differences between everyday blacks and their leadership. Seventy-four percent of everyday blacks were against divestment in South Africa, in contrast to the fifty-nine percent of the leaders for it; eighty-three percent approved of black leaders' influence on foreign policy, but sixty-five percent said they should work through the State Department instead of contacting leaders abroad directly. The percentage of blacks against discrimination in their favor on jobs and in college—"affirmative action"—matched the leaders for it: seventy-seven percent. Eighty-three percent were for prayer in public schools, in contrast to sixty percent of their leaders against it. Thirty percent approved of Reagan's conduct in office against thirteen percent of the leaders—despite a ten percent black vote for Reagan in 1984. The 105 black leaders questioned came from the civil rights and political organizations that received the most coverage on racial issues in *The New York Times*, *The Washington Post*, *Time* and *Newsweek* in 1984: The National Association for the Advancement of Colored Peoples (NAACP), the Urban League, the Southern Christian Leadership Conference, Operation PUSH, the National Conference of Black Mayors, and the Congressional Black Caucus.[15]

According to minutes of TransAfrica's meetings (which John Rees has seen), TransAfrica also strives to limit public and media attention to "the evils of apartheid" in order to prevent recognition of the facts: the increase in wages of blacks in South Africa (in contrast to the continuous decline in absolute terms in GNP in most of the sub-Saharan states since independence, except Zimbabwe); the limited but fundamental reforms; and above all the strategic importance of southern Africa—the minerals, important to the United States, crucial to Europe, otherwise available in some abundance only in the U.S.S.R., and the Cape sea routes.

Again the near success in silencing discussion and reporting of these facts, especially in silencing the government, needs explaining, not the attempt. This embarrassment in the face of facts that could make indignation more effective, or, at least less self-destructive, represents a chilling example of the capacity of ideology and misinformation to spread a climate of opinion that ignores the living world. Chester Crocker dismissed strategic considerations as beneath contempt in his article in Foreign Affairs in 1980. Alexander Haig spoke in vague unconvincing words of "a resource war." Government reports ring with hesitation,—all quite strange in the face of Brezhnev's well-known remark in a secret speech in Prague in 1973, soon reported in the West:

Our aim is to gain control of the two great treasure houses on which the West depends . . . the energy treasure house of the Persian Gulf and the mineral treasure house of central and southern Africa.

In contrast until the middle seventies, even those who wanted the West to act against South Africa publicly accepted its strategic importance. The embarrassed silence about realities came after the fall of Portugal in 1975, not to speak of the fall of Laos, Cambodia and Vietnam, and increased with the fall of Rhodesia five years later. The silence, as well as its ideology and misinformation, told of the unacknowledged fear of Soviet advances that even made the commonplace appreciation in the early seventies of South Africa as a loyal ally of the West, a "bulwark against communism and Soviet meddling," look quaint and naive.[16] The more danger made the basic truths about South Africa count, the harder they became to state,—and to comprehend.

Two months before the conference in Washington and New York, on March 31, 1981, the Soviet Union had openly called for "active measures" "to mobilize world opinion in the fight to eliminate colonialism, racism, and apartheid in southern Africa" in a statement in New York for the UN Special Committee Against Apartheid. A broad term for KGB and GRU secret actions besides collecting information, "active measures" here means the manipulation of Western media and public opinion—as John Rees who first called attention to this statement (in 1981!) observed.

In the same statement in its usual wooden language that you practically need to paraphrase to understand, the Soviet Union reminded the world that the UN approves "giving moral and material support and assistance *in every possible way* to the peoples fighting colonialism, racism and apartheid in southern Africa"—terrorism in short (Italics mine). The Soviets knew what they were talking about, as often, especially in juridical matters: On December 14, 1974, in Resolution 3314, the UN General Assembly had excused terror and violence against "colonial and racist regimes" in its definition of aggression.

The 1974 endorsement of violence had been preceded in 1973 by the General Assembly's resolution to call apartheid "a crime against humanity" and make individuals, states and organizations "legally" responsible for its persistence through an International Convention on the Suppression and Punishment of Apartheid that fifty-six states had accepted by 1980. The Soviets played an important part in the formulation of the convention. Its echo of the Greek and Roman concept of an "enemy of all mankind," in the phrase "crime against humanity," probably betrayed vestiges of Tsarist traditions of study of international law (*jus gentium*) in the Soviet Union. In 1977, the General Assembly had again reiterated the "legitimacy" of "armed struggle" that the Soviets had called for in 1969.[17]

The brashness of the Soviet statement,—the first open use of the phrase "active measures" according to Edwin O'Malley of the FBI,—probably was meant to get even with Alexander Haig's words, a few months before, about Soviet involvement in terrorism throughout the world,—the first public acknowledgment by a high government official. Bulgaria, Hungary, East Germany, the Ukraine, and Byelorussia (which enjoys independence only in the make-believe world at the UN) also openly supported the ANC and SWAPO. The UN then distributed the Soviet statement as a flyer, complete with black felt-pen ink circling and underlining, to introduce conferences against South Africa.

The Soviet hand also showed itself unmistakably in the "Conference in Solidarity with Liberation Struggles in Southern Africa" held a few months after the Washington and New York conferences, on October 9–11, again in New York. O'Malley called it an example of Soviet "active measures" in the United States before the House Intelligence Committee in July 1982. Its sponsors, besides TransAfrica and WOA, were well-known front organizations:

the International Association of Democratic Lawyers, the National Alliance Against Racist and Political Repression, the National Anti-Imperialist Movement in Solidarity with African Liberation, the National Conference of Black Lawyers, the National Lawyers' Guild, the Puerto Rican Socialist Party, the U.S. Peace Council, and so on. Among the individual sponsors: Bella Abzug, William Sloane Coffin, Coretta Scott King, and Ronald Dellums (who was to get a half-deserted House to order the withdrawal of all American investment from South Africa and prohibit further trade in June 1986).

In calling conferences in the United States and in shaping opinion throughout the world, especially outside Europe, the Soviets use the prestige of the UN for cover, and its committees for organization, much in the way Stalin intended after the war, especially the UN Special Committee Against Apartheid,: "We do not need the UN. What we need is a stage from which we can express any opinion we want." The KGB "basically" runs the UN Committee Against Apartheid,—according to Arkady Shevchenko, the Soviet with the highest civil service rank at the UN until he took refuge in the United States in 1978. The UN Department of Public Information is also crucial to Soviet disinformation, with its broadcasts and press releases. The latest ideological line from New York can undermine traditional conceptions of international law, outside of Europe, especially in Africa, in the swiftness of repetition. Many of the almost one hundred Non-Aligned nations more or less follow the Soviet ideological agenda. "The Whole Department of Information is mobilized"— again according to Shevchenko. The Soviets can manipulate these committees and departments because their employees from Non-Aligned countries—not necessarily only from Communist countries—owe their jobs to Soviet "infiltration" of the Department of Personnel "at the highest levels." About two hundred people work full-time at the UN against apartheid—and South Africa.[18]

Through UN committees the Soviets later began to manipulate campus opinion in the United States. In June 1985 the Special Committee Against Apartheid and the Council for Namibia, another UN committee, began to hear testimony from American student leaders about the campaigns for disinvestment on their campuses,—testimony the Department of Public Information distributes throughout the world. The Soviet UN civil service employee who gives out information to American high school and university students on Namibia worked as a "political commissar" in Angola indoctrinating SWAPO and refugees, sometimes kidnapped from Namibia, in Marxism-Leninism. He was trained in Kiev at the Institute for World History in disinformation and propaganda. The SWAPO notebooks published with the Denton Hearings, show this indoctrination. "I learned that the main job of the Soviet members of the UN staff was espionage and subversion of the U.S.," Igor Glagolev, another Soviet refugee, said in 1982 of his experience at the UN in the sixties.

From Repeal of the Clark Amendment to Aid to Savimbi

No longer faced with a Congress that prevented it from acting after the repeal of the Clark Amendment, the administration in the fall of 1985 had to face its own unwillingness to act. Repeal of the Clark Amendment undid the past. It meant also facing the dangers that the past had sought to avoid, especially facing the Soviet Union.

Kissinger had not fought publicly against the cut-off of aid to Angola at the end of 1975, and did not immediately after, in early 1976, seek "overt aid" to prevent a Communist takeover in Angola. These actions would have meant facing the Soviet Union. Most importantly, with their recognition that the war on the ground continued elsewhere, they would have limited the defeat to Indochina. They might have prevented the institutionalization of appeasement in Congress and the media.

The fall of Saigon in 1975 had not only made American intervention anywhere almost unthinkable, it had also made an issue, in 1975 and 1985, of public American support and aid for men willing to fight and die on their own in Angola, in Afghanistan, in Nicaragua, in Cambodia, and elsewhere,—the homemade Vietnamization that has occurred in many parts of the world since American defeat.

A few months after the repeal of the Clark Amendment, in part prompted by a constituency in Florida half made up of Cubans, Claude Pepper, who had led the repeal of the Clark Amendment in the House, introduced a bill for twenty-seven million dollars in "humanitarian" assistance to Savimbi's UNITA, quickly followed by another measure for military assistance. Pepper's Cuban constituents knew first hand in their flesh, the interconnections between the Cuban presence in Angola, Mozambique, Ethiopia, and in Nicaragua. They knew the Cubans and Soviets applied their method of controlling the MPLA in Angola to the Sandinistas, including transfers of experienced officers from Angola to Nicaragua.

The secretary of state wrote the House Republican leader in protest, because he feared these measures would upset negotiations with the Angola MPLA regime, Crocker's reasoning. Shultz did not realize that the MPLA's new-found *apparent* readiness to negotiate came because Savimbi had managed to survive a major MPLA offensive. The Soviets had exercised tactical control of MPLA units and Cubans had flown many of the airplanes, Savimbi claimed. All but ignored in the press, these battles that had lasted several months had been serious enough to show worry on Savimbi's face to visitors to Jamba in August 1985.

Visibly angered, the House Republican leader, Robert Michel, answered Shultz that support for UNITA "is not only a geostrategic but a moral necessity . . ." and went on to refer to a recent speech of Shultz's in London that had argued the necessary combination of force with diplomacy that Crocker would not accept. (That such things needed saying—and by a secretary of state—tells it all!) "You have quite correctly stated on many occasions that a mixture of military and diplomatic means is necessary to bring democracy to Nicaragua . . . We all want negotiations, in every area of geostrategic conflict, but I cannot see how we can argue that aid to democratic forces in Nicaragua helps the chance of negotiations while aid to UNITA somehow damages the negotiating process."[19]

Not only coherence was at stake but the immediate effect of success in one region on the wars in all the others, as Symms had pointed out in the Senate a few months earlier: "A success in Angola would be viewed around the world as a major setback for the Soviets and the Cubans, and a major psychological lift in places like Nicaragua, in Afghanistan, in Poland, in Southeast Asia, and other places, to those people who are resisting and are leaders of the resistance movement against the Communists."

For these wars, separate for the men that fight on their own, are all one for the Soviets and the Cubans. Their regimes are much more vulnerable to even minor setbacks than law-abiding countries: The American rescue of Grenada visibly shook Castro. Senator Denton also had not minced his words:

We share complicity for the famine in Ethiopia, the genocide in Cambodia and Afghanistan, the systematic use of physical and psychological torture in Vietnam, Eastern Europe, and other Communist nations, and most assuredly the continuing Communist exploitation and bloodshed in foreign-occupied Angola . . . The pattern of American and free-world misperception and folly is being observed with growing anxiety approaching despair by nations currently under Communist pressure . . . The United States is proving to be a dangerous friend and a helpless foe. Time is becoming short to avert a major disaster in world affairs . . . Critics of administration policy argue that a denial of aid to freedom fighters in Angola, Nicaragua, Afghanistan, and Southeast Asia, is intended to avoid violence and U.S. military involvement. History shrieks that such a policy is folly and makes U.S. military involvement more likely, more costly in lives and treasure, and less likely to succeed.

The turnabout in Congress prompted Reagan and Shultz, after some reluctance and State Department opposition, to receive Savimbi almost like a head of state several months later, in February 1986—quite a contrast to Savimbi's wandering practically alone in the streets of New York in 1979, his only interlocutors insomniacs on late-night talk shows. The White House announced seventeen million dollars in aid—not much in the face of two billion dollars of Soviet aid to the MPLA in the last two years, but a beginning, and after the announcement, a few weeks later, of the intention to ship Stinger missiles to Savimbi (as well as Afghanistan!), an important beginning.

In contrast to the president of the United States, the Whore of Babylon in New York, in her capital of make-believe, in her glass palace, as the Italians call it, knew obscenity in prudish shudders of disbelief at the suggestion of a visit from Savimbi, who had to move about a country that fancies itself "the freest in the world," with an unannounced schedule.

Open aid to Savimbi implied the United States' readiness to face the Soviet Union with the demand for the removal of forty-five thousand Cubans (or thirty thousand,—depending on who counts, Savimbi or the State Department, and how, from information inside the MPLA or air photographs of baseball diamonds). Removal of the Cubans had ostensibly been the cornerstone of the U.S. design for settlement in Angola and South West Africa since June 1981.

The United States had fled this confrontation at least twice, both moments of defeat for the MPLA: in 1975 just after the arrival of the first Cuban tanks, when Savimbi and a small force of South Africans was within thirty miles of Luanda. And again in November 1983, just before a major South African incursion of ten thousand men on December 6, when Soviet diplomats warned the South African ambassador to the UN (at the bar of the Algonquin Hotel in New York, no less!) that the Soviet Union would not tolerate defeat of the MPLA.

Without United States readiness to face the Soviets, settlement is probably not possible, in this war that diplomats still call regional, because neither the MPLA in Angola or the Front for the Liberation of Mozambique (FRELIMO) or SWAPO are their own men. "We are not certain whom we are addressing there, as the Angolan president does not seem to have the power of decision expected of a head of state. There are obviously at least two brains masterminding his policies—in Havana and Moscow," a French diplomat remarked at the end of 1983.[20]

The readiness to help Savimbi also implied United States acknowledgment that South Africa, with its aid to Savimbi and its incursions against SWAPO bases in Angola to protect South West Africa and with its air strikes in Savimbi's crucial battles, had played a responsible role in Angola after America's flight at the end of 1975, especially since 1978. But the United States' readiness to turn its back with sanctions and disinvestment on a South African government bent on the risks of reform, went on. It threatened to continue the abandonment of southern Africa, "two areas [Mozambique and Angola] of which the Soviets would rather the American people remain ignorant," as Symms remarked in 1985.

Unfortunately, Symms left off this forthrightness in 1986,—apparently on the advice of hotshot aides who think domestic politics more important than the situation on the ground throughout the world that could eventually determine, and already conditions, domestic politics, pathetic narcissism that infests Congress but not the country. He left Reagan to fight the renewed disinvestment-sanctions onslaught Reagan may have thought he outwitted in 1985, practically alone,—even against some of his aides and against the State Department. The State Department succeeded in making his July 22 speech endorse demands close to those of the ANC, despite Reagan's statement in the same speech that the South African government did not have to negotiate with organizations like the ANC—without naming it.

The Righteous Riot

But events were moving more swiftly than anybody realized. Even before President Reagan's executive order of September 9, 1985 coopting congressional sanctions, there were unmistakable signs of a transformation of American policy toward South Africa—and also thereby toward southern Africa—a transformation whose full significance was not apparent until late 1986. The recall of the American ambassador to South Africa, Herman Nickel, after the South

African commando raid on ANC bases in Gaborone, Botswana on June 14, 1985, was a willfully public gesture meant to embarrass. It marked the first break away from diplomacy that took South Africa for a foreign country,—and therefore dealt only with its government,—to confrontational activism that took South Africa for a United States domestic problem. By the end of 1986 this transformation had enmeshed the United States deeply in South Africa's domestic political life. The break's occurrence over foreign, not domestic, policy helped introduce a new propaganda theme: the "violence of apartheid" had also brought the wars in southern Africa.

The State Department Turns Against Itself:
The Heart of a Mighty Nihilist, Michael Clough

An article that appeared toward the end of 1985 by Michael Clough, who had served as study director of Secretary of State Shultz's Advisory Committee on South Africa, showed unmistakably the changes in thinking that were leading the State Department to treat South Africa as a domestic American problem, rather than a foreign country. Quite a change in stance for professional diplomats who notoriously, especially on the South Africa desk, have no first-hand experience of American politics, for instance, no experience in electoral campaigns. Clough's article shows the thinking that was to provide the basic structure for President Reagan's speech on July 22, 1986, and,—with the Eminent Persons Group Report,—for the CAA Act finally passed in defiance of a presidential veto on October 2:

These developments [the new constitution and the outbreak of violence] sparked across America a prairie fire [the nostalgic language is significant, especially for a State Department that takes Afrikaners for "cowboys" because they are straightforward] of anti-apartheid protest, the tinder for which had been steadily accumulating in response to the absence of serious reform efforts inside South Africa . . . Ironically, the past year's worth [September 1984 to September 1985] of South Africa-related political turmoil in America could enable the United States to exercise considerable influence over Pretoria. For the first time in U.S. history South Africa is viewed as an issue worthy of sustained, high-level attention. Moreover, a consensus has formed that nothing short of direct negotiations with credible black leaders, including representatives of the ANC, will resolve South Africa's crisis. The days of quiet diplomacy are gone forever. After the events of the past few months, white South Africans must realize that they have lost their last chance for comforting treatment by a U.S. president.[21]

Clough rejected reform categorically: "The past fifteen months have shown that white-led change cannot succeed." Support for the South African government meant support for apartheid: "Repeated comments by Reagan that seem to indicate an underlying sympathy with white rule have added doubts about how sincerely his administration abhors apartheid." "Abhorrence of apartheid," was to be the test of true belief—like making the sign of the cross.
Clough was ambivalent about civil violence because he cannot tell the

difference between violence and war, between the murder of citizens and the death of soldiers, and finally, between friends and enemies:

In the South African case, ideological engagement [engagement that distinguished between movements who openly preach violence and those who do not] would widen the chasm separating the United States from movements like the ANC, the UDF, the country's biggest black-led multiracial opposition coalition, and the Azanian People's Organization, an outlawed all-black opposition group.

The United States should become involved with all parties in South Africa and southern Africa—but not distinguish between them: "Talking with diverse regional actors will require a greater understanding of the question of violence as a means of promoting or preventing political change." Then he took it all back: "This does not mean that Washington should aid and abet violence."

The violence in the region was all one. The United States could not distinguish between the wars in Angola and Mozambique, the continuing violence in Zimbabwe, and the turmoil in South Africa limited to about thirty townships, that State Department cables took for the whole country ablaze with "revolution" because that meant defending the "violence of apartheid." Apartheid also requires no mention of South Africa's political and economic predominance in the region that could lead its nations out of poverty:

America's own ability to promote peace in Angola, Mozambique and Zimbabwe is severely limited by the widespread impression that US initiatives simply are veiled attempts to reinforce South Africa's regional hegemony and hence to protect apartheid.

Clough would not have the United States choose sides,—but he would also not have her withdraw and lose influence: "No matter how decent, non-involvement would leave the United States less prepared to deal with the onset and aftermath of a South African revolution." Clough did not mince his assurance: "Bitter, violent and anti-capitalistic this revolution will be."

Clough's goals was "accommodation," respect for democratic values without America's form of government:

Promoting accommodation and broadened political participation, however, does not mean imposing American political forms and ideas on other countries. US officials must be willing to support a wide range of alternative political formulas and structures in southern Africa—and elsewhere—so long as they are freely arrived at and broadly acceptable to the local population.

Clough's ambiguity led him to argue the plain contradiction that Mugabe's drive toward a one party state was of little importance as long as he came to reconciliation with the opposition he had been murdering (Clough did not say "murder")—as if the drive to a one party state was not itself leading him to murder.

About one matter Clough was indelibly right, any United States involvement in South Africa and southern Africa that made distinctions, that held that one world was better than another, that the violence in the region was about something important, would test United States will to the utmost, a test it has only undertaken gingerly in Nicaragua since its defeat in Indochina now more than ten years ago: "Pushing ideological engagement [engagement that distinguished between the ANC and UNITA] will create tests of will the United States is unlikely to win."

It would take Molière to do justice to the ambivalence of this article, to its Byzantine twistedness, that does not even have the dubious gusto of *raison d'état*: After all, southern Africa is not the Soviet Union. But nobody laughs in the United States, least of all at themselves, and least of all in the State Department, whose depression, and they have good reason to be depressed, the newspapers routinely mention.

This apparently naive policy of total involvement without force because the United States cannot support those who fight, meant to provide cover for joining the other side,—in either instance, a formula for drift and disaster.

After his recall in June 1986, the American Ambassador to South Africa, Herman Nickel struggled in Washington with the State Department bureaucrats whose thinking the Clough article betrayed six months later. A political appointee, not a career diplomat, once an editor of *Time*, who could think on his feet and write, Nickel could tell the difference between South Africa and the domestic politics of the United States—unlike some at the State Department. For four years he had dealt with the situation on the ground in South Africa—and kept control of his staff.

Nickel was alive to "the irony that the disinvestment campaign . . . [had] reached its highest pitch in the United States just as South Africa appeared to have turned the corner on the road to reform." He knew and, just before his recall, said in a leading South African magazine that "township unrest," not "dissatisfaction with the pace of the reform effort," had "touched off the sudden quantum leap in American anti-apartheid . . . activism." South Africa was an almost "cost-free" "no-win" issue in the United States.[22]

Several high officials of the Agency for International Development (AID) shocked at the plans to involve them in South African black political activity against the South African government, joined Nickel's resistance. In September the State Department's demand for the release of Mandela; Shultz's characterization of South Africa as "an evil empire"; instructions to American diplomats to attend black political funerals in South Africa, with their ANC and Soviet flags and their cries of "Long live the necklace"; and, a few months later, rumors a black was to replace Nickel, an inept and embarrassing move, all showed that Nickel's resistance had failed. Almost nobody noticed,—and nobody said "constructive engagement" was finished. The United States had entered the brave new world of Clough's article.

Clough's thinking soon showed itself in the raw in public, probably involuntarily. In testimony before the House Foreign Affairs Subcommittee on Africa on March 12, 1985, Crocker startled its chairman, Representative Howard Wolpe, and *The Washington Post* reporter by answering "Yes" when

Wolpe asked whether the administration endorsed "[black] majority rule," adding, disarmingly, that he did not feel "he was breaking new ground."

But Wolpe, his aides, and journalists, had no doubts—and said so: It was the first time any administration official had publicly endorsed "black majority rule"—a demand, Crocker knew perfectly well that Botha, the South African government, and almost all South African voters, would never accept.

Crocker also said outright that the ANC were "generically freedom fighters"—indistinguishable, that is, from Savimbi's UNITA or the Afghan resistance. (Clough had argued against support of all insurgencies because polarization in the United States made meaningful distinctions between them impossible.)

Tense, Crocker had suddenly cracked—according to an eyewitness. In the past he had resisted badgering. Crocker's collapse is a democratic equivalent of a confession in a Communist show trial. Except that instead of accusing himself, Crocker acted, and still acts, as if nothing has changed.[23]

The Eyes of the British Empire

The target of the Commonwealth Group Report, with its flashy title, *Mission to Africa*, was the United States, especially the Senate. The Group claims it settled down to write the report at Marlborough House in London on May 30 (candid snapshot included) after the May 14 South African raids in southern Africa broke down the negotiations.

But the Washington bookstores told another story: In mid-June *Mission to South Africa* was available. It was frequently quoted in the Senate. "I would note that the Commonwealth of Nations, of which South Africa has been a part, also agrees basically with what we are trying to do here today. Those are sister nations [of the United States?] within the Commonwealth. So it is not as though we, the United States were acting *solo* and *irresponsibly* in this situation," Senator John Glenn said on August 14, 1986. The underlying assumption of the Commonwealth Group Report that the "violence" of the South African government matched the violence of the ANC and other terrorist groups, and even some of its phrases, like temporary "suspension of violence" instead of renunciation of violence, appeared in Senate statements, and informed the CAA Act.

In contrast to the United States, and especially its Congress, in Britain the report did not make much impression: Poll after poll showed the British people were against sanctions, sympathetic to the South Africans, impatient of the Commonwealth. There were rumors even of a constitutional crisis with the Crown. Continental Europe paid only polite attention—but also spent a good deal of time figuring out exactly what the Commonwealth was, something the report itself despite a page of explanation did not answer. But in Washington, as often, they assumed they knew without asking. The State Department took the report for a full-fledged state paper.

The Commonwealth Eminent Persons Group Report could call Dickens up from the dead: He would know how to have a time with the title "Eminent Persons Group." After eighteen days in South Africa (jet-lag not included) on two separate visits, these worthies saw fit to say of themselves: "The range of contacts we made was probably unique, the frankness and openness of the discussion unlikely to be replicated in the near future." And to roundly declare: "The reforms implemented so far had not impressed the black community . . ."

About Nelson Mandela, whom they twice visited, the Group spoke repeatedly, almost in the language of youths with a crush, "of the consistency of his beliefs"; ". . . his physical authority . . . his immaculate appearance, his commanding presence,"—at the same time that they took the firmness of the South African government for "obduracy and intransigence." " . . . Of his [Mandela's] communism, either now or in the past, we found no trace"— despite a twenty-four page pamphlet, "How to Be a Good Communist," in his own handwriting, on Mandela upon his arrest.[24]

From their report you can learn the names of the best restaurants in Johannesburg and Durban, essential knowledge for the political tourist: ". . . Those blacks rich enough to dine at Johannesburg's Carlton Hotel or Durban's Maharani are very few in number [!] . . ." The former prime minister of Australia's candid snapshot of toilets in a workers' dormitory in Soweto,— stripped down to the porcelain, without covers!—precedes this remark.

"We believe we acquired the confidence and the trust of all the principal black leaders and organizations within the country, as well as the liberation movements outside." By blacks they mean, like the ANC, only urban blacks, dismissing the representatives of ten million blacks in the homelands with a twist of a phrase—except for Buthelezi who takes a paragraph without so much as an acknowledgment that he is an elected and hereditary leader of something like seven million Zulus, about as many men as in all but two of the states below Zaire: "With the exception of Chief Buthelezi, the 'homeland' [throughout the report quotation marks serve as epithets of contempt and involuntary condescension] leaders have no real political standing or following and would not, in our view, be credible parties in a negotiation to resolve South Africa's deepening crisis." After prescribing, the Group blandly denies it prescribes: "It is not for us to prescribe or advise who the parties to a genuine negotiation might be . . ."

This casual reading out of roughly half of the blacks in South Africa, and their leaders,—in unstated accordance with ANC hostility to the homelands,— amounts to silent acquiescence to the future murder of peoples: "If there were four million of us left after the revolution, that would be better than the present situation," Johnny Makatini, formerly ANC representative at the UN, in charge of ANC "international relations" in Lusaka until his death in late 1988, told an American visitor recently. And even then he was only echoing Lenin's "winged words" in 1918: "Even if ninety percent of the people perish, what matter if the other ten percent live to see the revolution become universal?"[25]

The Group took murder for self-government, for blacks taking responsibility for *their own affairs,*—a phrase lifted from the new South African Constitution, no quotation marks here: "In frustration at those who have aided the system by joining government-backed 'town councils,' 'collaborators' have been hounded out of office—frequently out of house and home and often 'necklaced' as angry black residents have vented their fury and assumed responsibility for their own affairs."

"Catalysed in particular by opposition to the Tricameral Parliament, [black resistance] has resolved into a new telling strategy to make South Africa ungovernable and apartheid unworkable,"—a description of events since 1984 that turns UDF and ANC slogans like "Make the townships ungovernable" into impersonal third-person narrative without saying so.

Botha's groping toward a federal constitution is not enough because "[It] would enable whites to prevent the *economic and social restructuring* of South Africa that is essential if the legacy of four decades of apartheid—and three hundred years of discrimination—is to be remedied." "Restructuring" means violent seizure of power and the destruction of capitalism and individual initiative: Three hundred years of history are to be undone in an instant! Wild ignorance, in any case, since only a hundred and fifty years have passed since the first contacts with Africans.

The Group was overpowered by the notion that there was no difference between the murder of the terrorists and of the police seeking to protect lives, including their own, and property,—sometimes with ineptness exposed in South African courts and newspapers. Over and over they equated the "violence" of the government with terrorism: "We were struck immediately by the government's attitude to the question of violence . . . There was no recognition that apartheid itself was sustained through violence and that the inequities and injustices it perpetrated fostered violence"; "For the government to attribute all violence to the ANC, as it was now doing, was to overlook a situation in which the structures of society, dominated by a relatively small group of people, were founded upon injustice and inevitably led to violence."

Only once did the Group mention the duty of governments to enforce the law, only to deny it to the South African government because it had not extended one-man, one-vote to peoples it had defeated in battle in the nineteenth century—without, of course, mentioning those defeats: "All governments have coercive powers, and regard the maintenance of law and order as their first duty. If the government of South Africa was a democratic government, its claims in this regard would command respect."

Like a good deal of the West, the Group could not remember the meaning of the word conquest, although the division of Germany and Europe lies before their eyes to teach them its consequences. Buthelezi, in contrast, understands, like Alan Paton, that South Africa is now undoing conquest—the effects of the past: "The massacre of Zulus at Blood River in 1838 was also an attempt at solving a problem which was no solution. The whole idea of keeping blacks out of decision-making ever since they were conquered, has been no solution."[26]

The denial of the distinction between law enforcement and terrorist murder led the Group to argue again and again that the government should negotiate with the terrorists as equals. The South African government ought to negotiate with the ANC and other terrorist groups without insisting on a permanent renunciation of violence,—but, only at best on a "suspension of violence": "To ask the ANC or other parties, all of them far weaker than the government, to renounce violence for all time here and now would be to put them in a position of having to rely absolutely on the government's intentions and determination to press through the process of negotiation."

It reprimanded the government for seeking "consistently to dictate both the content and the pace of change," for striving to keep change from degenerating into chaos. It even argued that the government should negotiate in the midst of violence: "We reiterate that the Lancaster House negotiations [the negotiations in London that led to the undoing of the Muzorewa government in Zimbabwe-Rhodesia, elected in a one-man, one-vote election that excluded terrorists because they would not renounce violence] continued without the suspension of violence as have many others in situations of conflict."

In a letter welcoming the "Commonwealth initiative" on Christmas Eve 1985, P.W. Botha had agreed "that a suspension of violence is a requirement for dialogue." He had not made it unmistakably clear that the South African government distinguished good faith negotiations between parties that renounced violence from negotiations that masked surrender. He had also written ". . . We want to get moving with negotiations. The sooner this can be done the better, for *this is the key to the solution of our problems.* Our political programme provides for power sharing, subject only to the protection of the rights of all minorities, *and we are reconciled to the eventual disappearance of white domination*" (Italics mine). But he had also warned that the Commonwealth Group could do "incalculable damage" if it took itself for a "pressure group" meant to extract concessions from the government and to prescribe "solutions to problems which are the sole concern of South Africans,"—the last, words that recall the thinking of the UN Charter, Chapter 7.

In contrast to P.W. Botha, the foreign minister, R.F. Botha, made the position of the South African government unmistakably clear in conversations with the Group on May 16 and in a letter on May 29, 1986—after South African commando attacks on ANC bases in Harare, Lusaka, and Gaborone on May 19 showed the government could tell the meaning of sovereignty, self-defense, not only in words the Group could not understand, but in actions it could not deny. On May 16: "He [R.F. Botha] questioned the term 'suspension of violence' as it appeared in the concept [the Group's plan for negotiation] . . . The government's understanding was that this meant a cessation, an end for all time. If the notion was that violence could be resumed because of differences at the conference table, then the Commonwealth initiative stood no chance of success." And in the letter of May 29 more directly: "The South African government is prepared to negotiate with South African citizens about a new constitutional dispensation which will provide for power sharing. *It is not interested in negotiation about transfer of power*" (Italics mine).

He went on in unmistakable allusion to the UDF and ANC: "In contrast [to the South African government], others are on record as wanting a diminished democracy in the form of a one-party state with restricted personal and other freedoms." R.F. Botha meant South Africa would not countenance the spread, within its borders, of the Soviet-Leninist tactic of "fight and negotiate, negotiate and fight,"—used against the United States in Indochina. Upon the United States' promise to see to the removal of the Cubans from Angola in 1981, he had already negotiated with the MPLA in Angola and FRELIMO in Mozambique, and had allowed negotiations between the provisional government of South West Africa and SWAPO.

The Group coolly answered that unless the government disregarded its strength, and acceded to at most a temporary cessation of violence, the violence would increase: "Unless the cycle of violence is broken, full-fledged guerrilla warfare as practised in other parts of the world, in which 'soft' civilian targets become prime targets in a reign of terror and counter-terror may come to pass." The group here almost literally repeated the threats of the President of the ANC, Oliver Tambo, in Lusaka on January 6,—but they did not say it.

That the ANC should turn negotiations on and off to weaken the government but not to settle,—the Group's underlying attitude,—was spelled out in a SACP Politburo directive of March 1986 that P.W. Botha released upon declaration of the State of Emergency on June 12: "We must continue to make clear that our 'bottom line' for negotiations is the transfer of political power to the majority in a one united democratic South Africa."

The SACP feared good faith negotiations for settlement because they would undermine its drive to seize power: "We must not play into their hands by working out compromises (or being seen to work out compromises) for some hypothetical negotiating which constitutes a retreat from the main aims of the national democratic revolution." But toying with negotiations, the SACP directive went on, especially through the Commonwealth Group and other organizations, brings the whole society into question and divides the "ruling class" both within South Africa and abroad: ". . . The struggle in our country is creating a situation in which the white power bloc is beginning to lose its cohesion. Sections of the ruling class in the imperialist countries, which were previously quite ready to underpin the apartheid system, are also beginning to lose faith in its capacity to protect their interests."[27]

On May 19, the day of the South African raids, Shridath Ramphal, the Commonwealth secretary-general in London, got the mood of the report just right: "Those who are supine now must never speak again in righteous terms in the name of justice, morality or freedom, especially those whose policies help apartheid."[28]

Those who are not for us are against us. An observer suddenly back from the past might have taken such demands for unanimity for evidence we were at war. And we were at war, but we did not recognize it because our minds were at stake, not our bodies. To break the mind, and let the body exist on, but not live—that is totalitarian war, the war that makes you bear witness against yourself. "'Bullets kill. Words prolong the death by giving false hope. It is worse to prolong.'"[29]

The Mediafest: Blut und Erde

In the meantime, as the Group's Report dazzled Washington the media were having the time of their life with South Africa—or, to be more exact, the time of their careers, the poor man's substitute for the love of life. What a price we pay for niggardliness in recognizing greatness!

A doughty warrior of the pen, in a country whose public men and media fear words more than bullets, and abuse them more, Reed Irvine, counted two hundred stories on race in South Africa published in *The Washington Post* and *The New York Times* from May to July 1986, in the newsletter he edits that keeps after the media, *Accuracy in Media.* About a quarter of them in each newspaper ran on the front page, the rest with big headlines, on important inner pages. The stories gave the "overwhelming impression" that South Africa was not in earnest about change.

There was also little perspective, especially in *The New York Times.* Coverage of the rest of southern Africa enjoyed neither space nor prominence with the exception of several substantial stories in *The Post*: Angola, eighteen stories (only two in *The Times*); fifteen on Zambia; Mozambique four (all in *The Post*); one on Tanzania, about lions devouring ten people.

The Post's attention to Angola comes of understanding Savimbi's importance: In 1977 and 1981 it published a series of articles on UNITA among the most important of the handful of first-hand accounts. The 1977 series, the extraordinary work of an American, Leon Dash, who hiked seven-and-a-half months, 3,400 kilometers off roads, mostly away from villages, through forest wilderness, with UNITA guerrillas, first showed that Savimbi had survived the extensive Cuban campaign to destroy him in 1976.

In the same months, the *Times* and the *Post* paid little attention to the killing in Sri Lanka, three to four thousand dead in three years, and to the rioting in India between Sikhs, Moslems and Hindus. They supported the Indian government's strict emergency measures as a matter of course.

Two crucial stories that would have helped put the situation in South Africa in context were all but suppressed: the SACP Politburo directive of March 1986 I have just quoted that shows a concerted Communist strategy to seize power, mentioned fleetingly in the *Times*; and a UPI Story of June 12 on *Médecins sans Frontières*, charging that international agencies like Live Aid, UNICEF, and Save the Children, were allowing the Communist regime in Ethiopia (only nine stories in three months) to use their stations as "bait" to draw hungry people from their homes so they could be transported in brutal conditions away from rebellious territory.[30] The South African government's release of the SACP directive represented a startling break with its previous refusal to reveal sensitive information lest it compromise sources.

On June 24, 1986, *The New York Times* concentrated on discrediting South African government evidence of large numbers of Communists on the ANC Executive Committee,—an update of information in the Denton Hearings. Besides the usual unnamed "critics," the story quoted Tom Lodge, a well-known apologist for the ANC (also the Eminent Persons Group's only cited source besides the ANC), calling him "South Africa's principal white academic expert on the Pretoria government's exiled foes,"—as if the government had some personal grudge against the ANC that had nothing to do with the country.

In contrast, in those days in the wake of the South African government's insistence, and President Reagan's hints in his July 22 speech, the serious European press, including Milan's *Corriere della Sera*, and above all *The Economist*, to its great credit, finally looked the question of Communist control of the ANC in the face. *The Economist* soberly pointed out that the past taught that one-third Communists in a national front were enough to take it over "when the time is ripe."[31]

In contrast to a story eight months earlier (December 1, 1985) on the ANC from Lusaka that had spoken vaguely, quoting an ANC official, of "military actions," the *Times* reporter on June 24 identified the ANC in his own voice, and matter-of-factly, "as the most prominent of the guerrilla movements seeking the overthrow of the government,"—as if it was a well-known fact barely in need of repetition. The story quoted Lodge: "There is no question the ANC is prepared to use violence and that it receives help from the Soviet Union and is generally supportive of Soviet foreign policy."

The *Times* article on the first of December had referred in its last sentence to supplies and training from the Soviet Union as something that "officials in Pretoria say," without making any judgment,—words the editors knew would be dismissed because of contempt for South Africa. It had also spoken in vague terms of "disparate ideological banners" within the ANC as if the ANC were medieval Siena with its flags,—"a spectrum that ranges from Western-oriented liberal democrats to Marxist-Leninists."

After quoting a government pamphlet's description of the ANC as a "Communist-steered terrorist organization" that "does not differ at all from the PLO, IRA, and the Red Brigades," the June 24 story went on to cite the usual unnamed "critics" who took the government's facts and judgments for propaganda—without the word "propaganda" that would have taken the strength from the critics' and the *Times*' quiet aspersions:

But the impressions the document sought to create, critics said, were oversimplified, from selective quotations drawn from Congress documents, and designed to counter *the idea among many blacks that, at some stage, the organization might provide a workable government for a South Africa ruled by the majority* (Italics mine).

My reader will, I hope immediately recognize that the italicized words betray the line of the Eminent Persons Group. The Commonwealth Group's and the *Times*' reporter's source, his unnamed "critics," are UDF and ANC spokesmen. This story neither mentioned the Denton Hearings on Communist infiltration of the ANC, nor the murder, several months later, of its chief witness, Bartholomew Hlapane.

The *Times* went on in its belittlement of Communists in the ANC in its account on August 1 of the celebrations of the sixty-fifth anniversary of the

SACP in London, with the ANC sharing the stage. The story quoted the new chairman of the SACP, Joe Slovo, ridiculing the "Communist bogey" in a rare public appearance, without mentioning that the independent South African press has for years identified Slovo as a KGB agent and that he is head of the terrorist wing of the ANC: "The Communist bogey is being exploited in an attempt to weaken the major force of our liberation, the African National Congress."

The secretary-general of the ANC, Alfred Nzo, went on in Slovo's vein speaking of "hysterical and maniacal anti-communism" that sought to undermine "the drive for liberation of the black majority." Slovo openly argued for "no let-up in 'revolutionary violence' as international pressures grow for compromise,"—an exact paraphrase of the March SACP Politburo directive of March 1986, also, of course, not mentioned.

An article on the ANC in the *Times* Sunday Magazine section on October 12, 1986, based largely on interviews with ANC leaders in Lusaka, finally noted the South African government's "assertion" that Joe Slovo was a colonel in the KGB—without judgment. Finally it noted the Denton Hearings in passing. It stated outright that Slovo was chief of staff of the military arm of the ANC as well as chairman of the SACP,—a connection it described "as a propaganda bonanza . . . for the Pretoria regime,"—as if the question of its truth did not count.

This reporting dreads responsibility for ascertaining facts until it is too late for their significance to make a difference. Once it were too late for choice, the *Times* would immediately matter-of-factly recognize the ANC as a Communist organization trained and controlled by the Soviet Union—because freed of the responsibility of choice. The media chose to hear strong voices against sanctions only after their passage—for instance, from the black Episcopal Bishop of Washington.

The remarkable Mr. Alan Cowell, the *Times*' man in Boerland, who hardly ever made a judgment in his own name, betrayed his cover when he finally tried to deal with black violence against blacks, instead of police brutality, in a major story on necklacing on June 29, 1986. He called the murders "fiery executions," without quotes,—a matter of course in a newspaper that for twenty years had called teenage gang murders in the United States "executions" without quotes: "The tire is filled with gasoline and ignited. The person [not the victim] dies, and a statistic is added to the nation's pain." Mawkish passive language, passive to the point of paralysis, and vague except for one detail: The tires ignited are "used." Mr. Cowell went on:

South African officials often complain that what is depicted in the foreign press as protest is, in fact, largely what they label "black-on-black" violence.
   The term seems designed, the government's critics say, to absolve the white authorities of responsibility for some of the bloodshed and to support the notion that the national State of Emergency is justified not as quelling dissent but as quelling random violence so as to permit political change.
   By official accounts—all that are available under the press restrictions imposed

by the emergency decree—hundreds of the 1,900 fatalities recorded in 21 months of violence and protest have been caused by "black-on-black violence."

Yet the term, the government's critics say, is misleading since in many instances feuding among blacks in the townships reflects not so much the savagery implied by the official view, but the results of a bitter war between those who style themselves anti-apartheid freedom fighters and those they see as stooges of a white authority standing in the way of black majority rule.

I ask my readers to reread these "winged words." They need to be read as carefully as a classical text. They are the unnamed prayers of our times—just as the gulags and the concentration camps are its cathedrals.

Our man Cowell, or rather his unnamed informants, take the horror that gripped the South African government and South Africa at these murders for "an official view" that mistook a "bitter war" for "savagery"—a "bitter war . . . between *anti-apartheid freedom fighters* [Crocker's phrase before the House Subcommittee on African Affairs on March 12] and . . . *stooges of white authority* standing in the way of black majority rule." Not much space for the government there, or for plain murder,—a stunning confirmation of Hobbes' understanding that without governments you cannot say the word *murder*. The government's determination shown in the State of Emergency to end "random violence" in order to go on with reform that is already moving the whole society, black and white, in its depths, is merely a pretext for crushing "dissent." "Bitter war" excuses atrocity, although the *Times* took to righteousness at the hint of inadvertent atrocities in the resistance in Nicaragua, let alone from American troops in combat. Cowell's story went on with several paragraphs of quotes from unidentified blacks justifying murder.

Winnie Mandela got to the heart of Cowell's complicated paraphrase. Because blacks were murdering blacks, the government and South African whites had no cause for horror or words like "savagery." The blacks could take care of themselves, and did: "I know of no white victim of necklacing, and yet that was where the hysteria came from,"—a remark that took the breath away from its reporter.[32]

Just after these remarks Cowell identified his "critics" as "anti-government activists." In other words, members of the UDF and the ANC he did not name, to imply they were disinterested experts. "What does the UDF stand for?" "Uniroyal, Dunlop and Firestone"—a joke passing from lip to lip in the eastern Cape at the time of Cowell's story.

After the cancellation of the limited State of Emergency in February, black murders of blacks, mostly burnt to death, had exceeded the dead in police actions to control rioting: 87 to 57 in March; 58 to 11 in April; 114 to 35 from May 1 to 18,—according to official statistics that Cowell did not report.

A State Department Cable; Reagan's July 22 Speech

Reagan's speech on July 22, 1986 showed that the White House could not recover the ground it had lost the year before when it chose preemption of sanctions instead of fighting outright that would have forced the issue into the open. Both *The New York Times* and James Reston remarked that Reagan wanted it both ways: He wanted to argue against sanctions he had already imposed.

But wanting it both ways went much deeper than *The New York Times* and Reston dreamt: A cable from the State Department, to all major embassies sketching Reagan's speech against sanctions ten days before delivery, turned the themes of Clough's article and of the Commonwealth Group Report into policy that amounted to an outline of the CAA Act that Congress passed a few weeks later.

The gravity of the situation in South Africa and southern Africa,—the cable ran,—had led the President to reassess policy and suggest "specific actions" to end apartheid and to establish a "democratic form of government." The President would call upon the South African government for a timetable to eliminate "*all* apartheid laws" (including presumably, the Group Areas Act and The Registration of Populations Act, named in the CAA Act); to release Nelson Mandela and "all political prisoners" (despite the absence of that category in South African law, and Amnesty International's refusal of it to Nelson Mandela); "to begin serious dialogue about a democratic system of government,"—all demands of the Clough article, the Commonwealth Group, and the CAA Act.

The instructions also called for "intensive consultations with key allies and South Africa's neighbors [the "Front-Line States"] to encourage regional trade, private investment and transport in southern Africa, with a focus on its landlocked states now *overwhelmingly and artificially* dependent on South Africa," and for the continuation of the two-year, forty-five million dollar program for black political and community groups. The United States would "use its full influence . . . in concert with its friends to push for change in South Africa"—except for "punitive economic sanctions."

The railway lines meant in the vague reference to "transport in southern Africa" are the Benguela line in Angola, the Beira line and road in Mozambique kept out of commission most of the time by the resistance. The organization meant is the Southern African Development Coordination Conference (SADCC) that Mugabe founded, right after assuming power, to counter Botha's offer of a plan for southern Africa,—an organization that exists on the dole and has little private business backing. The instructions' use of the adjective "artificial" echoes SADCC propaganda denying South Africa's actual economic predominance.

By linking the end of apartheid, not only to the coming of democracy in South Africa, but also to the end of the war in southern Africa, the instructions called for the United States to join the other side, not only in South Africa but throughout southern Africa—all themes hinted at, in blank disarming terms, in Reagan's speech ten days later. Castro made the connection between the war in southern Africa and apartheid only a few weeks later, at the Non-Aligned meeting in Harare on September 1 when he announced that the Cubans would not leave Angola "for as long as apartheid exists."[33]

The instructions differed from Reagan's speech, in fact undermined it, in one crucial matter: They ordered American embassies in southern Africa *to open up contacts with the ANC.* In his speech, in contrast, Reagan mentioned the ANC in name twice, first with details of its terrorism and then to identify its Soviet arms. He referred to it, without naming it, in the most important sentence in the speech, a line that Patrick J. Buchanan, an intelligent White House aide, managed to insert just three hours before delivery. This sentence went to the heart of what Reagan really thought, unlike the rest of the speech whose framework came from the State Department: "But the South African government is under no obligation to negotiate the future of the country with any organization that proclaims a goal of creating a Communist state, and uses terrorist tactics and violence to achieve it." Apparently Reagan himself added "and violence."[34]

Immediately spotted by intelligent reporters, like the Washington correspondent for the *Neue Zürcher Zeitung*, the sentence made an uproar. Shultz was apparently furious—and for good reason: The sentence was the last gasp against the destruction of "constructive engagement" that Shultz's cable had made plain ten days before,—without public acknowledgment.

Two or three days later the White House ate its words. President Reagan had not wanted it in two ways: He had wanted it in one way, the State Department and Congress in another.

Before the State Department cable and Reagan's speech, the SACP Politburo directive in March 1986 had taken the full significance of these overtures to the ANC and of this commitment to change. But the SACP did not expect the United States to outflank, not only the South African government, but also South African liberals, with a position barely distinguishable from "one-man, one-vote, once"—as they call it in Africa:

... There appears to be a proliferation of new groupings which consider themselves to be part of the *forces for change* but which cannot necessarily be embraced as part of what we regard as the *revolutionary force* ... It is [the "liberal" bourgeoisie] and their likeminded imperialist friends which triggered off the current series of talks and dialogue with the ANC ...

Sensing the inevitability of change, important sectors of the white power bloc and some imperialist strata [the United States and Great Britain] are themselves beginning to seek transformation involving mainly extension of varying forms of political democracy within the framework of capitalism.

The Eyes of the British Empire Upon It, Congress Plunges

The State Department cables that transformed American policy were secret, but the CAA Act that turned them into law, and added sanctions, is public. But it might as well have been secret: The United States, and the world, knows as little about the law as about the cables, except for sanctions.

Upon first reading the law, I could not believe my eyes, before the almost indescribable tangle of juridical incoherence, complete with violations of customary international law now taken more or less for granted, of the UN Charter, and of United States laws, especially the laws that forbid discrimination by color or race.

In a confusion of last hope masking as doubt, I showed the text in the *Congressional Record* to a reference librarian at the Columbia Law Library who with the aplomb of a Roman jurist, the light of recognition glancing in her eyes, asked me what authority else I wanted—besides the voted text! The law reads like it had been written by undergraduate "activists" in the sixties,—and it probably was, for former "activists" have been everywhere in the government for the last ten years.

I asked myself how it happened that nobody noticed: *Time, US News and World Report, The New York Times* had run not even a mention, *The Washington Post* little more than a hint, of the fighting over sixty-five amendments that possessed the Senate for several days in the middle of August,—and which had turned the law into a patchwork of contradictions.

How was it that Congress had not noticed the frequent sloppiness, the tell-tale slips that showed they could not distinguish between a legitimate government, a phrase only the ANC and the totalitarians use, and thugs? For instance, the repeated characterization of necklacing (Sections 108, 211) as "executions by fire," without quotes. The truth is that Congress had counted more on the anonymity that passes for respect of privacy now pervading much of American life than the State Department had. They had sensed that public words and acts anybody could read now provide more cover than secrecy because the media fat on indiscretions despise anything the plain day can see. Besides, who cares about a law whose passage, and whose override of the presidential veto, was taken for granted,—even by the White House?

The law repeatedly calls for an end of the State of Emergency (Section 101,b,1; 106,d,1; 310,a,2), making it one of the preconditions for lifting sanctions, a provision, like other provisions, that flies in the face of Chapter 7 of the UN Charter that prohibits interference in domestic affairs: "Nothing contained in the present Charter shall authorize the United Nations to intervene in matters which are essentially within the domestic jurisdiction of any state . . ."

I asked myself why on earth in the face of obvious violence, Congress and even the President of the United States, who had accused the government's State of Emergency of exceeding "the law of necessity," an obscure phrase, reminiscent of the Commonwealth Group's attitude, went up in arms at the State of Emergency? They seemed incapable of understanding Foreign Minister R.F. Botha's words: "The intimidation and killing of people must stop. Unless you do that, normal democratic rules that we are all attached to, will be eroded to such an extent that nothing will remain of democracy . . . So there are times like that for us, when those very norms which are so dear to Americans, and, I believe to us, are threatened, and when the normal procedures at your disposal are inadequate and insufficient, then the government has the painful decision to take."[35] R.F. Botha might have been paraphrasing Lincoln.

Did the Congress and the President no longer know the Constitution of the United States provides for the suspension of *habeas corpus* (Article I, Section 9) ". . . When in cases of Rebellion or Invasion the Public Safety may require it." Barely more than a hundred years ago, on July 4, 1861, the men who then held their offices, had heard Lincoln in special session:

. . . [The issue] presents the question, whether discontented individuals, too few in numbers to control administration, according to organic law, in any case, can always, upon the pretences made in this case, or any other pretences, or arbitrarily, without any pretence, break up their Government, and thus practically put an end to free government upon the earth. It forces us to ask: "Is there, in all republics, this inherent and fatal weakness?" "Must a government of necessity, be too *strong* for the liberties of its own people, or too *weak* to maintain its own existence?"

. . . The attention of the country has been called to the proposition that one who is sworn to "take care that the laws be faithfully executed," should not himself violate them . . . Must [the laws] be allowed to finally fail of execution, even had it been perfectly clear, that by the use of the means necessary to their execution, some single law, made in such extreme tenderness of the citizens' liberty, that practically, it relieves more of the guilty, than of the innocent, should, to a very limited extent be violated? To state the question more directly, are the laws, but one, to go unexecuted, and the government itself to go to pieces, lest that one be violated? Even in such a case, would not the official oath be broken, if the government should be overthrown, when it was believed that disregarding the single law, would tend to preserve it? But it was not believed that this question was presented. It was not believed that any law was violated. The provision of the Constitution that "The privilege of the writ of *habeas corpus*, shall not be suspended unless when, in cases of rebellion or invasion, the public safety may require it," is equivalent to a provision—is a provision—that such privilege may be suspended when, in cases of rebellion, or invasion, the public safety *does* require it. It was decided that we have a case of rebellion, and that the public safety does require the qualified suspension of the writ which was authorized to be made . . .[36]

Without the authorization of Congress, that the Chief Justice ruled necessary for Lincoln's suspension of *habeas corpus*, Lincoln in 1861 arrested many members of the Maryland legislature to prevent their vote to secede, clearly not a response to "invasion," at best, an anticipation of "rebellion." More than three hundred newspapers were suppressed, at one time or another, and more than fifteen thousand men were arrested without charge or published evidence in the North in the following years. There was uproar and scandal, and cries of "military usurpation," that strengthened the government after trying it,—because the attacks provoked public support. In a famous instance in 1863, Clement Vallandigham lost an election for governor of Ohio by one hundred thousand votes, in the face of a campaign in newspapers and pulpits throughout the country against his arrest, in defiance of a writ of *habeas corpus*, for exciting desertion and resistance to conscription.

But public support did not make these actions legal. It only showed some people understood the reasons that drove Lincoln beyond the law. James Stockdale recently saw into the character it takes to make this sort of decision:

> It takes a strong man, and one who has confidence in his cleverness and sense of humor to hold . . . the position that democracy has limits of applicability in the face of you-know-what kinds of ridicule . . . What do you rely on in those cases? A heritage, a sense of values, common sense, and your own willingness as a leader . . . to realize and not kid yourself, but face the fact that what is just and what is moral cannot be achieved easily, if at all, within the constraints of what law you have. And then to act on that realization, on your own cognizance, without the protection of any "approval from on high," and make order out of chaos by your own best lights . . . How do you sleep at night? You just live on hope that history will treat you well.
>
> "My gosh," you say. "If the world can get like this, what's to protect us from tyrants?" The short answer is that you just have to hope that the man who finds himself in charge, is well brought up—well enough brought up to handle it.[37]

But the past does not count for much now in Congress. Neither the American nor the South African past—the past that affords the best self-knowledge for any time, and, thereby, the best measure of its love of life, and the only sure guide in distinguishing policy from illusion.

Sanctions, the prohibition of loans to the South African government, of any further investment by United States nationals in South Africa, of import of textiles, agricultural products, iron, steel, uranium, coal, sugar, Krugerrands, the cessation of all air connections by both American and South African companies between the two countries,—a provision conceived simply to humiliate the Republic,—all well-known measures, are the least of the law. Comprehensive, in all senses of the word, the CAA Act entangles the United States in all aspects of domestic political life in South Africa, and encourages it to play a leading role in southern Africa against South Africa.

The first words of the law, repeated again and again throughout, betray its deep changes in American policy, for they obliterate the distinction between reform, or the dismantlement of apartheid, a process that once started, common sense men would understand, needs time, and introduction of one-man, one-vote—the very distinction Julian Amery called crucial in Parliament a few months before: "The purpose of this Act is to set forth a *comprehensive and complete framework* to guide the efforts of the United States in helping bring an end to apartheid in South Africa and lead to the establishment of a *nonracial, democratic* form of government . . ." (Section 4, Italics mine). "Nonracial" means the United States will not countenance federal solutions that recognize ethnic differences but that provide against their economic exploitation and, to some extent, against their social reinforcement. "Democratic" means one-man, one-vote: "The United States policy toward the government of South Africa shall be designed to bring about reforms in that system of government that will lead to the establishment of a nonracial democracy" (Section 101a).

Almost immediately after the law holds that "the establishment of a nonracial democracy" will mean not only negotiations "with representatives of all racial groups in South Africa" about "the future political system in South Africa," but also the "end" of "military and paramilitary activities aimed at neighboring states" (Section 101a, 5 and 6). In other words, no aid to Savimbi,

RENAMO, or defense of South West Africa, which will have "independence" and a "nonracial democracy" in accordance with UN Security Council Resolution 435 (Section 104b,1). Resolution 435 facilitates a SWAPO takeover, especially without the unmentioned withdrawal of the Cubans.

The United States will pursue negotiations both at home and abroad. Within South Africa: "United States policy will seek to promote negotiations among representatives of all citizens of South Africa to determine a future political system that would permit all citizens to be full participants in the governance of their country" (Section 106a,1). Abroad, the United States will take the place of the South African army "by encouraging, and when necessary strongly demanding [!] that all countries of the region take effective action to end crossborder terrorism" (104a, 5).

Instead of soldiers, words with everybody, Clough's world: Hostilities fifteen years old are simply to disappear upon the United States' request. In addition, there are hints, here and there, of a policy against the homelands, for instance, in the prohibition of help for law enforcement to their governments (Section 304a, 8) and in the refusal of "any recognition" (Section 605).

Within South Africa, the law calls "suspension of violence by all parties" (without recognition of the sovereignty of the South African government), an "essential precondition . . . for negotiations" (Section 106b). "Suspension," not renunciation, the words and thinking of the Commonwealth Group.

At the same time, the law does what it can to weaken the government it urges to risky negotiations. It forbids aid and the sale of equipment: computers, spare parts and weapons to, and cooperation with, the "military," the "police," the "prison system," "national security agencies," and "armed forces"—except for intelligence, the last a bit of sanity the act owes to the US Navy (Sections 304a; 318a ii; 322). To speed change, through negotiation, the law impatient of its prize like an inexperienced seducer urges meetings of "high-level officials," the president, the secretary of state, "with the leaders of opposition organizations of South Africa, particularly but not limited to those organizations representing the black majority" (section 106a, 2). This means the White House should receive the president of the ANC, Oliver Tambo—but may still talk, if it must, to the South African government. In the footsteps of the Commonwealth, the United States ambassador should visit Nelson Mandela in Pollsmoor Prison (Section 109). Should he make the pilgrimage three times—like the Group political tourists?

The United States in the anticipation of change, speed again, should challenge the system, not only negotiate: "In anticipation of the removal of the system of apartheid and as a further means of challenging that system, it is the policy of the United States to assist those victims of apartheid as individuals and through organizations to overcome the handicaps imposed on them by the system of apartheid and to help prepare them for their rightful roles as full participants in the political, social, economic, and intellectual life of their country in the post-partheid South Africa envisioned by this Act" (Section 103).

Section 202b provides for not less that 500,000 dollars (of $1,500,000) for each fiscal year for outright political activity, for "direct legal and other assistance to political detainees and prisoners and their families, including the investigation of the killing of protestors and prisoners, and *for support for actions of black-led community organizations to resist, through nonviolent means, the enforcement of apartheid policies* . . . An additional $175,000 shall be made available to black groups in South Africa which are actively working toward a multi-racial solution for the sharing of political power in that country through non-violent constructive means" (Italics mine). Section 205a,b provides for ten million dollars in 1987 for housing for black employees of the United States government, called "victims of apartheid," in "neighborhoods . . . open . . . to . . . other employees of the United States government in South Africa," presumably in white areas in violation of the Group Areas Act that the South African government is loosening.

Section 511a provides for forty million dollars in "fiscal year 1987, and each fiscal year thereafter," to assist "disadvantaged South Africans" in "activities that are consistent with the objectives of a majority of South Africans for an end to the apartheid system and the establishment of a society based on non-racial principles. Such activities may include scholarships, assistance to promote the participation of disadvantaged South Africans in trade unions and private enterprise, alternative education and community development programs."

This section (511b) also provides that no money shall be given to "organizations or groups . . . financed or controlled by the government of South Africa,"—a provision that might lead to the exclusion of Buthelezi's Inkatha, the only large black grassroots organization (1,300,000 members), and the only one that somewhat bridges the gap between homelands and townships.

Several provisions foresee obvious abuse nobody will do anything about: For instance, Section 211 forbids money "to any individual, group, organization, or member thereof, or entity that directly or indirectly engages in, advocates, supports or approves the practice of execution by fire, commonly known as 'necklacing.'" A witless and uninformed Senator, Claiborne Pell, disingenuously but rightly questioned enforceability: He wanted no obstacles to the march of time. In the same breath that it weakens the capacity of the entire South African government to enforce the law, Congress also (Section 312) bears witness to its abhorrence of "necklacing."

A schoolboy reading this farrago of provisions, and protestations of good intentions, would rightly assume the United States wanted to overthrow the government of South Africa. Buthelezi seized upon this theme, the law's exploitation of the desire to end apartheid to justify the undoing of the South African government, in an unreported speech at Boston University on November 17, 1986, barely a month after passage of the CAA Act.

Buthelezi said the South African government had started a process that would not allow apartheid to survive. Activists who knew nothing of the hard labor of day-to-day, face-to-face political work, and international organizations abroad, wanted to turn the hatred of apartheid against South African institutions essential for liberty: ". . . Apartheid can now no longer possibly survive for any length of time. South Africa is in the process of radical transition . . .

Success in the real struggle in South Africa is now not dependent on whether apartheid can be eradicated . . ."; "[All too many] fail to see that the way in which apartheid is eradicated holds vital implications for the future . . . It is as though any means are good enough"; ". . . [The purveyors of violence] clamour the most for sanctions because they want more poverty. [They] do not have to permeate black power into South Africa's institutional life. They want to break that institutional life and they want to do it by breaking the economy." The last, almost a paraphrase of Lenin's remark that destruction of its currency was the quickest way to overcome a country.

"South Africa is slowly but surely developing a revolutionary climate in which *applauded radicalism* threatens to destroy the very foundations on which any real democracy will have to be built." Buthelezi had a more likely view of the future the CAA Act "envisioned" than Congress: "I do not strive to produce a future in which I will have to govern by the gun."

Western audiences', and especially Western media's, yearning for thrills at the cost of other people's blood, made them a patsy to extremists' exploitation of apartheid to justify violence:

. . . And close to the heart of the problem those of us face in moderating the hideousness of violence in our midst, is the fact that the media raise sentiment to indignant heights and endow radicals with praise and moderates with reserve and even condemnation . . .

Sensational reporting minimizes the efforts of middle-ground leadership and maximizes the efforts of leadership in violent confrontation. Newspapers with occasional strokes of the pen create celebrity leaders. TV cameras flash myths about black leadership and carpets are rolled out in the United States for fast-talking, midstream horse-changing jockeys. It is as though there is a Western hunger for heroic freedom fighters, *regardless of what the consequences of all this is in terms of the destruction of the foundations of true democracy* (Italics mine).

The ANC and its "surrogate" the UDF that the CAA Act seeks to turn into the government's principal interlocutors use violence to intimidate— because they do not have the following that comes from day-to-day political activity without intimidation:

It is insufficiently realized in countries such as the United States that at the heart of the turmoil in South Africa there is a *life and death struggle* taking place which is, bluntly put, a power struggle. The African National Congress Mission in Exile regards itself as a *government in exile*. It has observer status at the United Nations, the OAU, and at meetings of the Commonwealth and Non-aligned countries and everywhere it represents itself as the sole, authentic voice of the people of South Africa. It constantly talks about itself as the vanguard movement in the struggle for liberation. It arrogates unto itself the right to plan the struggle, to conduct the struggle, and to direct events in it. It is hungry for power that it will need if it has to achieve *the position in reality which it now claims in its propaganda.*

For the ANC Mission in Exile the primary means of liberating South Africa must be violence. It has moved from conducting the classical armed struggle against South African security forces and the South African government to initiating what in their own words is a people's war. *The violence which is reported in black South African townships* is more often than not violence perpetrated in the black South African power struggle. The plight of the responsible black leader in South Africa is that this is just not sufficiently recognized. "Necklacing," streetcorner butchering by mobs, hand grenades thrown into black houses, are all too often reported as black anger against apartheid when they are no more than dastardly deeds of power-hungry forces (Italics mine).

In another unreported speech, several months before, to the National Urban League in San Francisco on July 21, 1986, Alan Keyes, then still assistant secretary for international organization affairs, anticipated Buthelezi's argument against the connection between the end of apartheid and the overthrow of the South African government drawn in the CAA Act. He knew that only the government responsible for the past could cope with greater freedom:

No one can say that the whirlwind of violence will not give birth to a tyranny of violence, rejecting racism only so that it may oppress all equally . . . without the sense of a positive good to be preserved and realized, the struggle against evil is determined and defined by evil itself . . . Strange as it may seem, in that future South Africa—the very community that today maintains a system to repress freedom in South Africa— could be the anchor and shield against repression.

Keyes could have written the speech President Reagan deserved. He understood you had to be for something, not only against things.

The ANC, the UDF, and the SACP, in contrast, count on the connection Buthelezi wants to cut, and the CAA Acts makes, between the hatred of apartheid and the overthrow of the South African government through unconditional negotiations during "suspension of violence." Suspicious of negotiations, they also know that negotiations at the right time can lead to the seizure of power, as the March 1986 SACP directive put it:

[The liberal bourgeoisie and their external allies] seek transformation through negotiation and not the kind of conflict which would culminate in a revolutionary seizure of power . . . to implement this tactic, they, together with their external allies, can be expected to attempt to push the revolutionary forces into negotiations before they are strong enough to impose the basic objectives . . . At the same time we must not mechanically dig in our heels against any further possibility of negotiation or compromise with other forces. We must remember that virtually all revolutionary struggles in the post-war period (Algeria, Vietnam, Angola, Mozambique, etc.) reached their final climax at the negotiating table. But the question of negotiation usually arises at a time of major revolutionary climax involving the transfer of power based on massive strength of the people's offensive. At such a stage we have to judge what interim compromises are historically justified and take the people with us. *The main thrust of our present strategy remains a revolutionary seizure of power.*

The discussion in the Senate, really only a medley of declarations, that surrounded the crucial Helms amendment on ANC violence, made it clear that Congress could not draw a meaningful distinction between the South African government and terrorists. This confusion showed in the CAA Act's equation of the end of apartheid with the introduction of "democracy" rather than with evolutionary change.

Teddy Kennedy argued that the Helms amendment sought to take advantage of "the instincts of the American people, who deplore violence . . ." to "disrupt" the "legitimate purposes" of the CAA Act, after stating that he, like nearly everybody else, was against violence:

Mr. President, I yield to no one in this body and to no one in the Congress of this United States and to no one in America or any other person in this world about the issue of violence.

Just before he voted against the amendment despite revisions, Kennedy went on:

All of us, for example, deplore terrorism. But this amendment does not include any mention of the terrorist activities of the government of South Africa, with its government policy of torture and beating and killing—of men, women and children . . . There is no mention about other forms of government terrorism—about detainees being separated from their families—some detainees as young as 12, 13, and 14 years old.

After calling the secretary of state's offer to talk to leaders of the ANC "that represents millions of black South Africans," "a glimmer of light," Senator Charles Mathias gave what amounted to a gloss of the final Helms amendment: "I would agree with the Senator [Helms] that little progress can be made as long as anyone resorts to violence and terrorism in whatever form—including the Government of South Africa whose armed forces often rely on firepower to enforce the will of a discredited political system."

These statements and others that equated law enforcement with terrorism led to revisions that reversed the Helm's amendment's intent and won it passage by a large margin (67–31): "If the South African government agrees to enter into negotiations without preconditions [again the language of the Commonwealth Group], abandons unprovoked violence against its opponents, commits itself to a free and democratic post-apartheid South Africa under a code of law; and if nonetheless the African National Congress, the Pan African Congress, or other organizations refuse . . . to abandon unprovoked violence during the negotiations [again, not renunciation, but a truce] . . . then the United States will support negotiations which do not include these organizations" (Section 311c). Helms' original draft did not refer to the "violence" of the South African government at all, and spoke simply of the "violence" of the ANC without the qualification "unprovoked."

As I was writing the preceding words, I came across "An Appeal to the World Community" issued by the ANC at a conference openly called a "Council of War" in Lusaka, Zambia from June 15 to 23, 1985:

Apartheid cannot be reformed. It has to be destroyed. To wipe out this crime against humanity requires a sustained and determined campaign on the part of our people and the international community. There must be no "constructive engagement," only total opposition to the racist regime and active support and solidarity for our struggle and the ANC, . . .

- Intensify the campaign to isolate racist South Africa in the economic, political, diplomatic, military, educational and cultural fields (Section 106d; 401b(1); 501c2; 506a).
- Impose mandatory sanctions through the UN Security Council (Section 401be).
- End all nuclear collaboration with apartheid South Africa (Section 307).
- Demand the immediate and unconditional release of Nelson Mandela and all other political prisoners (Section 101,2; 311a1).
- Increase diplomatic, financial and material support and develop solidarity with the ANC (Section 106a2; 109, and elsewhere throughout the act, despite some limitations).
- Demand the immediate independence of Namibia (Section 104b1).
- Demand that the racist regime stop its aggression against the Front Line States and Lesotho (Section 101a6).
- Give all forms of support to these innocent victims of fascist aggression and expansionism (Section 104a7; 210).

Every one of these demands appears in the Comprehensive Anti-Apartheid Act either as a provision or as an expression of "the sense of Congress," as the CAA Act sections numbers I have added to each "demand" show.

Through the thousand and one "academic experts," through "think tanks" in Washington like the Institute for Policy Studies, through political tourists like the "Eminent Persons Group," through the divines, through astrologers, through unemployed kids on campuses, through the UN, especially through the UN Special Committee on Apartheid, through the OAU, through the media, especially *The New York Times*, through the many lobbying groups, especially through TransAfrica, WOA, ACOA, FSAM and on and on in the forest of acronyms, through SADCC, the transmission belt from Lusaka to Washington has spun back and forth over the ocean,—a belt that speaks for nobody, except the top ANC, because it pretends to speak for everybody. The Congress of the United States had passed a law largely conceived in Lusaka,— and in more well-known capitals beyond. It might have, at least, concocted its own recipe for the destruction of South Africa.

In the sorry spectacle of this act's passage, there was only one voice of unmistakable opposition: Denton's. He was the only man to use the word sovereignty in a chamber of men who never ceased to talk as if the South African government was not sovereign but never said so outright: ". . . Not withstanding our unanimous desire to effect the elimination of apartheid, at least in passing one must note that the United States possesses neither the right nor the power to impose forthwith its own standards on other sovereign nations."

Of all the senators who spoke in the struggle over the amendments, only Denton betrayed the seriousness of the situation. The Senate is not made for debate. The design of its chamber, roughly the same half-moon shape of the UN General Assembly shows its function: a meeting place for ambassadors from the states to make statements, statements directed, with the formality of another time, in the third person, to the presiding officer.

But Denton talked as if he was in the House of Commons, as if he could persuade, like an American Cervantes. His intelligence leaves its imprint because it is bigger than his words, always. You would think his words would have counted, you would think the other senators, most of them with little experience of foreign affairs and knowledge of the world outside the United States, would have listened to a colleague with eight years in Vietnamese Communist prisons and concentration camps at his back who knows something about the way the world that threatens us really works,—who has had the "short course."

But Denton did not count, not for Weicker, not for Kennedy, not for Moynihan, not for Sarbanes, all men who cannot bear their own words, let alone those of a man with incomparably deeper knowledge of war and peace, and of South Africa, in the scars of his own flesh and soul. Denton sounded like a man in a crowded subway station at rush hour, with everybody determinedly on their way, a station that he happened to know was afire, who could not get anybody to listen without choking smoke:

Mr. President, I beseech my colleagues at this time to agree with me that each side needs to listen to the other.
Mr. President, may we have order?
The PRESIDING OFFICER. The Senator from Alabama is going to be heard on his amendment. Will those Democratic Senators engaged in conversation retire to the cloakroom? Will Democratic staffers please take their seats or retire?
On the Republican side, the same request is made. Will those Senators engaged in conversations in the aisles please take their seats?
Mr. DENTON. Mr. President, I beseech my colleagues to agree with me that each side needs to listen to the other—listen carefully, because the issue of economic sanctions against South Africa will have major effects not only on the people in South Africa, but also on people elsewhere and on the interests of the United States and other Nations. Never before have the words "deliberative body" been more needful of real application to the mood and method which should be applied to the Senate's disposing of this issue. Let us deliberate on facts, on opinions and on likely consequences of proposed U.S. actions.

There has been a strange silence about the enormous largess of the United States to blacks in South Africa, colossal sums of money that even in the United States, let alone in a foreign country, would invite abuse—especially in the hands of inexperienced diplomats, some of them "activists," under a new ambassador without the experience for such a crucial post. In South Africa P.W. Botha began to break this silence in the fall of 1987. In the United States it persisted throughout 1988. The silence about these great sums of money comes, in part, because CAA Act money changes hands almost covertly,—in contrast to conventional aid programs administered with the knowledge of the country's foreign minister. Uneasy, but not uneasy enough to break through the "activist civil-rights" preconceptions they got with their education, American reporters keep silent because they sense something wrong in this meddling.[38]

The provisions for money caught the South African government off-balance in 1986: In October 1986 it forbade foreign funds to the UDF without mentioning the money it probably meant was American. Reliable reports from Americans who have visited South Africa indicate some of this money goes, not to the UDF, but to UDF-ANC approved individuals and organizations,—not openly on political grounds.

To my knowledge, only Buthelezi has spoken out, in 1986 in Boston, without making it clear he meant money from the United States government: "All too frequently . . . both in North America and Europe aid springing from the goodness of heart of noble democrats is used by black South Africans to favour the forces of violence . . . I who seek a radical turning of South Africa on its head to bring about a true democracy, am more often black-listed by donor agencies and donor governments because this label 'moderate' is hung around my neck."

But soon, especially after the passage of legislation forbidding foreign funding, the Republic may have to start expelling meddling American diplomats,—a sorry sight that no uproar will dispel. In early 1987, it refused a visa to a State Department official "who was to examine health conditions . . . to determine the extent of starvation and malnutrition . . . in the 'homelands' areas" (Section 503)—with the pertinent rebuff that other countries in Africa deserved his attention more.

In South Africa, just after the passage of the CAA Act, a professor at Rand Afrikaans University in Johannesburg, Carl Noffke, guessed United States largess might reach one hundred or one hundred and fifty million dollars a year in the next years. He had no illusions about the overriding conception of the CAA Act that first showed itself in Clough's article: "Its intent is clearly to shape black politics for the present, to press black majority rule upon us and then to ensure a government friendly to the United States afterward . . . Naturally there are questions about whether any of this will be to our benefit or whether much of it should not be stopped."

The repeated provisions of the CAA Act that insist on funds only to non-violent organizations serve only to beguile the naive to the cruelty of the disingenuous. Demonstrations, consumer boycotts, work stoppages, school strikes, American-financed in part, and political funerals in the black townships are the other face of the necklace—just as the UDF is the ANC's other face. The thugs rounding up for demonstrations and boycotts showed a matchbox, terror's mace, to reluctant kids.

The law's provisions against abuse of funds betray Congress' flight from responsibility for what it knows will happen. They amount simply to wearing a sentimental mask to exorcise cruelty and murderousness. There is no way of controlling these funds.

The same evasion through outspokenness showed itself in the plaintive remark of an American official in South Africa, unidentified, as usual, just after passage of the CAA Act: "After liberation, we want to see a politically pluralist society in South Africa. Frankly [a word that tells it all], we don't want apartheid replaced with some system modeled on East Germany or Bulgaria." Not what he wants counts, but what he does—especially with actions plain in their consequences.

The gathering uproar about funds may center on black education, a top priority of the South African government. But it has made it clear it will not countenance its politicization. In the chaos, especially in 1985–1986, among black schoolchildren overpowered by the slogan, attractive to schoolboys anywhere, "liberation now, education later," informal schools sprang up, sometimes funded with United States money,—"People's Schools" with political indoctrination. At a conference at Michigan State in late 1986 to promote funding for these "People's Schools," in South Africa, sponsored by the Mott Foundation, State Department and AID officials talked of "math, reading, writing, plumbing." But SWAPO, UDF, ANC radicals from South Africa backed Soviet-style indoctrination. The conference had first defined "People's Education" as any education "not supporting counter-revolutionary values."

A few weeks after final passage of the law, with the override of the President's veto on October 2, 1986, the Washington Office on Africa (WOA) announced: "The fight for sanctions against South Africa has just begun"; "The United States cannot at once abhor apartheid and finance its regional expansion." In other words, the United States was to join the "Front-Line States" in their attack on the "external face of apartheid," the Commonwealth Group's name. It was not only to break the Republic at home but also abroad. Next on the WOA's agenda: resumption of the struggle for the independence of South West Africa, lately "overshadowed by events in South Africa"; the prevention of United States' aid to RENAMO in Mozambique; and above all, the cutoff of United States' aid to Savimbi, who may be not only a fighter but an honorable man, something harder to forgive—or forget.

By the end of 1988 the CAA Act, and especially the threat of further sanctions, had played its part in some of the WOA's goals: South Africa had agreed to withdraw from Namibia before the Cubans withdrew from Angola; American aid to RENAMO, probably faltering, was out of the question; aid to Savimbi was at risk despite assurances from President George Bush and support in Congress.

But even in 1986 the CAA Act was not to be outdone by the WOA, TransAfrica, and the almost innumerable other lobbying groups that conceived it. It called for a report from the president every twelve months "on the extent to which progress has been made in ending the system of apartheid and establishing a nonracial democracy" and, in the absence of "significant progress," for further sanctions, including a provision against the importation of strategic minerals (Section 501).

The braggadocio of an almost immediately following provision (Section 504) underlines the blatantly suicidal character of the prohibition on the future importation of strategic minerals. It instructs the president to "develop a program which reduces the dependence, *if any*, on the strategic minerals from South Africa" (Italics mine)—minerals the drafters know only the Soviet Union possesses.

But this legislation that entangles the United States in the domestic affairs of a foreign land, a European land outside Europe, like the United States and Israel, that sacrificed the lives of twenty-five thousand of its sons in the two

World Wars and the Korean War, will ultimately harm the United States more than South Africa. It will undermine respect for its institutions and its elected officers in the world and in the United States. "All violent policy, contrary to the natural and experienced course of human affairs, defeats itself."[39]

Without much notice the Soviets have opened a front within the United States in the war throughout the world whose target is the United States—and Europe. So much for "politically safe" domestic issues.

The United States has been in a constitutional crisis for more than ten years,—a crisis that never comes to a head but shows hints of itself in scandals and farce and suspicion, and in bizarre legislation like the CAA Act that no novelist would dare invent.

Absence of confidence,—and a reckless sense that domestic life can go on as if the rest of the world did not exist, except for countries like South Africa that are treated in a fit of apparent sudden passion as if they were a part of the United States,—too, tells of this creeping crisis, of a war that destroys without knowing itself as war. This incapacity to even remember that South Africa is a foreign country that hardly anybody in the United States, certainly hardly anybody in Congress, knows anything about, this inability to show elementary respect for strangers, is the most astonishing and most terrifying characteristic of the campaign against South Africa that has now turned into American law. Terrifying because it makes the United States complicit with the Soviet Union. It is the Soviet Union that knows no frontiers; that acts with the same lawlessness abroad, mostly with impunity, as it does at home; that maintains parties in many countries that openly attempt to undermine their governments, something unheard of *in all Western history*.

Strangely, if we lived in less danger, we would experience danger more,—and, thereby, learn modesty and sobriety. Of all peoples, the United States should appreciate what it means to have made a new country in a little more than three hundred years—and in Africa!

The CAA Act is the fruit of a revolt of the Congress and the State Department against the president and the secretary of state, who are meant to lead them in foreign affairs. This revolt against responsible authority that has spread through the institutions of the entire society has been going on since the fall of Saigon, really since 1973 when Congress passed one law after another undermining the president's ability to enforce the accords between South Vietnam and the Communists,—legislation that might have been stopped by Kissinger's resignation or even the threat of his resignation. But Kissinger only spoke his mind on the day Saigon fell,—and his words so late sounded out of place.

Individuals in high office have allowed this revolt to undermine their capacity to make decisions and act. They go along with it, and, thereby, prolong the crisis without facing it. Shultz did not lead the State Department, he consulted it like a patient a doctor,—and he did not seem to get a second opinion.

The Constitution of the United States gives the burden and the responsibility for foreign affairs to the president and the secretary of state,—except for the declaration of war by both Houses and the ratification of treaties and appointment of ambassadors by the Senate, in their time radical limitations meant to distinguish the president of a republic from a monarch. The founding fathers knew individuals had to make decisions in foreign affairs,—not legislatures. They knew that unless individuals took responsibility, nobody would:

> They who have turned their attention to the affairs of men must have perceived that there are tides in them; tides very irregular in their duration, strength and direction, and seldom found to run twice exactly in the same manner or measure. To discern and to profit by these tides in national affairs is the business of those who preside over them; and they who have had much experience on this head inform us that there frequently are occasions when days, nay, even when hours, are precious. The loss of a battle, the death of a prince, the removal of a minister, or other circumstances intervening to change the present posture and aspect of affairs may turn the most favorable tide into a course opposite to our wishes. As in the field, so in the cabinet, there are moments to be seized as they pass, and they who preside in either should be left in capacity to improve them. So often and so essentially have we heretofore suffered from the want of secrecy and dispatch that the Constitution would have been inexcusably defective if no attention had been paid to those objects.[40]

3 Who Knows What's Going On?

For at least a year after the passage of the CAA Act the search for the moral fix went elsewhere. The scandal about the administration's dealings with Iran, to help the resistance in Nicaragua, the severe criticisms of Israel because of disturbances in the West Bank and Gaza more or less kept South Africa off the front pages. Indignation can only stand one issue at a time, narrowness that tells of its self-preoccupation.

Defiance, violence and terrorism touched off both the 1987 campaigns as they had the campaign against South Africa in 1984. In Iran terrorism brought the United States down to its level, a blow to the confidence and authority of the Reagan administration, especially because of the administration's violation of its public professions against dealings with terrorists. The campaign against the administration showed, like the executive's attempt to coopt sanctions against South Africa in 1985, that understandings, to avoid open fights with Congress, do not work: The administration had acquiesced to the Boland amendments prohibiting public aid to the resistance in Nicaragua on the understanding that this did not mean the end of all help. Congress did not want to undermine resistance in Nicaragua without the complicity of the administration.

In the midst of the two campaigns an act of real policy intervened: the American intervention, in the name of classical international law, freedom of the seas, in the Gulf of Persia in the summer of 1987 that by the fall had brought the cooperation of all the major European nations except Germany. A year later, in the summer of 1988, this intervention, especially the American destruction of half of Iran's navy, showed its effect, perhaps decisive, in the first break in a war the West had more or less ignored for eight years: the cease-fire between Iran and Iraq. The euphoria about Mikhail Gorbachev, the underbelly of the moral fix, dulled the appreciation of this consequence of effective free-world policy that the Soviet Union had opposed. American initiative had brought Europe that like Japan, and in contrast to the United States, could not survive without Middle-East oil, to act for itself.

The renewed move for sanctions began punctually in October on the first anniversary of the CAA Act. It was followed in December by a passage of an undebated amendment, slipped into the budget reconciliation bill, forbidding tax credits to firms for taxes paid in South Africa, an increase to 72 percent from 57.5 percent in the corporate tax rate that puts South Africa in the company of Iran, Libya, North Korea, Albania and Syria.

In January 1987 the secretary of state's Advisory Committee on South Africa that President Reagan had appointed in September 1985 had prepared the way for renewed congressional action: It called for more sanctions in the the event of South Africa's intransigence despite minerals that it held should not determine policy. America should also lead other nations to isolate South Africa with sanctions, including sanctions "on newly mined South African gold."

The new "Dellums-Wolpe" bill that passed the House on August 11, just after the Republicans decided against including sanctions against South Africa in their platform in part because of the Angola cease-fire, showed the Democratic party's desire to make South Africa an election issue in order to win black, and above all, white votes: 244, including twelve Republican votes, for; 132 against, 122 Republican with 59 absences, a very high number on a crucial vote. The new bill called for the end of all American investment and loans in South Africa within 180 days; for the end of most trade, not only of imports, already achieved in part by protectionists in 1986, but also of exports with a few exceptions including some minerals; and for a break in all cooperation in intelligence, crucial especially for the Navy. It called for the president to take reprisals against Great Britain, Germany, France, Italy and Japan for increases in trade with South Africa that resulted from their refusal to adopt similar sanctions.

Until the House passage of the "Dellums-Wolpe" bill discussion in congressional circles in Washington had appeared to center on mustering thirty-four votes to uphold a presidential veto in the Senate—without public discussion of sanctions despite elaborate testimony from the administration against sanctions. It was clear that some in the Senate, especially Richard Lugar and Nancy Kassebaum, who had backed the 1986 CAA Act did not want further sanctions.

The general sense was sanctions might be slowed, they might even be stopped, but they could not be argued against openly. In an important report that concentrated on facts, finally, *South Africa, the Dynamics of Isolation*, published by the Economist Intelligence Unit in January 1988, Merle Lipton, tactfully told of her bewildered discovery of the discrepancies between public and private words: "For those engaged in research on this question, it is disconcerting how frequently public utterances of participants in this debate differ from their private, off-the-record assessments, because many people feel constrained from saying publicly what they think."

The malaise this silence betrays, Lipton rightly argued, came because the motives for sanctions are not above suspicion, not only because of demagoguery in the United States, but because of mean miscalculation that took propaganda for irresistible strength, as if words could not be dismissed: ". . . Sanctions are a relatively cheap way of doing something to show Western goodwill towards the Third World as well as distancing Western governments from a government and system they believe will fall."

These unacknowledged motives explain, as Lipton also pointed out, the little attention paid to the political changes sanctions might actually bring. Nobody had seemed much interested in definable results. The urgency of "the large new constituency" for sanctions, a pretty polite word for people who allow themselves to be maneuvered by organizations they do not know, came in part because nobody took these people on in words: "[The misguided belief that a button pressed on Capitol Hill] will automatically lead to the required response in South Africa (or indeed elsewhere) . . . has become an important factor in the sanctions campaign because of the entry into the debate of a large new constituency, which knows little of the historical evolution and internal dynamics of South Africa, and therefore has little basis for interpreting its behavior and anticipating how it might react in the future."

The reluctance to consider sanctions outright showed itself in a crucial *Washington Post* editorial in June 1988 that argued simply against further sanctions because the South Africans were tough enough to resist them despite their costs. Only in its last sentence did it admit doubts about sanctions in general: "But we don't think any new sanctions are justified while such doubt exists about whether the old ones were wise."[41]

Something equivalent to Lipton's readiness to think on her own about sanctions also began to show itself on local levels during the spring and summer of 1988 in the judgments of students, tourists, businessmen who had gone to South Africa to see for themselves. But these voices, really from the grassroots for a change, moved slowly,—they were not programmed,—through word of mouth, in sporadic bits of conversations and in letters to local, and sometimes, in national newspapers.

A letter in 1988 in *The Washington Post* from a visitor to South Africa from Annapolis pointed out that Tutu, the ANC and the UDF represented "only a small number of blacks." "The many blacks I talked to in various parts of the country did not support the UDF or the ANC either." "The uneducated blacks" looked to "tribal leaders," the "educated" said "the reforms of the Botha government, though slow, are the only reasonable answer to eventual political equity": "Whites and blacks need one another and not 'sanctions' was the main theme I heard from blacks."[42]

Reporters were too impatient for such casual, obvious, prosaic talk that anyhow needs the warmth of confidence and privacy, now difficult to distinguish from anonymity, of private encounters among strangers out of the tangle of headlines telling them what they want and think.

Also in 1988, the Annapolis *Evening Capital* printed a letter from a member of the Cape Town City Council in a response to a story it had run on damage of sanctions to the United States that said that despite their differences all thirty-four councillors were "as one in encouraging our government towards reform and an integrated government in South Africa": ". . . But the majority of us want reform in an orderly, peaceful manner and not in a chaotic, violent way as has happened in the majority of African states since the colonial rulers . . . We South Africans are not really vindictive people, I don't think we would impose any restrictions of USA imports from our country."[43]

Such blows for truth were enough for the Canadian government to expel South African Airways and the South African Tourism Board in 1986 after it ran ads urging Canadians to "come see for yourself" on "fact-finding trips" to South Africa, not an action that reassured everyday Canadians. The Canadian prime minister and external affairs minister who in 1985 had pretended they were in Jamaica in order not to receive Buthelezi were not about to countenance information that contradicted the ANC, their main source on South Africa.[44]

Savimbi also made it plain on a visit to the deep South for two daring days of his week in the United States at the end of June 1988 that at the grassroots blacks also thought enough not to all think alike, especially after they heard another side: "We want you to understand both sides so black leaders communicate with Angolan leaders to stop the war." His supporters, outnumbered three-to-one, largely by organized Jackson pickets, shouted "We are against communism." A clergyman: "I hate communism more than apartheid." Blunt, raw words, obvious enough to embarrass, especially against a background of MPLA ads in major newspapers in those days that called Savimbi, "South Africa's Secret Agent,"—courtesy of Fenton Communications whose clients also number the ANC, the Sandinistas, the Salvadoran Farabundo Marti National Liberation Front.[45]

In the same week Savimbi on television's *Nightline* let Randall Robinson get away unchallenged after he asserted that the South Africans had entered Angola before the Cubans, crucial falsification that showed itself in the media also during Savimbi's 1986 visit to Washington. This lie had first won its place in the media after *The Washington Post* in January 1977 reprinted a series of articles by the novelist Gabriel Marquez, soon after their publication in an official Cuban publication, that repeated Castro's assertion in March 1976 that "Cuban military units" first entered Angola on November 5, 1975.[46] Robinson had reportedly received thousands of dollars for TransAfrica from the Cuban Interests Section in Washington in the weeks before Savimbi's visit.

Despite these doubts stirring perceptibly enough to hear, and Lipton's facts, Dukakis yielded to Jackson's demands that the Democratic Platform call South Africa a "terrorist state" in May 1988. "We have no problem calling South Africa a terrorist state because it is a terrorist state," said Representative Robert Matsui, one of Dukakis' members on the platform drafting committee, a man who obviously knows he speaks prose, to preclude the discussion he opened.[47]

Two weeks later, at TransAfrica's eleventh annual banquet, the mayor of Washington called South Africa a "terrorist state," "a major theme of TransAfrica," *The Washington Post* reporter acknowledged. The mayor went on to make it clear the end of apartheid meant "one-man, one-vote,"—"in our lifetime," he added mercifully: "We are going to see one-man, one-vote." With a haughty reminder that no Democratic candidate could win the presidency without the black vote that he assumed TransAfrica could deliver, Randall Robinson called for the next president to move all major nations to isolate South Africa. A month later the mayor of Washington said Savimbi should be treated "as the scourge of the earth he is."[48]

Dukakis' foreign policy advisor wished away Jackson's victory without a fight as "symbolic," because the phrase "state terrorism" came from the 1979 Export Administration Act whose sanctions against nations involved in murder throughout the world like Libya and Iran were much milder than the "Dellums-Wolpe" bill that Dukakis supported. But Jackson's advisor who knew the change of a phrase means "you change the whole political climate" had it right.

As usual, Jackson had not invented the phrase "terrorist state" that the newspapers, also, as usual, did not fathom. Even our demagogues are programmed. The term "state terrorism" had surfaced alongside such phrases as the "illegitimacy of the apartheid regime" at the ANC's conference at Arusha in Tanzania in 1987 to signal the opening of an ANC campaign for international recognition, perhaps precipitated by Canada's hints that it might break relations with South Africa.

The ANC had not invented the phrase either. It had taken it, not from the Export Administration Act that did not use it, but from the Soviets. The Soviets had forged the phrase "terrorist state" in response to the United States' announcement of its readiness not to let terrorism go unpunished that showed itself first in the Export Administration Act. By calling the readiness of free nations to defend themselves against terrorism with preemptive and punitive strikes across frontiers "state terrorism" the Soviets meant to confound the United States' definition, and turn it against the West. This classic totalitarian technique also shows in the ANC's and the Soviets' use of "legitimacy," the word that allowed Talleyrand to explain the impossibility of peace in Europe with Napoleon undeposed to Alexander the First.

The ANC's use of the phrase "state terrorism" for South Africa amounted to a call to the leading nations of the world to recognize it, not as they had before as the alternative equal in violence to the South African government, but as the only "legitimate government," a phrase also much on the lips of ANC spokesmen at the Arusha conference. Above all, the ANC wanted a place at the UN, like SWAPO and the PLO, as the "sole, legitimate representative" of the people of South Africa. The ANC that had up to then enjoyed diplomatic recognition from the Soviet Union, Rumania and East Germany, also wanted some sort of diplomatic recognition from the twenty-six capitals that entertain its offices. In April 1986, it opened still another office, in Tokyo, that some

African countries had the nerve to ask the Japanese government to fund because the money from a well-known Japanese Communist front organization did not suffice.[49]

ANC spokesmen at Arusha were nothing but explicit about their new claims for sole recognition. "There is at the moment dual power in South Africa—the Botha regime and the ANC. If Botha power is declared illegitimate, then you have to confer recognition to whatever power is legitimate."[50]

The overcoming of "dual power,"—Trotsky's phrase to describe the six months between democracy and the Bolshevik seizure of the government in Russia,—here means that the ANC judged the divisions the SACP 1986 directive had analyzed deep enough for it to claim to replace the South African government, at least abroad.[51]

The ANC's urgency in seeking the international recognition that Jackson got Dukakis to support with his acceptance of the designation "terrorist state" showed that the ANC realized, in contrast to Western governments and media, that Botha was in earnest about negotiations after the government's reopening of discussion of the National Statutory Council and the release of Govan Mbeki in the fall of 1987. The ANC wanted to use recognition from nations abroad to exclude all other black organizations from the negotiations that it meant to turn into a masked "transfer of power" through insistence on one-man, one-vote. Recognition from abroad, it knew, would also mean support for one-man, one-vote because Western nations were incapable of distinguishing one-man, one-vote from the "dismantlement of apartheid."

As usual also, it took Buthelezi to realize the fear of change that drove the ANC to seek international recognition and the intensification of sanctions in the United States: "Those who want victories by violence fear democratic developments, and they will scream and protest the loudest on the very eve of victory through negotiation," he wrote the Reverend Leon H. Sullivan six months before the ANC conference in Arusha.[52]

Buthelezi, who wanted to persuade Sullivan not to abandon his Sullivan Code, realized that the resort to violence, including sanctions, feared living strength, almost envied it: "Violence now strives to delay progress through negotiations because the politics of negotiation has a potential power which violence does not have."

Buthelezi also understood that P.W. Botha can deal with ANC violence at home and sanctions abroad much more easily than with reform, the "challenge he in fact set out to meet": "Those who want to bring about the downfall through violence attack P.W. Botha where he is strongest."

In order to avoid this unwitting collusion between the ANC, the US Congress and P.W. Botha, the profoundest criticism of Botha I know, the strength of the Africans had to make itself felt without the violence that undermines it:

Please hear me when I say that the way forward is not through confrontation . . . when we meet intransigence, or when we meet racism and when we meet the terrible poverty that we as the dispossessed ["dispossessed," the very word Smuts used in his letter to

Merriman in 1906] of South Africa suffer, we can neither turn left nor right nor can we go backwards. We must stand where we are and forge forward with everything we have got, or die where we stand.

Violence meant fear of change, of actual strength and its self-respect. Buthelezi did not distinguish sanctions from violence, for sanctions also meant to bring down the South African government. They both closed doors that were ajar, and that the whites could not entirely open of themselves, Van der Merwe's dilemma, another way of saying the heart has reasons the mind cannot fathom: "The punitive isolation of South Africa favours the forces of violence. Were it not so they would not be crying out the loudest for it. They know that punitive isolation increases the prospect of bloody revolution finally dictating the course of events in South Africa . . . The going may get a lot tougher yet and we will yet see one Westerner after another withdraw from trying to do something to help the cause of non-violent negotiations in South Africa because disgust deepens."

Buthelezi's use of the word "disgust" betrayed the depth that allows him to perceive the fear of change in the organizations at home and abroad that cry out most for it. No other campaign against any other nations stirs such disgust,—"revulsion" Lipton calls it,—even in, especially in, people who have not seen the country. In one way or another almost every speaker who wants to say a word in favor of South Africa tries to exorcise this disgust, usually by confessing his own disgust with apartheid. Public men from abroad do it unashamedly to the South Africans' faces in their own country. But such disgust so freely exhibited betrays not simple conviction but conflicts deeper than comprehending that people cannot simply tolerate and that will not go away.

Buthelezi's depth also allowed him, the example of southern Africa especially before his eyes, to defend the sovereignty of South Africa, in contrast to *The Washington Post*, not because its government is tough enough to resist those who want to undo it, but because no change, except for the worse, would be possible without it: "Everywhere in the Third World, political victories which have been followed by deepening poverty have not led to decent democracies."

Helen Suzman, in contrast, on the op-ed page of *The Washington Post* on the day of its editorial against further sanctions, wrote ambiguously enough to allow a reader to think she might be for a revolution that might succeed: "But given the obduracy and the military strength of the present government, it must be conceded that any prospect of a transfer of power by the National Party government is just not on the agenda."[53]

The reason the going was getting tougher, the forces of violence more desperate and insatiate, was that "Time is running for us." Like Biko eleven years before, Buthelezi sensed the change the ANC wanted to stop and the United States Congress dared not trust because it meant trusting a sovereign government, and a largely white one at that. Like an oncoming birth this change would call its own time: "Let us struggle our way, let us employ that bargaining power the way it should be employed in the ripeness of the time that could descend upon us with amazing rapidity. Be with us when that happens."

Sullivan, a few weeks later, forsook his own guidelines for the call for total withdrawal and the isolation of South Africa, the ANC's line. Sullivan's good intentions did not go deep enough to resist intimidation despite Buthelezi's classic words. The "good works" Sullivan had persuaded, and coerced, from American companies had served to spread illusions about American companies' political, instead of economic, power that reinforced demands for their withdrawal. The South Africans took the destructiveness that had surfaced from beneath the good intentions, for destructiveness excited by them that had led Sullivan to embrace the positions he had sought to resist. For instance, *Business Day*, in words barely comprehensible in Washington:

> ... Archbishop Tutu never explained to us what benefit the impoverishment of South Africa might bring, and few other people could see much benefit in the sanctions campaign. Sullivan's code of conduct for American corporations seemed, therefore, a sensible way to moderate the pressure for withdrawal. From the start it had its limitations. American businesses pay worse salaries, and maintain more exploitative practices, in other parts of the world than they ever did in South Africa. If they did not do so, they would have to pack up and go home, because they could not hope to make a commercial profit. But nobody would complain if their South African wages were a little better, if they trained more black people than whites, if they provided education for their workers' children, and if they set aside a little of their profits for good works. The more profitably they operated, the more they invested, the more they—yes, say it—exploited the local conditions, the more jobs and training and prosperity they brought to South Africa. Beyond that, the efforts of the corporations to foster change in South Africa were futile. Whatever they did, government could easily counter or forbid or undo. No extra pressure from abroad could make of such weak instruments an effective weapon against a sovereign state. As an alternative to withdrawal, the Sullivan Code had some propaganda value; as an instrument of pressure on the South African government, it was useless. The Reverend Sullivan, in calling for total withdrawal, has succumbed to the folly which he tried at the outset to moderate. The irony is obvious.[54]

In Britain, Margaret Thatcher managed to give her government's refusal of "further punitive sanctions" more bite than administration officials in the United States. In a major speech in May 1988 the British foreign secretary reiterated the stand against sanctions because they were ineffective,—a stand he had taken in September 1987 after talks with the Canadian prime minister and secretary for internal affairs. He made the important points that "opposition to sanctions does *not* mean support for apartheid"; that "the lead for change must come from inside South Africa"; and that ". . . change will *not* be rapid."

But he buried these points in a litany that undermined Thatcher's bluntness before forty-nine states,—thirty-three sharply criticized for violations of human rights by Amnesty International,—at the Commonwealth conference in Vancouver the previous October. Thatcher had called the ANC a "typical terrorist organization" like the PLO and the IRA and said she would "have no talks with those organizations." This plain speaking had told especially because, a year before, Thatcher had wanted the unbanning of the ANC because of its importance to South Africa's future.

In his May 1988 speech, however, Sir Geoffrey Howe spoke of keeping "open our channels of communication with all the representative black opposition organizations" despite indications from the foreign office in November 1987, after Thatcher's bluntness in Vancouver, of no further contacts with the ANC: "We acknowledge [the ANC's] role in any negotiation and we shall maintain contact with them as well as with others." He called also for the unbanning of the ANC, freedom for Nelson Mandela and the end to the State of Emergency. He endorsed the Eminent Persons Group's report including its phrase "suspension of violence" with its refusal to distinguish between the ANC and the government. He implied that Britain backed one-man, one-vote: "The majority must be granted full political rights." To top it off, he started with a Soviet official's characterization of Soviet reporting on South Africa as "a caricature, not a living image of a multifaceted, dynamic, extremely complex and confused reality,"—as if to conjure up *"glasnost"* to still criticism, *captatio benevolentiae* Soviet-American style.[55]

A few weeks after Howe's speech, about thirty young conservatives distributed their program, "Mandela speaks," for a ten-hour release-Mandela pop concert in London that drew seventy thousand. The booklet reprinted Mandela's and the ANC's statements refusing to renounce violence and pictures of necklacing. One of the groups exposing the concert, the Conservatives against Apartheid, out of Scotland, pointed out: "Thousands of ordinary, politically moderate young people, who abhor terrorist violence, will this coming weekend be duped by attending the Mandela concert into filling the coffers of the Anti-Apartheid movement." One of the concert's hosts, the Anti-Apartheid Movement, the leading activist group in Britain founded in 1959, had refused to condemn ANC violence, for instance, the explosion in Johannesburg the week before, four dead, three black, twenty injured.

Members of the Conservative Party and the South African government also feared that the estimated sixty-million dollars in television rights from the concert, broadcast to about fifty countries, would end up with the ANC, a suspicion the BBC, attacked for carrying the live concert despite laws against BBC political broadcasting, denied. Earlier in the same week, the BBC's board of directors had stopped publication of an article on the Mandela concert in the BBC's weekly, *Radio Times*, because it was too political.

Oliver Tambo and other ANC comments blamed the booklets on the South African government, an oddly comic accusation that showed their servility: They could not believe anybody, especially abroad, would criticize them on their own. They had learned their tactics that the *Observer* called "dirty-tricks" from the left at the universities, said the youths as they explained that they opposed both racial discrimination and the ANC's pretense to speak for all blacks.[56]

In the United States the companies that syndicated the concert cut some of the propaganda to a pop singer's whine that called the broadcast "anything but free" on the op-ed page of *The New York Times*: "Comments that I made calling South Africa a *terrorist state* and urging sanctions were heard and seen in Britain-but somehow did not get across the Atlantic" (Italics mine). He had not read the Democratic platform.[57]

"Sanctions are *not* the last peaceful option," not the substitute for, but the other side of, the ANC's "armed struggle,"—this was perhaps the most important point buried in the equivocations of the British foreign secretary's May 1988 speech. The realization that sanctions did not work speedily for "peaceful change," that they did not persuade, for after all they were not words, had brought home their violence to him. It had not, however, brought home the unpredictability of their consequences,—because unpredictability betrayed kinship with war he was not about to acknowledge.

An example of unpredictability: The sanctions on coal in the 1986 CAA Act,—blocked in the EEC that buys about fifty percent of South African coal exports by Great Britain, West Germany and Portugal,—cost American mining companies two hundred and fifty million dollars and the miners between three and seven thousand jobs in 1987 and early 1988. South African mines had cut the costs of coal in over-supply in the world, like all other minerals sanctioned, from thirty-eight dollars a ton in early 1986 to a guessed price of just under twenty-five dollars in a major deal with Japan for steam coal in early 1987. Next in importance after gold, South African coal exports may have dropped to under forty million tons, in contrast to forty-four million tons in 1985 and forty-five in 1986, out of 250 million tons traded in the world yearly outside of Comecon countries in 1985–1986, before the bans.[58]

In South Africa too some of the organizations that had mistaken sanctions for persuasive words, came to their senses. In January 1987, a report commissioned by the Southern African Catholic Bishops' Conference that in 1985 had held sanctions "justifiably imposed to end apartheid" called sanctions "very hurtful to the economic and therefore social fabric of the country" and politically "totally counterproductive . . . on government thinking."[59]

Abroad, in Europe especially, people interested in actual results began to doubt, especially after Lipton's concentration on consequences. Before 1988 even the economic difficulties South Africa faced without sanctions were kept from people's eyes, in part because of the reticence of business in South Africa: the growing population, the fall throughout the world in the prices of raw materials and the competition increasing from industrializing Asia. In explanation of their reticence business organizations said they could not match the resources of the "activists."

The lack of attention to consequences, especially outside South Africa, came because sanctions had been imposed on governments by activist organizations working with the ANC that wanted only the world's mobilization in complicity with it. Complicity only works when people go along with something they do not know they want but dare not argue against. Almost everybody who wrote and spoke about South Africa said things they knew were not true they did not want to say.

In contrast to previous bans that aimed at South Africa's self-defense, the 1985 and 1986 embargoes,—South Africa's severest test so far,—aim to cut its give-and-take with the world, its material and spiritual life-blood. For South Africa takes its relationship to the world, not only its economic relationship, seriously because it knows that what makes it different from the West also shows that it belongs to the West. It is unique because it is part of the West in the face of African realities, and is, therefore, willing to acknowledge its faults, and not afraid of bluntness. Besides, South Africa is open to the world in a way Americans can barely imagine, for the realities of other countries do not reach the United States.

The present attempt to isolate South Africa completely bears the same relationship to the previous attack on its capacity and will to defend itself that classical war bears to total unlimited war that does not distinguish between military and civilian targets. That the present sanctions are slow-acting and partial does not make them any less total than low-intensity guerrilla warfare, for they are indiscriminate in their targets, and have no specific aims besides breaking the will of the country. Like guerrilla warfare they confound war and peace: We continue diplomatic relations with South African in the midst of humiliating hostile measures. This confusion of war and peace is also characteristic of total war, of the slow-death twentieth-century style that the characters in *Waiting for Godot* rightly name:

VLADIMIR: Christ! What has Christ got to do with it? You're not going to compare yourself to Christ!
ESTRAGON: All my life I've compared myself to him.
VLADIMIR: But where he lived it was warm, it was dry!
ESTRAGON: Yes, and they crucified quickly.

South Africa's response to the previous attack on its self-defense markedly increased its self-sufficiency without making it invulnerable, especially in oil and air power. It can replace the airplanes it loses only slowly, at great cost and not with the latest designs. In the years from 1973–1984, after the Organization of Arab Petroleum Exporting Countries' oil embargo on behest of the OAU and the UN Security Council's mandatory arms and nuclear weapons technology embargo in 1977, in the wake of the Soweto disturbances in 1976, South Africa spent almost eleven billion dollars for relative autarchy in oil. This very high figure has been questioned, because it is not clear whether it includes the costs of mistakes and of the corruption endemic in sanctions-busting and, above all, of the SASOL coal-to-oil plants decided upon in the years when many countries searched for oil substitutes. The costs for the domestic development of the arms industry, not available, may be in the same range. On the black market arms mark-ups range from twenty to one hundred percent.[60]

In these years South Africa reduced its dependence on oil to twenty to twenty-five percent, a very low figure in contrast to other countries. The rest of its energy comes from coal and nuclear plants. Of the oil requirement, thirty-five to forty percent comes from the three SASOL plants, with perhaps three years' supply of oil in reserve in addition. But an effective oil embargo could decisively weaken, impoverish, and fracture the country because transportation that consumes three-quarters of liquid oil, the army and police, both highly motorized, and agriculture, as well as Savimbi, cannot move without oil.

By 1980 South African companies manufactured three quarters of South African arms, including some aircraft, under contract to the state corporation *Armscor*. Development of the South African mechanical and components industry as well as the sale of South African arms abroad somewhat compensated for the economic distortions self-sufficiency in self-defense necessitated. These distortions could in any case be justified because self-defense took absolute precedence, as Adam Smith argued.

But the 1985 and 1986 sanctions that attempt to cripple movement in the entire country tempt South Africa to join the countries that sanction it, in the repudiation of free trade. They tempt it to attack its free trade itself. Such an attack would amount to an attack on its own confidence, for South Africa believes in free trade. South Africa did not take the adoption of some protective tariffs in the summer of 1988 easily. The central bank governor called "inward industrialization" suicidal, a newspaper accused the finance minister of himself resorting to sanctions.[61] The protective measures had been taken in the face of the first trade deficit since 1984: In 1987 exports to the United States had dropped to just over half the yearly average in 1983–85.

About sixty percent of South Africa's trade is usually considered invulnerable to sanctions except in an outright blockade, and with concerted action by many nations against gold. Besides gold, this invulnerable trade includes: platinum and the two strategic minerals, vanadium and chrome; also wool, of high quality, with many disparate customers, totaling four percent of world production; and paper and pulp, competitive in many markets, including east Asia.

The income from gold, forty-two percent of export earnings in 1985–1986, sometimes as much as sixty percent, crucial for earnings in trade, fluctuates sharply: A change of fifty dollars an ounce price translates into a gain or loss of one billion dollars in balance of payments. But the dumping of gold to lower the price that *The Economist* frivolously suggested in the summer of 1986 would damage all trade, especially the credit of small nations, the majority. For small nations still measure their viability in gold despite the United States' renunciation of the gold standard in 1973.

The remaining forty percent of export income—from coal, iron, steel, agricultural products and manufacturing—is more vulnerable, probably mainly to reduction in prices, estimated as little as five to fifteen percent, in order to hold on to markets in the face of sanctions. A drop in half the value of the forty percent at risk,—twenty percent of total export earnings,—could mean a nine percent drop in a GNP, in 1986, of 141 billion rand.

Besides coal, agricultural production, which exports twenty-five percent of production and brings in twenty-percent of trade income outside of gold, is exposed. The fruit industry, mainly in the western Cape,—four hundred and fifty thousand mainly African and Colored workers, 11,400 producers,—is most exposed. Sixty percent of deciduous fruit, eighty percent of canned and sixty-six percent of dried fruits are exported, about seventy percent to the EEC, especially to Great Britain and West Germany, which appreciates fresh fruit from South Africa's summer in its winter. Sugar,—twenty-five thousand cane growers, two thousand white, the rest black small holders, with one hundred and fifty thousand mainly African workers,—exports three quarters of a million tons, out of just over two million tons normal yearly production. It lost its quota for twenty thousand tons to the United States and for one hundred and twenty thousand tons to Canada, worth about thirty-four million rand, in 1986. Manufacturing exports only about ten percent of its production, in any case easily relabeled to disguise origin. The steel and coal industry estimated that the 1986 sanctions, if effective, could cost fifty thousand jobs. Each worker supports six to eight other people. Operation Hunger, an organization out of Johannesburg active throughout South Africa, found itself with forty-eight thousand people to feed after the return of eight thousand dismissed coal miners to their villages in the northern Transvaal.[62] No mere "economic readjustments," these homecomings also mean a return to a life partly outgrown.

These slow-working sanctions pick off the weakest in numbers small enough to go unnoticed, unskilled workers in enterprises with little capital that face hard quickly-changing competition, in contrast to minerals and gold. They might add two million workers, mainly blacks, to the unemployed by the year two thousand—to bring down the African share of total income to twenty percent from twenty-nine percent in 1985 and the thirty-six percent that had been expected for the turn of the century. They would deepen the differences between blacks with unions to protect them and those entirely at mercy of markets. They tend to break down the economic unity of the country and the growing interdependence of blacks and whites that the present government accepts for the fragmentation the CP wants.

Western governments' disregard of the consequences of sanctions, their incapacity to make them serve defined policy, means they serve to reinforce the ANC's denial of change within South Africa to show the South African government illegitimate, and therefore worthy of destruction. Lipton said sanctions tempted the South African government to behave irrationally in order that it then could be attacked for its irrationality. But in the midst of her words she went, almost inadvertently, deeper than the spiteful provocation of irrationality. She said outright that the tendency to isolate South Africa is dangerous: "[The strategy of delegitimizing and isolating the South African government] involves a dangerous tendency to treat South Africa as a special case to which no rules apply."[63]

But this strategy is dangerous not only, and not especially, because it tempts the South African government to act irrationally, a temptation it had the confidence to resist until the 1988 negotiations for Angola and South West Africa. It is dangerous because it sets major nations to outlawing a nation, to turning it into an *extorris gentium,* a *communis gentium hostis* in accordance with the 1973 General Assembly's resolution calling apartheid a "crime against humanity." It sets a precedent that can be turned against other small tough nations in difficult circumstances who still know they have enemies.

The President's Advisory Committee on South Africa referred to the "broadly held view that Israel is South Africa's major trading partner," an innuendo it then took back as "impossible to confirm." Israel's trade with South Africa in 1985 ran to 383 million rand, without arms sales, in contrast to South African trade of 6.2 billion rand for the United States, with Great Britain, Japan and West Germany a little behind.[64] After the Democratic platform called South Africa a "terrorist state," the Washington correspondent for *Neue Zürcher Zeitung* remarked the phrase might one day go for Israel since it also fights terrorism across its borders.

4

The War for Southern Africa

—l'oeil chargé d'un pleur involontaire,
Il rêve d'échafauds en fumant son houka.

There is no making sense of the situation within South Africa without keeping the violence and the war throughout southern Africa before your eyes. It is a war that knows differences in intensity but not frontiers,—in a territory nearly two-thirds the size of Europe, the Europe of the Urals, or three-quarters of the United States. In this huge land the Republic of South Africa numbers the most people, both black and white, a total of 32.5 million with 24 million blacks (including the four independent or quasi-independent homelands).

In contrast to the rest of southern Africa, South Africa is an old country, the only government that has lasted more than a generation. But it is a young country in contrast to Europe and the Americas, its world also as well as Africa, as Savimbi, with an ear for plain facts people do not know well enough to remember, recently remarked: ". . . South Africa . . . became a state only in 1910, and an independent republic in 1960 . . . It took one hundred years after Lincoln and the Civil War before blacks in America had full civil rights: Why cannot we be equally generous, or patient with South Africa . . .? South Africa is clearly changing."[1]

But the paradoxes run deeper. The British seizure of the Cape was comparatively recent. The Dutch and Huguenot ancestors of the Afrikaners now baffling the liberal Western world that apparently cannot conceive of men changing their minds except in the face of a gun, somebody else's gun, actually, no change of mind at all, first came to the Cape, the Dutch in 1652, the French Protestants a generation later, after the revocation of the Edict of Nantes in 1686, more than 150 years before the Congress of Vienna in 1814–15 finally confirmed British possession of the Cape Colony. The British who had first taken the Cape in 1795, in the wake of the French Revolution, had seen its restoration to Holland at the Peace of Amiens in 1802, and taken it again in 1806.

Never easy, the relations between the relative newcomers, first the British governors, and then the English-speaking colonists, and the descendants of the original Dutch and French Huguenot settlers, broke down in two great events in the nineteenth century: the Great Trek that started in earnest around 1836 and brutal war, the South African War or the Anglo-Boer War of 1899–1902.

Both events showed the depth of the worlds at stake and, the Great Trek especially, the contrast between the new European ideals that came both out of England and the French Revolution and the realities of life in Africa. Then and now this contrast can be coped with politically but does not allow easy solutions. It goes to the heart of Western civilization and Western doubt and self-doubt. After thirty years of British government, with tensions between London and the colonists, and British governors in the middle, the colony had doubled in area but numbered only thirty thousand souls—an "ill-peopled and unprofitable colony," James Stephens, permanent Head of the Colonial Department (1836–1847), called it in 1841.

Instead of rebelling openly within the colony, the Dutch farmers, then called Boers, their descendants now Afrikaners, took off beyond the frontiers first into Natal, and then across tremendous mountains into the High Veld, beyond the Orange River and beyond the Vaal, into the entire area that became the Union of South Africa in 1910,—a move in some ways comparable to the secession of the plebs in Rome with two essential related differences. Those who left made no political demands for incorporation into a body politic but wanted simply to be left alone, and they moved in the confidence of a faith that brought them to compare their exodus to the entrance of the Hebrew tribes into ancient idol-worshipping Canaan. Their numbers were small, a few thousand, perhaps finally six thousand, their losses severe: In 1838 in Natal they lost 362 men, women and children to the Zulus, 200 Colored and Bantu servants and 13 English allies among them.

The migration immeasurably intensified contacts between the Europeans and the Bantu peoples who before had only been allowed into the Cape Colony with passes. The Boers did not want to conquer the natives; they wanted to live among them without much contact. They knew they had to take care of themselves because nobody else would take care of them.

For decades their governments were not strong enough to serve justice among them, let alone among the native peoples. Only Britain could have done that. But despite Parliament's passage, before the Great Trek in 1836, of the Cape of Good Hope Punishment Act that meant to save the "sovereign" rights of tribes and their chiefs and made Europeans beyond the frontiers of the Cape Colony, south of twenty-five degrees latitude, the latitude of Delagoa, now Maputo Bay, subject to the Cape laws,—an area that includes most of present day South Africa;—despite the annexation of Natal in 1845, and after a decided effort in the early fifties, the government in London vacillated. For almost two more generations, it put up with a situation it would do little about in spite of the intentions its laws showed. "Informal Empire," historians call this vacillation.

The vacillation of the British government in the enforcement of its laws precipitated the exodus of some of the Dutch farmers. It did not cause it. The cause ran deeper. The frontiersmen who took off, in contrast to the Dutch-speakers who remained behind, were not about to accept the same juridical position as the Natives. They reacted with horror to *gelijkstelling*, not only because it contradicted the African realities they lived, or because the British government did not energetically enforce the new laws that strained their authority, but because it went against all they were and had made of themselves. Differences counted, especially thousands of years of differences in customs and religion. Left to themselves, they were not about to be talked into something they could not comprehend: the obliteration of the distinction between master and servant, and European and savage. Somebody had to rule.

In their territories, they accepted the abolition of slavery that the British had brought to the Cape in 1834. After the British annexed Natal in 1845 in order not to recognize Boer independence, some of the Boers in Natal accepted British sovereignty. Later they took off over the mountains and across the Orange River. Before their flight these Boers had accepted the proclamation of 1843 that ran:

There shall not be in the eye of the law any distinction or disqualification whatever founded upon mere distinction of color, origin, language or creed, but the protection of the law, in letter and in substance, shall be extended impartially to all alike.[2]

The Anglo-Boer War turned, not on the status of the Natives that had precipitated the Great Trek, but on the independence of the two Boer republics that came of it—which the British had never entirely recognized. The fierce war finally took four hundred and fifty thousand British troops, English-speaking South Africans, Canadians, Australians, against eighty thousand Boers. It came less than a generation after sudden wealth,—diamonds had been discovered in Kimberley in 1867, gold in the Witwatersrand in 1876,— and after staggering immigration of tens of thousands, largely from Europe, mainly from Great Britain. By 1900 the Europeans in South Africa numbered about a million, against one hundred and eighty-five thousand in 1865. The war turned on the political design for a region which Cecil Rhodes envisioned would eventually include southern Rhodesia and the whole plateau through Tanganyika and Kenya.

Only eight years after the victory, impossible without the might of soldiers from all over the Empire, the formation of the Union of South Africa,—possible because a liberal victory in Britain in 1906 changed policy,—undid the conquest and set a political framework for the reconciliation of Afrikaners and British-speakers who were all to become South Africans. The settlement that the First World War tested to the utmost a few years later, turned the region of South Africa into a Western nation in the making. This settlement remains a remarkable example of political foresight, and a telling contrast with the incapacity of the allies, a few years later, to settle the First World War, and of Great Britain and the United States to end the Second World War—a failure that has prevented the political, but not the economic recovery, of Europe.

Like the United States and Israel, South Africa is a new European nation outside Europe, the only one in Africa. By European nation, I mean peoples with institutions and men vigorous enough to make the rule of law survive war, violence and disaster,—a somewhat paradoxical assertion since after 1917 the incapacity of the rule of law to survive war in some of Europe has allowed the war for Europe to take over the world.

European nations outside Europe are hard to understand,—as anyone who has lived in any one of them knows. Their history is a continuous groping in the dark, an alternation of euphoria and disappointment, of self-discovery and delusion, of arrogance and humiliation, of confidence and self-doubt. These European nations outside Europe, who have difficulty knowing others because they do not have a long enough past to know themselves, are now among the most hated and isolated in the world: Israel has diplomatic missions in 40, South Africa in 25, of the 159 countries in the United Nations, in contrast to Ethiopia's 68, and Tanzania's 53.

South Africa and Israel are hated because they know they have to take care of themselves, because they are tough and little, because they fight and sometimes win, and because they do not take the word "republic" for appeasement; the United States is not trusted because it once fought and won,—but did not settle,—and because, unable to use the strength that it has, and even to say a forthright word most of the time, it now unwittingly betrays its friends and helps its enemies.

A good deal of the destiny of the world now turns on these three European nations outside Europe. Each is crucial to the survival of freedom, especially in the remains of Europe which means also the whole world. For Europeans discovered political freedom and still, despite their exhaustion and incapacity to defend freedom, understand it best, especially its relation to excellence, and to the capacity to distinguish one thing from another, and to speak to each other. Europe is both the heart of the crisis and of the capacity to overcome it. Without Europe the United States would not be able to distinguish itself from the Soviet Union. The wide currency, in the United States, of Zbigniew Brzezinski's foolish "ideas" about "convergence of the two systems" in the sixties, complete with recommendations that the police should use gangs to keep order, shows the depth of this ambivalence among Americans with heavy responsibilities who should know best, quite the opposite of the doubt that comes of rough give-and-take of argument.³

1 The Start and Spread of War

The War for southern Africa, the violence and terrorism, broke out: in Angola in 1961; in Portuguese Guinea and Mozambique in 1964; in South West Africa in 1966. It began to really take off in 1974, after the collapse of the Portuguese, and especially in 1976, after the Communists tightened their control of SWAPO. In Rhodesia it started more or less in 1967, and broke out full-scale in 1974, after the departure of the Portuguese isolated the country.

In Angola a civil war that overcame the entire country broke out in March 1975 in Luanda, almost a year after the Portuguese collapse on April 25, 1974. In Mozambique, the terrorism and resistance that now plagues the entire country broke out in early 1976, much less than a year after independence on June 25, 1975. After the end of the civil war, with the failure of the South African intervention at the end of 1975, and after the Cubans failed to exterminate Savimbi in 1976, a guerrilla war that gradually turned into a mixture of guerrilla and conventional warfare took hold of Angola.

In South Africa, the ANC recommenced full-scale terrorism in 1980, after training many of the black youths who had fled South Africa in the wake of the 1976–1977 disturbances. On January 25, 1980, three ANC terrorists with AK–47 rifles and grenades took twenty-five hostages, and murdered a bank teller in cold-blood in Silverton, a suburb of Pretoria. They demanded the release of terrorists, including Nelson Mandela. The police shot all three after an ANC grenade killed another hostage and wounded eleven. On June 1, 1980 the ANC attacked three installations of the South African Coal, Oil and Gas Corporation (SASOL)—seven million dollars in destruction.

Abroad, Mandela won currency. "A sixty-one year old lawyer regarded as the most probable head of a black government if one is ever established in South Africa," a newspaper called him. The terror meant to divide the country. An SACC member said: "The black man saw and interpreted the Silverton episode as heroic, the white man on the other hand labelled it as an act of terrorism."

Two years later, on June 6, 1982, Jorge da Costa, the escaped head of Mozambique security who knew both Joe Slovo and Samora Machel, said Slovo had planned the attacks: "There is no doubt in my mind that Slovo is behind every operation launched by the ANC against South Africa. He has a brilliant mind and is one of the best-informed people about this country."⁴

The terror on the ground in southern Africa, and now in South Africa, is closely related to the huge international campaigns: Terrorist groups use violence to master international attention.

The international campaign against South Africa, and the instigation of violence among blacks within it, represented a political response to the military successes on the ground and the heroic tenacity of the resistance movements in Mozambique and Angola: Savimbi had been fighting for twenty years, since he returned to Angola to stay in 1968. It meant to end South Africa's tough limited policy of supporting the resistance movements and itself fighting in the region.

Unable to win on the battlefield, the Soviet-Cuban directed liberation movements now sought to break the will of South Africa, and further compromise the West, through the world of make-believe: the media, crowds in the the streets, and the pressure of international organizations. This pantomime amounted to a speeded-up rerun, to the point of ritualization, of the techniques used in the United States during the Indochina War. It put on the equivalent of a Communist show trial on the international stage. Ronald Reagan and Margaret Thatcher, the accused, testified against themselves before the whole world, without appeal to the "fifth," the very name of totalitarianism.

The successes on the ground of the resistance and of South Africa had shown their bite in three sets of negotiations in 1984, before the outbreak of disturbances in South Africa: an agreement with the MPLA regime in Angola to withdraw South African troops from Angola in exchange for a commitment to prevent SWAPO attacks on South West Africa from Angola that held until sometime in 1985; a working statement of accord between SWAPO and the political parties of the South African-sponsored government of South West Africa, first accepted and then, after consultations with the Soviet Ambassador, rejected by Sam Nujoma, the president of SWAPO; and the only enduring concession, the Nkomati accords, Machel's commitment to remove ANC bases from Mozambique,—bases forced upon him in 1980 by the Soviet ambassador, head of the KGB for Africa, in Lusaka,—in exchange for an end to South African raids against the ANC and of aid to Mozambique resistance. The South African military observed this last not-too-honorable commitment, reluctantly and perhaps fitfully, only after flying in two years of supplies.

Reflections of South African and resistance successes on the ground, these negotiations,—held at American insistence and dependent upon the United States' promise to see to the removal of the Cubans,—also bought time for the MPLA and FRELIMO in a war they could not win but would not negotiate. They also advanced the Soviet strategy of breaking South African support for the resistance, for they excluded the resistance movements from the negotiations. The resistance movements bore this exclusion with grace. One of the leaders of the Mozambicans said he regretted only that Machel had not signed with RENAMO instead of South Africa.

The Communist tactic of using these negotiations not for bona fide settlement, but to continue the war by the diplomacy of piecemeal surrender, worked better with the Americans,—at least with the State Department and Crocker, drawn on by the mirage of the "peaceful" settlement in Rhodesia,— than with the South Africans, until the negotiations of 1988.

In February 1985, in the very days when the risk of a "paper settlement" in Angola and South West Africa that masked a Soviet-Cuban takeover drove

Symms to seek repeal of the Clark Amendment, and a few weeks before violence in a few of the major townships in South Africa brought a State of Emergency in the industrial Transvaal and in the Cape, Crocker took the breath away from the South African government with a demand that it send regular soldiers and arms to Machel to crush the resistance, by then, probably, deprived in earnest of South African arms.[5] The policy of "stability," in polite "expertise," at any cost. The negotiations in 1988 between the MPLA, the Cubans and South Africa, under American, and indirectly, Soviet, auspices, renewed the danger of a "paper settlement" that would undo both Savimbi and South West Africa.

Alan Paton, who had helped found the South African Liberal Party in 1953, the first party in South Africa open to all races, in the "hope" of opening "the doors of our society to *all people who are ready for it* no matter what their race or color" (Italics mine), sensed, almost a year before the violence actually broke out in the townships, that the war had spread to South Africa. He sensed the new war within South Africa was meant to undermine the South African Defense Force (SADF) beyond the frontiers, especially its support of Savimbi in Angola and of the resistance in Mozambique: "He [P.W. Botha] and his military advisors know that the battle for Afrikaner survival could not be won on the border if there was unrest at home."

More than a year later, in May 1985, the defense minister, General Magnus Malan, openly drew the connection between the war abroad and at home: "[It is South Africa's policy] to defend and safeguard itself *offensively with all the might at its disposal against any form of foreign aggression or internal revolution.*" South Africa meant, "not to 'destabilize,' but to prevent the build-up of any hostile terrorists—or of conventional forces in neighbouring states which may pose a threat" (Italics mine).[6]

2 The Unseen War: Infiltration, Terror—and Words

I call the violence in southern Africa a war, not because of pitched battles, because except for Angola and the South African raids on SWAPO camps, there are few pitched battles. I call this violence war because it serves a total strategy, a total strategy that knows it cannot win militarily before it wins psychologically. I call it war because it makes its fear and intimidation and terror felt, not only throughout southern Africa and South Africa, but in the entire world.

The strategy of terror means to set up the rudiment of a totalitarian state even before the seizure of power: the paralysis of fear and the words that spread it. The means are infiltrations, sometimes in groups of two or three, sometimes in groups of a hundred. The goal: the murder of the defenseless. ". . . SWAPO knows perfectly well that the security forces in Namibia always make use of anti-mine vehicles. Thus we can assume that in laying mines, their prime target is the civil defenseless population." This viciousness came as a shock even to a young soldier who had seen the undoing of Mozambique, when he visited South West Africa, a few months before he bore witness at the Denton Hearings in 1982. He went on: "I saw, specifically, the result of a landmine explosion which had destroyed a civilian ambulance transporting civil patients from Eeenhana base hospital to a large one equipped with better medical and surgical material."

Not only are the defenseless victims murdered, they are sometimes tortured and mutilated beyond words, not for brutal gratification as newspapers in the United States too often assume, but to spread terror: "We want to make the death of a collaborator so grotesque that people will never think of [collaborating]," said an ANC member of the "necklace" at a meeting at California State University on October 10, 1985.[7] In Rhodesia between roughly 1974 and 1980, there were about thirty thousand men murdered, mainly African women and children; ten thousand maimed; one million homeless. And never an open battle. No open battle meant the world could wear the face of peace in the midst of murder and its siege of Rhodesia, one kind of peace.

South Africans now sometimes tell visitors to stay away from parks, shopping centers, crowded places. "What [the South African government] is fighting [in Angola and Namibia] is the Communist infiltration into southern Africa, and they feel strongly that the ultimate objective of the Soviet Union is South Africa itself . . ." These are the words of Jariretundu Kozonguizi, another witness before the Denton Hearings.

The totality of the war for southern Africa shows itself, not only in infiltration everywhere, in the integration of the ANC and SWAPO men in the MPLA army to fight Savimbi. It also shows in repeated statements by the leaders of the Front-Line states, the name itself tells much, and by the OAU, an organization as crucial in Africa as the UN in the world for blinding the leaders of these countries to realities, and for reinforcing their irresponsibility towards their own people. "But while peaceful progress is blocked by actions of those at present in power in the states of southern Africa, we have no choice but to give the peoples of those territories all the support of which we are capable in their struggle against their oppressors," ran the Lusaka Manifesto, approved by the OAU heads of state in September 1969. In 1974 when violence against the defenseless took hold in Rhodesia, the Zimbabwe African National Union (ZANU), the organization that later came under Mugabe's control, argued for terror all at once in all the countries still not seized (Rhodesia, South West Africa and South Africa). Its rival the Zimbabwe African People's Union (ZAPU) wanted a step-by-step escalation of "the struggle for the liberation of southern Africa," first Rhodesia, then South West Africa . . .

The sinister Julius Nyerere, who uprooted eighty percent of twenty million Tanzanians in the sixties before the eyes of a West his self-righteousness paralyzed, said in 1974: ". . . If the West supports these racialist and fascist states [South Africa, Rhodesia, South West Africa, the Portuguese territories] southern Africa will become a part of the world ideological conflict—as it is now wrongly alleged to be."[8]

The man who said these words knew all about the "ideological conflict" he sought to blame on the West. Soviet weapons came through Tanzania. Besides training terrorists for all the wars of southern Africa, Tanzania was the nerve center for planning the war against the Portuguese. It was, and still is, the transit center for guerrillas from all over southern Africa on their way to advanced training and indoctrination in eastern Europe and the Soviet Union. "Most of the others who had left [Rhodesia] had been trained in [Tanzania] which remained one of the strongest supporters of the anti-White revolution on the continent," a soon-to-be-shot Rhodesian terrorist told the South African journalist, Al J. Venter, who can tell the grandeur of events in a single detail, at about the time of Nyerere's statement.

The next year in a speech at Oxford during a state visit, Nyerere went on: "We very much regret the need for war. It can only bring dreadful suffering to the people of Rhodesia—both Black and White [He did not, in contrast to Savimbi, emphasize that the Africans would suffer most]. . . . but we can no more refuse support to the Rhodesian freedom fighters now than Britain could have refused support to Resistance Movements during the 1940's."[9]

He had not only "supported," he had trained and commanded them. In 1976 Nyerere started to train both ZANU and ZAPU in the huge Nachingwea camp in southern Tanzania that FRELIMO no longer needed that could turn out five thousand terrorists every six months. There was also training in Mozambique, and for Joshua Nkomo's ZAPU men, in Zambia and Angola. There were three thousand ZANU terrorists in Rhodesia, in the east, north and south, by the middle of 1977.[10]

In conjuring up nazism, Nyerere conveniently forgot a little detail: Tanzania was not at war with Rhodesia, in contrast to Britain at war with Germany at the time of its support of the resistance. But Nyerere knew his audience: The analogy still paralyzes in the West despite its absurdity. For what on earth does fascism and nazism have to do with independence in Africa unless you are a disciple of the Third International in Soviet Moscow in 1919–1920 that first connected the European War with "wars of liberation" in Asia and Africa.

But Nyerere meant something much uglier than the open hate of the Third International: He meant we would become the Fascists and Nazis we had triumphed over unless we yielded to terrorism and its wishes.

Machel's successor, Joaquin Chissano gave the theme of total war in southern Africa a new twist on the day he took power, November 6, 1986, a twist already implied at the conference of the Non-Aligned in September 1986 and in the CAA Act finally passed barely a month before. He called South Africa the aggressor, the "Fascist, Nazi aggressor," in all of southern Africa, and blamed it for the resistance in Mozambique.

It is about time we understood that the recent past of Italy and Germany is more than enough for them to suffer alone, and not for us to curse. This ideological cursing serves only to make us liable to the emotional blackmail of the weak, who will not fight those they take for their enemies face to face.

The outbreak of terror and terror's intimidation within South Africa—

coordinated with a political campaign by the UDF and other front organizations within South Africa bent on destroying reform—and the corresponding international campaign initiated by the Soviets and the ANC and SWAPO through TransAfrica, the UN and many other groups, some of them Communist fronts, some not, that took off first in the United States and Britain,—show the Soviets and the Cubans, the ANC and SWAPO, and Mugabe's SADCC are well aware they cannot win in battle on the ground against the vastly stronger South Africans. They know they cannot win even against the scantily armed but deeply motivated resistance groups in Mozambique and Angola who, in contrast to the discouraged and coerced soldiers of FRELIMO and the MPLA, know what they fight. They know they can only win in battle *after* they succeed in breaking American and European, and more importantly, South African, will.

They know they can win if the West adopts sanctions that undermine the economy, in contrast to the present ones. Especially they know they can win if they get so-called international public opinion, especially the heads of Western governments, and finally even some South Africans, both black and white, to blame all the destruction on apartheid—the current theme of the "Front-Line States" and the CAA Act. This propaganda calls "victims of apartheid": the men the ANC and SWAPO kill; the dead in the MPLA's and the Cubans' war against Savimbi; the murdered in Zimbabwe; the starving in Mozambique. The billions of dollars SADCC manages to extract from the West measure the effectiveness of this theme. Instead of earning their money through hard trade through, and with, South Africa, they get it by blaming others, and making them feel guilty. Finally, they know they can win if they demoralize the SADF, if they force it to spend its energies in keeping order in the townships, not exactly a soldier's vocation.

This confession of weakness knows that violence at home against civilians, and above all words and negotiations, both at home but especially abroad, are dirtier and more effective than open battle, or even guerrilla warfare, because they can undo the intelligence of men, especially of leaders, that alone can make the courage of soldiers effective: Think of the American secretary of state calling South Africa "an evil empire," in the fall of 1985.

As the ANC and the Soviet Union openly stated in January 1986, this combination of the war of words and terrorism is calculated to paralyze Botha's two-pronged policy of fighting and negotiating for leadership of southern Africa abroad and fundamental limited reform at home,—and then to turn it in upon itself, to divide the whites against themselves. "A serious revolutionary movement always tries to divide the enemy and to broaden the base of opposition to the enemy. This implies the need for ever-widening varieties of opposition some of which may not be motivated by revolutionary intentions . . . We are justified in helping by all means (*including talks*) to advance the process of breaking the cohesion and unity of the ruling class and to isolate and weaken its most racist and politically reactionary sector," runs the SACP March 1986 Politburo directive South Africa released on June 12, 1986 (Italics mine).

But you do not need secret documents to know this: ANC speakers on

American campuses in the fall of 1986 spoke in palpably regimented words of dividing the "Afrikaners" and even the famous Broederbond. In Lusaka, two weeks before his visit to the United States early in 1987, Tambo announced the ANC's plans to turn on the whites: "We must pay the greatest possible attention to the mobilization and activization of the white population."

One day he reassured the State Department that ANC violence was not meant for whites, the next he said he wanted to make whites, like blacks, "used to bleeding." Meanwhile, back in Lusaka, another ANC leader showed the starting thesis of Tambo's synthesis, the "mobilization and activization" of the "white population": "We, the black people, are everywhere. We are in every household. We cook their food and make their beds. We can use this to our advantage."

Because the State Department would not draw the obvious conclusion these ambiguities,—the dialectic naked,—indicated, it aped the contradictions that the ANC and the Soviets mean to use to divide the Europeans of South Africa and the West against themselves. The secretary of state would meet Tambo a few days later, it reassured, at the same time that it remarked, primly: "This [the call for violence] is exactly the kind of thing we need to keep our distance from."[11]

The intimidation also showed its traces in the United States, in the media, but probably not in the public who did not have to be told what to make of "necklacing": "And yet it is hard to fashion a more realistic means of achieving black liberation in South Africa," wrote William Raspberry, a regular *Washington Post* columnist of Tambo's insistence on violence against the defenseless. Roughly a year later Raspberry came out against sanctions.

Infiltration means to prepare for outright conquest, once the West's and South Africa's will is broken, not substitute for it. The Soviet arms build-up in Angola and Mozambique, including most recently SAM missiles and MIG strike aircraft,—two billion dollars worth to the MPLA in Angola alone in the two years before 1987 by State Department estimate!—outstrips any conceivable needs of terrorism, as Kozonguizi also testified of Soviet shipments to SWAPO, also in Angola before 1982: ". . . Equipment which no guerrilla movement, in my view, sir, can be expected to use, but I think equipment which is in preparation for an entry of the Cubans or the Russians or the East Germans who can use this equipment . . . This equipment, in my view, cannot be said to be within the ability of a guerrilla movement to handle, but rather it is indicative of a potential conventional war . . ."

In August 1985 the chief of the South African Air Force, Lieutenant General Denis Earp, said that the building of a Soviet radar "air umbrella as formidable as those in eastern Europe or the Middle East" underway in southern Africa would mean heavy casualties in strikes against terrorists. On November 23, 1985, the Johannesburg *Star* reported the arrival of much radar equipment and large numbers of SAM–8 and SAM–9 missiles in southern Angola, near Menongue and Cuito Cuanavale—the latter on the road to Savimbi's headquarters. These weapons helped bring the deadlock in the fierce fighting in 1987 and early 1988, the third Soviet-Cuban-MPLA attempt in three years to wipe out Savimbi, that led to the negotiations in 1988 that excluded Savimbi.

This build-up shows an able South African general knew what he was talking about when he said in 1983 that South Africa faced a low-scale war that at any moment might turn full-scale. I first took this statement for outlandish. But it is the real-life version of Conor Cruise O'Brien's bizarre call for a UN sponsored Soviet-United States armed intervention in South Africa. "The question today in Africa and elsewhere is not one of defensive or piecemeal actions as in the past, but it is one . . . of carrying out a total offensive against imperialism and world capitalism as a whole in order to do away with them," a Soviet official said in 1985,—words that recall Brezhnev's remark in Prague in 1973 that by 1985 the "correlation of forces" everywhere would allow the Soviet Union to dictate its will.[12] Soviet apparent encouragement of negotiations in 1988 marked a change in tactics, not in strategy.

3 The Fall of Portugal and Rhodesia

The collapse in Portugal in April 1974 that lasted until September 1975, but that brought the announcement of "self-determination" for the overseas territories at the end of July 1974, tested the policy of concentrating on diplomatic relations with Africa and the countries beyond its borders that South Africa's prime minister John Vorster adopted almost immediately after assuming office in 1966. It forced South Africa to concentrate on the actual situation on the ground.

Vorster intensified negotiations, especially with Zambia's Kaunda. But at the same time, little more than a year after the collapse of Portugal, and a few weeks after the unmistakable signs of recovery of stability had shown themselves in Portugal, in the last week of October 1975, three South African armored columns, about two to three thousand men, entered Angola,—a fateful intervention that had it succeeded would have given Vorster's initiatives in Africa new bite and confidence. Events had forced South Africa, against all Vorster's instincts, to fight as well as negotiate.

Everybody, vividly in southern Africa, dimly in the rest of the world, sensed the momentousness of the fall of Portugal. After five hundred years of presence, beginning largely on the coasts, that had turned into colonialism right and proper after the Berlin conference of 1884–85 divided up Africa and forced Portugal to stake out frontiers in Angola and Mozambique, the Portuguese in Africa became a memory almost overnight,—a collapse nobody, least of all those closest to events, expected. For Portugal had all but won the war on the ground: In Angola, the terrorists were dispersed and active only in a small strip of territory north of Luanda; in Mozambique, FRELIMO, the most successful of the guerilla that fought the Portuguese, had made some gains in the northern reaches, and to a somewhat lesser extent, in Tete,—the very areas where Chissano, Machel's successor faced his greatest challenge at the end of 1986 and in 1987,—but they had never come within one thousand kilometers of Lourenço Marques, had never taken a town or threatened a city. In Washington, a few Congressmen started to look at maps, reluctantly, for the nation of Alexander Hamilton and Mahan now finds it painful to remember that it is just one nation among others, located in one place, not everywhere. Geography's hints of destiny make it uncomfortable.

The collapse of Portugal occurred not on the battlefield, not in Africa, but in Lisbon. It was occasioned of all things by a book that meant to avert it, and should have: General Antonio de Spinola's *Portugal and the Future*, published on February 3, 1974 with the tacit approval of the prime minister of Portugal, Marcello Caetano, who, in 1971, without the notice of almost anybody outside Portugal, had managed to get the Assembly to adopt a constitution that provided for self-determination of overseas territories.

The suddenness of the event shook people, especially of the abandonment of the overseas territories, and Vorster did not underestimate its seriousness. Thirteen years of fighting in Angola, ten in Mozambique, of skillful heroic fighting, sixteen thousand Portuguese dead, black and white, thirty thousand crippled, had come to nothing. "I believe that southern Africa has come to the crossroads. I believe that southern Africa has to make a choice . . . between peace on the one hand and an escalation of strife on the other," Vorster said in the South African Senate on October 23, 1974, barely a month after Portugal had agreed to hand over Mozambique to FRELIMO on June 25, 1975, despite Chissano's and other FRELIMO leaders' demands for a phased withdrawal.

In the face of the previous decade of "violence," Vorster persisted in calling for "the way of peace": ". . . the way of normalizing relations, the way of sound understanding and normal association," that had been his policy in earnest since 1972. "Discrimination based solely on the colour of a man's skin cannot be defended and we shall do everything in our power to move away from discrimination based on race or colour," R.F. Botha, then South African ambassador to the UN, told the UN on the next day.

At the same time Vorster's resort to the word "détente" instead of "dialogue," the word he had previously used, showed his awareness of the seriousness of the new situation. South Africa would provoke no incidents,— and offered a nonaggression pact to any country that desired,—but it would defend itself, self-defense that he might have added the UN Charter that Jan Smuts helped to draft called a right (article 51): ". . . South Africa has the elementary right to defend itself with all the power at its command, and South Africa's power in that regard is not inconsiderable."

He was modest and straightforward enough to add that the "toll of a major confrontation" might be "too high for South Africa to pay,"—an admission that should have made his interlocutors pause, for it showed Vorster was not blustering.

"African countries will not take up arms and fight South Africa. The people of South Africa will face the primary task of shaping their own destiny," Kaunda answered Vorster's "voice of reason," as he called it, on October 26th in words whose arrogance nobody bothered to notice because they brought the appearance of relief: Kaunda had no such armies.

The collapse of Portugal added geographic isolation to the political isolation of Rhodesia that had begun in November 1965 when Ian Smith had broken with Britain. Rebellion at first had not come easily to Ian Smith, an RAF pilot during the Second World War, who had fought in an Italian partisan group with his newly-learned Italian after crashing in the Po Valley. In words that echoed the American Declaration of Independence, he broke with the British government of Harold Wilson that had reversed traditional British policy toward Rhodesia—but not with the Crown. In 1970, however, Rhodesia became a republic, a change first discussed in 1968.

For South Africa the collapse of Portugal meant the exposure of the frontier of South West Africa and of the Eastern Transvaal. It meant the possibility of direct terrorist infiltration into South West Africa and South Africa. It also meant the exposure of Rhodesia to infiltration on all sides of its 2,964 kilometers of borders except for the relatively short 222 kilometer frontier with South Africa along the Limpopo River,—a fact that impressed Vorster much more than Ian Smith who argued bravely, and perhaps rightly in the immediate military sense, that the situation had not changed dramatically. Smith probably meant that the fundamental problem was the political isolation of Rhodesia, and of all of southern Africa, that had begun in 1965. The situation needed the political will of Rhodesia and South Africa to make Rhodesian fighting effective.

4 Vorster's "Outward Reach" Policy

Vorster's concentration on Africa, like P.W. Botha's policy of reform ten years later, surprised everyone. But like P.W. Botha's reform, Vorster's policy that appeared to break decisively with the past, had actually begun with his predecessor, Hendrik Verwoerd. It had its roots in Verwoerd's transformation of *apartheid* into separate development that was to lead to independence for the Transkei in 1976 in Vorster's prime-ministership,—a momentous event in South Africa, now all but forgotten.

Verwoerd had really meant it about segregation of the races, but he had also meant it about independence for the homelands, about granting the various black tribal groups political respect. Verwoerd's readiness to begin the political recognition of the various black groups within South Africa gave Vorster the confidence to approach the new African states outside South Africa.

In a remarkable tribute to Verwoerd upon his assassination in 1966, Alan Paton, who had been enough revolted by Verwoerd's intensification of segregation after he assumed office in 1959 to compare him to Stalin and Hitler, admitted that "separate development" had been real enough to change Verwoerd and get things moving in South Africa. "Separate development" despite its cruelty and self-deception had made a return to the previous brutality of outright domination, *baaskap*, impossible: "[Verwoerd]—and the changing world—made it virtually impossible for any politicians to return to the *baaskap* of Mr. Strijdom [the previous prime minister]."

Paton realized that because "separate development" substituted constructive action for the simple assertion of white dominance it made future change possible,—more or less the position of the black homeland leaders who accepted separate development, at the same time that they criticized it, because with all its defects it provided a way of working with whites, within the system, to improve the lives of blacks: "Dr. Verwoerd liberated Afrikaner idealism from the sterile narcissism in which it was captive, and by so doing strengthened Afrikaner progressivism, and weakened Afrikaner reaction."

Verwoerd had gotten South Africans to do something, instead of simply denying,—he had gotten them to move. That movement might mean they would keep on going, it might mean change. "Separate development" had been real enough to lend Verwoerd a "benignity" and confidence he had not enjoyed upon the assumption of office: "In a peculiar way [Verwoerd] changed remarkably: In his later years he showed an impersonal geniality toward black people which was entirely absent in his earlier life. But racial consultation remained for him a matter for group leaders, not for persons . . ."

The change in Verwoerd showed itself in others: "The transformation that Verwoerd wrought in himself had its effect on others." At the same time, Paton knew the change had cost increased segregation in areas not set for independence: "The independence of the Transkei was the price Dr. Verwoerd persuaded white South Africa to pay for the right to deny to Transkeians and all other Africans any prospect of achieving permanent residence or attaining quite ordinary freedoms of movement, employment and so on, in so-called white areas." All these limitations P.W. Botha's reforms were gradually to abolish.[13]

The confidence Paton saw in Verwoerd before his assassination showed itself in Vorster's readiness to approach the African states almost immediately after his election as prime minister: "We strive for friendship and peaceful coexistence which are possible even between nations whose internal policies are not necessarily the same," he had remarked in 1968. Friendly relations meant economic and technical cooperation: "We have a measure of self-interest—and I do not attempt to hide this—in the development and prosperity of Africa, but it is not self-interest alone that motivates us. We have a sense of mission in respect to Africa . . . The principle of self-determination is strongly rooted in our national life. What we ask for ourselves, we do not begrudge others." He had gone on to state an obvious truth that like many obvious truths needs repeating: "Conquest has never been our policy." In 1968, also, he told *US News and World Report*: "We wish to avoid the dangers of neo-colonialism in any pattern of assistance which may be agreed upon, but we expect in return a recognition of our own sovereignty."[14]

Vorster meant that the new nations conceived by the UN had to make their way in the world and the region like older nations. He was asking them whether they were serious enough about independence to concentrate on realities, to pursue traditional diplomacy instead of relying on the UN and OAU, a more destructive African version of the UN, and their ideological wall of violent words that spoke to everybody and nobody, without accountability to anybody. He meant, in short, traditional relations between states not at war.

Vorster meant to show the states beyond South Africa's borders that he took their independence seriously, he meant to show them that South Africa recognized there was a new world around it it could deal with directly,—not through Europe,—on condition that this world took itself seriously.

A new note informed the policy of "mission" that had also been Jan Smuts' and Cecil Rhodes' before the formation of the Union of South Africa: The sense that South Africa's leadership in Africa, especially in southern Africa, would take precedence over its relations with the West, especially Europe—a daring break, for Europe had always counted for more for South Africa than Africa. For Europe no longer looked outwards toward the world. Success in Africa could dispel the hostility towards South Africa in Europe and the West generally: "To the extent that we establish right relations with Africa, to that extent will our problems diminish," Vorster had remarked in 1969.

Vorster's initiative won response in northwestern Africa: In 1969, the prime minister of Ghana later overthrown, and in 1970 the president of the Ivory Coast, Felix Houphouet-Boigny announced their readiness for dialogue with South Africa. At home Vorster ran into serious opposition from South Africans that held recognition of black states would force loosening of policy towards its own black peoples: In 1970 Vorster had to expel four MP's from the National Party, who founded the Herstigte National Party (HNP) that never won a seat until a by-election in 1985, to lose it in 1987.

There was loosening too that sometimes recognized change that had already taken place of its own and that foreshadowed P.W. Botha's reforms,— and that showed the justness of Paton's intuition upon Verwoerd's death: equal pay for equal work in government jobs; greater bargaining rights for black workers; the gradual undoing of "job reservation" that protected certain jobs for whites; more common facilities for men of all races; the beginning of acceptance of home ownership in the townships—by 1975 about thirty percent of blacks owned their homes, 132,992 out of a total of 447,733 homes; the administrative acceptance that black workers in the townships were not "temporary sojourners"; and advisory town councils in the townships.[15]

In his "outward reach" Vorster insisted only on the renunciation of subversion, not on formal diplomatic recognition,—a strange concession that betrayed both lack of confidence in South Africa and the harshness of illusion in Africa and the rest of the world.

Kaunda had a price for calling Vorster "the voice of reason,"—a price that meant transformation of Vorster's "opening toward the world," and the abandonment of Rhodesia. The collapse of Portugal drove Kaunda to imagine he could use Vorster's goodwill, and the West's indecisiveness, for his purposes: "There is no doubt at all the southern African minority regimes are really led by Mr. Vorster," Kaunda remarked toward the end of 1974, gracelessly, just in the days Vorster had shown his good faith in negotiations for settlement in Rhodesia and South West Africa.

At the time of Kaunda's remark Vorster was about to pressure Ian Smith and the rest of the Rhodesian government into three fateful concessions. He was also about to concede the independence of South West Africa with the sensible reservation that left rejection or acceptance to the South West Africans. Vorster had persuaded Smith to accept a cease-fire with the guerrillas at the end of 1974, at a moment when the Rhodesians thought they had seen the face of victory; he had begun to remove the South African Police who had volunteered, since around 1967, for service in Rhodesian units to prevent ANC infiltration across the Zambezi from Zambia; and most fateful of all, he had convinced Smith and his government to release sixteen black political leaders, including Nkomo, Sithole and Mugabe then almost unknown, some of whom had been in prison for ten years.

Vorster's concession on South West Africa amounted to acquiescence,— with the crucial reservation that distinguished between independence and SWAPO seizure of power,—to the International Court of Justice's rejection in 1971, with a vote of thirteen to two, of South Africa's case against the UN Security Council resolution in 1965 that, with the abstention of France and Great Britain, had "terminated" the League of Nations mandate for South African administration of the territory. South Africa had argued her case with juridical coherence that had won the admiration of jurists in a world that could still distinguish between arguments based on traditional international law and the past's facts, and ideology.

Vorster's concession of independence in principle on condition that it not mask a SWAPO seizure of power under UN auspices overturned South Africa's traditional position on South West Africa—a country ". . . over which [South Africa's] claim to rule is as good as ours over any of our territory—certainly west of the Alleghenies . . ." Dean Acheson had remarked a few years before. Acheson had perhaps meant to quietly remember that the political consequences of the United States' expansion to the west coast had caused the Civil War the spread of slavery had precipitated.[16]

A few weeks before Britain announced it no longer recognized SWAPO as the sole representative of the people of Namibia, in September 1975, the South African government called a constitutional conference that led to the Turnhalle alliance, a coalition of South West African tribally-based parties.

More or less at the same time that he made major concessions on Rhodesia and South West Africa, Vorster showed his determination to maintain relations with southern African regimes, regardless of their way to power, and their exercise of it. He acquiesced to the situation in Mozambique in defiance of expectations of intervention, especially at the time the Europeans attempted a coup in September 1974, because of the breakdown in diplomatic relations: The South Africans operated the port of Maputo and supplied most of the little food in its shops.

The hesitation almost at the core of Vorster's "outward reach" showed itself in his acceptance of secrecy in his dealings with the southern African states, especially Zambia, and most fatefully of all, in his insistence on secrecy in his daring intervention in Angola in October 1975. Secrecy allowed Kaunda to prevaricate, to make hard deals for peace in the quiet of traditional diplomacy, and to alternate between threats of peace and war in public,—in a world that mouthed the word "peace" but thought war and "instability."

Already by April 1975, after Vorster's major concessions and something like fifteen meetings between South African and Zambian officials in Lusaka and South Africa between October 1974 and February 1975, Kaunda's foreign minister at the OAU made the end of "white minority rule," and not "dialogue" and "détente,"—Vorster's new word for his "outward reach" policy after the collapse of the Portuguese,—the condition of further negotiations. In September 1974, a few weeks before South Africa's intervention in Angola, that Kaunda had approved and perhaps requested, a new Zambian foreign minister attacked South Africa before a packed cheering UN General Assembly and accused "certain Western powers . . . of sustaining the racist minority regimes in southern Africa [including South Africa]." Vorster's word "crossroads" on his lips, he said change had to come either by "peaceful means" or "through armed struggle." He meant both: violence and beguiling demands to justify it,—a hendiadys for terrorism.

The secrecy about the intervention in Angola that both tested Vorster's policy to the limit, and that might have strengthened it, is much harder to understand than the secrecy in diplomacy. Vorster may have told himself that sticking to traditional reserve might eventually teach the new nations common sense despite their untraditional provocations that he had said he would not tolerate. But secrecy about a major intervention? Vorster had imagined he could do right in the dark,—a telling measure of the intimidation international propaganda could work,—despite the Israeli example of straightforwardness in fighting that until Beirut in 1982 had always won a measure of acquiescence and admiration. The South Africans kept the Israeli example before their eyes but did not dare follow it. The contempt for South Africa, taken for granted almost everywhere, had made them ashamed of even their noble acts, of their readiness to risk their lives for others. Besides inept, the policy of secrecy was also impractical: The world was going to find out about the intervention.

The secrecy about negotiations and interventions had two bad effects: It kept Vorster's and Rhodesia's concessions from making an imprint on the world and, thereby, facilitated abandonment of Rhodesia; and it kept the world from knowing catastrophe in Angola. The combination of secrecy about the negotiations, especially with Zambia, and concessions made South African and Rhodesian public opinion suspect betrayal and the sacrifice of tough straightforwardness in the pursuit of a constructive solution: "The paranoia and hypocrisy which characterizes relations between Salisbury and Pretoria are not the least factor in the rapid decline of white morale in Rhodesia," a British journalist, James MacManus of *The Guardian* remarked in 1976.

The denial of the intervention in Angola made it possible for the rest of the world,—in contrast to the South African government that knew the facts,— to continue to ignore the undoing of Angola—not a sight eyes met readily a few months after the vision of helicopters rising like dragonflies, Vietnamese clinging to their feet, from Saigon. "It would not be unfair to say that, apart from a couple of cover stories in *Time* and *Newsweek* which were centered more on the strife of civil war than on the plight of the Portuguese refugees, together with several lead articles in the British and European press, the 1976 Montreal Olympic Games received bigger, better and more wide-spread coverage than the human tragedy which unfolded in Africa the year before," Al J. Venter remarked a few months later of a denial that continues.[17] Nobody knows the number of the dead in the violence that broke out in March 1975, and lasted more or less nine months in Angola: Guesses run from 125,000 to 250,000. More than 500,000 men fled.

Even after the plain failure before the whole world of the South African intervention, it took Savimbi who had pleaded with South Africa to remain in Angola until the OAU meeting in December, to name names: Zambia, Zaire, and the Ivory Coast, but, significantly, not the United States that, itself no longer willing to fight, would not support others that fought. Vorster clung doggedly to his discretion in a speech in Parliament on January 30, 1976,— impressive loyalty but shortsighted for it prevented recognition of the exploitation of his "outward reach" policy: "South Africa's involvement was not an isolated involvement; others were involved. I am not going to mention names."

Savimbi had hoped in vain that the continued South African presence in Angola might encourage the OAU to vote for the enforcement of the Alvor accords' three-way settlement that the Portuguese had suspended about two months before they abandoned Angola to the strongest on November 10, 1975—or, as they put it, in bloody understatement, "to the Angolan people who should decide the forms of the execution of independence." But even the fight they left the country was not fair: The Portuguese left all their military equipment behind, most of it to the MPLA.

The prevarication that secrecy encouraged made it possible to ignore South Africa's strength, its readiness to fight as well as to negotiate,—the other side of Vorster's "outward" policy that had led Verwoerd, a few months before his assassination, to appoint P.W. Botha defense minister to make South Africa capable of defending itself without reliance on others. Prevarication's words meant not only to wish South Africa's strength away but eventually to turn it against itself, to make South Africa an accomplice in its own destruction.

Only Hastings Kamuzu Banda of little poor Malawi said it like it was. Almost a year after Harold Wilson, victor in a close election, overturned Great Britain's traditional policy toward Rhodesia and two days before Rhodesia broke with the British government, but not the Crown, in November 1965, Banda sought to bring southern African leaders to their senses with words straightforward Western leaders or the South Africans might have said. He concentrated on Rhodesia, the crucial issue of the day whose consequence Banda understood more deeply than Vorster or Smith, but he meant South Africa also:

Military force? African military force? O.A.U. military force? Let me really laugh again. What single country in Africa today . . . from north to south, east to west, has an army that can take on and beat the Rhodesian Army? Not one!

> The Rhodesian Army, next to the Army of the Union of South Africa, is the strongest and the most efficient . . . in the African continent, and I mean just that. Don't deceive yourselves. . . . It is all right to have these uniforms. . . . It is one thing to impress, but it is quite another on the battlefield. . .
>
> Mr. Smith knows the quality of this so-called army that some of my colleagues praise. . . . Ten mercenaries will fix a five thousand so-called army, you know. Do you think Mr. Smith is afraid of that sort of thing? He is not a fool, you know . . .
>
> Let me be blunt. . . . The Rhodesian Army, if Smith pushed, would conquer the whole of East and Central Africa in a week. . . . the Rhodesian Air Force would reduce to ashes and dust all the capitals of East and Central Africa—Zomba, Lusaka, Dar es Salaam, Nairobi, Leopoldville, Brazzaville—within twenty-four hours. Within twenty-four hours I mean, and neither Ghana nor the Nigerian Army, could do anything to rescue us . . .
>
> We must not beat about the bush. Even our friends in North Africa, the United Arab Republic, Libya, Tunisia, Algeria, Morocco, all of them couldn't help us. . . .They wouldn't even get here.[18]

Banda did not conceive terrorism and its "armed propaganda" could paralyze the will to use that force, that weakness and cruelty could undo strength.

5 Banda's Importance

Vorster got the formal diplomatic recognition he did not insist on from Malawi alone in 1967. Banda had opened up relations not only with South Africa, but with Portugal and Rhodesia, all countries he had attacked mercilessly in the struggle for independence. Diplomatic relations with Portugal, Rhodesia and South Africa, and contacts, meant he knew their destruction would make things worse,—not that he approved entirely of them. It meant he knew many people in these countries did not agree with their governments—that they might change:

> I do not agree with [Portuguese policy in Africa], and I dare say there are many Portuguese in Lisbon now who do not agree with it—or even in Lourenço Marques or in Beira.

"Shouting at each other will not help," he had said upon Vorster's visit to Malawi in May 1970, the first trip abroad in nine years, the first to an independent black state, of a South African prime minister: "You, in the Republic of South Africa have your way of life . . . we . . . have our way of life . . . Am I to be the judge that yours is bad, ours is good, or that ours is bad and yours is good? No. *No one knows . . . No one knows.*" Times are bad enough that I have to add that Banda, like Savimbi, pleading for time in South Africa did not mean he approved of *apartheid,* only that he was not about to turn race discrimination into a pretext for the destruction of a state and its peoples, all its people.

Banda was practically the only new leader who would even talk to these countries openly, because, as Dean Acheson put it, he realized they were "more important [to his sub-Saharan neighbors] than all the rest of Africa put together," for the realization of actual, instead of illusory independence. And more important to the United States and Europe in their struggle for change with stability, Acheson added.

In contrast to his relations with Portugal, South Africa and Rhodesia, Banda who wanted to deal with all countries around him, managed only an exchange of prisoners with the black states in those years—with Zambia: Two captured Portuguese soldiers for five Zambians arrested illegally entering Mozambique. The newly independent states could not take the practicality of his straightforward refusal to interfere in South Africa's domestic affairs, and above all his readiness to take responsibility for himself and his country without blaming others.

Instead, after Vorster's rejection of the Lusaka Manifesto, endorsed by the UN General Assembly in November 1969, because of party pressure, but more importantly, because of the Manifesto's interference in domestic affairs,—the interference Banda rejected and the UN Charter precluded,—the leaders of the East and Central African States in October 1971 declared "no way [left] for the liberation of southern Africa except by armed struggle." The Manifesto had primly agreed to settle for sanctions and economic boycotts from countries too squeamish to violate traditional international law in order to support openly subversion and terrorism in the name of "humanity": "But it appeared that for many countries international law takes precedence over humanity."

The responsibilities of office, the responsibility for four million people, had made Banda drop the ideological preoccupations of the time before independence. They changed him deeply, matured him,—like a Prince Hal with the age of a Falstaff who knew himself, nevertheless, to be somewhat of an usurper. Responsibility made him see the actual world around him: "I have to do what I think is in the best interests of my people, the people of this country. Not what some theoretical white-headed professor in a college says . . . I have four million people to look after, four million. And to look after these four million I must not be swayed by theories either from the West or from the East because these theories, while they might work in Europe and Asia and other countries—or even other countries in our own continent—they may not work in Malawi, and it is Malawi that counts." Buthelezi in Washington in the fall of 1986 spoke the same words,—words that betray the daily responsibilities of office.

Banda's concentration on realities and common sense also brought harsh words for the international organizations, especially the UN, the OAU and the Commonwealth that baited African leaders' flight from responsibilities. They were words that baffled, most of all, the men who should have said them, the leaders of the West: "I will not be guided by people thousands of miles away from Rhodesia . . . people whose ignorance of conditions and the situation is greater than their ignorance of the situation and conditions in the planets Mars and Venus," he told African leaders upon his return from the Commonwealth Conference in London in January 1966. He went on a few months later: ". . . That is the trouble in Africa today—too many ignorant people who do not know anything about history and if they do know anything about it, they do not know how to interpret and apply it. That is why Africa is in a mess . . . *That is the tragedy of Africa: Too many ignorant people are in a position of power and responsibility*" (Italics mine).

Banda also sensed the ambivalence and guilt in the West's innards that paralyzed it in the face of terror and violence in the name of change. Antonio de Spinola was to name this ambivalence outright in 1974: ". . . [The attitude of Western democracies] varies only between a declared support of the anti-Portuguese subversive movements and a courteous official reserve concealing an indirect support in order to ensure the status quo."

Banda did not have to tell himself that subversion of his neighbors would undermine him as well. He had the decency to shrink from it instinctively: It horrified him. It did not make any sense to undermine his neighbors at the moment he assumed responsibility for his own country; besides he understood that stability in his own country, a black country, would reassure his neighbors, and make talk easier. He knew instinctively that the insistence on ideological uniformity in all governments would in time bring the destruction of all of them.

He saw through Nyerere at a time when Nyerere's moralistic posturing paralyzed the West. Nyerere feared the responsibilities of office because the British had handed him the country "on a silver platter," or "in wholesale lots," as Acheson put it. He had not earned his office. His readiness to support so-called "liberation movements"; to mastermind terrorism against the Portuguese and all of southern Africa; to allow Chinese and Vietnamese instructors to train guerrillas; to stock and distribute Soviet weapons; to coordinate and arrange the flights for Africans from all of southern Africa to the Soviet Union and eastern Europe and China for advanced training in terrorism, sabotage and indoctrination,—all that simply betrayed Nyerere's flight from responsibility for twenty-million Tanzanians: ". . . That man is simply suffering from a sense of inferiority, an inferiority complex that makes him . . . pose as a champion of Africa . . . when he is *no fighter at all but a coward*" (Italics mine).

Banda knew about Nyerere's subversion first hand. Nyerere had ignored Banda's letters of protest after Malawian police caught infiltrators trained in Tanzania by the Chinese and with weapons from Nyerere, barely a half-year after independence. "I am just waiting to hear Banda make the same accusation against President Johnson because Chipembere [a conspirator against Banda] is studying in the United States," Nyerere told a world, already in 1965, no longer willing to distinguish condescension and arrogance from confidence,— another way of saying it could not tell weakness from strength.

Kamuzu Banda is the only southern African leader, with the exception of Savimbi, who knows the West as deeply as his country's Africa, and not merely as a scholarship student, but as a professional, a medical doctor, who earned his living in competition with whites in Scotland and in London. An African

Odysseus, he had returned home to address crowds in English with an interpreter because he spoke his tribal language haltingly and in outdated phrases,—and because chiefs traditionally spoke through third parties,—after almost fifty years abroad: three in South Africa, twelve in the United States, the rest in Great Britain. He knew the world like few men but with an innocence that baffled the men he met. He knew English well enough not to let it lie to him,—in contrast to Nyerere and Kaunda. Banda shows that straightforward common sense counts for more than resources because without it resources can only promise. Besides, he had one advantage he did not flinch from knowing: His country was poor. Banda recognized the world Vorster's foreign policy wanted, the only one there is.

6 Rhodesia: The End Begins

The cessation of all terrorist activities had been Smith's condition for the cease-fire and the release of African leaders towards the end of 1974. But already by the end of 1974 there were reports of terrorists beating, murdering and kidnapping villagers refusing to assist them, and of terrorist propaganda claiming the cease-fire as a proof of victory.[19] The Victoria Falls talks failed in August 1975 because Smith would not grant the return of all leaders with unconditional guarantees against arrest, prosecution and execution of sentences, to attend the constitutional congress Smith had agreed to call at the end of 1975. Two months later Smith gave a television interview in South Africa that caused an uproar. But for South Africa's "détente exercise" Rhodesia would have already brought the war to an end, he said. At the time of the cease-fire with almost daily "contacts" and terrorist losses of up to twenty a day, the remaining terrorists numbered, in Rhodesian reckoning, no more than a few hundred, an estimate the terrorists confirmed after the war.

A few months earlier, in early 1975, Smith had called the actions just before the cease-fire "the greatest successes of the security forces": "We were on the brink of dealing a knock-out blow . . . In our minds the détente exercise [a clear recall of Vorster's echo of Kissinger's language] undoubtedly saved those terrorists remaining in Rhodesia because our security forces abided by the terms of the cease-fire,"—and the terrorists did not.[20]

After the breakdown at Victoria Falls, Vorster doggedly persisted in negotiations despite Kaunda's and Nyerere's open hostility in early 1976. He would not accept disappointment, and Smith went along.

Vorster called in Kissinger, who had just failed him in his intervention in Angola, a few months after his 1973 accords in Vietnam had gone to oblivion,— a call of desperation masked in euphoria that took itself for hope. Kissinger came to Africa, a continent he knew little about, in the spring and summer of 1976. On September 12, Ian Smith accepted Kissinger's terms: majority rule in Rhodesia with temporary guarantees for the white minority.

The following talks in Geneva that again brought Smith face to face with some of the men he had released from prison barely two years before, failed largely because Mugabe and Nkomo insisted on the immediate hand-over of power *sans ambages*. The main result of the negotiations: the association of Mugabe and Nkomo in an opportunistic alliance—the so-called Patriotic Front (PF) that gave them the political leadership of terrorists who had fought for almost ten years without them, and who now came under the direct military command of Machel, Nyerere and Kaunda.

Terrorist infiltrations now broke in upon Rhodesia from almost all sides, from the long frontier with Mozambique, from Zambia, including the opening of a new front in the northwest, and later from Botswana,—just the isolation that Vorster had feared in 1974 after the collapse of Portugal. In contrast until 1971, when FRELIMO had allowed them a few bases in Tete province, in areas near the Rhodesian frontier beyond Portugal's weakening will or in impassable country, the terrorists had had to cross the Zambezi to attack Rhodesia.

The intensity of renewed terror in 1976 showed its masked face in a region of the eastern front: Colors;—red, amber, or white,—marked all roads on maps to show degrees of land mine danger more deadly than anything the Portuguese had faced. Losses averaged two vehicles a day. Limping mutilated animals became a common sight, the victims of poisoned spikes, whiplash devices and booby traps meant to kill and maim men,—Vietnam's contribution to the war effort.

In short, every concession of Vorster's to pressure brought renewed attacks and demands: He had wanted a negotiated solution, but the yearning for negotiated solution was leading to the abandonment of Rhodesia, with Rhodesia's apparent compliance. The war was coming closer to South Africa, just what Vorster had wanted most to avoid by opening up more or less straightforward relations with Africa.

In 1976, after a visit to Mozambique to show "solidarity" with FRELIMO, Kaunda called for the violent overthrow of Smith, and for talks in South Africa with "all leaders": "The Mandelas and the Sisulus in jail and the Tambos outside to help map out the future of the country together."

His earlier distinction between the end of apartheid and one-man, one-vote disappeared: "Today it is Mozambique and Angola, and tomorrow it will be Zimbabwe and Namibia . . . All around them White South Africans will have countries with majority rule [he did not add, *in name only*] . . . There is no alternative to majority rule," he added mercifully, "before the end of the century."[21]

A decade earlier, Harold Wilson's Great Britain and the United States had begun the isolation of Rhodesia, and also of South Africa, that Vorster and the collapse of Portugal only completed,—after terrorism broke out in Angola and Mozambique *but before its start in Rhodesia*. In 1965 and especially in 1966,—after the ineffectiveness of sanctions Britain imposed after Rhodesia's declaration of independence in November that Wilson expected would overthrow Smith's government by November 1966,—Wilson turned to the UN Security Council with United States support: in November 1965, voluntary sanctions; in April 1966, a call on Britain to use force to stop oil to Rhodesia through Beira; in December 1966, selective mandatory sanctions, "the United Nations term for economic warfare," Acheson called them. To justify sanctions the UN had to hold that Rhodesia's defiance of Wilson's government but not the Crown, threatened neighboring states, for the UN Charter forbade interference in the internal affairs of members. The UN Security Council's decisions subverted the UN Charter's distinction between external war and rebellion or other disturbances within a country.

A few weeks after the Security Council's third measure against Rhodesia, on December 8, 1966, in the House of Commons Wilson coolly blamed his obduracy on the UN obliteration of this distinction, he did not add at his and the United States' behest: ". . . Rhodesia insists on remaining, not in an imperfectly multi-racial condition, but in a state of illegal rebellion, *and the United Nations has voted this is a threat to the peace*" (Italics mine).

Wilson had been franker, before he assumed office on October 14, 1964, and adopted the language of high-principled disingenuousness, the smoldering mark of our day, that eventually allowed him to blame the UN for his heart's desires. A few days before he took office he had made it pitilessly clear that he meant to use negotiations between all parties to overthrow Rhodesia's sovereignty with its consent,—the present goal of the media; the bureaucracies; the lobbying groups that presume to speak for the "grassroots," both African and white; the CAA Act; the Eminent Persons Group in South Africa:

The Labour Party is totally opposed to granting the independence to Southern Rhodesia so long as the Government of that country remains under the control of a white minority. We have repeatedly urged the British government to negotiate a new constitution with all of the African and European parties represented in order to achieve a peaceful transition to African majority rule [not simply, *majority rule*].[22]

Harold Wilson's Britain and the United States that "followed along in the Children's Crusade to universalize one-man, one-vote," Acheson's words, had brought the obliteration of the distinction between external war and domestic disturbances,—at the core of Communist dogma since the Third International,—upon the UN in violation of its charter. The Soviet Union must have stood amazed at this unwitting complicity in its goals despite its ostensible confidence that democracies were bound to undo each other in spite of their strength,—overwhelming in southern Africa.

"The United Nations policy is thus, ironically, the chief threat to the peace and security of southern and central Africa," Acheson said in 1968 in a plea to President Johnson to overturn his policy against Rhodesia in the last days of his administration: ". . . The United States will bear the responsibility for a continuance of this mistaken quarrel with Rhodesia—and secondarily with South Africa and Portugal—by continuing encouragement of measures taken in the United Nations . . . We will bear responsibility for the growing political isolation of southern Africa which these emotional and ill-considered measures are bringing about . . . It is the height of folly to sacrifice these desirable ends to an aggressive reformist intervention in the internal affairs of these states, an intervention designed to force upon them electoral practices that none of black African or Communist states and few of the Asian accept."

These imperishable words tell with even greater force against present American, Commonwealth and UN policy toward South Africa.[23] For the strategy, not the countries, are strikingly similar,—and with good reason. Mugabe, who now leads the attack on South Africa in southern Africa, devised it against Rhodesia in ten years in Rhodesia's comfortable prisons. He knows nothing else. Besides it worked, in Rhodesia.

Harold Wilson's application of sanctions and his recourse to the UN against Rhodesia brought, not only a fateful undermining of the UN Charter, but also a reversal of the previous, historically accurate, position of the British government that it could not impose a solution on Rhodesia because it had always governed itself. In fact until the ninety-eight days that followed the conclusion of the Lancaster House talks on December 21, 1979, Great Britain had never administered Rhodesia directly as a Crown Colony.

First administered by Cecil Rhodes' British South Africa Company (BSAC) under a Royal Charter of 1893, the Rhodesians had showed the political confidence to chose self-rule instead of union with South Africa in 1923, the burning question of those years, after petitioning the Crown in 1920 for "responsible government." From 1889 Rhodesia had been responsible for its own defense, and from 1923 it had its own consuls in a few countries. It had never received money or aid from Great Britain. Without South Africa's experience of tragedy and with a past of barely two generations, Rhodesia had one thing in common with it, and incidentally with the United States: Political organization preceded the formation of a nation that would take generations and centuries.

The BSAC had provided not national identity but enough stability,—the Rhodesian police went about unarmed,—to attract immigration of both Africans and whites that started almost immediately after the cessation of tribal wars in 1897, the first great achievement of the BSAC, and which increased markedly after the Second World War. Between 1946 and 1951 whites increased from 82,000 to 135,000, to number 225,000 by 1965. By 1960 African population had reached an estimated 3,400,000 from an estimated 500,000 in 1901, 850,000 in 1920, 1,430,000 in 1940, 2,820,000 in 1954.

Introduced in 1961, after British prompting, to gain independence for Southern Rhodesia upon the expectation of Great Britain's unilateral dissolution of the Federation of Rhodesia and Nyasaland (1953–1963), the new constitution that Wilson sought to undo, besides continuing a modest property and literacy qualification (enough to read the ballot) for African voters, had reserved one quarter plus one seat for African representatives, elected by Africans, in each house. This racial discrimination led Ian Smith to break with the ruling party and turned him into a national figure: "Our policy in the past has always been that we would have a government in Rhodesia based on merit and that people wouldn't worry whether you were black or whether you were white . . . In a diabolical way a more racialist constitution it would be difficult to find."[24]

At the time Harold Wilson and the United States turned the UN against Rhodesia, the Rhodesian government wanted time for gradual extension of the franchise to Africans it expected would outnumber whites on the common roll by 1975. "All we are asking for is a little bit of time to prove our case," Smith told *Life* in 1966, a few weeks after his government committed itself to universal primary education by 1969 and a full four years of secondary education for thirty-seven percent of African children by 1974. By 1979 sixty percent of African children were in primary school, with thirty-four percent finishing and places for twenty percent of them in secondary school. In 1977 a study of the Division of African Education argued the African birth rate made primary education for all African children unrealistic.[25]

"Once you start lowering standards, then you are on the slippery road down," Smith added in explanation of property and literacy qualifications far less stringent than Lord Selborne's.[26] Similar provisions, especially the property qualification, determined the electorate in some of the thirteen states upon their formation of the United States. They were far more necessary in twentieth century Rhodesia with five thousand years telling the difference between Europeans and Africans: Of Rhodesia's four million Africans in 1966, fifty percent aged eighteen and under, about seventy percent lived permanently in Tribal Trust Lands, sometimes in "Neolithic conditions," Acheson still dared say in 1968, only six hundred thousand in townships outside the major cities and towns.

The commitment of Europeans to gradual responsible change met with rejection, soon violence's rejection, from the "Black Nationalists" after Nkomo in 1961 first accepted, then rejected, the new constitution, a reversal Banda did not forgive him. "White-man stooges" they called the thirteen black representatives elected under the new constitution in the 1962 elections they boycotted,—the slogan and intimidation of the ANC and the UDF in South Africa since 1984. They kept Africans from registering, and those that registered from voting, either through outright intimidation or through the excitation of distrust: Of 10,623 registered African voters, only 2,396 voted. Five thousand more African voters would have kept the United Federal Party (UFP) that had sponsored the 1961 constitution from defeat by a new party, the Rhodesian Front (RF). Roughly sixteen months later, an RF Cabinet revolt against the previous prime minister, Winston Field, for not making progress on independence with the British, made Smith prime minister.[27]

In the year before the elections: Six Africans, one a policeman out of uniform, another a woman taken for a police informer, burned to death, in a township outside Salisbury; a fire-bomb badly damaged the house of the secretary of the youth branch of the multi-racial UFP. October, roughly six weeks before the election, saw 193 incidents of serious violence, 34 of them fire-bombings. Not called "necklacing" then, murder by fire became the "hallmark of nationalist attacks."[28]

In the following year, 1963, Mugabe broke with Nkomo because he doubted his commitment to violence: "We broke with Nkomo . . . because we believed he was not for armed struggle [and] was half-hearted about it at the time," Mugabe recollected in 1976.[29] The year 1963 also brought the first proof that African "Nationalist" groups received arms from Communist countries.[30]

In the seven weeks in 1964 before the banning of the two African Nationalist Parties, Nkomo's ZAPU and Mugabe's ZANU, and the arrest of the leaders Smith was to release at Vorster's behest ten years later, there were 1,725 incidents of thuggery including 20 gasoline bomb attacks, 68 assaults on police, 5 murders, 205 arson attacks, the victims nearly all Africans. On August 20 a letter in the African newspaper, *The Daily News*, said: "Life in the townships has now become a Hell. Fear is ruling our lives because one does not know who is the next man to be attacked."[31]

"As far as we are concerned the time has come for African rule. We are not for gradualism . . . It is an insult to the African people. There is no compromise on the one-man, one-vote issue," Mugabe had announced to the world in the same days just before the banishment of his organization.[32] Three months earlier, in May 1964 just after Smith became prime minister, Rhodesian intelligence learned that both ZANU and ZAPU had decided on "armed struggle" with any available means.[33]

But the Africans showed in their actions they thought differently from the men who claimed to lead them, as any sensible man would expect: They informed on thugs; later in the Security Forces, they killed and captured a large percentage of terrorists. The rejection of the constitution by the African "Nationalists," who had resorted to intimidation to muster the appearance of support, betrayed their dread of responsibility for actual change—like ANC and UDF violence in South Africa. Actual change, gradual and responsible, was too much for the "radical" self-appointed leaders of the Africans who needed intimidation to reassure themselves, and most importantly, for headlines abroad.

In 1962 the United Nations created a subcommittee of the United Nations Committee on Colonialism to investigate Southern Rhodesia. In 1963 Britain had to veto a Security Council resolution not to "grant any power or attributes of sovereignty . . . [nor] to transfer the armed forces and aircraft [of the Central African Federation to Southern Rhodesia]."[34] This attention abroad reinforced the African leaders' dread of change.

Unfortunately Smith had been right about the "diabolically racialist constitution" he had opposed: The introduction of racial quotas in the 1961 constitution had served to incite the appearance of racial passion, to stop gradual change and to impugn the Europeans' good faith. The incitement of the appearance of racial passion had a future because it served to blind regard for realities of daily life that alone could restrain violence: " 'Anti-racism' has become a code-word for socialist transformation since, according to Marxist-Leninist ideology, 'racism' is endemic to capitalism and will be eliminated with the abolition of classes." These words of two South African writers describe Mugabe's propaganda mastering Zimbabwe since 1980. It had started with the African boycott of the constitution.[35]

A few weeks before Wilson overturned traditional policy toward Rhodesia, the secretary of state for commonwealth relations, Duncan Sandys, in words Alec Douglas-Home, the prime minister, echoed, had indicated that the British government would acquiesce in Rhodesia's independence under the 1961 constitution if Smith's government could "prove—and I underline the prime minister's scepticism on this point—that the Africans will accept the present constitution without any enlargement of representative institutions . . ." At a traditional Indaba on October 21–26, 1964, that Smith argued reflected the "will of the people" more accurately than "somewhat burlesque polling methods with the use of pictorial symbols [because of widespread illiteracy] together with physical intimidation," about seven hundred chiefs and headmen unanimously declared for independence; on November 5, enfranchised voters, 58,091 against 6,096 (including 13,333 Africans) voted for independence. Douglas-Home might have accepted this "proof" that Wilson rejected out of hand—without "the courtesy and fairmindedness to listen to the evidence," Smith remarked.

The Conservative government had, however, made it clear that the Indaba Smith had announced the day before the British election "would not provide conclusive evidence of the wishes of the people" and had refused to send observers. In early March 1965 the chiefs told two ministers Wilson sent to sound out opinion in Rhodesia, who asked them to show they had majority African support: "It is not our custom to use a ballot or a piece of paper. It is a foreign custom."

Settlement may have been within grasp, except for the unexpected, the British vote, very close also. *Fortuna*, "the way things go," ancient historians might have called it; "contingency," philosophers since the seventeenth century. Both words mean the uncertainty, the disappointment of plausible expectations, that make the experience of tragedy inseparable from freedom,— in contrast to immolation in the "inevitability of history," which will know no tragedy.

Banda knew seriousness in the face of these events:

Who is right and who is wrong in this tragic affair? . . . We do not know and *we may never know*. But which ever of the two men [Harold Wilson or Ian Smith] is to blame . . . on his head will be heaped the curses of generations for the suffering of millions of innocent people that will inevitably follow in the wake of this tragedy (Italics mine).

That was in 1965. There were not many men in high office then, and there are fewer now, who can use the word "tragedy" and mean it, and who can say they do not know.

7 Angola Catastrophe

The three South African armored columns, somewhere between two and three thousand men, that entered Angola in the last week of October 1975 almost reached the Cuanza River,—with probing groups thirty-five miles outside of Luanda,—with a speed, a few weeks, that took the breath away from the South African government. In the crucial days, perhaps four, the South African government hesitated before ordering withdrawal, in part because of American failure to support an attempt to take Luanda.

Entrance into Luanda might have transformed the situation, not only in Angola, but in all of southern Africa. For it would have meant the South Africans would have undertaken enforcement of the Alvor accords just after the Portuguese abandonment on November 11. They also would have made it impossible for the world to continue to ignore the situation in Angola; they would have shown the United States could face realities despite defeat in Indochina. All the countries in southern Africa had taken seriously the Alvor agreements of January 15, 1975 that had provided for elections and transfer of sovereignty to the three Angolan "liberation movements" on November 11th, with some Portuguese soldiers to remain until February 1976. But the Soviets, the MPLA and foreign observers judged them a recipe for chaos and partition because they were without provisions for enforcement,—like the agreements between South Africa, Cuba, and the MPLA in 1988.

Vorster's decision to withdraw showed again the limits of his Africa policy, limits of political confidence, not of military strength. As in Rhodesia, South Africa would not go it alone,—without the United States and the West.

American refusal to supply South Africa with weapons and ammunition to match Soviet armor, may have also prompted Vorster's withdrawal despite few South African losses, perhaps no more than forty-three: "Only big powers can offset the arsenal, above all the 122mm rockets. It is beyond our limits," he remarked in December 1975.[36] Besides the dreaded 122mm rocket, the Katyusha, with a range of forty miles, and destruction of everything within a radius of forty meters, mounted in groups of forty in the "Stalin Organ," that sometimes landed in hundreds, Vorster meant weapons like the Sagger antitank missile, wire-controlled and compact operated directly by Cubans, or under supervision of Soviet and East German officers.

Even so the South African attempt to do the obvious won them a measure of respect. They had at least tried—in contrast to the United States unable to act itself, and unwilling even to support the daring of others. "Soviet leaders were overjoyed by America's lack of response," in spite of UN Ambassador Moynihan's "outrage" overruled by Washington "that could be felt all the way from Moscow," remarks Arkady Shevchenko in *Breaking with Moscow*.[37] Above all, the South Africans showed how easy it would have been to set the situation right with a little political confidence. The totalitarians exploited this lack of confidence to make self-defense and succoring others look like aggression.

The South Africans entered a country in total breakdown. At least half of the Portuguese, about 300,000 had fled, some by air to Lisbon, others on foot without food to the South West African border. Refugees, children without parents, wives without husbands, at the mercy of any kid with a weapon, blocked traffic on the roads south. "Perhaps the biggest fear among those of us who covered this war was that so many of the troops, the majority of whom were armed with the most sophisticated weapons available on the market, were only in their early teens. And most of the time they were within shouting distance of the firing line or of any real or imagined enemy, they opened up without provocation."[38]

There were murders, not simple deaths, but agonies in torture, mutilation and emasculation, deaths that paralyzed the country in the terror of flight and in the euphoria of killing and dying. Europeans fought in all groups mixed up with Africans against other blacks and whites, fathers against sons, brothers against brothers, in apparently aimless violence that had a purpose its instigators knew: not the "nuclear holocaust" but unlimited total war with a "personal touch," the destruction of the living core of the country. ". . . Unlike other wars, there are no real sides. Firing is indiscriminate. Huge quantities of firepower are being let loose and even distant bystanders are being wounded and killed," a *Time* photographer, Don Stefan, got the appearance without recognition of its purpose.

People could not believe their eyes. They denied what was going on, the same denial that smote the West, with much less reason, for present danger did not excite its fear. Some of the people who had believed "it would never happen here," crowded the airport in Luanda, "a city of real fear and death": "Perhaps the most tragic sight in this already desperate city was at the Luanda Airport. There, in long straggling lines, one could observe the hopelessness of the situation created by the over-enthusiastic and politically motivated young army officers in Europe. Children, parents, the pregnant, the aged and crippled all waited, pathetic in their eagerness to get away from this land of shattered illusions." In Luanda frequent random shooting broke out. The *Jornal de Angola* ran daily advertisements with photographs of men, women and children who had disappeared.

Those who remained are still stunned: "For ten years, we can not get anything—clothes, wine, food,—we aren't used to living like this," an Angolan told an American reporter in 1987.[39] Almost nothing moves, not even money, except stray cats and dogs, now in Luanda: A few tomatoes cost thirty-three dollars at the "official" exchange rate.

In this savagery the young South African conscripts and professionals brought something like order: The young disciplined soldiers of the Republic did not just kill anybody they came upon, a sentence that would make almost any other time blush. Their very presence meant protection for the unarmed. The kids turned murderers and thugs melted back into the bush. The MPLA under Cubans sometimes stood up to the South Africans. But without the Cubans, ten to sixteen thousand by the end of 1975, who shot MPLA soldiers lingering behind, who manned the tanks; without the Soviets and their weapons that started arriving systematically six months after the coup in Portugal; without East German advisors,—there would have been little resistance.[40]

To foresee the chaos Portuguese abandonment brought that the West refused to see, you did not have to be a Communist: All Western experience since the breakdown at Corcyra Thucydides described taught its expectation.

But to know its difference from Corcyra, to understand the will to make it worse, in order to pulverize the souls of those who did not die outright in Angola, and throughout the world, you had to know the world the Communists take for granted.

In contrast to Corcyra, the nine months of killing in Angola were instigated from the top to prepare the new world, in typically totalitarian fashion that makes plain murder and hate appear quaint, old-fashioned, homemade and "human," a word that now so often reeks of the blood-thirstiness it denies. The Soviets needed the real confusion of collapse,—the confusion Clough, in his article, "Beyond Constructive Engagement," and the United States State Department now so devoutly wish on South Africa. But they could not do it alone.

To precipitate the bloodshed that would destroy the country five hundred years had made the Soviets needed Portuguese soldiers and officers to provide passion and illusion, and Portuguese Communist cadres to exploit it. The victim had to be made to do himself in, as always. They needed idealism and innocence.

The conscripts and the professional officers sometimes learned this idealism and innocence from the diaries and Marxist propaganda they found on the terrorists they had killed or captured. This readiness to listen to the men they fought shows there was something to the Portuguese claim, so often mocked, that they took the Africans for Portuguese.[41]

The Soviets also needed the disingenuousness of a few high officers who unable any longer to stand bravery's simplicity would seek refuge in ideology from the contradictions their comrades had lived, and died with, as best they could, for years. These were men who knew the answers.[42]

Two moves from the top precipitated the massacres: The announcement of "self-determination," Woodrow Wilson's fateful words, for the overseas territories and the decision to disarm the Europeans in Mozambique and Angola. The "self-determination" announced to the world in July 1974 by Prime Minister General Vasco Gonçalves, later identified as a Communist,— Spinola had been forced to appoint him after the failure of his first government in May 1974,—turned out to be nothing more than a code-word for the "immediate independence" demanded in the Portuguese Communist Party's (PCP) 1965 Manifesto. (The Manifesto had been drawn up under the chairmanship of Alvaro Cunhal who returned to Portugal immediately after the coup to take over Communist operations, at the same time as Mario Soares and other exiles, after fourteen years of planning and preparation in Czechoslovakia and the Soviet Union.)

In early September, Spinola announced he would take over the Angola negotiations, to prevent precipitate abandonment: He meant to give the Africans a choice. But his resignation on September 30th with a warning of a danger of new tyranny broadcast live to the "Portuguese nation in Europe" turned his intentions to nothing. Mozambique and Guinea Bissau had already been abandoned.

The first Portuguese high commissioner after the coup, Rosa Coutinho, nicknamed the "Red Admiral," knew his business in disarming the Europeans in Angola. "Terrorize whites by all means," he had written his brother-in-law, Agostinho Neto, an *assimilado*, an African with the earned status of a European and Portuguese citizenship, who had seized control of the MPLA, on December 24, 1974, barely three months before the first breakdowns in Angola.

Coutinho had minced no words in the letter he never repudiated, published in a Portuguese language newspaper in Johannesburg scarcely a month after the South African intervention: "We shall uproot the whites so completely that with their fall the whole capitalistic structure will be demolished making it possible to establish the new socialist society."[43]

Portuguese soldiers even took hunting guns from farmers that needed them for protection from marauders and animals: "Thousands of people were slaughtered because they were defenseless, killed by groups of armed bandits who would have fled at the first sign of resistance."

Savimbi's UNITA and Holden Roberto's FNLA, some of whose men were to fight alongside the South Africans ten months later, had already gotten to Coutinho. They represented a threat to the spread of "communism from Tangiers to the Cape and from Lisbon to Washington," words hardly as extravagant as they first appear.

Coutinho meant terror to break men's minds. The words from the notebook of a South West African youth in terrorist training in Angola published in the Denton Hearings best show the mind of the Coutinho that ordered the Europeans disarmed: "Indeed difficulties—hunger, death, encirclement, economic blockage, sometimes no food, ammunition, clothes etc.—are not bad: *They force us to think differently*" (Italics mine). But Coutinho, in contrast to the training terrorist, meant sufferings for others, not for himself.

The order to disarm the Portuguese turned the junior officers from idealists who wanted to give the war a new significance into accomplices in murder. The order robbed the conscripts who carried it out of the self-respect that defines a soldier. The complicity showed itself in the young officers who overnight turned into their opposite, a change Spinola had sensed and sought to avert and overcome in his book. All the old words lost their meaning: "Individuals who were regarded as part of the establishment before became vocal propagandists for a radical cause, sowing dissension and confusion."

Some even turned into the enemy: FRELIMO's chief instructor of Mugabe's terrorists was a Portuguese who had come to live for the destruction of white rule in southern Africa,—killed in a Rhodesian incursion into Mozambique in 1976.

The conscripts' loss of self-respect showed itself in their bedraggled stunned appearance: "In the Portuguese armed forces, more than anywhere else, one could detect all the signs of a nation torn by revolt within the ranks. To me it was all the more poignant, for I had seen these fighting men at their best. But that was long ago," Al J. Venter wrote. Long ago means two years before: This kind of breakdown has a speed almost quicker than thought.

The MPLA and Cuban seizure of Luanda under Soviet and East German direction in August 1975, not only the capital, but a port crucial for the shipment of arms and troops to conquer the country, intensified Portuguese complicity because Portuguese passivity in the face of the takeover amounted to cooperation.

The often brave Portuguese officers' readiness to own their responsibility for the deaths of others because of their illusions, just a few months after, argues their goodwill, goodwill the Communists exploited to turn them into accomplices,—a contrast to the persisting silence that takes its toll in present disingenuousness of many of the men responsible for the abandonment of Indochina in the same year: "I feel that I am a murderer for all the bloodshed I have caused," Major Vitor Alves, one of the important brains behind the collapse of Portugal, told Venter in 1976. He would add no other word, another kind of silence, respect for words.

"I do not understand why you are so frightened of the Communists. They don't eat babies, and it is a political party like any other," Alves had said barely two years before in the comparative safety of Lisbon.[44]

In the months from January roughly to May 1975 in the face of the spreading violence, Savimbi alone had the assurance to call on Angolans to stop killing and respect the Alvor accords, not the transitional government, not the MPLA, not the Portuguese. He toured the country, a powerful speaker who preferred campaigning to fighting. He was determined, as he still is, to go through with the elections the Alvor accords promised. His words showed the confidence of that commitment, they brought some steadfastness to crowds. Polls in March through May showed UNITA ahead of the FNLA and the MPLA, with twenty-five percent of the vote, a plurality that in part reflected the numbers of Savimbi's tribe, the Ovimbundu, thirty-five to forty percent of the population. Savimbi's UNITA and the FNLA would have won the elections.

These were the hardest days for Savimbi. They taught Savimbi who had probably assumed that things would take care of themselves once the Portuguese left that the fight for independence had started in earnest because of Portuguese abandonment,—and against much crueler and hypocritical masters, the Cubans, East Germans and the Soviets who worked through the Angolans, and whose words denied their actions and fascinated the media. "I have been seven years in the jungle. I did not spend them there to be dominated after independence by the Russians," he told the British reporter, Fred Bridgland, in January 1976.

Events were now showing him the enormity of his rebellion against Portugal, the most questionable decision of his life. He did not flinch them. Always independent, he now began to learn what it really took to stand alone. One of Roberto's associates broke into tears before the South African generals who informed Roberto and Savimbi on January 16, 1976 of South Africa's withdrawal from Angola:

Chipenda began crying in front of the South African officers. I said no, it is just that: they came in, they want to go out, so let them go. Then when we went outside Roberto asked me what made me so confident that I had troops who could replace the South Africans. I said I didn't have any, but I wasn't going to cry in front of the South Africans. If they want to leave us, they leave. If we have to die, let us die. This is our country.

What can we do? We were not part of the arrangement when they came here, so we have no power to persuade them to stay. The one who sent them in is sending them out, so we have to accept it.[45]

Events were teaching him distinctions, for instance, between Angolans and Cubans, that make for common sense, a quality rarer than genius. In the months after the South African withdrawal Savimbi had only one policy: "Kill Cubans! Kill them all!," he told a French journalist in the latter half of 1976. UNITA groups even allowed MPLA fighters they met on the roads to pass without fighting.

He had the capacity to learn from events, to mature in their face,—in contrast to totalitarians who sought only to exploit them, to make things worse in the name of making things better, the so-called inevitability of history. He did not take flight from events into ideological immolation.

8 Spinola's Book—Lev Davidovich Bronstein's "Dustbin of History"; Savimbi's Lesson

Leur [of the Seleucids] *régime ne constituait cependant nullement un régime colonial dans le sens où nous l'entendons aujourd'hui. Comme ils n'avaient aucun zèle missionaire et ne cherchaient à améliorer ni la religion ni les égouts de leurs sujets, mais laissaient les indigènes aussi crasseux et aussi heureux qu'ils l'avaient été auparavant, la dynastie ne donna jamais lieu à aucune insurrection de leur part.*
E. BICKERMAN

In his book *Portugal and the Future*, Spinola sensed the polarization threatening the minds of his officers, and in his country, between the yearning for victory's grandeur and old authority's reassertion and the Marxists' and materialists' sympathy for the enemy and the abolition of the past. To overcome this polarization, he meant to get at the rational core, for Portugal, Africa and Europe, of the war he had fought brilliantly in Portuguese Guinea for five years,—Portugal's most serious guerrilla war. He knew the contradiction provoking the polarization: "We cannot, in fact proclaim a multiculture and, at the same time, attribute to the Portuguese of European origin a superior aptitude for the exercise of power."[46]

He called Portugal's bluff, especially the Portuguese government's bluff. It had to risk its confidence in the Africans' choice: "If a free choice prevails, and having clearly explained to them the various options, the evidence at hand indicates that the great majority of our Africans would choose to remain in the Portuguese nation . . ."

The Portuguese, both Africans and Europeans, were fighting for something important. Their reluctance to explain their fighting, and take the consequences, drew them to misunderstand themselves and the world to misunderstand them: "It should be recognized that, if we are not really what we are accused of being, we sometimes appear to be so or we act in such a way that our detractors can turn an appearance to their advantage."

The Portuguese, especially Spinola's officers, had come to believe in the propaganda against them that held they were fighting against the blacks, not for the Africans,—that the war at its core was racial, or turning racial, because it was inconclusive, apparently endless. This propaganda had shaken them because the war was without the limited political design or goal that might make its end visible and possible and above all, comprehensible. In Angola and Mozambique a past was at stake, a past of a Europe that counted, of the Europe that had not known the Second World War, barely the First World War, the past the totalitarians wanted to destroy, the very power of memory.

The war prompted Spinola's concentration on political coherence: "It seems therefore, that we must exclude victory through the physical extermination of the enemy owing to his possibilities for the constant renewal of his forces." Portugal could not win but it must not lose.

He renounced conquest: The international organizations would not have it, he did not believe in it, he thought it was impossible,—an admission that some South African and Rhodesian men who know war called "appeasement." But fighting meant precious time "for finding those political solutions which are the only ones which can put an end to the conflict": "The forces of law and order can always lose a subversive war, but they will never win one for the simple reason that the construction of victory does not lie in their sphere." Fixation on military victory meant "anticipation of defeat" unless a country had the unlimited facilities to turn war into an "institution": The war consumed forty percent of Portugal's budget at the time Spinola wrote.

Spinola knew what he meant: Men, both Europeans and Africans, had fought and willingly died for him because of his words. Governor-general and commander-in-chief in Portuguese Guinea in the previous years (1968–73), he had led the most successful of Portugal's three wars, and the only one that did not lead to disaster after independence, because he had talked as well as fought. He had converted many "insurgents." He had developed social services and fashioned the African Congress that sought to respect tribal ways but give the Africans a political voice that counted in decisions. From 1961–1964 he had served in Angola.

A young American officer sent from Vietnam to Africa to study Portuguese counterinsurgency was astonished to find this general, a man of dramatic appearance who wore a monocle and carried a riding crop, who in the depth of the tropics refused air-conditioning, who had learned his tactics and strategy from the Germans on the Russian front for two years during the Second World War, talk more about politics, about reaching people, than about war, with words that belied his appearance.

And words did not come easily to him: His book is turgid with the turgidity of a man who has finally decided to talk in a world that respected silence; who does not even know the word "glib"; who has read others but who does not say anything he has not rediscovered in his own thought.

His words burst with the energy that comes only when a man writes in the face of his actual experience and success, when he writes only what he has seen, lived, done,—especially done. I shall not call him sincere, a word that we have come to use for men you know are not telling you what they think, or who are not thinking at all. Some journalists took his straightforwardness for naiveté, an inadvertent tribute.

   It would be cheap to say that Spinola was a dreamer, naive, a man given to his illusions, who was saying the truth too late. He did not come to see things too late because it was too late—like the American diplomats who argued against supporting the South African intervention in Angola in 1975 because the Portuguese war for dominion was not part of the "East-West" conflict,—after the collapse of Portugal had made it a part of that conflict.

   Salazar's words, at the outbreak of the first massacres in Angola in 1961, preceded by Portuguese atrocities quickly stopped, "The fatherland is to be defended, not argued about," were not enough: "The time for dogmas and doctrines has passed . . . The era of epics, stirred by the thirst for glory, heroic deeds and respect for traditional honor, or based on romantic love or passion is definitely past." Not easy words for a general with dead soldiers before his eyes: "We defend this theory because we are pro-Portuguese and above all out of respect for the memory of those who died in Africa, their last thoughts being for the fatherland."

   The objections, the *rational* criticism of Portugal, had to be taken seriously to prevent their exploitation: "[We live in a world] from whose norms of behaviour we cannot escape. To lay claim to the opposite is to undermine the solidarity of the human race. And in our case to ignore the present is not only to concede that our attackers are right, but, more importantly, it is to lend them strength."

   About the totalitarian exploitation of these criticisms he suffered little doubt: "Subversive movements do not represent the African spirit of emancipation; they use it." The witnesses before the Denton Hearings repeat and repeat this understanding that glows like an unheard-of truth in much of the West.

   Western ambivalence paralyzed it: "On the Western side there is the conviction, shared by responsible members of the governments of the great powers, that the process of the emancipation of Africa is inevitable; and convinced of this, they cannot but avoid giving support to subversives, even if only indirectly . . ." This paralyzing ambivalence reduced the West to Soviet positions: "The subversive movement seeks in this manner to enlist their sympathies [the West's] and to draw them into their orbit."

   The war continuing in Angola and Mozambique divided people's minds throughout the world, it turned them into willing and unwilling instruments of totalitarianism in southern Africa, and elsewhere: "The Communist bloc is not interested in immediately putting a stop to the conflict, for otherwise it would already have provided those movements with the possibility of effective intervention which would have been very difficult for us to counter . . . In their view, the destruction of the centers of international tension would not be logical, for the existence of these latter are extraordinarily well-suited to the spread of their ideology and the maintenance of their situation as opponents." In southern Africa their eyes and minds were turning against South West Africa, Rhodesia and South Africa.

Just this "spread of ideology" that obliterates the perception of differences in nations and individuals drove Machel in May 1970 to declare that the war would lose sense unless Rhodesia followed Mozambique: "Some of us, when we look at the situation in Mozambique, realize if we liberate Mozambique tomorrow that it will not be the end. The liberation of Mozambique without the liberation of Zimbabwe is *meaningless*" (Italics mine).[47]

These words do not mean one war sets off another, the chain of wars that baffled ancient historians, for instance, in the East after the Second Punic War. They mean the violence cannot stop because it lives in the mind. Not lust for power, not greed, comprehensible passions, but the more deadly fear of disappointment of illusions drives violence to overcome everyone. Within Angola too Spinola wrote, "The people cannot, even should they wish to, remain indifferent" to the violence because it was "total."

The wars' intensification after Portuguese abandonment supports Spinola's understanding that the Soviets wanted violence but not decisive violence. The war really started after the Portuguese left but it never approached conquest outside of Mozambique and Angola. It spread to Rhodesia and then to South West Africa and South Africa, relentlessly, but slowly enough to avoid the confrontation with South Africa that an attempt at direct conquest would provoke. With Angola and Mozambique, and then Rhodesia after 1980, the slow continuation of violence grinds up the countries like the Second World War with all its attendant civil wars ground up Europe before totalitarianism. For totalitarianism is not the creature of a day. It means to transform not only people but the face of a country, to make villages and towns look like Soviet towns and villages the way they do in Cuba. For this pulverization the means are uncertainty and terror, and in Mozambique and Angola, hunger and starvation.

The violence made Portugal doubt, doubt that could rot into the ambivalence that eats at a good deal of the West: "At home our people question our future, the general atmosphere is one of doubt and insecurity. Abroad we are almost totally isolated: Only a few faint voices are raised in our defense. Our few friends give us but feeble support." Spinola wanted to cease "to feel that we are a foreign body in the world about to be rejected." But he wanted only to acknowledge the club's principles in a way that would recognize Portugal's difference, not join it. Only by doing everything publicly could Portugal overcome its isolation abroad and the doubts everywhere at home. The Portuguese had been remarkably effective in keeping their war out of the media.

Portugal's war was not a part of the "East-West" conflict's prolongation of the Second World War despite Portugal's membership in the UN (1955, late for an old nation) and NATO but significantly, not in the Common Market: "We will have to explode the myth that we are defending the West and Western civilization"; "If to defend the West is to defend the way of life of the Western nations, it is permissible to conclude that we are being, for example, more Swedish than the Swedes, or more Dutch than the Dutch . . ."; "NATO seem thus to feel themselves to be more embarrassed than protected by our presence in Africa, and there is nothing more ignominious than to defend those who do not wish to be defended"; "The truth is that the interests of the West, which we take it upon ourselves to defend, have not in recent times coincided with our own." Spinola did not mention an important reason for Portugal's standing apart: It had not fought in the Second World War.

He did not want to join the warring club, but he wanted to win its free members' respect. The arrival of Vietcong instructors in Angola had bared the spread of war that started in 1917 he wanted to stay out of. The spread of "East-West" conflict meant failure, the abandonment of responsibility and the stability that the settlement of limited wars can bring.

The past had helped keep Portugal out of the "East-West" conflict and true to itself. Spinola insisted on facts,—the five hundred years the Portuguese had lived in Mozambique and Angola. Facts had a meaning. He was not about to countenance the use of an "internationalist" version of history,—the fictions of international organizations and the Communists that probably reflected no people's experience,—to obliterate Portugal's actual experience: ". . . It is difficult to understand that any group should attempt to rely on a reality more authentic than of another, or which comes to the same, should arrogate to itself the position of the holder of truth . . . History is made by marshalling answers that are obtained by examining facts . . ." He meant Europe was greater than the war of 1917 and the international institutions it had produced to overcome it that prolonged it.

The independence of the "new" African nations amounted to little more than abandonment: "Then came the rise of the more or less fictitiously independent states." This clarity did not prompt him to underestimate the yearning "for the emancipation of Africa, the rejection of the colonial domination."

Spinola had read all the books; they had visibly shaken him. Books, like Basil Davidson's *In the Eye of the Storm*, that denied everything Portugal had done; that ridiculed the reforms, the abolishment of the slave trade in 1838; the decision to abolish slavery within twenty years in 1858; that argued that the introduction of free paid-labor amounted merely to a continuation of slavery under the mask of forced labor; that insisted the worst mostly came out to Africa, criminals, ex-convicts, greedy cruel adventurers; that reviled the settlers' resistance to the reforms liberals in Lisbon imposed because they were utopian and out of touch with the realities overseas; that at most conceded the benefits of Portuguese introduction of new crops; that quoted Portuguese sources to document Portuguese inefficiency, cruelty, greed, without any acknowledgment of Portugal's readiness to stand self-criticism,—humorless books that less grim times, times more willing to face their own cruelties and betrayals, would not have taken seriously, would have dismissed as foolish, obviously mischievous, even funny. These books that readily dismissed the

European past,—for they had convinced themselves, and they took their refusal to doubt for conviction, that everything would set itself right once the Portuguese left,—had prepared for the Soviet and Cuban attempt to destroy this past, to substitute Europe's self-destructiveness for her endurance.[48]

These books had taught Spinola something more important than the distinction between Portugal's war and the "East-West" conflict. They taught him that force alone could not account for Portuguese endurance in southern Africa. Force could account for first settlements, it could not alone account for their persistence. They taught him that continuation counted, not numbers, always small, still barely nine thousand in Angola in 1900, and that continuation meant confidence, confidence reflected in the readiness of some of the Africans, almost from the beginning, to fight alongside the Portuguese.

The task of continuing that Portugal faced in its war had always asked more than beginning. Going-on told more than beginning, going-on was the meaning of Portugal's war. Spinola meant something like Lincoln's remark, in different circumstances, that he faced "a task . . . greater than that which rested upon Washington" in his farewell to Springfield after the election of 1861.

Continuation meant something deeper than "colonialism" and "imperialism." It meant something that made Europe different from any other peoples. It meant the readiness to voyage, to hug the coastlines but stay on the sea, that had marked Europe since the Greeks and Phoenicians had voyaged the Mediterranean in the eighth and seventh centuries B.C. Frogs around a pond, Plato called the Greeks four centuries later.

This readiness to go out, and go back and forth across the seas, to face the unknown, and live with it and keep on living with it, to reencounter the state of nature, as the seventeenth century named it, this courage, not only to reproduce one's kind, but also the framework of social and political life of the world they left, to know the way one lived counted more than life itself, distinguished Europeans from others.

They had a confidence nobody else had known, a confidence that baffled others, that first showed itself in the *Odyssey*, and then Herodotus, the first great texts of international law and manners, on welcoming strangers, besides the Bible. Like these texts, they knew the world was always bigger than any people's thoughts, than any individual's understanding.

This confidence dreaded self-delusion. It had the courage to remember but it knew no amount of intelligence could keep understanding free of self-delusion. It went out to encounter the unknown, for the same reason it remembered, because it sensed the unknown, and the past, alone could show it its delusions,—the things it denied or no longer would remember.

All that daring sensed its unsureness and wanted to uncover it because it drew its energy from it. There was a kind of rapture in it. No governments alone, no individuals alone could have gone out. It needed both individuals and governments. It was the rapture of those who could leave, could say goodbye in some sense forever, just because they kept up contacts and went back and forth, but at the same time became something else than they had been before, still recognizable but at the same time unmistakably different.

An African king recognized this difference without understanding it in the seventeenth century when he told the Portuguese that with ships he too could have beaten them. He thought they took to the sea because they had ships, but they had ships because they had the confidence to go. He did not conceive the ships showed the difference he wished away.

This readiness to live in daily uncertainty, in the presence of the unknown, at its edges, meant also living in contradictions,—the contradictions that made the Portuguese call Africans "brutes" and at the same time know better,—and in the knowledge that contradictions could not be resolved, but that you had to go on making choices and decisions, and running the risks of failure that alone was perfect and without contradictions. Never final, never without blemishes, success lived in the face of tragedy but showed itself in the capacity to take the next step, to keep moving.

For living in these contradictions, for continuing, for taking failures and success, for distinguishing the perfectness of failure from the imperfectness of success, Catholicism was crucial because it looked horror and betrayal in the face. It somehow knew how to get at insides, the real mark of Europe, the mark that distinguished it from its parents, Greece and Rome, the insides that showed themselves on the face in European portraits in the seventeenth century that took in the earth in their recognition at a glance,—a glance also of self-recognition, a glance with the unmistakable clarity and confidence in judgment that comes from looking inside as well as out: no flight in the eyes. Those men, individuals and governments, called their own outrages. They had no need to keep thugs to tell them, the thugs that now make them incomprehensible to us.

The five hundred years of unbroken presence Spinola kept before his eyes, meant above all the Portuguese living in his time in the overseas territories. They were the continuation of the five hundred years of presence and could not be separated from the Africans. The living, and the dead, in thirteen years of violence, both African and European, some sixteen thousand, had to mean something, they must not disappear into oblivion: "We cannot abandon those Africans and Europeans who built their lives overseas and nurtured their hopes under the shadow of the Portuguese flag as this could only be seen as a criminal resignation, as would any solution that aims at purely and simply substituting the present institutional structures by those of revolutionary parties who do not represent the African populations nor their legitimate interests."

Spinola's recall of the past was not a conceit, a fancy. The Portuguese actually made their decisions, not simply in terms of expediency or future aspirations, but with their eyes on the past. Portugal remembered both Britain's support for India's seizure of Goa in 1961 and Wellington's support for Portugal in the War in the Peninsula and the "Ancient Alliance" before it decided on close contacts with Rhodesia after its declaration of independence.

Goa counted for more despite their loyalty to Britain, not only because it was more recent, but also because the Portuguese took their possessions from Mozambique to Macao for centuries for one state, *O Estado da India*, that the sea united instead of separated. The chief of Rhodesian intelligence, who came to know the Portuguese in a way only a stranger, especially a Protestant could, remarked profoundly that to survive in Africa they should have abandoned the sea. But he did not understand that their energy and confidence, their sense of unity that surpassed place, had come because they were a thalassocracy. They had never "colonized" in the real sense of the word.[49]

To allow the Africans choice, the Portuguese too had to choose, Spinola argued: "It is one of two things: Either we, from the metropolis, really want to intermingle in the new nation that we wish to build of full equality with Africans and Asians who are likewise Portuguese, accepting as natural the preponderance of the territorial and ethnic majority, in which case we will be in agreement with the theory of integration, or we shall not succeed in reconciling what we proclaim with actual intentions, and then we shall never attain that desired unity, nor can we hope for any favorable development in the understanding of those outside."

The embarrassed readiness to call the Africans Portuguese, the butt of ridicule outside of Portugal, was too important to be new. It too was the work, not of Spinola's fancy, but of centuries. It had not been new even in the early seventeenth century when the Council of India in Lisbon counseled the Crown:

India and the other overseas territories whose government is the concern of this council, are not distinct nor separate from this kingdom, nor even are they joined to it in a sort of union, but they are actual members of this same kingdom, just like the kingdom of the Algarve and any of the provinces of Alemtejo, Minho e Douro, etc., . . . and thus anybody who is born and lives in Goa, or in Brasil, or in Angola, is just as Portuguese as is anyone who is born and lives in Lisbon.[50]

Spinola also kept African realities before his eyes. The Africans might turn out to be Portuguese, once they had choice, but they were also Africans: "We know the Africans sufficiently well to know what they believe in. The African believes not in the written or spoken word, but in the expressions which he, with remarkable perspicacity, detects in the face and look of the speaker."

This remarkable confession of the common ground of the perception of their differences showed its other side in the inadvertent remark of a much more sophisticated black from one of the large townships in South Africa in 1977: "If the whites went I would feel as if someone had taken my clothes away from me."[51]

The mirror the Africans held up to Europeans, and assimilated Africans like Neto, reflected also their deeply different ways of life: "The tribe is still the true African nation, characterized by an egalitarian and very collective distribution of the fruits of production. The pre-capitalist state of development of the tribes cannot be ignored, noting that they have lived in relative harmony even when grouped in confederations, empires or kingdoms, so long as the central power was exclusively of a political-religious order, not extending to the distribution of producer goods."

Western influence, both "the concentration of economic power" and the support of the "more cooperative tribes" had disturbed this balance, disturbances that the "Communist bloc," the transformed UN, the OAU had exploited but not precipitated. The Portuguese had made their own problems. "And over and above being Portuguese, the Africans were and are Africans . . . We have no illusions: It is a fact that the Africans want to be Portuguese—but they want to be so in an African way, not in a way that a certain sector of the metropolis claims they do . . ."

Savimbi's Lesson

Savimbi and RENAMO are now on their own before these African realities, above all the tribes, with sixteen languages in Angola alone, that the Portuguese presence defined and brought to awareness, realities that startled the eyes of the Canadian journalist, Peter Worthington, upon a visit to southern Angola in 1985:

> I watched a strange, rather touching meeting of local chiefs with Savimbi. While he sat on a grass throne with his fingers adorned with huge gold rings, toying with his ivory-handled cane, a pistol on his hip, and a Soviet AK–47 assault rifle leaning against his chair, a succession of chiefs in a peculiar wardrobe of mismatched socks, angle-length skirts, shirts and ties, pith helmets, cowboy hats, and even a US confederate Civil War hat, pledged undying support to Savimbi, *which may last unless UNITA loses* (Italics mine).[52]

Savimbi has to emphasize these realities that the Portuguese disturbed, but also took for granted, because he now faces enemies that want to obliterate them immediately instead of merely disturbing them. All "liberation movements," including the ANC and SWAPO, demand immediate "detribalization." The MPLA forbids membership to anyone who "believes in any religious ideas" and FRELIMO forbids church attendance to youths under eighteen, the majority of the population,—both in deeply religious lands. Impatience that promises murder and its slow substitute, the Gulag. In contrast Savimbi and RENAMO respect the chiefs and the traditional life of the eighty-five percent illiterate "peasants," as Savimbi calls them for lack of a better word.

Savimbi is in the awkward position of trying to teach the West facts he had known well enough to forget until the Portuguese abandonment, and until the totalitarian members of the West's warring club brought them home again to him: "UNITA's sympathy is with the West, in economy and politics. In other areas national ideas must be followed."

He means, *Les hommes sont étrangement faits*. These words almost escape comprehension in a West that has not heard them since at least 1848 when the inebriation of aspiration, and envy, began to atrophy the experience of differences. Almost nobody knows the meaning of the word "primitive" or dares say it, except the Communists: "Their [the Angolans'] level of development is not very high—we only try to set an example," a Cuban in Angola told a *New York Times* reporter in early 1987 who probably would not have dared such a thought, let alone say it.[53] For an African to have to recall these realities to Europeans, including Americans, torn apart in their innards in their struggle with totalitarianism,—a struggle that shows the soul of a whole time, as Hegel knew,—shows the depth of European and American abandonment of Africa. We will no longer understand what we do. Acheson foresaw and feared, Savimbi now has to cope with, this abandonment that he, in part, brought upon his country.

In courage, in vigor, in respect for the past, Savimbi and Spinola are alike. The difference in their goals is more apparent than real. Savimbi's is to fashion a new nation, Spinola's to transform and continue an old one.

Portuguese, the only living thing the Portuguese could not take away, remains the "common language." Savimbi insists on its instruction in the UNITA's schools to overcome tribal loyalties and focus eyes on Angola. In Mozambique a survey in 1970 showed only ten percent of adults in the country knew Portuguese. At a steel factory in Maputo in 1977 only about fifteen percent of workers could write, the Production Council used mostly Shangaan, the local language, in meetings.[54]

Savimbi knows the new needs the past; Spinola knew that Portugal needed to face the present, both in Angola and Mozambique, and in the Free World, to remain true to the past,—the same knowledge from different perspective with one difference. Savimbi means something more difficult than Spinola: real independence, and in the midst of conflict between free and totalitarian countries. The Portuguese fought, in contrast, to keep Angola and Mozambique out of the Second World War's continuation outside Europe, especially Africa.

Savimbi also knows Spinola's straightforwardness: "[The Portuguese] put almost no emphasis on the political side of waging war, and they had no international support,"—Spinola's thought without his style. Maybe Savimbi learned this straightforwardness from the Portuguese, from Spinola, and men like him. For Savimbi is a worldly man despite, and because of, the time he spends in his thatched-hut fighting capital, lost in southeastern Angola, a roadless land, "The End of the World," its Portuguese name, where the sand blows up like snow. He knows how to learn from everybody.

Out in those wastes Savimbi, who instructs his officers and soldiers to listen to the world news every day on their transistor radios, understands more about events than many of the inhabitants and leaders of the great cities of Europe and the United States, mired in ideological slogans and lost in a maze of arguments about nuclear strategy that make you long for the distinctions of scholasticism Descartes thought he had done away with. "The yakety-yak world," James Stockdale calls it.

This worldliness that shows itself in the capacity to learn from others and to pay attention to facts cannot live without common sense. And the best place

Bronstein's "Dustbin"

Spinola argued that the Portuguese had to allow the Africans to govern themselves because they were African as well as Portuguese. Portugal should commit itself, before the world with a plan with deadlines, to the gradual introduction of the vote, perhaps on a qualified franchise. On this point Spinola was not clear. In addition the African territories would elect representatives to a central federal government distinct from the government of Portugal in Europe that would in time enjoy no constitutional predominance. Spinola even hoped Brazil might join.

Portugal must no longer hide. The coherence of the new plan that introduced a new nation, the first European nation not entirely in Europe, might convince people and give them the strength to resist ideological slogans, to distinguish between thought based on actual realities and on mere aspiration, on wishes but not desires. For wishes serve to justify subjection and often violence and destruction and above all terror and intimidation. Spinola meant confidence. Geography would no longer define a nation.

Not only might the plan bring Portugal back into the open world on terms that challenged its presuppositions at the same time that Portugal accepted the world's principles but acted on those principles to transform the past, not break with it. It might also open up Europe to the world; it might bring it to act in the world, not only to trade with it. It might put the UN, the OAU, the Commonwealth in perspective and bring some sobriety to the fantasy world of these organizations. Because instead of nominal independence for nations of arbitrarily defined frontiers without a conscious past, independence that amounted to abandonment, it suggested a solution that combined the advantages of independence with the strength that comes of continuity: rejection of the past, and fear and longing for it, would not define the new.

Time was essential. For changes could only come gradually, like any real change. But Spinola also knew that to win this time, the commitment to change had to be deep and fundamental, otherwise Portugal would lose the loyalty of the Africans:

And we believe that we can affirm, with the authority of experience, that the majority of African peoples are on our side, as is the majority of the population of Guinea. But they were certainly not always so, and they may at any moment cease to be so, but then irrevocably. It would be more correct, therefore, to state that the peoples are still with us, but that they will cease to be so when they feel that they are precluded from the realization of their legitimate hope of a better life and of a full participation, at all levels and with complete equality, in the political and administrative life of the nation to which they belong. One cannot ask them to feel Portuguese in a different set up.

Daring words that today appear like illusions, even disingenuous illusions, because they precipitated the events that led to abandonment. Even at the time their self-evident goodwill made them hard to believe. For we have learned this much from the totalitarians, who are incapable of regret, never to trust anyone who admits he was wrong,—and before the whole world,—like Spinola.

But Spinola's plan failed only by a few months because in his concentration on the overseas territories he had paid little attention to Portugal in Europe. He had written of a profound constitutional transformation without understanding that it could not occur without a deep change in Portugal, a change, it turned out, that occurred with great swiftness but not swiftly enough to prevent the abandonment of the overseas territories. Spinola had forgotten that Portugal in Europe also had to choose.

There was one thing more Spinola knew, knew it so deeply that he could not even conceive of abandonment. He knew what any sensible man used to know, before the new and the future had come to baffle men's eyes,—Spinola knew that the collapse of any age-old authority brings cruelty and savagery worse than the state of nature because it is the cruelty and savagery of men who know they are evil, who are destroying themselves, the lesson Hobbes meditated on all his life with Corcyra and Thucydides before his eyes. And he knew one thing more that Hobbes could not know, that distinguishes the breakdowns Hobbes feared and sought to avoid from contemporary seizures of power,—a twentieth century first.

He knew that in our times these breakdowns are programmed, the work of professionals; that war nowadays aims at the destruction of governments; that these breakdowns that serve the seizure of power are not even the outbreaks of depraved but genuine passion; that they are cold and efficient; that the absence of passion makes them worse than plain murderousness, human in comparison. He knew that these breakdowns are irreparable. There is no going back. Hobbes who had spent his life taking up Thucydides' challenge that unless human character changed Corcyras would repeat and repeat had, it turned out in the twentieth century, helped fashion states susceptible to mechanized rebellion, to the mere appearance of passion and rebellion. Spinola knew that there was little rebellion in Angola and Mozambique.

Spinola knew Portugal had to hold on, he could not even conceive it would not. But he also knew it had to let go to hold on. There had to be change but change that would show that there was little actual rebellion in Mozambique and Angola, and that that rebellion could be reached. He had reached it in Portuguese Guinea.

He meant change that would show the twentieth century something about itself: show it the pettiness of its fascination with violence; show it the extent of the agreement, within the warring club, between "East" and "West"; show it the healing strength of the past. The past would show it the difference between strength and force, and confidence and exhilaration—and, perhaps most important of all, would show it that not everybody was the same, not individuals, not nations, and that respect for individuals could not tell without the respect for the differences in nations.

9 Portugal Joins the Warring Club that Calls War Peace

On September 19, 1975, barely a month before the South African Defense Force secretly entered Angola, the formation of the sixth provisional government in Portugal began to control Communist influence in Portugal, now more or less exposed to the world. The turning-point that made this government possible had occurred in April and July 1975.

The elections for a constituent assembly on April 25, 1975 made it unmistakably clear that the Portuguese people, six million, seventy percent registered to vote, who exactly a year before had turned to the streets to celebrate the Armed Forces Movement's (AFM) seizure of power, were moderate and quite capable of distinguishing between leftist Socialists and Communists,—a distinction that had come hard to the Socialist leader, Mario Soares, in January 1975 when the government and the AFM put the newly-formed Communist-infiltrated unions under direct Communist control. Soares had said he could not conceive of a government without Communists upon his return from exile immediately after the coup.

In January 1975 also, after polls gave them ten percent of the vote, the Communists had sought to postpone the elections the AFM had first promised in October 1974. In the elections, the Socialists and Social Democrats won sixty-four percent of the vote, the Communists something less than thirteen percent, the Popular Democratic Movement (MDP), a party close to the Communists that openly called for abandonment of the overseas territories already in May 1974, four percent.

In July, crisis followed the elections. The AFM voted power to a three man junta that announced it would substitute direct participatory grassroots democracy for elections of representatives. The three, General Costa Gomes, a close friend of Spinola, and a Communist sympathizer, General Vasco Gonçalves, the Communist responsible for the loss of the territories overseas, and General Otelo de Carvalho, who had directed the coup and formed the new secret police in July 1974, rejected a proposal for elections for local councils to replace the Communist-appointed members of 1974.

On July 11, the resignation of Soares, and a week later of the PPD, the Social Democrats, left the Communists alone in the government that was dissolved. After Soares' charge upon his resignation that AFM was moving towards "a police state run by a new class of bureaucrats," tens of thousands of angry people took to the streets in protest. In the north and elsewhere they broke into PCP buildings. On July 18, despite Communist roadblocks and barbed wire, seventy-five thousand people came to Oporto in the north to hear Soares say: "The PCP is engaged in a totalitarian adventure."

The AFM movement openly split into three factions. Crowds in the streets had shown the three men at the top and the AFM the true face of participatory democracy, but in the defense of elections, not to undo them,— with the Church in a crucial role, especially in the north.

A few weeks before in an interview in Italy that took the breath away from the Italian Communist Party, then in inch-thick democratic make-up, the most visible of the Portuguese Communist leaders, Alvaro Cunhal had made it clear that Communists wanted to take power despite elections: "I could not care less about elections . . . We Portuguese Communists need the military . . . We have already signed . . . [a] pact with the AFM."[55]

Army uniforms, ready-to-wear, the crowds discovered in some party buildings in July, showed he meant his words. The Communists had counted on the army because they feared to count on the people, correctly it turned out. The AFM had not been able to face up to the Communist infiltration it had known about before July 1975, until the people did. Abroad no one demonstrated for the people of Portugal in Europe. But the world, and its governments, sensed that, for once, the demonstrations in Portugal were for real, the rage real and spontaneous, and, therefore, somewhat embarrassing. It was also embarrassing because it did not have international propaganda behind it.

The people, after the show of their will and the choice of their leaders in the April 1975 elections had saved the first soul of the army that had almost from the beginning promised elections from its second soul. The Communists had sought to exploit the second soul that toyed with direct democracy. The two souls had struggled with each other in secret until the AFM openly split into three factions in July and August 1975.

Not Communist, but often leftist and Marxist, and above all idealistic, with the real idealism that came from years of dangerous service to their country, innocent, politically inexperienced, and gullible, the men in the AFM were willing instruments of the Communists infiltrating them, especially their leadership, until the people, foreign press, and their elected leaders woke them up. They were especially drawn by notions of direct democracy, easier to understand than representative democracy. But like Savimbi in Angola, they were determined to be their own rebels and idealists, not pawns, especially after they were made to recognize Communist manipulation. Like Savimbi too, they loved their country enough not to betray themselves: They did not murder each other. But they undid the army, reduced in 1976 to about 26,000 men from 210,000 a few years before.[56]

Their cloudy notions led them to put up with all sorts of "experiments": They allowed workers' committees, largely controlled by the Communists that, as in Mozambique a few months later, weeded out managers they did not like, the notorious *saneamentos*. Something like a thousand were dismissed, including the directors of the telephone, electric companies, postal service and national airlines, sometimes for trivial reasons like not smiling at subordinates. They nationalized the banks, a measure that allowed the Communists to use credit for political purposes, even with shopkeepers; to make election funds scarce for anti-Communists; and to exercise some control over the newspapers—since the banks held many of their shares. For fifteen months leftist notions and propaganda dominated the media with the exception of *Republica*, taken over by Communist workers in May 1975, and *Expresso*. They allowed "Parents-Teachers" committees, like those in the townships in South Africa today, to take over the education of their children and see to the introduction of textbooks prepared in Czechoslovakia. They closed the stock exchange. They took majority control of the defense industries and interfered in other major industries—all measures that crippled enterprise in the country.

But these men also provided the stability Spinola had taken too much for granted. They kept events from breaking down into violence. Confused, ambivalent about elections and their role after them, they saw to the order that made them scrupulously fair. And they learned from events, quickly, even though they sometimes regretted what they learned. "In retrospect, our biggest single mistake was to have allowed the elections to go ahead. Our downfall can be traced from then," Otelo de Carvalho later said of the elections that Soares at the time had called important "because they give us a platform."[57]

The only organized political force in the last forty years, clandestine but active, the Communists were in a formidable position to take advantage of the dangerous, good-willed confusion in the AFM. Communist infiltration was long and carefully planned, in its rudiments as early as forty years before the coup. The AFM had seized power bloodlessly in part because the Communists had cut all communications, merely telephones, between the police and Republican Guard units. Almost immediately after the coup, Communist operatives began to move in, more than 250, perhaps more than 300 trained in Czechoslovakia, mostly Czechs, but fluent in Portuguese, in some instances learned in Brazil. In addition there were several thousand Chileans, Spanish Communists and so on, armed, and something like fifty thousand activist leftists of every imaginable persuasion, at loose, mainly in Lisbon, quite a crew of the world's first and only proletariat. The previous decades had seen a net of Communist party cells cast over the country.

The danger the Portuguese people had looked in the face and dispelled in anger,—in rage that could know death but not denial, after elections had shown their minds to them,—had brought them within inches of the vast world of the living dead—but they had shrunk back at the first glimpse. Geography had helped,—the support of a living Europe around them,—the same geography, with lines of communication longer than between the United States and Indochina that had made for the abandonment of the peoples overseas, an "amputation," Spinola had written, that would prove the Portuguese nothing but "imperialists" after all.

Because there was no meaningful middle class, the discontent of the junior officers remained isolated within the army. It had not ignited much of the society outside. The resistance focused in the north with sixty percent of the population, and first of all, in the Church. But also among peasants who owned land that provided them with an adequate living in an economy not oriented to cash and consumers. These small holders, more than half in the north, had been frightened by the activist seizures of land in the south. The AFM and Portugal's other revolutionaries "were transfixed to discover that the impoverished Portuguese people were anything but revolutionaries, and capable even of fighting against revolution."[58]

The courage of the people and their elected leaders in achieving the freedom they had imagined the AFM had given them fifteen months before showed Spinola's confidence in change that would renew Portugal had been realistic. Spinola had known he needed time, only a few months it turned out, but he had not counted on turmoil in Portugal,—turmoil he should have expected after forty-seven years of authoritarian rule, and because the changes he wanted abroad had to mean fundamental transformation at home.

Spinola had assumed that thought alone would be strong enough to overcome the polarization in the army's attitudes. He had not realized that Communist infiltration had put some officers beyond the reach of argument, officers who immediately understood they could use his thinking and its openness to their advantage, to deprive him and Portugal of the time they needed for its realization.

Spinola could not act effectively upon his understanding because he did not have the resilience to deal with the duplicity that comes of infiltration. In Guinea he had learned to talk as well as fight, but always from a position of superiority that came of the readiness to fight and die.

Back in the metropolis, the mother of them all, he had to deal with individuals face-to-face, as equals, whose duplicity he could not even imagine, who meant to use him and his courage. He had no sense of the hard give-and-take necessary with equals who do not know what they think or who know all too well what they think but will not say it. He was innocent, gullible in the good faith that marks real soldiers in Clausewitz's description.

The transformation of Portugal in Europe was swift, but too late for Angola, in the grip of uncontrollable violence, and Mozambique, independent on June 25, 1975,—by a few months. Close—like almost all Western losses, especially when you remember what was at stake: a taste of reality and constructive statesmanship for the "international system," and what has happened since. What the Portuguese had managed in Portugal in a few months, would take years of cruel fighting in the bush of Mozambique and Angola—without any end in sight.

Unable to steal the heart of a country in the vulnerable moment of its rejection of a previous regime—in contrast to Cuba in 1959, a country without the depth of history of Portugal—the Communists had got most of what they wanted, not Portugal in Europe, but the peoples overseas, more important in the long run for breaking not only Portugal, but all of Europe, and the encirclement of the United States.

Agostinho Neto, who eleven years later would say "We would even take aid from the Devil himself to win our independence," already in 1958 understood that Portugal was vulnerable in Europe, not in Africa. Savimbi, just arrived in Lisbon, asked him why he was not fighting openly for independence; he replied that change in Portugal would decide the situation in Africa. Lisbon had taught him that. At the time of his meeting with Savimbi, Neto was a secret member of the Communist party-influenced youth movement against Salazar, the *Movimento de Unidade Democratica-Juvenil*.[59] He was probably more interested in revolution than in independence. In any case he did not distinguish between the two—in contrast to Savimbi. Neto, and the MPLA, seized power in Angola in 1975—with the Cubans and the Soviets, at the cost of a civil war they had not expected: Neto knew Portugal's weakness but not the fight in his country.

The reduction of Portugal to merely local European status, to another province of a Europe without a center, meant it no longer counted in the world, and that Mozambique and Angola lost the authority and confidence that only can come from centuries,—all things Spinola had dreaded. It also meant that almost exactly a generation after fighting had ceased in Europe, the Second World War had taken its toll in Portugal,—the real significance of the shameful shameless abandonment of the overseas peoples, the main consequence of the coup.

The arrival of the Second World War betrayed itself in Portugal in an attack on the previous fifty years, to cow the present and still the stirrings of shame for the abandonment of Africa, that won the approval of a world which would suffer its consequences. The tiresome codeword for this intimidation: fascism. Fascism meant support for the previous authority. Communist saturation propaganda called any opposition to the right of Socialists fascist. This slander would work, nobody then realized, to the immediate advantage of Soares because the devoutly Catholic people could tell the difference between indifferent secularism and Communist insufferance of worship. They knew things could be much worse than under Salazar because they could make this distinction.

Communist groups and the new regime denounced men who had shown allegiance to past authority. The AFM banned a succession of right wing parties. Parties that cowed conservatives later supported took on bewildering leftist airs to exorcise this slander.[60] Outside of Portugal, Raymond Aron and a few other *honnêtes hommes* had to argue the differences between Salazar's Portugal and Franco's Spain and Mussolini's Italy. The Portuguese were made to fear their own past, in the way Europe had feared, and been made to fear, itself in the thirty years before. And this at a time when Europe betrayed the first largely unnoticed signs, they became unmistakable ten years later, of outgrowing this intimidation.

Of these events, the founder of nations, Kaunda of Zambia, gave this weighty judgment upon Machel's arrival in Lusaka for the talks that gave him Mozambique in 1974: "Freedom fighters in Africa have freed the people of Portugal."[61]

10 The Triumph of the West and Mugabe over Rhodesia—a Model that Counts

After the failure of the Kissinger intervention in the Geneva talks at the end of 1976, Ian Smith resumed talks with Bishop Abel Muzorewa, the only African political leader not arrested in 1964, on the terms he had accepted from Kissinger. Nkomo's destruction of an Air Rhodesia Viscount in September 1978,—forty-three dead, ten murdered after the crash,—undid even secret contacts with Smith. Alarmed at the exclusion they had brought upon themselves, the terrorists, who refused to negotiate except for the immediate transfer of power, especially Mugabe, began to seek attention from the United States and Britain and also the Soviet Union. In 1977 Nkomo and Mugabe opened an office in East Germany and Mugabe saw the Soviet chief of state Podgorny in March upon his visit to Mozambique. In April 1978, after a preliminary meeting in Malta in January from which Britain deliberately excluded Muzorewa and Sithole, Mugabe and Nkomo met with the American secretary of state Cyrus Vance, and the British foreign secretary David Owen in Dar es Salaam.

Just a year before, after the failure of Smith's face-to-face talks with the terrorists, again in Dar es Salaam, Mugabe alone had probably shocked Owen with the demand that Britain exclude the other "black nationalists" and Smith from a settlement. But Owen still called the Patriotic Front (PF) "men of peace forced into violence." Mugabe had meant to remind Britain that it alone had authority for final settlement—a Communist reminding, as often, a Western statesman of fundamental realities of international law which Owen had forgotten because Britain in practice had blunted them. Until Wilson's victory in 1964, and his turn to the UN in 1966, Britain had insisted that it could not impose the settlement that would allow it to grant Rhodesia independence.

Vorster's pressure on Smith to turn his back on Britain, and to negotiate directly with the terrorists, barely two years before, had made it possible for the terrorists to appeal directly to Britain, over Smith's head,—after Smith had excluded them from talks because they would not renounce violence. They had turned Vorster's initiative to their advantage,—to "legitimize" violence, the deepest goal of their totalitarian mentors in the world-wide struggle. In a visit to Cuba in late July 1978, Mugabe made an agreement with Castro for intensification of the terrorist "liberation war."

All this attention helped Mugabe, practically unknown before 1975, to undercut much more well-known, more experienced, in appearance less ruthless and extreme, "nationalist" leaders like the Reverend Ndabaningi Sithole and Joshua Nkomo, whose terrorists operated out of Zambia increasingly under Soviet direction. Nkomo actually was as brutal but, true to Soviet style, less consistent and more cunning than Mugabe who took his lessons from the Chinese. In contrast, Sithole's public renunciation of violence, first in 1969, eventually cost him the leadership of ZANU, which he had founded in 1963.

More importantly, this attention helped Mugabe isolate, dwarf and discredit, especially in the media and international organizations, the "home-based stooge and reactionary leadership" that dared negotiate with Smith. (For Mugabe first-hand knowledge of Rhodesia, he had had none for more than ten years, deserved scorn for it got in the way of rigidity that the West could not distinguish from firmness: "The main principles of socialism do not vary but the application varies. Yes, we are Marxist-Leninist," he had said in 1977.)[62]

Even before Smith came to an agreement with Muzorewa, the West's readiness to talk to the terrorists distanced it along with the Soviets from the people of Rhodesia, both European and African,—and incited the intransigence of the terrorists outside Rhodesia. It helped them make people abroad forget the readiness to negotiate of Africans within the country,—even after murderous intimidation really took hold in 1976. "The blacks in Rhodesia have proved preponderantly cooperative rather than recalcitrant toward the regime," Acheson had observed in 1968, correctly.

Despite the nothing-will-do mood outside Rhodesia, Harold Wilson's legacy, Ian Smith reached a settlement with Muzorewa on March 3, 1978. The so-called internal settlement kept Kissinger's majority rule with full adult suffrage but also guaranteed white seats,—twenty-eight out of a hundred for at least ten years and a white veto on constitutional changes. There was also a Declaration of Rights and provision for an independent judiciary.

Smith had yielded the qualified franchise but he had excluded terrorists who did not renounce violence, like the ANC in South Africa today,—his condition at the beginning of the negotiations in 1974 that Kissinger had wished away in 1976, probably because he hoped "progress" in talks with the PF would make it unnecessary. But Nyerere, speaking for the PF, in Dar es Salaam just before Kissinger met Smith in South Africa, had not fed Kissinger's illusions: "I am not a trade unionist. This is not a bargaining point."[63]

In April 1979 Muzorewa won sixty-two percent of the vote in an election that a delegation of observers from the Conservative party in opposition judged fair. The UN Security Council immediately, the OAU in July, called the election invalid because of the exclusion of terrorists.

Recognition of the new constitution and the Muzorewa government was the first big foreign policy decision that faced Margaret Thatcher, who had become prime minister after the Conservative party victory on May 2, just after the Rhodesian election. Malcolm Fraser, then the prime minister of Australia, sent two messengers to London to tell Mrs. Thatcher, barely in office, that he would not support her at the Commonwealth meeting in August in Lusaka if she recognized the Muzorewa government, lifted sanctions and granted Zimbabwe the independence the Rhodesians had wanted since 1961. Seven years later almost to the day, Fraser was to play a key role in drafting the Eminent Persons Group report whose plan for the overthrow of the South African government informed some of the thinking and wording of the CAA Act.

Thatcher yielded, apparently unfamiliar with the almost twenty years of negotiations that preceded the choice she faced, against her best instincts but under the pressure of her foreign secretary Lord Carrington, whose self-deceptiveness was to show publicly two years later, in his neglect of intelligence pointing to the Falklands War.

Conversion or collapse? Probably collapse that took itself for conversion, in the face of threats from Tanzania, and possibly Zambia and Nigeria, to leave the Commonwealth. Diplomatic recognition of Muzorewa would not easily have won international acceptance, it would have meant abuse at the UN and elsewhere, and above all it would not have ended the war Britain, at least Lord Carrington, could not bring itself to support. In these circumstances, the argument that recognition of Muzorewa would have increased Communist influence, not diminished it, took its toll,—the classic argument for appeasement, Kissinger's in Africa in 1976. Trade also probably counted, two billion pounds of exports to "black Africa," almost half of it to Nigeria, against almost a billion pounds to South Africa. On August 1, just before the Commonwealth meeting in Lusaka, the president of Nigeria, General Olusegun Obasanjo, who was also to play an important part in the Eminent Persons Group seven years later, had suggestively seized British Petroleum's assets.

But above all, tongue-tiedness did its work. Nobody since Acheson had been able to make the case for Rhodesia, even after acquiescence to terrorism was clearly at stake in 1979, in contrast to 1968. Nobody could say the rule of law, not indiscriminate "one man, one vote," defined republican freedom. The Rhodesians also were tongue-tied, in part because of their respect for Britain and the United States. Rhodesian defiance had meant to bring these countries to their senses, not repudiate them.

From the beginning, the Rhodesians had counted on reaching public opinion in the West, especially in Britain and the United States. ". . . The truth can be something of a shock treatment. Get one piece of incontrovertible truth through to a brain-washed zombie, and you may well suddenly turn him back into an angry human being—angry at the way he knows he has been fooled," the Rhodesian minister of information had told the Rhodesian Parliament in 1966.[64] He had meant Western public opinion, and above all governments.

There was support in the United States and especially in Great Britain, strong, unorganized but difficult to measure. Everyday people, in contrast to their governments, could distinguish between actual defiance and the myth of "revolution." Besides, the European Rhodesians were underdogs, a handful of men against the world, enough to take your breath away, as a British MP told the head of Rhodesian intelligence on a visit to his country:

It seems ludicrous but with an effective population smaller than Bournemouth you run a country over twice the size of Britain, man an Army and Air Force, and now defy Britain, the Commonwealth and the rest of the world![65]

But this support unnerved Rhodesian intelligence, more than the deadly "orchestra of hate," because it was spontaneous and based on judgment, not ideology,—because it could not be taken for granted. It had to be seen with one's own eyes, only continuing forthrightness could reach it.

Margaret Thatcher's acquiescence completed the reversal of British policy and practice Wilson had begun when he had acted as if Britain could impose a solution on Rhodesia through economic siege-warfare, as if it were a Crown Colony, like any other, almost without anybody's notice. Except Mugabe's. Mugabe condescended, reluctantly, to negotiations to take power instead of terrorism because of the pleas of Kaunda and Machel. Their countries suffering more from sanctions than Rhodesia, could no longer take the Rhodesian, and South African, incursions against the terrorists they organized and trained.

To the surprise of the world, and to the astonishment of the South Africans,—but not to the negotiators at Lancaster House, especially Lord Carrington,—in new elections on February 29–March 2, 1980, the blacks of Zimbabwe voted for the practically unknown Mugabe instead of for Muzorewa. Muzorewa had won Zimbabwe's first one-man, one-vote election that had excluded terrorists less than a year before,—and won a sixty-four percent turnout, a serious setback for the terrorists. Mugabe's symbol for the illiterate: a rooster. He had made only two or three appearances during the election campaign because of fear for his life.

The surrender that showed itself in the elections had actually occurred at the Lancaster House negotiations when Muzorewa had resigned office upon British endorsement of a PF demand that the head of Rhodesian intelligence called "preposterous." He told Muzorewa "standing aside" would bring certain defeat and charges of betrayal since no African leader had ever willingly left office. But he did not advise Muzorewa against resignation he knew would be taken for weakness, despite his assurances before the conference that the British would not betray him.[66] The readiness of the South Africans, including the government, to believe Muzorewa would win the election after his surrender shows the capacity of negotiations to turn the heads of men who know better, the danger that faced South Africa in 1988 in Crocker's negotiations.

Exhausted by the years of murder and atrocity they knew Mugabe had the power to continue, the African Rhodesians sensed nobody had the will to resist anymore. They were right.

The terrorists had used the election to penetrate the country further and tighten their hold on it. *Mujibas*, kids with rusty weapons, not terrorists, appeared at the Assembly Points of the Cease-Fire Monitoring Group, a token British-led Commonwealth force of fifteen hundred, as even the British governor admitted on January 16, 1980. Outside the Assembly Points, the terrorists, seven thousand or more in the central and eastern election districts, hid their weapons and intimidated the Africans. In the south-eastern region, around Fort Victoria, men campaigning from parties other than Mugabe's among the uncommitted Karangas, the largest ethnic group, did not survive. A few years later a ZANU leader said on television: ". . . We had a very large army left [besides those at the Assembly Points] who remained as political commissars in the country simply to ensure we would win the election."[67]

The intimidation reinforced the terror that had gone deep enough before the elections for children openly to justify the terrorists' murder of their parents. "He deserved to die. He clung to his bad ways. We tried hard to warn him but he was proud and stubborn. He hit me so hard over the ear that I couldn't hear for three days . . . They killed him with axes and iron bars, then they warned us to leave him there, lying in the open. 'Let the government come and bury him,' they said. 'Let Smith come from Salisbury and bury him,'" a daughter told an English journalist of the murder of her father, an

African district assistant who had seen to the arrest of youths who helped the terrorists.[68]

The Romans had known what they meant when they called revolution and conspiracy, *parricidium*. Terrorist gangs had hit mission schools for money, drugs, liquor, indoctrination in "liberation," recruits and sex:

> The poorly trained, under-equipped young men that fought in the rural areas from March to July 1978, after several months of being hunted in the bush, were often nervous wrecks, emerging startled into the tranquility of the mission complex, trigger-happy and needing tranquilizers from the dispensary, or drink, before they could begin to relax. Hospital staff began to dread the frequent demand for drugs or drink which made a travesty of the missionaries' hope for genuine liberation. The price of cordial relations might be serious exploitation of the mission, priests commandeered imperiously to drive guerrillas in the mission car, demands for the *best* drink, good meals cooked by frightened girls while the local population went hungry. . . .[69]

The young girls in their care who went with the terrorists or "ran with them" across the border into Mozambique sometimes fascinated their priest schoolmasters. They took them for "idealists."

The Rhodesians could not bring themselves to renew the fighting after the election because they could not face the slaughter it required. The witticism that made the rounds in heavy fighting before the Lancaster House "cease-fire" betrays Rhodesian sensitivity to the atrocities the terrorists had drawn them into, not callousness: "If we carry on this way the country will soon have a white majority and its political problems will be solved."[70] They had tried to fight a war until atrocities like Nkomo's destruction of the Air Rhodesia Viscount on September 3, 1978 "broke any illusions they might have retained that they were fighting a war, not terrorism."[71]

Already in July 1977 the Commander of Combined Operations, Lieutenant-General Peter Walls told the *Daily Telegraph*, "The whole of Rhodesia must be regarded as an operational area."[72]

Just after the end of the Lancaster House talks in December 1979, Rhodesian intelligence estimated; 4,055 ZAPU and 10,275 ZANU terrorists in the country; 16,000 ZAPU, and 3,500 ZANU trained terrorists outside the country; 2,950 ZAPU and 14,000 ZANU terrorists in training, also outside the country. In June 1976, in contrast, it had estimated sixteen hundred guerrillas in the country, two thousand in training outside, with possibly ten thousand waiting for training. Any resumption of fighting after the elections that allowed Mugabe to take power would have required killing on a scale the Rhodesians were not about to imagine.

The raids into Mozambique on Nyadzonia on August 9, 1976, that mistook a staging-camp for elementary training for an attack base: one thousand men, women and children dead, mostly unarmed and untrained; the spectacular raids, again into Mozambique, in December 1979 against Chimoio and Tembue, well-defended terrorist bases for recruits on their way north for training and for trained terrorists about to infiltrate into Rhodesia: vast quantities of arms destroyed, two thousand terrorists dead, more than four thousand wounded or deserters, had shaken some Rhodesian leaders more than the terrorists:

Hitherto, Operations Coordinating Committee (OCC) had confined itself to facts when issuing communiqués on enemy casualties, recording as "kills" only the deaths of trained guerrillas, armed or identified and with the "kill" confirmed. From the time of the Nyadzonia raid onwards, however, we had to cook the books . . . as far as the OCC were concerned, things were never quite the same again . . .[73]

In contrast the terrorist leaders were indifferent to the slaughters of "the masses," Mugabe's name. They only looked to their military and political consequences, as a casual remark explaining the failure of the British initiative in 1977 by writers close to Mugabe shows: "[The April 1977 initiative] could not succeed because the pressure of war was not yet sufficient to make the Rhodesians capitulate to reality, but it would add new links to the chain of events begun by Kissinger and, as it ran its two years course, the war would spread across the country . . . encircling the cities and dampening white morale."[74] For these writers, and for Mugabe, negotiations were merely "events" that measured terror's work.

The visible general relief at Mugabe's taking office without massacres betrayed the hollowness of the insistence on "diplomatic triumph"—but embarrassed no one. The unembarrassed relief at absence of slaughter showed that the West could not conceive of seizure of power without flights of refugees and fighting in the streets; that it did not understand that the take-over of a state intact, not blood, counted; that it could not see that Mugabe was much more dangerous than Machel or Neto because he seized power with the West's rejoicing at a "bloodless" invasion of armed terrorists entering a country to "vote."

It did not see that Mugabe's renunciation of vengeance did not mean "reconciliation," a word much about in the following years, but only persistence in "revolution," "an ever continuous effort," Mugabe had called it a few years before, Lenin's words. To judge Mugabe you had to use your own eyes on your own.

In contrast to the wars of Angola and Mozambique that cannot be ignored, Mugabe's way may be the way of the future, and not only in southern Africa: the transformation of a government from within, without much notice despite the evidence, with those most opposed trapped in ostensible cooperation. In Harare in September 1988, Pope John Paul II repeatedly called Mugabe's regime "a model for all of Africa . . ."[75]

At the opening of Parliament it fell to Ian Smith to guide Mugabe, a former schoolteacher like Kaunda and Nyerere, with no experience of political responsibility, to the government benches. The provision that, in contrast to Angola and Mozambique, left the Europeans and the farms the war had turned into fortresses armed, served to underline Mugabe's unwillingness to protect them. At Mugabe's and the West's independence ceremonies one of the representatives of the United States, Andrew Young, haughtily remarked that

South Africa was next: "I would like to see South Africa learn the lesson of Zimbabwe."⁷⁶

Mugabe rejected Botha's suggestion that Muzorewa had enthusiastically accepted, for a regional common market, and a few weeks later broke diplomatic relations with South Africa whose soldiers had been ready to enter Rhodesia to defend Muzorewa's expected re-election. The approval of the United States showed in immediate recognition and aid that ran to a half billion dollars at its temporary interruption in 1986.

The refusal to appreciate Mugabe's use of the state Britain and the United States had given him, to take over the country, the most developed in southern Africa outside of South Africa, meant also that no one paid much attention to Mugabe's violence not only in Rhodesia but in Mozambique, and to his prosecution of the war against South Africa in threats and words in the second half of 1986 and in 1987, with more or less unwitting Western complicity.

In 1977, a little before Ian Smith began to negotiate in earnest with Muzorewa, Mugabe had called this violence both within and outside the country, "the determined struggle against imperialism and its thorough and complete destruction" that "alone would make it possible to establish peace in the world."

The Rhodesians were free to remain in Zimbabwe. One hundred thousand out of 270,000 did. But who were the Zimbabweans? Nobody knew, and Mugabe was not about to find out. What became of the Rhodesians? They disappeared overnight with their name, obliteration without slaughter, but obliteration nonetheless, and without the rewriting of history. They simply went—they who in fifteen years of brave independence had won the recognition of no one in a world promiscuous in recognizing nations most people have never heard of—not of the South Africans, not of the Portuguese.

Truth to remember, the South African government from the beginning had sought to keep the Rhodesians from defiance. It would not break existing links or support sanctions, it said. But it also would not grant diplomatic recognition or acquiesce to popular support for Rhodesia in South Africa. At one point the head of South African intelligence, a man close to Vorster, called Smith's continuation of discrimination that the United Federal Party (UFP) had sought to undo, "an embarrassing anachronism."⁷⁷ He had meant apartheid also.

In the toughest situation, the Africans, three thousand volunteers at any one time in the Rhodesian African Rifles and in the militia, "the territorials," made themselves scarce. In October 1978 Muzorewa's government had instituted conscription, not for lack of volunteers but because "blacks must accept a major role in defending the agreement [the "internal settlement" on March 3, 1978] which confers power upon them," Sithole's words.⁷⁸ Black students in high schools in Salisbury and Umtali and at the University of Rhodesia had marched and signed against conscription, but the government had stood firm. In the fall of 1975, the government had rejected the increase of African volunteers in all units of the Armed forces and promotions to commissioned rank that Rhodesian intelligence suggested to hinder terrorist "recruiting."

Abroad, the European Rhodesians kept their mouths shut, even in South Africa,—the stiff upper lip. There was no place to remember, no language anybody could understand to write their history. A novelty, surely, even for the twentieth century, a young nation in history's count but old by contemporary standards, almost a hundred years old, gone, lost, swiftly as a dream, so completely hardly anyone can say its name,—and without exiles yearning to return.

The Rhodesians could not, at least publicly, even recall their defiance, they repudiated it in their memory. A letter in the *Umtali Post*, soon after Mugabe's victory, published under the headline, "Mugabe has shown tragic war was futile," argued that for eighteen years the people of Rhodesia had been "subjected to the most gigantic confidence trick in modern history . . ."[79] This exaggeration betrays the despair it seeks to deny.

The memoir of the former head of Rhodesian intelligence, Ken Flower, published in 1987, shows the same disbelief in a past he lived firsthand, and called "the locust years" in the deepest moment of the book, its dedication. He will not hear of what he saw. He cannot say a good word for Smith, but he served him fifteen years, a greater compliment, not merely the professionalism of a civil servant. "The deception of the Rhodesian public, through a Goebbels-type propaganda was by now well under way," he characterizes 1964, a sentence Nyerere would like. The reader has to fight against the writer's repudiation of his past with the facts he provides, but the book is honest enough to invite the struggle, similar to the struggle that drove Ken Flower to write it.[80]

The silence of the Rhodesians met a match in the silence that took hold of the West. In Zimbabwe, the West ignored events because it feared disappointment of its triumph, in Angola and Mozambique because it knew they were going badly. South Africa became the place to concentrate on because it was strong and rich, and more importantly, one of us: It still spoke our language.

Once in office Mugabe infiltrated his party into the government and in much of the land. Already before he took office, Mugabe had seen to it that nobody's illusions would break at the realities of power, the story of FRELIMO: In 1977 he had already purged his party of "counter-revolutionaries,"—a purge he had called "the negation of the negation," broken Hegel to justify ruthlessness. Individuals in the party "must comply with the orders laid down by the group." Party cells and gangs covered the country. A party school, Chitepo College, was set up to train cadres. Men with old ties to the Soviet Union were put in positions that allowed them to infiltrate the expanding army. Later, the minister of home affairs took "a private unit" to use against men labeled political opponents. At the opening of Parliament, President Canaan Banana, a Protestant minister, said those who stood in the way of "a truly Socialist state" would be "crushed." In his first year, Mugabe made trade agreements only with Communist or "Socialist" countries.

In early 1981 the Zimbabwean Media Trust under government direction acquired shares in major newspapers. The minister of information took to calling independent journalists and editors "racists" and "fascists." The party took control of the Zimbabwean Broadcasting Corporation. The Soviet ambassador signed a Tass cooperation agreement with the state-controlled Media Trust, "to break the monopoly of global news supplied by the Western press,"— as the trust director put it. In early 1982 Mugabe announced private and public sectors "must move forward as one, regardless of their ideological differences, and continue to exist side by side during the three-year national development period toward socialism." Also in 1982, the map took on a new face, to mark the second anniversary of independence: Salisbury became Harare; Fort Victoria, Masvingo; Umtali, Mutare and so on. Mugabe feared the past.

In 1981 North Koreans started to train and equip the five thousand man Fifth "Whirlwind" Brigade to terrorize ZAPU, Nkomo, and the Matebele. Mugabe had not disarmed them. He was not about to insist on "loyal opposition," unheard of in Africa. Already in 1981, the regime mouthed the war against enemies at home and abroad that the world heard at the Non-Aligned Conference in September 1986. Mugabe rejected the withdrawal of Cuban troops from Angola,—the new condition the United States made in June 1981 for implementation of UN Security Council Resolution 435 for the independence of South West Africa. He called the US rescue of tiny Grenada in 1983, "an act of wanton aggression" and helped sponsor a UN Security Council Resolution of condemnation. He accused the United States of "destabilizing," and wanting to destroy "progressive governments in Latin America, the Caribbean and Africa." In a visit to East Germany, Czechoslovakia, and Hungary,—examples, Mugabe said, that inspired his party in its fight against "colonialism, imperialism and fascism"—Mugabe's and his party's victory was characterized as the "victory of the whole Socialist community." Just this sort of subordination, *Gleichschaltung*, shocked some of the youths before the Denton Hearings who in training in the Soviet Union realized they were to lose their country, not only themselves. "There [is] no holier dogma than the philosophy of Communism," Mugabe said, in Parliament in 1983, in answer to Ian Smith's description of Soviet manipulation of Cubans in the Caribbean, a situation, less grim, but otherwise not unlike Mozambique and Angola. Marx, Lenin, Tito, Mao Tse Tung, Kim II Sung, Mengistu Haile Mariam name the streets of Harare.

In 1982 Mugabe, who had never hidden his desire for a one-party state, moved openly against the opposition. Nkomo was forced out of the government after the discovery of huge caches of Soviet arms on lands Nkomo and his associates owned. Two thousand former ZAPU terrorists left the army with their weapons. Nkomo was arrested. Muzorewa was arrested. After the 1985 election, with much violence against Nkomo's followers,—they were tortured, Nkomo almost murdered by unidentified gunmen,— Mugabe took major steps toward a one-party state. He spoke contemptuously of the 1980 constitution that guaranteed twenty seats for the diminishing Europeans. Nkomo, the only leader capable of opposition, remained tangled in the violence of his followers, violence he did not entirely accept or reject. This ambivalence has enmeshed him since his rejection of the 1961 constitution.

In April 1987, the Zimbabwean Parliament suspended Ian Smith for a year for a speech he had given in February in Johannesburg urging South African unity in the face of sanctions that would hurt Rhodesia more than South Africa. The motion condemned Smith for statements "calculated to give encouragement and succor to a foreign power so hostile to Zimbabwe,"— touchiness that betrays the regime's fear that criticism might show the self-destructiveness of the propaganda war it wages at home and throughout the world. More than anything else Mugabe fears alternatives, reason's limits on his power, especially at home. He fears public statement of facts he acknowledges in private, that show his ideological rigidity, his entrapment in the fanaticism he wishes upon the West. Mugabe's health minister Sydney Sekeramayi indulged "racism": Smith was "basically a racist who despises the African people in general and African people in Zimbabwe in particular."[81] "Beliefs, abilities, and behavior are all irrelevant to a man's status; everything depends on race. Manhood is irrelevant." This was the Lusaka Manifesto's description of South Africa in 1969.

Between 1980 and 1986 at least twelve thousand were murdered, mostly Africans as usual. In 1982 alone there were three thousand "political" arrests according to the State Department that openly acknowledged it had no information about Mugabe's secret prisons and camps. On the streets of Harare, sensitive visitors notice Africans keep their eyes to the ground, the sullen fear of a police state,—in contrast to the straightforwardness between blacks and whites in central Johannesburg.

By the end of 1987 more Europeans had died at the hands of gangs since Mugabe took power than in the fourteen years of terrorism before, a time *The Economist* now calls the "black-white war" that brought a "more legitimate regime."[82]

"A built-in time bomb," a Western diplomat, as usual unidentified and, as often, fatuous, called rivalries in the Shona, Mugabe's collection of kinship groups, not a tribe like the Matebele, in Harare in September 1986.[83] He was wrong. Mugabe's violence is not a resurgence of the wars Rhodes ended almost immediately after he came to the land. It is state-initiated and controlled murder, the irresistible continuation of the terrorism that brought Mugabe and Nkomo to power. It is the violence of men without the confidence to face harsh words of opposition, not the violence of a state breaking down. "Mugabe—he is the one to watch," Derek Robinson, then a plain detective, later head of the Rhodesian Special Branch, said in 1961. He is still right.

In December 1987, Mugabe turned himself into the executive president of Zimbabwe, abolished the office of prime minister and the twenty-seats reserved for whites and turned his country into a one-party state. He appointed eleven whites to Parliament, among them several leading men in Ian Smith's government, a tactical alliance. "Now rather than saving my face, I am saving the face of my country," Nkomo said of the new "one-party unity" that undid opposition in Parliament to overcome tribal differences and to establish "a socialist society." The presidents of Tanzania, Uganda, Ethiopia, Botswana, Mozambique and Zambia and leaders of the ANC, PAC and SWAPO attended

Mugabe's inauguration. Later, Mugabe did away with the time in Parliament set aside for questioning the leader of the government. *L'avventura* continued.

Because it still draws the United States and Great Britain on in the hopes of a negotiated settlement with terrorists that does not mask a seizure of power, a mirage that still flees before their eyes, and because it increased Soviet influence, the Rhodesia-Zimbabwe settlement of 1980 is the most important event in southern Africa since the Portuguese abandonment of Angola and Mozambique, and the almost immediately subsequent arrival of the Soviets and Cubans brought in Soviet ships and airplanes in 1974—and before the Cuban, South African and MPLA agreements in 1988.

It is also the least understood. On the fourth of July 1986 President Carter left a party at the American Embassy (!) in Harare because of the insults of one of Mugabe's men, an incident reported in the press without a hint of the world it momentarily betrayed.

Increase in Soviet activity after the "settlement" that turned Rhodesia into Zimbabwe showed itself not only in the appointment as ambassador to Zambia of the head of the KGB for southern Africa, Soldovnikov, who pressured Machel to take ANC bases in Mozambique, and in the shipment of arms to Kaunda, but also in the words Kaunda no longer dared say. Kaunda who as late as ten years ago had spoken out against the suppression of Dubcek in 1968, who at independence in 1964 had talked of blacks and whites living together in southern Africa, began to toe the party line, like Nyerere before 1980, and to call in blood-thirsty threats, for instance, in June 1986 upon the declaration of the State of Emergency, and in the first days of August at the little Commonwealth conference in London, for the immediate dismantlement of apartheid, in Soviet propaganda a transparent codeword for the destruction of the South African government.

The "settlement" led also to the immediate increase in tensions, now directly along South Africa's border. The victory of the terrorists Mugabe and Kaunda help and back, of FRELIMO in Mozambique, of the MPLA in Angola, of SWAPO in South West Africa, not to speak of the ANC in South Africa, would destroy all but the appearance of independence of Zambia, Tanzania, and Zimbabwe and bring the whole region more or less under direct Soviet-Cuban control,—an irony that does not escape Savimbi who is against revolution in South Africa because it "will spill over in the rest of southern and central Africa in unpredictable ways."

I say independence, not freedom,—a fragile independence that depends on the world of make-believe, especially the Commonwealth, the UN and the OAU,—for none of these "majority-ruled" countries, as Mugabe calls them, allows political opposition: Nyerere, who resigned in October 1985, has sometimes had as many as seven thousand political prisoners in his jails.[84]

Zambia, Tanzania, and Zimbabwe depend not only economically but also politically, for their independence on the country they say they hate most, the government of South Africa, which also alone has the authority to keep the blacks of South Africa from tearing each other apart.

Kaunda alone, whose personal goodness leaves its mark, or used to leave its mark, on whites and blacks,—but the political suffering of the blacks from southern Africa I have talked to has begun to teach them to resist its fascination,—senses this self-destructiveness, in contrast to Mugabe and Nyerere who are possessed of the paralyzing rigidity of former schoolmasters. ". . . But I have fears that while trying to build up Zambia, I am myself unleashing forces . . . which will prove more difficult to deal with than the former colonial masters," Kaunda once confessed, overwhelmed by his true thoughts in the casualness of conversation with the sensitive South African political writer, A.P.J. van Rensburg.[85]

11 South West Africa: A Largely Untold Tale of Dangerous Progress

The world ignored the progress in South West Africa, especially since 1978. It ignored it because it fears responsibility for supporting constructive action of the South African government and African and European Namibians—actions that ask it, like the reforms in South Africa, to choose resolutely between lawful change and transformation, and violence in the name of change. This lawful change means risk because it shows real respect for the West's principles, especially the principle of the self-determination of peoples. In South West Africa the South Africans and the Africans and Europeans did the possible,—a partial success like all successes. For only failures are total.

Since 1978 South Africa, and increasingly African and European Namibians, under South African leadership in war, in domestic politics more or less on their own, fought a war that first showed its face in 1966, and built the rudiments of self-rule.

I call the territory two names, interchangeably, because the land does not have one name but two: Namibia for some of the Germans and Africans; South West Africa for the South Africans who shouldered heavy responsibilities for it, an alternation of names meant to remind the reader of the ambiguity and complexity in a territory that is by no means a country.

The name that the Kho-Khoi or San peoples wandering in its desert wastes centuries ago gave the region is not known; the tribes later settled in the more-watered grazing lands did not think of the present territory as a whole. The Germans meant their name, South West Africa, to identify a country that had no name. SWAPO before it became the terrorist organization that gave the name wide currency, especially through the UN, made up the name Namibia to suggest an identity for the region. It comes from the word for enclosure, "namib," the Nama and Damara tribes used to identify the long desert that isolates the territory from its coast. The word Namibia is about all most of the people who insist on its independence know about the country.

Made up of at least twelve different peoples and groups that speak sixteen languages, the land, in contrast to Rhodesia, has never known self-rule, not even European self-rule, since the Germans first came in 1884. In such circumstances, progress has an unreal, almost utopian quality that tests Western, and South African, in their way idealists, too, capacity for common sense realistic thinking to the utmost.

The reluctance to acknowledge and support progress in such circumstances betrays something more than Western ambivalence about professed ideals. It shows that somewhere the West knows that independence for such a territory is, and will be, for a long time, impractical,—impracticality, however, that the West will not acknowledge, because nobody in our world can say a land is not ready for independence, least of all the Namibians who have already suffered some of the likely consequences of that independence. In private Namibian leaders will admit such things, or at least acknowledge they cannot say them publicly. The truth is that nobody cares about Namibia except some Namibians and Savimbi's UNITA,—and above all the South Africans who have fought and died for South West Africa, in part because they cannot defend themselves without it, and also because they take their responsibilities seriously, words that do not come easily in a time of mob-thinking.

"There has never been a serious endeavor to consider what Namibians want or what is in their best interest." This is the judgment of the former chief director in the office of the administrator-general of South West Africa, Sean Cleary, one of the men most responsible for changes in the territory.[86]

The American connection of Cuban withdrawal from Angola to independence for Namibia in 1981 that the South Africans accepted, besides putting another country at risk, shows this readiness not to think of South West Africa in its own terms, the proof of seriousness about independence. The point was to get the Cubans out of Angola, not to make the Namibians' independence dependent upon them.

By 1987, really already by 1984, the terrorists of SWAPO had been more or less broken. This important success, also ignored, showed in a huge increase in 1984 through 1986 in reports in South West Africa to security forces about terrorist infiltration and plans, a measure of the drop in intimidation. South African officers, in contrast to South African diplomats and most Namibians, knew this advance might turn out to be temporary, especially because SWAPO continued to speak for Namibia on the international stage. The Soviets are not so easily undone, and especially not on the battlefield alone. They know the use of negotiations in turning setbacks to advantage. There are two ways out of an impasse, military or political, wrote *Red Star*, a Soviet military review, in 1988 of the negotiations between Cuba, South Africa, and Angola's MPLA.[87]

By 1987 also, the Transitional Government of National Unity (TGNU), about eighty percent African, completed a constitution that excludes parties which used violence and that would substitute mixed local government for the "second tier" ethnic authorities,—a provision that made for difficulties between the TGNU and the administrator-general in 1987 and 1988. The provision excluding violent parties tells all anybody needs to know, to imagine the unreality in Namibia.

Since 1975 the country had begun a slow political, social and economic transformation that needs stability. 1978 saw a national government elected through one-man, one-vote without regard to tribes or groups. This gradual change made it clear to many Namibians that they needed the South Africans more than they could do without them.

1978 was a fateful year above all because it committed South Africa, and Namibia, to independence without ever putting the question of whether the Namibians actually wanted it. In 1974–75 Vorster had wanted, not only to prevent the exploitation of the yearning for independence for seizure of power, so-called revolution, but also to preserve choice about independence itself. He had wanted to keep the choices open.

The transformation of the struggle since 1978 into a struggle about the conditions of independence without ever putting the question of independence itself, represents a victory for SWAPO and the Soviets and, perhaps, an unwitting concession of the South Africans to terrorism and what passes for world opinion.

The imminence of independence meant also a much heavier burden for South Africans than the defense of a territory in practice annexed, a burden even heavier after the 1988 negotiations. It demands they not only fight, but also preside over changes that have made the country more vulnerable at the same time that they promise greater strength in a generation or more.

In the face of orchestrated world opinion that knows little about Namibia and cares less but thinks it knows what it wants both for South West Africa and for South Africa, the South Africans have excited aspirations within Namibia, not only with their encouragement of self-government, but also with programs in health and education and with lavish road-building, in part for the army and mining. These improvements have led the country to live, and more importantly, think beyond its means. The country is not rich despite mines and diamonds. Seventy percent of the population depends directly or indirectly on agriculture that yields nine percent of the GNP.

Vorster's concession of the possibility of independence came, it should not be forgotten, only a few years after Dean Acheson, the last American secretary of state, with the possible exception of Dean Rusk, who could think in terms of traditional international law (*jus gentium*),—instead of in the terms of the lawyers' codification of international law that started after 1917 that undoes customary international law in the name of preserving it,—argued that South Africa's title to South West Africa was as good as the United States' to most of its territory.

In 1920 when the League of Nations granted South Africa a class C mandate over South West Africa, statesmen expected South Africa would soon annex the territory, not annexed outright because of American reservations about "self-determination." South Africa had taken South West Africa from Germany in 1915 upon orders from Great Britain, in an expedition that provoked resistance approaching insurrection among the Afrikaners in the barely five-year-old Union.

Like Ian Smith, Vorster discovered that conceding the possibility of change meant more fighting not less, for the terrorists took it for appeasement,—but dreaded it might succeed. The year 1978 began with South Africa's decision again to intervene aggressively in Angola, and ended with South West Africa's first one-man, one-vote election,—fighting and nation-building inextricably intertwined. To his credit Vorster and his defense minister, P.W. Botha, did not shirk the intensification of the war, and they involved themselves openly, barely two years after the political failure of the secret intervention in Angola that had brought South African soldiers almost within sight of Luanda, and in full awareness of the consequences of openness: uproar and indignation, and underlying respect, even admiration few would acknowledge. In the effort to bring independence, but not abandonment, South Africa ran great dangers, the risk of all-out war or collapse that showed in 1988.

The change in the war that brought Vorster's and P.W. Botha's decision to cross the Angolan border in preemptive strikes first betrayed itself on October 27, 1977: a three-day fight, at least sixty terrorists dead, after eighty SWAPO guerrillas crossed over from Angola ran into a small group of South African soldiers who stood their ground. Until that October day, the war that had started in 1966 after SWAPO's turn to Moscow and the UN's revocation of South Africa's League of Nations' Mandate over the territory,—and intensified after South Africa's final withdrawal from Angola in March 1976,—had meant SWAPO infiltration in small groups that met "sections" of ten South African soldiers under non-commissioned officers, the so-called "corporals' war." In 1977 it had averaged a hundred "contacts" with terrorists a month.

The first relatively large-scale South African intervention, "Operation Reindeer,"—an airborne attack that destroyed several SWAPO bases, left some of a village in ruins and hundreds of terrorists dead,—occurred in May 1978, just after South Africa had accepted the proposals of the Western Contact Group (the United States, Canada, Great Britain, West Germany and France) for a South West Africa/Namibia settlement, and after six months of continued SWAPO violence had shown that the three-day fight on October 27, 1977 had not been an incident.

The events that followed the October 1977 fight aimed to terrorize the population, especially in the north, the most fertile region in the country with eighty percent of its population, and to destroy all leadership: the murder of a minister in the Ovambo tribal government, Toivo Shiyagaya on February 7, 1978; the abduction of a teacher and 119 children from an Anglican mission on February 21; the murder on March 27 of Clemens Kapuuo, chief of the Hereros, an important leader, long an opponent of the South African government; the near-murder of another Ovambo minister, Tara Imbili, on April 21; 73 hijacked on a bus the next day; the mining of the tribal legislative building at Ongwediva to murder other leaders from the Ovambo tribes on April 29 and 30; a clash with one hundred SWAPO men, two dead on April 28.[88] SADF captured SWAPO documents, printed along with the Denton Hearings, show a concentrated plan to eliminate leaders, the same murder the Vietcong largely completed in South Vietnam by 1965 before extensive American involvement.[89]

A statement of SWAPO's leader, Sam Nujoma, to the South African

Broadcasting Company (SABC) in New York on February 28 that caused a sensation in South Africa made it clear that SWAPO's increased violence against people and leaders came because it feared the elections that the negotiations underway might bring: "The question of black majority rule is out. We are not fighting for even majority rule. We are fighting to seize power in Namibia, for the benefit of the Namibian people. We are revolutionaries. We are not counter-revolutionaries . . ." These words match almost to the letter SWAPO indoctrination notebooks printed in facsimile in the Denton Hearings.

Nujoma blamed the SWAPO atrocities he denied on the SADF. "The people would do away with traitors" after they seized power. Traitors meant the Namibians fighting along with the South Africans and the "puppets" of the "internal parties" that might run in the elections,—the slander, and the murder, the ANC and the UDF adopted in South Africa just five years later.

SWAPO insurgents numbered 300 in the operational zone in northern South West Africa, 2,000 in Angola, 1,400 in Zambia, the low guess of a South African major-general at the time of these events. Others later acknowledged over 16,500 cadres in 1978.

The non-binding resolution, like all General Assembly resolutions, that first named SWAPO, the "sole and legitimate representative of the Namibian people," in 1976 explains the, at first glance, reckless words of Nujoma in 1978. He knew he had the international bureaucracies behind him, and in *Gleichschaltung*, like the movement against South Africa that led to the CAA Act in the United States.

Like many resolutions, the 1976 General Assembly resolution did not simply come out of nowhere. The Soviet Union had started to campaign openly for the General Assembly's exclusive recognition of Soviet "liberation movements" after the OAU had adopted a similar resolution upon the insistence of a leading funder and his threat to cut off money and supplies to the OAU's African Liberation Committee: Muammar al-Quaddafi. Quaddafi had acted at the behest of a conference in Khartoum the Soviet Union organized through the SACP out of London in January 1969, for the ANC, SWAPO, ZAPU, MPLA, FRELIMO and other terrorists from Guinea-Bissau and the Comoros. Savimbi's UNITA, the FNLA, ZANU and others were excluded from the conference whose members called themselves the "authentics."[90]

SWAPO's insistence on the withdrawal of all South African troops from South West Africa and the cession of Walvis Bay,—the only port on the long treacherous Skelton Coast, a part of the Cape Colony since before the arrival of the Germans,—after the passage of the UN Security Council Resolution 435 for Namibia's independence in September 1978, forced South Africa, already committed to elections, to hold them under her own auspices on December 4–8. She hoped that elected leaders might win international recognition through the UN Special Representative. But the Five Nation Contact group that had implicitly accepted South Africa's refusal to withdraw before elections, in consultations in South Africa on October 15–18, refused to recognize the "unilateral" elections held on December 4–8, 1978 despite SWAPO's plain attempt to use the UN resolution to take over the country.

Seventy-eight percent of the registered voters, an estimated ninety-three percent of the eligible turned out: 324,264 (out of a population of roughly one million with about seventy-eight thousand Europeans, estimated at about sixty-five percent literate) in 1,094 polling places with 375 election offices, some mobile,—a considerable achievement for a country with a widely-scattered rural population living in simple primitive conditions But that made little impression on the world, despite 65 invited foreign observers and 235 journalists. Polling in the north, SWAPO's main target, was consistently high. The Democratic Turnhalle Alliance (DTA), made up of the openly tribally-based parties, led after the murder of its founder Chief Clemens Kapuuo, by Dirk Mudge, a widely respected white stock farmer, outstripped all the other parties with 268,130 votes and 41 seats: The Aksiefront vir de behoud van die Turnhalle beginsels (AKTUR), 38,716 votes, 6 representatives; the Herstigte Nasionale Party (HNP), 5,781 votes, 1 representative; the Liberation Front 4,864 votes, 1 representative; the Namibia Christian Democratic Party (NCDP), 1 representative.

The new government's weakness came of its apparent strength, the predominance of the DTA, not a party but a coalition of parties. After working a remarkable change in the climate of opinion in South West Africa, among whites and blacks, with its dismantlement of some of apartheid on the national level, the DTA fell to quarreling about tribal distinctions in politics that masked personal rivalries,—quarreling that led to the resignation of several crucial Herero, Damara tribal groups and especially Peter Kalangula's Ovambo Namibia Democratic Party in February 1982.

In February 1983 the South African Government decided not to hold new elections after executive and legislative authority had reverted to the South African administrator-general, upon Dirk Mudge's resignation in January 1983,—a hard decision. It was taken probably in dismay at the outbreak of the maze of domestic strife and bickering that betrayed little appreciation of the real dangers South West Africa ran both from SWAPO's violence and from its monopoly, and the Soviet's manipulation, of international organizations,— South Africa's burden in war and diplomacy.

The strife that brought the collapse of Namibia's first elected government in the beginning of 1983 showed there was no ignoring the deep differences centuries have made in a country that never thought of itself as a whole. At first glance, the bewildering number of parties, more than anybody could count, guesses went from thirty to fifty-four for half a million possible voters, testified to appetite for self-rule. But with a few exceptions all these groups, including the seven that could be called parties because of their programs and contacts with constituents, coincided with tribal differences. In most cases they made up small tribal and kinship groups with no appeal beyond themselves. The DTA had organized an alliance, not a party, with some tribal and special interest groups, to cope with this situation, but not to change it.[91]

These differences that the attempt to fashion political unity turn into fragmentation show themselves starkly in languages and agriculture. The spread of English or Afrikaans measures political unity. Children, eighty percent between the ages of seven and seventeen, learn these languages in some kind of school, their main contact with what there is of a society that is more than a territory. But learning these languages is no easy matter: It means a break for children with the joys of childhood that will sustain them throughout life, and also distance from parents who taught them the African language that first showed them the world. Out in the country the large majority of parents speak only rudimentary Afrikaans or English, they cannot express themselves in them. "Non-formal" instruction for adults that aims at functional literacy, apparently fairly well-attended, shows that the changes in children work on parents. Twenty-four percent of all the population receives some sort of instruction, in contrast to an average of less than ten percent in Africa. Some better-educated blacks insist that all instruction should begin in English because it is an "international language." In contrast, some Europeans rightly argue for reaching children first through their mother-tongues, reasoning that can easily be made to look like "racism."

To begin to cope with this situation, the TGNU that came out of the breakup of the elected government in 1983 wanted a year for six year olds to prepare them for the contrast between their traditional family and tribal life and Western technological education that will test them throughout their lives. The TGNU also realized that to overcome discrimination in education it would have to produce children capable of coping with no-holds-barred English or Afrikaans in the schools, an impossible task with all but extraordinary youths.[92]

These difficulties have met a "People's Education" movement SWAPO manipulates. Like the NECC and other groups in South Africa, it incites evasion of the hard realities and humiliations of simple learning that show in high dropout and failure rates. The schools and the past, not the children, are to blame. The answer: ideological indoctrination, to reinforce flight from responsibility that allows the political exploitation of children. A question of one of the sensible and practical men in the TGNU responsible for the rapid expansion of education betrayed the effects of this agitation in 1986: "Should we allow past colonial blunders in the education of our children to overshadow our desire to return to honest, down to earth education? Should revenge and destruction preached by radicals be a part of the process?"

The five months of school boycotts in the north and in the townships around Windhoek in 1988, organized through the SWAPO infiltrated mining unions, show SWAPO's exploitation of the difficulties in the schools. The school children wanted schools, originally built near army bases to protect them, moved away because of SWAPO mortar attacks on several bases. And because the soldiers had sometimes abused them. These attacks occurred in the winter and spring months of negotiations that saw eleven to sixteen thousand Cuban troops, with SWAPO members integrated into some of their units, move near the South West African frontier for the first time.

The traditional life that gives the country stability, but also impedes unity, also persists in agriculture. Almost forty-one percent of the land, the most fertile, in the north, with the highest rainfall in a country of vast arid regions is, and has been for centuries, maybe thousands of years, tribally owned and cultivated, like some private land also, only for subsistence. The rest of the cultivated land, about forty-four percent, employing more people than any other occupation, almost three hundred thousand, is commercially farmed with comparatively high production. Private ownership of the now communally owned lands would eventually turn South West Africa that now exports eighty percent of its meat but depends on South Africa for almost all of its wheat and half of its corn, from a country that cannot grow its basic foods into an exporting land. Nobody knows how to initiate this change, let alone guide it.[93]

After the breakup in 1983, the administrator-general proposed a state council that reduced the parties to advisory status. But the eleven parties that remained in the DTA and other parties, *on their own initiative but without new elections*, sought to turn the break in domestic self-government into an interruption, and preserve some of the momentum of the first government. The Multi-Party Conference (MPC) these groups formed, after a secret meeting in September 1983 and a public meeting in November, came to public agreement on basic principles on February 24, 1984, and on April 18th on a Bill of Rights that distinguishes sharply between political rights and economic and welfare goals. It endorses, but does not guarantee, the latter. The Bill of Rights also distinguishes clearly between political activity and violence, between "freedom of expression" and "the advocacy of ethnic or religious hatred and incitement to discrimination, hostility and violence." It allows restriction of peaceful assembly and freedom of association for the sake of "national security" and "public order."

For something like eleven months the MPC sought "reconciliation,"—a key word in the preamble to the Bill of Rights,—with SWAPO. This effort came to a head in two sets of talks in the first half of 1984 between the administrator-general and Nujoma in the Cape Verde Islands and in Lusaka from May 11–13, in talks between the MPC and SWAPO in separate rooms, with the administrator-general and Kaunda going back and forth, for neither side will talk to the other directly. In both talks Nujoma refused to renounce violence. In the crucial Lusaka talks upon Kaunda's pleading, he first agreed to sign a joint communiqué that made clear areas of agreement and disagreement between SWAPO and the MPC, but after the intervention of the Soviet Ambassador, reversed himself and "launched a vitriolic attack against certain members of the MPC"—P.W. Botha's words.[94]

Nujoma could not face the recognition of men who wanted independence but renounced violence. He cared about power, not Namibia, as African leaders and Western diplomats readily say in private.

More important than the formal sessions, the private contacts between SWAPO members who wanted to return home and the MPC at Lusaka deepened the MPC's resolve. Nujoma's taunt that talks between SWAPO and the MPC made no sense because the MPC had no power also did its work.

After its return the MPC asked South Africa to make good on its commitment not to stand in the way of Namibia's self-determination. In little short of a month, P.W. Botha agreed to "reinstate the legislative and executive authorities" broken in 1983 and to turn the MPC into the Transitional Government of National Unity (TGNU) on June 17, 1985. In addition to the Lusaka talks, MPC consultations with Namibia had satisfied Botha that the MPC had done all it could "to involve all the parties of South West Africa/Namibia in its deliberations." But the Ovambo tribes, the largest population group, and the one most vulnerable to SWAPO, were not in the government which represented most of the other minorities in South West Africa. The Damara tribes that together with the Namibia Democratic Party of the Ovambo leader, Peter Kalangula, had brought down the previously elected government were also not in the TGNU. Botha had apparently decided a beginning was better than nothing, especially a little beginning because it would keep things from moving too fast. Defense and foreign affairs remained South Africa's responsibility. The administrator-general could only refuse to sign TGNU laws that he took to violate the proclamation of the new government.

At the inauguration in Windhoek on June 17, 1985, Botha flatly stated he preferred a new election to an appointed government but an election would at that moment disturb "current efforts to achieve internationally acceptable independence for South West Africa and Namibia." At the same time Botha reiterated Vorster's policy for peace in southern Africa: no foreign troops, no support for bases for terrorists, respect for different constitutional arrangements. Twenty thousand people attended the ceremony, less than two thousand, a SWAPO rally against the TGNU elsewhere in Windhoek.

The inability of the United States to deliver on its June 1981 commitment, first publicly announced by Vice-President Bush in Africa in November 1982, to prevent implementation of Resolution 435 until the forty thousand Cubans left Angola had prompted South Africa to go on with a settlement on its own,— rather than do nothing or abandon the country. "The challenge is now yours to make a success of this venture,"[95] Botha told the politically active Namibians of the TGNU who also would no longer wait on the UN, the Cubans, the Americans, and SWAPO and the Soviets, and in his way Savimbi, to decide their future.

They knew waiting meant losing, because waiting means doing nothing and doing nothing weakens the will: "After eleven fruitless months of negotiation, both in Namibia and under international auspices, had led only to increasingly strident attacks on the [Multi-Party] Conference by SWAPO, and an attempt by that organization to shift the focus of its struggle in Namibia to a campaign of urban terrorism, the MPC decided to call on the South African government to transfer the executive and legislative powers exercised by the South African-appointed administrator-general to a Transitional Government of National Unity, constituted by the parties which comprised the Multi-Party Conference,"—this is the description of the birth of a new government by a leading member of the MPC and a witness at the Denton Hearings, Jariretundu Kozonguizi. ". . . We cannot wait to improve the lot of our people in terms of human rights until such a time as [UN Resolution 435] is implemented after the Cuban departure from Angola. SWAPO says it will wait for fifty or even a hundred years—the Namibian people will not wait for SWAPO! . . . We, however, are not prepared to achieve independence only to launch the nation into a nightmare of destruction and bloodshed," said another member of the TGNU, also a witness at the Denton Hearings, Andreas Shipanga, at a conference in London in 1986 that meant to show men like the former British Ambassador to the UN, Lord Caradon, SWAPO's true face.[96] Kozonguizi also called the new unelected white and black government "inconceivable five years earlier." Progress, but who is interested in progress?

By November 1985 the TGNU with a National Assembly of sixty-two men, fifty-one African; and a Constitutional Council, sixteen men, fourteen African, had unconditionally released twenty-two prisoners: South African courts had imprisoned these men, seventeen for life, for crimes the TGNU considered politically motivated,—in contrast to South African law that does not recognize political prisoners. These were men, including Toivo Ya Toivo, a well-known SWAPO member, sometimes called "Namibia's Nelson Mandela," harder to catch than to release. This act of unpredictable consequences showed the South African government's determination to respect the TGNU's decisions, perhaps at the expense of prudence. For these releases lent SWAPO justification within South West Africa and increased confusion that men had died to clarify.

The TGNU National Assembly cannot take harsher measures, it can only weaken terrorist detention laws it inherited because of the new Bill of Rights. By 1986 the Constitutional Council was at work on a constitution and the design for elections, a more difficult question, under the chairmanship of a South African jurist, not a field to underrate in South Africa.

The South African administrator-general struck an American official upon a visit to South West Africa in 1986 as a man "energetically engaged in working himself out of a job who represents Pretoria in Windhoek and Windhoek in Pretoria,"—not an entirely reassuring description, for as everybody knows, but few say, the South Africans cannot leave without SWAPO seizing the country. Of more than forty thousand civil servants, thirty-four thousand are African.

The South African government has turned over to the administrator-general and the TGNU, the majority voting-right on the board of British (majority stock), French, German and South African owned Roessing Uranium, the largest uranium mine in the world with ten thousand dependents, and the ownership of the railways with one billion dollars in assets. The future's uncertainty has slowed investment, for instance, in the Kudu gas field discovered off the coast more than ten years ago. Since 1984 South Africa has spent about a half billion dollars a year, more than a billion rand on South West Africa a year, not including military expenses, a total of 2.2 billion rand up to the middle of 1988, in contrast to 2.3 billion from 1969 to 1984. In addition, the territory owes about three-quarters of a billion rand. Who will give this money after Namibia's independence, the South African foreign minister asked at the beginning of August 1988 upon announcing South Africa's readiness to begin withdrawing from South West Africa on November 1, at President Reagan and Gorbachev's behest. He meant to test the West's seriousness. On top of this, the realization of Resolution 435 might cost three-quarters of a billion dollars. Independence would teach the West South Africa's generosity, a word the foreign minister did not dare use, and Namibia, thrift, if not poverty. Without increasing subsidies from South Africa, and with diamond mining taxes, its only important income,—personal income taxes, eighty percent white, go to local government,—the new government will have to cut health, education and other services and subsidies. The least of a rude awakening.

Despite South African and South West African political and military achievements, the war going on in the country continues to show its traces, both inside the country and on the "international stage," especially in the disregard of the TGNU, as the first six months of 1988 showed. Terror persists after murder relents, and takes only a few atrocities to renew. Towards the end of June 1988, a group of lawyers, journalists, farmers and academics journeyed to Stockholm for two days of "informal talks" with Sam Nujoma and SWAPO. One of these men publicly called for a "common front" to "force South Africa to leave our country," words that betrayed the real face of the negotiations and the Cuban build-up that had frightened the men to Stockholm.[97] The reality of their own suffering has come home to individuals,—but not in public life that turns individual experience into the reality of all. South West Africa, perhaps, is not enough of a nation for that.

At the UN in 1985, predictably, the Committee on Apartheid, SWAPO and the President of the Security Council dismissed the TGNU in contempt as South Africa's "puppet," a condition in any case better than Soviet-Cuban-SWAPO pulverization. In response to the institution of the TGNU, the UN Council for Namibia, the supposedly *de jure* government of the country, stated flatly that there were only two forces that counted in South West Africa, SWAPO and South Africa, and called on the Security Council to impose "comprehensive sanctions against the racist regime . . ." if it persisted in its obstruction of UN Resolution 435: ". . . There [are] only two parties to the conflict in Namibia, namely the Namibian people, led by SWAPO, *their sole and authentic representative*, and South Africa, the *illegal occupation regime*" (Italics mine). The acting president of the Council of Namibia called the TGNU, "the latest maneuver by the apartheid regime . . . facilitated" by the United States policy of "constructive engagement." Its institution represented "yet another blatant violation of Security Council Resolution 435, the only internationally accepted basis for peaceful settlement in Namibia."

The representative of the Non-Aligned countries called South Africa's and South West Africa's defense of the country, "South Africa's continued illegal occupation of Namibia, its massive militarization of the territory, its use of Namibia as a base for aggression and subversion against independent African states . . ." He "reaffirmed" the Non-Aligned's support for violent seizure of power. "The inalienable right of the Namibian people to self-determination and independence by all means at their disposal, *including armed struggle*," he called it (Italics mine). He blamed the United States for subordinating Resolution 435 to the withdrawal of the Cubans from Angola, an "extraneous issue" that had, he implied, led to "Pretoria's decision to install a so-called internal administration at Windhoek" that the Non-Aligned "strongly condemned." SWAPO called the TGNU "a puppet administration . . . of the apartheid regime" and the Namibians who backed it "either puppets of South Africa or misguided."

The president of the Security Council echoed most of these themes, except "the armed struggle," in somewhat vaguer words: Members of the Security Council had "directed international attention to the obstinate attitude of South Africa and expressed indignation and grave concern at the decision taken in Pretoria to establish a so-called interim government in illegally occupied Namibia," a "maneuver . . . contrary to the expressed will of the international community" that the Security Council "declared . . . null and void."[98] "Indignation and grave concern" is hardly a name for this hate.

A "well-informed champion of civil liberties," in the words of the Namibia Council of Churches, an American who apparently knows little shame, Senator Edward Kennedy on a visit to Windhoek, a few months earlier, on January 12, 1985, had encouraged these extravagances that the United States government sought to limit. Just days after the murder of five people in a bomb explosion in a post office in northern South West Africa on December 31, 1984, blood Nujoma claimed for SWAPO from Tunisia, Kennedy met publicly with members of SWAPO he called the "brave sons and daughters" of Namibia, and openly refused to meet with any other leaders from other Namibian parties, parties the United States recognizes without recognizing the TGNU.[99] Extravagances routine enough at the UN to pass for the air we breathe long before 1985. Days after assumption of the office of secretary-general at the UN on January 7, 1982, Perez de Cuellar had praised SWAPO's "valuable cooperation," attacked South Africa's policies and blamed it for slowing South West Africa negotiations. The UN's official information kit on Namibia wears SWAPO's colors and carries its constitutional and political program and a color poster of Nujoma.

All these themes that showed themselves in the UN after South Africa's institution of the TGNU upon initiative of the MPC, flooded the newspapers of the United States, especially *The New York Times*, at the end of 1986 and the beginning of 1987, after they had won currency at the conference of the Non-Aligned on September 1, 1986 in Harare and endorsement in the CAA Act.

But for the moment, in 1987, realities won out over words. After four days of debate on April 9, the United States and Great Britain, with West Germany voting against, and Italy, France and Japan abstaining, vetoed mandatory sanctions modeled on the CAA Act that members of the TGNU had pled against in Washington. At the UN Thatcher and Reagan could halt the havoc that overcame Reagan in the United States and that threatened Thatcher before the Commonwealth.

These actions, like Great Britain's and the United States' veto, with West Germany, France and Japan abstaining, of milder selective sanctions against South Africa seven weeks before, on February 20,—and like South Africa's intervention in Angola in 1975,—won public vituperation and private thanks. We abuse words, and put up with their abuse, too much, and lack the courage for public respect. Kaunda, especially after he yielded to the humiliation of food riots that forced him to break his agreement with the IMF; and maybe Mugabe, in the deepest recesses of his coldness, where his heart might flinch; and surely, Mugabe's men responsible for the economy, do not want the world they shout about in public,—as long as somebody else decides for them. Call it independence.

But the struggle within South West Africa/Namibia is even more dangerous than on the international stage. For there, in that vast land with few people that might be better off had it never heard of independence, the entertainment of illusions as promiscuous but more naive than any outside, weakens the TGNU. The flight into the future from a present more disappointing the more it changes,—and from terror's whip,—blunts the embarrassed dread of responsibility. This embarrassment shows in ridicule of the TGNU. Belief in South African and Namibian constructive actions that otherwise serve to increase the unreality that marks Namibia requires belief in oneself. Nujoma takes the absence of this confidence for granted especially because organizations that pass for the whole world, and governments that do make a world, ignore or ridicule the TGNU. SWAPO divides Namibia despite its suffering and because of it, into two camps,—in the name of "reconciliation."

Words, words of hate that dress in aspiration, and mask Soviet purposes, threaten to undo life before Namibians' eyes. These words come, strange to tell, and yet these days all too commonly throughout the world, from the churches, not from their worshippers in this deeply ninety percent Christian land, but from those who take themselves for their representatives,—from their ministers, especially from the Namibian Council of Churches (NCC). "Even the Churches have gone absolutely crazy," Mburumba Kerina, a founding member of SWAPO in 1959 who broke in 1966, wrote me of the situation in his country in 1987: The NCC knows the embrace of the World Council of Churches that gave something like eighty thousand dollars to SWAPO in 1986.

Within South West Africa and throughout the world, in key organizations, like the UN and TransAfrica and the Black Caucus in the United States Congress, that receive its newsletter, issued in London by the "Namibia Communications Centre," the NCC makes its voice heard in support of SWAPO and the UN's contempt for the TGNU. This voice tells because it appears disinterested, above politics, and from the "grassroots."

In its open endorsement of the "liberation movement" SWAPO, "the largest political party in the territory," ("We don't believe the propaganda which says they are Communists and Marxists instead of Lutherans, Anglicans, Roman Catholics, Methodists"); in its attacks on the United States for "constructive engagement" and linking the Cuban withdrawal with implementation of Resolution 435 that "retards the negotiations and postpones independence"; in its contempt for the TGNU, "South Africa's appointed government in Namibia," because it is "unrepresentative of the wishes of the people of the former German colony,"—in contrast to the churches that "represent seventy percent of the population,"—the NCC not only does not distinguish,—like SWAPO, the ANC, Clough, the CAA Act, the Commonwealth Eminent Persons Group Report,—between the violence of SWAPO and the fighting of the soldiers of South West Africa and South Africa. It also blames the South Africans more than SWAPO: ". . . We reject the whole debate on violence as *hypocritical and even racist*. We are concerned with the violence of a system which has been destroying people for more than a hundred years in our country"; ". . . The occupation of our country by the South Africans and the violence they have done to our people to continue that occupation . . . is [the] root cause of this violence." Unless the South Africans withdraw, there will be widespread murder, "genocidal civil war." Just the words Kaunda and the OAU, the fall of Rhodesia in their sights, took up in the late seventies. The NCC argues that this murder increased after Resolution 435 in 1978. But it does not say it increased because SWAPO feared free elections for independence.

The timing too matches the propaganda of the ANC, SWAPO, their lobbying organizations in the United States, and the UN. "We do not know if it is deliberate, but it seems as if the world is getting more silent on the Namibian issue, an issue which is costing lives," said the president of the Namibia Council of Churches, head of the Anglican Church in South West Africa, in London in late 1986. This renewed call for eyes to turn on South West Africa after world-wide media obsession with the ANC and South Africa, matches the statement of the WOA in Washington immediately after passage of the CAA Act two months before.[100] But it took negotiations, and especially the Cubans herding SWAPO south to the South West African frontier in 1988, to turn faces again against South Africa's "occupation of Namibia and its apartheid policy"— Nujoma's words.

The NCC uses the deepest experience of South West Africa's short conscious past, its European past, that antedates South African rule by a generation: the conversion to Lutheranism, now the country's largest denomination: 380,000. It calls up the memory of that past, not to bring out whatever unity the country has, but to weaken the TGNU's and its parties' fragile allegiance among the scattered fragmented people of South West Africa, and to reinforce SWAPO.

This exploitation of the faith of simple people for political purposes leads the NCC to twist the deepest teachings of Protestantism on faith and works, and on top of that, to equate works with political action, called the "theology of doing." Terrorists are martyrs or, as the president of Zimbabwe the Reverend Canaan Banana put it in 1980: "When I look at a guerrilla I see Jesus Christ," a remark that did not keep Mugabe in the same days from removing mention of God from his constitution.[101] "Statements and decisions in themselves are nothing unless they are backed up by action," the Anglican Bishop Kaluma said in a sermon in London on St. James' "faith without works is dead,"—a statement that gave Luther trouble.

Faced with the SWAPO violence they justify, the Namibian Bishops react with casual indifference: "People are already fighting and that is a decision they have made. They did not need the encouragement of a church or to be told by a church. They did it on their own, as human beings with a desire to be free . . . and they are still doing that without any encouragement from the churches." Not a word about SWAPO abductions or the murder of men who leave the organization.

In contrast to such emptiness that denies the terrorism it justifies, soldiers fighting terrorists in the face of international contempt show that good faith lives at the risk of one's life. Aware of the workings of this good faith on people that see it, the South Africans, in contrast to the Rhodesians, have known the confidence to recruit from the populations in the north: from the seven tribes of the Ovambo, more than half the population of the country, almost 600,000; from the Kvango, 110,000; from the Caprivi, 40,000. In the two most feared units, the 101 Battalion of the South West Africa Territorial Force (SWATF) and the South West African Police Counterinsurgency Force (SWAPOLCOIN), eighty to ninety percent of the men come from the country they fight in. Led by white South Africans, but also by a growing number of Ovambo junior officers, they know the languages, the customs and the terrain: "The picture of even-handed and well-armed paid Ovambos in security force uniforms is not lost on a local population accustomed to often brutal intimidation at the hands of wandering bands of shabbily-dressed and unpaid insurgents." No Ovambo from 101 Battalion or from SWAPOLCOIN has ever gone over to SWAPO, in contrast to the at least thirty men from SWAPO that track for them. Information from rural Ovambos led to over half the "contacts" with SWAPO in 1987.[102]

The Namibian Bishops' turn to "political activism" apes some South African divines, like Allan Boesak, a Calvinist no less, and a patron of UDF, who confessed he took up "politics" to get across to South African black youth after the turmoil in 1976 in Soweto:

This new political consciousness, and the consciousness of black humanity, have brought a new sense of responsibility in the black community. This new sense of responsibility and the active involvement of the black community in the struggle have taken away almost completely the traditional deference to the church. *Church officials are no longer judged by their office and the authority it represents.* [Whose? God's?] *Their office and authority are now measured by their active participation in the struggle for liberation* (Italics mine).[103]

But in relatively quiet Namibia seeing reform, it did not take turmoil and turmoil's face on the front pages of the world to break Church leaders. It took only fashion that spreads like a cancer in the absence of theology that bites, South African fashion. In June 1981 the NCC received a "Report on Namibia" from the South African Bishop's Conference, written in part by Denis Hurley, Archbishop of Durban, that called SWAPO "first and foremost a national liberation movement" that was "Marxist" only because it received help from Russia and other countries under Soviet control. This familiar leftist reasoning holds that "liberation movements" come under Soviet control because the West will not give them weapons.

The report listed six instances of alleged South African Security Force brutalities. It did not interview any of the many surviving victims of SWAPO atrocities it admitted. In South Africa, tough criticism met the report's insistence on the "popularity" of SWAPO and the "unpopularity" of the SADF.

Bishop Hurley told the newspapers he had "merely communicated the attitude of the Namibian people . . ." A few years later, with the same casualness of the Namibian Bishops, he admitted the report's endorsement of the demands of SWAPO and the UN "could be dangerous": "We could be backing a dangerous horse, I don't know, but this is what the majority of people are backing, [despite the result of the 1978 election with heavy voting in the north that Bishop Hurley apparently knew nothing about] and we are warned that majorities can be led astray, of course they can . . . If SWAPO wins, SWAPO wins, and we'll live with them somehow." These words' readiness to make those they mean to help responsible for decisions taken without their consultation, foretold the thinking in the State Department and the Congress that led to recognition of the ANC in January 1987 with Tambo's visit to Washington and the 1988 negotiations.

There is also a book behind this confusion, a charitable word for disingenuousness, printed, in of all places, Mugabe's Zimbabwe in 1982. Entitled *Marx-Money-Christ*, it was written by a Catholic Priest, Oswald Hirmer, with a preface by, of all people, the Archbishop of the Anglican Church of South Africa, Nobel Peace Prize Laureate, Desmond Tutu. Tutu, who publicly gave thanks for Mugabe's seizure of Rhodesia, is a lot clearer about money than he is about Christ: "I am a socialist . . . I detest capitalism. Capitalism is exploitative and I cannot stand that."[104]

In contrast Rome, at least the Apostolic Vicar in Windhoek, did better: "If SWAPO came to power in Namibia, I'd pack up and go *unless Rome ordered me to stay* . . . The internal wing of SWAPO now says there is only one organization, with one program, which means they too subscribe to violence. And this is unacceptable to the Church," he said in 1979 (Italics mine).[105] "The internal wing of SWAPO" means the so-called political arm of SWAPO,—it calls itself a "revolutionary vanguard party" and "a liberation movement,"—that the South Africans did not ban within Namibia, in contrast to the outlawed ANC in South Africa.

Within South West Africa, the NCC, in its words "the representative" of the wide majority of Namibia's population, takes advantage of the liberty of South West Africa to take on the TGNU and the last of the South African administration. In 1986 it sued in the South African Supreme Court in Windhoek against the curfew in the "operational area in the north" and attacked the National Assembly for its discussion of an investigation of church leadership. After the court's dismissal of the suit, the NCC said the "one-sided" decision,—apparently it thought "yes" or "no" could mean "yes" and "no,"— went against the will of "the majority of the people of the north": "There is no freedom here, the majority does not rule." These words betray thinking that could bring courts like Mozambique's and the ANC's peoples' courts to independent Namibia. ". . . Interim government will not bring a peaceful solution to the problems of Namibia," the NCC said in its attack on the TGNU when it so much as dared discuss an investigation of the NCC. This investigation might have uncovered evidence for the allegation—I have not been able to confirm—of a knowledgeable Namibian that East German agents with West German passports have infiltrated the Lutheran pastorate.

The NCC gives currency to every bit of evidence, usually court evidence, of South African police and military brutality. It ignores South West African soldiers and police because it will not recognize Namibians fighting for their country. The evidence that often involves members of the dreaded and highly effective Kovoets ("crowbar") special unit, disbanded in 1985, its uncompromised members reintegrated into other units, shows the predicament of soldiers and police, caught in the middle, that need to get Ovambos, including children, to talk quickly to find hiding terrorists: beatings, threats to life, sometimes carried out, and prosecuted. Brutality, no policy of systematic and prolonged torture. In January 1987 there was an uproar that shows the decency, and the innocence and gullibility, of Namibians, after a Windhoek weekly newspaper *The Namibian*, that backs SWAPO, showed an army truck with three killed terrorists strapped outside. The truck had passed through *one* village in the north. "A Christian organization, such as the South African Defense Force, would not publicly exhibit the enemy's dead," the police replied after first denying the "parade of dead." Living soldiers and ammunition had taken up the space needed for the dead in the Casspir. In his situation, I might do worse than the man in charge who *may* have decided on the spot to put the fear of death in the village. In any case the police were too apologetic: Christian Europe did not hesitate to exhibit the bodies of criminals because salvation, not death counted, as François Villon's "Ballade des Pendus" shows. The story made the rounds in some newspapers abroad like a *Time* magazine version of a Homeric epithet.[106]

The NCC also broadcasts stories, hilarious stories except for their consequences that South African soldiers in the integrated army units '"paint themselves black'—apparently a common practice of white soldiers in north Namibia." These stories mean to forget that black Namibian volunteers, now sixty percent of soldiers fighting SWAPO, have taken the place of South African soldiers. In 1985 the SWATF numbered 21,163 against an estimated 8,500 SWAPO terrorists, at war-costs of about four hundred million rand a year for South Africa. Three thousand responded to a call for 225 soldiers.[107]

The NCC propaganda knows no restraint because it wants extremity to paralyze common sense and the courage it takes. It wants continual mental panic. According to Bishop Dumeni, the leader of the Lutheran Church in Namibia, in Munich on July 7, 1988, "The killings are continuing simply because of the South African government's refusal to sign a cease-fire between her troops and those of SWAPO." The night curfew, necessary "to protect the local population," in the north, the judge-president's words in the Supreme Court, "threatens life" and violates "freedom of religion, movement and assembly," according to the Catholic, Lutheran and Anglican Bishops.

The NCC campaigns feed on, and incite, the sense of unreality that intimidation and outright fear, and too much change and too much responsibility, make. They want to make the country appear it thinks like one man in order to reinforce its division. This reinforcement of polarization in the appearance of unity is also the technique of the ANC, the Commonwealth Group and the State Department in South Africa,—Michael Clough's world. It means to prepare the way for negotiations, like the negotiations in 1988, that will allow SWAPO to seize the country. More than half the members of NCC also belong to SWAPO.[108] Still another front.

The unreality in South West Africa wishes away the truth about SWAPO Namibians know in their own flesh: Almost every family in the north remembers a relative or a child SWAPO murdered, abducted or enticed to willing flight.

For a year and a half the men and women of these families torn apart for ever, the Namibia Parents' Committee (NPC), organized in the middle of 1985, made only *private* inquiries about their children and relatives who disappeared into SWAPO's embrace. SWAPO did not answer at all, except obliquely, at a press conference in London, with a remark on war's necessities. The NCC, also without a word, dismissed the leading members of the NPC from their posts on the Council. SWAPO and the NCC wanted to keep the outrages "in the family" out of loyalty, really fear, to the "liberation of Namibia."

Their failure at home drove the NPC abroad, to Europe. But in Europe too, they went at first only to politicians who supported SWAPO. Their reply from the parliamentary group in West Germany with the closest ties to SWAPO: "This is a matter between Namibians," or "We cannot help, because we support SWAPO."

After this rebuke, one of the mothers brought herself to speak out: "These people say they support SWAPO, we tell them of SWAPO's tortures and killings and they tell us they support SWAPO. I am angry because our liberation has lost its soul and with it the souls of many other people."[109] The shock of this lesson, the true name of the fancy Western word "independence," can break men, especially men who suffered allegiance to SWAPO in words. A Catholic priest from Cape Town went to pieces after he saw a SWAPO camp in Angola in 1986, and later died.

The terror of SWAPO reaches far beyond South West Africa. In the great cities of the Western world and on the campuses of obscure American universities, young and strikingly open refugees from SWAPO, well-informed about Namibia through an astonishing worldwide grapevine, live isolated and alone, their mouths shut, among students who demonstrate against South Africa but who have never even heard of "South West," as the South Africans call it. Even the way home through a South African consulate, watched by God knows whom, in cities where Sam Nujoma lunches with prominent bankers with inept eyes on the future, can lead to intimidation. "But, I would like to add, that the terror is not limited just to Africa. I found that out when I travelled with the ladies from the [Namibia] Parents' Committee. They are afraid of SWAPO forces here, not SWAPO forces in the way as you will meet them in Angola and Zambia, but other types of SWAPO forces. I know many cases of this fear of SWAPO. Many people are not prepared to step into public life here as a result of SWAPO threats. They are so much afraid of what might happen to them . . . It is not only an African problem anymore . . ." "Here" means London; the speaker, Jorn Ziegler of the *Internationale Gesellschaft für Menschenrechte* of Frankfurt in March 1986.

At the European Parliament in Strasbourg in May 1987, Nujoma slapped the face of one of three women from the NCC who had asked what had become of their children. He also threatened a former SWAPO terrorist accompanying the women, Phil Ya Nangoloh, "We will kill you."

A man with the courage to tell facts both within Namibia and abroad, Nangoloh saw SWAPO murders and torture during his imprisonment as a "Rhodesian spy" in a SWAPO camp in Oshatotwa in Zambia from January to the middle of February 1975. He had escaped to the United States through Switzerland after training in radio operations in the Soviet Union after SWAPO "rehabilitation." Two SWAPO representatives in Western Europe warned him SWAPO murdered many who returned.[110]

This terror both within and outside South West Africa mocks "reconciliation," a word that figures prominently in the TGNU preamble to its bill of rights. SWAPO cannot recuperate.

Like the Africans of Rhodesia and the Angolans and the South Vietnamese, the South West Africans have been forced to quaff from the cup of programmed revolution before tasting of independence. Before the seizure of power, SWAPO has sought to pulverize the minds and hearts of the country, and of "international opinion," for the war in one place goes on everywhere also, not only to seize power,—but also to blame the destruction on the West and South Africa; to absolve SWAPO of responsibility; to turn South Africa and the West into accomplices who have shown themselves and the rest of the world they have no confidence in lawful change. After independence SWAPO means to use this guilt to get the West to pay its bills.

The South Africans have looked into the empty core of this attempt to divide the country forever, especially families, children and parents, wives and husbands, brothers and sisters, in order to destroy the living. Like the Portuguese before them who used more rough-and-ready methods, they have sought to turn captured SWAPO terrorists, men the Communists would kill or grind to death in camps without a second thought, men Rhodesia tried with a mandatory death sentence for armed invasion, into soldiers to fight SWAPO. The method: the choice between long prison sentences and fighting against SWAPO after rough "debriefing procedures" of various length to test their trustworthiness to fight alongside white and black soldiers, bold dangerous work.[111] The result: The dreaded Kovoets unit numbered ninety percent former SWAPO terrorists before its disbandment.

But loyalty does not mean a remade human being: The involuntary expressions of horror on the faces of South Africans who have fought alongside these men told me more than any words I could have heard to answer my naive questioning. Those faces told me the real name of "reconciliation." Whatever else it may do, and it may do much, the TGNU will not have the stuff for generations to lead an army capable of reconciling and defending the land.

There is also a more straightforward story: The 32nd Buffalo Battalion stationed in the Caprivi Strip, made up in part of FNLA veterans who left

Angola after the South Africans withdrew in 1975, with Portuguese one of its three languages, has the best fighting record in the SADF since World War II.

The Namibians I have met are warm intelligent gentle men, not without the bluntness and ferocity that comes of real gentleness. Their words filled with foreboding betrayed an unmistakable but unspoken sense of what had hit them since the fall of the Portuguese. They know the courage of soldiers needs leadership that takes generations, not just a few years to produce. The soft dread about their words showed they knew they were not ready for independence, but they did not say it outright, like almost everybody else who might think it. The flood of half-truths turns silence into eloquence.

Throughout 1988, especially after South African negotiations with the Cubans and the MPLA took hold, tensions built between the TGNU, in some sense an anti-SWAPO coalition, and the administrator general. They led in April to Botha's reassertion of the administrator general's powers under the South West Constitution Act of 1968 that the TGNU said reduced South West Africa again to direct South African administration. At the end of June 1988, the TGNU upon presentation of a draft constitution declared it wanted national, regional and local elections before the end of the year. The head of TGNU said he had enough of the incessant charges that the TGNU enjoyed no "democratic legitimacy."[112]

For the South Africans, the TGNU's request came more than a year too late. They were determined to surrender Namibia to the UN and SWAPO upon success of their negotiations whose failure might mean war. Namibia had for too long wanted it both ways, it now would learn the harsh lessons of independence—this was the mood in the South African government. Botha made harsh cuts in South African subsidies to Namibia. South Africa meant to dissolve the TGNU before the UN constituent assembly elections, a dissolution like Muzorewa's "standing aside" at the Lancaster House talks, except that the TGNU is unelected. The TGNU, which knew the full meaning of the Cuban build-up close to its frontiers, wanted agreement on a constitution before the UN elections. Even by September it could not believe the South Africans meant to give up the country.

More than a year before the administrator general had wanted regional, "second tier" elections not necessarily on a tribal basis to reach the groups that rejected the TGNU, among them, the crucial Ovambo leader, Peter Kalangula, who oscillated between SWAPO and South Africa because he refused to recognize the TGNU. South African thinking at that time, at least the thinking of the South African supreme court justice Victor Hiemstra, working with the TGNU, and of the administrator general, countenanced even the abolition of the second tier entirely. They meant to leave only municipal and national governments in order to avoid dealing with differences in Namibia's peoples. It is difficult to tell whether this position was prudent or merely evasive, whether it was a practical way of not exacerbating tensions or a way of not dealing with them. In any case the TGNU and the administrator general could not come to an agreement on replacing proclamation AG-8 that in 1968 had provided for second tier elections separately for each of the eleven population groups.

From the beginning the TGNU had been committed to abolishing AG-8. First accepted even among Africans because it made for self-government, the provision later appeared unthinkable in the face of propaganda against South Africa that called it also "apartheid." Hiemstra already in 1986 called the charge "to a large extent well founded [that] did the image of the country no good." He should have worried less about the country's reputation, for realities count more for survival than appearances, and realities do not aim to please. Later, South West Africa's highest court called AG-8 a violation of the TGNU's bill of rights. Wide differences between the funds available to whites and other groups, because AG-8 allowed each group to tax itself for itself, also made the provision unpopular. Even after Botha declared against abolishing AG-8 in April 1988, the TGNU could not agree on the geographical districts to replace the eleven groups for the elections it wanted quickly. Despite the threats of some ministers, including the head of government, the TGNU decided to remain in office to the end, as the minister of mines, Andreas Shipanga, put it.[113] But the real question, it became clear at the end of 1988, was would the TGNU, or anybody else, have the stuff to campaign effectively against SWAPO in the UN election scheduled for November 1989?

12 The Fighters: Savimbi's UNITA and RENAMO

Neither Savimbi's UNITA in Angola nor the resistance in Mozambique wants the total defeat of its Soviet-controlled opponents, the MPLA in Angola and FRELIMO in Mozambique. RENAMO's rare statements call for the dissolution of the Communist government "without any spirit of vindictiveness." They speak of the "the peoples' right to choose and freely vote for the country's political, social and economic system." In the face of such demands, Machel would not, and his successor Chissano will not, negotiate but cannot govern,— desperation that first showed its full face in 1982 when Machel bartered away all his country's mineral rights in exchange for an immediate increase in Soviet military aid, six months after he had ignored RENAMO's offer of a truce in exchange for a commitment to free elections.[114] Even in 1988, the MPLA refused to negotiate with Savimbi, stubbornness the Soviets openly encouraged.[115]

In Savimbi's conception, the war that gradually took shape after the Cubans failed to exterminate him in 1976 is a war of limited aims, not a fight to the death. From the beginning Savimbi called the fighting "this externally induced war" and concentrated on ridding the country of the foreigners who impeded agreement, who had replaced the Portuguese, the "thousands of East Germans, Poles, Czechoslovaks and North Koreans" and above all the Cubans,—also the cornerstone of the Reagan administration's engagement in southern Africa since 1981, and of South Africa in the negotiations in 1988: "Our military strategy is designed to inflict casualties on Castro's troops, and not when possible on the MPLA." For some Angolans fight unwillingly in the MPLA: "Some true Angolan nationalists have been forced by the Cubans to fight in the MPLA."

Even before the collapse of the Portuguese in 1974, Savimbi had subordinated fighting to the fashioning of "national consciousness," and citizens, as UNITA explained in 1972: "Our army is not an instrument of power. It must above all protect our educational work and agricultural cooperatives. To liberate territory is of no interest to us, we want to liberate consciousness."[116] In 1969 Savimbi, with the bluntness that eyes on realities yield, had said guerrillas without discipline and responsibility "would not be working for the people, but rather the people would be working for them": "If the man who has the gun in his hand does not understand why he has the gun, he is going to abuse the power of the gun against the people."[117]

Savimbi had learned the ways of winning people, in part, from the Portuguese, who in turn did not crush him because they feared the hatred of the people he had won over, as a Portuguese officer on the eastern front said in 1974. Savimbi's subordination of violence to constructive ends won him accusations of "collaborator" from an MPLA bent on "liquidating" both the FNLA and UNITA,—but it made the Portuguese think they could one day negotiate with him.[118] These expectations and this restraint show Spinola did not reason merely from his own experience. Savimbi too, in December 1967, little more than six months before he would enter Angola secretly and for good, expected negotiations, not victory, his position later also in the face of the MPLA: "We are to create such pressure that the Portuguese will have to negotiate."[119]

From the late seventies and especially in the eighties, Castro's fear of Cuban reactions at home made Savimbi hope for his withdrawal. Castro sent the badly wounded to East Germany to stay, he did not bring the corpses of the dead back home. In late 1986 and 1987, after the failure of a daring South African commando raid in 1985, Savimbi also tried to destroy the Chevron-owned installations that provide five hundred million dollars a year to pay for the Cubans at a thousand dollars a month: "These mercenaries can afford to stay in our nation only as long as they are paid"; "The goals of UNITA are clear and open for the world to see. We will drive the Cubans and the Soviets and Eastern-bloc personnel from Angola."[120]

But letters from Savimbi to Senator Symms published in the Congressional Record of 1985 show that UNITA has begun to doubt the feasibility of separating the MPLA from the Cubans. But UNITA has never said outright that only victory would bring the end of violence, because outright victory goes against Savimbi's grain and because victory could not be achieved after 1981, and especially after 1985, without South Africa unless the Cubans left. Savimbi kept talking about reconciliation. But the MPLA, even when it hinted at negotiations, made it clear it wanted to destroy UNITA. "We have no alternative but to liquidate UNITA," Jose dos Santos, the leader of the MPLA, said at a rally in a southern port on June 15, 1984 immediately after negotiations with the South Africans that foreshadowed the negotiations in 1988.[121]

Even before the collapse of Portugal, Savimbi had constantly talked of reconciliation between the FNLA, the MPLA and UNITA. In these years the MPLA fought both the FNLA and UNITA: In 1972 a deserter from the MPLA said his group fought mostly against UNITA; Portuguese officers said MPLA informers "often" betrayed FNLA positions.[122]

Savimbi's belief that UNITA could force the MPLA to negotiate meant "a protracted war for national liberation relying on our own efforts," as the fifty-five delegates, twenty-five of them soldiers, at UNITA's second policy-making congress voted in 1969.[123] But a "protracted war," as the intensification and spread of violence throughout the country in the eighties showed, risked irremediably dividing the country into sides that could not talk to each other, it risked turning UNITA into the MPLA's accomplice, just the division Savimbi's greatness sought to avoid. It risked catching Savimbi in the tangles of the violence he had sought to limit, in contrast to both the MPLA and the FNLA. In 1983 South Africa tripled its arms and supply shipments to Savimbi. Above all UNITA's use of land mines, that did their work against the Portuguese, and even more against Rhodesia and Afghanistan, draws UNITA into the MPLA's indiscriminate terror: "Visit either side in the Angolan war and the large and growing numbers of limbless people is startling. Others abound with even more vital parts blown away or who have been hideously disfigured."[124]

The grinding up of the country that risks turning UNITA into the MPLA's accomplice hit an English journalist, Fred Bridgland, who knows the difference between UNITA and the MPLA, after UNITA's destruction of the town of Cangonga in 1983. UNITA drove six hundred men and women, among them two hundred children, for resettlement and political "re-education," two to three families to a village, into "areas of UNITA's control":

We spoke to the civilians. But though many of them told us they were UNITA supporters who had been taken to Cangonga against their wills, our conversations, through a UNITA interpreter, can have had little meaning. One man busily showed us a small photograph he had used on his UNITA membership card. Another poured out complaints about how bad the MPLA school was for his children in Cangonga—and we had certainly seen for ourselves that it had no furniture or books and that all the washbasins were cracked and filthy. One woman claimed once to have belonged to LIMA, the UNITA women's movement. But how do Europeans on fleeting visits assess the real feelings of peasant people, caught in a terrible war, whose language and culture and perspective are so different? If any one of the civilians were unhappy about being taken off to a new life in the forest, they were keeping quiet about it. And why not? In their situation, I'd wave the flag and sing the anthem of whichever movement was momentarily in control.

However, we'd got a crude basic picture. The civilians looked bewildered rather than happily liberated. And no wonder. The MPLA rounds them up from the countryside and concentrates them in towns from which they can till the surrounding fields to feed the garrison. UNITA moves them out and scatters them around its areas where they learn a new line in political slogans. Of course, it's very easy and morally comfortable to sit on the fence and say each side is as bad as the other, and I know where I believe the best hope for the Angola peasantry lies. But at the stage of warfare I've been describing above, the peasants are as helpless as chaff in the wind.[125]

The protraction of the war that has also intensified comes because Savimbi cares about human life, but it helps the MPLA use negotiations for masked surrender. Murder gets to Savimbi in contrast to the MPLA. Despite his experience of exile brutality in the sixties, he probably never expected his rebellion against the Portuguese would draw him into such killing. "The situation inside Angola is very difficult. People cannot understand why they should continue to die even when our independence is near," he said in 1975.

With Neto and the second-in-command of the FNLA in April 1975, Savimbi saw the *musseques*, the African districts of Luanda, after three days of fighting between the MPLA and the FNLA had left about seven hundred dead and more than a thousand hurt. The killing had also hit towns in the north and the east. "Savimbi was shocked. He feels for the people . . . But Neto was cold. After the tour Savimbi turned to the MPLA leader and the FNLA representative and said: 'You have no place in Angola,'" the Portuguese high commissioner, General Antonio Silva Cardosa, who had accompanied them told journalists afterwards.[126] "My answer is: Politics is too difficult to survive on all the time—too painful. There has to be something else," Savimbi said of his profession of Christianity in the United States in 1979.[127]

A few months before he saw the dead in the *musseques*, at the end of 1974, just before conclusion of the Alvor accords, the strength of Savimbi's desire for reconciliation had reached foreign journalists, for instance, the African correspondent of the *Guardian*: "UNITA, long ignored and attacked by the other movements, has emerged as the binding force in the new nationalist union. Dr. Savimbi in particular is striving to dampen the tribal and personal animosities that divided the liberation movements so deeply during their thirteen-year war with the Portuguese."[128]

UNITA's harshest experiences deepened its leaders' capacity for reconciliation at the same time that it taught them the impossibility of reconciliation without victory. "The march was the most profound experience of my life. You felt you needed to love your brother as yourself. Alone, you couldn't survive. When colleagues died you truly felt diminished. All of us who were on the march believed by the end of it that *the war could really be won*" (Italics mine).[129]

With these words, years later, Tito Chingungi, UNITA's representative in Washington in 1988, recalled the six months from February to August 1976 when the Cubans hunted Savimbi and about one thousand followers through three thousand kilometers of forests. Only seventy-nine, among them nine women, made it to the end. But these lessons have never shown themselves in UNITA's public policies. The same indecision marks South Africa and the West.

Both RENAMO, in the more desperate situation in Mozambique, and UNITA do not intend to carry the war they are fighting beyond their frontiers. They fight for their country, unlike the MPLA, Mugabe and Machel, and his successor, Chissano, who serve "history" at the expense of their countries,— and will not stop until the "violent apartheid state of South Africa has been destroyed," as Mugabe scribbled in 1988.[130] "Mozambique will not discriminate against any country on account of its internal system," runs a statement of

RENAMO's, sometimes taken for proof of its obsequiousness toward South Africa.

With Savimbi the sense for limits comes from his respect for living facts. This respect for reality showed early in his readiness to alternate study for a doctorate in international relations in Switzerland with the heady treacherous world of Angolan exile politics in the early sixties, no trivial proof of discipline. "We always talk in concrete terms and repeat constantly that the road to success is long and hard," Savimbi said in 1973 at the same time that he admitted UNITA concentrated on peasants that had had contacts with the Portuguese to get "at their smouldering resentment."[131] UNITA instructs its officers to follow the news on their transistor radios, not because they are part of a "worldwide revolution," but because their fighting has consequences for everybody. Savimbi speaks of a practical foreign policy and face-to-face negotiation:

I would invite Mr. Botha to my own capital and receive him as head of state. Kaunda meets him on other peoples' borders, but I will challenge him on my own ground. And when he visits me, I will not, I cannot become less black than I am already. And because I am willing to talk with South Africa does not mean I believe in apartheid. I cannot. Things must change in South Africa . . .

In August 1985, in Jamba, Savimbi showed his impatience with American policy to a straightforward intelligent legislative assistant from the Senate: "The Americans have got the wrong man. Botha is not Vorster. He wants change, not the status quo." More than a year earlier, he had told a reporter from the Johannesburg *Star*: "The participation of Indians and Coloreds cannot be ignored—it is important. And no leader in South Africa has ever said it is the end of the road."[132] Again in 1986: "Even in South Africa everyone talks about how to move away from apartheid,"—a remark that shows his capacity to grasp what stirs in a country. He says he has never dealt with the ANC, a sobering contrast to the United States government, and Chester Crocker whose "freedom fighters in a generic sense" turn out not to talk to each other.

From a man with unsurpassed experience in the wars of our time, this confidence in negotiations with South Africa and its reforms should have counted,—especially among Congressmen whose ambivalence about violence shows in their readiness to encourage with money the violence they denounce. But Savimbi's words do not count, not only because he was an underdog, and an underdog without the formidable totalitarian "orchestra of hate," Banda's phrase, behind him,—but also because the moment he gained "visibility," a word that tells something of the anonymity of life today in the United States,— the Communists labeled him a puppet of South Africa. *The New York Times* that never fails in such conjunctures, practically turned "South African supported" into Savimbi's epithet,—as if it could not tell friendship from manipulation, another inadvertent acknowledgment of the "quality of life" in the United States. A shift Savimbi sought to expose: "A new tactic is to claim that UNITA is tied to the South African government . . . This claim may fool some in the West, but the nations of black South Africa know the truth. [Savimbi did not add they do not dare tell it.] They know Nigeria offered to replace the

Cuban and Soviet-bloc troops with Nigerian troops. But the MPLA leadership refused, showing the whole world that their real fear is not the South Africans, but UNITA, the Angolan people and nationalists within the MPLA [the Angolans in the army against their will]. Yes, UNITA receives aid from the Republic of South Africa. We have also received support from China, Arab nations and other black African countries, and much of that support has been shipped across the Namibian border." The Republic of South Africa, not the "white minority regime" another *New York Times* and *Washington Post* epithet.

The South African withdrawal in 1976 before his eyes, Savimbi suspects that South African support of UNITA depends on his usefulness in fighting and diplomacy neither he or the South Africans or the MPLA can entirely control, quite a worry for a "puppet." He knows he is expendable without successes in fighting,—successes in a situation where UNITA is too weak for direct confrontations with the Cubans. Before South Africa stopped its aid in late 1988, he had looked that situation in the face in 1983 after UNITA informers in the MPLA sent him documents that showed South Africa and the MPLA were negotiating a cease-fire and the withdrawal of South African troops from Angola and of Cubans and SWAPO three hundred miles north into Angola that would have meant an immediate cutoff of diesel fuel for UNITA. His response was to spread UNITA throughout the country like mosquitoes, a further intensification of the war:

The fact is that our friendship is something the South Africans can dispose of overnight. It is why we need to devise a strategy which ensures that we cannot become disposable material. If we can give a sign that we can win, we will not be disposed of. If we cannot give that sign, we will be disposed of. However, it will not be easy to sell out UNITA because there are many elements in this situation which are not controllable either by South Africa or the MPLA. In 1976 we had to disperse and accept that we might die. But in 1983 the situation is different. We don't have enough forces to make direct confrontations everywhere with the Cubans and the MPLA: If we did that, we would break our forces. We are confronted by forty thousand Cubans, but if we avoid taking them on in fixed positions, if our activities force them to spread through the whole country, they are an obstacle we can overcome.

Savimbi's common sense born to some extent out of the disasters his illusions brought him, shows the same respect for realities as Kamuzu Banda of Malawi who already in 1968 remarked "do gooders do more harm than good": "South Africa threatens no one. She is a peaceful country . . . [It is] . . . all [the] African states . . . [who] are shouting . . . threats against South Africa"; ". . .Already because of our attitude here [in Malawi], the attitude of South Africans toward their own Africans is changing. They are becoming more liberal." "But," he added, "they won't change overnight."

In contrast to Banda who saw through totalitarianism from the outside, Savimbi, in part because he was a generation younger, had to go through totalitarianism. He does not have Banda's grasp of history, and unlike Banda who became a statesman after many years as a physician, he gave up his dream of studying medicine after a turbulent, and largely unknown, year in Portugal.

From his arrival in Lisbon in 1958, at the age of twenty-four, he mixed in the destructive element but kept his head because of his studies in Lausanne and because of his integrity and independence, and maybe, because of his faith. In 1964 he publicly stood up to Che Guevara, at the cost of cries of "CIA stooge," in Dar es Salaam. He told him that the fight was against "colonialism," for independence and not for the "revolution" in the already independent Belgian Congo that Che Guevara wanted because it would give the totalitarians all of Africa,—Mao Tse-Tung's thought: "If outsiders like you bring along all their formulas of revolution and try to impose them on us then you are coming with the same kind of superiority complex as the colonialists in Africa," he told Guevara the next morning.[133] In Cairo, he met Malcolm X who taught him "the links, long camouflaged by the enemy, that are bound to exist between the struggle of Blacks in America and Blacks in Africa."[134]

Also, in 1964, at thirty years of age Savimbi met some of the most destructive men the world has ever known, Mao Tse-Tung and Chou En-lai, who told him "frankly they could not trust him" because he had criticized China a few months before. But they agreed to train him and some of his men. He visited the Soviet Union, Czechoslovakia, Bulgaria, Hungary, General Vo Nguyen Giap in North Vietnam and the North Koreans—who all received him coldly.[135] In July 1965, just after completing his degree in Switzerland, he left Europe "for good" to fly to China for four months of guerrilla training. In September eleven UNITA leaders, the so-called Chinese eleven, joined him to train until May 1976. Eleven members of ZANU under the leadership of Josiah Tongogara, later Mugabe's military commander, followed in November.[136] Again, in 1967 he spent an hour with Mao Tse-Tung who promised arms and money; not much it turned out, about five thousand pounds by 1970.

But not even Maoist indoctrination full in the face shook Savimbi's belief, and his respect for elders and parents, as he wrote from China in 1965: "Political and economic theories which are supported in atheistic attitudes do not fall in line with the feelings of Africa. The African believes in a higher Being whatever his name may be or whatever the place where he is worshipped. There is an ancestral force which transcends man."[137] Yet in 1969 UNITA's Second Congress praised the "cultural revolution" for turning China into the "center of World Revolution."[138] By 1971 an Austrian journalist who walked two months to reach Savimbi's camp in Angola wrote, "Mao's political doctrines are not Savimbi's."[139]

Savimbi learned how to fight from China, and even more questionably, how to "politicize" the peasants he knew were not easily convinced to leave land, sometimes in their families for generations, to fight: "Once you've convinced a peasant, he will not divide in his loyalty. You've written on a clean sheet of paper." "Our Chinese type was winning more support" than the MPLA's "Russian type organization" that murdered chiefs to trap the youth in "revolution," Savimbi said of Angola in 1969, eleven years later. The MPLA had guns, but they had no "techniques for mobilizing the people," they murdered UNITA supporters more than "our soldiers" because they wanted "them to turn to the MPLA": "The MPLA killed a lot of chiefs because they thought that to make a revolutionary movement they had to get rid of the chiefs so that they could build up the youth to become revolutionaries. They said the heads of villages were feudalists. But by doing it they turned the people against them."[140]

Savimbi did not say the persistence he had learned in Nanking had led in China to intimidation much more pervasive than *comparatively* straightforward Soviet brutality that permitted everything it did not forbid, the reverse of the situation in China. "Shouting and screaming" and "revolutionary theories" that promise to "change their plight overnight" would not help: "You must never talk down to them . . . It may take us months or even years to convince one particular set of villagers to come and join us." The test of effectiveness was whether the peasants told the Portuguese UNITA had broken in upon their village,—another way of saying the Portuguese had helped keep him honest.[141]

Years later, the authority Savimbi would not attack directly came home to the sensitive British journalist, Fred Bridgland, when he saw elders costumed in old clothes and solar topees; one in a dinner jacket, the shine blanching on its lapels, at a UNITA rally in Cago Coutinho: "The village elders had stoic enduring faces which seemed to contain much fundamental wisdom not lightly shared."[142]

It was the Soviet-Cuban invasion after the collapse of Portugal that brought the distinction between independence and "revolution" that had always hovered in Savimbi's mind to the fore: "The Cubans are killing our country, so we have to defend it as other peoples have defended themselves against invasions."

After 1975, his readiness to take responsibility for the catastrophe he had helped bring about made Savimbi face the difficulties of change he had always acknowledged, more straightforwardly: ". . . We have to work for progress, and in modern times we cannot apply all our traditions without changing them or adjusting them, but we have to keep the *essence* of our values in order to remain a people with an identity. If we cannot do this, as a political party, we are going to speak a language that our people will never understand. No ideological system exists in a vacuum. And you cannot hurry people along a road that they do not want to follow. That is why a genuinely African revolution requires a willingness to learn from the peasants, and a patience as well, because—how can I put it—peasants are naturally *reluctant*. When you bring them a new idea they are reluctant to change. They say the life they are living—well, it is not very good, it is not very pleasant, but they are afraid to change because they say the future is unknown. So if you want to transform their lethargy into action you must understand their aspirations."[143] Spinola knew that also.

Both RENAMO and UNITA do not want to make a new man,—a crucial contrast with Nyerere, Kaunda, Machel, Mugabe, SWAPO, and the ANC who all took independence, not merely for self-government, but for an occasion for the transformation of man. Kaunda, who takes the state for an "institution of violence," said at his inauguration in 1964, ". . . The sky is the limit to what can be achieved by individuals as well as by the nation . . . Where we once had doubts, fears, and hatreds, we shall have confidence, courage, and love. In short, independence could act as some sort of magic wand . . ." And Machel (to the *Wall Street Journal*!): "Marxist materialism simply means I have confidence in my own strength, in my own ability to transform the world." In pursuit of the transformation of man through "villagization," Nyerere moved eighty-five percent of the population, some at gun point, six million souls in 1974 alone, with the result that major export crops fell in the seventies: sisal nearly sixty percent, cashews nearly fifty percent, cotton almost thirty percent.[144]

The heavy dull responsibility of effective rule did not interest these men. It was not enough. They would do more because they feared their actual responsibilities. Mao in 1967 coolly told Savimbi he expected Kaunda would let the Chinese arms Nyerere would accept for UNITA pass through Zambia.[145] These men not only allowed terrorists and guerrillas to use their countries as bases, they also directed the wars, and their diplomacy, more important and more twisted than terrorism, for it made it respectable, against Mozambique, Angola, and later, with Machel, against South West Africa and Rhodesia, while the world took them for disinterested lovers of peace,—quite a distraction from failure.

For good reason they dread criticism that might bring them to their senses. Kaunda forbids open criticism of himself or his "philosophy of humanism" with a penalty of up to three years in prison. "People who think Tanzania will change her cherished policy of *Umjamaa* [usually translated socialism] and self-reliance because of the current economic difficulties are wasting their time. We shall never change," Nyerere remarked in the face of International Monetary Fund conditions in 1980.

With their goal to make a nation without remaking man, UNITA and even more, RENAMO want to separate self-rule from violent revolution. "RENAMO's objective has been, and still is, to break the grip of foreign arms and ideology imposed on our people."[146] A young South West African I interviewed, intelligent, blessedly unsophisticated, who had managed to escape SWAPO's forcible embrace, drew the same distinction almost involuntarily: He wanted to trade and move about his country freely but not go into peoples' homes. He had seen, after the first indoctrination in SWAPO camps in Angola had taken the breath out of his eyes momentarily, that the formulas repeated against his ears went against the grain of everything he knew.

The truth these fighters show, a truth so bare and simple it can hardly bear words, is that most men want to live the way they want to live, or manage to live, and not be told by any party on any pretext how and what they must do and think: "FRELIMO imposed a political regime alien to the Mozambican understanding of life."[147]

Most astonishingly still, for a West that, for the most part, cannot conceive of rational reasons to fight, or even to help others fight, they are willing to fight and die for this simplemindedness. They taught the world, before the Afghans, that some men, even without a state, will fight against communism and foreign domination, the two are practically indistinguishable, almost with their hands while we look on, distractedly. They show the true price of self-determination, in contrast to the formalistic imposition of independence from the outside the UN and the State Department are now imposing on South West Africa.

RENAMO wants to preserve the life it had before Portuguese abandonment because it knows change will take care of itself. Barely six months after independence, one resistance group called FRELIMO "so atrocious that it has made people wish they were under Portuguese rule."[148]

There are also real differences between UNITA and RENAMO that come in part because of the courage and intelligence of Savimbi and because of the differences in the Portuguese terms of abandonment. The Portuguese left Angola fighting. In Mozambique, they disregarded other resistance groups, the "several healthy nationalist parties" and the groups that did not want the Portuguese to leave at all, and handed power to Samora Machel and FRELIMO without any provision for elections to discover the peoples' will, the ANC goal in South Africa.

The resistance in Mozambique came, and almost immediately, from inside the party,—from former members of FRELIMO who had seen the face of the new regime after arrest in the purges of 1975 in its concentration camps, the "reeducation camps," the Gulags, called "Centers for Mental Decolonization." This name, funny to anybody outside, betrays the euphoria of the cruelty in Mozambique, and the confusion in Portugal and Europe in those days. The PCP, the other face of Portuguese abandonment, saw to it that Marxists trained in Algeria that include many of the men still at the top of the regime took over FRELIMO. FRELIMO also had close contacts with "student leaders," especially in Italy, some of whom had been trained in Czechoslovakia.

The most shocking measures, besides the camps, were the nationalization of land and shipment of children, called "the property of the State," to Cuba to work on the land, to the Soviet Union for political training, and to East Germany to work in the mines and steel mills and cleaning streets. The parents who had stood by to see their children taken away received no letters,—but FRELIMO received thirty percent of their wages in desperately needed hard currency. In Germany they soon numbered ten thousand, twelve thousand in 1988.[149] FRELIMO members who spoke out against these measures like Andre Matessangaisse, a FRELIMO commander since 1972, were sent to concentration camps to await "execution."

In October 1976 Matessangaisse and others took the weapons from the guards they overpowered and broke out of Sacuze concentration camp. They started attacking other camps for weapons and to free their men,—the beginning of the resistance, according to RENAMO. Also in October, on the night between the thirtieth and the thirty-first, the secret police the KGB had organized and the East Germans trained, arrested more than three thousand people in Maputo, Beira and elsewhere, for the camps. The young who soon made up most of RENAMO learned fast. "I didn't like the Communists' system. I saw the people suffering as they suffer now. So I deserted and joined RENAMO," said a young man who had fought with FRELIMO until his escape in 1977 at the age of nineteen. The resistance turned to Rhodesia.

Already in the five years before 1974, the Rhodesians had used Mozambicans as the eyes and ears of their intelligence, and encouraged them "to do their own thing in Mozambique without having to rely on support from Rhodesia." The Rhodesians' astonishment at the readiness of Mozambicans to resist shows the FRELIMO front's claim that their terror, for instance, their systematic murder of the tribal chiefs north of the Zambezi from the end of 1971, spoke for the people had captivated the Rhodesians also, as an intelligence report in 1974 just after the coup in Portugal, shows:

> The undoubted success of the movement [the Rhodesians already called it the Mozambican Resistance Movement] also signified that FRELIMO in Mozambique . . . lacked the essential measure of support that they needed from the population: or the Portuguese had acted too hastily in transferring power to a liberation movement which could not establish popular support through free elections.[150]

In other words there was already strong resistance from outside FRELIMO that may not have wanted independence at all before leading FRELIMO commanders broke with the organization in 1975 and 1976.

In part in reaction to this resistance from both within and without, FRELIMO turned itself from a broad front into a tightly-knit "vanguard" party in February 1977. Besides all members of FRELIMO before the independence agreement in September 1974 who still met party requirements, the new party admitted only men put up by party members after a one-year trial. By 1983, the first available figures, the party numbered 110,000 members, at least half from the country, and mostly illiterate, and 4,200 cells.

Radio Free Africa organized by FRELIMO moderates started broadcasting into Mozambique from Umtali in Rhodesia, first for five minutes, then for hour-long lists of the arrested and deported unavailable to relatives and friends in Mozambique, on July 5, 1976, a few months before Matessangaisse's escape, and a few months after Machel showed he cared more for Mugabe's terrorism than his own country by closing the border with Rhodesia on March 1, 1976. But Rhodesia limited supplies, actions and men: 917 trained men carried out operations in December 1978.

The closure of the border showed Machel's self-destructive preoccupation with destroying others. It cost FRELIMO five hundred million dollars a year in hard currency, in addition to the loss of eighteen to twenty million dollars in remittances from Mozambicans in Rhodesia and the paralysis of the port of Beira with thousands out of work,—a paralysis that was made the occasion of a rage of propaganda, ten years later, in late 1986 and 1987, after the CAA Act precluded United States objection.

The Rhodesians knew this self-destructiveness, and suspected only a "classical war across borders" they dared not undertake could show it its face, as an intelligence analysis of July 1977 shows: "Mozambique and Zambia are determined to support the Patriotic Front regardless of the consequences to themselves . . . Tanzania will continue to maintain and intensify the terrorist offensive."[151] But it worked, for the time being.

In contrast to the fighters that left FRELIMO, Savimbi has had to live with his former self, not rebel against disappointment. But his past despite the near destruction it brought upon him, also gave him strength. He continued to govern in rudimentary fashion as well as to fight, to control territory and organize it with schools, clinics,—in short the subordination of fighting to politics he insisted on years before the Portuguese collapse. In 1977, at the time of perhaps its greatest military weakness with only largely inexperienced guerrillas often without proper arms in its ranks, with few if any nations supporting it after United States abandonment,—days that still bear in upon the South African officers who saw them, as if they were not in the past,— UNITA had the political stuff and confidence to muster its Fourth Congress with 1,600 delegates. In contrast 221 delegates had attended its previous congress in 1971 that agreed, among other things, to turn its guerrillas into more organized forces.

In 1986, UNITA numbered 6,941 primary schools with 7,127 teachers and 224,811 pupils; 9 secondary schools with 80 teachers and 1,860 students,— rudimentary thatched-hut schools out in the bush where teachers, and the confidence in the future their work shows, count most. Medicine too is simple: Only three doctors in Jamba, no dentists, but *Médecins sans Frontières*, men of imperishable courage, has sent doctors and nurses to train Angolans and organize inoculations. Every battalion has men trained to treat and evacuate the wounded.

Savimbi's resilience after the collapse of Portugal, his capacity to stand alone, did not spring up overnight. It came of a crucial decision, the most crucial after his decision to take up arms against the Portuguese in 1964 and 1965, after he broke with the FNLA: to return to Angola and fight from within the country without reliance on foreign support. He returned to Angola in 1966, and for good in 1968, from Egypt where he had fled after his expulsion from Zambia because of UNITA's sabotage of the Benguela line in 1967. The decision to return meant he would live among the people he fought for and capture his weapons from the Portuguese. It meant he would be his own man, self-reliance he had only in part learned from the Chinese. It meant farewell to the treacherous and murderous exile politics that had punctuated his student years since 1958. Above all, it meant the subordination of violence to rudimentary governing, the distinguishing mark of UNITA.

Savimbi's decision also meant that the world outside ignored UNITA. From 1966-1974 Savimbi says he received help from only one country in Africa, Egypt.[152] No other guerrilla or terrorist organization in southern Africa has operated entirely from the land it sought to seize. The leader of the FNLA, Holden Roberto, who enjoyed the protection of Zaire, never set foot in Angola until 1974-75. Neto and the MPLA talked of putting their headquarters in the country but never went beyond a few excursions.

Self-reliance has made UNITA resourceful to an extent that defies imagination. This resourcefulness has given it confidence in coping and improvisation, almost as if it had to invent the world, or civilization, from the ground up all over again. A reporter in Jamba in 1986 saw Savimbi's men at work: on a T-34 tank with parts from another wreck; on a Soviet truck engine with

German spare parts to convert it to diesel and increase its power; and even on a rocket after a Soviet model. To get its trucks that sometimes travel not on roads, but on tracks through rough dusty terrain, across the unfordable Cuando River UNITA dismantled them and ferried them across on a small troop ferry with an outboard motor. A Ural truck takes eight days, a Star three days, a British Land Rover twenty-four hours.[153] In 1983 UNITA sent a man to Europe to learn the legendarily secretive diamond business so it could get the right price for the diamonds it captures in the northeast: six million dollars worth from one attack in 1986. With pride that betrays a man who knows how to live off booty, Savimbi says no rifle matches the Soviet AK-47. The South Africans gave him enough to fight with but not enough to turn him into a client. They value Savimbi's resilience.

Savimbi has a sense that war is not only the roughest but the deepest political education; that a disciplined army is the first expression of a people, something he may have learned with his own eyes as a doctoral student from the Swiss militia that also served as an example for the Israeli army. UNITA photographs show smartly uniformed soldiers drilling—in contrast to RENAMO snapshots of heavily-armed kids, barefoot and barely in dirty T-shirts. But even in 1971 when UNITA soldiers lived and died barefoot and in rags, the Austrian journalist who had traveled two months to see them called them, "disciplined, more disciplined than any other guerrilla group I have come across."[154]

Savimbi's sense of order runs deep,—not compulsive order, but the order that distinguishes a people from a crowd, an army from a gang. In the extreme conditions of the "Long March," he kept notebooks with the names of everyone, their skills, their illnesses and deaths; at every halt he listened to the count of the weapons and ammunition each guerrilla carried. In the years when he moved bases every few months he had papers his secretaries typed buried in metal trunks until the new base was secure. He knows appearance counts, as reporters' frequent notice of the well-pressed uniforms of UNITA's soldiers shows. "It was immediately clear that UNITA was an organization of a very different calibre than the FNLA," the CIA chief in Angola said after a twenty-four hour visit.[155]

From the time of the breakdown in Angola and his retreat to guerrilla war in the bush to survive, Savimbi has striven to create a conventional army that also labors, in order not to live off the population. After the capture of Cazombo in 1984, and the repulse of a Cuban counter-attack that cost one thousand UNITA dead, Savimbi had his soldiers plant nine hundred acres with corn and cassava. Divided in four categories, the steps of an army in the making, UNITA's forces ran, in E. P. Cain's estimate in 1986, to something like: two thousand regular troops; eighteen thousand semi-regulars that sometimes number battalions of five hundred; twenty thousand in company size units for ambushes, mine-laying and sabotage; and as many as thirty-five thousand dispersed guerrillas.

Savimbi's soldiers, who mostly walk to war, live under strict discipline: Abuse and pillaging of local population means "treason," probably execution.

This discipline keeps the groups scattered throughout the country from breaking down into thuggery and in some kind of coordination: "We have engaged the Cubans in virtually every province, and our support comes from every region and tribe in Angola." Even urban bombings make a clear limited point, for instance, the attack on the East German embassy and the Aeroflot offices in Luanda in 1979. Since 1975 the war had cost the country seven billion dollars in destruction of roads, bridges and factories according to an American estimate in 1983.[156] In the years before 1985, UNITA claimed two thousand MPLA-Cuban casualties a month in something like twenty ambushes and "encounters" a month. Training, the Roman word for army, is constant: "Sweat lost in training is blood saved in battle."

Despite open enthusiasm, all American visitors to Jamba I have met betray unacknowledged unease. They are startled by the huge posters of Savimbi, the commissars, "political officers," in every army unit and village, the discipline and the rallies with chants of "Savimbi." Questioned, they reluctantly say: "China, an African China" or "cult of personality,"—despite their knowledge that the indoctrination emphasizes respect for property, individual initiative, free enterprise and opposition and despite their own experience of Savimbi's presence. "The first impression is one of formidable strength. In his well-pressed jungle green uniform he looks, physically, even bigger than he really is, and when he talks it is easy to understand how he has captured the imagination and the loyalty of the fifteen thousand guerrillas who make up UNITA," Lord Chalfont described Savimbi in 1977, his hardest time.[157]

Self-evident greatness makes men uneasy—and with good reason, for it lives in daily presence of its opposite, on heights that know the temptations of the depths. Greatness, especially among statesmen, who have responsibilities for millions, always lives close enough to self-destruction to know its presence. Savimbi's hardest test will come after the relief of settlement or victory—if it comes.

Unlike UNITA, RENAMO has never sought to rule, at most to administer, and to disrupt and destroy, to show the weakness of FRELIMO, not its own strength. Two crises mark its development: the Lancaster House agreements that brought Mugabe to power in Zimbabwe in 1980 and South Africa's Nkomati accords with Machel in March 1984. Mugabe in power meant the death or capture of almost six hundred guerrillas in June 1980 reducing RENAMO to three hundred fighters; the cessation of broadcasts from Zimbabwe; and the transference of RENAMO's headquarters, including its broadcasting equipment flown out in a South African C-130 to the Transvaal. Before the transfer of RENAMO headquarters to South Africa, Rhodesia had sought to disband it, and discovered RENAMO was not Rhodesia's creature, a lesson the media, and FRELIMO, have yet to learn: "To my great surprise, the vast majority [of RENAMO] not only preferred to continue in the field but took no exception to being placed under South African control."[158]

The Nkomati accords meant the end of South African ammunition, weapons and training,—an abandonment that provoked continuing tension between South African soldiers and the government, especially its diplomats, some of whom openly call RENAMO "thugs." This tension showed itself to the world in the resignation of the Chief of the Army, Constand Viljoen at the end of 1985, a loss comparable to Israel's loss of Sharon.

By 1988 South Africa's promise to spend fourteen million dollars training and equipping, everything but weapons, as many as three FRELIMO battalions to guard the power line of the Cabora Bassa dam showed it might turn against RENAMO. This move, unthinkable a few years before, followed Crocker's overcoming conservatives in Washington who had wanted the United States to insist on negotiations between FRELIMO and RENAMO, in accordance with the "Reagan Doctrine" that originally wanted help for RENAMO as well as Savimbi, the Afghans, the Nicaraguan resistance and even Cambodia.[159] At a dramatic meeting at the Cabora Bassa dam in September 1988, with Botha, who apparently hinted RENAMO should surrender, Chissano admitted South Africa had made "important reforms," the new Soviet line.[160] At the time of the Nkomati accords in 1984, RENAMO had been within six months of victory over FRELIMO, South African military briefers said after South Africa signed a similar accord with the MPLA and the Cubans in 1988.

Nkomati forced RENAMO to operate almost entirely from within Mozambique, to capture its weapons and ammunition, largely Soviet, from FRELIMO and to control some territory,—necessity's self-reliance. "Our morale was shattered. My men said we couldn't win. But I told them to trust me . . . We staged a general offensive, captured huge stocks of enemy weapons and started taking territory," remarked the present leader of RENAMO, Afonso Dhlakama in 1986 of 1984.[161]

RENAMO thrived, it turned out, on self-reliance: three times more attacks and control of twice as much territory within a year of Nkomati. Two thousand in 1981, the guerrillas numbered twenty thousand in 1988. By 1986, a reporter from *Jane's Defense Weekly*, after four months in Mozambique, said RENAMO appeared to control all the territory north of the Zambezi, more territory than FRELIMO had ever controlled before Portuguese abandonment. More importantly, it seemed "to be winning over the local population in many parts of the country."[162]

In the years after 1980, and especially 1984, RENAMO "seemed to go from strength to strength, and I began to wonder whether we had created a monster," Ken Flower wrote.[163] The word "monster" betrays not only Mugabe's Rhodesia and the workings of FRELIMO propaganda that blamed every RENAMO success on South Africa, a label that stuck the more RENAMO attacked. It also shows that, like Chissano, Flower took resistance not under some government's control for uncontrollable resistance, a fearful thing. Flower succumbed to FRELIMO propaganda despite the "intense" fear of RENAMO he saw in Chissano already in 1980. In 1980, Chissano could not conceive of resistance against FRELIMO, for it showed mighty forces overcoming the theories that provoked them,—and called RENAMO, and the Rhodesians to boot, "South African puppets." An assertion that might have made Flower smile, in days not meant for smiling, since South Africa had refused Rhodesian requests for involvement with Mozambique fighters.[164]

The few reporters that dare go into RENAMO country have seen no signs of South African weapons: "The only weapons I saw were dated AK–47 Kalashnikovs, Soviet and Chinese made 82mm anti-aircraft guns and a collection of grenades and land mines, some dating from the independence war against the colonialists."[165] And another reporter on a RENAMO base with about a thousand people, mostly not fighters, many children, twenty-five kilometers from Maputo: "They only have small arms such as AK–47 rifles and platoon weapons such as RPG–7 rocket launchers, RPD machine guns and 82mm mortars."[166] In November 1987, the International Institute for Strategic Studies in London said, "RENAMO has no significant outside source of major military supplies for its war against Mozambique's FRELIMO government . . . Contrary to claims that South Africa continues to supply equipment to RENAMO, it relies for the most part on material captured during its raids"—to little effect despite its authority.[167]

In the spring of 1988 a French journalist just returned from a trip in RENAMO areas, who also remarked on the fighters' "lack of virtually everything: few arms and less equipment," said they were disciplined and drew on noticeable support in their territories, in part, because they had allowed traditional village life to return.[168] FRELIMO had imposed collective villages with people from different tribes "to impede the reproduction of colonial/traditional relations of production into the new society," without distinguishing between tribes.[169] "Under FRELIMO it was like living in a prison. We were forced to work in communal villages, and we were whipped when we didn't produce enough."[170]

FRELIMO accusations overcame the few available facts because by 1987 and 1988 it had succeeded in getting other countries, sometimes through the State Department, to repeat its propaganda, most strikingly in a shocking atrocity report Crocker released in April 1988.[171] This report accused RENAMO of murdering "a conservatively estimated one hundred thousand civilians," a figure extrapolated from about eighty eye-witnesses, interviewed in languages the investigator could not understand. *The Washington Post*, in a lead editorial, immediately and without a word of analysis turned the figure into "at least a hundred thousand people" under the heading "Pretoria's Victims in Mozambique."[172] With the authority of the United States behind it, the report did its work in Europe.[173]

"More alarming than FRELIMO's brutality is the conscious attempt by State Department bureaucrats to obstruct and falsify the flow of information to American policy-makers in the Congress and the White House," RENAMO's office in Washington had said, almost a year earlier, of an unsigned State Department white paper, "Mozambique: Charting a New Course."[174] Chissano had meant just this sort of campaign done by others with words, to make negotiations between it and FRELIMO unthinkable, when he said, after Reagan received him in October 1987, that to save lives,—he cares,—his Party meant to defeat RENAMO, not "militarily," but by other "methods of persuasion" and "political means." Chissano claimed Reagan had not dared mentioned RENAMO by name,—by implication not to embarrass Chissano who cannot bear mention of RENAMO, a bald-faced lie, I hope.[175]

At the same time that it made RENAMO attack harder, South Africa's cutoff also further weakened RENAMO's never strong capacity to make its conditions for settlement known in the world,—the necessary condition for a cease-fire. Even before the Nkomati accords, South Africa had always been ambivalent about its goals in Mozambique, had always alternated between diplomacy and fighting,—in contrast to Angola where failure in 1975, the Cubans and Savimbi's unbroken leadership taught it the confidence of direction until 1988. Even after the short-lived agreements with the MPLA in 1984, South Africa showed its loyalty to Savimbi: Malan flew to Jamba, Botha invited Savimbi to his inauguration as state president at the beginning of September 1984. Savimbi accepted Botha's invitation because he wanted to show support for reform, after visiting Africa's most able and courageous leaders, King Hassan II of Morocco and Houphouet-Boigny of the Ivory Coast.

Also in contrast to UNITA, RENAMO has not sought to make a conventional army. More mixed than UNITA, made up of (in addition to former FRELIMO members that make up perhaps three quarters of its leadership) blacks and whites who want their property, especially their land, back and of youths that have seen what has become of their country, RENAMO seems almost a movement of restoration: It wants its country back with the change Spinola wanted but without Portuguese sovereignty.

Its conditions for settlement are much the same as Savimbi's: removal of the estimated thirty thousand foreign troops and agents from Zimbabwe (15,000), Zambia (3,000), Tanzania (5,000), Cuba (2,202), East Germany (1,038), the Soviet Union (2,261), and most recently, even from Ethiopia; and internationally supervised elections. "Peace will only come through a respect for religious freedom, private property, human rights and political tolerance."[176]

In the short range more desperate and more modest than UNITA, and more realistic, for it seems to know in a more immediate sense than Savimbi that the country cannot function without the return of Europeans, RENAMO is more short-sighted about the long-term difficulties of independence and self-rule. Savimbi has never wanted to go back, he has sought a rudimentary state in the readiness to fight and die,—and govern. RENAMO, instead, does not seem to realize there is no going back, and that taking up centuries of Portuguese dominion requires more than an adjustment.

The absence of a RENAMO program, often criticized in the West, in phrases that seem picked up from one newspaper to the next, as if we did not know the ravages of ideology, might argue these fighters do not need future promises to live and die off, as the South African photographer at the base with a view of Maputo noted with relief: "One thing that struck me was that there were no propaganda pamphlets, no parades, no political speeches. Now and again they would just let the troops get together and shout 'Viva RENAMO' or 'Down with Chissano' and a returning patrol has the strange ritual of mustering and doing a short hand-clapping routine before they disperse to their shelters."[177] FRELIMO propaganda, an infection of the language, has taught them to get along without explanations.

RENAMO makes its presence felt in much of the country because of its network of support bases, scattered in thousands of square miles of rough, thick vegetation, scarcely inhabited or uninhabited, broken here and there by lonely run-down towns. It has not imposed itself, and manages its presence in rudimentary fashion,—a blessing but for its terror. It has concentrated on cutting communications throughout the country, on railroads and roads, few and vulnerable, on military installations, barracks, convoys, munitions depots, lightly-garrisoned towns. Even through the "Beira Corridor," guarded by a string of soldiers never further apart than the sight of each other, trucks move in convoys. The guerrillas operate almost everywhere in groups as small as four or five, appearing out of nowhere like ghosts. "When we attack a town, our objective is not to hold it, but to scatter the enemy, capture their material, destroy their infrastructure and then withdraw," Dhlakama told an English journalist, Sharon Behn.

RENAMO's claim of control of eighty-five percent of the country means fear of its ambushes has made normal life uncertain except within a range of twenty or thirty kilometers of towns and large villages. At nightfall, people from the outlying suburbs come into Maputo to sleep. Most travel by air, and, since 1987, by ship. Ships carry UN World Food Program aid because the highway north from Maputo requires convoys, and has in parts reverted to bush. RENAMO's war takes place everywhere and nowhere. It constantly makes its invisible threat felt. The only guides to its bases,—local peasants.[178]

In 1987 "reliable" sources told *Africa Confidencial* RENAMO was gaining influence in the country, especially in areas that saw its activity. "A serious threat to survival of the regime," the Pentagon called it.[179] "If it weren't for the Zimbabweans and other fighting forces, RENAMO would have won the war by now. Harare runs that war, not Maputo," a businessman, not about to give his name, however, told Behn.

FRELIMO makes itself heard abroad, in Great Britain, the United States, Italy and West Germany. But in Mozambique, its voice reaches only Maputo and the provincial capitals. Even in the capitals Machel and Chissano reshuffle the government and the army to prevent RENAMO sympathizers and infiltrators from coming together. But FRELIMO passes for one of the "stablest" regimes in Africa. "RENAMO's political weakness is further illustrated by the fact that it is not supported by any country in black Africa or by any Western country," runs the State Department 1987 white paper. What on earth does this State Department judgment mean? It means the West cannot see through bluff, and fears the meaning of its own words. Ken Flower saw this posturing, he noticed Chissano resembled the bust of Lenin behind him.

The war's suffering only began to come home to the world in late 1986 and 1987 after propaganda suddenly turned on the "Beira Corridor," and after the crash of Machel's plane on October 19, 1986 like lightning showed RENAMO and refugees all over northern Mozambique, suddenly and for an instant, in its ghastly light. The propaganda meant to make the West pay instead of insisting on negotiations between RENAMO and FRELIMO. Long before, Machel had admitted to seven hundred thousand cases of malnutrition, bureaucratese for starvation, and to a hundred thousand dead of starvation, in the three years before 1986. From 1970 to 1980 the yearly growth rate *declined* 8.6 percent a year.

In contrast, in the decade before the Portuguese collapse, the economy grew, after the Portuguese allowed foreign investment and trade in 1961. From 1960 to 1970, manufacturing production increased eleven percent a year; investments thirteen percent overall, twenty percent in mining, machine construction and transport. Construction more than tripled to almost sixteen hundred buildings a year. Almost twenty-five million dollars were invested in food processing, before done abroad, mainly in India. Tarred roads also tripled to three thousand kilometers. Local electricity production tripled. Cashew production, one of Mozambique's most important exports, doubled in 1966. The introduction of industrial fertilizer, instead of cow dung, increased coconut production ninety percent on some farms in Zambezia, the most fertile province. The increase in manufacturing made Mozambique the eighth industrialized country in Africa. The overall growth rate ran to 2.6 percent.[180]

The expansion may have been too much for the country, and the Portuguese. It may have distracted them from the murder in far off unreachable places; it may have made Marxism more tempting to soldiers: Poor property owners saved Portugal in Europe from communism. "We are not facing reality discussing our war here in Lourenço Marques when the nearest scene of action is over a thousand miles away in the African bush," an officer told Ken Flower in the sixties. The expansion was certainly too much for FRELIMO.

FRELIMO's destruction of the small farmers it forced into collective farms, communal villages and state cooperatives is responsible for the famine in Mozambique, nothing else. "And FRELIMO despite its preconceptions didn't have to 'free' the country at all," a Swiss reporter remarked in the face of this desolation in 1988.[181] One of the young European university Marxists who came to Mozambique to try his theories on Africans, says almost the same thing. But in two hundred pages of prose still in the grip of FRELIMO, he never mentions force, terror or murder. Even in retrospect he would not see the life and death struggle before his eyes he had ignored that would have shown him the meaning of his words: "The question poses itself, if conditions, internal and external were there for such a rapid and radical transformation as was envisaged in FRELIMO's strategy . . . Not only were external conditions adverse to such a change, but it is possible that history itself was not potentially pregnant with these changes."[182]

These words do not mean he would not try it again, just as Machel did not mean he was going to stop when he remarked in 1976: "The colonial structures persist. Here was our mistake. We did not strike a mortal blow against these structures."[183] Machel meant there still was not enough dying. The readiness to allow small shops and farmers to sell their own produce in 1987 does not mean FRELIMO "has moved away from Soviet-style socialism," as the State Department claims. It only means it is learning totalitarian hypocrisy. Russian farmers on collective farms grow a disproportionate amount of the Soviet Union's food on the small plots they cultivate on their own. By 1983, two years before the State Department said Mozambique had begun "to shift its policies towards promoting production in the private sector, particularly in the agricultural sector," FRELIMO directly controlled almost all economic activity, between seventy and one hundred percent, according to one eye-witness.[184] Eight years before, at independence, it had turned all land into the property of the state. A month later, it had taken over education, legal and health activity and funeral homes,—the last, probably, to bury its victims without public funerals. The estimates run to seventy-five thousand dead and two hundred, maybe, three hundred thousand in concentration camps in the years of take-over that turned the country into a prison.[185] A representative in the Australian Parliament got it right: "The trouble the FRELIMO government finds itself in is largely of its own making. However, they continue to blame everything and anyone but themselves."[186]

Only the readiness to negotiate with RENAMO and hold free elections would show recognition of responsibility, the only test of FRELIMO's "turn away from the Soviet Union." But FRELIMO, like the MPLA, could not survive the negotiations, and it knows it. It can only be defeated, like the MPLA.

But blaming others, especially RENAMO, gets FRELIMO places. In 1988 more than a hundred Western organizations delivered food and other necessities of daily life, with the rarest exception, to FRELIMO, not to the population directly. The FRELIMO leaders who heard these organizations trying to warn them they could not count forever on foreign help to bring them through, listened to their actions, not their words. In the meantime, men from the totalitarian countries continued to mind their business: key positions in the police and secret police; ideological indoctrination and training of party cadres; and education, largely in the hands of East Germans.[187] In 1985, on the occasion of Machel's visit to Washington in October, the State Department had argued for just over one million dollars in "non-lethal military" assistance . . . [to] help demonstrate that Mozambicans need not rely on the East bloc for their total security."[188] "Dialogue between the United States and the Soviet Union is the new element of international relations," said the Mozambican foreign minister in Washington in October 1988, to get the United States to pay more than the only "symbolic" ten million dollars it gave in 1987.[189]

RENAMO guerrillas fight under harsh conditions, some with few medical supplies; only a few diarrhea and malaria pills and antibiotic ointments at one base a reporter visited,—but they could not operate at all without support from the highly varied population, probably fear's support. People are forced to carry food and weapons, in sparsely settled country with only family hamlets for a few hours with little abuse; in more populated areas with more RENAMO control, sometimes for a week with beatings and murder of those too tired and weak to go on. RENAMO moves almost always on foot, sometimes,—to avoid mines,—not even on paths because in contrast to UNITA it has no trucks or jeeps and very few motorbikes. In sparsely inhabited areas, it takes flour and food grain at its will with some regularity, once a month or once a week. In others, people cultivate for it, with one day a week to grow for themselves. In areas where it has allowed the return of private ownership, it takes a good deal of the crop. Women are at its disposal. It exercises enough fear to keep the *naturales*, the local people, and the people it has marched into its regions from elsewhere from escape,—not enough to provoke their escape except on harsh portering trips: "The only reciprocity the captives appear to receive or to expect is the opportunity to remain alive . . . Not until death becomes a real possibility in their minds do the captives consider risking the dangerous escape attempt." These details, taken from the State Department's RENAMO atrocity report, ring true despite the investigation's reliance on witnesses largely in camps in FRELIMO's Mozambique or in Zimbabwe and Tanzania. "There is almost no reported effort to explain the purposes of the insurgents' efforts, the nature of its goals, or to enlist the loyalty, or even neutrality, of the population," the report also confirms.

Conditions are also rough in the territories under RENAMO's direct control. There is rudimentary instruction in Portuguese (like UNITA, RENAMO knows a future depends on the language the Portuguese left behind) and first aid, "but people too ill or badly injured to be treated are sent to isolated camps where they await their end without affecting the morale of others."[190] A bad situation, but not much worse than in FRELIMO towns, for instance in Mocuba, where at the end of 1986 a French reporter saw one Indian surgeon operating on badly wounded soldiers with only local anesthetic without running water or electricity,—a result of FRELIMO's nationalization of private medical practice that a year after independence had reduced the 366 mostly anti-Portuguese doctors registered in 1974 to twenty.

RENAMO gets little press, mostly bad: atrocities and lawlessness,— accusations, difficult to evaluate, that often use the words "bandits" and "monsters," from FRELIMO propaganda. In 1987 and 1988, the accusations, true or not, reached a climax because they served a political purpose in Washington, the prevention of an American policy of weapons and aid for RENAMO and of insistence on negotiations. This struggle centered on the confirmation of an ambassador, Melissa Wells, openly against recognizing or even talking to RENAMO,—"bandits," she called them,—that took eleven months.

In the midst of this struggle to discredit RENAMO, the Catholic Bishops of Mozambique, in a pastoral letter on April 30, 1987, distinguished between the country,—the Mozambicans who have no firearms,—and the fighters. They called for negotiations between those most responsible for the killing, "in the first place" on FRELIMO and RENAMO, but also on those "who are *equally responsible* . . . who finance, feed and help direct the war in Mozambique" (Italics mine).[191] Besides Zimbabwe, Tanzania, the Cubans, the Soviet Union, the East Germans, the Bishops also meant Great Britain, the United States, West Germany, Australia, Italy, and the more than one hundred international organizations active in Mozambique. In early September 1988, the Pope in Mozambique called for a "union of forces" between Rome and FRELIMO, not for negotiations, in accordance with the State Department's attempts to characterize the Mozambican Bishop's defiance, more than a year before, as one of several "positive developments in relations between the government and the church."[192]

The Western media pay more attention to "rebel" than to regime atrocities, especially in Mozambique. In the United States especially, they take killing by regimes that seize power for granted because they get practically all their information from them, in Mozambique, from FRELIMO,—like the State Department's atrocity report. They do not insist on the same reporter going back and forth between both sides. *The New York Times* reporter for the MPLA, and sometimes for FRELIMO, told a UNITA lobbyist in Washington in 1988 he would not visit UNITA because it would compromise him with the MPLA. In Angola, this one-sidedness amounts to a newspaper's recognition of regime in a country where the United States recognizes neither side but openly helps the fighters against the regime. This timidity serves the MPLA's and FRELIMO's refusal to negotiate. It also makes it impossible to make out events: Almost every battle and killing in Angola and in Mozambique is in dispute. Who has heard of FRELIMO's public "executions" after secret "trials"?

In 1983, after seeing seven RENAMO prisoners shot, cheering crowds carried Joaquim Chissano, the present leader of FRELIMO, then foreign minister, and other party members on their shoulders. At another rally Machel mocked fifty-six ragged RENAMO youths before crowds screaming blood: "Those who supply the bandits with information must die with the bandits. Those who feed the bandits must die with the bandits. Those who deal with the bandits must die with the bandits. Our mission is not to wound, but to kill!"[193]

In a crucial appearance before the Senate Foreign Relations Sub-Committee on June 25, 1987 unnoticed, as far as I know, except in the Australian Parliament, a former FRELIMO fighter Jose Francisco, gave testimony I wish I never heard. Francisco's testimony about the years just before and after Portuguese abandonment shows FRELIMO first murdered its own before it murdered others, and that the war of few limits that later overtook Mozambique started within FRELIMO, as Ken Flower's analysis in April 1974 also shows.[194]

Francisco once saw FRELIMO murder one hundred and twenty of its cadres the Soviets had in secret identified as "unconverted Communists." These bayonetings "after sexual dismemberment," a regular occurrence, meant to assure Communist control of FRELIMO in the years before the Portuguese collapse. Upon their arrival in Dar es Salaam from terrorist training and indoctrination in the Soviet Union, the marked men received orders for "special missions" to their deaths in "operational areas" in Mozambique.

Francisco also witnessed his unit's torture to death of another FRELIMO "moderate," Silveiro Nungo, on orders of the present minister of interior Mariano Matsinhe, an informer for the Portuguese before FRELIMO came to power, according to Jorge da Costa, Chissano's man in the secret police until he fled in 1983.[195] "Possibly the most shocking story I have ever heard," an Australian MP called these words:

I saw my officers take diabolic glee in flogging Nungo repeatedly for twelve hours. He was left overnight tied to a tree. The next day he was beaten again until unconscious. The third day after he regained consciousness, the most gruesome part followed. Nungo was dismembered, joint by joint, starting with his fingers going up to the shoulders. Using crude machetes to do the hacking, Nungo died by mid-day.

Francisco also testified that Alberto Chipande, the first man from the Maconde tribe to join FRELIMO in 1962, defense minister under Machel and Chissano, murdered his father before one thousand FRELIMO cadres "by stabbing him in the stomach and ripping upwards until his viscera spilled to the ground." Chissano, in charge of security during the war and "de facto head of the state secret police," even as foreign minister, called this public parricide and the other murder Francisco witnessed "a teaching method" to show "the new order" to cadres.

"A soft spoken FRELIMO veteran" with "a quiet, unassuming style, honed through twelve years as Mozambique's foreign minister" and "the charismatic and dynamic FRELIMO leader," *The New York Times* respectively called the two men most responsible for these crimes, Chissano and Machel, a few months after this testimony.[196] "The closely guarded front of formality . . . of a sinister man who has no friends," da Costa in 1983 had called Chissano's velvety exterior that took in the *Times*: "He wants power so badly, he can taste it."

Chissano has had experience of both worlds that sometimes seem to deserve each other, the mark of the most dangerous and the most extraordinary men since 1945, for instance, Savimbi: He studied law in Portugal for two years after high school in Mozambique before he fled through France and Algeria for training and indoctrination in the Soviet Union. Stalin and Lenin, in contrast, turned one world into the other but never lived in both. "My priority is to destroy terrorism and at the same time to develop the economy," Chissano told the *Times* reporter who could not see the arrogance of these words. Chissano meant he and his crowd would kill, and we would pay.

Nobody much heard Francisco's testimony because the "orchestra of hate" was not behind it, and because other men are embarrassed to believe their ears. The executive editor of *Commentary*, a New York monthly, Neal Kozodoy, told me when he refused to print an account of the Denton testimony in early 1986, individuals special plead. He meant he did not trust himself. But the only testimony that counts about totalitarianism comes from individuals.

The atrocity campaign against RENAMO centered on the "Homoine Massacre" on July 18, 1987 and the State Department Report released in April 1988. The major newspapers in the United States frightened their readers with the news of the massacre they admitted came from FRELIMO which had not allowed them to visit the site: 386, then 388, then 408, then 424, FRELIMO kept upping the count, men, women, and children, had been murdered when RENAMO men attacked a hospital after firing on the police station without fighting. RENAMO shouted: "We want to finish off the people of Samora Machel." Less than twenty survivors, interviewed by Western reporters five days after the massacre, in a hospital thirty miles from the farming village, told of a woman murdered with her baby strapped to her back; another woman beheaded; still another, pregnant stabbed in the stomach.

Besides the timing,—on July 12, the day *The Washington Post* and *The New York Times* published malicious lead editorials against RENAMO, and the day Secretary of State Shultz saw Senators Jesse Helms and Robert Dole, the minority leader, to get them to stop opposing the nomination of the anti-RENAMO ambassador to Mozambique,—and besides FRELIMO's refusal to let reporters visit Homoine; RENAMO's shouting self-betraying slogans; no fighting at the FRELIMO police station,—the most important detail that makes the story doubtful came from an eyewitness, a thirty year old Mennonite farm worker first interviewed by FRELIMO's news agency, AIM, then in some detail by Western reporters. He said there was "no question" RENAMO attacked because the soldiers wore "brand-new uniforms and shiny boots," unlike FRELIMO soldiers. Nobody has ever seen RENAMO in anything but rags. The details about dress point instead to Zimbabwean soldiers, well-dressed and well-equipped, at least in comparison to FRELIMO. The soldiers spoke Ndau, a dialect of Shona, a language spoken in Zimbabwe, according to survivors that talked to RENAMO. FRELIMO's release of the news three days after the massacre, with most of the victims already buried, points to the improvised exploitation of unexpected killings for propaganda, rather than to planned misinformation,—"disinformation."[197]

The State Department's report betrayed its political motives in the statistical extrapolations that end it; in its refusal to talk to RENAMO and visit its territories; in its omission of FRELIMO and Zimbabwean atrocities and destruction, well-catalogued in the State Department's own annual human rights report. No report that did not investigate and visit both sides in Mozambique could avoid political exploitation, even if everything in it was true. The naiveté or disingenuousness of the investigator shows in his readiness to use US AID agricultural mission translators FRELIMO could easily control in three of the five countries he visited: Tanzania, Zimbabwe and Mozambique itself, and possibly also in Malawi, in short in all except South Africa. He should not have undertaken such work without at least knowing Portuguese, the only European language used besides eighteen native languages or dialects, a distinction not drawn in the report. The investigator noticed the refugees in Mozambique said not a word against FRELIMO, to remark they made up only 54 of the 196 men he saw,—seventy percent of them interviewed in three countries he does not name. The men interviewed outside Mozambique knew anything they said, certainly in Zimbabwe and Tanzania, would get back to FRELIMO that would not hesitate to wipe them out in good "liberation movement" style.

A week after the report's release the State Department showed its political purposes unmistakably at a UN conference to raise 380 million dollars for FRELIMO,—a hundred million pledged by Crocker,—in Maputo. One of

Crocker's men, the man who persuaded him to persuade Shultz to support SADCC several months before the CAA Act, Deputy Assistant Secretary of State for African Affairs Roy Stacy said that RENAMO's atrocities "had emerged as one of the most brutal holocausts against ordinary human beings since World War II,"—language that struck the *Times*, not to be undone, as "surprisingly blunt." "A horde of criminals created by the South African government," Chissano had called RENAMO just before. The *Times* story that identified RENAMO as "right wing rebels," a label I'd like to see them explain in the jungle, routinely recited RENAMO's Homoine massacre without a hint of the doubts it had stirred in a good article in *The Washington Times* and in Congress from Representative Dan Burton and Senator Jesse Helms.[198] There is no novelist bad enough to invent this tale I can only tell because it is true,—and, for worse, the stuff of our lives.

But there is no denying there are RENAMO atrocities. The war is brutal. The point is to prevent the political exploitation of this brutality. Already in 1985, E.P. Cain, a South African missionary in Mozambique for ten years, and nothing but sympathetic to RENAMO describes typical RENAMO political meetings in villages: "Goods, taken from raided stores, are distributed, and those suspected of FRELIMO sympathies are killed or mutilated."[199] Afonso Dhlakama, educated in mission schools, who once wanted to be a priest, and who knows the traditional life FRELIMO seeks to eradicate because he is a chief's son, has taken measures against these atrocities. But it is not easy to restrain raw hungry youths with nothing but rusty weapons,—cleaning oil is scarce,—scattered all over the country and constantly on the move in small groups in jungles that can hide divisions without a wink. The youths move without maps they could not read or compasses, often without watches. They wear their rags until they disintegrate. Dhlakama manages to keep in daily contact in code with provincial commanders, but in the field radios are also worn-out, hand-cranked, nothing like UNITA's sophisticated equipment that can monitor MPLA communications.

Dhlakama and the State Department Report both agree that most of the atrocities occur during the destruction of towns and villages, sometimes villages of forty families, sometimes of a hundred, especially of towns and villages with FRELIMO troops in them.[200] Like UNITA, RENAMO usually destroys villages, it does not take them, especially in disputed territory. Dhlakama says FRELIMO uses "pseudo-operations," a Rhodesian term for government troops masquerading as guerrillas, to pin atrocities on RENAMO, and to drive refugees, over a million by 1988, away from RENAMO into camps,—in order to then extract aid from foreign countries, and above all to erode popular support for RENAMO. In 1987, *Africa Confidencial* confirmed Dhlakama's charge that FRELIMO, and above all the Zimbabweans, fear people's support of RENAMO: They never expected to have men, fighters like themselves, fighting against them. "Zimbabwean experts in terror are convinced that RENAMO's successes come because of the support of the population they live among."[201] The State Department report says that RENAMO groups attack especially villages and towns with FRELIMO troops and officials in them. They gather intelligence about these villages and towns through questioning farmers and abductions of villagers who sometimes never return. In villages, they come in and kill FRELIMO officials and their wives and children before the villagers unarmed with firearms. The forces attacking defended villages in earliest morning are divided between looters, fighters and men firing the thatched huts. They kill more people than crossfire can explain: "A large number of civilians in these attacks and other contexts were reported to be victims of purposeful shooting deaths and executions, of axing, knifing, bayoneting, burning to death, forced drowning and asphyxiation, and other forms of murder where no meaningful resistance or defense is present."

There must be some truth here, but exaggerated both in number of instances and victims, especially since "most of the refugees could not count accurately above the number of ten." The villagers do not flee before the attacks because "they are most reluctant to abandon homes and land, with which they seem to identify very closely." Why was the State Department investigator surprised that they stuck to their lands? FRELIMO cannot understand their attachment to the land because violence feeds on denial of the obvious, but the State Department? "Refugee" is a word from Europe, born first probably in the Anglo-Boer war.

The State Department not only did not mention FRELIMO brutality, it did not mention the Zimbabweans known for their greater brutality against suspected RENAMO villages according to *Africa Confidencial* and other sources. On April 6, 1986 the Zimbabweans ordered two helicopters to bomb the village of Maneira, killing and injuring "dozens" of unarmed locals; another similar attack was reported in Chavundire, also in Zambezia province; and earlier, in March, Licuare suffered intensive bombing, apparently by FRELIMO. In a three hundred man RENAMO attack on Inhaminga, the district capital of Sofala province, in 1986, RENAMO suffered several days of repeated MIG–17 and Mi–8 helicopter raids after it attacked the garrison that had fled the town to its barracks. On April 28, 1987, Zimbabwean soldiers beheaded rounded-up suspected RENAMO sympathizers after they retook the town of Morrumbala. Zimbabwean brutality broke into violence between FRELIMO and the Zimbabweans in Mutarara on July 4, 1987, according to RENAMO; four Zimbabweans dead including the commander.

In contrast to FRELIMO who have turned themselves into foreigners in their own country, and call in the whole world, Dhlakama does not take the presence of foreigners for granted: "The Marxist FRELIMO regime . . . has brought foreign armies to dominate our people." Jose Francisco in Washington also spoke of foreigners overrunning the country: "Unfortunately for Mozambique, Chester Crocker has not taken into account the extent of Mozambicans' contempt for foreign meddling in their affairs." And some Zimbabwean soldiers, not officers, also know Mozambique is not their country, unlike Mugabe who cannot stop fighting until the destruction of South Africa for fear of seeing his own face: "We are very far from home. Why should we be killed in someone else's war? First we were told just to guard the pipeline. Now we seem to be fighting the whole war," they told an English reporter.[202]

Reporters with the guts to visit RENAMO all remark on the guerrillas' buoyancy. "Confident," "spirited" are adjectives they use. "Their confidence is unshakeable," remarked a writer for *Jane's Defense Weekly*: "The rebels usually succeed." In part this confidence comes because RENAMO calls FRELIMO's bluff. They know totalitarianism gives way before determined resistance, as Houphouet-Boigny told the United States and Western Europe in 1976 after the failure of the South African invasion of Angola. "When we attack, the enemy usually runs away after a few minutes," a daring commander said recently. The buoyancy also shows in Dhlakama's sense of his limits: "RENAMO will maintain guerrilla tactics, we lack training and equipment for large operations." This buoyancy points to something at work despite, and beyond, brutalities.

This spirit beyond brutality shows in RENAMO's readiness to allow people to feed themselves instead of forcing them to starve like FRELIMO. People do not starve in RENAMO's territories, RENAMO claims, and reporters who have been there agree. Only malnutrition because there is no milk, no vitamins, very little salt or oil. In some areas RENAMO controls, maybe 2,200,000 souls in early 1987, especially near its headquarters in Sofala province and across the Zambezi, reporters saw tillers growing their own food on condition they not deliver it to FRELIMO towns: "An unexpected sight was that of sweeping fields of corn and manioc *machambas* or farms which contrasted dramatically with international aid organization warnings that Mozambique is swiftly becoming a second Ethiopia. Private property is one of RENAMO's keystone principles. Local communities have their own well-tended and productive *machambas*, and they also grow rice and peanuts. Such fruit trees as banana, orange, papaya and grapefruit practically grow wild." International Committee of the Red Cross (ICRC) airplanes fly food into FRELIMO areas, but mostly blankets, clothes, soap and medicine to RENAMO areas. Quite a contrast to the four million wandering about the country or hoveled into FRELIMO towns,—fifty thousand in thatched huts surround the deserted center of Mocuba,—that depend on Europe, the UN, Great Britain, at least $153 million in 1987, the United States, $48 million, for "humanitarian" food.

RENAMO's buoyancy gets to its enemies. It is the reason FRELIMO dreads RENAMO. It even gets to Zimbabweans: "All behind us is RENAMO. As far as we are concerned, they have already won this war. All that is left is for them to announce it. These RENAMO are good. They control the countryside. The local people support them," a Zimbabwean sergeant told a British reporter at the southern tip of Malawi reaching deep into Mozambique. The Malawians also on this frontier know the meaning of his words, they see Zimbabwean soldiers sneaking across the frontier at nightfall to sleep for fear of RENAMO ambushes: "They [the Zimbabweans] are not strong in their hearts." But this buoyancy does not get to the West. Why?

The West, especially men like Chester Crocker, who calls Chissano, and called Machel, "moderates" will not even see, let alone act, in recognition that both sides are both wrong and right, the classical terms of international law in the eighteenth century before wars masquerading as revolutions broke upon the world. He will not even talk to both sides. Even the more than one hundred international and national agencies at work, with the exception of the ICRC, the only organization to visit both sides in both Angola and Mozambique, do not have the guts to insist on evenhandedness, on visiting both sides. Apparently they fear the displeasure of Chissano, as if their charity was his. Peace probably cannot come without the victory of RENAMO; it certainly cannot come if the West fears to deal openly with both sides.

In contrast, FRELIMO and the Zimbabweans and the rest of their crowd know there is something more than fear in the supporters of RENAMO, and that they can only offer fear in retort. They know that, not only are both sides right and wrong, but that FRELIMO is more wrong than right. That is why they insist the West and the totalitarians together give them victory,—like the Portuguese. RENAMO may even make Zimbabweans doubt that brutality can do everything, something they did not learn in their terror against African and European Rhodesians because it succeeded, nor afterwards because it managed to still criticism, even abroad.

The deep differences between RENAMO and UNITA show themselves: in Soviet concentration on UNITA,—they can tell a real threat;—in Savimbi's distance,—RENAMO was noticeably absent from the meeting of representatives of the resistance from Nicaragua, Afghanistan, Laos in Jamba on January 12, 1986;—and in Savimbi's readiness to face the world almost from the beginning of his second war, from 1977 when King Hassan of Morocco "made his friends, our friends," and allowed Savimbi to do his quiet diplomacy from Rabat. Savimbi's readiness to face the world also shows in his public trips abroad, to remind the West that its voice counts, trips that also show Savimbi enjoys loyalty that allows absence: "We need you to insist at the United Nations and other international forums that the Cubans and Soviets leave Angola and promised elections be held. With your military and political support, other nations will follow your lead and give us aid," Savimbi recently told the West.

Besides showing Angola's strategic importance,—because of its minerals and because of South West Africa, and also Zambia, Botswana and Zaire,—in the war against South Africa, Soviet concentration on UNITA shows Savimbi threatens the Soviets because he fights them to some extent with strategies learned from totalitarianism, not the case with RENAMO. Savimbi may have even prompted the Soviets, and the rest of the world in their wake, to underestimate RENAMO's straightforward successes that have, arguably, made themselves felt through more of Mozambique than UNITA's in Angola.

Savimbi will not forget news-coverage black-outs: "Little television footage gets out of Kampuchea and Afghanistan . . . The Cubans do not permit newspaper or television coverage of their atrocities in areas they control." He contrasts this Western passivity with totalitarian readiness to seize words: ". . . When the Cubans and Soviets seized power in Angola, sympathetic propaganda outlets immediately sprang into action in the OAU, the United Nations and other front organizations around the world." These organizations turned their loudspeakers on the "Beira Corridor,"—the State Department called it the "liberty corridor," in a passage the White House managed to strike out of Reagan's July 22, 1986 speech,—in late 1986 and early 1987, *once they saw the West and the UN would go along.*

To get governments to yield him the recognition of talking, Savimbi uses decently-treated hostages both from eastern Europe and the West. For instance: sixteen British subjects taken on February 23, 1984, at Cafunfo, eleven hundred kilometers from Jamba, released on May 12 at Jamba in a midnight ceremony, after the arrival of a British under-secretary. Savimbi used the occasion to restate his commitment to the Alvor accords: "We seek peace and reconciliation, as we did in 1974. We shall firmly hold on to our arms and maintain our hearts open to dialogue." In these and other encounters with journalists, Savimbi's presence makes something stir in men of good will: His "strange humility" got through to bluff but sensitive South African journalists in Jamba in 1984.

In contrast RENAMO shunned the world, except Portugal, until in 1986 United States' Stinger rockets sent to Savimbi and the worldwide concentration on the "Beira Corridor" stung it to words and to open a Washington office with uncertain communications with Dhlakama who fights without radio contact with the world outside, in a country usually without telephones or radio connections in its rural districts: "Perhaps, if we had launched our diplomatic offensive earlier, we would have Stinger missiles . . . By giving assistance to the Maputo government, the United States and other Western Nations are actually paying for Soviet expansion in southern Africa."

RENAMO's isolation and secretiveness comes: of the desperation of survival in a war of terror that divides sons from fathers, and sons from sons, and feeds on one family after another; of guilt; of South Africa's ambivalence; of instability of leadership that showed itself blatantly in the murder, on a RENAMO base in the Transvaal in 1983, of Dhlakama's predecessor, Orlando Cristina, a white who had organized the crack Portuguese black units after infiltrating FRELIMO in 1964. Cristina had resisted American and South African pressure in the months of negotiations before Nkomati, according to RENAMO's Washington office in 1988. The isolation and secretiveness intensifies the internecine privacy of the violence.

Savimbi has made the transition from guerrilla war to a combination of conventional and guerrilla war RENAMO has not attempted. But guerrilla warfare remains UNITA's resort in crisis, as Savimbi stated in a tense moment in September 1988.[203] The turning point for UNITA came in 1979–1981, in E.P. Cain's judgment, when UNITA fought something like thirteen "significant" engagements that cost the MPLA about sixteen hundred men. For the first time UNITA showed it could fight face-to-face, like a conventional army, as well as in hit-and-run guerrilla attacks of thirty to a hundred and fifty. By 1982, it claimed to control territory with two and a half million inhabitants. In January 1983, Savimbi announced he had doubled the territory under his control. Later in the year the focus of the war began to shift to provinces north, east, and south of Luanda, with operations sometimes within two hundred miles of the city. An attack on Luanda with the support of ten thousand South

African soldiers might have brought the victory in sight. But the Soviets headed the South Africans off with their threat in November to unleash the Cuban-piloted MPLA airplanes against the South African Air Force.

The Soviet threat may have been a turning point,—a guess, not a judgment. In 1984 UNITA seems to have held on to the third of Angola it controlled and to have operated throughout the rest of the country, with some intensity in another third of it. But in 1985 it faced a major Cuban MPLA campaign under Soviet officers—to destroy it, or at least its headquarters, that reached deep into southeastern Angola before it was halted in several ferocious open battles with the help of South African air strikes.

The arrival of the Soviet general Konstantin Shaganovitch, thought the highest ranking Soviet officer outside Europe and Afghanistan, in Angola in 1985 showed the Soviets were not about to take the MPLA setback a few months before. Intensive resupply in subsequent months and again in 1987, showed they meant to pursue their 1985 strategy: the capture of Mavinga that would deprive UNITA of the supplies the United States and South Africa fly into Mavinga's airport and open the road to the destruction of Savimbi's headquarters at Jamba. In the six months before the offensive's outbreak at the end of May there were as many as five to six Soviet flights a day into Menongue, Cuito Cuanavale and Luena,—the last two, the jump-offs for the attack. In 1987 Luanda saw as many as twelve Antonov-24 flights a day for some time. These airplanes carried T-62 and T-67 battle tanks, PT-76 amphibious tanks, BTR-60 and BRDM-2 armored personnel carriers, and SAM anti-aircraft systems. By the start of 1986, the MPLA's air force numbered twenty-seven MIG 25s, twenty-three MIG 23s, seventy MIG 21s, twenty-two MI-17 assault helicopters, ten Sukhoi 22s, according to Western intelligence.[204]

This build-up aimed at South Africa's resolution, not only at UNITA, Savimbi correctly observed. The actual sight of sophisticated arms in the field took the breath away from SADF officers who had before only seen them on paper lists. In May 1986, the MPLA admitted it had Soviet officers, including a Soviet "counter-insurgency expert," General Mikhail Petrov, at headquarters and in the field. In 1987, seventy Soviet advisors were reported attached to the twenty-two MPLA brigades of eleven hundred to sixteen hundred men, a total force of over twenty thousand. In the 1987 offensive that started very late, on August 14, with fighting that continued through the rainy season, there was at least one platoon of Cuban soldiers with each brigade.[205] In all 125 Cuban soldiers, 4 Soviets and 882 MPLA were killed in 412 "contacts" in other areas of Angola in April through June 1987, before the major offensive in the southeast.

The small number of UNITA fighters facing these forces, roughly eight thousand regular troops and many guerrillas, makes strategy in this war decisive, the case probably in any war. It also makes South Africa's role in this strategy crucial. "Don't think of this war in conventional terms," Botha said in 1988. Savimbi skillfully combines guerrilla harassment with direct engagements. Also, operations throughout Angola especially in the northwest, and bombings in Luanda, for instance, of the Cuban airline office in early 1986, serve to weaken the MPLA behind the front. UNITA's guerrilla groups in the northwest forced the MPLA to withdraw four of its twenty-two brigades from the fighting in the southeast in 1986. Frequent guerrilla strikes along the road from Bie to Menongue and from Menongue into Cuito Cuanavale forced the Soviets to air-resupply in 1986. The frequent harassment, especially the attacks on watering spots, and minefields slow and discourage the MPLA: In 1986 youths escaped conscription across the borders to Zaire and Zambia and warrants for the arrest of MPLA deserters appeared in Luanda's daily newspaper, according to the *Guardian*.

The crucial battle, perhaps the most important of the war so far, according to Savimbi, occurred when UNITA forced its way across the Lomba River, the most important natural defense of Mavinga, in a ten-hour fight on October 4, 1987. South African artillery, air strikes and a "mechanised element" numbering up to four battalions were crucial in this battle, and in six fierce battles on September 13 and 14 that stopped an MPLA bridgehead. "Mechanised" meant South African tanks, in action for the first time since the Second World War. South Africa's effectiveness came from its unpredictable interventions at crucial points at crucial moments. The Soviets and the Cubans never knew what to expect. On October 31, SADF and SWATF attacked SWAPO in southern Angola, near Cuvelai, about 180 kilometers from the frontier: a seven-hour battle, 150 SWAPO dead, 4 South Africans, to prevent SWAPO infiltration into South West Africa at the start of the rainy season.

The international response to this fighting, immediately after the South Africans on November 11 for the first time admitted fighting in Angola to help UNITA, not only to prevent SWAPO infiltration, was a Security Council Resolution on November 25 that the United States ambassador Vernon Walters apparently wanted to veto. The resolution that repeatedly called South Africa a "racist regime" demanded the withdrawal of the South Africans without mention of the Cubans, an absence of evenhandedness that Walters immediately pointed out in a press release. But what counted was the vote, not Walters' following criticisms that showed one of the best American statesmen alive caught in a situation that went against the best in him—and against American policy since 1981.

The resolution misnamed and misperceived the situation on the ground and provided justification for undoing it politically in negotiation, the Soviet and Cuban strategy in 1988. Its refusal to mention the Cubans, and for that matter, the Soviets, continued in the readiness to ignore the Cuban build-up in southern Angola in 1988.

The South Africans had in some sense contributed to the drive for negotiations the Security Council put at center stage: In 1986 Botha had said in Parliament that South Africa might leave South West Africa, not after the Cubans left Angola, but after a Cuban commitment to withdraw, a reversal of position that sent Savimbi to Cape Town. In 1987 the government hinted it would accept a coalition government in Angola without elections, an abandonment of the Alvor accords that defined Savimbi's policy, and South African support of him.

No longer in sight of victory, the man who came to Washington in early 1986 had been struggling to hold on. It tells something of Savimbi's buoyancy that nobody suspected. United States aid may turn out to have been too little much too late, especially since it came without bold diplomatic support.

13 A World Uncovered: The Death of Machel

The crash of Machel's plane on October 19, 1986 showed not only that RENAMO operated more or less with impunity throughout the entire countryside, even with land mines on the beaches at Maputo, and that FRELIMO hung on only in refugee-crowded cities and towns mainly supplied by air and sea. It showed that Mugabe was more important in Mozambique than Machel, that Mugabe needed the Beira corridor not only because of his dependence on its pipeline for oil but because he wanted to use its rehabilitation and defense to bring the West, especially the United States, over to his side in the total war against South Africa and RENAMO. Documents found in the wreckage of Machel's plane showed this total war wanted the destruction of Malawi and the remarkable Kamuzu Banda, the only country in the region, Zimbabwe's increases in GNP notwithstanding, slowly to improve itself since independence.

Mugabe's commitment to Mozambique also helped to explain the ease of succession, and Machel's and Chissano's obduracy in the face of the desperation of their land. "The survival of Mozambique is our survival. The fall of Mozambique will certainly also be our fall," Mugabe said in Parliament in Zimbabwe in unabashed admission of the self-destructiveness he cannot live without.[206] He is self-destructive because he will not put his responsibility for his country first—in contrast to Banda. Taking responsibility would mean breaking with his past, especially his past dependence on Mozambique for the conquest of Rhodesia.

A few days later, in his inaugural speech on November 6, Chissano laid out this desperation's flight into total war in the wooden bureaucratese that turns suffering into an ideological poster: "The aggression against our country [unnameable RENAMO] is also an undeclared war against Zimbabwe, Botswana, Zambia and other countries of the region . . . The unity achieved within the Front-Line states is a guarantee that the independent countries of the region have understood the dimension of the sacrifices that are demanded of us by the war being waged against us by the warmongers and criminal forces of the apartheid regime. Also, on our side is the OAU, as well as all peace, liberty and progress-loving countries worldwide." He thought blaming desperation on South Africa might serve to intimidate the confused and reluctant Western governments, who want to be on all sides because they dare not choose, to join his side.

War defines "independence," not minding your own responsibilities because Chissano, Machel before him, and Mugabe take Malawi's actual independence for a threat. Chissano knows his past: "In their origin and nature, the armed bandits [RENAMO] continue the historic links between Portuguese colonialism and fascism, southern Rhodesia's racist and illegal regime, and the apartheid system . . . The armed banditry was born as a means of perpetuating colonial domination and exploitation." These are almost all themes of the Third International that meant to turn the West against itself, Chissano's goal in southern Africa.

Mugabe was right: Settlement or reversal in Mozambique and Angola would have had immediate effect, not only in southern Africa, but throughout the world, especially in Nicaragua, and in South Africa where it would have renewed confidence in reform. Mugabe also meant it: He put close to half his army in Mozambique, a Mozambican equivalent to Angola's Cubans, at an estimated cost of about 350 million dollars a year.[207]

Mugabe and Chissano got away with their desperation, they boasted of it, they used it to intimidate the pity of the West's helplessness, especially of Britain and the United States. They calculated the West would not dare make negotiations with all sides for free elections the condition of aid,—despite the readiness of some FRELIMO generals to deal with RENAMO. Even Mugabe hinted at negotiations, probably not in good faith but to gain time.

The "prestige press," especially in the United States, but not *The Economist*, *L'Express* in Paris, *Il Giornale Nuovo* in Milan, the *Neue Zürcher Zeitung* in Zurich, the *Frankfurter Allgemeine Zeitung* in Frankfurt, reinforced Mugabe's and Chissano's recklessness with their suspicions of the October 19th crash, and especially with the disregard of the planned coup against Malawi. The immediate accusations of South African sabotage from Zimbabwe, Mozambique, the ANC and "peace-loving" Kaunda, who has the knack of bewildering journalists with his tears, complete with "demonstrations" in Harare and Maputo before various embassies, took the space in major newspapers. They overcame the common sense surmise of almost any man on the street until contrary evidence: an accident. Apparently, apartheid had the power also to banish chance from the world, at least in southern Africa, and to win acquiescence to slander, as long as it comes from "heads-of-state," against South Africa.

The United States government went along with its press: The State Department did not answer the Republic's immediate request for the United States' participation in the customary international inquiry. This silence passed for tact but it betrayed an unwillingness to face the truth that alone can give the confidence to act effectively.

The report of the South African Board of Inquiry nine months later found numerous pilot and crew errors caused the crash but had little impact outside South Africa. The board counted an American astronaut, Frank Borman, a British test pilot and chief of the British Aviation Accidents Branch, and a retired British Lord Justice of Appeal, besides three South Africans: two aviation experts and a judge from South Africa's Appellate Court.[208]

On the day, November 6, 1986, South Africa showed the evidence for

Machel's and Mugabe's plan to destroy Malawi's independence, Vice President Bush received Mugabe's foreign minister without comment on the revelations. Who can defend a country almost nobody had ever heard of? Besides, what was new about a coup, especially of blacks and against blacks, and in Africa! The South African foreign Minister R.F. Botha's plain startled words before simple evil sounded quaint: "I am dismayed, disappointed, shocked and I did not expect this."

A few weeks after Machel's death, articles on southern Africa began to flood the American press, especially *The New York Times* which had run few stories on Angola and Mozambique the year before. Even the *New Yorker* ran a long story with many inaccuracies and blurred hasty accounts of crucial events. For the graduate schools, the Indiana University Press brought out Joseph Hanlon's dull catalogue, *Beggar Your Neighbours*, that blames South Africa,— "destabilization," the code-word,—for the fighting that will not cease in southern Africa.

The New York Times' sudden concentration on southern Africa at the expense of South Africa came, in part, because of the Republic's refusal to renew the visa of its reporter, and for a time to grant a visa to his replacement, in the instance of Allan Cowell, a well-earned humiliation: Reuters and AP dispatches about South Africa apparently were not good enough for *The New York Times*.

New York Times reporters wandered about the bush capitals of southern Africa, the slogans of these regimes like the "Beira corridor" and their international conferences more on their minds than the sights in the streets and in the countryside. Until January 1988, they wrote little of the dramatic situation in Maputo and the towns of Mozambique that met the eyes of reporters from *The Economist* and the continent: a FRELIMO soldier shot in Mocuba for trading his gun for two cartons of cigarettes; refugees camping in six abandoned high-rises, bare skeletons of the past's confidence that hulk like ghosts over the skyline in Beira; the price of an essential, a homemade water-bucket, forty percent of a laborer's weekly wages, again in Beira; the empty shops; the request of embarrassed bureaucrats who earn three times the minimum wage to foreign reporters to buy them a bar of soap in the hard currency stores reserved for foreigners and Party members. In the countryside: the destroyed railway tracks, the blown-up bridges, the terrified refugees on the roads in flight from the guerrillas, seventy to a hundred thousand in camps in South Africa by 1986,—and the visions of torture and death, for instance, six corpses, their ears and noses cut off in a truck trailer in an officially "secure pacified area" four hundred kilometers from Maputo.

The stories in *The New York Times* and some other American newspapers and magazines betrayed, more or less inadvertently, the agenda of Mugabe and the United States Congressmen who had driven the campaign against South Africa since 1981: The articles saw rehabilitation of the port of Beira and the Beira line already underway with private investments, and the object of a financing conference of Western countries including the United States, in Brussels on October 23–24, 1986, as the first step involving the West in the "defense" of southern Africa either through individual troop commitments or through the UN and the Commonwealth. ". . . Anyway, I have lots of reasons for hope, including our growing ability to defend the corridor. If it's worth having, it's worth defending. The possibility of setting up some sort of international force has been discussed—during the [Non-Aligned] conference. It was mentioned in the hallways and in some speeches," Dennis Norman, a close friend of Mugabe, former minister of agriculture and leader of the Zimbabwean businessmen seeking European and American investments in the "Beira Corridor," told Robert Shaplan.[209] He guessed that three billion dollars over the next four years would do.

By 1986, the British government had been training FRELIMO officers in groups of sixty at Nyanga, just inside Zimbabwe from Mozambique. In late 1986, it gave approval to a British company to train and equip a six hundred man battalion to guard the Nacala railroad to Malawi between Nampula and Cuamba, at a cost of 1.6 million pounds, and to use former British special forces men to train FRELIMO in Mozambique. Protection of the Nacala line helped Malawi, whose soldiers also guarded the line, but it also reinforced FRELIMO. In early 1987 Britain announced further aid to Chissano, already doubled to 8.4 million pounds the year before.

These measures prompted the *London Times* and eight MP's to insist on negotiations between FRELIMO and RENAMO instead of the Foreign Office's seemingly futile attempt to save the Chissano regime, an effort born, in part, of an "exaggerated sense of gratitude" to Machel for persuading Mugabe to accept the Lancaster House settlement. Britain was beholden to the same past as Mugabe but for a different reason, its refusal to recognize failure.

This opposition came at roughly the same time, before the "Homoine Massacre," as the calls for evenhandedness in the United States Congress I have already mentioned: In May 1987, Dan Burton, the intelligent representative from Indiana, had gotten a promise from Reagan to consider calling on FRELIMO to negotiate with RENAMO; in indirect support of Burton, Robert Dole, Senate minority leader had asked for distribution of US food to RENAMO as well as FRELIMO.[210]

At the closed-door seventeenth annual African-American Institute Conference in Gaborone, Botswana in January 1987 reported-in-detail in Washington, the African delegates left American Congressmen from the Black Caucus,—including the nonvoting delegate to the House from Washington D.C., Walter Fauntroy,—and their aides, to make money for "rehabilitation" dependent on the defense of the "Beira Corridor." Congressional aides, in contrast to the Africans, who said not a word about "security," repeatedly pointed out that money for the "Beira Corridor" made no sense without "security arrangements": a UN or "multi-national" or Commonwealth "peace-keeping" force. Fauntroy promised a campaign to focus "American public opinion" on South Africa's "destabilization" of the "Front-Line" states. Black Caucus members said they would seek one hundred million dollars for SADCC, in part for the "Beira Corridor," in accordance with the CAA Act. This appropriation would also mean "logistical aid," equipment for communication and "rapid deployment," for FRELIMO, and the cutoff of aid to Savimbi, the hidden agenda.[211]

The American press' exaggerated attention to the "Front-Line" states' slander of South Africa after Machel's death betrayed the reverse of the bad faith of its passivity in the face of the revelation of Machel's and Mugabe's plan to destroy Malawi. A word against the planned coup would have offended the "Front-Line" states. Worse still, it would have looked like respect for South Africa's word, a country that can do nothing right.

On the strength of this paralysis, Mugabe and Chissano denied the conspiracy they did not renounce. Their denial provoked a warning from the foreign minister of South Africa who had rightly wanted apology: "I think they [Mugabe and Chissano] have a pretty good idea of how far they could go without inviting severe trouble."

In January 1987 the United States went from silence about the attempted coup to scolding: A high State Department official, Michael A. Armacost, on a visit to the "Front-Line" states warned Malawian officials to cooperate with Mugabe's SADCC, and to stop supporting RENAMO and dealing openly with South Africa as if it were a normal nation. Armacost probably did not know that Banda knew the United States better than Armacost knew any country in the world including his own. That's the way the State Department treats some of the United States' friends these days, and the government of a man who had the respect of Dean Acheson.

Revelation of the plot was important not only because it showed that Mugabe and Machel bring the destruction they blame on others upon themselves, but above all because it saved Malawi and prevented the spread of death, starvation and chaos. Supplies may have come to RENAMO through Malawi, as Machel and Mugabe charged with no hard evidence, and guerrillas may have gone back and forth among the thousands of refugees fleeing into Malawi across its two-sided thousand miles of thick jungle frontier that thrusts deep into Mozambique. But this charge was merely a proximate cause for the conspiracy.

From independence in 1964 Malawi alone in the region has shunned *le avventure*, and lip-service to the propaganda war of the OAU, the UN, and now of a good deal of the West. Banda did not aim to please, courage neither Mugabe or Machel, or Nyerere for that matter, were about to forget,—it makes them uncomfortable.

14 Malawi, the Cost of Another Way

On the day that South Africa made evidence of the conspiracy public, quoting from unreleased documents from the wreckage of Machel's plane, the Malawi news agency undid Mugabe's and Machel's resentment in cool words: "It would appear that the problem with most people in other [neighboring] countries is their inability to understand the open daylight, front door, above-table Malawi-South African relations . . . Almost all countries within the region maintain diplomatic relations with the Republic of South Africa. However, because of wanting to appear saintly, these relations are termed 'trade' relations."[212]

Except for Angola and Tanzania, the SADCC countries depend on South Africa, Lesotho almost entirely, the six landlocked states for fifty percent of their imports, cheaper in South Africa than elsewhere. Except for Tanzania that does not trade with South Africa, each of the SADCC countries has more trade with South Africa than with all the SADCC countries combined. In contrast, South Africa's trade with all Africa, about half to SADCC countries, ran to 7.5 percent of its exports in 1984, according to official estimates; to almost 10 percent, and about 20 percent of its exports outside gold, about 1.7 billion dollars, according to unofficial reckoning. In addition, more than two million Africans outside South Africa depend on money from relatives working in South Africa, many illegally. South Africa has supplied oil to Zimbabwe when RENAMO stopped shipments for a few days.

Not only Malawi's independent non-ideological dealings with its neighbors, its open relations with South Africa, angered Mugabe and Machel. They were also not about to forget Banda's freespokenness, his frequent attacks on their "way of life," terror and subversion. They were after the truth: "Because they believe strongly they know what is best for Africa . . . some of the African leaders are actively encouraging and even organizing subversive activities in those countries where leaders hold different views from those of their own. While calling other leaders at the OAU meetings or in letters brothers and colleagues . . . they are actively working for the overthrow of the governments led by those very leaders," Banda had said in 1965, and again in later times.[213]

Yes, Malawi is not a democracy—nor a "revolutionary" state that feeds on destruction of itself and others. Once in office he had not sought or wanted, in the beginning he even tried to keep up his medical practice, Banda dropped the aspirations for democracy that led him in the fight for independence. After the attempt to overthrow him almost immediately after independence, he reintroduced British laws on detention without charges; he turned Malawi into a one-party state which made him life-president since he was president for life of the party; he put youth into organizations that beat up rebels in the dangerous situation in 1965. But he limited strong-arm methods, despite some ugly excesses, through his outspokenness and prosecution. He knew that fierce and swift action could alone preserve the precarious stability of a nascent state in Africa.

He dared concentrate on agriculture despite the insistence of experts, who in the sixties knew they had the answers, on rapid industrialization. His education, largely self-taught, from experience as well as books, deeper than the training of experts, especially his memory of history, his grasp of facts, allowed him this defiance: "Without food independence means nothing." He prohibited the miniskirt and women wearing trousers, and men long hair, measures so astonishing to Western eyes, in 1968, that for a time they made

Malawi a mentionable name. Worse still, he told his people they had to work to prosper,—none of Kaunda's "magic wand":

> At every stage of . . . civilization, there are certain institutions, certain traditions, certain laws and [a] certain code of behavior that hold that particular civilization intact. Once you let these . . . go by the board, that civilization itself is gone to the dogs.

The practical problems, the responsibilities of office, taught him Malawi was not England, let alone Switzerland. He knew that less than a hundred years of colonial presence was not enough to overcome a difference of five thousand years:

> There was a time in Britain when they did worse things than we are going to do to these people [the rebels] now . . . Britain is tolerant only because the Government has been established for centuries . . . Therefore we have to do things here which in Britain and America [at] the stage they have arrived at in their own history, [are] repugnant to their idea of freedom and justice, but [to us], [at] our stage of development are the normal thing to do.[214]

The tough decisions he took did not lead to aimless tyranny like Nyerere's in Tanzania because he respected men enough not to want to remake them, and because he did not fly from responsibility. Character as usual was decisive, it gave him decency. Like himself Malawi had to live in the face of both Europe and Africa: "We are here just a little different, we do things in our own way."

He was not afraid to disappoint everybody, often the price of effective rational action. He did not think he could get rid of the tribes, ever, only make them loyal to Malawi. He knew one thing clearly: Malawians were used to respecting their leaders. No state could enjoy stability unless fierce enough, but not cruel, and straightforward enough to keep the respect the men in the land had lived for thousands of years. He knew the natural reserve and modesty of Malawians that prompts Western reporters to call the country "somnolent" could not take bare-faced Western political life straight all at once, or maybe ever.[215]

There are no Western adjectives to describe his accomplishment. But authoritarian will do better than totalitarian, with this one reservation that Banda deserves the respect he receives. He has never wanted, or needed, subjects to fear him. But he has made his country depend on him too much, and now he is aging, ninety years old, age Mugabe and Machel wanted to show their respect.

15 The Captive Mind in Africa: The Planned Coup Against Banda

In contrast to Banda's practicality that disappointed nearly everyone, first of all himself,—but he is used to disappointment,—Machel's and Mugabe's coup to undo him and his country betrayed all the dreariness of European totalitarianism.

First. The demand for imperviousness, confused with strength, for "coldbloodedness" that would allow no suffering to penetrate the soul, funny in its posturing. For these men would collapse before statesmen bold enough to call their bluff: ". . . The victory is being planned . . . It demands cold-bloodedness . . . We have some special forces for the special operations, we have about 41 MIG-21 [jet fighters] . . ."

A hospital orderly with no education to speak of, Machel knew about cold-bloodedness. He meant the same woodenness an ANC leader thought he recognized in one of the most remarkable of the Denton witnesses, a young woman, who after seeing two murders, looked at the butchering of a third youth: "You seem to be strong. You are not affected."[216]

Second. The attack on the whole population, especially women and children, to break the core of their living, to turn them into starving wanderers like the Mozambicans, and their country into a prison: "If we destroy the bridges to Tanzania and Zambia, we have Malawi in our hands." The bridges Machel meant had taken years to build.

Third. Secrecy, the expectation, perhaps not unrealistic, that the country could be taken; the Malawian police and security forces infiltrated; troops invade, without anybody's notice, without the world's notice: "I don't want to increase enemies . . . I can't do that."

Last, the finishing touch that unmistakably betrays intimacy with European totalitarianism: The victim was to cooperate in his own destruction, like men who "confess" in show trials before "execution," or like "necklace" victims sometimes made to light the gasoline that will burn them to death. ". . . They [Mugabe and Machel] were going to force President Banda to give them permission to move their troops, Zimbabwe and Mozambique troops, across his territory quite clearly to assist in the overthrow of his government. They would have gone in and, under pretext of assisting President Banda to repair certain of his roads, blown up his bridges . . .," R.F. Botha said outlining the contents of the notes found on Machel's plane.

16 The "Winged Words" of Vladimir Ilyich Ulanov and Yosif Djugashvili ("Soso"): The Third International and the United States' and Europe's War in Africa

Banda in the courage of his foreign policy and his outspokenness; Savimbi and the fighters in Mozambique; and South Africa in its readiness until 1988 to see that independence in South West Africa not mask a terrorist seizure of power as in Rhodesia, have been asking the West, and the UN, for something like twelve years, in the instance of Banda, twenty-three years, whether it is serious about independence, in deeds not in words. Can it distinguish between actual independence and its masquerade, to wipe out a country in all but name,—destruction worse than subjection under an empire because of its hypocrisy? Can it distinguish its ideals from totalitarian exploitation of them, the exploitation that occurred at Yalta and Potsdam? Yalta and Potsdam ostensibly guaranteed free elections and the self-determination of all Europe,—except the Soviet Union, a contradiction that told all,—and the unity of Germany. They turned out to serve the "legitimization" of the division of Europe and Germany, a division that shows 1945 brought a truce, not a peace. A truce limited to Europe.

The fighters in southern Africa,—and in South Africa Buthelezi who fights with words because he knows he lives in a country capable of slow change, the only change not a pretext for destruction,—are asking the West to understand that hostilities ended in Europe in 1945 but the war went on elsewhere, outside of Europe: The war for southern Africa, the wars in the Persian Gulf, and Afghanistan as well as the war for Central America, that all broke out in earnest more or less in the wake of the fall of Saigon, are a prolongation of the Second World War. They may decide not only Pakistan's, India's, Mexico's, but Japan's, Europe's, and finally the United States' fate. The United States campaign against South Africa, a war without the responsibilities of war, as well as its precipitate embrace of *glasnost*, show a country already isolating itself from a world not about to isolate itself from the United States.

Europe, but especially the United States, the country most responsible, do not see these wars continue the Second World War, they will not conceive their encouragement of "independence" in the name of peace precipitated them. They assumed independence, like Kaunda's "magic wand," would of itself bring peace, not a continuation and spread of the war whose horror had taught them evasiveness they took for hope. For who could be against independence?

They assumed independence meant no risks, an astonishing assumption much history belies. They took up the word "independence" but they were embarrassed by the men and the countries,—like Savimbi in Angola; RENAMO in Mozambique; Banda in Malawi since 1964; Rhodesia from 1961 to 1980; and South Africa, in its relations with Malawi since 1967, and in South West Africa since 1975,—who took their words in earnest, and were willing to fight and die, and to negotiate, for independence. They were baffled by men and countries who took them seriously, they did not support, encourage, or speak up for them.

The United States did worse, it acted without prudence, in disregard, in unwitting contempt, for its own past. It acted as if it had forgotten that its independence had had to stand the test of a merciless civil war, the first total war after Napoleon's wars spent the French Revolution in the conquest of Europe, the first war of unconditional surrender of our times. It spoke and acted as if self-rule was easy, as if anybody could do it. And it took up this confidence at a moment when Europe lay broken in the ruins of its self-destructiveness and incapacity for self-rule. These centuries of dedication to excellence and daring that had produced accomplishments equal to those of antiquity, the antiquity Europe did not forget and in whose face it had grown up; this confidence that had opened up the whole world,—"the greatest event since the creation of the world, apart from the incarnation and death of its creator," a sixteenth century Spanish historian had called it,—no longer trusted itself even to doubt itself, to know the other side might also be right, the real meaning of the division of Europe.[217] It wanted angels because it feared men, above all itself: "He labors in vain who tries to make the savage heathen Tapuias, eaters of human flesh, angels before making them men," a famous Indian-fighter, a *Paulista*, operating on his own mainly with Amerindian followers wrote the Crown in Portugal in 1694.[218]

At this moment, the United States said to the rest of the world, "You try," without regard for Europe's failure, obscured somewhat in the euphoria of victory, but palpable in its hunger, rags and rooflessness: Europe nearly succumbed to the harsh winter immediately following the cease-fire in Europe.

The message in many instances reached countries in name only, whose frontiers Europeans had drawn arbitrarily, but no more arbitrarily than some of the frontiers it knew in Europe. They drew these frontiers in the confidence that Europe would see to the preservation of these countries, countries with no conscious past as countries before the Europeans—like Zambia with its seventy-three tribes and at least six languages, seven million people in a land almost the size of France and West Germany.

The history of black Africa since Ghana's independence in 1957 takes the measure of this foolhardiness: seventy-two violent seizures of power; twelve wars; thirteen murders of heads of state; seventy cabinet members murdered or jailed since independence in Guinea alone; seven hundred thousand murdered in Uganda, about half before and half after Amin, a country once called a paradise; two hundred and fifty thousand, eighty thousand the lowest estimate, murdered in Burundi in 1972; not to speak of the murder and expulsion of peoples in Nigeria, an estimated million dead in the thirty-month civil war from 1967 to 1970, seven thousand dead in unreported riots in 1981; and in the present, the untold death and murder in Ethiopia, a nation with a long history in contrast to most sub-Saharan African countries. And again in Burundi in August 1988, at least five thousand dead, one hundred thousand people homeless, the flight of more than fifty thousand into Rwanda,—and the government's rejection of an EEC request for an international inquiry. "Burundi is an independent state which has the situation under control," the foreign minister said, to ask the UN for an immediate fifteen million dollars.[219]

Future historians will be aghast at the West's, above all the United States', readiness to abandon a good deal of the world to its own cruelty, and to clothe this abandonment in the magnificence of its own past and call it "independence," as if people could imitate the history of other nations at will. I said future historians but there may be no historians if the West loses, now a real possibility.

The shows of hatred of colonialism, a form of ideological cursing, and the refusal to remember the way it was, the accomplishments and the faults, show we sense the foolhardiness of this abandonment but will not admit it. Hating the past blunts our perception of the present horrors and of our responsibility for them. But it atrophies resilience, and the appetite for life. It traps us in impossible contradictions no thinking can resolve. We blame the past because we will not blame ourselves: "There is also a widespread reluctance to give any public credit to the South African government, partly because of the bad things it continues to do; and partly, it is argued, because it should not be given any credit for measures to relax a system—apartheid—which should never have existed in the first place. This argument, if consistently applied, would mean there would never be any welcome or credit for the removal of any injustice or disability—slavery, child labor, sexual inequality—because these too should never have existed in the first place."[220]

The United States had public men, during the war and after, men like Forrestal, MacArthur, Bedell Smith, Stimson, Turner Joy, Acheson, Wedemeyer, and others, who did not flinch from the crisis, from the knowledge that the war continues. But they were not able to impress their sobriety, their appreciation of danger, their resolution on the public. There were no historians true to their depth, who could face tragedy, instead of exulting in its misapprehension, only professors and journalists.

Hobbes knew the true name of independence Europe and the United States tried to forget after the War. He knew like the ancients, their words before his eyes, that founders of states were extraordinary and rare, not to be had at the asking. He knew there was no difference in kind between the destruction of a government formed freely in social contract and one conquest imposes like the colonial dominions. He would have known that "independence" would mean in most instances violent seizure of power that the twentieth century still enthralled with the French Revolution calls "revolution," especially when it occurs in the wake of war.

He knew that the man-made violence that follows upon either, upon any breakdown of government, outdid in cruelty and terror, in bloodthirstiness, the original state of nature of man before he called himself by name and could lie. It made the original state of nature appear mild in comparison because it did not serve theories: It did not rage against what it had been, it came before history, before man remembered.

The Soviets and their Communist parties throughout the world know this difference between violence that serves the mind and the original state of nature, also. In contrast to the West that reads everything but does not understand much, they can learn from essential books without reading them, through formulas and manuals. For instance, they live Clausewitz more deeply, in distorted fashion, than the West that only misunderstood Clausewitz to forget him. They knew almost instinctively already in 1920 that "independence" equaled "revolution" because it meant continuing the war, and denying it. They knew the destruction of the previous government counted in the yearning for independence, not palaver about the future useful only to undermine the present.

The Third International in 1919 for the first time made the seizure of power "in advanced capitalist countries" dependent on the so-called Third World: ". . . It is the breaking up of the colonial empires together with the proletarian revolution in each home country that will overthrow the capitalist system in advanced capitalist countries."

Lenin added in a speech to the second congress of the Third International in 1920: "World imperialism shall fall when the revolutionary onslaught of the exploited and oppressed workers in each country, overcoming resistance from petty-bourgeois elements and the influence of the small upper crust of labor aristocrats, merges with the revolutionary onslaught of hundreds of millions of people who hitherto stood beyond the pale of history, and have been regarded merely as the object of history"; ". . .The freeing of oppressed countries from the imperialist yoke certainly contains unexhausted revolutionary possibilities that . . . can be utilized for the overthrow of our common enemy, for the destruction of imperialism."

Wilson's "self-determination" of nations was to serve to provoke demands for "complete severance," Stalin's name for independence: ". . . Self-determination must be understood in a much wider sense, as meaning that inhabitants of colonies and dependencies have the rights of complete severance, the right to independent national existence."

Lenin and Stalin used the world "severance" instead of independence because the total break counted for them. They regarded the sovereignty that would follow merely as a first step to "socialism" and the "voluntary union of peoples" or "the fusion of peoples": "The cooperation of the bourgeois nationalist revolutionary element is useful for the overthrow of foreign imperialistic capitalism, which is the first step toward socialist revolution in the colonies . . . The masses in the backwards countries may reach communism, not through capitalist development, but directly under the leadership of the class-conscious proletariat of the advanced capitalist countries [The Third International]."

The slogan "self-determination," used against the rich nations that promoted it, would undermine "cultural autonomy" or "home-rule" that sought to preserve some link with previous authority instead of a complete break: "[Self-determination] becomes a touchstone for the detection of imperialist leanings and chauvinist machinations, and a means for political enlightenment of the masses in the spirit of internationalism." "Internationalist fighters," Castro called the Cuban pilots UNITA shot down after their release in August 1988.

In his comments in 1924 on the Third International, Stalin clearly grasped that the obliteration of the distinction between "severance" and "revolution" meant that the "proletariat [the Communist Parties]" could not support "any and every nationalist movement, at all times, in all places, but had only to support nationalist movements which tend to weaken and subvert imperialism, not those which tend to strengthen and maintain it."

This distinction reappears in the SWAPO notebooks that call Savimbi's UNITA and RENAMO "reactionary": "I and my colleagues are going to be killed and have been killed in Namibia, I want to know that I am dying or sacrificing for a real revolution, not just for a change in regime like there has been in the Ivory Coast or the fighters who sacrifice in a reactionary cause, e.g., UNITA, FNLA."[221] The leader of the MPLA in Angola, dos Santos, drew the same distinction in a haughty remark to a *New York Times* reporter discovering southern Africa in early 1987: "Yet everyone knows that there is no true national liberation struggle in the world which does not have the support, direct or indirect, of the Soviet Union or Cuba."[222]

Stalin focused on actions, not only words: ". . . Unless the proletariat parties [the Communist parties] *give direct support* to the oppressed nationalities in their struggle for freedom . . . the talk about 'equality of nations' is false and empty declamation . . . For the revolution in the Western world the path to victory lies by way of revolutionary alliance with the struggle of the colonial and dependent nationalities to throw off the yoke of imperialism" (Italics mine).

In the Manifesto of the Third International, Lenin held that the European nations did not understand the tremendous violence that had overwhelmed them and, therefore, would not be able to stop it. They had never comprehended the war they fought relentlessly. He was right, as Smuts saw.

Lenin concentrated on the colonies, because immediate seizure of power in Europe, especially in Germany had not occurred. The way to Europe was through the colonies and other countries outside Europe. The continuation and spread of the war outside would show Europe could not cope with itself. The First World War had brought the war outside: "The imperialist war has drawn the dependent peoples into world history." The European nations had conscripted their native subjects: "The last war, which was not least a war for colonies, was at the same time a war fought with the help of colonies. The colonial populations were drawn into the European war on an unprecedented scale, Indians, Negroes, Arabs, and Madagascans fought on the European continent—for what?"

Lenin thanked France and Great Britain for teaching these people to shoot: "They taught them the use of arms, a very useful thing, for which we might express our deep gratitude to the bourgeoisie . . ."; ". . . We are more and more becoming representatives and genuine defenders of this seventy percent of the world's population, this mass of working and exploited people." "For what?" is the key question.

In 1924, Stalin also described this division of the world between the "small minority of civilized nations and the rest of the world" in succinct brutality that focused on racial differences,—already hinted in the call of the second congress of the Third International "to support the revolutionary movement among the subject nations, [for example] the American Negroes!" Stalin divided the world into two camps: "The camp of the civilized nations . . . no more than a small minority, though they control financial capital and exploit the overwhelming majority of the inhabitants of the globe; and the camp of the oppressed and exploited peoples in colonial and dependent lands, far more numerous than their exploiters."

Stalin attacked the Second International in 1889 in Paris for dividing the Europeans from the rest of the world in "occasional insipid resolutions" that "glossed over" the fundamentals of the position of colonial and dependent peoples" and kept "whites and blacks, 'civilized' and 'uncivilized' " in "different categories." Racial differences defined the division of the world into two hostile "camps" and would turn the Asiatics and the Africans into a decisive force: "The Asiatics and the Africans who, to the number of tens or even hundreds of millions, were subject to the most outrageous forms of oppression, were [at the time of the Second International] for the most part beyond the horizon of vision." Communist parties must realize "the closest possible union between all national and colonial liberation movements."

The breaking down of the distinctions between Europeans and the rest of the world also would mean the further blunting of the distinction between nations and their sovereignty the war had begun to undermine. Lenin had an uncanny sense for the exploitation of the yearnings for international cooperation the war brought. These yearnings showed themselves in the formation of all sorts of international organizations like the League of Nations after the First World War, and the UN, the World Council of Churches, the Commonwealth, the OAU and so on, the list is almost endless, after the Second World War.

Lenin called this process "fusion of nations": ". . . We see the formation and strengthening of all sorts of ties between the nations; the breaking down of the barriers that separate them; the establishment of international unity in capitalism, in economic and political life, in the field of science, etc." Lenin appreciated the enormous difficulties in establishing sovereignty or "viable independence," as the experts call it, that Hobbes thought nearly impossible. Slogans like "international unity," "the spirit of internationalism," "self-determination" invited exploitation of these difficulties. By "fusion of nations" Lenin said he meant a worldwide "Soviet republic" in a speech at the second congress: "If our comrades in all lands help us now to organize a united army, no shortcomings will prevent us from accomplishing our task. That task is the world proletariat revolution, the creation of a world Soviet republic (Prolonged applause)." The "fusion of nations" made violence the necessary, but not sufficient, cause for masked conquest. Just this distinction implied in Spinola's remark that the Portuguese could neither lose nor win in battle had inspired his book.

The Soviets decided to move in southern Africa at the end of the sixties according to Igor Glagolev, who before he fled the Soviet Union in 1976 had taken part in Soviet organization of terrorism in southern Africa: "The decision to begin an offensive for the conquest of southern Africa was taken by the Politburo of the Communist Party of the Soviet Union near the end of the 1960's . . ." And Arkady Shevchenko in *Breaking with Moscow*: "For more than two decades Africa was viewed by Moscow as the most turbulent outpost of the capitalist world, and therefore the weakest. Exploiting local turmoil created opportunities to expand Moscow's zone of control without incurring high costs. Some money and advisors and a supply of relatively cheap weapons could buy disproportionate influence with new and shaky governments or anti-colonialist guerrilla forces."

The dogmas of the Third International fossilized Marx's thinking in *Capital*.[223] But Marx had also sometimes known more sensible thoughts. In articles on India in the New York *Daily Tribune* on June 25 and August 8, 1853, he had argued Europe's presence abroad meant progress, not exploitation, for societies stagnating for centuries. Political organization; the recruitment and training of native armies; individual ownership of land; printing and freedom to express opinion, for the first time "in Asiatic society"; the telegraph; steam; irrigation; the railroads, with their demands for skill and industries throughout an immense land, were bringing India together and into close frequent rapid communication with Europe.

Change meant tension, just the tension that now reaches throughout South Africa, tension that stirred age-old passivity. This tension did not precipitate, it overcame violence and cruelty:

You must not forget that this undignified, stagnatory and vegetative life, that this passive sort of existence evoked . . . wild, aimless, unbounded forces of destruction and rendered murder itself a religious rite in Hindustan.

The superiority of the European nations made for this tension and change: "The British were the first conquerors superior, and therefore, inaccessible to Hindu civilization."

More than a hundred years afterwards, Stephen Biko, in a trial in South Africa in May 1976, spoke openly of the almost unbearable anxiety of South African blacks in the universities face-to-face with superior culture. But Biko spoke, in contrast to Marx, in a world where free Europe and the United States no longer have the confidence to both doubt and act. Their sense that totalitarianism is their child, a bastard child, but their child nevertheless, paralyzes them. They no longer know the confidence of knowing they do not have all the answers, not quite the same thing as not having the answers. For this modesty, and willingness to face tragedy, has moved Europe's strength.

To read the propositions of the second congress of the Third International in 1920 today is an astonishing experience. They show you you do not speak prose. Veiled and more disguised, especially in the notion that the riches of the few nations depend on the poverty of others, these propositions now make up the ready assumptions of a good deal of the non-totalitarian world. Anybody who uses the expression "Third World" unwittingly embraces some of the ruling thinking of the Third International, as Carlos Rangel remarked in his classic book, *The Latin Americans*,—a book that changed thinking about the world outside Europe, and even the terms of discussion about France, in France, after its first publication in Paris in 1976.[224]

Race would give the Third International bite the division of the world between rich and poor could not, Stalin realized. It made for irremediable conflict. But black and white conflict between "blacks" and "whites" is to some extent an imposed attitude that feeds on the dread that takes it for granted especially outside southern Africa. In southern Africa, both Europeans and Africans resisted, and still resist it.

In South Africa, there may be a reason to talk of "whites" and "blacks," though I doubt it, but in Rhodesia there was not. There in the large majority, there were Africans and Europeans, with Rhodesians somewhere in between them: The Europeans, many more of them, proportionally, than in South Africa, spoke the native languages. South Africa appears like a *concursus gentium*, not like the one in the United States because it will not pretend there are no differences when there are, but a *concursus* nevertheless, and just as artificial. But all European governments outside Europe are to some extent artificial, for they presume a past not entirely theirs. In Angola and Mozambique, the Portuguese baffled everybody, the Rhodesians, the South Africans, themselves and most of all the guerrillas. FRELIMO was so baffled that it tried to tell a British MP, Iain Sproat, before 1970 "that racial discrimination [in Mozambique] was . . . different in detail from South African apartheid but no different in results . . ." Savimbi too is at his pettiest about the Portuguese: He blames them rightly for abandoning Angola, he insists also rightly that RENAMO is not a "liberation movement"—but his illusions also helped bring disaster. The world, the world outside Africa, did not even understand enough to know the Portuguese baffled it.

The Portuguese could talk about the exploitation of race more openly because they were more innocent and less deeply entangled with the Africans than the South Africans. In a book, *The Portuguese Answer*, published in 1973, another leading Portuguese general, the commander in Mozambique, argued that the Soviets incited racial passions in blacks, passions the Portuguese had provoked in the past, because they wanted to isolate "white" Europe and the United States in a "black" and "colored" world: "Racism, or to be more exact, the neo-racism of the nonwhite man against the white man" was the "first cause" of the "strategic political upheavals which we see occurring in so many different parts of the world."[225] He meant the Third International he did not name.

Kaulza de Arriaga's clarity about Soviet incitement of racial hatred made him want to fight it out in Africa, in contrast to Spinola. He argued not that the war in Mozambique could not be won or lost, but that "it cannot now be lost" and that "it is only a question of time before it is fully won."

In his remarkable memoir, one of the first terrorists in the ANC's Umkhonto we Sizwe in the early sixties, Bruno Mtolo, a Zulu whose ancestors had taken refuge from King Shaka's cruelties among the Xhosa in the Transkei, showed Kaulza's analysis in the story of his life. "It never occurred" to him that he had occasionally clashed with Europeans, he did not call them "whites," "just because I was black and the other man white": "Up to this period I was not at all politically minded. I used to hear people, even when I was working at the camp, say a lot about the wickedness of the Europeans. Nevertheless I seemed to be getting on very well generally. Naturally I had clashes with *some* Europeans but they were not important" (Italics mine).[226]

Mtolo's transformation, imperceptible except in retrospect, had taken almost fifteen years, roughly from 1945 to 1960, "The road to the left is long." It had started in a night school history class with a teacher who had said blacks born equal to the whites had less opportunities because the whites had "overpowered" them, Paton's "conquest." It had gone on in political indoctrination meetings Mtolo first casually attended.

In Rhodesia too, blaming the "whites" did not come naturally to Africans. A Catholic lay teacher, one of fifteen children of a father with two wives who owned a seventy-three acre farm, ran into FRELIMO guerrillas at a mission hospital. Unarmed and disguised as locals, the FRELIMO guerrillas who had come across the border for food and clothes and to recruit for ZANU, pretended to want to become catechists too, and had him run errands,—his first orders. They taught him the words they used he did not understand, like "oppression," through examples: For instance, at a chief's court, the innocent who did not pay for a hearing usually did not win. With insistence that amounted to bullying, they again almost imperceptibly turned him into an accomplice who compromised a good deal of the region: He hid over four hundred refugees from Mozambique in local kraals. Police looking for him precipitated his, and his wife's, flight to the guerrillas. "She insisted on coming: She told me that I was not the only one who was oppressed. We all were. And we were all suffering." Brand-new words.[227]

In South Africa the incitement of racial passions to seize power, now more than two generations old, started before the Bolsheviks seized power. In 1917 the International Socialist League (ISL) which had broken with the South African Labor Party because it backed the war, started to indoctrinate blacks in Johannesburg. At its first conference in 1916, it called for "equal rights for Africans and abolition of the pass laws" and for treatment of "the natives as part of the working class," as one of its leaders said. In 1920 the ISL followed its unprecedented recruitment from all races with open defiance of the government in its newspaper, *The International*: "The ISL will continue its work of agitation and organization of the masses, irrespective of race, color or creed, on class lines, to fight and destroy the system [capitalism] responsible for the present world misery, peacefully if possible, by force if needs be."

Before the foundation in 1921 of the SACP, then called the CPSA, the ISL, the core of the future party, had taken up with Lenin's Zimmerwald group, the Third International's predecessor. Leading ISL members, especially the English-born, Sidney Bunting, put the Soviets on to race in South Africa. They were at the second congress of the Second International in 1920. At the third conference of the SACP in December 1924, the touchiest subject was blacks. "Up to that time the party had concerned itself chiefly with European workers; in the future the 'liberation' of the black man in South Africa would be regarded throughout as the most important task of the CPSA," wrote Gerard Ludi, the plucky South African youth who infiltrated the SACP in the early sixties. In 1925 a Party night school opened in Johannesburg that trained many of the leading African Communists.

This indoctrination reached blacks who fought Communist infiltration with open courage like Clements Kadalie, the founder of the first black labor movement in South Africa in 1915: The Industrial and Commercial Workers Union. "There will be no peace in South Africa till the black man triumphs over the white man," Kadalie wrote in *The Worker's Herald* in 1927, at the same time that he called "Russia, the only government kindly disposed to the workers." He meant war to undo conquest, not what the SACP had in mind.[228]

The real question is to what extent the SACP's exploitation of race rigidified customary attitudes and impeded change. One of the first acts of the National government long before apartheid legislation was the suppression of the SACP in 1950. The decision to suppress the SACP came in part because of a detailed report Smuts had commissioned that showed the SACP was secretly organizing strikes to provoke confrontations with the government, especially the miners' strike in 1946. The SACP provoked these confrontations because they incited agitation abroad crucial, in its judgment, for the seizure of power within South Africa. The "masses" the SACP could move were outside South Africa. To what extent did the SACP succeed in reinforcing the attitudes of South Africans it claimed it wanted to overcome but actually wanted to exploit to overthrow the state? To what extent did it impose "the racial problem" on South Africans—and on a government that rightly judged it was locked in a life-and-death struggle with totalitarianism? Like the rest of the world, but more acutely and blatantly.

The sheer rigidity of the Communists is amazing: The notebooks of SWAPO guerrillas, published along with the Denton Hearings, show that SWAPO and ANC indoctrination literally reproduces the Third International's every nuance, and with the same brutality. Nothing has changed, not a word. This amazing rigidity comes because the dogmas of the Third International feed on the dread of racial hatred which few not face-to-face with the situation can cope with. Totalitarian, in contrast to classical, wars are done in a dream—in a nightmare.

I have seen the same rigidity in ANC speakers on American campuses in 1986 and 1987 and in Oliver Tambo at the Foreign Policy Association in New York on January 22, 1987. They speak of South Africa in a glassy eerie way as if nothing has changed since 1960. They outrightly deny the repeal of the pass laws in July 1986. They ignore questions. They assume total ignorance in their audiences. They talk of a country that has never existed on heaven or earth, with no living people in it, only slogans, violence and death,—a country to be wiped off the face of the earth because it does not exist.

The youths who testified in the Denton Hearings came up against this rigidity in the terrorist training camps in the Soviet Union and eastern Europe. They were startled, the shock of unassuming intelligence before bizarre presumption, to be thrown in among youths of all nations, to fight one enemy, in one war. They were astonished to discover their Soviet and eastern European instructors meant to ruin their worlds and call it independence. They knew the unremitting hardness of the "fusion of nations" and "the spirit of internationalism" in their flesh. They knew they were being used.

This rigidity means something. It betrays unwillingness to react to anything that happens. It is resigned and trapped, the so-called "inevitability of history" raw. It dreads change, and grows desperate in the face of actual change, the change now occurring in South Africa. It is not mere incompetence or rage or conviction, least of all repetition of the truth. For the truth has to be rediscovered in facts, in reality, continually, and these slogans and formulas are now more than two generations old.

Lieutenant General Peter Walls, commander of the Rhodesian Army, gave an unwitting description of this rigidity: He said terrorism precluded negotiation because it was an end in itself, not a means to an end. This rigidity and isolation that will not see the world before its eyes makes terror the only out.

The dogmas of the Third International spread this rigidity to prepare the way for terrorism. A whole climate of opinion makes the spread of the assumptions of the Third International appear irresistible. In the universities, in the prestige media in the United States, these attitudes reinforced through demonstrations serve to precipitate enough rigidity in "thinking" individuals, politicians and nations who are not Communists, not to make them terrorists, but to paralyze them before terrorism, to make them unwillingly acquiesce to terrorism. Open apologists for terrorism are less dangerous because they are more straightforward. ANC and SWAPO speakers mean this largely mental rigidity when they say the inherent "violence of the system" justifies their violence.

This rigidity turns Savimbi, Banda, Buthelezi, P.W. Botha, Alan Paton and other men of their stamp—perhaps I should add Afonso Dhlakama,—into an embarrassment, the embarrassment Chester Crocker wishes away. We fear nothing more than greatness because its resilience undoes rigidity. But to come up against this rigidity in yourself is painful, it makes you feel all the life you have not lived. And Africa in contrast to Europe and the United States has great public men in part because greatness comes harder in the war called "peace" than in fighting.

The resistance in Mozambique and Angola also tells something about Portugal. Whatever else the Portuguese did, they did not break the men they ruled. The worst they did was to abandon them to themselves, and to the worst of Europe. The Mozambicans and the Angolans will never have to ask themselves why they did not fight back. They will never have to say as a sensitive Cambodian did: "The worst thing was that the killings seemed so normal. Maybe not normal, but inevitable. The way things were . . . Demoralized, split apart, like atoms removed from their chemical compounds, we let the Khmer Rouge do what they wanted with us. We didn't fight back. In the fields we were two thousand men and women with hoes, and Angka [the Khmer Rouge organization] was only two or three brainwashed teenagers with rifles. Yet we let the soldiers take us away. Why? Because it was in our nature to obey leaders. Because we were weak and sick and starved. Because it was *kama* [fate]. We did not even know why, but we submitted to them."[229]

The worst off in our world are the highly developed civilizations that are not European, not the "savages." "Marx himself spoke of the difficulty of applying his theories to savages. I suppose it was people like us he was talking about," Savimbi said in 1983. But the West is not far behind. The West will also have to ask itself the questions the Cambodian asks, not the Angolans and the Mozambicans.

Savimbi and other fighters in southern Africa want to rebuild the governments destroyed in the war the Third International and the Soviets decided to continue and spread, the war of 1917. The ANC wants to bring this war to South Africa, SWAPO to South West Africa. Hobbes and Rousseau thought rebuilding almost impossible even without organizations like the Soviet Union that want to prevent it. But rebuilding governments destroyed in war means ending the phase of the war of 1914 that began in 1917. It means taking all we have said and done since 1914 seriously, especially the fighting and dying of men who trusted themselves enough to trust others:

> I think it must be the Third World that has to give the West the courage to oppose the Soviet Union and stand up for its ideals, not the other way around—to provide a cure for what Solzhenitsyn calls the "western disease." That is why, we say, "UNITA is the key to Angola, Angola is the Key to Africa, Africa is the key to the West."[230]

These are embarrassing words because they respect us more than we respect ourselves. "We fought and carried on while the West went through a crisis of faith wondering if its traditions, values and civilizations were worth fighting and dying for," Savimbi recently said. So did the Afghans. How I wish we knew our passivity for a "crisis of faith."

Call him Sertorius, Sertorius of Africa.

17 Bear Hug, Grand Maneuvers: South Africa Strives for Credibility at the Risk of Abandoning South West Africa, Savimbi—and Itself

1988 saw the culmination, but not the consummation, of Chester Crocker's efforts to resolve the wars of southern Africa on the basis of the condition of 1981: the withdrawal of Cuban troops from Angola. The South Africans accepted Crocker's mediation but they also took the diplomatic initiative in Africa. Both in the negotiations Crocker mediated, and in their initiatives in Africa, the South Africans strove to give preference to the situation on the ground in Angola and to the desires of many African leaders for a reconciliation between the MPLA and UNITA. In some sense, they wanted their negotiations in Africa to overcome the ambiguities of East-West considerations in Crocker's mediation that might allow the Soviet Union to continue to use the West to prolong the violence in Angola. The test South Africa undertook was more dangerous than outright battle for it ran the risks of entertaining illusions that could undo individuals and nations more completely than defeat in battle.

The South Africans meant to test the unreal atmosphere of *glasnost* then sweeping the United States and Western Europe. Reagan had even repudiated his phrase, an "evil empire," for the Soviet Union at the Reagan-Gorbachev summit at the end of May, 1988, a phrase that had marked his administration. *Glasnost* had found consummate expression in Georgi Arbatov's boutade, at the Washington summit in December 1987, that the Soviets were going to deprive the West of its Enemy. The Soviet Foreign Minister Eduard Shevardnadze spelled out Arbatov's remark at the UN in September 1988: "The Soviet Union supports a de-ideologization of international relations and the exclusion of an overwhelming component of ideological differences from foreign policy and diplomacy." He added the haughty admonition that the Soviet Union "expects and wishes that others will do likewise," meaning that the West suffered as much from ideology as the Soviet Union, Stalin's assumption at Yalta that had angered Churchill. Shevardnadze also threatened: The Soviet Union "had the means to make things fall in place" in Afghanistan in the face of "a non-stop production line of violations" of the Afghan accords after Soviet troops began to leave Afghanistan in the spring of 1988.[231]

The South Africans knew they could only test *glasnost* if they took it at its words, and negotiated in good faith, and did not break off negotiations in the face of provocations to fight, as they had in the past. The South Africans hoped, they did not merely wish, that their good faith might make a strong enough impression, first of all, on Africa, and then on the world, to overcome the propaganda barrage that had always discredited all their efforts. But to do this they had to mean it, and also to distinguish between reasonableness and appeasement, a much harder task. Good faith also meant the South Africans had to keep their mouths shut in the confidence that actions spoke for themselves to plain-thinking men.

South African silence for months left Savimbi finally to take the measure of the strengths and dangers of South African policy at an extraordinary press conference at Jamba on September 3, 1988. Savimbi was practically the only man in the world at that moment who could speak about Crocker's negotiations, and UNITA's and South Africa's diplomacy in Africa, with enough openness to make his reticence obvious. The newspapers should have been able to make Savimbi's analysis on their own but they had been too much blinded by the presuppositions of totalitarian propaganda that the Soviet Union was just then arguing it had abandoned, the latest twist of the Sphinx's riddle. Savimbi understood South African policy best because he, and Angola and Namibia, stood to lose or gain most from it.

The international negotiations, in contrast to Savimbi's and South Africa's diplomacy in Africa that stressed Angola before Namibia, concentrated on "free and fair and democratic elections" and independence for Namibia. But they were not talking about elections in Angola, "They are talking about finding a cosmetic solution which leaves UNITA and the MPLA fighting." Savimbi was not about to commit suicide for Crocker, a warning that went for Namibia, and also for South Africa, and ultimately also for the United States: "However, we also want the world to understand that we are not going to help those who want to do us in. We are going to help those who want us to be free . . ."

Crocker was working against his country's policy. The State Department's policy was not the policy of the White House, the Senate and the country, a distinction that showed the patience dealings with the United States required in 1988: "Dr. Crocker is playing into the hands of his enemy . . . What is Dr. Crocker trying to do—save the face of his enemies and dig the graves of his friends?" Crocker's negotiations might intensify the war in South West Africa, in Angola, and ultimately spread it to South Africa, an accurate description of the risks the South Africans were taking, and making Namibia run, especially the TGNU, and Savimbi; "Is [the aim of the international negotiations] to find a peace or is it to increase the possibilities of a continuation of the war?"

But the South Africans had run these risks because they wanted to show their good faith. They meant what they said, "They are like that": "We [UNITA] are alone because they want to comply with the spirit of the negotiations, but we see the other side, the Cubans building up more and more." It was up to the West, especially the journalists he addressed, to see facts that spoke for themselves, "now that UNITA is still alone to face the Cubans, FAPLA [the acronym for the MPLA army]": "What is the new attitude of the international media now? Now that there are no more South Africans here . . . What is now your attitude? Is it still the same, that we are here surviving because of the South Africans. All this is going to change your attitude. To become more objective." Refusal to see the South African withdrawal from Angola meant journalists would be responsible for the continuing killing: "And you give again reasons to the MPLA, to the Cubans to kill our own people."

Like the South Africans, Savimbi understood there could be no peace unless facts overcame ideology. The Soviets, in contrast, pretended they no longer needed ideology as long as the West also went along. They wanted their new ideology that denied it was an ideology, that substituted "peace" for "class warfare," a substitution that Stalin had begun long ago, just after the Second World War, to continue to overcome the facts.

In a speech, exactly a month later, Savimbi also named the countries in Africa South Africa could not name that wanted reconciliation between the MPLA and UNITA before independence for Namibia. Crocker instead was fudging a settlement in Angola in the international negotiations despite his promise to Savimbi eventually to include him in the negotiations, a promise Savimbi thought Crocker no longer meant to keep:

We could say, without fear of being contradicted, that Congo-Brazzaville, a former ally of the MPLA, Zaire, Gabon, Senegal, Nigeria, also a former MPLA ally, the Ivory Coast, Morocco, Egypt, Togo, Cameroon, Mozambique, also a former ally, Guinea-Conakry, Equatorial Guinea, Niger, also a former MPLA ally, Zambia, a former MPLA ally, Botswana, a so-called Front-Line State, Burundi, Rwanda, the Central African Republic, Somalia, Malawi, Lesotho, Swaziland and a number of other countries support the initiative of national reconciliation between UNITA and the MPLA.[232]

The newspapers had not even suspected the extent of South Africa's and Savimbi's diplomacy in Africa that this list shows. They had been unwilling to see that Savimbi could work for the same goals as the South Africans independently of them because they were rational goals that could strengthen all of Africa.

Their obtuseness had even led them to take P.W. Botha's visits to Mozambique and Malawi, and a few weeks later, to Zaire, in August and September 1988, for an entirely new development instead of for a renewal of

Vorster's "outward reach policy." Everything Botha did, as usual, built on past policies that had received classical formulation, in this instance, in Vorster's remark in 1969 I have already quoted: "To the extent that we establish right relations with Africa, to that extent will our problems diminish."

The newspapers could not conceive South Africa had a past, and Botha enough regard for his predecessors' actions, to allow him to distinguish measured boldness, the only boldness that might count, from impulsiveness that cannot master the drift that leads to disaster, and in the meantime undermines confidence. Impulsiveness marks Western policies toward southern Africa the Soviet Union exploits, not South African policy, or Savimbi's, each rooted in facts.

Savimbi gave voice to those facts in his speech in Portuguese over the UNITA radio to his followers and the other Angolans within reach of UNITA's radio a month after his press conference. He said peace meant peace, not this kind of peace or that: "There is no such thing as a UNITA or MPLA peace, a Soviet or Cuban peace. Peace has a single name everywhere."

He pleaded for the Church in Angola to speak out simply for peace like the bishops in Mozambique, in a relatively rare reference to Mozambique's courage in its suffering. People in Angola could not simply even say the word "peace" in their own name, only anonymously, because the MPLA took "peace" for a code-word for sympathy for UNITA, a measure of terror. He did not need to add that the MPLA secret police trained and directed by the East Germans would rub out anyone it even suspected of UNITA sympathies. But not to say "peace" meant Angolans did not dare remember their thirteen years' suffering, it meant existing as if they had not suffered or as if they deserved to suffer.

The way out of the impasse was for people to say the word peace anonymously, to scrawl it on walls, anywhere. Savimbi called for "mobilization," a word that betrays all the past that brought him and Angola the disaster that has shown his greatness. Even the anonymous expression of the word "peace" was a "major contribution": "UNITA must use all means to try to mobilize those who have suffered deeply in the past thirteen years, so that their voice can be heard. Writing a simple word about peace and national reconciliation on a wall, a road, a carriage, a school or desk would be a *major contribution* in the present circumstances" (Italics mine).

The South Africans concentrated on Africa because they too wanted to strip the word "peace" of the qualifications that made it serve war by another name. But letting the word have its meaning meant facing the fury that sought to deny its meaning with qualifications. It meant risking losing themselves in the qualifications they wanted to strip away from the international negotiations. In the rest of the world also peace without qualifications, peace that is not simply a truce, Stalin's name for Yalta, or worse still for surrender, means fighting and dying, and worse still, entering into negotiations that mean to undo you in the name of *la force des choses*.

Before they accepted Crocker's mediation, the South Africans turned to the Soviets in March 1988, a startling move. The South African turn to the

Soviets meant to match Soviet realism with South African realism, it meant to call the Soviet's bluff outside the framework of *glasnost*, because on the ground the Soviets counted in southern Africa, not America. The bold initiative showed the South Africans wanted to face up to the Soviet Union because the Americans could not, just what Europe, also caught in the middle, dared not do. In some sense South Africa wanted to break threatening Soviet-American collaboration, to bring the actual situation on the ground in southern Africa to the fore. For there could be no peace until the actual situation in Angola took precedence, as Savimbi kept pointing out.

The South African government turned to the Soviets first, because it thought the Afghan accords showed the Soviet Union might also face realities in southern Africa. ". . . I believe that Mr. Gorbachev thinks that previous Soviet leaders miscalculated the chances for revolution in South Africa. He now knows it's simply not on," P.W. Botha said in his interview in March 1988. The Soviet admission of miscalculation in South Africa, a miscalculation the West, except the United States, also admitted in the wake of the Soviets, prompted Botha to hope the Soviet Union would also leave southern Africa, not a necessary connection: "If [Gorbachev] is a wise man, which we are told he is by many experts in the West, then surely he will make use of this opportunity to get out of southern Africa where he knows Russia is not wanted." The last words meant to suggest vaguely South Africa's, and Savimbi's, diplomacy throughout Africa for reconciliation between the MPLA and UNITA. South Africa, however, in contrast to Savimbi, set reconciliation in terms of a coalition government, not of the elections of the Alvor accords, for paradoxically the same reason Savimbi wanted the Alvor accords: the desperation of the situation in Angola that made the utterance of the word "peace" so deadly. The desperation of the situation in southern Africa also made Botha hope the Soviet Union might, at least, not oppose South Africa's economic leadership of southern Africa: "New Soviet leaders also know that the destruction of our economy would be a disaster for the entire region."[233]

In other words, Botha took the Soviet's realism for change in attitude, not for a change in tactics meant to disarm those who had foiled their previous tactics. At least he meant to act as if the Soviets had changed, to find out whether they had.

The South Africans, however, had few illusions about Soviet withdrawal. They knew it would not be swift or clean-cut. They knew the Soviets meant negotiations to give them what they had been unable to win in battles, especially the destruction of the resistance that in Angola, Mozambique, Nicaragua and Afghanistan had shown the world after the fall of Saigon that there were men in the world who would fight alone with the free nations looking distractedly on. But with all these doubts South Africa calculated the Soviets really wanted out, perhaps the greatest illusion of all. For the Soviets even before Botha's interview, had made it indelibly clear that in Angola they would not accept the "non-alignment" they pretended to accept in Afghanistan because Angola was different from Afghanistan.

The Soviets rejected South African readiness to deal with them alone because they preferred to work through *glasnost*. Working through *glasnost* did not mean a joint Soviet-American initiative. It meant the United States, really Chester Crocker, would mediate while the Soviets remained in the background, manipulating. Americans were to give assurances of Soviet good intentions, they were to act as go-betweens, a dangerous role that could lead not only to the undoing of the Namibians, a Communist victory in Angola, but eventually also to the undoing of South Africa and the United States, as Savimbi pointed out on September 3.

The Reagan-Gorbachev summit in Moscow at the end of May moved South Africa to accept the international negotiations within the framework of *glasnost* it had sought to evade a few weeks earlier.[234] It set September 29, 1988, the tenth anniversary of UN Security Council Resolution 435, for the start of Namibian independence and the withdrawal of Cuban troops from Angola within twelve months, as *The New York Times* reported one day, only to call its report an "error" the next. The Soviets were saying the South Africans would have to deal with illusions before the Soviets would recognize facts. These illusions might again overwhelm facts, or at least, put the South Africans in a situation of having to negotiate and fight, the tactic that had not only broken Vietnam but deeply divided, almost polarized, the United States.

The Reagan-Gorbachev summit meant the South Africans could either defy both the Soviet Union and the United States in a world where no other country, even in Africa, would back them in public, or acquiesce to negotiations. They acquiesced. "South Africa has been squeezed between the superpowers," Savimbi told an American visitor to Jamba in the middle of December.

At the same time the South Africans continued their diplomacy in Africa which they hoped would at least make realities on the ground compete with *glasnost*, and even perhaps show its limits, show the distinction between facts and illusions Shevardnadze was to complain several months later no longer determined Soviet policy. A dangerous decision but the only alternative to even more intense isolation. The Soviets had refused the South Africans' turn to them in March because negotiating with them directly would have made the Soviets squarely responsible for events they wanted to make the responsibility of the West. They knew the West wanted Namibian independence, but not enough to intervene directly, instead of the UN, to see that independence would not mean a SWAPO take over. Mark Antony's "Let it work," only not half so honest.

The South Africans had already abandoned a good deal of their classical position, a month before the Reagan-Gorbachev summit when they talked to the Cubans under American mediation in London. The readiness of the South Africans to negotiate with the Cubans as well as the MPLA, meant they recognized the Cubans' presence in Angola, and worse still, it meant they would no longer insist on the complete withdrawal of the Cubans from Angola *before* they negotiated. Only a few weeks before the South Africans met the Cubans in London, Botha had reaffirmed South Africa's classical position that it would not leave Angola until the Cubans left: "We are staying there until the

Cubans leave." He had not even mentioned negotiations with the Cubans that turned their withdrawal into a negotiable matter.

The South Africans' readiness to negotiate with the Cubans, as well as the MPLA, meant also they would no longer fight them, for in contrast to the totalitarian regimes the South Africans took their own refusal to fight while negotiating for proof of their good faith. The totalitarians, the Cubans said it openly, took this good faith for weakness: It meant the South Africans no longer had the nerve to fight. The assertion had enough truth to bite, for the South Africans knew that breaking-off negotiations to fight would bring another tidal wave of propaganda, and perhaps also, the United States Senate's passage of drastic sanctions.

The readiness to talk to Cubans also made it look like South Africa might abandon Savimbi. From the time Crocker had judged negotiations a realistic possibility in February 1988, the MPLA had made it indelibly clear, first in February 1988, and then again in slightly more oblique terms in Washington during Savimbi's visit at the end of June, that besides Namibian independence the cutoff of aid to Savimbi was a necessary condition for Cuban withdrawal.

Crocker responded to this rigidity by excluding aid to Savimbi from the international negotiations, evasion that cut both ways but not in an evenhanded manner. It suggested the abandonment of Savimbi it denied, it frightened Savimbi, it put the South Africans in a bind, and it encouraged the totalitarians who know that illusions are violence's children. To show his loyalty to the United States', but not the State Department's, decision to aid Savimbi, Crocker had promised to include Savimbi in the negotiations, as Savimbi revealed on September 3. But neither Crocker nor the South Africans, for different reasons, held to the truth that Savimbi was crucial both for a settlement in Angola and to ensure independence for South West Africa would not simply mean a Communist SWAPO takeover. Neither would speak for the man each had helped for the sake of Cuban withdrawal, a mirage.

On September 3 Savimbi had said the Cubans, now sixty thousand,—the State Department had admitted fifty thousand in July,—had no intention of withdrawing from Angola: "The Cubans are massing their troops in Cuito Cuanavale, immediately after the South Africans have left. I don't see that when you have to leave, or you have the intention of leaving, you have to bring thousands of troops to wave at us, to tell us goodbye, one man is enough." The Soviets, he went on, are not interested in peace but in fighting as they have shown in practice. He did not say, thank God, "Have a nice day."

The efforts at settlement probably were at their most intense in the middle of July and August 1988. Confidence waned after the killing of Zia and the American Ambassador and the chief of the US military aid mission and twenty seven other men on August 17 showed the Afghanistan accords might mean the continuation of war by other means. But as late as November 1988 the South Africans insisted on their readiness to surrender South West Africa provided the Cubans agreed to a reasonable time schedule for withdrawal from Angola.

South Africa still wanted others to draw the conclusions it would not draw, conclusions that Savimbi announced a few weeks later to a world that did not listen. Its good faith had made enough of an impression, not to still the attacks against it, but to rob them of their vehemence. The credibility it had won showed itself in boredom—who could follow the negotiations?—not in any straightforward acknowledgment of their good faith. South Africa had produced a situation where none of the old arguments stuck, where its friends feared it might abandon rational positions for an eventual war without any other goal but survival, a war it might lose at home before South Africa fought it, the real strategy of the totalitarians.

The fourteen points the Cubans, the South Africans and the MPLA agreed on in New York on July 13, approved by their governments on July 20, reiterated all the classic points of Vorster's policy with the addition of the withdrawal of the Cubans: independence for South West Africa; respect for borders and self-determination regardless of the form of government; no subversion; no terrorist or guerrilla bases for attacks on neighboring countries. These provisions meant the South Africans would cut off aid to Savimbi. The agreement left Cuban withdrawal to negotiations between the MPLA and the Cubans, like the Afghanistan accords a few months earlier. The Afghanistan accords had not made the withdrawal of Soviet troops part of the international agreement but left it up to the Soviets and the regime in Kabul without provision for enforcement or verification. The omission of Cuban withdrawal from Angola from the international agreement showed the ambiguity of South Africa's negotiations with the Cubans for it denied the plain fact that the brunt of the negotiations had been between the Cubans and the South Africans. The provisions did not directly connect Namibian independence with Cuban withdrawal, although the South Africans said in November that the transcript of the talks would show that the Cubans had accepted the connection.[235] In other words, they did not spell out the crucial condition that kept the sides from coming to agreement later, and that finally led the South Africans to agree to withdraw from Namibia before any significant withdrawal of the Cubans from Angola.

More importantly, they also continued the uncertainty of conception in Vorster's policy that had led Vorster to violate it with the intervention in Angola in 1975. For only democratic governments respect different forms of government; totalitarian regimes do not forsake *le avventure* abroad, their uneasy substitute for confidence at home. On August 2–5 in Geneva, the three countries agreed on November 1, a date the final agreement postponed to April 1, 1989, for the beginning of independence in Namibia and set September 1 for agreement on a timetable for withdrawal of the Cubans from Angola. They approved the draft of a treaty for submission to their governments that made the July 13 principles binding.

The single most important fact during these negotiations was the continuing Cuban build-up. In November 1987 when it appeared that Savimbi and the South Africans might take Cuito Cuanavale, Castro had clearly decided on reinforcing the 40,000 Cubans in Angola with soldiers from one of the best

Cuban divisions, the fiftieth. Its airport made Cuito crucial in the campaigns to destroy UNITA, or at least Jamba, since 1985.[236]

The UN Security Council Resolution on November 25, 1987 that called for South African withdrawal from Angola without mention of the Cubans had been timed to keep Savimbi and the South Africans from taking Cuito. The South Africans had for the first time admitted their presence in Angola not only to prevent SWAPO infiltration but to support UNITA, a few weeks earlier. After arguing against the UN resolution, the South Africans had foregone victory by agreeing to a "tactical withdrawal" from Angola on December 5. This withdrawal was completed by August 20, 1988 after the South Africans on their own on August 2, had set the final deadline for it in order to make the MPLA and the Cubans put up or shut up in Geneva. Capture of Cuito might have given Savimbi control of all Angola south of the Benguela railroad, roughly half the country, the most populated half.

South Africa's tacit renunciation of the conquest of Cuito showed its most threatening consequence in the movement of troops south of the fifteenth parallel, roughly the latitude of Cuito, after the MPLA invited the international press to Cuito on March 1 to show the town was securely theirs. The Cuban build-up almost in sight of the Namibian border: 12,000, soldiers at least, and maybe 200 tanks by September 1988, according to Savimbi, was not really publicly recognized until May and June. It was a direct consequence of the South Africans' acquiescence to the Security Council resolution toward the end of November 1987. The resolution set the stage both for the international negotiations and for the build-up.

Provocative words accompanied Castro's provocative build-up, especially his move south. On March 17, Cuba's Armed Forces Ministry called the foiling of South Africa's,—they did not mention UNITA's,—capture of Cuito "decisive." In mid-July 1988, Castro said Cuba and Angola "have been willing to take the risks of a serious, big confrontation." He boasted that South Africa was "too weak, too weak politically . . . to cause a confrontation": "They might not only lose Namibia, they might lose apartheid . . . [The regime] has too many oppressed people. It cannot risk a big military defeat. It cannot risk a big military disaster." And then again on August 16, 1988, he said "reinforcements sent by Cuba; the support we gave Cuito Cuanavale; the advance of Cuban-Angolan forces toward the Namibian border in the western sector of the southern front; and a significant change of the balance of power in our favor," had caused South Africa to negotiate. He stressed the importance of military means to achieve a political solution. He also said, especially abroad, that Cuba would withdraw if the MPLA wanted but he showed his reluctance because of the "bellicose nature of apartheid": "Once those troops are totally withdrawn, no one will be able to prevent new actions against Namibia, possibly against Angola." Castro threatened to attack Namibia directly.[237]

On May 22, the Angolan defense minister and the first deputy chief of staff as well as the defense minister of Tanzania arrived in Havana for a week of talks with Castro, Raul Castro and important generals. Sam Nujoma, the leader of SWAPO, and his men were received in Havana like heads of state after a visit to Moscow in April where they saw Crocker's chief Soviet interlocutor, Deputy Foreign Minister for African Affairs Anatoly Adamishin, and a visit to the United States. The presence of Tanzania, never a reassuring sign, meant to make new diplomatic way for Castro's policy among the "Front-Line" states and in international organizations, Tanzania's role in the war against Rhodesia.

To top it all off, the *International Herald Tribune* broke a story on August 11, 1988 that held that Crocker had "given the nod" to the Cuban build-up six months before and quoted a "senior Cuban diplomat": "The Reagan administration was fully aware since last March that our strategy was to hit the South Africans hard—on their own turf." The story took up all the clichés: The South Africans had negotiated because they feared losses on the battlefield, and the Cubans had sent forces to Angola, and then moved them south, against the "Soviet Union's advice," the good-cop, bad-cop routine.[238] The South Africans took this probably Cuban misinformation in the silence Savimbi broke on September 3.

Despite these words and the build-up they accompanied, the South Africans continued to negotiate. They fought twice, once immediately after a SWAPO terrorist attack against civilians on a bank in Oshakati on February 18: twenty dead, thirty wounded, twenty-eight seriously,—the worst SWAPO attack in roughly twenty years of war that has cost an estimated twenty thousand lives. They fought again after the Cubans with SWAPO integrated into their units attacked toward the Calueque dam a few days before June 28, 1988, the day South Africa made the attack public. The attack near the Calueque dam followed by a low-altitude attack of eight MIG-23's on the dam itself that also hit the water pipeline for Namibia, showed the Cubans' disregard for the MPLA. For the MPLA had agreed to keep the complex of dams out of the fighting at the talks in May with the South Africans in Brazzaville, Congo that the Cubans and the Americans had not attended. The Cuban attack on the originally Portuguese-South African project to provide water and electricity to the entire border region, showed their desire to pressure the border region of Namibia, the most populated in the entire country, Ovamboland, not only with terror but with the threat of a cutoff of water, and that in a year of drought. Although the South Africans fought back with an estimated two hundred Cuban and Angolan dead, the Cubans retained control of the dam, and, thereby, of the capacity to threaten Namibia.

Both attacks showed the Cuban renewal of SWAPO all but destroyed in 1985, and its capture of territory in Angola close to the border that the South Africans had controlled since 1978. There were three mixed Cuban SWAPO battalions of 200 to 250, with 150 to 200 Cubans in addition, officered by Cubans,—"mechanized forces . . . not the guerrilla type of SWAPO that we have been involved with in most of our operations," a SWATF major reported on the BBC on June 16. More than a year before, a seventeen year old boy abducted into SWAPO at the age of nine, had reported the training of SWAPO men in motorized warfare and anti-aircraft at Lubango, SWAPO and Cuban headquarters about 185 miles from the frontier that the South Africans had attacked after the explosion at Oshakati. In October 1988, a South African officer at the front said there had been incidents involving 349 SWAPO terrorists in Ovamboland between September 1 and October 10. On August 30, a SWAPO terrorist confessed in court to the attack on the bank in Oshakati. In February, the NCC, Toivo Ya Toivo, the SWAPO leader the TGNU had released, and Peter Kalangula, the Ovambo leader not in the TGNU, had blamed the attack on South African "agents" renewed proof of SWAPO's capacity to maintain the divisions in Namibia its terror had wrought in the past.[239]

"Castro's dangerous games," serious enough not to be over-dramatized, Savimbi had called Cuba's build-up in a sober analysis a few days before the attack on the Calueque dam and his departure for Europe and the United States. Savimbi's sobriety, the sobriety that comes from years of measuring annihilation, showed in his refusal to choose between the many possibilities the Cuban build-up might portend: an attack on Namibia, the most dangerous possibility; an attack on UNITA; facilitation of SWAPO infiltration into Namibia; influence over Crocker's negotiations; delay of the negotiations until after the American elections,—any of these could be the motive for the Cuban build-up.[240] Savimbi meant the Cubans themselves did not know what they were doing, another word for bluffing.

South African actions showed they had made a similar analysis: Almost anything was possible, and there was no way of deciding. They were determined not to be provoked beyond reprisals to all out war. They responded to overt attacks but they did not break off negotiations. They too realized the Cubans probably did not know what they were doing. In its way, South African persistence in negotiation in the face of continuing evidence that the Cubans were not serious was more daring than an outright military response and breaking off negotiations because it showed they no longer wanted to fight the way they had in the past.

The South Africans knew that a military response, especially in the face of a Cuban build-up that overturned the balance since 1978, meant taking Luanda, undoing 1975, on their own this time. Their readiness to negotiate alone with the Soviets in March probably meant also to show the Soviets they knew they were on their own.

Besides, fighting meant uncertainty, always the case in war. The Cubans were heavily armed, they might have air superiority. But the Cubans and the Soviets did not know the terrain, they relied on heavy firepower, not the swift-moving scattered tactics of bush warfare in vast spaces the South Africans have known for generations and UNITA had learned in almost a generation of fighting. Since 1976 when they had first tried to finish off Savimbi, the Cubans had not done well in fighting. In 1976 they feared to get off the roads into the country, in 1987 they and the Soviets had fled the fierce fighting. The only thing not uncertain was the words Castro would say.

South African persistence in negotiations ran the risk of turning into appeasement, a real risk, a risk that the foreign minister R.F. Botha sometimes appeared to confirm in careless statements that South Africa would have been better off abandoning South West Africa ten or fifteen years before. For instance, at a Nationalist party meeting in Johannesburg in October 1988: "I do not think we did the right thing when we took over South West Africa. It is not ours. Just think what we could have done [with the five billion rand spent in South West Africa] inside this country."[241] Thrift, thrift, not a good disguise for regret for past generosity.

The South Africans repeatedly said they would not fight and negotiate, as the defense minister said again on September 3, pointing to the Cuban build-up nobody would really notice. They were not fighting and negotiating, the Cubans were, at least they could not make up their minds whether to negotiate or fight, the indecisiveness of bluff waiting upon Western irresolution.

All the nastiness behind Soviet foreign policy had shown itself unequivocally in Gorbachev's open threat at the Reagan-Gorbachev summit at the end of May 1988 to undermine the resolution of other "regional conflicts" if Pakistan continued to aid the Afghan resistance. He meant the actual wars actually on the earth, in contrast to the future war in men's minds. The killing of Zia on August 17, 1988 showed Gorbachev meant the retaliation he threatened. The deep silence of Western governments and newspapers that met the crash of the Hercules C–130 showed we already live in a world that left plain surmise to the privacy of individuals, the true face of *glasnost*. Two months later, the former editor of *The New York Times* had the nerve to blame the silence on the American people and the government of the United States, not on the newspapers, let alone his newspaper.[242] For a year before, a terrorist campaign struck Pakistan, the clear target, in addition to the resistance, of the Afghanistan accords signed on April 14, 1988. Just before the American election, the Soviet Union announced the halt of troop-withdrawal from Afghanistan, and hinted it might not meet the deadline for complete withdrawal, February 15, 1989, because of Pakistan's "glaring violations" of the accords with the support of the United States. A few days before, Scud-B missiles, a range of 170 miles, had passed before the American embassy; backfire bombers from the Soviet Union and something like thirty MIG-27's just arrived from the Soviet Union attacked the resistance outside Khandahar no longer protected by Soviet troops.

Gorbachev knew he had Pakistan, and even more the United States, in a bind: The weapons the United States had promised the resistance in the face of the Afghanistan accords had to go through Pakistan but the United States had pressured Pakistan to commit itself to stop aid to the resistance, to save the Soviet Union from "humiliation" with Kabul about to fall. But Kabul had not fallen, neither had the other cities. By August the Soviet strategy the accords had made plain showed itself on the ground: to break Pakistan, besides the resistance, by holding on to the cities that only a conventional army with artillery like Pakistan's could take, not the resistance. "We don't want [the Soviets] to get through delays and negotiations, what they failed to get through sheer brute military power," the Pakistani Ambassador to Washington said.[243] In the face of these attacks the United States State Department continued to tell the resistance that it said had sufficient arms not "to humiliate the Soviets."

Shevardnadze and Gorbachev had made this strategy, not only in Afghanistan but also in southern Africa and Nicaragua, plain to the German conservative leader, Franz Josef Strauss, on his visit to Moscow on December 28 to 31, 1987. They said nobody could stop events in Mozambique, Angola, Nicaragua and Ethiopia, events they pretended to distinguish from Afghanistan only because the Soviets were more involved, and the strategy was more advanced, in Afghanistan.

The undoing of colonialism, a tough process, had its own momentum nobody could control. They meant the West did not have the will to control the violence the Soviets did not want to stop, much the same answer the South Africans received when they faced the Soviets directly a few months later. But they did not want an "explosion in South Africa," only a step-by-step undoing of apartheid.

This line that Botha had called the Soviet miscalculation of "the chances for revolution in South Africa" in his March interview showed itself little more than six months later in full battle dress in the remark in Moscow of a man the South African press took for Gorbachev's spokesman on South Africa, the Soviet Ambassador to Lesotho: "Those who continue to believe that South Africa is entirely comprised of confirmed racists and opponents of radical changes and talks with the black majority are mistaken." *Business Day* said the Soviet Ambassador thought Afrikaners were destroying "apartheid with the help of P.W. Botha's reforms." Earlier, in South Africa, the ambassador had protested even more: "The Soviet Union is not going to destroy South Africa . . . Our policy as I see it is aimed at establishing peace and stability in southern Africa, preferably by peaceful means. We want to see a prosperous South Africa without apartheid."[244] Shevardnadze's silence before Strauss's remark that the departure of white South Africans,—he probably meant the consummation the CAA Act devoutly wishes, the fall of the South African government,—would unleash a cruel war among blacks showed the face behind the Soviet mask.

The unreality behind *glasnost* showed in Gorbachev's complaint to Strauss that he could not understand why people ascribed an aggressive character to Marxist-Leninism. Marxist-Leninism had never hurt anyone, it could not be exported artificially, it never went where it was not wanted, only to countries where it fitted realities through authentic events. Besides, he valued the Soviet Union as part of civilization, a pathetic statement, true enough unfortunately, not to need stating. The Soviet Union did not philosophize, it only had realities to offer. You could only become a Communist after you had understood everything. The words came from Lenin, Gorbachev said, to hide his arrogance. Margaret Thatcher just would not understand that everything had changed since Churchill, a statement Strauss in some sense confirmed with a remark that the world had changed as much since 1917 as it had since the Stone Age, rough on seventy centuries.[245]

In his press conference in September and especially in his speech to Angolans a month later, Savimbi hit the Portuguese hardest, and not only in small-minded fashion. Their recognition of the MPLA violated their own Alvor accords. Finally, somebody was paying attention to the Portuguese because the Portuguese were finally paying attention to themselves. More than a year before, members of the Portuguese Parliament from the Social Democratic, Socialist and Christian Democratic parties had visited UNITA in Angola.[246] Leading figures in the Portuguese government, including apparently Mario Soares, the president, had wanted to receive Savimbi in Lisbon during his visit to Europe and the United States at the end of June 1988, a visit that would have brought the Alvor accords to the fore. Apparently, the thirty year old minister for international cooperation, Durao Barroso, attacked strongly by Savimbi in his speech in October, who had not seen the worst of the previous history with his own eyes was opposed. It was too obvious, too right, too courageous—he did not want to offend the MPLA. But Portugal was beginning to move, movement of incalculable importance because Portugal knew Angola best and had the most responsibility, especially for the Alvor accords, the only possible basis for unqualified peace.

In late October 1988 the Senate refused to vote on money to pay for UN forces in South West Africa despite pressure from the White House because many Senators feared that a regional settlement meant an abandonment of Savimbi. Support for Savimbi in the Senate ran deep, fifty one Senators signed a letter to Reagan. It had already shown itself in a unanimous consent resolution on October 6, 1987 reminding Reagan before the scheduled discussions between Shultz and Shevardnadze and the summit in Washington between Reagan and Gorbachev that "the United States is committed to supporting democratic forces in Angola until democracy is achieved."[247] The loyalty to Savimbi in the Senate showed that the Senate's decision to repeal the Clark amendment had not been lightly taken. It had gone deep enough to make the Senate wonder whether the "regional settlements" *glasnost* promised might bring the "paper settlement" that in 1985 had prompted repeal of the Clark amendment. But the Senate's action also showed again that foreign policy, for better and for worse, had become a part of domestic politics, a telling indication of present danger.

In the same days the laconic answer of an Afghan resistance leader to an American reporter's request for advice for the American people told something of the risks of "paper settlements" not only to the South Africans, but to the United States: "Not very much. Just do not trust very much the Soviets, and to look at what they did to us. If they have the same chance, they will do the same to you."[248]

At the signing of the agreement in New York on December 22, 1988, the South African foreign minister remarked that he could name many black African presidents that had asked South Africa not to leave Namibia until the last Cuban left, an outburst of inadvertent self-criticism no other criticism could match. Little more than a month later UNITA said it "profoundly laments that the South Africans signed an accord they don't believe in," and announced an offensive in every province of Angola, especially in the north.[249]

Anyone who studies these negotiations in the bits and pieces of hundreds of newspaper articles throughout the world will learn that statesmen and nations in public life are both much worse and much greater than everyday individuals in private life, the core of Western tragedy and its greatness that both Savimbi and the South Africans dared to take on.

Upon UNITA's resumption of fighting in February 1989, offensive deployment Savimbi stopped without declaring a cease-fire a few days later against the bitter opposition of his commanders in the field, Savimbi made it clear that UNITA would be fighting for survival in the next two years until the completion of the Cuban withdrawal on July 1, 1991. To expect SWAPO would not prevail in Namibia was a delusion, especially because the UN backed it. Castro's recent statements showed no acceptance of Cuban withdrawal from Angola. UNITA was broadcasting throughout Angola in tribal languages, transmissions the MPLA called the "second Stinger." With the South Africans gone responsibility for supplying Savimbi with artillery and anti aircraft guns, and above all fuel after UNITA's year's suppy ran out, centered on the United States, Savimbi indicated without saying outright.

5

Gulags for Southern Africa: The Denton Hearings

For five days in March 1982, Senator Jeremiah Denton, chairman of the Subcommittee on Security and Terrorism, held hearings on "The Role of the Soviet Union, Cuba, and East Germany in Fomenting Terrorism in Southern Africa."[1] The committee heard nine witnesses, all black Africans, one from Mozambique, the rest from South Africa or South West Africa. Six of the nine were in their early twenties.

Three of the witnesses, Nokonono Delphine Kave, a young South African woman, Lieutenant Adriano Bomba, a young man from Mozambique, and Bartholomew Hlapane, a mature man who had been at the top of the South African Communist Party in the early sixties, gave extraordinary testimony.

I could not believe my eyes. The testimony reminded me vividly of the European experience of totalitarianism, but it was also unmistakably different. Even the language was different, fluent and clear. I knew I had never heard it before. It had a daring fluidity of syntax and a raw straightforwardness. It came to me that this must be the English of people who still thought in part in the intimacy and privacy of their native tongues. The witnesses had spoken this free-spoken language, not only in the relatively august Senate hearing room, but throughout the bush and capitals of southern Africa, to Soviet and Cuban instructors in guerrilla training camps, and in the Soviet Union and eastern Europe. Their assurance in it showed they knew they lived irrevocably in two worlds, and that the world of the English-speaking, in Washington and South Africa, or in the Soviet Union and eastern Europe, could decide their lives.

Usually you get this sort of information long after a disaster, not before or during it.

The notebooks of South West African students in terrorist training camps captured by the South African Defense Force in Angola, reprinted in facsimile in the hearing volumes, showed more legible English than some of my students write in the United States. It smelled of small no-nonsense mission country schools that still know that penmanship tells almost as much as neatness of appearance about the soul. But the language of these bush notebooks was the language of Soviet propaganda throughout the world. I told myself, against this uniformity of lies and distortion that reached even the bush, we haven't got a chance.

The hearings show with clarity that the Soviets, Cubans, East Europeans, and now most lately the North Koreans, are active on a face-to-face basis throughout southern Africa,—implementing a specific strategy on the ground that needs young men ready to kill blindly on orders, and die, in addition to the magnificent campaigns in the media and in international organizations like the UN, OAU, the Commonwealth, and the Common Market. They show that the Soviets and the others train South African blacks for terrorism, sabotage, and political agitation, especially manipulation of the media.

The story of these witnesses who spoke at the risk of their lives, to be ignored by press and television, may be the story of the future of southern Africa. Their testimony shows the rudimentary apparatus of an entire totalitarian state, including gulags, already in existence, scattered in dismantled parts in the small guerrilla training camps and schools that riddle all of southern Africa, especially in Angola and Mozambique, but also in Zambia, Zimbabwe, and Tanzania.

Besides the routine of totalitarian violence and the extent of Soviet and Eastern European penetration of all of southern Africa and their determination to manipulate international organizations and the media, these hearings show something that goes to the heart of the history of our times. They show that SWAPO, the ANC, the SACP and, behind everything, the Soviet Union and its satellites will stop at nothing to break the defiant individuals of real stature among the blacks of southern Africa. They show that the blacks the Communists fear most are the blacks who want change, who have the guts to fight for it *on their own*. These individuals have the courage to defy the government of South Africa but they also know they must take responsibility for themselves before they can demand of others rights and privileges they do not have. These individuals know that, unlike the civil-rights movement in the United States, they are not fighting for rights already constitutionally guaranteed but for "a new dispensation," the South African government's phrase, that will overcome their conquest in the last century.

They realize that flight into foreign ideologies is no way to overcome past defeats, as Bruno Mtolo, the SACP and ANC terrorist who testified against Mandela and his associates in 1963, already wrote in 1966: "Many were still viewing the conditions in South Africa as Shaka, Dingane and Cetshwayo [Zulu kings in the nineteenth century] did. They did not realize that today a country must be seen as part of the world. Nothing could be returned to the days of our great-grandfathers, nor could one import ideas from other countries and think they could be applied successfully in this country . . . We are still dominated by the white man, but the weapons that were taken up by our great-grandfathers we can never touch. They are so dangerous today that they can backfire, and make us slaves for the rest of our days in this world."[2]

The hearings show that there is, or was, a real rebellion among the youths of South Africa that is angry, defiant, but also at bottom sensible. It is "nationalist," it does not want to be part or pawn of the "international liberation movements" supplied, supported, and manipulated by the Soviet Union, it does not hold that fundamental gradual change requires a "Socialist" totalitarian revolution, it does not believe in violence, except in some instances, as a last resort.

These hearings show that the Communist terrorist organizations dreaded this disorganized and, in part, spontaneous rebellion, because it threatened their power. They wanted to exploit it—but above all to break it. Envy is the best word to describe their feelings in the face of all these extremely young blacks flooding across South Africa's frontiers in 1976 and 1977 after the upheaval that quickly turned to riot in Soweto on June 16, 1976, and continued intermittently in other black townships for more than a year. The youths who fled South Africa numbered somewhere between five and ten thousand.

The exodus from South West Africa, in contrast, started earlier, in the year SWAPO turned to terrorism, 1966, and took off with the collapse of the Portuguese in 1974–1975. The wanderers trapped abroad now number seventy thousand, mainly women and children, some abducted, some children born in captivity in Angola, but also youths who left in the hope of higher education then not available in South West Africa. SWAPO insists on more than one hundred thousand "refugees" in Angola because the UN and Europe, especially the Scandinavian countries, pay by the head.

These youths were astonishingly daring in their readiness to wander, and unsuspicious in their trust of SWAPO promises of education in Zambia broadcast from Lusaka. They still talk of their flight from home and family in matter-of-fact almost casual words,—as if the reasons for it were self-evident, as plain as the day.

The success of Communist terrorist organizations in coopting, and destroying, the defiance of these blacks who fled South Africa and South West Africa is shown in *The New York Times*' disingenuous, naive, or merely incompetent claim that the founder of the ANC's terrorist wing, Nelson Mandela, is an "imprisoned black nationalist leader" as late as July 1986, a characterization Secretary of State Shultz echoed on July 23, 1986.[3] The omissions tell in this label: no mention of Mandela's membership in the SACP and of his responsibility for the ANC's turn to violence.

The *Times* does obeisance to Mandela's secretiveness before his trial almost a generation after it. Already in 1962, when ANC and SACP youths first went abroad for terrorist training, Mandela had ordered silence on SACP membership because "the African states said they were prepared to help us, but only if we were not Communists." Mtolo also wrote that he had been warned not to tell "even my best girlfriend I was a member of the Communist Party."[4]

The murder of blacks capable of rational defiance who are not Communist, and do not want to submit totally to the ANC or SWAPO, mirrors, in the innards of these organizations, the violence against orderly reform in South Africa that has shown itself to the world since 1984. This violence seeks to pass itself off as an irresistible spontaneous uprising of all the blacks which will know no reason, the fulfillment of the cherished fantasies of some of the West.

These hearings show what is happening right now in South Africa to thinking feeling individuals who want change, are willing to fight for it, but who can tell the difference between defiance and suicide. They tell what is happening to the best, the men of good will, who know they are in part responsible for their condition.

The real, the feasible, the imperfect, the possible, the not easily possible, is under murderous attack. The struggle is a deadly one because the totalitarians realize they are fighting for their existence. The victory of reform in South Africa that would show fundamental but limited change is possible without destruction of the South African government; the victory of the United States' policy of constructive engagement over disinvestment; of actual independence over the appearance of independence in Mozambique and Angola, and, eventually in the rest of southern Africa, would show the strength of the feasible. It would show the strength of governments that respect their own laws, and the weakness and ruin of totalitarianism that only survives by spreading, by feeding on the strength of others, and by exploiting their weaknesses.

The new Soviet line in 1987–88 that speaks of "reconciliation through reason not force," in southern Africa as Soviet spokesmen touring universities, think-tanks, and foundations in the United States in 1988 put it, recognizes the strengths of this feasibility. It seeks to use it, in part because the United States has rejected it. It seeks to help the South Africans, UNITA and the Namibians do themselves in through negotiations, as Savimbi best recognized. The closer the goal, the more intense the masquerade to unarm straightforward men.

The raw material of defiance, the youths that the ANC, like SWAPO, tried to break because they frightened it, and that lent the ANC the appearance of new life and determination, had fled their country, homes, and family, wanderers intoxicated by a will to change; they had sensed the possibility of deep transformation, the readiness of some of the whites to listen to them. Stephen Biko had announced this new mood in the South African government to the world as witness in court a few weeks before the outbreak of the Soweto riots. These youths wanted to do everything they could to bring about this change. Some of them wanted to fight, some had been in the "Black Consciousness" movements, all had known its influence, its hope, its euphoria, its sense of possibility. The years 1984–1986 precipitated uncounted other flights of youths abroad and into the ANC, this time with fewer illusions and more obviously coerced.

One event that will either destroy this region or lead to the beginnings of living independence for its countries runs through all the testimony of the Denton Hearings: the failure of Portuguese dominion after more than five hundred years and the continuation, spread and intensification of the war Portugal had managed to contain. The disappearance of Portuguese dominion, and the consequent arrival of the Cubans and the Soviets, set everything loose in the world of these witnesses. Only sixteen at the time of the Portuguese collapse in 1974 and taken up with guitars and pop music, Bomba was sensitive enough to realize the euphoria that surrounded him spelled trouble he was too young to fathom:

I was then in the first year of high school when Mozambique came to grips with the coup d'état in Portugal [April 1974]. FRELIMO was no longer in the forefront of our themes during this period. Another trend had, in the meantime, emerged: that of pop music and guitar playing. When I heard about the coup d'état, nothing changed in me, as I could not possibly grasp the full impact of its meaning . . . *only the euphoria of others*, and the comments of the more politically enlightened, made me realize that *something awful had, in fact, happened* (Italics mine).

Another older witness, at that time a leader of SWAPO, Andreas Shipanga, described the war-frenzy that possessed the leaders of Zambia and Tanzania, the already independent states of southern Africa, and which helped the Communists complete their seizure of SWAPO, in the same days that the schoolboy Bomba felt the earth give way under his feet:

But anyway the tensions started coming up and up until, again, because of geopolitics, you know, the change in the Portuguese, when the Portuguese colonies collapsed, then they became these front-line states, they came in too big, and obviously men like President Nyerere or President Kaunda, they felt, well, they got now the destiny of the whole of southern Africa in their hands, they can make or break. And so they decided that those of us—not only me, we were over 2,000—we must be sacrificed [to the Communists] so that Sam Nujoma [the present Soviet-controlled leader of SWAPO] will be leader of Namibia.

The euphoria Bomba described in Mozambique also showed itself among black university and secondary school students in South Africa and South West Africa, an elite that history will remember, and contemporaries should not forget, the South African government has fostered. In 1974 almost 250,000 blacks were in secondary school, 25,000 in the top grades, in South Africa,—in contrast to less than 50,000, and less than 2,500 in the top grades in 1960.

In 1966, Mtolo had already sensed this world coming: "At no stage before the advent of the National Party Government were schools for the Africans built by the government. We were left as we were, without any schools or educational institutions, except those built by the missionaries. But today we have schools throughout the country, in every reserve, built and maintained by the government. We have our own universities. All these plans have been ridiculed as 'tribal colleges in the bush,' but it is obvious that the government is determined to educate the African people and that it is succeeding."[5]

By 1980, a year after the South African government introduced the beginnings of compulsory education, there were 515,138 black youths in secondary schools; by 1982, 615,149, the last, a figure that does not include secondary school students in the quasi-independent homelands of Venda, Transkei and Bophuthatswana. In contrast to the 919 black students at universities in 1960 there were 8,220 in the four black universities in 1980, 11,010 by 1982, and 1,479 blacks at white universities, all full-time students. In addition, 11,656 blacks took part-time correspondence courses. In 1983 the government opened four branches of a new university for blacks that appear to resemble American community colleges, at Mamelodi (Pretoria), Bloemfontein, Soweto, and Port Elizabeth. The government sent the Africans to school, the ANC took them out.

The euphoria in South Africa broke out in a rally, in defiance of a ban, upon the withdrawal of Portugal from Mozambique on September 25, 1974. The euphoric mood also showed itself in the "Black Consciousness" movements and in the South African Students' Organization (SASO), inspired in part by a black medical student whose unassumingness left its mark on everybody he met but who remained obscure until his horrible death in police custody in September 1977, an event that shocked the world, and South Africa.

Stephen Biko showed this mood at its best. He was the real thing. He was alive and unassuming enough to recall Melville's *Billy Budd*. He was against violence. He kept his distance from the ANC. He would have nothing to do with the Communists because he knew they mean Soviet domination. But everything he did or said brought change, his presence, his words made people different. Most of the time he avoided leading because he knew people had to find their own way themselves. Born white, he would have led a turbulent life in any free country on earth. With the perlucidity of youth he saw through political systems, but he did not hate them. He thought the blacks had to change first.

In May 1976, although already banned, he gave evidence for five days at the trial of student leaders from SASO and "Black Consciousness" who were responsible for the rally on September 25 for Mozambique. His testimony, several hundred pages, is a remarkable document.[6] Just weeks before the situation degenerated into violence in Soweto on June 16, the Court had to find whether SASO and "Black Consciousness" were revolutionary organizations. It had to decide whether words that might lead to violence intended violence.

Almost everything that Biko said at this trial shows the mood of black elite students. There was real hope as well as dread, more dread than anger. "And I think the outside world is merely tackling this [discrimination in sports] to bring to the mind of white South Africa that we have got to think about change, and change is an irreversible process because, as I say, I believe in history moving in a direction that is logical to a logical end."

Biko had an uncanny sense of the change in thinking at the top of the government that was to show itself a few years later in a slow steady stream of government commissions and reforms: "The government itself has started to make moves which are calculated to offer some kind of solution"; ". . . The whole sort of political system throughout South Africa is vibrant with change right now . . ."; ". . . At the same time one must understand that there is a progressive change in attitudes which constitutes what I called a historical process yesterday. I think white society now is not at the same point as it was in 1960 . . . So that whereas perhaps at that time white society was against change, nowadays you know they may be considering listening to what the black man is saying."

"The process in fact may take well over twenty years of dialogue between Blacks and Whites. We certainly don't envisage failure. We certainly don't have an alternative. We have analyzed history. We believe that history moves in a particular logical direction, and in this particular instance the logical direction is that eventually any White society in this country is going to have to accommodate Black thinking."

He understood, not only that the blacks he worked with wanted negotiation, but also that the whites were getting ready to negotiate without knowing it:

I said to you that the whole bargaining process is not supposed to start at a particular point in history; it has started right now. You know, when we speak in these strong terms, we accept the trend of thinking of White people. When the international world condemns South Africa they accept the trend of thinking. At some point South Africa itself will begin to want to bargain in a realistic fashion other than through Bantustans. We want to be ready for this sort of thing. We want to continue mounting criticisms and pressure as a people on South Africa, so that when a period of negotiation, which is inevitable in terms of our looking at history, comes, we are there to be talked to.

When the Court asked him bluntly whether he thought "the white man in South Africa" was afraid he answered the government was ahead of the electorate:

I think the general White population may very well be under the influence of propaganda to a point where they do not realize just how inevitable change is, but I think the White leadership, especially the leadership of the three main parties in this country, is aware of the inevitability of change, and I think there is a certain fear which is gnawing at them about which direction this change should take. Okay, they certainly do not want to find themselves overtaken by events. They want to be moving with the events.

He mistook the government's readiness for some change, but its insistence on order, for mere ambivalence of men divided against themselves:

He [the white man] does two things if he is in government. On the one hand he carries out repressive measures against spokesmen of the Black people; this is why, for instance, we call it a struggle. We know that if you speak on behalf of Black people things happen to you, not because you are legally wrong, but just because you represent proper aspirations of people. You get banned, okay, you get arrested, you get detained for two years before you appear in a court like this one. On the other hand he also begins to open up, he tells Koornhof to "hamba gashli" ["Go carefully" in Xhosa] on the question of multiracial sport. All right, you begin to see two Blacks in the rugby Springbok team. He also tells somebody else to open up Nico Malan theater. In a sense it is a two-way thing.

He was unequivocally against violence because it undid consent:

Now we don't believe it [violence] is the only alternative. We believe there is a way of getting across to where we want to go by peaceful means. And the very fact that we have decided to actually form an above-board movement implies that we accept certain legal limitations in our operations.
I don't believe the whites will be deaf all the time.
When you weaken the System you can weaken aspects of the System, physical aspects, right? You can weaken the economic order. You can weaken the whole social order by creating panic amongst people, for instance, and throwing bombs like the IRA are doing in London and so on. That is now weakening the System physically. But if you are applying yourself to change the minds of the internal support, the only result and effect can be a weakening in the resolve of the governing power to continue governing as they are. Now certainly this we are interested in doing. We are interested in changing this almost stoic stance of the government to continue ruling as things are going on now. But we are not interested in weakening the physical aspects of the country, if you see what I mean.

He also took demonstrations for violence, the demonstrations the U.S. government now encourages: "We are not interested in armed struggle. We have stated clearly that we are not interested in confrontation methods—by that meaning demonstrations which lead to definite breaking of existing laws . . . Now, our operation is basically bargaining, and there is no alternative to it."

The Court asked him whether the transformation of black attitudes would lead to uncontrollable "antagonizing of the Black people": ". . . On the contrary, what I would say is that our methods do in fact give hope. I think it must be taken in the context of a situation where Black people don't have any hope, don't see any way ahead. They are just defeated persons. They live with their misery and they drink a hell of a lot because of their misery. . .":

I think the central theme about Black society is that it has got elements of a defeated society. People often look like they have given up the struggle . . . Now, this sense of defeat is basically what we are fighting against; people must not just give in to the hardship of life.

The blacks were also responsible for their depression, not only the whites, depression that could be overcome in everyday actions, not through symbolic demonstrations that blamed others justifiably but did not build strength: "Let us talk about the guy we were talking about yesterday, the [white] man who insulted his assistant . . . If the Black man had from the very beginning objected, that kind of relationship would not have developed so that . . . the White man in that situation is to blame for insulting the Black man. The Black man is also to be blamed for allowing the situation to develop . . . If he had said, No, you can't refer to me like that, I am also a father of four like you, then I am sure the White man would have thought seriously about it. But because there is no response—because the Black man just keeps quiet and accepts everything, you know—prejudice tends to build up against him, and certain practices become entrenched."

Biko was often bold. He knew the courage of words that did not miss could melt the hardness that led to self-destructive violence. He thought the blacks could overcome their fear without suicidal explosions of uncontrollable violence. He did not mean the instigated violence that sought to appear uncontrollable and spontaneous in some of the black townships, especially in 1984–86. "I am against the kind of fear that there is in the Blacks—this bottled-up fear. In a sense I am trying to get Blacks to look at issues more positively, and I am also against the kind of mentality that emanates from White society which seeks to promote that fear in Black society." Only simple everyday actions would overcome that fear:

. . . you know, the way the police rides around the townships, for instance. There is no need for them to speed at the kind of pace at which they speed normally, but somehow, as a sign of authority, as a sign of saying, "We are there," police vans just loom through townships and everybody has got to run away from the police van because it is authority. Now, this is sort of inculcated fear in Blacks, you know a fear against authority, and I am saying this is an unhealthy fear because it is the kind of fear which, if it goes unchecked, generates an uncontrollable response, some kind of blow-up . . . One gets the impression that white society wants to continually remind us of our position.

Biko also understood Vorster's turn toward Africa, begun already in 1969 but with open diplomacy in 1972, could not make sense unless it had repercussions in South Africa's domestic life. The fear of the domestic changes Vorster's foreign policy might bring had already made a break in the National Party in 1969. The Europeans, too, not only the blacks, would have to live in two worlds. Otherwise Vorster's proud words, "We are of Africa and our destiny is in Africa," would amount only to a hollow boast, a remark that shows he took South Africa's public life seriously in the way only a man who does not desire destruction can:

What we are saying now is that at the present moment we have a culture here which is a European culture. This country looks, My Lord, like a province of Europe. You know, to anybody who perceives the behavior pattern it looks like a province of Europe. It has got no relationship rootwise to the fact that it happens to exist in Africa. And when Mr. Pik Botha says at the United Nations, "We are Africans," he just doesn't know what he is talking about. We don't behave like Africans, we behave like Europeans who are staying in Africa. So we don't want to be just mere political Africans, we want to be people living in Africa. We want to be called complete Africans, we want . . . social Africans. And we don't have to go far. We just have to live with the man here, the Black man here, whose proportionate contribution in the joint culture is going to sufficiently change our joint culture to accommodate the African experience. Sure, it will have European experience, because we have Whites here who are descended from Europe. We don't dispute that. But for God's sake it must have African experience as well.

Biko might have been paraphrasing Spinola.

Biko's testimony also showed the tremendous anxieties secondary and higher education unleashed in blacks, anxieties that precipitated uproar in 1976, and, in some instances, flight from South Africa. He told of what it was like to live at the behest of three languages, a tribal language, then Afrikaans, and finally English, a remark that astonished the court because of Biko's eloquence in English:

You do not grasp enough and therefore you cannot be articulate enough, and when you play side by side with people who are more articulate than you, you tend to think that it is because they are more intelligent than you . . . I am not complaining against the language. I am merely explaining how language can help in the development of an inferiority complex . . . You grapple with the language to . . . *matric*, and before you conquer it you must apply it now to learn discipline at university. As a result you never quite catch everything that is in a book, you certainly understand the paragraph . . . I mean, I am talking about the average man now, I am not talking about exceptional cases . . .

You understand the paragraph but you are not quite adept at reproducing an argument that was in a particular book, precisely because of your failure to understand certain words in the book. This makes you less articulate as a Black man generally, and this makes you more inward looking. You feel things rather than say them. And this applies to Afrikaans as well—much more to English than to Afrikaans. Afrikaans is essentially a language that has developed here . . . It relates much better to African languages, but English is completely foreign, and therefore people find it difficult to move beyond a certain point in their comprehension of the language.

Not only living with two languages that demand unceasing back and forth between two worlds prompts insecurity. The world that the new language brings provokes despair, and sometimes anger, to deny the despair. The blacks know that world is superior, and not theirs. It makes blacks doubt they know what they want. Their own is not enough, but the other world is too much for them:

As a Black student, again, you are exposed to competition with White students in fields in which you are completely inadequate. We come from a background which is essentially peasant and worker. We do not have any form of daily contact with a highly technological society; we are foreigners in that field. When you have to go to write an essay as a Black child, the topics that are given there tally very well with White experience, but you as a Black student writing the same essay have got to grapple with something which is foreign to you—not only foreign but superior in a sense. Because of the ability of the White culture to solve so many problems in the sphere of medicine, various spheres, you tend to look at it as a more superior culture than yours. You tend to despise the peasant culture, and of course you despise the worker culture. And this inculcates in the Black man a sense of self-hatred which I think is an important determining factor in his dealings with himself and his like.

Despite their superior accomplishments, the Europeans also lack something, and know it,—something Biko senses more than says.

To some extent because of this extraordinary testimony that at moments turned into dialogue with the Court, the Court found that the organizations Biko helped inspire were not revolutionary.

The Denton Hearings tell the story of the black youths around Biko, and of the youths all over South Africa and in South West Africa they inspired, especially of the youths that fled South Africa and South West Africa after the disturbances of 1976, and came into contact with the ANC and SWAPO abroad. The hearings focus on Soviet and eastern European, and in the instance of the ANC, SACP infiltration and manipulation of these two terrorist organizations against the spreading background of war in southern Africa.

Denton began the hearing with the severity of a prince that, I am told, provoked the derisive disbelief of some of the press:

For those of you who may not realize the cost to these witnesses in testifying before this subcommittee, it is important to know that they are marked, marked for assassination. They are not simply outcasts among former associates.

After carefully weighing the risks, each made an individual decision that they would testify publicly because they realize the need to expose what is happening in southern Africa and to expose the activities and motives of the Soviet Union in that part of the world.

He went on to show a prince's grace. He had often thought, he said, that women in general could endure more suffering and pain than men, but until he encountered Miss Kave he had not understood that he had "actually encountered a woman who has undergone more suffering than I have or any of my colleagues."

Those words mean something. Denton spent eight and a half years in North Vietnamese Communist prisons, five of them in torture and under the constant threat of torture, with continual indoctrination in Marxist-Leninism, with long spells of solitary. At any moment he could have walked out "free," at the price of public repudiation of the United States. By "colleagues" Denton means James Stockdale and other American flyers who did the same life in the Communist prisons of Hanoi.[7]

Denton counts as much as the witnesses in these hearings. He suffers no involuntary condescension in their presence, the involuntary condescension that sometimes possesses people in the face of suffering they have not experienced. His respect is self-evident. He knows the world of the victims with the uncanny familiarity of a mature man returning to the cities of his youth. He knows instantly when the victims cannot say what they want, when they are leaving something crucial out. He knows also the mind of the torturers, how the torturers think. You can almost hear them breathe in his words. His interjections are sometimes unnerving because they show you how little you understand of a world that is at the same time familiar and totally alien to Denton.

The ANC and SWAPO tried to recruit the youths once they had fled abroad. Some joined willingly, others refused, others were kidnapped into the organizations.

The youths from South West Africa who found themselves in SWAPO had even less of a notion of what they were getting into than youths from the black townships in South Africa. They had wanted an education beyond high school, not available then in South West Africa. The SWAPO radio from Lusaka had said they could get educated in Zambia. Their pastors encouraged them to leave. These were youths who for the most part had never seen a city, but had had good elementary education. They knew the Bible. Some spoke in both Afrikaans and English.

All of the youths who joined the ANC or SWAPO discovered they could not leave without risking their lives. Once in the organizations they were horrified by their regimentation, their cynicism, and their intolerance of open discussion and questioning. They broke with them, often in circumstances their testimony does not reveal, only after they crossed clandestinely into South Africa or South West Africa on SWAPO or ANC terrorist missions. In some instances the South African police caught them, in others they surrendered willingly. The South African government did what it could to encourage those who had fled to come home.

Well, from my own experience and some of the people whom I met, the government in South Africa is prepared to accept young students, even those who were involved in the African National Congress, if they had returned to South Africa.

For instance, immediately after June 16, 1976 [the Soweto disturbances] erupted, there were some arrangements that were done between parents of students or children involved and the South African government that if they have any other way of making contact with their own children to come back to South Africa, this will be accepted and welcome to the South African government, and this is what is happening today.

Like many policies of the South African government, this policy of recovering youths trapped in terrorism by their defiance is not new. It started a few years after the ANC began "recruiting" for terrorism in late 1961, probably after the arrest of Mandela in 1963, as Mtolo reported in 1966:

The government has now made certain concessions for the release of young people convicted of sabotage if the parents apply for the release of their children. Unfortunately, some of the parents do not even know where their children are, as many left without their knowledge. In other cases the parents are uneducated people who do not know what procedure to follow in order to obtain the release of their children. The people who did the recruiting are of course lying low, or are safely overseas, while the boys have to suffer. When these recruits come out they will not even be able to explain that they were not politicians but were drawn only by the chances of visiting foreign countries.

Mtolo who had drawn unsuspecting youths including his only brother into the terror network, could not get the faces of these youths out of his memory: "I have met some of the boys from other provinces who were arrested and it upset me to learn that the leaders had not even told them that they were going for military training. They were quite innocent and went into the thing innocent of all political implications. I heard of a boy suspected of being a police informer, who was told that he was being sent for further education. When he arrived in Lobatsi he was told he was now a soldier and was to be sent for military training. He was forced into it and had no choice but to submit. Later he was arrested with others."[8]

Two former members of SWAPO told Denton they had operated as terrorists because they had no choice. They were free because the SADF had released them after capture and rough debriefing. They adapted to circumstances but they had learned the difference between a terrorist organization and a government.

Like the youths Mtolo remembered nearly a generation earlier, these young men and women were the cannon fodder of these organizations, and they sensed it. Shipped in some instances half-way around the world, they never left the underworld of the small guerrilla camps with their incessant political indoctrination and training in sabotage and violence. They never saw headquarters, or talked to the leaders whom they heard on their occasional visits to the training camps. They feared even to talk to each other.

Ready to fight if it was necessary, they were not about to let themselves be turned into professional killers who would murder blindly upon orders. They knew the difference between a soldier and a murderer, the distinction Buthelezi drew when he rejected the ANC's violence publicly in 1983. But they had become completely dependent on the organizations for food and livelihood: There is no way out except at the risk of one's life. They realized they were in prison, in a moving prison that would spread to the whole of South Africa and South West Africa if these organizations won.

In their testimony in Washington, their strong feelings were evident in their will to speak out, but their words still bore traces of the bureaucratese of their indoctrination. They still did not call the killings of members who objected or tried to leave *murders*. Instead they said that you could only leave the organization in a "military way," which means "the person has to be killed" by stabbing in the kidneys that brings instant death. They speak of "orders to execute secretly" and "confirmation reports."

The words of these youths have the distance and the bureaucratic coolness of men who once believed and then turned into unwilling accomplices—who still fall unawares into the newspeak of the indoctrination they cannot forget.

The second man who I know was killed was a man by the name of Pedro, who belonged to the machinery of the African National Congress in Botswana. And he was dissatisfied and disillusioned about the ANC, and told ANC members that he would no longer take part in any activity of the ANC.

But then the report was sent to headquarters and the head of the military department, of which I was a member, decided that the man must be executed secretly and buried in Botswana. And this was done, and I reported the confirmation report that the man had been killed.

People did not hear about the murders. The killings are mostly secret. Men who wanted to leave or objected simply disappeared. The uncertain threat of death always hung in the air,—the dreadful creature of ideologies that dread doubt most of all, the doubt that in its different characters in Socrates, Montaigne, Shakespeare, Descartes, and Hume is the deepest expression of the modesty of freedom in the West:

With my own experience, it [to leave the ANC] is an offense punishable by long-time prison or by death, because I know several people who attempted genuinely to register their dissatisfaction and disillusionment about this. But unfortunately, a majority of them are in prison or are *killed secretly. Nobody can ever know* (Italics mine).

The murders may look "spontaneous," but they are always ordered from above, as Denton had learned of the even apparently casual brutalities and humiliations of his prisons.

Another witness, a young man from Soweto, who discovered in Angola in a camp near Luanda, that the education the ANC promised him was actually training in the use of explosives for sabotage, told Denton refusal would have meant jail:

Well, normally [upon refusal of training] what they do is they would call you a traitor or they would lock you into jail somewhere in Angola.

The youths from SWAPO told the same story: "If a person wanted to leave SWAPO, it could only be done in a military way: that means the person has to be killed."

There are also routine murders, also reported in the youths' familiar newspeak. One witness told of an order from the Lusaka headquarters of the ANC for "execution" of an ANC cadre who had killed another cadre with a clearly Russian sounding name, Zabochev, but not identified as Soviet in the testimony, supposedly "over a woman." The ANC had abducted the man to Lusaka from Botswana where he had fled for refuge from Zimbabwe.

... And he gave me orders that I must instruct the administration staff in Zimbabwe to dig a grave, and I must transport this Pismo to an agreed spot where the administrative staff would be waiting, and the man must be stabbed in the kidneys and immediately be thrown in the hole and buried, and that was done.

The readiness to murder, to turn the youths in terrorist organizations into accomplices, only continues the force and deceit that originally trapped the youths into these organizations. They told of raids into northern South West Africa to abduct school-children into SWAPO. In 1977, a group of 100 kidnapped 150 children near a military base:

Many of the children were crying because they did not want to go to Angola: it was not their willingness. And after that we bring the students in Angola, up to Vietnam [a SWAPO base attacked by the South Africa Defense Force in its incursion into Angola in

1978] where the regional commander stayed. And when Nakada [the commander] saw the students he called his political commissar so that he could speak to the students: it means to give them some politics. I know all the students were trained as military men or cadres.

Another witness told of a brother kidnapped by SWAPO:

One of my brothers was kidnapped by SWAPO. He was at school at Odibo and then he was taken to Angola where he was sent to the GDR [East Germany] for training.

In 1983, there were 278 such abductions; in 1984, 106, according to a report of the South African administrator general of South West Africa of January 22, 1985.

The abducted were taught to return home and abduct others. They were taught to operate in small groups for the purpose of terrorizing the tribes in Ovamboland, in northern South West Africa just across the border from Angola, into submission. This meant raids, not only to abduct children into SWAPO, but also to murder individuals, especially tribal leaders. Some of their fellows were as young as fourteen, one was ten years old. One of them in a group of twelve was sent to the Soviet Union for six months to "study underground work and intelligence." In Angola they were instructed with sticks for the most part instead of guns because the leaders feared they might desert with real weapons.

Denton put his finger on the significance of the murder of ANC and SWAPO members. The war was not only against supposed enemies but against everybody, and, therefore, he implied, of increasing intensity, unlimited and irresolvable:

I have watched the citizens of North Vietnam, for example, and now Vietnam, show their hatred and contempt for the system in which they had to live and perform.
Would you think it is fair to say that in the case of the ANC and your association with communism as it is being applied in Africa, that not only do they apply terrorism against their perceived enemies—those whom they want to defeat—but they apply terrorism within their own ranks to rule those who are considered their own people, their own servants?

The murder of members in the camps scattered throughout the bush promises the sealing of frontiers, the trapping of "citizens" behind frontiers, that occurs after Communist seizure of the state, an imprisonment unheard of before in human history, another twentieth century first.

The huge portraits of Che Guevara, Fidel Castro, and Lenin in Angola baffled these youths. In preparation for their obliteration in the world terrorist movement, they were made to celebrate Communist, but not ANC, holidays:

On July 29, 1977, we celebrated an important Cuban day. The instructors told us it was the day in 1953 when Fidel Castro attacked the Moncada Barracks, which eventually led to his accession to power. The Cubans presented a play that evening which symbolized the attack.
On the 17th of October 1977, we had the afternoon off to celebrate the Great

October Socialist Revolution Day. During our training no big ANC days were celebrated, and that led to considerable dissatisfaction among the recruits.

The morale of the recruits at the camp was very bad. Many recruits wanted to go back to South Africa. In March of 1977, one of the instructors shot himself as a result of poor conditions.

These holidays also meant to prepare them for training in the Soviet Union and eastern Europe. But in the Soviet Union they also had to keep up more conventional appearances. They were to tell the local people in Russia they were students, in short, to profess, almost as at a show trial, that they had realized the dream that had enticed some of them into SWAPO and the ANC. A guerrilla training camp near Rostov in eastern Germany betrayed little out of the ordinary: "The appearance was civilian and, from outside, it looked quite innocent, except for the high security fence."

When they left South Africa, these youths left their parents and brothers and sisters, but they did not mention any of this, because they fled without leave-taking. You only hear of parents and friends when they return to South Africa after training on ANC sabotage missions, and sneak off to visit them. The youths returned home to their parents and relatives before they surrendered to the South African police. They needed their parents' confidence to surrender. It was on these visits to relatives they had not mentioned even missing that they remembered their names. They had been stripped of their names upon "recruitment," in typical Communist fashion.

The world made of flights from Botswana to Lusaka, from Lusaka to Dar es Salaam and Angola, and then to Berlin and Moscow, in which everything seemed possible and they were in control of nothing, disappeared as quickly as a nightmare. The years of indoctrination that sought to master and immobilize their thought, to make it impossible for them to listen even to what stirred of its own in their minds, to make it impossible to consult everyday common sense, went dumb.

Even in the distance of their words you can sense their relief, and the glow of familiarity and of shame they perhaps do not know they feel because these things are too deep and embarrassing for words, especially for youths fresh from a world in which their words had known everything; understood everything; and never ceased from abstraction; in which, the crowning abstraction, they had not known the names of their commanders.

When these youths say, ". . . One of the most serious problems that we used to face in sustaining our operation within the country was the lack of political sympathy from the people," they mean the faces of their parents, sisters and brothers, and the friends they saw upon their return to South Africa as secret agents. In the soberness of safety, these youths barely in their middle twenties speak a language not too different from P.W. Botha's:

So, I came to the conclusion that the only solution left for all the people involved was to sort of secure a free, systematic, evolutionary change so that all the parties involved should come together and solve their problems peacefully.

One of the most important points that pushed me into this decision was that the aims and the objectives of the ANC, in reality were one and the same thing with the objectives of the Communist Party in South Africa.

The other problem which led to my decision [to leave] was the ANC involvement with Communists. We subsequently were to sort of bring a situation where the ANC would be irrelevant to South African politics and would even complicate much more the immediate problem that the African people are facing in that country.

Like the SACP, the ANC wanted a "socialist revolution" to succeed the "liberation of the black people":

And this [the "socialist revolution"], in my opinion, is going to complicate a lot of historical development and political economy, because history has proved that it has cost the lives of millions of people. Many people are killed in the process of what they may call the dictatorship of the proletariat, and a lot of suffering and killing of democratic forces who are opposed to this type of system.

Twenty years earlier Mtolo had also come to realize his violence, he had been involved in twenty-eight sabotage attempts in and around Durban in 1962, made things worse, not better:

I knew that if I was arrested it would be the end of my days in this world, but it was even more torturing to think that I was in this mess, because I had thought I was doing something good for my people. In reality, as I was beginning to realize, I was doing something which was not going to do any good but which brought misery and hardship to them. The people who engineered this were somewhere safe, moving around Trafalgar Square in England addressing meetings, or sitting in posh offices in North Africa, Moscow and Peking, or having tea parties as VIP's . . . I came back to Durban [after a meeting with the "High Command" of Umkhonto we Sizwe in Johannesburg] more disillusioned than ever. The very people who were supposed to be fighting to end the misery and hardship among the black people were worse than imperialists.[9]

In 1985, seven former members of SWAPO testified before the *Internationale Gesellschaft für Menschenrechte* (IGFM) in Frankfurt.[10] They not only confirmed in all important details the testimony of the youths before the Denton Committee but also gave much more information about the SWAPO training and punishment camps all over southern Africa, but especially in Angola and Zambia. These descriptions, the indoctrination, the repression, the murder of men who criticize or want to leave, apply also to ANC camps. For in Angola, the ANC and SWAPO often train together in the same camps. They also fight UNITA in FAPLA (the MPLA's army) units. These witnesses also make it clear that in Zambia, and sometimes in Botswana, the governments are unable to control the ANC and SWAPO who murder and abduct with impunity.

The witnesses before IGFM tell the same story of enticement, deception and finally force that trapped them in terrorism. For one witness it had all started more than ten years before in October 1975 when she had left secondary school in Windhoek, a naive outspoken girl of sixteen: ". . . I did not feel like staying in Namibia any more, as was the case with many others . . . In those days we did not know the full truth and did not know what was awaiting us."

Anything seemed possible, and it was: "For us it was something like a matter of prestige to get out of Namibia. We wanted to have a better education, wanted to go to schools outside Namibia because we had better chances there."

In Lusaka she had taken a course at the UN Institute for Namibia in Management and Development Studies. At the Institute she had come into contact with SWAPO members who attacked her because she was a member of the South West African National Union (SWANU), an organization that had challenged SWAPO with a declaration at the UN and at the OAU that it would fight, even with arms, any government in South West Africa not democratically elected. "Time and again we had trouble with SWAPO, were bothered and vilified by them. They insulted us with names such as 'reactionaries,' 'puppets' and 'paper tigers.'"

Political indoctrination started as harassment: "We were constantly under pressure from SWAPO in the Institute as well as during our leisure time." There were blows.

In January 1979, she joined SWAPO because she could no longer stand it: "I joined SWAPO later, because I merely wanted to be left in peace." The pressure let off despite underlying unease: "Well, it was better then." She could concentrate on her studies. "But I never had the feeling I was really accepted [by SWAPO], because I was a former member of SWANU."

In January 1981 she was ordered to Angola: "It was an order by SWAPO. I did not dare to oppose." She was to get, it turned out, not the education she wanted but the education that counts in the twentieth century, but that few, except those who have had it first hand, take seriously.

In Angola at the Tobias Hainyako Training Center in Lubango she immediately saw through the life she had embraced for the sake of a little peace: "I was thunderstruck . . . I only met with mistrust and rejection, it was unbelievable: They knew that earlier I had been with SWANU. They said that I had been sent by SWANU in order to destabilize SWAPO. I was put through a political rolling press and was eternally being indoctrinated. I very quickly regretted that I had joined SWAPO." For the first six months in Angola she had military training.

A nurse who had gone abroad, not in pursuit of a dream, but only to see relatives:

I left Namibia in February or March in 1980 to visit relatives in Botswana. First I was in Gaborone and then in Francistown. Here SWAPO people talked to me and invited me. The people in the SWAPO office in Francistown persuaded me not to return to Namibia. In Namibia I would not only be exploited, badly paid and would have no work opportunities. It was easy for them to get the better of me. It was the first time I had been outside Namibia and was certainly easily impressed. In any case they promised me that SWAPO would organize better education for me—in fact in Dar es Salaam. There was I to take courses at an institution for SWAPO supporters, this training would be free of charge. I agreed to that.

Once she agreed, "everything happened very quickly." The SWAPO men who had talked to her assumed she was "a spy for the Boers." They more or less abducted her at the airport in Francistown, Botswana, on to a plane for Lusaka, not Dar es Salaam. "But suddenly I was aboard a plane to Lusaka, there was no talk anymore about Dar es Salaam . . . I was scared":

We drove to a house of SWAPO in the suburb of Lilanda. I resisted and wanted to go back. Nobody wanted to hear about training. I was locked into a little room and was interrogated for hours. I was under suspicion of being a spy that worked for the South Africans. I was totally confused and became more and more frightened. I do not know exactly anymore for how many days I was detained in Lusaka. Until today I do not know why I was specifically under suspicion.

She thought they suspected her because she was a Herero, a tribe of ninety thousand, not an Ovambo. SWAPO is made up almost all of Ovambos:

SWAPO is very suspicious of Hereros; they do not like us. It was psychological terrorism, always the same questions and threats. Everywhere in the house were posters and slogans "Be alert," "Watch our for spies."

These posters will line the streets of Windhoek should SWAPO manage to seize power.

After this interrogation, she was shipped to a camp in Nyango in western Zambia four hundred kilometers from Lusaka, called a "Health and Education Center." "The guards there told me that I had to be re-educated,"—the same phrase used in Vietnam, Cambodia, Laos. Officially a refugee camp administered by SWAPO with money from the UN and European nations, Nyango was actually a prison:

But first and foremost it is a prison. For me it was hell on earth. Only there I realized that I was a prisoner of SWAPO for whatever reason that might have been. In Nyango, they first of all took away my watch and radio for the reason that I would not be able to make contact with others. Together with other prisoners they locked me in a cell, actually a wooden cage, primitively assembled. They still could watch us the whole time through the wooden bars that formed the walls of the cell. We had to sleep on the bare floor and had no blankets. No toilets were in the cell, only holes dug into the earth. The stench was terrible. At five o'clock in the mornings we had to wash ourselves in the river, it was bitterly cold. During the day we, as women, had to lift and clean latrines and dig trenches. We as women had to do heavy labor. All my nails broke off and I was totally exhausted and I permanently had a cold. At five o'clock in the evenings they took our clothes away so that we could not escape. Yes we had to sleep naked, so that we could not escape during the night. We were kept like animals. And in the night it was often so very cold. I was glad when it became warm again in the day, when I could work.

After two months she was judged broken enough to return to Lusaka and a bit of the education she yearned for:

Apparently my political re-education was over. For a time I was even allowed to attend a course in Public Administration at the UN Institute for Namibia in Lusaka. But time and again I was harassed by SWAPO, I was watched and interrogated. I had to tell whom I met, to whom I wrote letters, what I was doing. They were still very suspicious and threatened me with all possible things should I spy for South Africa. I then left the course at the UNO Institute because I could no longer bear the spying and threats.

She went into hiding in Lusaka. A SWAPO commando of four men found her:

In panic I jumped out of the window from the fifth floor. I could have broken my neck. But I fell on a shrub or onto the lawn and crept away and hid in the dark. My foot was broken, teeth had fallen out and my skin was torn. I am so disfigured that people would not recognize me anymore.

She jumped because she had feared they would take her back to the camp at Nyango.

Like many people fleeing SWAPO or the ANC, she had gone to the Zambian police who advised her to go to the UN High Commissioner for Refugees (UNHCR): "The police did not even take my statement, they are powerless. They only advised me to turn to the UNHCR." SWAPO tried to abduct her in front of the UN official's house. After two months SWAPO found her on a farm of Dutch aid development workers, ten kilometers outside of Lusaka. Again, she went to the police who told her to go to the UNHCR:

But that was pointless [at the police]. They only told me that I should turn to the UNO offices. The office of the UNHCR refused any help. They did not want to do anything against SWAPO. One man of the UNO even told me that I should go to SWAPO and work as a nurse in a camp.

She did not know where to turn when she found the organizations supposed to help, did not believe her:

It was unbelievable. Nobody wanted to help me. I was so desperate that I even thought of suicide. Once I even ran into the way of a car because I did not want to live anymore, but the driver managed to swerve the car around.

The callousness of UN officials on the spot betrays the same rigidity as their home office whose resolutions, broadcast daily to all of Africa, are taken for international law, not mere propaganda. Both will not acknowledge living facts. They act as if the world were made of words,—contemporary magic. The UN officials in the bush would not see what was before their eyes, or believe the words of suffering. They would not see realities the UN in New York denied.

Another witness, a teacher who had almost been shot by the tribal police in Ovamboland in South West Africa who "were always ready to shoot," joined SWAPO willingly in 1977. At first SWAPO welcomed him "with open arms": "They even promised me a place to study so that I could at last get a good training as a teacher . . . I must say, at the beginning SWAPO was very concerned about me. They especially tried to get the teachers on their side because we had better training and could draw other people with us."

But then he was told by "SWAPO functionaries" there was a war on: ". . . After independence you can study, not now." He had not imagined it that way:

But then all of a sudden everything was different: I had to go to the Tobias Hainyako Training Center in Lubango for military training . . . That was not what I had visualized. Then I realized: You have no rights in Angola, you are at the mercy of SWAPO. I had no choice, I had to go along with military training. I went along with that because I thought, you can still study later. Because they had promised that to me.

Military training also meant "political schooling" that turned the teacher who had wanted to learn more into a "political instructor." For a while he operated in camps in Angola. In 1979 still dreaming of the education promised him, he was sent to East Germany for ten months, to Wihelm Pieck High School in Bogensee near Berlin, for "political education":

Actually at first we were optimistic. We thought, here we shall get a clean, decent education, that will help us later in our occupation. They had told us that with this education we should later belong to the leadership stratum when Namibia became independent. We were proud that we had been selected. In Bogensee there were many students from Africa, comrades from the South African ANC, from ZAPU of Zimbabwe, from Mozambique, Zambia and Madagascar.

But the reality again disappointed his expectations, harshly. He received only dogmatic political indoctrination that showed its true face to him, not so much in its words, but in the prohibitions that accompanied it: They could not go where they wanted, or look at what they wanted. They were not to go to church,—an order that more than anything else showed him the world he was trapped in. He had taught in mission schools in Namibia. He had probably never imagined that somebody might try to keep him from worship. He saw that the dogma of the phrases repeated and repeated betrayed the same rigidity as the prohibitions against looking and seeing; he was neither to think or move on his own:

But the education was not what we had expected. We had classes in Marxist philosophy, scientific communism, the history of revolution and political economy. The political training was very exacting. It was pure theory without practical use for our people in Namibia. Again and again we heard the same sentences and slogans. Apart from that we felt imprisoned. Every day we had political schooling about the advantages of Socialism. But we did not have the right to move freely, to go where we wanted to. We saw very little. Once there was an organized tour through the GDR, when they wanted to show us how well the people live in a Communist society. It bothered me that we were not allowed to go to church. I am a devout Christian and was a teacher at mission schools. Then I understood how they wanted to eliminate Christianity. I dearly would have liked to attend a church service, but we did not dare to do so.

The attack on God during his years of indoctrination into the SACP moved Mtolo, who unlike the SWAPO teacher had never believed, towards God as he sought his way out of the violence that had trapped him, a slow conversion he is too bashful to tell in detail that underlies his whole account. "Suddenly God seemed very real to me," he recalled his arrest that he expected would bring torture, and death, swiftly, not regeneration: "My mind was blank while they [the police] were talking to me. I was not interested in anything in this world . . . I was thinking about my own personal sins, because I had no doubt that I would never see the Supreme Court. That afternoon I was going to die, I felt sure, because there was no force in the world which would make me talk."

But his courage was not made only of desperation and hardness of soul: "God would never punish me for what I had done. He knew how I was dragged into it and He would understand. I preferred to die."

The SACP's attack on God had been essential to turning him to violence, he came to realize towards the end of his account:

The idea [in SACP indoctrination] is to condition the minds of students in such a way that when they want something they will not kneel down and pray, or expect some miracle to happen, but will fight even if it demands the spilling of blood, until they achieve their aim. This must be done without any fear of God.[11]

After ten months, the SWAPO teacher returned to a "Health and Education Center" in Angola, in Cuanza-Sul province, a deputy political commissioner. A mission teacher transformed into an apparatchik, a "new man." He understood that political indoctrination, to stifle all opposition, was the other face of the constant spying and surveillance: "Time and again people are gathered for political meetings and have to listen to Marxist propaganda for hours on end . . . It is torture if you have to listen to these speeches on an empty stomach."

He learned to recognize the prototypes for the world SWAPO was building: "SWAPO has learned a lot from the methods used by the Soviet Union and the GDR"; "Those who are merely under suspicion that they are against SWAPO are put into prison, just simply disappear." "Political education" needs spying, for spying seeks to detect the deviation indoctrination means to prevent: "The camp leadership takes political education very seriously. Everything is regulated according to the Communist example. Everyone is watched and spied on. The camp leadership has its eyes and ears everywhere to sniff out the politically unreliable people among the refugees."

The indoctrination and spying make opposition unthinkable: "The people realize very quickly that resistance is very dangerous. He who is against SWAPO is finished. He who opens his mouth is dead":

In August 1981 three men from our camp were shot because they were dissatisfied and did not shut their mouths. They interrupted a speech by Nujoma with interjections. They used swearwords, I do not know precisely anymore what they shouted. Be that as it may, they were led away by the military police, interrogated and later shot in Lubango. That was also a disciplinary measure so that everyone knew what would happen to him if he criticized the leadership. In this way any opposition is suppressed. Everybody is afraid.

Another witness testifying anonymously who had joined SWAPO in 1974, told how he was taken for a spy because he criticized. "I opened my mouth widely. I criticized the bad equipment and supplies. SWAPO then arrested me and maintained that I was a spy and agent of the Boers, who had to instigate the people." He was sent away to a concentration camp for "dissidents and spies,"—hendiadys,—the camp of Mboroma in Zambia:

> Many of my comrades there died of starvation. It was unbelievably terrible. We were so weak that we could not walk anymore. There were women there who gave birth to children that died the same day due to their weakened state. I was imprisoned there for eleven months. Dear God, it was hell on earth. The people were as thin as skeletons and crept through their own feces like animals . . . Once a week we received food, only mealy meal, beans and Kapenta [dried fish], which they threw into the earth holes where we were kept. SWAPO and the Zambian army guarded the camp. Those who tried to escape were shot.

He told how nobody has seen these camps in Zambia "because they are concentration camps." Besides Mboroma he mentioned Nyango and another camp in Senanga in the Western Province of Zambia.

Without time or money to build prisons that would attract attention, SWAPO casts its prisoners into the earth: "The people are imprisoned in earth holes up to six meters deep and they have to climb down with the help of ropes." He approached the OAU instead of the UN. But the OAU too cannot see facts for words:

> I tried to smuggle letters to Kassiber which were then to be sent to the Liberation Committee of the OAU. In these letters I described the conditions in the camp, starvation, misery and the death of people. But I never heard a thing. Nobody reacted. I thought, this is the end of you. Here you will kick the bucket. After my release I was destined to go to the front again, but I escaped and disappeared.

Like the nurse this anonymous witness pointed to tribal hatreds, and also murder within SWAPO:

> In any case, the important roles in SWAPO are only played by Ovambos. Other tribes are systematically discriminated against and eliminated. I say this, although I myself came from Ovamboland. For instance, many people of the East-Caprivi were shot dead, because the Ovambos did not like them . . . Also in PLAN [SWAPO's terrorist organization] only Ovambos can get to the top and have positions such as commanders. These are the rules of the game in SWAPO.

Another witness betrayed no regret. He had joined SWAPO in 1974 because he wanted an education he could not afford in South West Africa: "SWAPO promised me that I could have free studies outside Namibia." Instead of education, he accepted terrorist training because "he did not want to hang about in the refugee camp":

> I was surprised when I heard that I should go to the Soviet Union for my training. I received my travelling documents and, together with fifty or sixty other recruits, was

taken by truck to Dar es Salaam. Here we flew with an aeroplane of Aeroflot to Moscow. Then we were taken to a training camp in the Krim, thirty kilometers away from Simferopol on the road to Yalta. Here we met people from the liberation movements in Mozambique, Zimbabwe, Angola, Guinea-Bissau and Oman. For ten months I stayed in Russia. We were mainly trained in the handling of artillery weapons, for instance the 122 millimeter rocket-apparatus, but also the smaller grenade apparatus and aiming mechanisms and anti-aircraft defense weapons. August 1975 I returned to Zambia.

In 1981, South African soldiers captured him in Angola.

All former members of SWAPO and the ANC who took to hiding in Zambia, often in Lusaka, and even the few who hid out in Angola, speak in terror of SWAPO and ANC squads and spies that roam with impunity in supposedly sovereign Zambia whose leader is treated with respect in Europe and the United States. These refugees number hundreds, perhaps thousands, according to the anonymous witness.

Hundreds have deserted SWAPO in the last few years, perhaps even thousands. In the last few months at least seven people who were formerly with SWAPO have been abducted from Zambia to Angola [in 1985]. This is practically their death sentence, but I want to stay alive.

Such numbers mean constant turmoil within SWAPO: The gulag does not come easily to Africans. These refugees who flee know something of the stuff of freedom they took for granted. They did not have to be taught it. But in their flesh and blood they had to be taught the history of Europe, of the other Europe since the War.

They wander about like ghosts often without the papers that count for life in the chaos just underneath the surface of daily life, ghosts that have tasted the possible future of southern Africa. For nineteen months the woman who had fled secondary school in Windhoek, a young girl, ran and hid in her own make-shift prisons in Kaunda's Zambia: From January 15 to July 25, 1983, "I did not see the sun once."

Some of these witnesses still live this life even as I write. For instance, the anonymous:

I am continuously on the run, since I left SWAPO. I disappeared so that they cannot catch me . . . For a long time I have been outside of Lusaka and have been hiding in the copper-belt or in the north-western province or other provinces of Zambia. They hunt dissidents and deserters, they are damned powerful here and have many spies. A special unit, the Discipline Squad, searches hotels and bars and other meeting places to look for us. They have weapons and lots of money. This is a killer brigade against "enemies" and dissidents, who, with the help of a black list, search for certain people. They drive fast cars and have good connections. They are very dangerous. Their leader is a certain James Awala, a nasty character. They can interrogate and torture people, also shoot them or lock them up. Here they may do everything. They approach a woman if they suspect her husband of being an agent for the enemy. They offer drinks or give money or send a woman to you. They know all the tricks. Everyone who has criticized Nujoma is finished off by them. They have learned a lot from the Russian KGB . . .

The nurse: "I live in constant fear that they will still abduct me. Before this discussion [her testimony was apparently taken in Lusaka] I was also afraid, I thought that it could be a trap of SWAPO"; "Even today I am all nerves. In Lusaka I cannot move freely anymore, or at best if friends take me somewhere and protect me. I myself never go shopping and hardly dare to leave my hiding place."

She described the pursuit gangs that roam the streets and bars of Lusaka: "They spread terror and fear among the refugees from Namibia. They finish everybody who does not cooperate with SWAPO unconditionally. I say to achieve this they shall stop at nothing: torture, abduction, murder." Unlike the Congress of the United States these ghosts do not call murder "execution."

Her description betrayed the same world as the anonymous. But she added that the pursuit squads hunt not only "deserters" but also those who help:

They also pursued the people who helped me. I may not mention any names or details about this. Also my friends who hid me were hunted by SWAPO. One of them was interrogated outside in the bush: They wanted him to divulge my and other refugee's whereabouts. Somewhere near him they gave two shots and then said: "The third one is for you, if you do not talk!" The gang responsible for these criminal acts is the "Discipline Squad," as SWAPO calls them. Their leader is a man called James Awala. It is sort of a special unit that goes for the so-called "dissidents," unreliable elements and all sorts of suspicious people. They have weapons, more than enough money and full powers granted to them by the SWAPO leadership. Even, should one of them be arrested by the Zambian police, he for sure will be free the next day due to pressure from above. This gang combs the bars and hotels of Lusaka and search for people who do not want to have anything to do with SWAPO any more. James Awala and his men are very powerful. Nothing can happen to them, it doesn't matter what they do. They will stop at nothing in their hunt for dissidents, so-called spies and traitors. This James and his people are devils, they act by order of the SWAPO leadership.

The woman who had left parents and school in Windhoek in 1975 testified that the Zambians in their own capital, Lusaka, also fear the SWAPO and ANC killers. To find cover until nightfall after she had escaped from a SWAPO "safehouse", "scantily dressed with a T-shirt and a curtain which I had wrapped around me," she knocked randomly and desperately at the houses in the neighborhood: "The woman was just as scared as I was: She said they will shoot us all if they find you here. She had often heard shots from the SWAPO house." Four days before, the woman from Windhoek had been abducted in the middle of Lusaka: "They said that I was a spy of the Boers—and that I should finally admit it." She managed to stay in the house she had fled to until dark despite the Zambian woman's repeated requests she leave: "Since then I do not dare to leave the house, so that they do not catch me again and lock me up."

She had the SWAPO gang, the "commando unit" roaming the dusty bush capital, before her eyes always:

The special commando unit of SWAPO do not have anything to fear here in Lusaka. They know the police will not interfere. The police in Zambia cannot hold their own against SWAPO and do not want to have anything to do with the problems of the refugees. Here this gang can achieve anything with money or through force of arms. They have a free hand in all their assignments, no matter whether it is murder, abduction or torture.

The UNHCR had as usual been of no help after her abduction: "There nobody could help me."

SWAPO and the ANC get by airport officials who in pantomime of the formalities of airports in law-abiding countries meticulously stop the men and women fleeing SWAPO and the ANC because they have no papers:

They have repeatedly abducted Namibians from Lusaka to Angola. These people are just taken to the airport and put on the plane to Luanda, either the Aeroflot or the machine of TAAG, the Angolan airways company. At the airport they arrange everything through bribery. There they pay 100 Kwacha or more when they drag someone onto the machine to Luanda.

At the end, she said:

In SWAPO there is no justice or freedom, only the contrary: terror, control, suspicion, spying and violence. Those who want to survive in SWAPO may not ask questions, must only act according to orders and must keep quiet. SWAPO is a terrorist organization. If Sam Nujoma takes over in Namibia then it will be worse than it was under Idi Amin in Uganda.

The witnesses of IGFM also gave a much more detailed picture of the camps in Zambia and Angola than the Denton witnesses. Except for the outright punishment camps that are hidden, the camps seek to appear like the usual refugee camps. The areas UN, OAU and other visitors see are mainly for women and children and wounded terrorists. The other areas are for those who oppose, criticize or "desert," and who are not murdered outright, to die in.

The camps also produce children for SWAPO. In Zambia, children are a by-product of rape and degradation; in Angola, at least in the notorious camp in Cuanza-Sul province, three or four hundred kilometers south of Luanda, the women are bred cold-bloodedly like cattle.

But even at the camp in Cuanza-Sul they keep up appearances: "Children and young people attend schools, the sick and injured are looked after in hospitals. Old people are nursed here, there are kindergartens, doctors and teachers. SWAPO always says, here is shelter for all those who have fled from the war and oppression in Namibia. That is true, but it is only part of the truth." These words may betray the witnesses' former training in political indoctrination. For according to another witness, even in these areas open to visitors the conditions are grim, but perhaps no more grim than in many other refugee camps in the world. The rain, wind, mist and sun rot the tents of the refugees to tatters. Only the camp personnel live in brick houses: "The people were ill and apathetic. Many small children had bloated bellies because of malnutrition. Many became mad in this misery, especially the women who were totally weakened. There were women who lost their minds and ran through the camp without clothes."

But there were areas visitors never saw that made these conditions look like the rosy description of the former political indoctrinator:

However, almost nobody saw the most horrible areas of the camp. Those were the holes in which the "traitors," "spies" and so-called dissidents had to stay . . . Here people who are regarded as politically unreliable or have at some time or other criticized SWAPO, disappear without a trace, but also men who didn't want to fight anymore.

The prisoners spend the night in these holes deeply dug into the ground, the day in labor to exhaustion:

The prisoners are kept in underground cells: holes deeply sunk into the earth, like a cage. During the day the prisoners have to work very hard, up to the point of exhaustion. Digging out trenches, carrying water, collecting and piling up wood. In the evening they have to go back into the earth holes. They are kept there in the most cramped conditions, men and women together. One dozen people are cramped into one room of two by four meters. The stench is horrible. Many suffer diarrhea or colds. The latrines are only emptied once a week.

In Nyango in Zambia the word prostitution still has meaning,—in contrast to the camp in Angola. "In Nyango prostitution was a matter of course. Nobody took any notice." Like flight, or speaking your mind, to resist was barely thinkable: "Those who were new might still have resisted, but then the women were simply raped." There was no saying "no": "You cannot say 'no' to a commander or camp officer if he wants you. But later they actually did not have to force the women anymore. There were fourteen or sixteen year old girls who had children by SWAPO officers." The camp officers and guards gave food, "many times even sugar, salt, mealy meal, milk" to the women who went along:

I was also raped, not just once . . . It was actually madness. The women had to bring children into the world, but in camp one could not feed them properly and look after them . . .

In the camp in Angola, there is not even the hatred and violence of rape, a desperate sign of life, but a sign of life nevertheless—just mere flesh: "For the women the camp in Cuanza-Sul is a prison where they have to get pregnant as often as possible and have to bring children into the world. The women are treated like breeding stock so that SWAPO can get a new generation"; "All pregnant women go into the so-called A-camp. It is what one might call a 'breeding farm' for Namibian children . . . The women are down-rightly locked up, they have no choice. Also the pregnant women get beaten. Many women are forced to sleep with the men of SWAPO." In this camp there were doctors from Finland, East Germany, and technicians from Sweden. Those caught escaping, for in this camp in Angola there is resistance, are accused of betraying SWAPO:

They try to run away and hide with the local population, but most of them are caught and are imprisoned for six months in a prison where they are treated badly. The prison is surrounded by deep trenches and is guarded by two or three platoons of PLAN [SWAPO's guerrilla army]. Three machine guns were installed.

Many of the children of prostitution do not live long: "During my imprisonment in Nyango, about two months, at least fifty children died of measles. The children were dying like flies, they were so weakened. There were many sicknesses like measles, cholera and I think, also typhoid fever. Others continually suffered from diarrhea, cried through the whole night or were mere apathetic human bundles. I could not take this misery any more, although I had seen quite a few things myself during my training as a nurse."

The children belong to the Party: They have no parents. "Then [when the children reach three] the mothers have fulfilled their duty towards the Party, the children are practically the property of SWAPO. The women are misused as mothers and betrayed, only the aims of the organization count. The women have to produce a new generation but they cannot influence or educate it." The children are taken away from their mothers and taken to the children's camp in Talatado, about fifteen kilometers away from the main camp, a short distance to cut off a life time. They call it "kindergarten." A member of the Central Committee of SWAPO, a woman, Libertina Amadhila, SWAPO's vice-secretary for health, education and welfare, runs it. "The mothers take the separation from their children very badly, because often they never see their children again. They have to give birth to the the children, look after the babies and then they are taken away."

Even this drama keeps up the appearance of normality most of the time: "They do not know any other life and obey the orders, otherwise they are punished. Opposition is pointless, and the women are in the hands of SWAPO. They can only cry"; "They are afraid. They have to go along with it, even if they want to keep their children"; ". . . They are forced to give their children away, even if they are secretly against it. The women suffer . . . Many are desperate and tragedies take place . . ."; "Even before they can read or write the small children are politically educated in the idiom of SWAPO. The children are already prepared for the war in Namibia and learn unconditional obedience to SWAPO. Later functionaries came into the camp [at Nyango] and handpicked certain children for school. These children were then taken away to other SWAPO camps, perhaps also to Angola."

At fifteen they begin military training: "Here too, they have no other choice, they are forced . . . Many children are also sent to foreign countries for political education, especially to Cuba. When I was in Angola, sixteen hundred children were sent from the SWAPO camps to Cuba."

There must be no ties of affection between individuals because such ties are unpredictable and threatening. There must be no lovers or husbands and wives, above all no mothers with children. SWAPO breaks up the liaisons of youths recruited with their girlfriends.

SWAPO has not only totalitarianism's gulags and indoctrination, it also already has its bureaucratic corruption. Its *nomenklatura* stays in Luanda and Lusaka, it rarely shows itself in the bush camps and at the "front":

> While we who had to fight in the bush almost starved, the high functionaries sold everything possible and embezzled. Top people from SWAPO were in partnership with hotels and nightclubs. They divided the provisions and monies [that came from the UN and Europe] among themselves and only a fraction was given to the refugees.

Zambia's incapacity to control this continual violence and threat of violence between members of terrorist organizations it allows to operate on its soil became as much of a public issue as Zambian political life can take in the year following the killing of Herbert Chitepo in Lusaka on March 18, 1975. Chitepo's death along with his bodyguard and a child playing in the next-door garden,— his car exploded backing out of his driveway,—occurred at just about the time some of the witnesses before IGFM knew SWAPO violence in Lusaka and the rest of Zambia in their flesh. A leading member of ZANU, the terrorist group that later under Mugabe's control won power in Zimbabwe, Chitepo had masterminded terrorism against Rhodesia since it started in 1966.

Chitepo's death came because he had refused to renounce violence in the preceding months; "We have not been fighting to bring Smith to the talking table. We are fighting for majority rule."[12] This announcement used the codeword "majority rule" for seizure of power, immediately after Smith had released African leaders in jail and agreed to a ceasefire upon South Africa's insistence.

Carnage within ZANU at the end of December had preceded the killing of Chitepo: four hundred murders, according to the commission of thirteen African nations and representatives of the OAU that released its report on Chitepo's death almost a year later; two hundred, according to Rhodesian intelligence; sixty according to ZANU.[13] In December 1974 and in early 1975 ZANU gangs armed with submachine guns and hand grenades moved in and around Lusaka with impunity.

In the weeks immediately following Chitepo's death the Zambian police arrested a good many of the leaders of ZANU and thirteen hundred ZANU terrorists, a reaction that took the breath away from Rhodesian intelligence. Zambia admitted its responsibility for order in a speech a few weeks later, on April 8, 1975 in Tanzania, before the OAU that had withdrawn recognition of both ZANU and ZAPU on January 8: "We will not allow now or in the future the spilling of blood on our soil." But in the same breath the Zambian foreign minister reiterated Zambia's "support" of "the liberation struggle by whatever means" and called the killing of the Zambian bodyguard with Chitepo "Zambian blood" lost in the fight "to achieve independence for our oppressed brothers around us." He blamed Rhodesia for the killings, without evidence and promised to "rid the liberation movements of enemy agents."[14]

Both the Zambian investigation in those weeks and the African commission sworn in in July sought to blame the death of Chitepo on the ZANU leadership despite the impulsive interventions by the head of Rhodesian intelligence that made it clear to Zambian security that ZANU had not killed Chitepo: "Suddenly, I got the hell in me—Chitepo was dead and Tongogara [the most important ZANU leader after Chitepo] had suffered enough, so surely Rhodesia could afford to be magnanimous."

Ken Flower could live with the killing of Chitepo "who was directly responsible for the murder of a considerable number of black and white Rhodesians," as the Rhodesian government put it on March 20, 1975. He could not take reports of Zambian beatings and torture of ZANU leaders,—Tongogara's back had been reported broken,—to get them to confess to Chitepo's death.

Flower could justify the killing of Chitepo as an act of war, he could not live with the torture of his colleagues who had been responsible for as much murder as Chitepo. ZANU, and the Zambian government, could not conceive such distinctions let alone reciprocate. In typical Communist fashion he had learned in China, Tongogara could not conceive of defiance within his own group let alone of magnanimity from an enemy. "There's been a coup! Couping who? Because if you conduct a coup you're couping the Party and now what are you?" he said upon first report of the rebellion within ZANU a few months before its harvest of four hundred dead before the death of Chitepo a few months later.[15] In contrast Flower could fight on his enemy's level—but he shrank in horror from reducing himself to his level. He wanted to strengthen the Zambian government, not weaken it.

Kaunda did not have the heart for the truth. A year later the investigating commission exonerated Rhodesia and South Africa for responsibility for the killings. Kaunda later admitted that his main objective was to clear Zambia's name, not to get the truth. He had lost the confidence and self-respect to keep order at home because he had encouraged men to commit every sort of atrocity beyond Zambia's borders.

The handwritten notebooks of young blacks in SWAPO, captured by the South African Defense Force in Angola, reproduced in facsimile in the Denton Hearings, show the rigid political indoctrination that goes on incessantly in SWAPO and ANC camps and in eastern Europe and the Soviet Union: "I was put through a political rolling press and was eternally being indoctrinated"; "Time and again people are gathered for political meetings and have to listen to Marxist propaganda for hours on end."

Both intructors and "pupils" work in a language foreign to them: English. The instructors are often Soviet: "We were taken to Lubango, where we received military training for six months, taught also by Russians." The strangeness of tongues serves also to stifle discussion and induce rigidity. For the Africans English is sometimes twice removed from them, as Biko pointed out. In South West Africa, and sometimes in South Africa, they learn Afrikaans before English. At first, often the barrage of words they take for European "science" overwhelms them. There are also notebooks reprinted that show the details of military training: laying mines, sabotage, ambushes, infiltration of territory, first-aid (with instructions for frostbite!) and so on.

The witnesses before the Denton Committee make it clear that ANC indoctrination is the same as SWAPO's. The Soviets consider the organizations twins: At the demonstrations against the declaration of the State of Emergency in South Africa in London on June 28, 1986 the crowds carried signs of exactly the same printed format, to show "solidarity" with either the ANC or SWAPO.

The indoctrination notebooks make for astonishing reading: The straight Communist line unabashed in detail, with a coherent view of history since 1917, is taught in the furthest reaches of the bush where, except for these words, there is little but trees and sand. The notebooks stress a comprehensive world-view, Hitler's *Weltanschauung* in bush dress:

What is happiness and how is a society to be created where all people are happy? What is the purpose of life? Is there anybody not interested in the following question? . . . Experience teaches us that only a person who guides himself by a correct world outlook can answer those questions properly, i.e., can correctly understand what is happening around him (us) but what is a world outlook? A world outlook is the sum total of views of life, phenomena and events—World outlook plays an enormous role in life—not to have a correct world outlook is indeed not to have a soul—LENIN wrote a socialist must have a well thought-out and steadfast world outlook to master events, so that events will not master him. N.B. Marxist-Leninist Philosophy is a dialectical materialism and is directly opposed to idealism and metaphysics.

They make it clear that a "world outlook" means the obliteration of all the differences the flesh is heir to:

[The aim of SWAPO is] to combat all reactionary tendencies of individualism, tribalism, racism, sexism, and regionalism.

After obliterating the individual, an obliteration that betrays itself literally in the terrorists' loss of their birth names, a "liberation movement" proves its seriousness by losing itself in violence throughout the world. This interchangeability upset many youths because they knew they came from one country, not any place:

To cooperate to the fullest extent with all the genuine national liberation movements, progressive governments, organizations and individuals throughout the world towards complete elimination of the colonial system of imperialism.

The notebooks want violence, instead of reform, to menace everybody and obliterate all differences. The South African government's use of its strength to enforce the law justifies this violence:

An army is a main component of the state—born for the people and fight for the people. Whoever wants to seize power and maintain it must have it. Especially for the oppressed, colonized peoples who want to liberate themselves from oppression, this liberation is not possible, without people's army so it is impossible for the working class to win power through parliamentary changes, e.g., peaceful means, e.g., Allende of Chile, Indonesia, etc.

Whoever has an army has power—power comes from or through the barrel of the gun. That is why reactionary countries, e.g., Chile, can ruthlessly suppress the vast labouring people with their armies (small).

"Countries want independence, nations want liberation, and people want revolution." Mao Tse Tung. To liberate yourself we need a highly politicized genuine People's Army . . . N.B. Imperialism, reactionaries, atom bombs and other counterrevolutionaries, e.g., Kapuuo, are paper tigers.

This note refers to Chief Clemens Kapuuo, Paramount Chief of the Hereros in South West Africa, murdered by SWAPO on March 27, 1978 in Windhoek,—a murder, a South African murder some people still believe, that made a deep impression on South West Africa. A message to SWAPO in Luanda to a SWAPO base in southern Angola on August 8, 1977 published in the Denton Hearings reads in part:

He [the president of SWAPO, Sam Nujoma, in New York] instructed me to take a plane immediately to inform you that you send a message to the Front, that Kapuuo's group should end their lives in the North (killed). They should not leave the area alive.

A message from SWAPO army headquarters in Angola, named "Moscow," on April 9, 1978 congratulated SWAPO terrorists in southern Angola on the murder:

You performed the miracle of eliminating the most prominent puppet of imperialism in Namibia and note you did marvels by eradicating him exactly in the capital of Namibia.

The "people" must be forced to fight,—strategy that shows itself in the ANC's and UDF's cry, "Make the townships ungovernable," and in the ANC's threat to "necklace collaborators":

Make use of extensive (progressive) propaganda among the masses, organize and arm them. Make the masses support and actively participate in the armed struggle, and form a vast OCEAN of the people's war . . . Being war of the masses—People must liberate themselves.

Red and white tires hung in some of the "people's courts" in one or two townships, reminders of the penalty for resisting armed struggle. The ANC unequivocally talked of a "people's war" in Lusaka in January 1986 at its seventy-fourth anniversary, and again in January 1987 but in more blurred terms because of Tambo's impending visit to the secretary of state in Washington.

Like Clough in his article, "Beyond Constructive Engagement," that at the end of 1985 first sketched present State Department policy, the notebooks mince no words about suffering. They praise it, it will transform men:

In revolutionary war—come across various difficulties, even worse, e.g., hunger, death, encirclement, economic blockage, sometimes no food, ammunition, clothes, etc., but even then the struggle must continue!!! It depends on the masses and on self-reliance. Only by that can the war continue and remain invincible. *Indeed difficulties are not bad, they force us to think what was never thought of before.* In fact a revolutionary should experience difficulties and trials for the liberation of the fatherland to make a good and real revolutionary (Italics mine).

The terrorists can count on weapons, propaganda and instruction from the Soviet Union and East Germany. But they must fight and die alone, the Soviet Union will not fight for them. "Victory" will bring no respite. The terrorists will bring other countries the violence they do not say will also continue at home:

In fact no nation can win a revolutionary war without external help. But we must clearly understand that our friends can only help us materially and morally, but they cannot fight for us. We must fight ourselves. Freedom can never be bestowed on the oppressed people. Because when we win victory we were helped by others it will also be our responsibility to help the others.

The twenty-second Congress of the Communist Party of the Soviet Union in 1961 put just this "material and moral" support of "National Liberation Movements" outside of Europe at the center of its policy.

Even Emerson's "self-reliance" has found its way from Moscow to the bush in Angola and Zambia:

Preserve in self-reliance in carrying out revolutionary (war)—that is the political principle of revolutionaries, to put the revolution on one's own strength. Strive for assistance but not depend on it. In a word to win the victory, the political ideological line must be correct.

The future promises immolation in violence not only at home but throughout the world:

The Masses of the working people, the peasants of Colonial countries will have a very great Revolutionary role in the coming stages of the world revolution.

The National Liberation movement is a powerful Revolutionary force of the present day—and integral part of the World Revolution process.

During colonization thirty million American Indians [died].

The notebooks give a fairly accurate description of the consequences of the West's incapacity to bring peace after the First World War and to prevent the Second World War after the cessation of hostilities in Europe from turning into "a war called peace," as Brian Crozier has called it. The violence the the terrorists in southern Africa continue is the violence that first broke out with the Bolshevik putsch in 1917 and that spread in the wake of the "Victory of the Soviet Union" in the Second World War. The First and Second World Wars weakened free law-abiding governments everywhere. In Russia in 1917, the war brought the collapse of the government; in eastern Europe, the Second World War and the years immediately after destroyed governments. The war that broke out of the Second World War goes on everywhere, but especially outside of Europe, in the so-called Third World, Stalin's label. It avoids head-on attacks on the final targets, Europe, in any case already half-subjected, Japan and the United States:

Our epoch whose main content is the transition from capitalism to socialism is an epoch of struggle between the two opposing social systems. An epoch of socialist and national liberation revolutions, of the breakdown of imperialism and the abolition of the colonial system, an epoch of the transition of more peoples to the socialist path, of the triumph of socialism and communism on a *world-wide* scale.

In its development crisis of Capitalism passed through three stages. The first stage began in 1917. Thanks to the October Socialist Revolution.

The second stage is connected with the victory of the Soviet Union over fascist Germany and imperialist Japan.

The world socialist-system was formed, positions of capitalism were weakened.

The third stage is connected with strengthening of socialism; breakdown of colonial system.

The revolution of each country is a link in the chain of world revolution and its component part.

The twenty-second Congress of the Communist Party of the Soviet Union in 1961 had made "the transition from capitalism to communism" of these notes the guiding principle in the Soviet Union's support for "National Liberation Movements," along with the slogan, "peaceful coexistence," to reassure and distract the West.

Violence means unquestioning submission to the "party," the submission that made it impossible for Tongogara to even imagine defiance within ZANU:

Only if the Party possesses a monolithic ideological system will it be possible for Party members to follow orders and pledge their loyalty to the leader, so that the whole Party can crush all sorts of counter-revolutionary, pro-Western elements and enemy agents, and fully secure ideological unity, as well as organization unity—(only through this) the Party could overcome liberalism, anarchism and factionalism.

Independence will not mean the continuing of government under a new constitution. It means the undoing of the entire society, the "weeding out" of all "reactionaries," it means the making of the new man. All ideas more or less implicit in the so-called Freedom Charter in South Africa. The name of the new regime, People's Proletariat Democratic Dictatorship, amounts to a gloss of the Freedom Charter's claim to speak for all the people of South Africa: "We, the people of South Africa declare for all our country and the world to know . . ."

Here are the words of a terrorist upon his return from a mission in South West Africa:

Some of my comrades have returned to Namibia and been killed, others have been captured, jailed at Robben Island . . . I want a revolution as well as my colleagues do—not just a nationalist armed struggle. You can't have it half-way. I am a Marxist Leninist. However, the Party should control the whole movement military as well as political—If I and my colleagues are going to be killed and have been killed in Namibia, I want to know that I am dying or sacrificing for a real revolution, not just for a change in regime like there has been in the Ivory Coast—or like fighters who sacrificed in a reactionary cause as UNITA-FNLA.

Externally overthrow the exploitation and oppression of imperialism of the people, so as to accomplish national revolution. Internally overthrow exploitation of man by man and oppression, feudal and bureaucratic-capitalism so as to accomplish Democratic revolution. These tasks are closely linked. If imperialism and all foreign domination is not overthrown, it will be difficult to crush feudal-bureaucratic-bourgeoisie and other reactionaries.

To establish the Popular (People's Power) aim is to weed out from the grass-roots (masses) the old political machinery (colonial mentality). In order to establish a Grand new People's Proletariat Democratic Dictatorship. It is a life and death struggle. World revolution can only take place with the participation of the broad masses of the people.

The notebooks openly acknowledge the terrorists face far superior military forces. They aim to win through propaganda and agitation like the Vietnamese Communists who as early as 1965 knew the streets of New York, not the battlefield, would bring them victory.

Judicious leadership. It is proved in the People's war that an insufficiently equipped army, e.g., PLAN [the acronym for the military wing of SWAPO] fighting the just cause with the correct strategy and tactics can defeat a modern well-equipped army, e.g., South African Army . . .

N.B. Workers, Peasants, revolutionary progressive students, (leftwing) intellectuals, and petty-bourgeois are the best elements in the revolution. In the war of liberation of all the oppressed people, history and experience proved that in the face of the powerful enemy as very powerful as he is cruel, victory is possible only by uniting the whole masses of the people within a firm unified party, e.g., (SWAPO) based on the worker-peasants alliance free from bourgeois and capitalist ideology led by the collective.

These notes are texts for memorization: "N.B. Learn it at Heart please," runs at the bottom of one page. The reader like myself caught before the aching lights of a microfilm machine reading this rubbish of preparation for future murder will have his surprises to start him from the words that keep on coming as in a trance: "To pluck a cherry to sleap with a girl who never sleap with a man."

This young terrorist hardly ever misspelled the dogma of words shot at him, he only stumbled over the letters of his fantasies.

In contrast to the youths who took these notes and the youths before the Denton Committee and before the *Internationale Gesellschaft für Menschenrechte*, two of the witnesses before the Denton Committee were not ANC or SWAPO cannon-fodder. They had seen the ANC operate at the top, in two crucial times, Hlapane in the early sixties when the ANC turned to terrorism, and Kave in the late seventies, after the collapse of Portuguese dominion in Angola and Mozambique and the outbreak of disturbances in South Africa.

Except in the things that count the most, they could not have been more different. Born in 1954, twenty-eight at the time of the hearings, Kave was young enough to be Hlapane's daughter—he was sixty-four. Hlapane's words were measured, sober, brief: He showed adults the respect that does not tell them what to think. To speak, for Kave, meant in contrast to relive all she had been through. She almost broke down during her testimony. Words that told were harder than the silence of the facts:

As I am speaking to you here, I am trying to be brave. I feel like crying. Everybody is dead from 1976.
. . . I cannot continue fighting alone against forces which are stronger. The outside struggle is no longer a nationalist struggle, but has become a struggle against the Socialist Countries, and now the Socialist countries have come out in the open to defend the South African Communist party, and our people are dead.

Hlapane wore the unnerving serenity of a man who knows the consequences of his actions. Just before his appearance in the relative quiet of the Senate committee room he took Denton aback: He told him he would be killed for talking.

Hlapane's face and posture in a photograph taken the moment he swore his oath before Senator Denton is striking. It shows intelligence, compassion, resilience—and surprising softness. It is the face of a man who has lived.

Nine months after the hearings, on December 16, 1982, Hlapane and his wife were murdered in their sleep in their home in Soweto. The killers left the one daughter they found at home for dead. She survived a paraplegic. On the floor of the Senate, Denton accused the ANC of the murders—to colleagues who did not bother to listen and to newspapers who, with the exception of *The Washington Times*, did not carry the story: Real blood does not taste as good as the blood of fantasy.

Why was Hlapane murdered after his testimony in Washington and not sixteen years before when he testified against Abraham Fischer? He had said everything he said in Washington, and much more, a half-generation before. His voice, "like peals of thunder" had exposed Fischer's fund-raising for the SACP abroad and his deadly work in Umkhonto we Sizwe. Hlapane was murdered, not only because his living voice meant more than printed words, but above all because of his readiness to retell his story *outside South Africa*. In South Africa, Hlapane's testimony was too well-known to bear repeating. Several books had dealt with it. But abroad his voice might tell. Besides, who reads South African books? His readiness to testify abroad might also help

South Africans remember events too blatant to live in anybody's memory,—except the government's.

In his account in Washington, Hlapane gave little account of what it had meant to turn state's evidence sixteen years before, and face his former comrades before the world. Fischer's trial had been the turning point in a slow regeneration that had made him into a man of few words who knew they would cost him his life.

Bruno Mtolo, who had testified, two years before Hlapane, against Mandela, tells something of what it probably also took for Hlapane to talk. "I felt as if I could penetrate into anyone's mind," he said of the clarity, depth's clarity, that possessed him after he decided to testify. Besides living with the continual fear of death, the decision to testify meant telling the truth, the only effective defense against cross-examination by South Africa's best lawyers, as the police told Mtolo: " 'It will depend on you. If you give satisfactory evidence you'll be released by the judge; but if you start telling things which you don't know, you'll be in trouble.' "

The "indemnity," almost a pardon, had to be earned: "When I thought about all the faces that would be staring at the 'traitor' who had turned against his leaders, it made me sick. I was convinced, though, that they had to have a dose of their own medicine."[16]

On his way to court he looked "unhappy" enough for the detectives accompanying him to reassure Mtolo that anyone appearing in court felt the same way, including the police: "One of them remarked that anyone who went to court felt like that, no matter whether he was a policeman or not. This remark gave me a bit of confidence. At least I was not the only one who was shivering."

But the fear kept at him:

I got into the box facing the accused, who were quite a distance away . . . I was shivering like a reed, and kept leaning against the box to stop shivering but it was useless . . . The judge granted the application of the prosecutor that my name should not be mentioned in the press. He warned me that, as an accomplice, I had to answer questions put to me according to my knowledge, but I would not be compelled to answer questions which might incriminate me. If satisfied that I had given truthful evidence the court could, however, grant me an indemnity from prosecution.

Testifying lent him some strength: "It took about four days to finish my evidence in chief, and I was feeling much better—not as scared as before."

But the test, the real trial, was the cross-examination postponed for three weeks: "Every member of the police force saw that I was in trouble. They thought that I would never stand up to cross-examination after three weeks, with such a long evidence."

During the first day of cross-examination, after a confident beginning, he had the ease to ask the judge for a recess without knowing he had right to relief. His confidence renewed the next day, he broke the cross-examination, "without anyone expecting it, and just when I was beginning to get used to his [the chief cross-examiner, Vernon Berrangé] bullying." The previous day he had "done his best to answer" before he felt "my mind would not take it" and asked the court for a break:

(Berrangé) asked, "Were you a member of the Communist Party?" I said, "Yes." "And were you a member of the ANC?" Again I said, "Yes." Then he asked me about the relationship between the Communist party and the ANC and SACTU [South African Congress of Trade Unions] and Umkhonto we Sizwe. He stood there for nearly the whole day hammering at me, asking me the policies of all these organizations and their interconnections. I gave him everything—my mind was now at ease because I knew that if he was trying to confuse me he would not catch me on this. I felt that my time as a Marxist student had not been wasted and everything was still fresh in my mind. He asked me about the historical and dialectical materialism and piece by piece I gave it to him.[17]

Mtolo also helps to understand why the ANC and the SACP murdered Hlapane after his testimony in Washington, and not sixteen years before when he testified in South Africa against Fischer. The Africans had simply not believed Mtolo's and probably Hlapane's testimony in South Africa, but they might believe it if Washington listened. People assumed the government had paid them to testify, especially after Mtolo made a success of farming after his release: "It was difficult to convince them that I had not sold my leaders but that in spite of the high ideals I had held, my views had changed. I had to leave home [and give up his profitable farming] and go out to work to disprove their beliefs."

They could not believe that he had turned his back on his former life:

Far from regarding me as a traitor other people insisted that I teach them how to make weapons. They believed that I had fought the government and had got away without being prosecuted because I was such a clever leader. They believed that it would take a lot of evidence and planning to send a hero like me to gaol. It was sickening! . . .

If it was difficult for the judges to believe that I had changed from an active supporter of Umkhonto we Sizwe to a man of peace, how much more difficult it must have been for my friends!

Mtolo too had needed the truth of experience to make him believe the words he said:

Before all this I would not have believed that I would be capable of changing my views so radically. I never dreamt that things would happen which would make me see the world through other eyes.[18]

He did not mean "other eyes" but sight itself, for his decision to bear witness brought the world before his eyes: "For the first time the thought struck me that you only appreciate your eyes after you have lost them."[19]

Before, he had not seen the stuff of everyday life: "I looked at the life I thought was so bad it had to be improved with bloodshed. It turned out to be not so bad at all. I thought about the days when I used to go to the beach on my bike with my camera."[20]

The change had come because Mtolo had recognized sovereignty, the sovereignty John Philip, more than a hundred years before, and Lord Selborne, several generations later, had said the Africans could not easily distinguish from force. Their times were happy enough not to have to know that not only Africans drew this distinction with difficulty:

When I told them of my experience with the Afrikaners, [my neighbors] were startled to hear that in all those months [after his arrest before he testified] not a finger was lifted against me. Some of them speculated that I had been given a slow poison and would not last long. They gave that as the reason for my release. I told them that I did not think so, because those days were over. If a man died today he had to be examined and the nature of his death would be revealed. In my case this was particularly so.[21]

Hlapane had joined the defiant but democratically-minded ANC in 1948, a year after the South African Communist Party (SACP) had begun to infiltrate it without his knowledge. Five years after the South African government outlawed the SACP, in 1955, Joe Slovo, a man still crucial in the SACP and the ANC, Kave repeatedly mentioned him, and more than once identified as a KGB agent by the liberal Johannesburg *Star*, recruited Hlapane into the Communist Party.

Hlapane's recruitment shows how the Communists infiltrated and then controlled political organizations which aimed at reform, not violent overthrow of the government. Unlike the ANC which was open to all, the SACP selectively went after leaders in important political and community organizations. Invisible in key positions in these organizations, the Communists were to further Party purposes and tactics:

Being a Communist, Mr. Chairman, we did not take anybody who wanted to join the Communist Party: its membership was strictly selective. It was a standing rule of the Communist party that all its members go out to all mass organizations or even community organizations to find out about people who are influential, who are clever, and who could be recruited as members of the Party, first of all getting these people interested in the Party by giving them pamphlets and some literature concerning the Party, and later getting them into some discussions, and then if we are satisfied that they have interest, get them into some lecture rooms.

[The main purpose of the Communist cell made up of three to five members] was to work amongst members of national organizations in order to influence their members to advance the aims and objects of the Communist party.

Mtolo also told both of the selectivity and the infiltration in roughly the same years:

In all our cell meetings we received directives which urged us to infiltrate every ANC branch with the object of taking over the leadership. We were given orders to join the nearest ANC branch and to obtain firm control over the branch committee. If no branch were in existence, we had to establish one, so we had to work hard.[22]

The moderate members of the ANC "knew nothing about the infiltration," they did not know the SACP's role in Umkhonto we Sizwe: "They thought we were fighting for them, but we were really advancing the cause of the Communist party."

"The Communists are very selective, they do not just draw anyone into the Party, no matter how great his understanding of Marxism. They want certain other qualities too." Mtolo had gone from the "trade union classes" to "Marxist classes" until the SACP tapped him after he organized workers in several hospitals and caused a strike:

While the student is attending these classes he is urged to enroll more workers into trade unions and also to join various organizations which are considered to be "progressive." By "progressive" is meant those organizations which, knowingly or unknowingly, further the aims of communism. In all these stages, the student is not yet a member of the Communist party nor does he know of its existence. He will know that of all the countries in the world, his true friends are in the Communist countries, but he himself will not yet know of any Communists in South Africa. It will only be after he has worked hard all by himself that he will be drawn into the Communist party.[23]

Gerard Ludi, the first South African intelligence agent to infiltrate the SACP, and with Hlapane the most important witness at Fischer's trial, doubted the SACP numbered much more than a hundred after it was suppressed in 1950:

To become a member of the South African Communist Party is to become one of the elite. Only people who are regarded as absolutely safe, who are experienced leadership material, are accepted. Convinced Marxist-Leninists are not absorbed into the Party proper if they do not come up to standard. Even at the height of its underground activity, I doubt if the South African Communist Party ever had many more than a hundred registered members, *but these CP members were the king-pins in all the massive fronts which operated on behalf of the Communist party* (Italics mine).[24]

Ludi even found joining the "numerous legal front organizations" that eventually led him to the SACP to be difficult. Anyone who simply asked to join was "automatically suspected of being an imperialist spy." Like Mtolo, he "soon discovered that the road to the Communist party was a long and laborious one."[25] At leftist parties talk concentrated on "racialism," the line of the fronts; socialism was barely mentioned. Before foreign visitors, the top SACP leaders were "strictly neutralist when discussing communism versus capitalism": "I lost count of the number of Americans, Germans, Britons, Scandinavians, and others that South Africa's top Reds duped into supplying Red fronts in South Africa with money and moral support, in the belief that they were in fact preventing them from going Red. Their claims of representing a free, democratic, multi-racial South Africa had been swallowed hook, line and sinker."[26] Ludi won admittance to the front organizations only after he published articles in the left wing press in South America, and told front leaders of Dag Hammarskjold's itinerary in the townships, closely guarded information he had from the police.

A word about Gerard Ludi, like Mtolo and Hlapane, an extraordinary man. He could listen to his own thoughts, he trusted himself enough for that, like Mtolo who told a comrade: "I have not got a mechanical mind which has to be set for me by someone else."²⁷ But unlike Mtolo and Hlapane, Ludi had not had to go through terrorism to discover his mind. He did not have to go through the struggle with his thoughts that Mtolo suffered for years: "Even to this day there are many things which I am trying to get out of my mind, which I cannot just throw out. I still need help from other people, otherwise I cannot rid myself of Marxism."²⁸

Ludi had gone through all this at the University of Witwatersrand. He had managed to get himself an education there at the cost of passing with average grades the first year, failing the next. He had come to the University with a conservative National party background and was shocked at the teachers who "openly sneered at the government during lectures, while an odd long-haired gnome-like character in class with me literally burst into tears of rage when I suggested to him I was a Nationalist supporter." At the same time that he rejected his "ideological tutors," he meant his parents and the National party, because "they had presented me with an ideology laced with half truth," he did not fall for the left. He resolved simply that he was "no longer going to accept anything I did not find out for myself." He studied native languages. He learned to "drink, race motor cars" and overcame "for the first time in my life . . . an innate shyness I had hitherto harboured towards women." He took real risks. In front of left-wingers he took up right wing dogmas, and with "a bit of effort managed to get them really hot under the collar." He taunted his father with "real hot left wing lines," who "would fly off the handle and mutter darkly he would no longer send me to that nest of pink liberals": "By the time I was in third year I had these clichés so well taped that I could fool almost anyone that I was anything from a left wing radical to right wing Neo-Nazi—and all the shades that existed in between." He read texts: Marx, Fichte, Hegel, Aristotle, Plato, Rousseau, Kant—but he liked Mill most of all: "And I must be frank. I had a completely open mind. Had Marxist-Leninism provided the answers I was looking for I would have stood by my convictions to this day." He saw through *On Liberty* to its good sense, not a common reading: "I felt complete political freedom is a sophisticated freedom, which can only be given to people whose political and other maturity warrants it."²⁹

In short, he gave himself a philosophical education, a real one, not only by reading texts, but by facing all sorts of views in argument. This education gave him a love of life, almost in Tolstoy's sense: He did not fear depths but he also loved the everyday nuance of the surface where most life unfolds in looks and slight intonations. He was sensitive with the matter-of-factness of common sense: He did not have to take himself for an artist to yield to his sensitivity. He knew that courage also needed cunning but in his cunning he remained open. "It was a difficult situation for me as morally I seemed wrong to dupe non-Communists into unconsciously becoming Communist puppets," he later wrote of his manipulation of fronts for the SACP.³⁰ He knew the world in the way a South African, but not an American usually can, for he never took his country as a paradigm for nations.

His description of his University friends who stuck by him when he was identified as a Communist in the newspapers, after the police ineptly arrested their own agent, perhaps best shows the education he gave himself: "Only a small group of university friends, who today are still my only close friends, virtually ignored the incident. They have a philosophy very close to my own. There is very little that can shock them. Life is just one vast, exciting experience."[31]

This appetite for life had drawn him to help the police when they asked him to work as an agent: ". . . Driving curiosity, the strong yearning to find out exactly what made the other man tick, was one of the main reasons why I had consented to being recruited as a Secret Agent." Smuts had just this driving curiosity, it had made him call the natives "the Sphinx problem" in 1906. Smuts knew the risks of that curiosity. So did Ludi: "I preferred the company [of nonwhites at Wits] to the very smug White extreme left wing liberals who were trying so very hard to prove to anyone with a dark skin that they were on HIS side. They were all so artificially intellectual." He had no training in intelligence, except the education he had given himself, probably the best preparation.

The balance that allowed Ludi to rebel against the National party and his parents but not to fall for the left,—the reason he could rebel against his parents without forsaking them,—came because he had learned essential things before he went away to university. As an adolescent on a visit to Germany in 1949–1950, he had seen the returning German prisoners:

As a high school boy I often saw first-hand examples of Red brutality in places like Germany and Austria. I will never forget how the returning German prisoners of war looked after doing a five to six year stretch in Siberia or Kazakstan—and the tales of horror they told. But what shocked me most of all was that most of the German POWs said the same: "It was terrible. Out of ten thousand entering the camp, twenty to thirty of us survived. We had no food, no clothes, no medicines, but by their standards they treated us well *because we were still far better off than the Russians imprisoned in camps near us.*"[32]

The South African government had no hard evidence of the reconstitution of the SACP after its suppression in 1950 until Ludi infiltrated it on May 12, 1963 after four years of operation in Johannesburg leftist circles and Communist front organizations, Ludi discovered to his amazement after he uncovered the SACP. For thirteen years, many South Africans including some men in the government had imagined the SACP no longer existed. But the police had thought otherwise, as they told Ludi when they sent him out: "Join the Communist Party. It exists somewhere and somehow, we don't know where and who the office-bearers are. Find them, even if it takes years."[33]

The excitement of hard facts was too much for the police: Barely a year after Ludi's infiltration, it arrested Fischer and the other Communists Ludi identified, and blew Ludi's cover. Too quickly. Ludi had just begun to approach the nerve center of Mtolo's world: "If they gave me a few more years I was sure I would penetrate to the heart of the terrorist organizations the Communist party had established in the country. Then I would have no objections to a trial," Ludi had argued, in vain, with his superiors.[34]

Towards the end of 1962, Hlapane had been coopted into the Central Committee of the Party. The "African members" were all in the ANC, most of them on the National Executive Committee: ". . . In this way, the South African Communist Party was able to influence and control the National Congress." The SACP approved, and often initiated, the ANC's major decisions:

During the period that I served in the ANC and in the SACP, no major decisions could be taken by the ANC without the concurrence and approval of the Central Committee of the SACP. Most major developments were in fact initiated by the Central Committee.

The Communist infiltration of the ANC Hlapane and Mtolo exposed had started before them, in earnest in the late nineteen forties. But the SACP had publicly stated its desire to transform the ANC in 1929, in words that echoed a resolution of the Executive Committee of the Communist International (Comintern) in 1928: "The work of the Party [SACP] in its turn has come to centre more than ever on native agitation, education and organization, political and industrial extension of the party's influence wherever possible in native bodies like the African National Congress . . ."

The resolution of the International in 1928 had stated that the SACP should participate in "embryonic national organizations among the natives" like the ANC, "to seek to broaden and extend their activity," but "[retain] its full independence": "Our aim should be to transform the African National Congress into a fighting nationalist revolutionary organization . . . developing systematically the leadership of the workers and the Communist Party in this organization."[35]

The twin themes of the SACP's independence but control of the ANC continues to appear in the SACP's March 1986 Politburo directive, released by the South African government on June 12 but ignored in the United States press: "It is also necessary to reflect on the profile of the PARTY [SACP] in the liberation alliance whose public head is correctly the ANC . . . We represent the short and long term political and social aspirations of the working class. We have always believed that our Party can only carry out its historic mission by ensuring that its vital role in the alliance *does not result in a negation of its role as a public vanguard of the working class.*" In contrast, the ANC had called itself and the SACP "two hands in the same body" in its monthly, *Sechaba*, in September 1985.

In 1963, Mtolo had read the same word "vanguard," and the same thinking, in an SACP pamphlet: "The Communist Central Committee issued a leaflet which made it clear to everyone that the Communist Party was in the vanguard of the struggle, and that it was prepared to carry on the struggle to the bitter end."

The year before Hlapane's cooptation into the Central Committee, 1961, had seen the organization of Umkhonto we Sizwe under the leadership of Nelson Mandela, despite serious disagreements with the delegates of other organizations, as Hlapane testified:

> The military arm of the ANC, also known as Umkhonto we Sizwe, was the brainchild of the SACP and after the decision to create it had been taken, Joe Slovo and J.B. Marks were sent by the Central Committee of the SACP to Moscow to organize arms and ammunition and to raise funds for Umkhonto we Sizwe.

Mtolo, not a member of the SACP Central Committee in contrast to Hlapane, had not realized the SACP's and Moscow's roles in the organization of Umkhonto we Sizwe. He had believed the "ANC executive in Johannesburg" had organized the terrorism until the panic of the local ANC men in Natal at the first "sabotage attempts" showed him they "were never consulted":

> Immediately we [the SACP members] saw the danger of their [the local ANC leaders] finding out who we were. They would not have hesitated to tell the police. They were not only scared of the new organization [Umkhonto] taking over the leadership, they were scared for their own skins. The movement [Umkhonto] was operating under the name of the ANC and it was quite clear to every one of them that the first people to be arrested would be the known members of the ANC, or rather the former members as it was by then banned and operating underground.³⁶

Mtolo had not understood the SACP role in initiating terrorism despite his awareness that Communists controlled Umkhonto in Natal: "In the Regional Command there was no genuine member of the ANC except our captain, Curnick Ndlovu, but he too was more of a Communist. We were all convinced Communists who would have nothing to do with the ANC unless it was prepared to toe the Communist line."³⁷ Call it the naiveté of desperation—Mtolo later named it blindness.

Barely a year after the shock of the first terrorism, the line between "sabotage" and murder disappeared: "At the beginning of our struggle we had been told to be careful of human life, but towards the end of 1962 and the beginning of 1963 this was no longer regarded as important."³⁸ The "complete" failure of a stay-at-home campaign Mandela organized for May 29–31, 1961 when South Africa became a Republic led to the turn to terrorism towards the end of the year, according to Mtolo: "A survey was made to determine the reasons for the failure. The leaders concluded that the main mistake lay in telling the people not to use violence in picketing in order to intimidate those who were inclined to go to work."³⁹

By 1963 terrorism compelled boycotts, for instance, a beer boycott in Durban, the pattern to this day: "The people did not respond to the boycott call, so we decided to scare them by exploding a pipe bomb in each of the three beer halls at Point Road, Victoria Street and Prince Alfred Street."⁴⁰

The turn to terrorism also brought much tighter organization of the ANC under the M-Plan, M for Mandela, and incidentally the substitution of the Communist clenched-fist salute for the earlier ANC greeting: "The locations or townships were divided into several branches, each of which were subdivided into zones, streets and cells. If there were matters to be discussed or leaflets to be distributed at night, the committee would instruct the zone leaders and the zone leaders would contact the street leaders, who would see that the work was carried out. The branch committees got their instructions from the ANC Regional Committee."

Hlapane also testified to the invisible hand of the SACP in the famous so-called Freedom Charter. Joe Slovo had drawn it up on instructions from the SACP Central Committee without the knowledge of the many African and Colored organizations that adopted it over objections of the ANC leaders in Natal, especially to its provision for "nationalization" of property:

The Freedom Charter is a document adopted at a conference held in Kliptown by the Congress Alliance. Let me go further to explain that it [the conference] consisted of organizations such as the African National Congress, the Congress of Democrats, the South African Congress of Trade Unions, Colored People's Organization, and the Indian Congress.

It is a document that I came to know about just having been drafted by Joe Slovo at the request of the Central Committee, and finally approved by the Central Committee of the Communist Party and sent down as a document that embodies all the demands of the people, as they were collected from all areas. It was placed before them for adoption, and finally it was adopted there.

The circumstances of the Freedom Charter's adoption confirm Hlapane's account. Neither the president of the ANC, Chief Albert Luthuli, nor his deputy, Dr. Wilson, nor the President of the ANC in the Cape, Professor Z. K. Matthews, saw a copy of the charter before the about three thousand delegates at the "Congress of the People" at Kliptown. Not even Luthuli knew the members of the drafting committee. A member of Alan Paton's Liberal Party, Peter Hjul, resigned in early 1955 from a local Cape committee, because he saw that the committee meant to endorse decisions already taken, instead of collecting grassroots suggestions for the charter. The delegates at the Congress acclaimed each clause with a show of hands without discussion or possibility of amendment.

Nothing in the ten provisions, not an accidental number in this deeply religious country, of the Freedom Charter directly betrays Communist ideology. It calls for redistribution of land ("The land shall be shared among those who work it.") and redistribution of wealth ("The people shall share in the country's wealth.") In the full text, not as often distributed as the ten commandments, there is a call for the transference of the "mineral wealth beneath the soil, banks and monopoly industry . . . to the ownership of the people as a whole" and for the control of "all other industries and trade . . . to assist the well-being of the people as a whole."

Most of the other provisions are anodyne, and at the same time exhilarating: They promise everything to everybody without a hint of how all this will come to pass: "There shall be peace and friendship."

They are commands—but they give no indication who is giving the commands. They are meant to fetch people of no political experience, and to keep them unrealistic.

In its simplemindedness and with its echoes of religious syntax, however, the Freedom Charter follows to the letter Lenin's instructions to appeal to the "masses" in the simplest terms,—a true grandchild of the Bolsheviks' *Land, Bread and Peace*. But simplemindedness almost promises violence and cruelty.

Despite,—and because of,—its vagueness, the Freedom Charter marks a turning point for the ANC: It replaces its traditional specific demands for constitutional reforms within the framework of democracy with the vague language of socialism and nationalization.[41]

The Freedom Charter also shows the SACP's ability to guide, manipulate and transform "native bodies," its name for the ANC and other organizations in 1929, a technique it has used in the last years to turn the defiance of some blacks against themselves and to reduce the Republic's readiness to change to violence.

The organizations that Hlapane said made up the Congress Alliance, organized in 1955 to sponsor the conference for the Freedom Charter, were Communist fronts. Two of them, the Colored People's Congress (CPC), first called the Colored People's Organization, and the Congress of Democrats (COD) had been founded in 1953, the year plans for the Freedom Charter were announced at the annual meeting of the ANC. The formation of the COD, CPC and later the South African Congress of Trade Unions (SACTU) showed the suppression of the SACP in 1950 had intensified the infiltrations the Communists had practised in South Africa even before the Bolsheviks seized power in Russia. To "prepare the ground for violent national-democratic revolution [in South Africa]," Ludi testified he had been instructed at secret SACP cell meetings, "we would have to work with the Congress Alliance and Liberal Party of South Africa."[42]

Already in 1960 after the ANC was banned and before he was inducted into the SACP, men he later learned were "practically all senior white executives of the underground Communist Party" put Ludi at the head of the COD's "secretariat of university affairs." He was to "infiltrate all leftist political student bodies or recruit their members for the movement," especially at the University of Witwatersrand. Student bodies were to be made to take up issues the COD exploited like total nuclear disarmament.[43]

The issue and the timing had to be right: "The students marched, *not* because they were Communist stooges but because they genuinely felt the law was wrong. But it took two Communists to provide the catalyst by coming up with just the right suggestion at exactly the right time."[44] COD leaders were "on the alert at all times for issues by which we could draw the entire left into ad hoc committees": "The main tactic of Communist organizations, wherever they are sadly outnumbered, is to form a 'wide front'—a front comprising all the left wing liberal elements they can persuade to work with them."⁴⁵

After the passage of the Freedom Charter, the COD distributed vast numbers of propaganda pamphlets against the "Bantustans" and so on printed in Great Britain. The leaders of the COD were almost all men from the SACP, suppressed in 1950, later identified in court as Communists, men like Joe Slovo and Abraham Fischer.

Probably in 1961, before he penetrated the SACP, Ludi had learned firsthand of SACP infiltration of the CPC from one of the CPC's few non-Communist leaders, Stanley Lollan. "I was nothing but a stooge in the hands of the Communists running [the CPC]," Lollan told Ludi driving with him to Swaziland on his escape both from the SACP and the South African police. After every important meeting of the CPC, Lollan had to report to Nelson Mandela: "In the end I felt as if I was working as a paid employee for the Communists . . . I had to report to [Mandela] like an office boy to his manager. He questioned me closely about everything said at the meetings and the decisions taken. He also gave me instructions to pass on to people in the CPC." Ludi had persuaded the South African police not to arrest the CPC leader crossing the frontier into Swaziland without a passport because he feared jail would turn him into a "hardened Communist."⁴⁶

Communist cadres also led SACTU, founded a few months before the Freedom Charter, in March 1955. SACTU's secretary, Leslie Massina, had "received intensive training in trade union organizations, with particular emphasis on the employment of strikes as a political weapon," in Czechoslovakia from November 1954 to February 1955.⁴⁷

In contrast to the recently organized COD and CPC, the SACP had used the South African Indian Congress (SAIC), formed in early 1900 out of three Indian organizations including Gandhi's Natal Indian Congress of 1939, for "joint protests" against the government, despite resistance from democratic Indian leaders driven out of the organization. The minutes of the district Committee of the SACP in Durban on June 21, 1946 confirm the Communist influence on SAIC in the "Passive Resistance Campaign" against the land tenure of Asiatics and representation of Indians bill, influence in any case evident to the naked eye by then:

> It was felt by the District Committee that the local Indian Congress [SAIC] must be forced by pressure to set up a Passive Resistance Council, and our Party members working in the Congress [are] to do everything possible to see that the whole Congress is activized—furthermore, that whenever and wherever it holds area or factory meetings it should point out clearly how the "Ghetto Act" [the land tenure of Asiatics and representation of Indians bill] affects all sections of the South African population.⁴⁸

SACTU recruited the fifty thousand members it claimed a few years after 1955 from all races, in contrast to the COD, SAIC and the CPC. But in the underground SACP that drew some of its members from SACTU, for instance Mtolo, "the Africans and Indians operated in racially segregated cells."

Communist manipulation of front organizations and other groups like local committees of Amnesty International astonished Ludi after his induction into the SACP in 1963 despite his experience. It was all too easy:

During the months that followed I really did experience at first hand how easily secret Communist Party members on front committees can run non-Communist bodies by good tactical maneuvering on a committee—with the non-Communists never guessing that they are in fact Red puppets.

When Ludi left his first Communist cell meeting he was made to turn out his pockets "to make sure you are not carrying any literature linking any of us with any of our front organizations."[49]

The SACP's turn to violence in 1961 gave the fronts more bite because then, as now with the UDF, NECC and its other fronts, the SACP had painted a non-violent face on them, as an SACP Central Committee decision of 1961 shows: "It was decided that the SAIC, CPC and SACTU should not do anything to jeopardize their legality by an open commitment to armed struggle."[50] The SACP meant the fronts to appear as an alternative to the violence that served them.

But a "non-violent" face, did not mean a non-violent mind, or body,—other people's bodies. Already in 1960, the COD had trained volunteers, not only in the distribution of leaflets and posters, but also in the "provocation of riots at public meetings."[51] This "action work" took off after Parliament passed the Ninety-Day Detention Law in May 1962. COD meetings always ended in riots, in contrast to merely rowdy Liberal Party, Black Sash and Progressive Party meetings protesting the law:

In order to provoke the riot COD always arranged for experienced street fighters from the ANC and the Indian Congresses. They did their part well. Surreptitiously they would melt into the crowd and start scuffles here and there. This was always done when opposing forces faced each other and the tension was high. The scuffle they started would erupt in an enormous free-for-all. By then the Communist would have extricated himself carefully and could stand back and watch smugly as relatively innocent White and non-Whites fought viciously and Red incited racial hatred reached fever pitch.[52]

The violence brought students the COD prompted into the streets to protest the detention law. The street teaches the world "international relations."

After Sharpeville in 1960 and the formation of Umkhonto, Ludi believed the Communists really expected to "take South Africa within two years." Long before the United States understood, probably already in 1965, the SACP had taught him the importance of Vietnam:

[The SACP] were certain that the country would become a second Algeria or Vietnam . . . In the towns the powerful ANC and PAC were expected to cause vast civil disobedience with continuous race riots and strikes flaring throughout the country. This, the Reds reasoned, would keep the army and police occupied 24 hours a day.

The sabotage and political assassination cells of Umkhonto we Sizwe would add to further confusion in the urban areas. They would also help bog down police and army units, as well as incapacitate the judiciary.

All this activity would give the guerrillas, who would infiltrate from Zambia over South Africa's vast uncontrolled borders at the rate of a few thousand a month, free rein in the bush country. A Vietnam situation would arise. The Reds would hold vast tracts of country, while the government under severe pressure managed to hold isolated urban regions and the surrounding countryside.

And to assist the three-pronged action assault the vast international Communist propaganda network dealing specifically with White dominated Africa was geared to rouse racial passions in an effort to persuade the West to help "liberate" South Africa.

Intensive care was taken to ensure that organizations such as the ANC were labelled "nationalist African" and that all Communist influence in these organizations was kept secret (viz. the big fuss over my credentials to the Moscow Peace Congress).[53]

These words of Ludi's written probably in 1967 sound surreal even today. But so does much twentieth century history. Outlandish or not these words reflect what Ludi learned as an undercover agent. They summarize the M-Plan, Mandela's plan, that Mtolo not at the center of the Party like Ludi knew, or at least only reported, in bits and pieces. This plan still guides the SACP.

Hlapane, who like Ludi was at the heart of the SACP in the same years, did not describe the M-Plan in Washington in 1982. Maybe he thought spelling it out would make his audience take him for credulous. Maybe he thought it was too obvious to need words. Mtolo, who did not know its total design thought he had discovered its weakness when he inadvertently uncovered its strength: "A planned war never comes to blows," he said repeating a Zulu saying. For the SACP, like the Soviet Union, will settle for victory without all-out fighting.

Ludi understood the violence better than Mtolo, "the typical Leninist tactic of aversion of guilt," he called it: "'We are arming ourselves to seize power from you. So hand over the country peacefully and without fuss. If you fail to do this we will start a war—*and then you will be guilty of starting a war*'"[54] Maybe, he understood too well: To defy bluff without getting caught up in it is difficult.

The violence counted for Hlapane, not the grand plan, its child. He knew without saying that violence was the end, the plan the means. He knew it because the violence betrayed his beliefs, and not only his beliefs, but the beliefs of thousands of Africans who unlike him did not know what was going on. He saw that another grand plan, the Freedom Charter, had begun the SACP's conversion of the ANC to violence:

And when people like Chief Luthuli pulled out in 1961 and said, "Now that you are entering in violence,"—1961 was when Umkhonto we Sizwe was formed—I felt that we no longer followed, really, what we told the people of South Africa.

I started thinking about all the presidents of the African National Congress. I can name them: Reverend Tansi, Dr. Moroka, and Chief Luthuli: none of them ever supported a policy of violence.

I joined this organization [ANC] under the understanding that whatever we are doing, we were going to achieve democratic rights by peaceful means, but we were now changing to violence and we intended now overthrowing the state of the Republic of South Africa: that was not the original aim.

But the violence had also done its work on Luthuli, it impugned him also, it had turned him almost into an accomplice. The demonstrators and the rioters in the Defiance Campaign Luthuli openly supported, made him famous and brought the ANC a hundred thousand fellow members. In 1952 Luthuli was elected president-general of an ANC whose executive committee numbered five Communists. Banned in 1952, and again in 1954 and 1959, he wrote several years later: "There are Communists in the South African resistance and I cooperate with them . . . Nobody in the Congress [ANC] may use the organization to further any aims but those of the Congress. When I cooperate with Communists in Congress Affairs, I am not cooperating with communism . . . I do not find within myself a blind terror of the 'communist menace.'"[55] In 1962, the year after the SACP turned the ANC to terrorism, Luthuli won the Nobel Peace Prize. Ludi's judgment, harsher than Hlapane's:

Luthuli was never a Communist. Luthuli was a very compassionate man and also a very devout Christian. Luthuli on his own probably was a very fine person. But Luthuli was not a strong character, nor was he extremely sophisticated, nor did he properly understand the intrigues of the political jungle . . . But all this does not alter the fact that he allowed the young turks, the Communists who really ran the ANC to dictate to him. Nor does it gainsay that he, as president-general, allowed the organization to switch to Castro-type terrorism.[56]

The South African government's ban on Luthuli after he had acquiesced to the ANC's violence in demonstrations, made it much more difficult for him to win control of the ANC.

Sabotage and terrorism also made the ANC more dependent on the Soviets, the beginning probably of direct Soviet control, not only because the Soviets supplied instruction and the mines and other weapons without payment—-but because the ANC lost the self-reliance that comes of give and take with members and of freely-given consent. Besides outlawed and abroad, it lost touch with the country. "The main attack on South Africa will come from the outside," Abraham Fischer told Ludi at his first cell meeting in 1963, reading from a Central Committee document he had probably helped write: "But it is essential that a strong local movement remains in the country. The task of the local movement is to help direct the outside attack—*and also to make it seem to be a local revolution and not a foreign aggression*" (Italics mine).[57]

On June 10, 1985 Denton summed up the main lesson of the Denton Hearings three years before: ". . . It has become absolutely clear . . . that two originally well-intentioned and even well founded organizations, the African National Congress and SWAPO are now totally coopted by the Soviet Union, and are used by them." He meant the SACP's conversion of the ANC to violence that made Hlapane desert both the ANC and the SACP.

The SACP's readiness to betray them hit Hlapane and Mtolo hardest. The leaders simply did not care about them, they did not even bother to warn them of imminent arrests: "The most annoying thing was that the people in Johannesburg [the leaders] were taking all precautions to avoid arrest but had never thought of giving us a warning," Mtolo wrote.[58] Hlapane's confidence in the SACP was undone after his arrest in 1963, and again in 1964, when the Communists broke their promise to look after his family and after the families of other arrested Communists:

Many men were locked up; women and children were starving. All the promises that had been made that they would provide food for them were never fulfilled. And those who had been arrested, we promised to pay for them in jail or even to defend them. Those promises were never fulfilled.

I personally found that the Communists were dishonest and most of them had run out of the country and left us in this mess. And the families of many people who were never released came to my house and demanded now to get food and help from me. I was left with this baby in my hands and I did not know where to turn to.

Hlapane could not stand the arrest of ANC members who had no idea the Communist controlled their organization:

And these are the matters that came to me strongly when I kept on going to jail and finding that the Communists were dishonest and they misled us. And to come to the rescue of many people, I decided to pull out and openly cooperate with the police, because innocent people were being arrested and did not know that the Communist party had, in fact, captured the leadership of the African National Congress. And the African National Congress could not do what they wanted, except to get permission from the Communist party.

Mtolo too was angered at the SACP for repeatedly breaking its promise to support his family. But above all he was undone to the quick by the arrests of his "recruits" for Umkhonto we Sizwe, and by the SACP's secretiveness,— the forerunner of censorship. It was the newspapers, and not the SACP, that told Mtolo some of these "recruits" for Umkhonto we Sizwe had been arrested in Northern Rhodesia, now Zambia,—an unwitting tribute to the freedom of the press: "The [arrests] were causing unrest to the public and to the parents of these youngsters. Some parents were told that their sons were just going to further their studies, because Bantu Education was not good enough. They handed their sons over with joy. Now [the arrests] had happened and how was it ever going to be explained to them? I took an oath that I would never recruit anybody from then on. Again we were not given any information from the High Command, but learned everything from the newspapers."[59] The Command had wanted two hundred "volunteer recruits" from Durban for training abroad by July 1963, two thousand from the country in Natal by October. "If [the High Command] was so serious about this military training, why had [Walter Sisulu] not sent his own son for military training," instead of to school in Swaziland, Mtolo asked himself.[60]

Mtolo had begun by recruiting his only brother in 1962: "My experience showed that some would sacrifice good jobs, not primarily because of politics—they had never even heard of the ANC—but simply for the experience." His brother had been so eager to see the world that "he had not even waited for my explanations."[61] He never saw his brother again. Recruits were not allowed to write home.

Mtolo could not stand the suffering he caused parents and sons who had no idea what was really going on, and who could not see through the leaders because they "just saw them on platforms during meetings":

Our people could not know what these men really were; even I had taken a long time to see through them . . . I felt that it was better to die on the spot than be hanged with them. I knew that I would then be identified with them, and in my heart I knew I was different . . . I could not think of any judge believing me, even if I were taken to him and tried to explain why I had done these things. No one on earth would believe that I had been hoodwinked, or brainwashed, though personally I knew that this was a fact.

Especially after the death of his father in 1964 he felt the presence of his brother's absence. His children also kept asking for him: "Today, when I think of my brother, I feel like crying. I have heard nothing from him since he left the country . . . I sometimes doubt whether he is still alive, because I am sure that he would not have been able to resist the temptation of writing. If he is still alive, I am sure that he would feel as I do. We grew up together and never had ill feelings between us," he wrote in 1968.

Ludi too knew the plight of the recruits, and the betrayal of the SACP:

Many of the trainees were semi-literate Africans tricked out of the country with promises of university bursaries in such countries as the USA. When "Fish," the ANC contact, met them at "Liberation Center" in Lobatsi, he carefully explained to the semi-literates that they would have to "free" South Africa first, then they could become doctors, lawyers and engineers. The poor misled Africans had little choice but to undergo an intensive three month military training course in Tanzania.[62]

A top SACP man had turned Ludi and several other young students out of his house after their arrest: "That evening I saw at first hand that Communists are prepared to be all fatherly if this benefits themselves—once you are in trouble they don't know you." Despite this betrayal, a girl in Ludi's group "always came back for more": "I have never seen anyone used and abused quite so blatantly by the Reds." Naive and idealistic, more or less tricked into joining, she could not leave the SACP because it "represented a security and comradeship she had probably never experienced before."[63]

Nkonono Delphine Kave, not only came from another generation, she had also never been in the SACP. More importantly, she had never testified in court. Unlike Hlapane, she had not had years to come to terms with her experiences. She told her story for the first time in Washington barely a few months after she had managed to pull herself out of the whirlwind. Her words rang like a confession. I owe this book most of all to her.

In contrast to many of the innocent newly-defiant black youths who had wandered across the frontiers in 1977, Kave had been deeply involved in the black student movements, in "Black Consciousness" and the South African Students' Organization (SASO) that many thought responsible for the disturbances in the schools in 1976–77. A close associate of Stephen Biko, she may have been politically innocent, the way any decent person is innocent, when she fled to Botswana on February 7, 1978,—but she was not politically naive: "I had been experiencing the political dishonesty of the black youth leadership and I was deeply disturbed."

Enrolled to study law at the legendary black university at Fort Hare in 1973, she belonged like Biko to the African elite that was well off enough to study instead of work. And she was well-connected: Lennox Sebe, the president of the Ciskei, the only homeland leader openly to support Botha's new constitution, was her uncle.

Unknown to South Africa and the world, like Biko until his death, she was famous among the black youths who were questioning everything: She helped organize, and spoke at Biko's funeral, attended without incident by a few hundred whites and twenty thousand blacks. Shrewd without being manipulative, she does not hate because she knows how to fight. She has something of Biko's unassumingness—vivid enough in Biko to recall Melville's Billy Budd.

Like Biko she would have led a turbulent life anywhere on earth, even born white in the United States or Europe. She has an inborn sense of authority, and does not equate change with the destruction of government. When Denton's chief counsel asked her bluntly about the possibility that the South African police "murdered" Biko, she, a fugitive from South African justice, said some ANC blacks had misrepresented Biko to the police:

. . . There was also a contribution [in the killing of Biko] by our very own people, because of differences in leaderships. Some of our own leaders gave false reports to the South Africans about what "Black Consciousness" stood for.

Everybody regarded the "Black Consciousness" as people who hated whites, and wanted to kill whites in South Africa, and people who were pro-ANC gave these reports to the South African security.

A few months before his terrible death in South Africa in police custody in September 1977, Biko had asked her to investigate information from blacks abroad that the ANC had been taken over by the SACP, "aided by the Socialists,"—just the information that brought Hlapane his death when he made it public to the deaf in Washington.

Denton was taken aback momentarily by the apparent contradiction. Despite detention by the South African police, Biko had resisted the Communists—and respected the law:

You say Steve Biko was detained by South African security and later died in detention? . . . And yet you indicated earlier that Steve Biko was really concerned about the Communist influence on the movement. So he was really caught between both sides, is that it?

Miss Kave was also caught between two sides, the South African government and the ANC, the SACP and, behind them all, the Soviet Union. But she, like Biko, did not equate them.

She experienced this conflict between the ANC and other blacks in full fury when she fled to Botswana. Upon her arrival the Botswana immigration authorities told Kave she had to choose between membership in the ANC and PAC, terrorist organizations illegal in South Africa that Botswana recognized. She chose the ANC, apparently without much thought: She did not insist on simple refugee status without ANC membership.

At the time she gave little importance to the ANC's Communist involvement: "In South Africa, I was always believing that the ANC is a national liberation movement. I believed that they had some working relationship with the Communist party but that not everybody within the African National Congress is a Communist." Luthuli's attitude, twenty-two years after.

The ANC agent who came to pick her up knew who she was. He told her "Steve Biko had been a CIA agent and was confusing the people inside South Africa,"—"unfounded accusations," Kave answered startled. The ANC wanted to use Kave's fame and influence among black students to take over the student movements in South Africa that had taken the ANC by surprise. They started immediately to indoctrinate her. At an ANC residence in Botswana a few days later, she was told she had "to realize that the ANC is not 'Black Consciousness' and we have to learn ANC politics": "After this day, we were getting lessons on Marxism-Leninism. [The texts were] 'The Fundamentals of Marxism-Leninism' and 'The Class Struggle in Africa' by Nkrumah."

The young African blacks with Kave refused to learn Marxism-Leninism and to "bake some fat cakes that ANC leaders were selling." She was accused of "inciting the others." She fled to the Botswana police in an attempt to escape the ANC. There was an uproar:

It was a big thing in Botswana. I even went to the police station trying to get away—some went to the police station to take me back to the African National Congress, and the following day I was told it was orders, to go to Lusaka, to the headquarters. I was following orders.

In Lusaka at ANC headquarters where she was flown just a week after seeking refuge with the Botswana police, she was again told Biko had been a CIA agent and invited to join the SACP. It was "a crime," she was told, "to be anti-Communist in the ANC, a person could be a non-Communist or non-Christian."

The ANC apparently made no headway in breaking her thinking. The alternation of intimidation and seduction did not shake her. She had an almost physical aversion to "Marxism-Leninism," to the indoctrination of the SWAPO guerrilla notebooks, and she had the invaluable gift of being able to distinguish between situations she knew something about and those she knew nothing about.

Later in the Soviet Union, she experienced almost physical disgust at being thrown in with terrorists from all over the earth because she knew nothing about them. She did not take to the destruction of elected governments. She sensed the Soviets meant to use her and the blacks of South Africa:

I felt really betrayed [when she learned the ANC worked with the PLO and many other "opposition parties in Africa"], and I felt I did not want to be a part of what I did not believe in . . . and I later found that in working together with the PLO and other southern African opposition parties that we are—you know, we are—undermining the stabilizing elected governments in southern Africa, not only, you know, in southern Africa, but northern Africa, and in the independent countries, and I realized I did not want to be a part of international terrorism, and communism.

But she only achieved this clarity months later. At the beginning in Botswana and Zambia she still trusted the ANC enough to expostulate with them.

By May of 1978, the ANC called her "a tribalist and an anti-Communist element," expelled her from its residence, and turned her over to a Danish Communist who was to turn her into a Communist. She was put to work translating scripts into Xhosa and broadcasting over the ANC radio *Radio Freedom* where on her own she attacked the leaders of homelands in order to foil an SACP attempt to use them against the whites of South Africa: "The president of the ANC, Oliver Tambo, was very annoyed, saying he had thought I was a relative of Lennox Sebe, and that I had placed him in a bad situation with the homeland leaders."

Exasperated at their inability to use her, the ANC told her that in August,—just six months after she had fled South Africa,—she would be sent to the Soviet Union to further her studies. Again she refused. She already had a law degree, she retorted, and besides ". . . I understand the legal degree in the Soviet Union is more political than legal."

But after she was made to learn the ANC would murder her in an accident in southern Africa if she did not leave for the Soviet Union where she would die also, but later, she left:

I got some information that they had arranged an accident for me on the way. These people said, "You are going to die in the Soviet Union, or die on your way tomorrow. You can choose whatever you want." So I felt that the one to the Soviet Union may take longer than the one tomorrow. I decided to go to the Soviet Union.

The ANC had kept her more or less captive but had been unable to break her. They expected the Soviets would deal with her. She had too many connections and was too well known among the young Africans both in Zambia and South Africa for the ANC to deal with her on their own. In the Soviet Union she continued to fight. Like the ANC, the Soviets tried to keep up appearances of normality that only Kave's bluntness exposed to her, and then not entirely. The Soviets wanted to break, not murder her.

In early September she was sent to Kishenev in Moldavia for language and political instruction. Almost immediately after her arrival, men came to her room in the evening and gave her injections:

At the language center at Kishenev in the Soviet Union, these three men were coming in the evenings, and giving me injections, and this went on from—at least September—it started on September 12, I think.

These injections went on until late November when one of the men who visited her in the evenings took the place of her sick mathematics teacher. At the sight of him in the light of day in a classroom, she ran to the door, and burst into tears:

One day our mathematics teacher became sick, and this man [one of the men who gave her injections] came to the classroom to teach mathematics, and he kept coming nearer to me, and he saw that I was very afraid of him, and one time, while I was sitting here he just came nearer, I do not know exactly, whether he took out a pen or what, but I just jumped from the chair, and I fell, and I ran to the door, and started crying. After that they called a doctor, but the doctor said there was nothing wrong with me.

She had endured the injections in silence until she saw one of the men who came to her in the evening in public; then she had broken down. Her political instructor too was shaken. She came to tell her she had received the injections because the ANC had told the Soviets she was a CIA agent:

When I was in my room, my political teacher came and said, "Do not think that we are giving this treatment to you because we do not like you, but we have got information from your Party, the African National Congress, that you are a CIA agent."

Apparently she was not to take it "personally." She asked her instructor, "Why do you think you should be teaching Marxism-Leninism to a CIA agent?" She was astonished that the ANC had told the Soviets she was a CIA agent.

Shaken, her teacher confessed she was a KGB agent. ". . . If the KGB ever know that I told you that you are a CIA agent, I will be killed."

Kave did not mince her words: "I do not care, I also will be killed. We can all be killed together." A burst of tears had let the truth out of a person used to mouthing words she did not think.

Kave now for the first time in the Soviet Union refused to go to classes in Marxism-Leninism. She hadn't done that since Zambia. She told her instructor, "Why do you not kill me quickly—I have had enough of this slow death. Why do you not kill me soon?"

They sent her boyfriend, a young African from Burundi, to tell her she needed a medical certificate to excuse her from classes. At the hospital the doctors asked her two questions:

"Why are you refusing to attend classes?" Before I could answer, another one asked me: "Why do you want to commit suicide?" I just looked at them, and some stood up and one said: "You need reeducation."

They left, two soldiers came to take her away. They had used her boyfriend and the pretext of a medical certificate to lure her to a psychiatric camp. They had not simply seized her from the school, they tricked her into walking to the camp herself, into handing herself in. They had kept up normal everyday appearances so she had no idea what was happening. She was now in the big time where the twentieth century really sings, and she had gone there the only way you can—docilely.

After some time I was taken—by the people there—they came and took some blood. They knew a little bit of English. And after some time, later in the evening, I was taken to a big room, and there was one bed, and some chairs, and I was left by the nurses—they call them nurses, but they all have the same medical coats. You cannot tell who is the nurses. I was left there by the nurses. Later that evening, many doctors, twenty—I realized twenty came, and they were about fifteen women and about five men—and after that they told me to take off my clothes. They could speak English as well. Very well.

She was now battling openly for her life—and she knew it:

. . . I was just left, and told to lie on the bed. They then asked me, they said they wanted to get my own opinion about the ANC leaders. ANC individual leaders.
First, I told them that I do not know much about ANC leaders. I had not been a member of the ANC in South Africa. I just met them outside the country. So they asked, "What you have experienced and what you think of them?" So I told them. This went on for about one week, they were now asking details and they were taking notes as I was talking about this.

SENATOR DENTON. They are interrogating you under increasingly intimidating circumstances?

Yes, she said. She told how they interrogated her only at night. During the day she was made to stay in her room and go to the inmates' mess. There was food, but only bread and tea without sugar or milk for her:

And they were saying I had to learn to be a revolutionary. So all the time I was at that place, I had only bread, you know, and tea.
They went on like that all that week, and during that week they also brought corpses in plastics.

SENATOR DENTON: Corpses in plastics?

MISS KAVE: Yes. And put them in my room—one would be near the door.

SENATOR DENTON: Put them in your room in various places? Put one in bed with you, did you say?

MISS KAVE: Later. But at first, they put one next to the door and put another one just next to the bed, and they would always be kicking them, saying, "That is what we do to reactionaries."
. . . And after some time, I realized that these were corpses, although I could not see through—it was not translucent plastic—I could realize. So, one day, I pretended that I do not realize that these are corpses. So one time they told the men to put one of them next to me on the bed, and they said, "Do you want to feel?"

She said yes and she felt. And they said, "You see, this is what we do to people."

Her steadfastness undid them: "Do you fear corpses?" She showed them her wit: "I do not usually fear corpses, I fear living people because they are dangerous." She did not scare.

She was astonished to discover they had detailed reports of her conversations with the Danish Communist after she had been expelled from the ANC residence in Zambia in May. They did not like what she had learned about Marx and Lenin from her white political science instructors in South Africa:

I said one time that I was told that they [Marx and Lenin] were utopian in their politics. That annoyed them very much. They were saying, "You should not listen to imperialistic lies from those whites in South Africa who told you what you are saying." And they said I had been brainwashed by the whites in South Africa, and that those whites told me that because they were supporters of Nazi Germany who fled to South Africa.

She parodied their propaganda back to them when they told her she should collaborate with South African Communists like Joe Slovo: "He is a white South African, and you said we are fighting the whites in South Africa."

Like everyday professionals they gave her shots of "calcium" because they said her blood was "weak," shots that made her slightly bleary, and then blinded her temporarily:

They tried to tell me that I seemed not to think that whites are people and they were going to reeducate me and show me that whites are also people. And I was given, you know, injections. I was given an injection here [indicating]. They said my blood is weak—they had been taking blood specimens from me—so now they were saying that my blood is weak and they are going to give me calcium.

They pretended again that they were everyday professionals who wanted to take care of her:

So the first day they gave me the calcium—they said it was calcium—I started not seeing properly. I became bleary in my sight . . . And they gave it to me the second time, and after the second time, I could not see anything. After that, they could come and, you know, make me have sex with whites, and say that I should know that whites are people also . . . that they are also people. Whites are also people . . .

Then they tried to make her ashamed of what they had done to her:

And after that, they would laugh and say, "We have photos of you, you know, and we are going to show these photos."

SENATOR DENTON: So they took photos of the sexual activity and said you could be exposed through blackmail by these photographs?

MISS KAVE: Yes, saying that now I have really become a revolutionary, I am having sex with whites.

To get out of the psychiatric camp after these rapes, she yielded, or pretended to yield: She said she would finally learn "Marxism-Leninism." She also promised to marry the Danish Communist who had told the Soviets of all their conversations about South Africa. She knew the Danish Communist, who would later turn out to be a KGB agent, was already married to a South African. But she promised nevertheless. The use of her wits without compromising her conscience that Denton praised would require several such "marriages." The Communists wanted the whole man, all of her: She pretended to yield.

By this time she was also probably curious about Marxism-Leninism,— the apparent cause of all the uproar and chaos that surrounded her underneath the wooden pretense of normality:

And also I wanted to learn Marxism-Leninism, to understand it. Because, you know, I knew that everybody knew Marxism-Leninism, and I did not know much about it from what I had learned.

Out of the psychiatric hospital and back in Moscow toward the end of December 1978, a man in charge of the "armed struggle in southern Africa,"— the Soviets never think of South Africa alone but of all of southern Africa,— asked her directly to work for the Soviet Union and KGB and "offered to pay any money I needed."

The officer, who figured she was broken enough to follow orders but had not taken her for a Communist, was taken aback when she refused money: "What would keep me from working with the Americans if they offered more money?" He called her a true revolutionary, "not like my leaders, Oliver Tambo and other ANC leaders, who had to be paid to be revolutionaries," and let her loose among the South African students in Moscow, where he said she now realized she belonged:

Now what they were trying to do was establish us—the youth—as a force. That is why they said that the youth was a force to challenge the adult members of the African National Congress. This was the aim, and I was still—they saw that I might be—useful.

Soviet slander of ANC leaders had confused and depressed the South African students. The Soviets called the leaders they did not like, "not true revolutionaries":

I . . . went to Lumumba University to join other South African students. I learned that the South African students were very frustrated. The Soviets were inciting them against some ANC leaders and many of them did not know how to cope with the confusion and Soviet teachings.

In February 1979, a year after she had fled to Botswana, she managed to leave the Soviet Union and return to Zambia,—in unclear circumstances and against the ANC's wishes. I surmise the Soviets took her for their agent, but they did not convince the ANC who had sent her away to disappear and die.

Upon her return to Zambia, she came upon a bloody stage: In the months of her absence, that with supreme irony had probably saved her life, five anti-

Communist members of the ANC had been murdered, two in Zambia, one in Tanzania, one in Botswana, one in Angola. The attempt to break her that had begun in the "psychiatric hospital" continued openly and brutally in Zambia.

In the next months on three successive nights the ANC made her assist at the murders of three young Africans suspected of informing the South African police,—murders that might spell the future of South Africa. They recited the deaths of anti-Communist ANC members to her. They told her some had been murdered because they had talked to her. Over and over again, they told her, she could not escape control of the ANC:

From 1978 several anti-Communist members of the ANC were killed under the direction of Reggie September of the ANC and SACP. Among these were Sonwabo Mlisane who was killed in Zambia, Majuba Yekiso in Zambia, Gwentshe killed in Tanzania, Panase in Botswana, Mavuso killed in Angola. Alfred Nzo [the present secretary of the ANC] warned me that I cannot try to outwit the SACP.

Upon her return to Lusaka the Danish Communist KGB agent, whom she had agreed to marry in the "psychiatric hospital," took her to the Cuban ambassador who tried to get her to join the SACP and fight for Communist control of the ANC. On a second visit she switched glasses with a Cuban and saved her life. After this incident, her "husband" assaulted her, "saying I was a bloody Nationalist and a CIA agent who had drugged and killed a Cuban revolutionary."

From March [just after she had left the Danish Communist's house] to June 1979, ANC and the SACP leaders joined hands trying to drive me to a nervous breakdown. I was helped by an old man, Mr. Mkwanazi, for moral and physical support.

In those months she was made to witness on three successive nights the ANC murder of three young Africans suspected of informing the South African police. (At the seventy-fifth anniversary celebrations of the ANC in January 1987, Tambo announced an "amnesty" for black spies who had infiltrated the ANC.)[64] As she watched these killings she was told she would soon see the old man Mr. Mkwanazi who had helped and comforted her die in the same way:

MR. LISKER [Denton's chief counsel and staff director]: Would you describe in detail the murders which you witnessed in the SACTU house, which is the South African Congress of Trade Unions, prior to June of 1979?

MISS KAVE: Yes. We were at the SACTU house. There is a plain house and seven squatters' huts in back. So the old man is Mkwanazi and myself, we are staying in one of those seven squatters' huts. We were taken the first evening—late in the evening—they came in, and we were told to go to the main house. At the main house there was Dr. Randaree, an ANC man, and Joe Modise. And they brought in a boy—they were working with this boy in the house—and we were sitting here with this old man. And after that, Dr. Randaree, who is an ANC member and in the Communist party, he started asking me if I think I am going to get away, after knowing about what he is doing here? He had asked me to do some research about loans before I left to go to the Soviet Union. He had asked me to make a report from Zambian local newspapers of loans which were given to Zambia by Western countries. So I had done that for him. So now he was mentioning those loans, do I think I am going to get away, and tell people about his activities? After that, Peter Mosemula, who is an ANC leader and a military man, started interrogating the boy and started asking him what message, "What message were you given by the South African security, to whom were you giving that message here in the organization?" This boy was denying that he had got any message from the white South Africans. And after that, Mosemula said, "You young South Africans, you think you are intelligent, or you think you are going to do what you like here within this ANC. Now, we are going to show you."

After that there were many things which they said which I do not want to go into detail about. They lifted the boy, and he was in a round chair, round wooden chair. So they came to him, and he was trying to get up. They held him, and Dr. Randaree gave him the injection, and after that, they took off his clothes.

MR. LISKER: Did the injection kill him?

MISS KAVE: No.

MR. LISKER: He was still alive, but he was unconscious?

MISS KAVE: Yes. He slowly went unconscious. He slowly went unconscious.
After that there was a table, a steel table—

MR. LISKER: Kitchen table?

MISS KAVE: Steel table. Yes, it is not steel but—

MR. LISKER: But this was taking place in the kitchen?

MISS KAVE: In the kitchen of the SACTU house, and they brought another table and put two tables together. They joined these two tables. And after that—after taking off the boy's clothes, they put him on the table, and then Modise went into another room and brought knives.

MR. LISKER: What kind of knives?

MISS KAVE: Big knives. And we were afraid because we did not know, although it was directed at the boy, it could have been us. And he started—he went—you know, to the heart, started from the heart, just cut the boy, and blood started falling from the table.

MR. LISKER: You were watching this?

MISS KAVE: Yes, I was watching, I was watching.
And after some time I was—I went—I was shocked, I just went and held the old man. And after then, when we were to leave the room, I saw that he was open from the navel upward to the stomach here. After they were telling me that I am going to see the old man—them doing the same thing to the old man. And the second day, they brought a girl. They brought a girl. The first boy, I had understood because in the interviews he was speaking to them in Sotho, a South African local language. So, the second night, we were again taken from the bed, and now they brought a girl, and the gentlemen who was the ANC military man was kissing this girl. They were talking with this girl in her language.

MR. LISKER: Did she know from the conversation what was about to happen to her?

MISS KAVE: No; she did not know. She seemed not to be aware of what was going to happen to her.
They were speaking in this language, which was the Zambian dialect, and I later asked the old man who knew Zambian, what the girl was speaking—it was a local

Zambian language—and after that talking Randaree also injected this girl, who was trying also to resist. And after that, it was during some killings of girls in Zambia that this thing was happening. And on the third night, they brought another boy, and with this boy they asked him—it was a different boy. I do not remember exactly what he was asked about now. He was also denying, saying I do not know anything, and also speaking in Sotho, which is a local language. The thing went the same way. By now, I was looking, and they were saying, "You seem to be strong. You are not affected."

I became angry. I felt that anything could happen to us. But the old man that evening, and some other people, they decided that we had to move from the house, from the SACTU house. And I and other people were also outside during all this time that these things were happening. So these people knew that they were killing them, and said if they die inside the house, we are going to fight right here in Zambia, and we will all die right here. But this thing was happening with people coming in the evening, and our own people watching from outside, saying we cannot do anything. These people have got the Zambian security and Zambian police who can go and report anybody.

So the old man told me to marry Chibeya, and that is how I made that sacrifice.

She attempted to establish a public life in Lusaka to escape the ANC. She married a young South West African, Chibeya, in flight from SWAPO, who had managed to win a three year position at the University of Zambia, canceled without explanation in a few months. The threats against her life continued.

At the time of the ministerial meeting of the OAU in Freetown, Sierra Leone in June 1980, she was told that all "independent" individuals like herself were to be wiped out: "I learned that Makatini, an ANC and SACP leader who attended the Freetown conference [Makatini, until recently at the UN, headed ANC "international relations" in Lusaka until his death in late 1988], had been given the go-ahead for the SACP to wipe out all reactionaries in the ANC . . . After this OAU conference at Freetown, Tennyson Makiwane was killed by the SACP inside South Africa. The firing and assassination squad was also sent after me . . ."

She described the three-tiered organization of the murder squads that roam with impunity throughout southern Africa, and that must also be involved in the murders of blacks who support the reforms of the South African government.

The second tier,—the "firing and assassination squad" Kave said was after her,—is made up of members of the SACP and other Communist parties including Western European parties. The first tier, the "security department," means simply a local ANC hit squad. The third tier, the most trusted, is simply "an extension wing of the KGB": "That group [the third tier] is usually dominated by the Palestine National Liberation Organization, because they are the best assassins." The PLO operates in southern Africa, because it understands Israel is next, after South Africa.

A little more than a year later, in July 1981,—less than a year before the Denton Hearings,—an official of the ANC threatened her with death in the middle of the capital of Botswana, Gaborone, a city of sixty thousand souls where she had fled from Zambia. He said nobody would believe her if she talked: "He was saying even if I outwitted him, I will not pass the Soviet Ambassador, Soldovnikov, in Lusaka."

The ANC sensed she would find a way to tell the world:

He was threatening me with death, saying nobody will believe my stories about the ANC. He was saying I am from a bourgeois family and they nearly killed my uncle [Lennox Sebe, the president of the Ciskei] inside South Africa.

She had in fact decided to talk. From the house of the United Nations High Commissioner for Refugees (UNHCR) who instead of helping abused her, weak unto death she called a journalist she knew in South Africa to tell him of the SACP and ANC killings. More or less imprisoned in the UNHCR's house, she had to hear him tell her he had seen the corpse of Mr. Mkwanazi, the old man who had kept up her strength and saved her life in the months just after her return to Zambia from Russia, especially in the days she had witnessed the ANC butcherings of the three youths:

The behavior of the representative of the UNHCR, Mr. Mkanda, shocked and disgusted me. He is abusing his position, and with what I experienced at his hands, as a representative of the United Nations, I gained a very negative impression of the United Nations in southern Africa. He locked me in his house, abused me sexually and mentally, *and did nothing to help those who were in danger in Zambia, Tanzania and Angola.*
On Monday following that Friday, I made a phone call to South Africa and told the SACP killings to a journalist friend, as I realized that I was getting weaker and may not leave Botswana alive. The phone call shocked Mr. Mkanda, as he thought I could not help myself (Italics mine).

Denton was visibly shocked at the allegations against a UN official that the witnesses before the *Internationale Gesellschaft für Menschenrechte* confirmed in 1985.
Kave's call to the journalist in South Africa began her journey to Washington. In Washington she spoke to the world,—but she wanted to be heard most in South Africa, both black and white. She wanted to tell them that many of the five to ten thousand youths who had fled South Africa in hope and anger in 1976–77, and had not returned, were mostly dead or wasting away in camps in Angola: The ANC and SACP had broken the defiant and rebellious who had refused to submit. They were attempting to blame murders and disappearances on the South African government. There was nothing left of "Black Consciousness":

I want to let the parents of these children, especially the ones who came in after 1976, and the other African National Congress members who came in the 1960's, know there is nobody who is left among these people. Those who are still alive, who had been sent for reeducation to prisons in Angola, and a number of our people have been killed. I want to let even the world known that I cannot reconcile my conscience with what the ANC is doing, because they are telling everyone for instance, that the South Africans raided the ANC bases in Matola [a suburb of Maputo] in 1980, [actually, January 30, 1981] and they gave a list of the people who supposedly died in that Mozambique raid. I can tell you that two of those people had been long dead. One died in 1978, and one in 1980 in Zambia, in my presence; and other people, from witnesses whom I know, I have learned that others had died even before that. So I do not want to be blamed by the parents of the children I worked with.

The Communists destroyed the non-Communist opposition in SWAPO in the same way as the ANC, but without open murder, in July 1976, roughly two years before the bloodshed Kave witnessed—according to Andreas Shipanga, a founding member of SWAPO, a member of the TGNU, the internal government of South West Africa, who also testified in Washington. The arrival of the Cubans and the Soviets in Angola precipitated the Communist takeover of SWAPO in 1976 that also betrayed itself in the removal at the same time of its headquarters from Lusaka to Angola. In contrast to the ANC, SWAPO had not succumbed completely to Marxist-Leninism before 1976, although it had begun to mix in the destructive element already in 1966.

In Moscow in 1965 Shipanga and other SWAPO leaders had told the Soviets they would not take sides in the Soviet-Chinese split: "And we say, well in the first place—and I say this truthfully—we are not a Communist organization, we cannot take part in ideological struggle between the Communist party of the Soviet Union and the Communist party of China, because we are not Communists."

"Peking," the SWAPO leaders told the Soviets when they asked where they were going after their Moscow meeting: ". . . And I can assure you, they didn't like it." They told the Soviets that Communists had to fight their own battles: "This thing will have to be solved by the Communist International, and we are not part of the Communist International." They repeated their words to the Communists in Peking: "While other movements, they clearly identified themselves to be either pro-Soviets or pro-Chinese, only SWAPO continued to have relations with both the Soviet Union and China." The Soviets had tried to bully them: "And they say, look, other movements, you know—Peking is only supported by small movements like SWANU, PAC, ZANU, COREMO, et cetera, but the other movements, you know, they are on our side." But they stood firm: "We continued until 1965, we continued with this policy."

The anti-Communist and non-Communist members of SWAPO realized something was up when Sam Nujoma, the current president of SWAPO, said in Prague in 1973, "He believes in scientific socialism." They asked him, "Where was this adopted as a policy of SWAPO?," and demanded a "congress" to thrash the matter out. Nujoma answered with an accusation of spying for South Africa, a frequent label for opposition in the ANC and SWAPO,—as the testimony before the IGFM also shows: ". . . We set the year 1974 to have a congress, and he starts saying that those who run the congress of SWAPO are South African agents, that SWAPO is not going to have a congress in exile, we will only have a congress in liberated Namibia. But everybody knew that that was a long dream." The members of SWAPO I have met still remember the uproar that reached the rank-and-file in those days with a shudder of pain and embarrassment at their ineptitude and naiveté.

Instead of murdering the opposition outright, Nujoma and the other SWAPO Communists had the presidents of Zambia and Tanzania order the arrest of about two thousand members of SWAPO, including thirteen leaders, who had fought against Communist control and Marxist-Leninist indoctrination. The thirteen leaders were sent from Zambia to the prisons of Tanzania. Almost a year later, Kaunda released six hundred from Zambia. Two years after their arrest, the thirteen leaders were released without charges or questioning. Nobody knows what became of the remaining roughly fourteen hundred who disappeared into Angola, as the witnesses before the IGFM testified:

. . . We fear the worst could have happened to them, but this is mere speculation. We really don't know. It is difficult to get any news from Angola or people out of Angola.

In 1986 there were renewed fights in SWAPO that showed some members again ready to risk their lives to break Communist control. About a hundred members, including men from SWAPO's Central Committee who wanted to negotiate with the South African supported government in Windhoek, the TGNU, were "arrested," SWAPO's first public admission of such "arrests."

These men had recognized the important changes in South West Africa since 1975 that the world had barely noticed. They wanted to negotiate with Windhoek because they believed South Africa was willing to grant independence to South West Africa as long as it was not a pretext for a Communist takeover.[65]

With something of aristocratic scorn Kave replied to a question of Denton's about United States newspaper coverage of South Africa:

You are poorly informed . . . And what information you are given, from what I hear, on what it is like in South Africa, the reports are prepared by the Soviets.

For an example of distorted coverage, she took the notorious "coup" against Kaunda that had baffled the most astute international press. In disbelief the *Economist* blamed Kaunda's suspiciousness, but wrote as if nothing had occurred: "He sees foreign plots in everything from union strikes to low turn-outs at political rallies. All this suggests a bad case of insecurity."

On October 15, 1980, the Zambian police in search of robbers, came upon about two hundred armed men on a farm south of Lusaka owned by a South African who had left Zambia three years before. Maps and notes for an attack the next day on the president's residence State House, the Lusaka radio station and the airport were found on gunmen killed in the police shoot-out. Gunmen picked up later implicated prominent Zambians. On October 22 a dawn-to-dusk curfew was drawn on Lusaka and other towns, but Zambians had to wait until the last Monday in October before they found out what Kaunda thought was going on: He blamed the South Africans who—the defense minister Magnus Malan and the foreign minister—denied the charge, a denial

The Daily Telegraph and the *Guardian* believed. Kaunda also accused the unions who were about to call a strike for political reasons to curb the powers of his regime, especially the Party Central Committee. Accomplished men were among the detained, rumored to number about a hundred, among them experts who had left the government in disgust because they could not get anything done. The story of the coup tempted the belief of discontented men with little confidence in Kaunda: "One-party states are coup-prone because their citizens have no other way of changing an unpopular administration," remarked one of the detained. A few of the accused still languish in Zambia's prisons awaiting trials for treason.[66]

Kave insisted that the SACP had tried to murder Kaunda when the anti-Communist Africans had fought back to resist their extermination and killed SACP and PLO men,—the only hint in her testimony of anti-Communist blacks fighting back. These Africans had not been able to get through to Kaunda helpless before all this murder, to tell him that the SACP had wanted to assassinate him,—not the CIA, not the United States, not the European countries, not the white South Africans, nor the Rhodesians. Misinformed by his Soviet-penetrated secret police, Kaunda had also expelled some baffled American diplomats without explanation:

What is happening in southern Africa, the Americans are not aware. Even when some American diplomats were expelled from Zambia, they did not understand, they did not know that we were fighting in Zambia, and they were said to be the ones organizing this net. The Zambians did not give reasons, they just told them then to leave the country. Many things which are happening in Zambia, which I was accused of being a part of—I was accused of trying to assassinate President Kaunda—it was actually done by the South African Communist Party, and later the story was changed. They changed the whole thing, and said it was the CIA and the Western countries you know, but with me having been persuaded to be part of that. I came to know of this. I changed—we changed—the whole thing, and some Palestinian Liberation Organization and SACP people were killed by our own people in Zambia. When the whole thing erupted, President Kaunda did not know who was trying to kill him, and he started saying it was the Americans, and we did not have access to him, to tell him exactly what was happening. His own security people have proven that they were working with the Soviets, and they said what sounded better—that it was the white South Africans and white Zimbabweans who were doing the SACP killings—when all the time it was our own people who killed the South African Communist members, and other Communist members.

Whatever the truth about this coup, Kave's account yields the same picture the witnesses drew before the IGFM of a Lusaka of violent commerce just underneath the surface of everyday life. Blaming the Americans, South Africans and the Rhodesians for the supposed coup,—and more recently the South Africans for the crash of Machel's plane,—without evidence in either instance, serves to distract Kaunda from the consequences of his one-party regime and of his support of terrorism. Kaunda cannot discriminate between violence, because he is against all violence, including the "violence" he considers inherent in the state: He presided over the seventy-fifth anniversary celebrations of the ANC in Lusaka in January 1987. He refused to help Mugabe and Machel overthrow Malawi, but apparently did not inform the president of Malawi of the conspiracy until after the crash of Machel's plane on October 19, 1986 betrayed it to the world.[67] Ambivalence that may undo him in the end.

There was something in the rush of Kave's words that Denton recognized instantly, the way lovers know things that need not be said. Not her suffering, but the attempt to deny that suffering drove Kave to speak. She dreaded the triumph of all that murder's purpose, the extermination of the truth itself, of the human voice itself, the voice that the dogma of the terrorist notebooks means to replace.

The distorted incompetent news accounts, and the taunting voice of the ANC official who told her no one would believe her even as he threatened her death, showed her a world of the living dead she feared more than the memory of her sufferings, and than death itself. Denton burst out:

Miss Kave, you have been talking rather rapidly . . . I talked rapidly when I was returned from a Communist country. Having had the experience hundreds of times of reading a report from Moscow, which I knew to be a lie, and then two days later seeing the same paragraphs in the English version of the Hanoi Communist propaganda and then less than a week later seeing similar paragraphs in the American press, I can understand the earnestness and rapidity with which you are testifying. I do not know why it happens. I went through a similar experience with a similar response of dismay and frustration.

She could not stand being used for other people's political purposes. She had an almost physical sense for the contempt of the Soviets that betrayed itself in their insistence on the interchangeability of "liberation movements"—for instance, in the integration of SWAPO and ANC members in FAPLA (the MPLA's army) units in Angola. "You must understand I had learned in Zambia . . . that the ANC worked with everybody who is from the National Liberation Movements assisted by the Soviet Union." Soviet insistence on treating all the "oppressed" as if they were the same helped the Soviets dominate and exploit them for their own purposes.

She was shocked by ANC collaboration with the PLO and with "the other opposition parties in Africa,"—she meant groups that want to overthrow governments,—because she knew she knew nothing about their countries,—uncommon modesty in a world that takes slogans for proof of its good conscience. She could not judge. She knew in a way few people know that South Africa was unique—like all other countries that have endured. This sense of the difference between one place and another gave her the guts to keep on fighting, and also the wit to know when she ought to pretend to go along that saved her life in the Soviet Union. That she was used was her deepest experience in the Soviet Union,—and in the ANC: *"Now I believe that people are blackmailed to be Communists* and the worst thing that I could not reconcile with was working with other known terrorist organizations. They may be fighting maybe for a just cause in their countries, but I do not have the facts about the history of those countries." The italicized words do not tell only Kave's story. They are the theme of this book Kave taught me.

She was taken aback when Denton asked her whether the information about SACP infiltration of the ANC Biko had gathered had been passed on to the CIA. She was not about to betray her country:

No, no we did not want to be influenced by any foreign country in South Africa. We did not want to—with America or with the Soviet Union. As nationalists, we wanted our struggle to be purely nationalist.

Like Savimbi she knows Africans have to remain true to their own lives and countries in their politics. They have only just begun to think politically, they need time above all, the time violence now seeks to rob:

We were against any foreign ideology. What we stand for should be a genuine, wholly African, political outlook, and the political culture, and our own African outlook, through politics *which is different from what Americans and the Western countries are standing for.*

We have this uniqueness of Africa, which we do not want to overlook, when we engage in politics, our background, our culture, we want to retain, this is why we are still moving into politics (Italics mine).

She insisted on differences, on arrangements that would take account of actual differences without exploiting them. Denton's chief counsel, Joel Lisker, asked her whether she wanted African blacks "to become a political force and a cultural force in the white man's world."

We do not become a lost force. The leadership, on certain occasions, can meet and work together, when they have to; groups can work separately because even among the Coloreds and Indians, and Africans, at times, we do not always have the same problems. We are acknowledging in South Africa that where we have similar problems we can work together, but in the political arena in South Africa, we felt that we could work loosely as the cultures would differ.

Each group could come in and work with its cultural group alone. She meant the blacks had to know themselves, talk to themselves in the languages they took on with their birth, as well as to others in the languages they learned at school and at work. Africans and perhaps also the whites—lived in at least two worlds, and there was no way of pretending they lived in one.

Hlapane hit differences head on in his remarks about the homelands where about half of South Africa's blacks live. He had been against the establishment of the self-governing homelands in 1960, the modification of apartheid into self-development. But the chiefs, who make up as much as half of the legislature in some of the homelands, had accepted them after the ANC turned to violence. The ANC could not claim to represent all the blacks. Whatever one thought of them, the homelands and their governments could not be dismissed or ignored in the way Clough's article, the Commonwealth Report and the CAA Act dismiss and ignore them. They are a reality, a reality that with the abolishment of the "Pass Laws" in July 1986 may slowly fade, but certainly not in one generation:

You have what we call these separate developments. That was the intention of the South African government, though I do not really say I agree with that. *But they have done something, and whether we like it or not, the situation is there.*

They have got this separate development, you know; they have got each tribal group in a position. For example, you take the Transkei, you take Bophuthatswana, you take Zululand, and you take other tribal groups—Basotho, and so on. They placed them in their own areas where they say, "Well, you can make laws to govern yourselves and you can do this for yourselves, and your own people control you," and so on. "We have the whites out of you," and so on.

And the chiefs have taken this up, and I can assure you, you will find it difficult if you go to South Africa today to try and say that the Prime Minister of South Africa is wrong by so doing. Some people may find it, you know, wrong to divide South Africa into portions and call them states.

I agree with them to some extent, but it is there. What do you do? These people now support the government of South Africa. In fact, if I may call upon my friend, Mr. Tambo [the president of the ANC] to go back to South Africa and try and say that he is a member of the African National Congress and he will be sending the ANC and doing away with all these legal things—say for instance, "Now Matanzima (Paramount Chief Kaiser Matanzima of Transkei, which chose independence in 1976), you do away with this nonsense; we want you to fall under the African National Congress." *He would be killed on the spot* (Italics mine).

The violence that began in July 1985 between UDF agitators and Zulus in Natal is a foretaste of the killing Hlapane meant. Almost twenty years before, Mtolo who could see the Zulus from the outside because his family had lived for generations among the Xhosas in the Transkei had not minced his words about these differences:

The situation is worse among the Zulus, who do not even recognize the other black tribes as their equals. The Zulus are very proud of their identity and their nationhood. If a Zulu gets married to, say, a Xhosa girl, his friends will always say that he married a Xhosa or a Basuto girl. They don't say he is married to so and so's daughter, even if the father is known to them. If he has done something wrong, he has done it because he married a Xhosa or a Basuto. Likewise with the Xhosa. They regard everyone who is not a Xhosa as someone whose brain is not ripe enough, not to mention Indians or whites.[68]

Lieutenant Adriano Francisco Bomba from Mozambique was in his way as admirable as Kave and Hlapane. Straightforward, fearless and modest, he had coped resolutely with a situation beyond his, and anybody's control. He never lost his attractive gaiety: "I have got my statement and I would love to read it." His testimony towards the end of the Hearings showed what had become of Mozambique since 1974.

In early 1979, upon his return after twenty-one months in the Soviet Union, he barely recognized his native land:

You look at the streets, look at the shops—empty; you only see queues, people sleep in the street to be first in the next day; they stay in the queues during the nights. Is that liberation? Is that development?

Shortages of people matched shortages of goods. Almost anybody who could do anything was gone. The government had taken the place of employers but handed out jobs on political grounds:

Mozambique had by now come to grips with a rather precarious economic situation: Shortages of raw materials had been aggravated by the exodus of skilled personnel. Hence the government started appointing newcomers to fill vacancies left by the Portuguese. The promotions and appointments were subject to adherence to and partisanship toward the ruling party. Thus the mediocrity of the promoted people and the economic chaos.

The private sector had been strangled by the newly implemented state-owned sector and collective farms. This proved to be detrimental to the economy, which started producing much less than before, and the whole bureaucratic machine started crumbling, too.

The faces of the missing came to him everywhere, absences that told not only of flight to South Africa, but of the camps lost in the bush, and of dying:

. . . From 1975 on, a lot of people in Maputo were taken just because they didn't have identification cards. They were taken to those reeducation camps, and when they arrived at those reeducation camps, they didn't see anything; it's just the bush, where there are animals—lions, snakes and other wild animals. The authorities said: "You must create here the conditions for your living; you are going to be reeducated here"— and they are guarded by soldiers. And they are very often tortured, and many of them die in these reeducation camps.

Three years before the Portuguese left, at the age of twelve, he had taken up with FRELIMO. He had been sensitive to little humiliating social discriminations that testified to the mixture of races,—but that hurt. The Portuguese had considered Mozambique and Angola an integral part of Portugal. Africans had numbered about sixty percent of the sixty thousand soldiers in Mozambique at the time of the collapse in Portugal: Maimed African veterans were conspicuous in wheelchairs at big soccer games in Lisbon in the early seventies.

Like Kave, Bomba did not fool himself about his ignorance, even when he joined the cause. "Due to the differences of social treatment between blacks and whites, I immediately identified with FRELIMO's national cause, in spite of my poor political knowledge":

I was able to air my views on FRELIMO and even hold discussions with Portuguese friends and colleagues, who obviously took an opposite stand as a result of their family upbringing. Despite our early age and bare political ignorance, when in the company of black friends, we used to refer to FRELIMO as "ours."

He had made no secret of his devotion to FRELIMO, but by 1974 he had been on to better things, "pop music and guitar playing."

But after it took over the country, FRELIMO did not forget about him. He submitted to the FRELIMO political action groups, the "Dynamizing Groups," in his school—squads meant to clean up the filth in the streets and factories that astonished South African visitors as early as 1975: the disheveled face of Lourenço Marques, renamed Maputo. Sweeping a floor had become a political exercise that left the floor dirty:

> These "Grupos Dinanmizodores," each with a specific mission, were in charge of promoting political awareness and of allocating to the people regardless of their social position, tasks that ranged from mop-up operations at schools, streets, et cetera, and the setting up of several collective farms. I took part in these campaigns although with some amount of aversion.

In 1976, a year later, he had the guts to refuse an "invitation" from his chemistry teacher to become a FRELIMO militant. The next year, 1977, there no longer was any school: "Amazed at these developments, we sought an explanation which was never given to us."

On March 8 at a meeting with President Machel, they were told that because of "the revolutionary realities of the country and of the pressing needs to form cadres," students from the tenth and eleventh classes "would be taken away from school and sent overseas where they would be trained in subjects and fields more suitable to the needs of the country."

On March 28, after medical examination, Bomba with seventy-four other students was flown to the Soviet Union. Like Kave and other ANC and SWAPO recruits, he beheld the sea of nations in the Soviet Union with astonishment: "I should stress that Mozambicans were not the only foreign military trainees, as there were also Angolans, Tanzanians, Congolese, Ethiopians, Somalis—they withdrew when the Somali government cut off diplomatic relations—Libyans, Chadians, Malians, Algerians, Yemenis, Afghans, Vietnamese, Cubans, East Germans, Bulgarians, Rumanians."

For almost two years he trained to fly the MIG–17 and other aircraft. In the Soviet Union he finally joined FRELIMO upon orders.

Upon his return he missed the Portuguese. Under the Portuguese he had been free to choose his profession: ". . . I didn't decide that I wanted to become a fighter-bomber pilot; I was studying only to become an engineer. But FRELIMO has got power. They decided that I would become a fighter-bomber pilot to defend the power of themselves." There had been enough food. He had been able to speak his mind:

> The Portuguese, they were not interested in developing Mozambique; they were colonialists. Despite that we had enough food, we could decide what we wanted to do, we were free to express our opinion—*of course, with some limits*. But now, with FRELIMO, it's this: What's not in this line, no place for it. That is the freedom that FRELIMO brought for us with the Soviet control (Italics mine).

Weapons had replaced food. "But with weapons nobody can produce food." The hunger Bomba saw upon his return brought the death of about a hundred thousand of starvation in the three years after his testimony, 1983–86:

> I can say . . . what they did to improve the life of the Mozambican people—for example, now one Mozambican can buy two kilos of rice per month—those are the limits they have. And who does not agree with the FRELIMO policy goes to reeducation camps. And many people die of diseases because they don't have enough hospitals, they don't have enough doctors. They have weapons, they have got many weapons—about that no problem . . . the Mozambican people don't need weapons; the Mozambican people need food.

People with weapons instead of food brought North Vietnam to Denton's eyes. The American flyers had pitied the Vietnamese people more than themselves after torture stopped in the last four years of their imprisonment—because they had had more food. Weapons without food, Denton knew, meant weapons would first serve against those meant to use them. He remembered Vietnam:

> But [instead of food] there were plenty of weapons, and, to encourage their zeal in communism, they were chained to their artillery pieces. This is the sort of thing that our people never learned about that conflict and about that nation.
>
> I watched one-legged men inducted into the armed services there, screaming and fighting. Over a period of days they were subdued until they could be fitted with an artificial—with what amounted to a peg leg and then, having previously been on crutches, they went into combat on the peg leg.

Bomba also got at the heart of the new world in Mozambique. You had to be for the new men or you were against them:

> You don't have to take an arm and fight against FRELIMO; if you don't agree with them, you are an enemy—just not agree. They don't accept even neutrality.

Bomba did not mince the hardest truth. Things could get worse:

> And after the independence, what happens is that the Soviets they replaced the Portuguese, and the Soviets are more cruel. I can say that before the independence in Mozambique the conditions of life were better.

All Bomba's missions after his return were against the resistance within Mozambique that renegades from FRELIMO started. On July 8, 1980 he flew his MIG–17 to South Africa. It had come to him that he had been destroying his own country:

> . . . It suddenly occurred to me that even though this system (FRELIMO) was to bring Mozambique down, I was in fact defending it. As it was impossible to resign from the armed forces, I decided to desert.

Four years ago, at the age of twenty-six, Lieutenant Bomba was killed in action in an attack on a railroad in Mozambique. Despite a grant of political asylum in South Africa, he had returned to his native land to fight in RENAMO. The professional rebels of FRELIMO had driven him to real rebellion,—the rebellion that had attracted him, briefly, at sixteen.

In Washington in 1982 his words had already shown the pull of the resistance on him,—resistance he knew had taken first breath in the gulags he had briefly defended:

And now there is a movement that is fighting in Mozambique against the FRELIMO government. The movement was created by one man that was in the reeducation camp of Ruarua. This man escaped from the reeducation camp and because of experiences he had there decided, no, I must fight against the Mozambican government.

Like Kave and Hlapane, Bomba saw clearly he and his country had been used. The Soviets did not care about him or Mozambique.

This clarity that came of his decision to stand alone gave him an unabashed common sense grasp of geography—of the consequences of the war for southern Africa for the whole world that will not do in public speech in today's West. Why is it almost always only those who fight, almost alone, who have to tell us these things?

The Soviets in Africa, they are not in Africa to help the African people. They use the intentions of the African people in their own—to their own plans; for example they convert liberation movements into their surrogates. It is just to have control of Africa, to control all that part of Africa, because the last intention of the Soviet Union is to control all the world. They want to kill the Western world by controlling the roots in Africa. If they can control—they have got now Mozambique, they have got now Angola, they are controlling Zimbabwe now, they want Namibia now, they are going to South Africa. If they control South Africa, this route of the Cape, good-bye to it.

And what does this mean? It means that all the stuff that is coming from South Africa and all the routes that pass the Cape won't come to the Western world, and the Western world won't have enough power to resist against the Soviet Union. That is their last intention; they don't want to liberate the African people. The African people must liberate themselves without the Soviets.

Not as eloquent as Mahan—but as intelligent.[69]

Jariretundu Kozonguizi, a man who has worked for the independence of South West Africa since the early fifties, who has lived long in Europe and who was a member of the South African sponsored internal government of South West Africa, the TGNU until its end in 1988, added a crucial dimension to Bomba's analysis. South Africa's readiness to defend South West Africa and to fight in Angola was essential to the freedom of all of southern Africa:

Whatever other things are happening in South Africa, whatever views one may hold on South Africa, there is something that is very clear about the stated position of the South African government, and that is they feel that they have to fight in Namibia or in Angola.

What they are fighting there is the Communist infiltration into southern Africa, and they feel strongly that the ultimate objective of the Soviet Union is South Africa itself, from which, as I have indicated in my testimony, it is hoped to build a strong foundation, to be able now to move strongly into Africa, no longer having to provide the African continent assistance from a distance as far as Europe.

They [the Soviets] want to come to where they want to, through Africa and the Third World, because they failed to do so through Europe.

I have no doubt that in a world where they have to fight for supremacy, definitely their final objective would have to be the country that really is the real frustrating element in whatever they really want to do, and in this particular case it is the United States of America, which I think has frustrated them to a very great extent in Europe.

Denton answered with the words of a Cuban Secret Service (DGI) agent who had testified before his committee a few weeks before:

. . . He testified that in Cuba they are taught that the Cuban involvement in Africa is only one phase of the attack upon the United States of America, which is the only major defender of freedom left in terms of strength.

But Europe comes before the United States.

Notes

Introduction

1 For the courts and newspapers, Edward Roux, *Time Longer than Rope*,² Madison, WI 1964 (first edition, the greater part of the text, 1948). An Afrikaner with a mother from Britain, Roux was an important member of the SACP, then called the CPSA, founded in 1921, from 1923–1936.
2 Aleksandr Solzhenitsyn, "Difficulties in the West with the Study of Russian History," Stanford 1988, 57–61.
3 Boris Asoyan quoted in *Front File*, November 1988.
4 *The New York Times*, January 8, 1989.
5 Jim and Sybil Stockdale, *In Love and War*, New York 1984, 394.

Chapter One

1 L.M. Thompson, *The Unification of South Africa*, 1902–1910, Oxford 1960, 168.
2 James Bryce, *Impressions of South Africa*,³ London 1899 (first edition 1897), 98.
3 Bryce, *Impressions*, 346–347.
4 Quoted in Paul Johnson, "The Race for South Africa," *Commentary*, September 1985, 30.
5 *Weekly Mail* (Johannesburg), May 15, 1987.
6 The two preceding quotations: Smuts to T. Lynedoch Graham, July 26, 1902, W.K. Hancock and J. van der Poel (eds.), *Selections from the Smuts Papers* (henceforth *SP*), Cambridge 1966, II, 13–16; "Memorandum to the Labour Commission," 1903, *SP*, II, 232. The passage directly footnoted, quoted in W.M. Macmillan, *Bantu, Boer and Briton, the Making of the South African Native Problem*², Oxford 1963 (first edition 1928), 95–96. This classic little book has become nearly a primary source, because a fire at the University Library in Johannesburg in 1930 destroyed the papers of the Reverend John Philip Macmillan quotes.
7 Kenneth Ingham, *Jan Christian Smuts, the Conscience of a South African*, London 1986, 41.
8 Smuts to E. Hobhouse, February 21, 1904, *SP*, II, 149.
9 For the distinction between Hobbes and Montesquieu, Pierre Manent, *Histoire intellectuelle du liberalisme*, Paris 1987, 119–142.
10 Alan Paton, "Dr. Hendrik Verwoerd—A Liberal Assessment" in Edward Callan (ed.), *The Long View*, New York 1968, 270, and "A Calm View of Change," *Contact I*, 5, April 5, 1968, reprinted in *The Long View*, 69.
11 Basil Hersov of Anglo-Vaal quoted in Richard John Neuhaus, *Dispensations, The Future of South Africa as South Africans See It*, Grand Rapids, MI 1986, 85.
12 Alan Paton, The New York Times, April 3, 1985.
13 Quoted in Neuhaus, *Dispensations*, 236 and 240.
14 Macmillan, *Bantu*, 73, 241–242, the second number refers to the preceding quotation.
15 Macmillan, *Bantu*, 347.
16 *Race Relations Survey 1985*, South African Institute of Race Relations 1986, 570–571.
17 Trevor Huddleston, *Naught for Your Comfort*, New York 1956, 139–142.
18 Bryce, *Impressions*, 459.
19 Bryce, *Impressions*, 453.
20 Quoted in Macmillan, *Bantu*, 122.
21 D'Urban quoted in Macmillan, *Bantu*, 156.
22 Macmillan, *Bantu*, 131.
23 Quoted in Macmillan, *Bantu*, 289.
24 Macmillan, *Bantu*, 117.
25 Macmillan, *Bantu*, 199.
26 Quoted in Macmillan, *Bantu*, 20.
27 Quoted in Macmillan, *Bantu*, 116.
28 Macmillan, *Bantu*, 196.

29 P.J. Joubert (the actual writer was Smuts), *A Century of Injustice*, Baltimore 1899, 66. Joubert was the vice-president of the South African Republic and commander-in-chief of the army.
30 Merriman to Smuts, May 12, 1906, *SP*, II 275.
31 Smuts to S.M. Smuts, May 12, 1902, *SP*, I 392–395, quoted in Ingham, *Smuts*, 40.
32 Bryce, *Impressions*, 374.
33 Merriman to Smuts September 5, 1905, *SP*, II, 198–201.
34 Macmillan, *Bantu*, 209.
35 Bryce, *Impressions*, 35.
36 Quoted in Macmillan, *Bantu*, 80.
37 Quoted in Macmillan, *Bantu*, 165.
38 Theodor Hanf, Heribert Weiland and Gerda Vierdag, *South Africa, the Prospects of Peaceful Change*, Bloomington, IN 1981, 335.
39 Quoted in Macmillan, *Bantu*, 289.
40 Bryce, *Impressions*, 95.
41 Quoted in Macmillan, *Bantu*, 97.
42 Quoted in Macmillan, *Bantu*, 66.
43 Marina Mapona, " 'South Africa in the Future,' the Problems and Challenges from a Black Woman's Point of View," in Gideon Jacobs (ed.), *South Africa—the Road Ahead*, Johannesburg 1986, 202–209, especially 206–207.
44 Bryce, *Impressions*, 375.
45 Bryce, *Impressions*, 353–355.
46 Quoted in Macmillan, *Bantu*, 97.
47 Bryce, *Impressions*, 377.
48 Merriman to Smuts, December 30, 1906, *SP*, II 311–314.
49 Huddleston, *Naught*, 57–58.
50 Alan Paton, forward to John W. de Gruchy, *The Church Struggle in South Africa*, Grand Rapids, MI 1979, xi.
51 Bryce, *Impressions*, 157–158.
52 Bryce, *Impressions*, 163–164.
53 Smuts to Graham, July 26, 1902, *SP*, II, 13–16.
54 Quoted in Macmillan, *Bantu*, 315.
55 Quoted in Macmillan, *Bantu*, 323.
56 Bryce, *Impressions*, 310.
57 Quoted in Thompson, *Unification*, 5.
58 Bryce, *Impressions*, 423.
59 Bryce, *Impressions*, 383–384.
60 Bryce, *Impressions*, 382–383.
61 Curtis to Smuts, January 7, 1907, *SP*, II 314–317.
62 Merriman to Smuts, December 18, 1906, *SP*, II 308–309; December 6, 1906, 306–307; March 18, 1906, 244–246.
63 Botha to L.T. Hobhouse, June 13, 1903, *SP*, II 100–107.
64 Bryce, *Impressions*, 455.
65 Quoted in Neuhaus, *Dispensations*, 18–20.
66 Smuts to Graham, July 26, 1902, *SP*, II, 13–16.
67 Quoted in Alan Paton, *Hofmeyr*, Oxford 1964, 85.
68 Smuts to Lloyd George, March 26, 1919, *SP*, IV, 83–87, quoted in Ingham, *Smuts*, 104.
69 Smuts to M.C. Gillet, April 9, 1919, *SP*, IV, 103–105, quoted in Ingham, *Smuts*, 107.
70 Smuts to Winston Churchill, September 27, 1948, *SP*, VII, 248–250.
71 Quoted in Neuhaus, *Dispensations*, 188.
72 M.C. Gillet to Smuts, May 31, 1906, *SP*, II, 279–281.
73 E. Hobhouse to Smuts, May 29, 1904, *SP*, II, 165–169.
74 The phrase is Thompson's, *Unification*, 5.
75 Smuts to S.M. Smuts, June 1, 1899, *SP*, I, 242, quoted in Ingham, *Smuts*, 27.
76 Quoted in Thompson, *Unification*, 16.
77 Quoted in Thompson, *Unification*, 16.
78 Lord Milner to Smuts, April 11, 1905, *SP*, II, 188–189.
79 Merriman to Smuts, June 4, 1904, *SP*, II, 171–173; March 18, 1906, 244–246; April 11, 1906, 256–257; May 12, 1906, 274–276.

80 Smuts to Merriman, March 13, 1906, *SP*, II, 242–243.
81 Merriman to Smuts, March 4, 1906, *SP*, II, 238–241; June 26, 1906, 289–292.
82 Merriman to Smuts, March 18, 1906, *SP*, II, 177–178. For Merriman, see Phyllis Lewsen, *John X. Merriman, Paradoxical South African Statesman*, New Haven 1982.
83 Paton, *Hofmeyr*, 151.
84 Smuts to E. Hobhouse, July 17, 1904, *SP*, II, 177–178.
85 Quoted in Paton, *Hofmeyr*, 85–86.
86 Lord Selborne to Smuts, January 9, 1908, with the enclosure, "Notes on a Suggested Policy towards Coloured People and Natives," *SP* II, 374–394.
87 "Memorandum to the Labour Commission" (1903), *SP*, II, 125–133.
88 Xan Smiley, "Misunderstanding Africa," *The Atlantic Monthly*, September 1982, 70–79.
89 Bryce, *Impressions*, 373.
90 Quoted in Neuhaus, *Dispensations*, 248 and 256.
91 Theodore Roszak, *The Making of a Counter Culture*, New York 1969, 105–106. For Roszak's attitudes in scholarship, see Peter Shaw, "Civilization and its Malcontents," *The New Criterion*, January 1986, 23–33.
92 Macmillan, *Bantu*, 152.
93 "Memorandum," *SP*, II, 125–133.
94 Macmillan, *Bantu*, 353.
95 Quoted in Paton, *Hofmeyr*, 226.
96 R.F.A. Hoernlé, *South African Native Policy and the Liberal Spirit*, Cape Town 1939, quoted in Charles Simkins, *Reconstructing South African Liberalism*, Johannesburg 1986, 26.
97 Quoted in *The New Yorker*, April 20, 1987, 66.
98 L.H. Gann and Peter Duignan, *Why South Africa Will Survive*, New York 1981, 79.
99 J.H. Hofmeyr, *South Africa*, London 1931, quoted in Paton, *Hofmeyr*, 180.
100 Paton, *Hofmeyr*, 470.
101 Gann and Duignan, *Survive*, 160.
102 Paton, *Hofmeyr*, 167.
103 On industrialization, Sean Cleary, "Is There a Revolution in South Africa?", *South Africa International*, July 1987.
104 Paton, *Hofmeyr*, 228.
105 Paton, "A Deep Experience," *Contrast I*, December 4, 1961, 20–24, reprinted in *The Long View*, 54–59.
106 Quoted in Neuhaus, *Dispensations*, 37.
107 Quoted in Neuhaus, *Dispensations*, 164–165.
108 George Findlay, *Miscegenation, A Study of the Biological Sources of Inheritance of the South African European Population*, Pretoria 1936, cited in Al J. Venter, *Coloured, A Profile of Two Million South Africans*, Cape Town 1974, 129.
109 Venter, *Coloured*, 120.
110 *Race Relations Survey 1983*, 302–303.
111 Venter, *Coloured*, 108.
112 For Sophiatown just before the removals, Huddleston, *Naught*, especially 117–136.
113 Venter, *Coloured*, 131–136.
114 Professor Edgar H. Brookes quoted in Venter, *Coloured*, 2–3.
115 *Race Relations Survey 1985*, 4–5.
116 *Race Relations Survey 1985*, 20.
117 Venter, *Coloured*, 533–534. Of Coloreds' lower status, Verwoerd said: "It is a fact which we must acknowledge if we want to overcome it."
118 Venter, *Coloured*, 496–497.
119 *The New York Times*, May 6, 1987.

Chapter Two

1 For the context of Mandela's statement, see the statement of D.J. Louis Nel, deputy minister of information, Cape Town, April 15, 1986.
2 *The McAlvany Intelligence Advisor*, April 1986.
3 Johannesburg *Star*, July 23, 1984.
4 *South African Institute of Race Relations News*, April 1987.

5 Steven Mufson, "The Fall of the Front," *The New Republic*, March 23, 1987.
6 *Race Relations Survey 1985*, 480–481.
7 "Inner Party Bulletin," facsimile text released by the South African government. See also *Sunday Times* (Johannesburg), June 30, 1985.
8 *Race Relations Survey 1985*, 446–455 and 495–496.
9 Don Foster with Dennis Davis and Diane Sandler, *Detention and Torture, Psychological, Legal, and Historical Studies*, New York 1987.
10 Pauline H. Baker, "South Africa: The Afrikaner Angst," *Foreign Policy*, Winter 1987–1988, 62, a useful article.
11 Johannesburg *Star*, April 2, 1988.
12 Andrew Kenny, "The Racism of Black Africa," *The Spectator* (London), February 6, 1988.
13 Jack Waldron, "Eyewitness to a Police Action," reprinted in *Family Protection Scoreboard*, 1987.
14 Steve Biko, *Black Consciousness in South Africa*, Millard Arnold (ed.), New York 1978, 25.
15 Cited in Gann and Duignan, *Survive*, 88.
16 *Survey of Race Relations 1986* (Part I), 123–124.
17 Mario Cervi, *Il Giornale* (Milan), June 27, 1987.
18 "Chickens' Return to the Roost," *The Daily Telegraph* (London), March 3, 1988.
19 The Sunday *Times* (London), August 3, 1986.
20 *The Economist*, September 8, 1984.
21 *The Economist*, October 5, 1985.
22 *Survey of Race Relations 1986*, (Part I), 89–97, 338–345, 347.
23 Not reported abroad, Tambo's remarks and other ANC statements left their mark on South Africa. See, *Business Day*, (Johannesburg) January 6, 9, 10, 16, 1986; *Sunday Times* (Johannesburg) January 23, 1986. In the same days on television Desmond Tutu with hints of support for violence made ANC demands his own without reference to the Lusaka celebrations: *The Citizen* (Johannesburg), January 10, 1986.
24 *The Economist*, December 20, 1985.
25 Nicholas Bethell, "An Interview with Nelson Mandela," Mark A. Uhlig (ed.), *Apartheid in Crisis*, New York 1986, 190–200; Makatini quoted in Neuhaus, *Dispensations*, 288.
26 *Race Relations Survey 1985*, 507–508. Formal offer made on February 5, 1985.
27 H.H.W. de Villiers, *Rivonia, Operation Mayibue, A Review of the Rivonia Trial*, Johannesburg, 1964.
28 *Foreign Broadcast Information Service* (henceforth *FBIS*), USSR International Affairs, Sub-Saharan Africa, January 16, 1986, broadcast on January 8, 1986.
29 Quoted in Clem Sunter, *The World and South Africa in 1990s*, Cape Town 1987, 98.
30 For the debate on the constitution, *Race Relations Survey 1983*, 71–98.
31 Johannesburg *Star*, January 24, 1987; *Race Relations Survey 1984*, 127–128. 62.5 percent of Coloreds voted in the Northern Transvaal-Pretoria region, eleven percent in the Cape peninsula, their area of greatest concentration. In contrast to registered voters, the overall percentage of estimated eligible voters ran to eighteen percent.
32 Quoted in Neuhaus, *Dispensations*, 206.
33 *Race Relations Survey 1983*, 17; *The New Yorker*, April 20, 1987, 74.
34 *Race Relations Survey 1983*, 88–89.
35 Quoted in *The Aida Parker Newsletter* (South Africa), 95, November 26, 1986, 20. *Isizwe* also put Mandela in the company of Ho Chi Minh and Fidel Castro.
36 *Race Relations Survey 1985*, 20, 550.
37 Tambo quoted in *The Aida Parker Newsletter*, November 26, 1986, 20.
38 The judgment is Michael Radu's in "The African National Congress: Cadres and Credo," *Problems of Communism*, July-August 1987, 58–75, an important article.
39 *The Role of the Soviet Union, Cuba, and East Germany in Fomenting Terrorism in Southern Africa*, hearings before the Subcommittee on Security and Terrorism of the Committee of the Judiciary, United States Senate, Washington, DC 1982, Volume 2, 201.
40 *The Weekly Mail* (Johannesburg), May 15, 1987.
41 *Business Day* (Johannesburg), July 17, 1987; *Sunday Times* (Johannesburg), July 6, 1987; *The Economist*, February 6, 1988; *Race Relations Survey 1986* (Part I), 178.
42 Quoted in Neuhaus, *Dispensations*, 244.
43 Remarks made before the International Conference on Personnel Management in Durban in October 1985, *Race Relations Survey 1985*, 20.

44 At a prayer meeting at the Jabulani Stadium in Soweto in May 1983, ten thousand people, *Race Relations Survey 1983*, 51. Buthelezi also said Inkatha had never condemned the "external mission of the ANC" for deciding on "the armed struggle."
45 Quoted in Neuhaus, *Dispensations*, 245.
46 Interview with Buthelezi, *News Weekly* (Australia), March 4, 1987.
47 "Storm Warnings Unheeded," March 1977, in *Power is Ours* (a collection of Buthelezi's speeches), New York 1979, 83–104, especially 101.
48 Quoted in Neuhaus, *Dispensations*, 249.
49 "Heartache and Treachery," speech on the funeral of Robert Sobukwe, April 9, 1978, in *Power is Ours*, 117–128, especially 123–124.
50 Nadine Gordimer quoted in Neuhaus, *Dispensations*, 122: "There is no forgetting how we could live if only we could find the way. We must continue to be tormented by the ideal."
51 Quoted in Neuhaus, *Dispensations*, 242.
52 *Institute of Race Relations Survey 1985*, 59–60.
53 "Building Alliances," January 11, 1978, in *Power is Ours*, 105–112, especially 111.
54 Hanf, *Change*, 300.
55 Hanf, *Change*, 299.
56 *Race Relations Survey 1985*, 550. For a good description of the ANC's radio propaganda, Louis Du Buisson, "South Africa After the Fall," *Penthouse*, March 1988.
57 *Race Relations Survey 1983*, 53.
58 Michael Massing, "The Chief," *New York Review of Books*, February 12, 1987, 15–22.
59 Jim and Sybil Stockdale, *In Love and War*, New York 1984, 179–181.
60 Michael Massing, "The Chief"; *Race Relations Survey 1985*, 21, 41, 391, 423, 538, 546, 548, 552.
61 *Race Relations Survey 1986* (Part I), 100–104; Edward A. Lynch, "South Africa's Federal Proposal: the KwaZulu/Natal Indaba," (unpublished paper), 1987.
62 The statement is from *The Sowetan*, quoted in The New York *Times*, November 9, 1987. For the violence, *The Economist*, November 7, 1987; January 16, 1988; *The Christian Science Monitor*, October 29, 1987.
63 Biko, *Consciousness*, 85.
64 Kent Durr, "Some Reflections on the Political Economy of South Africa," address at the annual European Institutional Investor Conference, November 15, 1986; Gann and Duignan, *Survive*, 163–165.
65 *Daily News* (Durban), February 10, 1987, reprinted in *South African Digest*, February 20, 1987.
66 *Race Relations Survey 1986* (Part I), 144.
67 Botha, quoted in A.P.J. van Rensburg, *Africa's Men of Destiny*, Johannesburg 1981, 308, 325.
68 Huddleston, *Naught*, 223.
69 Quoted in van Rensburg, *Africa's Men*, 303.
70 Piet Koornhof, quoted in van Rensburg, *Africa's Men*, 300.
71 Sebe, quoted in van Rensburg, *Africa's Men*, 308.
72 Paton, *Hofmeyr*, 180.
73 H.J. Wolstenholme to Smuts, April 20, 1906, *SP*, II, 259–260.
74 *Race Relations Survey 1985*, 401; *1986 (Part I)*, 218–228; *Business Day* (Johannesburg), March 28, 1988; *The Financial Mail* (Johannesburg), March 25, 1988; *The Economist*, February 27, 1988.
75 Peter Worthington, "A Canadian Journalist Revisits South Africa," *South Africa Forum*, 10, January 1987.
76 The Stellenbosch Professors' statement was published in South African newspapers on March 19, 1987. Botha's address to Parliament on October 5, 1987 came after a report of the President's Council on the Group Areas Act. See also *The Economist*, September 26, 1987 and The Washington *Times*, April 20, 1988.
77 *The Economist*, December 7, 1985.
78 *Race Relations Survey 1985*, 58–59.
79 *Race Relations Survey 1985*, 61.
80 Philip quoted in Macmillan, *Bantu*, 232; Seme quoted in Edward Roux, *Time Longer than Rope*,[2] Madison, Wisconsin 1964, 110.
81 Gann and Duignan, *Survive*, 60.
82 *New York Times Book Review*, November 9, 1986, 3.
83 Johannesburg *Star*, February 17, 1988.

84 *The Military Balance for 1985–1986*, International Institute of Strategic Studies, London 1985; also Deon Fourie, "The Climate of Security," in *South Africa*, 179–190.
85 Lawrence Schlemmer, "The Sanctions Surveys: In Search of Ordinary Black Opinion," *Indicator South Africa 1987*, in *Business Day*, January 7, 1987, reprinted in *South African Digest*, January 23, 1987.
86 *Race Relations Survey 1985*, 21 and 443.
87 Lawrence Schlemmer, "In Search of Social Equality in South Africa," in *South Africa*, 108–120, especially 110.
88 Annual Report of the Department of Education and Training, 1986, BBC Monitoring Service, Summary of World Broadcasts, February 28, 1987.
89 Huddleston, *Naught*, 159–160.
90 Jennifer Shindler, "African Matric Results: 1955 to 1983," South African Institute of Race Relations, Johannesburg 1984; "A Revolution in South Africa: The Rise of Black Education," *Southern African Facts Sheet*, March 1988.
91 Schlemmer, "Social Equality," 113.
92 *Race Relations Survey 1985*, 381.
93 Shindler, "Matric Results," especially tables.
94 *The Economist*, January 17, 1987.
95 *Race Relations Survey 1985*, 388.
96 *Race Relations Survey 1985*, 391.
97 *Race Relations Survey 1985*, 393–394.
98 Quoted in Du Buisson, *Penthouse*, March 1988, 44.
99 For the text of the resolutions of the conference, "People's Education for People's Power," South African Institute of Race Relations, Johannesburg 1986.
100 *Race Relations Survey 1985*, 443.
101 *Race Relations Survey 1985*, 442–443.
102 Affidavit of Major-General Steenkamp, the officer of the South African Police in charge of monitoring detainees, before the Supreme Court, Cape Town, in the case, PFP and K.M. Andrew versus the State President (Botha), April 1987; statement of Adriaan Volk, October 1, 1987.
103 Statement by the Minister of Law and Order, Mr. Adriaan Volk, Cape Town, June 2, 1987.
104 *The Weekly Mail*, April 24, 1987.
105 The Washington Times, December 11, 1986.
106 *Race Relations Survey 1976*, 57.
107 Huddleston, *Naught*, 88.
108 *Sunday Times* (Johannesburg), October 19, 1986.
109 Steenkamp Affidavit, Supreme Court, Cape Town, April 1987.
110 Interview in The Washington *Times*, May 14, 1988.
111 For instance, *The Economist*, September 5, 1987; February 27, 1988.
112 *Corriere della Sera* (Milan), August 14, 1987, *The Economist*, January 23, 1988.
113 *The Citizen* (Johannesburg), April 27, 1987; *Die Burger* (Cape Town), April 27, 1987; *Sunday Star* (Johannesburg), 1987; *Pretoria News*, April 27, 1987. See, for reprints of some of these articles, *South Africa Digest*, May 1, 1987. See also, Baker, *Foreign Policy*, Winter 1987–88.
114 Harald Pakendorf, "Independents and the Future," *South Africa Digest*, March 6, 1987.
115 C. Mulder, a leader of the CP, *Race Relations Survey 1986* (Part I), 144.
116 *Beeld* (Johannesburg), March 3, 1987, reprinted in *South Africa Digest*, March 6, 1987.
117 *The Citizen* (Johannesburg), March 1987; Letter of Buthelezi, *Africa Confidencial*, March 3, 1987. See also, *South Africa Digest*, March 27, 1987.
118 Hanf, *Change*, 439–440.
119 Quoted in *The New Yorker*, April 20, 1987.
120 Walter Hasselkus, "Telltale Signs," *Leadership* (South Africa) 6, 4, September 1987.
121 *Race Relations News*, April 1987. See also, Charles Simkins, *Reconstructing South African Liberalism*, for instance, 1: "If the past is depressing, many aspects of the present are even more so. One derives no pleasure from saying so, but the truth of liberal predictions that illiberal policies would lead to a progressive collapse of South African social institutions into a chaos impervious to reason is becoming steadily more apparent."
122 Venter, *Coloured*, 3.
123 Quoted in Neuhaus, *Dispensations*, 38–39.
124 Nic Wiehahn, *Rapport*, April 19, 1987, summarized in *South Africa Digest*, April 24, 1987.
125 *Race Relations Survey 1985*, 22, 182.

126 ANC-COSATU statements quoted in Thomas G. Karis, "South African Liberation; the Communist Factor," *Foreign Affairs*, Winter 1986–1987, 269–271. For the position of the COSATU Central Committee in February 1986, *Sunday Times* (Johannesburg), May 4, 1986.
127 *Financial Mail* (Johannesburg), December 26, 1986.
128 Interview with Jacob Zuma, member of the ANC National Executive Committee on Radio Freedom (the ANC Radio) from Addis Ababa in English, February 14, 1987, BBC Monitoring Service, Summary of World Broadcasts, February 17, 1987.
129 Quoted, without name, in *Business Day* (Johannesburg), November 11, 1986.
130 Quoted in in *The Weekly Mail*, March 6, 1987.
131 Johann Liebenberg, "Mine Strikes: Dealing with Militants and Violence," *South Africa Forum*, 113, March 1988.
132 *The Economist*, May 2, 1987.
133 Cyril Ramaphosa, "Organizing on the Mines," South African Institute of Race Relations, 1985.
134 *The Star* (Johannesburg) May 5, 1987; *The Citizen* (Johannesburg), May 5, 1987.
135 On "Perception of Wits," see Ken Owen, *Business Day* (Johannesburg), June 8, 15, 22 and the reply of the committee that wrote the booklet, July 1, 1987.
136 The Washington *Post*, October 16, 1987. A papyrologist might understand from this article that the government intended to preserve freedom of speech in the universities.
137 *The Citizen* (Johannesburg), April 23, 24, 25, 28, 1987; *Beeld* (Johannesburg), April 24, 1987; *Pretoria News*, April 26, 27, 1987, all summarized in *South Africa Digest*, May 1, 1987.
138 *The Citizen*, April 16, 1987, reprinted in *South Africa Digest*; also, *Frankfurter Allgemeine Zeitung*, May 4, 1987.
139 *Sunday Times* (Johannesburg) December 12, 1982; Johannesburg *Star*, December 10, 1982; *Paratus* (South African Defense Force publication), January 1983, 18–22, All quoted in Pike, *Communism*, 345.
140 Interview Stoffel van der Merwe, *Leadership* (South Africa) 6,4, September 1987.
141 Quoted in Du Buisson, *Penthouse*, March 1988, 44 and 113.
142 Henry R. Pike, *A History of Communism in South Africa*, Johannesburg 1985, 522–524. This admirable book manages to look the reality of the SACP in the face because the writer, an American clergyman who has lived ten years in South Africa, handles the facts including many photographs, as well as documents, straightforwardly, classic historical method rare in academic studies. He cites many primary memoirs, not often referred to outside South Africa. Available from Christian Mission International of South Africa, P.O. Box 7157, Primrose Hill, Germiston, South Africa 1417.
143 See also the statement on the release of youths in detention of the minister of law and order on October 1, 1987.
144 Press release of the minister of law and order, May 1, 1988; New York *Times*, May 12, 1988; *Beeld*, *The Citizen*, *Business Day* (all Johannesburg), May 16, 1988.
145 *Race Relations Survey 1986* (Part I), 117.
146 *Race Relations Survey 1986* (Part I), 118.
147 Du Buisson, *Penthouse*, March 1988, 44 and 113.
148 *Race Relations Survey 1986* (Part I). 122–123.
149 Worthington, *South Africa Forum*, January 1987.
150 *The Citizen* (Johannesburg), September 12, 1987.
151 Van der Merwe at a conference on freedom of the press, *Conflict and the Press*, to celebrate the centenary of the Johannesburg *Star*, *South Africa Digest*, October 16, 1987.
152 *Business Day* (Johannesburg), July 6, 1987; *The Sowetan*, September 10, 1987.
153 *Race Relations Survey 1986* (Part I), 175–176; *The Citizen* (Johannesburg), July 8, 1987.
154 G.C. Oosthuizen, Report of the Human Sciences Research Council, July 1986, conclusions reported in *Race Relations Survey 1986* (Part I), 311.
155 *The Sowetan*, *The Citizen*, *Business Day* (all Johannesburg), November 6, 1987. The New York *Times* did not run Mbeki's statement either in its story of his release (November 6, 1987) or in its later stories, on November 25, and on November 29, 1987. On November 25 it called the ANC's terrorism a "limited campaign of violent resistance."
156 Pike, *Communism*, 281–282 and 397.
157 The phrase is from a South African publisher's letter to the writer, April 5, 1988.
158 *Business Day* (Johannesburg), November 10, 1987. The doubts were about the SACP's relation to the ANC, not about ANC terrorism, as *Business Day*'s blunt criticism, on August 3, 1988, of Slabbert for his surprise at the Johannesburg car-explosion right after the "Dakar talks" with the ANC he sponsored shows.

159 See Mbeki's remarks to The New York Times, November 25, 1987: "Apartheid basically has not changed."
160 Quoted in Radu, *Problems of Communism*, July-August 1987, 71.
161 The Washington *Times*, May 14, 1988.
162 *South Africa Digest*, October 16, 1987.
163 For Sisulu's Marxism, Radu, *Problems of Communism*, July-August 1987, 70; for the rejection of Sisulu's appeal, The Washington *Post*, November 17, 1987, with juridical details muddled, as usual.
164 For adult reading at third-grade level, Gloria Miklowitz, "Why Deny the Children?," *Publishers Weekly*, October 9, 1987, 66.
165 "It staggers the human mind to think people could believe such nonsense," Pike writes of this statement. Gerard Ludi, the South African police undercover agent, *Operation Q-018*, Cape Town 1969: "Nelson Mandela (was) a top man in the Central Committee of the underground Communist party," quoted in Pike, *Communism*, 392.
166 Owen quoted in The New York *Times*, May 10, 1988.
167 The New York *Times*, March 23, 1988.
168 From an SACP pamphlet quoted in Eric H. Louw, *The Communist Danger*, Reunited National Party publication, 1943, 5, cited in Pike, *Communism*, 198–200. Louw mentioned 120,000 SACP pamphlets distributed on the Rand in March 1943 alone.
169 Reverend Arthur Lewis, The *Times* (London), March 24, 1988: "(Archbishop Runcie, the special envoy, and Archbishop Tutu) are not entitled to give the impression that they speak with the authority of their office—and on behalf of their flocks—on contentious and complex political issues. Anglicans who differ from them can and must speak out and be heard . . . Nothing is further from the truth than the ecclesiastical myth that Archbishop Tutu is the voice of the voiceless in South Africa . . . Many of us believe that the confrontational tactics of Archbishop Tutu—whose deeply divided Church numbers less than two million—are wrecking the hopes of reconciliation of large numbers of ordinary South African Christians in every race-group who lack the Archbishop's genius for exploiting the news media."
In response to the Reverend Lewis, two days later, the Reverend D.L. Scott, quoted Buthelezi, to explain "the Church has lost its authority" because it no longer "believed in its own message." P.H.B. Woods called the dispatch "to a foreign land" of "a high-ranking clergyman who within hours of arrival, publicly and defiantly, on Church land, challenges their police to arrest him . . ." a display of episcopal "vanity" in the service of "disobedience, if not violence."
170 Pike, *Communism*, 369, 384–385.
171 The Washington *Post*, April 13, 1988; The Washington *Times*, April 13, 1988.
172 On the NKG, 1986 synod, *Race Relations Survey 1986* (Part I), 312–315.
173 *Business Day* (Johannesburg), May 13, 1988; for Mtolo in the directly following quotation, *Road*, 126.
174 The new church did not expect rapid growth. *Rapport*, June 28, 1987; Johannesburg *Star*, June 28, 1987; *The Sowetan*, June 29, 1987; *Beeld*, June 29, 1987.
175 Quoted in Du Buisson, *Penthouse*, March 1988, 43.
176 Quoted in Pike, *Communism*, 375; on Fischer, 416–454.
177 The twenty-one points are reprinted in facsimile along with the constitution of the SACP that preceded them with the subheading on its title page, "South African Section of the Communist International," in the Denton Hearings, Volume 1, 596–600.
178 On the Springbok legion, Edward Roux, *Time Longer than Rope*, Madison, Wisconsin 1964, 196; on Beyleveld, Pike, *Communism*, 228–230, 301–302, 306, 422.
179 Quoted in Pike, *Communism*, 388.
180 Aleksei Myagkov, *Le Point* (Paris), March 16, 1977, cited in Pike, *Communism*, 468. See also, Myagkov, *Inside the KGB*, New York 1976.
181 Kurt M. Campbell, *Soviet Policy Towards South Africa*, New York 1986, 26.
182 Trotsky quoted in Pike, *Communism*, 186. For the Comintern orders and the order from Stalin, Gerard Ludi, the South African undercover agent in the SACP in the early sixties, quoted in Pike, 167 and 170. The Comintern slogan for a "Black Republic" amounts to a first statement of present ANC propaganda, *South African Worker*, November 30, 1928: "A South African Native Republic, as a stage towards a Workers' and Peasants' Government, with full protection and equal rights for all national minorities."
183 Dated February 19, 1943, quoted in Pike, *Communism*, 257; for the police report, Pike, 251–295; text of the report, *Hansard*, South Africa 1952, 7946–7968.
184 Pike's judgment, *Communism*, 242.

185 Testimony of Bartholomew Hlapane, Denton Hearings, Volume 1, 533; Radu, *Problems of Communism*, July-August 1987, 71- 72.

Chapter Three

1 The Washington *Post*, September 18, 1987.
2 Bruce Rickerson, "The Attack on Constructive Engagement," *American Review*, 5,1, (Rand Afrikaans University), 1–20. The preceding quotations are from this article.
3 *The Economist*, September 21, 1985; October 25, 1986; John H. Langbein, "Social Investing of Pension Funds and University Endowments: Unprincipled, Futile and Illegal," *Disinvestment*, Washington, DC 1985, (National Legal Center for the Public Interest), 1–28; Merle Lipton, *Sanctions and South Africa*, London 1988, (The Economist Intelligence Unit), a remarkable study, except for its readiness to dismiss the wars in Angola and Mozambique as "cold-war" exercises. Unless otherwise noted, the facts in the following pages come from Lipton.
4 The Wall Street *Journal*, January 5, 1988; *Race Relations Survey 1986* (Part 1).
5 The New York *Times*, April 4, 1988; for the text of the new disinvestment guidelines of United States anti-apartheid organizations, Lipton, *Sanctions*, Appendix 14; for ANC instructions, *Notes and Documents*, United Nations Centre Against Apartheid, February 1988.
6 Nat Henthoff, "Fighting Apartheid by Banning Books," The Washington *Post*, January 14, 1988; also, Gloria Miklowitz, "Why Deny the Children?," *Publishers Weekly*, October 9, 1987.
7 *The Economist*, April 27, 1976; The New York *Times*, April 27, 1976; for Houphouet-Boigny's remark, *Le Point* (Paris), April 24, 1976, cited in Fred Bridgland, *Jonas Savimbi, A Key to Africa*, New York 1987, 220–221, who taught me the significance of Kissinger's speech.
8 Conor Cruise O'Brien, "What Can Become of South Africa?," *The Atlantic Monthly*, March 1986; Amelia C. Leiss (ed.) *Apartheid and UN Collective Measures: An Analysis*, New York 1965, (Carnegie Endowment), cited in Campbell, Soviet Policy, 86.
9 Lipton, *Sanctions*, 54.
10 *The Economist*, March 30, 1985.
11 Chester A. Crocker, "South Africa: Strategy for Change," *Foreign Affairs*, Winter 1980/81, 324–51; for the second article, with Mario Greznes and Robert Henderson, "Southern Africa—a US Policy for the Eighties," *Africa Report*, January-February 1981; for the memorandum, The New York *Times*, June 1, 1981; for the statement of the South African commander in South West Africa, *The Financial Times* (London), February 11, 1981,—the last two cited in Bridgland, *Savimbi*, 302–306.
12 John Rees, *Red Locusts: Soviet Support for Terrorism in Southern Africa*, Alexandria, VA 1981 (Western Goals). All quotations that follow come from Rees' study. Also essential: Rael Jean Isaac and Erich Isaac, *The Coercive Utopians: Social Deception by America's Power Players*, Chicago 1983.
13 Henry Kissinger, *White House Years*, Boston 1979, 1028–1031.
14 Quoted in *TransAfrica, a Lobby of the Left*, Washington, DC 1985 (The Lincoln Institute for Research and Education), 15.
15 Linda S. Lichter, "Who Speaks for Black America?," *Public Opinion*. August/September 1985, 41–44, 58; for criticism of this poll, effectively answered: *Public Opinion*, October/November 1985, 58–60.
16 For this change, Lipton, *Sanctions*, 1, who does not however, connect it to changes in the "correlation of forces," to use the Soviet phrase.
17 Julian Stone, *Aggression and World Order: A Critique of U.N. Theories of Aggression*, Westport, CT 1976, cited in "The PLO's Valuable Ally at the United Nations," *United Nations Assessment Project Study, The Heritage Foundation*, December 17, 1985; Campbell, *Soviet Policy*, 77–87.
18 Juliana Pilon, "Moscow's U.N. Outpost," *United Nations Assessment Project Study, The Heritage Foundation*, November 22, 1983.
19 Fred Barnes, *The New Republic*, December 23, 1985.
20 Johannesburg *Star*, December 31, 1983.
21 Michael Clough, "Beyond Constructive Engagement," *Foreign Policy*, Winter 1985/86, 3–24.
22 Herman Nickel, "American Realities," *Leadership*, June 1985, 22–26.
23 The Washington *Post*, March 13, 1986.
24 Mandela's pamphlet is reprinted in the *Congressional Record*, August 14, 1986, S 11657–S 11660.

25 Makatini quoted in Neuhaus, *Dispensations*, 287; Lenin in Sergey Petrovich Melgounov, *The Red Terror in Russia*, London 1925, 33.
26 M. G. Buthelezi, "Dialogue or Confrontation?" (speech to an Afrikaner club on April 30, 1976), in *Power is Ours* (a collection of Buthelezi's speeches), New York 1979.
27 "SACP Directive/Discussion Document," published, with P.W. Botha's speech to a joint sitting of the three Houses of Parliament on June 12, 1986 by the South African Government's Bureau of Information, Johannesburg 1986.
28 The *Times* (London), May 2, 1986.
29 A Vietnamese peasant woman in James Webb, *Fields of Fire*, New York (Bantam Edition) 1979, 182.
30 *Accuracy in Media*, July-A, 1986; October-A, 1986.
31 *The Economist*, July 22, 1986.
32 Michael Radu, "Taking a Closer Look at Winnie Mandela," *The World and I* (Published by the Unification Church), December 1986, 134–139.
33 *FBIS*, September 3, 1986; The Washington *Post*, September 3, 1986.
34 For this sentence, Rowland Evans and Robert Novak, "Still Wobbling on South Africa," The Washington *Post*, July 28, 1986.
35 The Washington *Post*, December 9, 1986.
36 Abraham Lincoln, "Message to Congress in Special Session," July 4, 1861, *The Collected Works of Abraham Lincoln* IV, New Brunswick, NJ 1953, 421–441, especially 426 and 429–30. See also, "Proclamation Suspending the Writ of Habeas Corpus," September 24, 1862, V, 436–37. There is a good short account of the suspension of *habeas corpus* in John T. Morse's *Abraham Lincoln*, Boston 1893, two vols., better than in some more recent works.
37 James Stockdale, Speech at the Lincoln Memorial Banquet of the Peoria County Bar Association on February 13, 1988, printed in the *Congressional Record*, February 25, 1988, E 380—E 382.
38 For a rare story, Michael Parks, "U.S. Quietly Aids South African Black Activists," Los Angeles *Times*, November 11, 1986.
39 Alexander Hamilton, *Federalist*, 25.
40 John Jay, *Federalist*, 64.
41 The Washington *Post*, June 15, 1988.
42 The Washington *Post*, July 3, 1988.
43 The Evening *Capital* (Annapolis), June 19, 1988.
44 Peter Worthington, "Canadian Journalist Revisits South Africa," *South Africa Forum*, January 1987.
45 The Washington *Post*, June 27, 1988; Jeane Kirkpatrick, The Washington *Post*, July 4, 1988; for a typical MPLA advertisement, The New York *Times*, June 27, 1988; for Fenton Communications, The Washington *Times*, October 19, 1987.
46 For the falsification, Bridgland, *Savimbi*, 450–451; for Marquez on Castro, despite Armando Valladares' *Against All Hope*, New York 1986, see his introduction to Gianni Mina, *Il Racconto di Fidel* (a book-length interview with Castro), Milan 1988.
47 The Washington *Post*, June 13, 1988; The Washington *Times*, June 13, 1988.
48 The Washington *Post*, May 30, 1988; for the mayor of Washington on Savimbi, Jeane Kirkpatrick, The Washington *Post*, July 4, 1988.
49 The Washington *Times*, May 25, 1988.
50 The Washington *Post*, December 7, 1987.
51 Leon Trotsky, *The History of the Russian Revolution*, New York 1932, Chapter XI, "Dual Power."
52 Letter to the Reverend Leon H. Sullivan, May 8, 1987.
53 The Washington *Post*, June 15, 1988.
54 *Business Day* (Johannesburg), June 5, 1987.
55 Sir Geoffrey Howe, "South Africa, No Easy Answers," speech to the Royal Commonwealth Society, May 17, 1988.
56 The Washington *Times*, June 10, 1988; June 12, 1988.
57 The New York *Times*, June 24, 1988.
58 The Wall Street *Journal*, May 5, 1988; Lipton, *Sanctions*, 17, 46, 96.
59 Lipton, *Sanctions*, 120.
60 Lipton, *Sanctions*, 86. Most of the figures in the following discussion come from Lipton.
61 *The Economist*, August 20, 1988.
62 Phyllis Nickel, "Operation Hunger," *Radcliffe Quarterly*, June 1988.

63 Lipton, *Sanctions*, 81.
64 Lipton, *Sanctions*, 29.

Chapter Four

1 Quoted in Peter Worthington, "Angola's Secret War," *National Review*, November 1, 1985.
2 Quoted in MacMillan, *Bantu*, 214.
3 Zbigniew Brzezinski, *Between Two Ages: America's Role in the Technetronic Era*, New York 1970, 56.
4 Quoted in Pike, *Communism*, 492–493; Johannesburg *Star*, June 8, 1982.
5 Simon Jenkins, *The Economist*, March 30, 1985, 17–34.
6 For Paton, Johannesburg *Star*, January 6, 1984; for Malan, *Survey of Race Relations 1985*, 428.
7 For an example of this psychological approach, see the otherwise fairly well-informed article in *Time*, March 2, 1987, 36.
8 Quoted in Al J. Venter, *Vorster's Africa. Friendship and Frustration*, Johannesburg 1977, 14. All Venter's books are important because he saw the guerrilla war in Mozambique, Angola and Rhodesia first-hand. See also, Venter's *The Zambezi Salient*, London 1974 and *The Terror Fighters, A Profile of Guerrilla Warfare in Southern Africa*, Cape Town 1969, for the Portuguese war before the debacle.
9 Quoted in Venter, *Vorster*, 302.
10 David Martin and Phyllis Johnson, *The Struggle for Zimbabwe, The Chimurenga War*, Harare 1981, 246, 279, a valuable book, marred by obeisance to fanaticism, for it tells how the terrorists thought, not usually how they acted.
11 The New York *Times*, January 9, 1987; January 24, 1987; The Washington *Times*, January 14, 1987; The Washington *Post*, January 30, 1987.
12 For the South African general's statement, *Race Relations Survey 1983*, 575; for Conor Cruise O'Brien's article, *The Atlantic*, March 1986; for Brezhnev's remark, Brian Crozier, *Strategy for Survival*, London 1978, 76.
13 Alan Paton, "Dr. Hendrik Verwoerd—A Liberal Assessment," reprinted in *The Long View*, New York 1968, 268–275. In 1960, after the abolishment of African representation in Parliament, Paton had written in a tribute to Margaret Ballinger, representative for Africans in Parliament from 1938 to 1960: "We also have other liberals . . . who [have] . . . thought deeply about [political power], about how to use it, how to distribute it, how to tame it, how to prevent it in fact from eating people up, as it surely does when it gets into the hands of people like Hitler, Stalin and Dr. Verwoerd." "Margaret Ballinger," *Contact III*, 10, May 21, 1960, reprinted in *The Long View*, 159–163. See also, "An Open letter to Dr. Verwoerd," (1958) and "Verwoerd's Claim to Divine Guidance," (1958) also in *The Long View*, 72–75 and 76–79.
14 For Vorster's "outward reach policy," A.P.J. van Rensburg, *The Tangled Web, Leadership and Change in Southern Africa*, Cape Town 1977, 129–160; Venter, *Vorster*, especially 13–37.
15 Gann and Duignan, *Survive*, 80.
16 Dean Acheson, "Remarks to the American Society of Newspaper Editors," Washington, DC April 18, 1969, reprinted in *Dean Acheson on the Rhodesia Question*, State Department, Washington, DC 1969.
17 Venter, *Vorster*, 38.
18 November 9, 1965 in the Malawi Parliament, quoted in Philip Short, *Banda*, London 1974, 243. All subsequent quotations from Banda are from Short's good book. See also, T. David Wiliams, *Malawi, The Politics of Despair*, Ithaca, NY 1978.
19 *Race Relations Survey 1974*, 313.
20 Quoted in Venter, *Vorster*, 48. On Rhodesia, van Rensburg, *Web*, 94–110 and *Africa's Men*, especially 491–539.
21 Quoted in van Rensburg, *Africa's Men*, 483.
22 Quoted in A.J.A. Peck, *Rhodesia Condemns*, Salisbury 1967, 4.
23 Acheson, *The Sunday Star* (Washington, DC), December 22, 1968, reprinted in *Acheson on the Rhodesia Question*, 21–28.
24 Quoted in van Rensburg, *Web*, 97–98.
25 David Caute, *Under the Skin, The Death of White Rhodesia*, London 1983, 356, a remarkable achievement that wins Caute's scorn.
26 Quoted in *Life Magazine*, May 27, 1966.

27 James Barber, *Rhodesia: The Road to Rebellion*, Oxford 1967, 168.
28 Reg Shay and Chris Vermaak, *The Silent War*, Salisbury 1971, 11–13.
29 The New York *Times*, November 5, 1967, quoted in van Rensburg, *Africa's Men*, 516.
30 Shay, *War*, 19.
31 Quoted in Barber, *Rebellion*, 210–211.
32 Christian Science *Monitor*, August 19, 1964, quoted in van Rensburg, *Africa's Men*, 516. For the incidents of thuggery, Peck, *Rhodesia*, 9.
33 Ken Flower, *Serving Secretly, An Intelligence Chief on Record, Rhodesia into Zimbabwe, 1964 to 1981*, London 1987, 39.
34 Barber, *Rebellion*, 185.
35 Dirk Kunert and Colin Vale, "The Chimera of the 'Zimbabwe Solution,'" *Strategic Review*, 23–37, 30–31; Barber, *Rebellion*, 262, 297, for the following information on the Indaba.
36 Quoted in Venter, *Vorster*, 222.
37 Arkady N. Shevchenko, *Breaking With Moscow*, New York 1985, 363.
38 Venter, *Vorster*, 206. All quotations in this section come from Venter, unless otherwise noted. See also, "Angola after Independence: Struggle for Supremacy," *Conflict Studies*, 64, November 1975.
39 The New York *Times Magazine*, February 1, 1987.
40 Some State Department officials betray the bad conscience they will not acknowledge, in their attempts to minimize the numbers of Cubans in Angola before the South African intervention, or to deny their presence outright, and, thereby, to imply that the South Africans provoked Cuban "escalation," see, for instance, Larry C. Napper, deputy director of the Office of Southern African Affairs, "The African Terrain and U.S.-Soviet Conflict in Angola and Rhodesia: Some Implications for Crisis Prevention," in *Managing U.S.-Soviet Rivalry: Problems of Crisis Prevention*, Alexander L. George, editor, Boulder, CO 1983, 155–185. Evidence for Cuban troops in numbers before the South African intervention in *U.S. Involvement in Civil War in Angola*, Hearings before the U.S. Congress, Senate, Committee on Foreign Relations, Subcommittee on African Affairs, January 29, February 3–5, 1976, Washington, DC 1976, especially 8–13, 82–83, 172–177, 184–191. Also, Nathaniel Davis, "The Angola Decision of 1975: A Personal Memoir," *Foreign Affairs*, Fall 1978, especially 121–122.
41 Robert Harvey, *Portugal: Birth of a Democracy*, London 1978, 17, a book that renders the events and mood in Lisbon and Portugal in 1974–1975 with admirable nuance and sensitivity but that unwittingly reflects their self-preoccupation in its near total neglect of the abandonment of Africa, the "revolution's" most important consequence.
42 On Communist infiltration, "Portugal: Revolution and Backlash," *Conflict Studies*, 61, September 1975, especially section 2, "Communist Technique: Massive Infiltration of Agents," 21–25.
43 On this letter, E.P. Cain, "The Agony of Angola," in *Combat on Communist Territory*, Chicago 1985, 72–104, especially, 76–77.
44 For the first Alves quote, Venter, *Vorster*, 305, for the second, *Conflict Studies*, 61, 23.
45 Bridgland, *Savimbi*, 164–165.
46 Antonio de Spinola, *Portugal and the Future*, Johannesburg 1974.
47 Martin and Johnson, *Chimurenga*, 17.
48 Basil Davidson, *In the Eye of the Storm*, New York 1972.
49 Flower, *Service*, 34, 37.
50 Quoted in C.R. Boxer, *Race Relations in the Portuguese Colonial Empire, 1417–1825*, Oxford 1963, 70.
51 Quoted in Theodor Hanf, Heribert Weiland and Gerda Vierdag, *South Africa: The Prospects of Peaceful Change*, Bloomington, IN 1981, 350.
52 *National Review*, November 1, 1985, 53.
53 The New York *Times Magazine*, February 1, 1987.
54 Bertil Egeroe, *Mozambique: A Dream Undone, The Political Economy of Democracy, 1975–84*, Uppsala 1987, 63, 70.
55 For the Cunhal interview, that first appeared in *L'Europeo* (Milan), June 13, 1975, see *Conflict Studies*, 61, 27–31.
56 Harvey, *Birth*, 45, 103.
57 Quoted in Harvey, *Birth*, 50.
58 Harvey, *Birth*, 3.
59 Bridgland, *Savimbi*, 38.
60 Harvey, *Birth*, 39.

61 Quoted in van Rensburg, *Africa's Men*, 479.
62 Quoted in Dirk Kunert and Colin Vale, "The Chimera of the 'Zimbabwe Solution,'" *Strategic Review* (South Africa), Summer 1984, 27. Much of the detail about Mugabe's mastering of Rhodesia, and the quotations, unless otherwise noted, come from this important article.
63 Quoted in Martin and Johnson, *Chimurenga*, 256.
64 Quoted in Barber, *Rebellion*, 288–289.
65 Flower, *Service*, 89, 92.
66 Flower, *Service*, 237–239.
67 Flower, *Service*, 255.
68 Caute, *Skin*, 15.
69 Ian Linden, *The Catholic Church and the Struggle for Zimbabwe*, 272–273, quoted in *Skin*, 251.
70 Quoted in Flower, *Service*, 212.
71 Flower, *Service*, 210.
72 Flower, *Service*, 190.
73 Flower, *Service*, 151–152.
74 Martin and Johnson, *Chimurenga*, 264.
75 The New York *Times*, September 12, 1988.
76 Quoted in van Rensburg, *Africa's Men*, 492.
77 Flower, *Service*, 32, 157.
78 Quoted in Caute, *Skin*, 303.
79 Quoted in Caute, *Skin*, 434.
80 Flower, *Service*, 38. The scornful tone of two British reviews of this book (*TLS* November 13, 1987; *The Economist*, November 21, 1987) betray a similar malaise.
81 The Washington *Post*, April 3, 1987.
82 *The Economist*, November 7, 1987; November 21, 1987.
83 *The New Yorker*, February 2, 1987, 76.
84 Robert G. Mugabe, "Struggle for Southern Africa," *Foreign Affairs*, Winter, 1987–88, 314.
85 Quoted in van Rensburg, *Africa's Men*, 489.
86 Sean Cleary, "Path to Independence," *Internationales Afrikaforum*, 4, 1986, 355–362.
87 Cited in the Maldon Institute, "Strategic Implications of Cuba's Angolan Military Buildup," *International Freedom Review*, Fall 1988, 21–35.
88 For these incidents, "Operation Reindeer," and the following remark of Sam Nujoma, Willem Steenkamp, *Borderstrike! South Africa into Angola*, Durban 1983, especially 1–11 and 15–141.
89 By 1966, in the judgment of Douglas Pike, every person, every judge, every teacher, doctor, in South Vietnam, who had any capacity for leadership, had been murdered by terrorists who made a show of their "sentences" and "executions" as if already a "government": 21,400 kidnappings, 7,500 murders between 1957–1965. Douglas Pike, *Vietcong. The Organization and Techniques of the National Liberation Front of South Vietnam*, Cambridge, MA 1966, 249:

The common characteristic of this activity against individuals is that it was directed at the village leader, usually the natural leader—that individual who, because of age, sagacity, or strength of character, is the one to whom people turn for advice or leadership. Many were religious figures, schoolteachers, or simply people of integrity and honor. Since they were superior individuals these persons were more likely to stand up to the insurgents when they came to the village and thus most likely to be the first victims. *Potential opposition leadership was the NLF's most feared enemy.* Steadily, quietly, and with a systematic ruthlessness the NLF in six years wiped out virtually an entire class of Vietnamese villages. The assassination rate declined steadily from 1960 to 1965 for the simple reason that there was only a finite number of persons to be assassinated. Many villages by 1966 were virtually depopulated of their natural leaders, who are the single most important element in any society . . . By any definition, this NLF action against village leaders amounts to genocide (Italics mine).

90 Mburumba Kerina, "The Democratic Option in Namibia," *Institute on Religion and Democracy*, Washington, DC April 1984, 6; Martin and Johnson, *Chimurenga*, 14.
91 Sean Cleary, "The Origins of SWAPO," and "Facing Reality," *Leadership* (South Africa), 1985.
92 Andrew N. Matjila, "Essential Reforms in the Educational System of Namibia," *Internationales Afrikaforum*, 4, 1986, 373–374.
93 Eben van Zijl, "Probleme einer landwitschaftlichen Reform," *Internationales Afrikaforum*, 4, 1986, 380–382.
94 P.W. Botha, Statement to Parliament, April 18, 1985.

95 P.W. Botha, Speech in Windhoek, June 17, 1985.
96 *Human Rights and Namibia*, Internationale Gesellschaft für Menschenrechte, Frankfurt 1986. Proceedings of the Conference on Human Rights in Namibia, London, March 27, 1986.
97 The Washington *Times*, June 20, 1988.
98 Draft Annual Report of the United States Council for Namibia, United Nations, General Assembly, October 29, 1985.
99 Letter of Phil Ya Nangoloh, representative of SWAPO-Democrats, a party in the TGNU that broke with SWAPO because of its violence, The Washington *Times*, April 4, 1986.
100 Quotes, including the following quotes of members of the NCC, come from press-releases of the Namibia Communications Centre, P.O. Box 285, London WC1X OEL, for 1985, 1986 and 1987.
101 *The Herald* (Salisbury), February 11, 1980, quoted in Pike, *Communism*, 525, see also 298.
102 Jim Hooper, "Namibia's Bush War," *International Defense Review* 11, 1987.
103 Allan Boesak, "The Black Church and the Future," address to the South African Council of Churches, July 1979, reprinted in *Black and Reformed, Apartheid, Liberation and the Calvinist Tradition*, Maryknoll, NY 1984, 20–31, 25.
104 Quoted in Pike, *Communism* 298.
105 For the "Report on Namibia" and Hurley's and the Apostolic Vicar's statements, *The Whole Truth About SWAPO*, Position Paper of the American Society for the Defense of Tradition, Family, Property, Pleasantville, NY 1984, 49–61.
106 For instance, The Washington *Post*, June 19, 1987.
107 *Race Relations Survey 1985*, 429.
108 For SWAPO's hold on the NCC, see the remarkable interview with the former president of West Germany, Kaie-Uwe von Hassel, *Die Republikein* (South West Africa), November 6, 1987.
109 Quoted in remarks of Jorn Ziegler, *Human Rights and Namibia*, 31–33.
110 *Frankfurter Allgemeine Zeitung*, May 16, 1987.
111 For Rhodesian trials of terrorists, Venter, *Vorster's Africa*, 100–108, especially 107. For Portuguese debriefing, Venter, *The Zambezi Salient* and *The Terror Fighters*.
112 The Washington *Times*, June 1, 1988; *Frankfurter Allgemeine Zeitung*, July 1, 1988.
113 Victor G. Hiemstra, "Constitution-Making in Namibia," *Internationales Afrikaforum* 4, 1986, 363–367; Johannesburg *Star*, February 25 and 27, 1987; South African Press Association, February 27, 1987.
114 For RENAMO's political program, E.P. Cain, "Mozambique's Hidden War," in *Combat on Communist Territory* (Charles Moser, ed.), Chicago 1985, 38–71, especially 64–66, an important essay. FRELIMO and its supporters within the US State Department, for instance, Melissa Wells, nominated ambassador to Mozambique by the Reagan administration, (The Washington *Times*, May 5, 1987), frequently attack RENAMO for its lack of political program.
115 USSR Deputy Foreign Minister Anatoly Adamishin quoted in The Washington *Post*, September 23, 1988.
116 Quoted in John A. Marcum, *The Angola Revolution: Exile Politics and Guerrilla Warfare (1962–1976) II*, Cambridge, MA 1978, 217.
117 Quoted in Bridgland, *Savimbi*, 80.
118 Marcum, *Angola II*, 218.
119 Bridgland, *Savimbi*, 78.
120 Quotations, unless otherwise noted, from Jonas Savimbi, "The War Against Soviet Colonialism: the Strategy and Tactics of Anti-Communist Resistance," *Policy Review*, Winter 1986, 18–25.
121 Quoted in Bridgland, *Savimbi*, 431.
122 Marcum, *Angola II*, 123.
123 Bridgland, *Savimbi*, 87.
124 Bridgland, *Savimbi*, 449. A US intelligence officer told Bridgland who had seen the increase in supplies, South Africa had tripled its shipments, 434.
125 Bridgland, *Savimbi*, 377–378.
126 Quoted in Bridgland, *Savimbi*, 121.
127 *National Catholic Register*, December 1979, quoted in Bridgland, *Savimbi*, 290.
128 *The Guardian*, December 30, 1974, quoted in Bridgland, *Savimbi*, 114.
129 Quoted in Bridgland, *Savimbi*, 218.
130 Robert Mugabe, "Struggle for Southern Africa," *Foreign Affairs*, Winter 1987–88, 318. Mugabe also writes (316): "We are not militarily at war with apartheid but apartheid is at war with us."

131 Quoted in Bridgland, *Savimbi*, 97.
132 Johannesburg *Star*, April 9, 1984.
133 Quoted in Bridgland, *Savimbi*, 61.
134 "Who is Jonas Savimbi? A Short Political Biography," *Kwacha-Angola*, London, March 12, 1974, an UNITA publication quoted in Marcum, *Angola* II, 377.
135 Marcum, *Angola* II, 160–161, 230.
136 Bridgland, *Savimbi*, 67.
137 Quoted in Bridgland, *Savimbi*, 68.
138 Quoted in Marcum, *Angola* II, 419.
139 Fritz Sitte, quoted in Bridgland, *Savimbi*, 93.
140 Quoted in Bridgland, *Savimbi*, 81, 97, 98.
141 Bridgland, *Savimbi*, 365.
142 In 1983, quoted in Bridgland, *Savimbi*, 390.
143 *National Catholic Register*, December 1979, quoted in Bridgland, *Savimbi*, 290.
144 For Tanzania, Jannik Boesen, Kjell J. Havnevik and others, ed., *Tanzania, Crisis and Struggle for Survival*, Uppsala 1986.
145 Bridgland, *Savimbi*, 75.
146 RENAMO statement, March 30, 1988, released by the RENAMO representative in Washington, DC.
147 RENAMO's commander in charge of administering RENAMO's zones in Zambezia province, quoted in Sharon Behn, a reporter for the *Independent* (London) who spent four weeks in Zambezia, "Mozambique, the Unknown Side," *Africa Events*, May 1987.
148 The Democratic United Front, quoted in Cain, "Mozambique," 45.
149 Statement of Antonio Rocha who worked for the Portuguese and then for FRELIMO until he escaped in 1981, October 5, 1987, Washington, DC.
150 " 'Flechas' and the Formation of the 'Mozambique National Resistance,' " April 1974, published in Flower, *Service*, 300–302.
151 "Military and Police Implications of the Quarterly Threat: 1st July 1977 to 30th September 1977," July 20, 1977, published in Flower, *Service*, 308–310.
152 Marcum, *Angola* II, 228.
153 Bridgland, *Savimbi*, 363.
154 Quoted in Bridgland, *Savimbi*, 155.
155 Bridgland, *Savimbi*, 215, 218; CIA man quoted, 15.
156 Simon Jenkins, *The Economist*, July 16, 1983.
157 Quoted in E.P. Cain, "The Agony of Angola," in *Combat on Communist Territory*, Chicago 1985, 72–104, 86.
158 Flower, *Service*, 260–262.
159 Constantine C. Menges, *Inside the National Security Council*, New York 1988, 244, 231–249. The White House discussion of the "Reagan Doctrine," a fundamental turning point in American foreign policy since 1975, even since 1947, if seriously pursued, does not appear to have gone deep because of the unwillingness to face Secretary of State Shultz who opposed help to UNITA and RENAMO. Instead of having it out, the two sides sought to outmaneuver each other, without entire success and at the cost of confidence.
160 The Washington *Post*, September 13, 1988.
161 Quoted in Holger Jensen, "Winning the War Against All Odds," *Insight*, January 12, 1987, 33–35, a not entirely convincing article.
162 Almerigo Grilz, "Rebels of Mozambique," *Jane's Defense Weekly*, July 12, 1986.
163 Flower, *Service*, 262.
164 " 'Flechas' and the Formation of the 'Mozambique National Resistance,' " April 1974, Flower, *Service*, 301.
165 Behn, *Africa Events*, May 1987.
166 Cloete Breytenbach, quoted in the Johannesburg *Star*, January 7, 1988.
167 *The Military Balance 1987–1988*, International Institute for Strategic Studies, London.
168 Eric Gerard, quoted in *Inform Africa*, April 22, 1988.
169 Egeroe, *Dream*, 147.
170 A twenty year old, not a guerrilla but in RENAMO territory, quoted in Behn, *Africa Events*, May 1987.
171 Robert Gersony, "Summary of Mozambican Refugee Accounts of Principally Conflict-Related Experience in Mozambique," April 1988. Apparently Gersony cannot bring himself to say "war."

172 The Washington *Post*, April 28, 1988.
173 See, for instance, *L'Express* (Paris), June 3, 1988; *Neue Zürcher Zeitung*, August 24, 1988.
174 *Current Policy*, Number 980, United States Department of State, Bureau of Public Affairs, June 1987.
175 The Washington *Post*, October 6, 1987.
176 RENAMO Statement, Washington, DC Office, March 30, 1988.
177 Breytenbach, quoted in the Johannesburg *Star*, January 7, 1988.
178 *Neue Zürcher Zeitung*, August 27, 1988.
179 *Africa Confidencial*, April 16, 1987.
180 Egeroe, *Dream*, 53.
181 *Neue Zürcher Zeitung*, August 27, 1988.
182 Egeroe, *Dream*, 32.
183 Quoted in Egeroe, *Dream*, 137.
184 Egeroe, *Dream*, 72.
185 Menges, *Inside*, 234. The writer had access to American intelligence.
186 *Hansard*, House of Representatives (Australia), April 18, 1988, 1704.
187 *Neue Zürcher Zeitung*, August 27, 1988.
188 Assistant Secretary, Legislative and Intergovernmental Affairs, William L. Ball III to Senator Steve Symms, April 8, 1985.
189 The Washington *Post*, October 5, 1988.
190 Cain, "Mozambique," 70.
191 "A Paz que o Povo Quer," Pastoral Letter of the Catholic Bishops of Mozambique, April 30, 1987.
192 The New York *Times*, September 17, 1988.
193 Cain, "Mozambique," 53. The Machel quote comes from The Washington *Post*.
194 *Congressional Record*, June 25, 1987.
195 *Scope* (South Africa) February 11, 18, 25, 1983.
196 The New York *Times*, January 28, 1987.
197 Associated Press Wire, New York, August 6, 1987, see also, *Human Events*, September 5, 1987; for good criticism of the report, William Pascoe, "Hysteria Stirred by State," The Washington *Times*, May 4, 1988 and the editorial in The Washington *Times*, April 29, 1988.
198 The New York *Times*, April 27, 1988; for the criticism of the press treatment of Homoine, William Pascoe, "Massacre or Manipulation," The Washington *Times*, July 30, 1987, and also Donald R. Morris, The Houston *Post*, August 11, 1987.
199 Cain, "Mozambique," 66.
200 Afonso Dhlakama, "Response to the State Department Report on Mozambican Refugees," April 21, 1988 from RENAMO's office in Washington, DC.
201 *Africa Confidencial*, April 16, 1987.
202 Peter Godwin, *The Sunday Times* (London), April 5, 1987.
203 *FBIS*, Southern Africa, September 6, 1988.
204 Bridgland, *Savimbi*, 468–469; *Jane's Defense Weekly*, October 24, 1987.
205 "SADF Involvement in Angola," South Africa Defense Force report, May 1988; *Jane's Defense Weekly*, November 28, 1987; "South Africa and the Southern African Regional Imperative," *Southern African Facts Sheet* (Johannesburg), January 1988.
206 The Washington *Post*, November 19, 1986.
207 Peter Godwin, The Wall Street *Journal*, May 21, 1987.
208 "Extracts from the Report of the Board of Inquiry into the Accident which Claimed the Life of President Samora Machel and Others on 19 October 1986," released by the Permanent Mission of South Africa to the United Nations, July 9, 1987.
209 *The New Yorker*, February 2, 1987, 86–87.
210 For British involvement, *Jane's Defense Weekly*, October 18, 1986; for the letter of the MP's and an important editorial *The Times* (London), February 27, 1987; for Representative Dan Burton and Senator Robert Dole, The Washington *Times*, May 5, 1987.
211 The Washington *Post*, January 18, 1987.
212 For the statement from Malawi, The *Star* (Johannesburg), November 10, 1986; for R.F. Botha's presentation of the conspiracy evidence on November 6, BBC Broadcast Monitoring, November 8, 1986.
213 Quoted in Short, *Banda*, 248 and 233.
214 Quoted in Short, *Banda*, 281 and 256.

215 The Washington *Post*, September 12, 1988.
216 Denton Hearings, I, 383.
217 Francisco López de Gómara, quoted in C.R. Boxer, *Four Centuries of Portuguese Expansion, 1415–1825: A Succinct Survey*, Berkeley and Johannesburg, 1972, 1.
218 Quoted in Boxer, *Race Relations*, 94–95.
219 Christian Science *Monitor*, August 30, 1988.
220 Lipton, *Sanctions*, 81.
221 Denton Hearings II, 31.
222 Quoted in The New York *Times Magazine*, February 1, 1987.
223 *Capital*, I, Chapter 24.
224 Carlos Rangel, *The Latin Americans. Their Love-Hate Relationship with the United States* (a misleading title), New York 1977, especially 43–50, 106–112. For Lenin, "Report on the International Situation and the Fundamental Tasks of the Communist International," July 19, 1920, *Collected Works*, Moscow 1966, especially 232–234; for Stalin, "The National Question" (1924) in *Problems of Leninism*, New York 1934, 125–144.
225 Kaulza de Arriaga, *The Portuguese Answer*, London 1973, 17–18; for Sproats' account of his visit to FRELIMO, 7–15; also Harvey, *Portugal*, 16–17.
226 Bruno Mtolo, *Umkonto we Sizwe, The Road to the Left*, Durban 1966, 2.
227 Martin and Johnson, *Chimurenga*, 80–82.
228 Pike, *Communism*, 80–81. All quotations in the previous paragraphs come from Pike.
229 Haing Ngor, *A Cambodian Odyssey*, New York 1987, 230.
230 *Human Events*, July 7, 1984.
231 The Washington *Post*, September 28, 1988.
232 *FBIS*, Southern Africa, September 6, 1988, for the speech on September 3; October 4, 1988, for the speech on October 3.
233 The Washington *Times*, March 14, 1988.
234 The New York *Times*, June 1, 1988; June 2, 1988.
235 The New York *Times*, November 1, 1988.
236 The Washington *Times*, November 16, 1987.
237 See Castro's speech on July 26, 1988, *Granma* (English edition), August 7, 1988; for Castro's press conference in Quito, *Granma* (Spanish), August 13, 1988; also the Maldon Institute, "Strategic Implications of Cuba's Angolan Military Buildup," *International Freedom Review*, September 1988, with the unpublished update, October 1988, "The Military Situation in Southern Africa—Summary and Update."
238 International Herald *Tribune*, August 11, 1988, quoted in *Front File, Southern Africa Brief*, August 1988.
239 *Windhoek Advertiser* (South West Africa), April 10 and 13, 1987; *Windhoek Observer* (South West Africa), April 11, 1987; *Business Day* (Johannesburg), October 12, 1988; *The Citizen* (Johannesburg), October 12, 1988; *The Namibian* (South West Africa) October 19, 1988; BBC, October 19, 1988.
240 The Washington *Times*, June 20, 1988.
241 The Cape *Times* (Cape Town), October 6, 1988.
242 The New York *Times*, November 1, 1988.
243 The New York *Times*, November 8, 1988.
244 *Pretoria News*, April 9, 1988; *Business Day* (Johannesburg), August 9, 1988.
245 Wilfried Scharnagl (ed.), *Strauss in Moskau . . . und im südlichen Afrika*, Starnberger See (Germany) 1988, 21–29, 35–47. For *glasnost* and Afghanistan, Lev Navrozov, The New York City *Tribune*, May 23 to September 19, 1988, three columns a week.
246 *Africa Confidencial*, April 16, 1987.
247 *Congressional Record*, October 6, 1987, S-13566–13567.
248 Georgie Anne Geyer, The Washington *Times*, October 25, 1988.
249 The New York *Times*, December 23, 1988; February 3, 1989.

Chapter Five

1 *The Role of the Soviet Union, Cuba and East Germany in Fomenting Terrorism in Southern Africa*, Hearings before the Subcommittee on Security and Terrorism of the Committee on the Judiciary, United States Senate, Washington 1982 (Government Printing Office), 2 vols.

2 Bruno Mtolo, *Umkhonto we Sizwe, The Road to the Left*, Durban 1966, 128, 173.
3 Alan Cowell, reprinted in the International Herald *Tribune*, July 11, 1986.
4 Mtolo, *Road*, 12, 39.
5 Mtolo, *Road*, 185.
6 For the testimony, Stephen Biko, *Black Consciousness in South Africa*, Millard Arnold (ed.), New York 1978.
7 See Denton's account, *When Hell was in Session*, Alabama 1982, and also the classic account of Jim and Sybil Stockdale, *In Love and War*, New York 1984.
8 Mtolo, *Road*, 88.
9 Mtolo, *Road*, 54, 67, 87.
10 *South West Africa/Namibia: Human Rights in Conflict, Internationale Gesellschaft für Menschenrechte*, Frankfurt, a. M., Kaiserstrasse 72, 1985. The pamphlet is also available from the American branch, *International Society for Human Rights*, P.O. Box 90, Toms River, NJ 08754; see also *Human Rights Violations in SWAPO Camps in Angola and Zambia*, IGFM (British section), London 1988.
11 Mtolo, *Road*, 125, 181.
12 Quoted in Martin and Johnson, *Chimurenga*, 158.
13 For these incidents, Al J. Venter, *Vorster's Africa—Friendship and Frustration*, Johannesburg 1977, 100–123, especially 114–122; Martin and Johnson, *Chimurenga* 158–190; Flower, *Service*, 146–150.
14 For the full text of the April 8, 1975 speech of the foreign minister of Zambia, Venter, *Vorster's Africa*.
15 Quoted in Martin and Johnson, *Chimurenga*, 163.
16 Mtolo, *Road*, 146.
17 Mtolo, *Road*, 150; also 146–148.
18 Mtolo, *Road*, 171.
19 Mtolo, *Road*, 98.
20 Mtolo, *Road*, 119.
21 Mtolo, *Road*, 166–167.
22 Mtolo, *Road*, 64.
23 Mtolo, *Road*, 181.
24 Gerard Ludi, *Operation Q-018*, Cape Town 1969, 170.
25 Ludi, *Operation*, 17.
26 Ludi, *Operation*, 22–23.
27 Mtolo, *Road*, 119.
28 Mtolo, *Road*, 139.
29 Ludi, *Operation*, 10–15.
30 Ludi, *Operation*, 52.
31 Ludi, *Operation*, 60.
32 Ludi, *Operation*, 8–10.
33 Ludi, *Operation*, 14–15; 189.
34 Ludi, *Operation*, 212.
35 For these resolutions and for an analysis of the Freedom Charter in Marxist-Leninist terms, Keith Campbell, *ANC—A Soviet Task Force?*, London Institute for the Study of Terrorism, 1968, 19–20, 36–43.
36 Mtolo, *Road*, 23.
37 Mtolo, *Road*, 23.
38 Mtolo, *Road*, 55.
39 Mtolo, *Road*, 11–12.
40 Mtolo, *Road*, 56.
41 Gann and Duignan, *Survive*, 125–126; for the full text of the Freedom Charter, Thomas Karis and Gwendolen M. Carter, *From Protest to Challenge: A Documentary History of African Politics in South Africa, 1882–1964*, IV, Stanford 1977, 205–208.
42 Quoted in Pike, *Communism*, 288.
43 Ludi, *Operation*, 46–47; 53.
44 Ludi, *Operation*, 59.
45 Ludi, *Operation*, 51; 164.
46 Ludi, *Operation*, 30–31.
47 Ludi quoted in Pike, *Communism*, 303.

48 Quoted in Pike, *Communism*, 239.
49 Ludi, *Operation*, 190–191.
50 Quoted in Michael Radu, "The African National Congress: Cadres and Credo," *Problems of Communism*, July-August 1987, 63.
51 Ludi, *Operation*, 48.
52 Ludi, *Operation*, 57–59.
53 Ludi, *Operation*, 215.
54 Ludi, *Operation*, 64.
55 Quoted from Luthuli's book, *Let my People Go*, London 1962, in Pike, *Communism*, 288–291.
56 Ludi, *Operation*, 73–74.
57 Ludi, *Operation*, 195.
58 Mtolo, *Road*, 60.
59 Mtolo, *Road*, 66–67.
60 Mtolo, *Road*, 74.
61 Mtolo, *Road*, 52.
62 Ludi, *Operation*, 214–215.
63 Ludi, *Operation*, 68.
64 *The Washington Post*, January 9, 1987.
65 *Frankfurter Allgemeine Zeitung*, April 5, 1986, a remarkably well-informed article.
66 For the background of this attempted coup, A.P.J. van Rensburg, *Africa's Men of Destiny*, Johannesburg 1981, 456–459, 485; for the treason trial, Amnesty International reports on Zambia 1982, 1983, 1984, 1985, 1986; also, Country Reports on Human Rights Practices, Department of State for the U.S. House of Representatives, Committee on Foreign Affairs and U.S. Senate, Committee on Foreign Relations, Zambia for the same years.
67 The news that Kaunda confirmed the authenticity of the document found in the wreckage of Machel's plane to the the president of Malawi leads me to infer he had not told him of Mugabe's and Machel's plans to overthrow him before, *Business Day* (Johannesburg), January 13, 1987. For Kaunda's and Mugabe's blaming South Africa for the death of Machel, The New York *Times*, November 4, 1986.
68 Mtolo, *Road*, 140.
69 Captain A. T. Mahan, USN, *The Story of the War in South Africa*, London 1900, 1–4, better than any contemporary discussion of the strategic importance of the Cape, because Mahan knew the sea and the past.

Select Index of Names

Acheson, Dean, 241, 245, 249–50, 289
Adamishin, Anatoly, 365
Alves, Vitor, 258
Arbatov, Georgi, 358
Armacost, Michael, 342
Aron, Raymond, 275
Arriaga, Kaulza de, 353

Banana, Canaan 283, 300
Banda, Hastings Kamuzu, 243–47, 312, 338, 342–344
Beyleveld, Petrus, 152
Biko, Steve, 32, 73, 103, 352, 378–383
Boesak, Allan, 82, 86, 301
Bomba, Lieutenant Adriano Francisco, 377, 441–45
Botha, Louis, 14
Botha, P.W.:
  1988 Angolan negotiations 337, 361, 368;
  on the Commonwealth Group Report 189;
  defense minister 112, 290;
  on 1987 elections, 123;
  on foreign funds, 143;
  on Mandela 78;
  reforms 61, 75–76, 80, 102, 104, 105, 107–108, 126;
  on religion and Tutu, 145, 146–47;
  on South West Africa 295;
  on violence 91
Botha, R.F., 189
Bridgland, Fred, 309
Bryce, Lord James, 12, 28–29, 31–33, 35,
Brzezinski, Zbigniew, 228
Burton, Dan, 341
Buthelezi, Chief Mangosuthu: 91–102;
  on aid to organizations, 207;
  and ANC/UDF 88, 93, 95–99, 215;
  on Botha, 105;
  on the CAA Act, 201–2;
  character of, 92;
  on demonstrations, 94;
  on Mandela, 100;
  Natal Indaba, 94, 100;
  on 1984 constitution, 81, 83;
  on past conquest, 18;
  on political opposition, 49;
  on West's complicity, 50

Cain, E.P., 331
Campbell-Bannerman, Sir Henry, 40
Carrington, Lord, 277
Carvalho, General Otelo de, 271, 273
Castro, Fidel, 365
Chingungi, Tito, 310
Chipande, Albert, 329
Chissano, Joaquin 233, 321, 323, 329, 338, 342–45
Chitepo, Herbert, 401
Christina, Orlando, 335
Cleary, Sean, 288

Clough, Michael, 183–5
Costa, Jorge da, 229
Coutinho, Rosa, 256
Cowell, Alan, 193–4
Crocker, Chester: 169–71;
  1988 Angolan negotiations, 357–64, 366;
  on majority rule, 185;
  and RENAMO, 231, 322, 334
Cuellar, Perez de, 298
Cunhal, Alvaro, 272

D'Urban, Benjamin, 23
Dash, Leon, 191
Denton, Senator Jeremiah, 181, 205–06, 383–384, 422, 444
Dhlakama, Afonso, 321, 324, 331–33, 335
Dhlomo, Oscar, 100
Dole, Senator Robert, 341
Dube, John, 52
Dukakis, Michael, 213–14
Durr, Kent, 14, 103

Fischer, Abraham, 150–1, 152
Flower, Ken, 283, 321, 402
Francisco, Jose, 328–29, 332
Fraser, Malcolm, 277

Glagolev, Igor, 351
Gogotya, John, 121, 140
Gomes, General Costa, 271
Gonçalves, General Vasco, 271
Gorbachev, Mikhail, 368–69
Grey, Earl, 34
Gumede, Archie, 87

Haig, Alexander, 170
Helms, Senator Jesse, 204
Hendrickse, Allan, 82, 123
Heunis, Chris, 75, 80, 83
Hlapane, Bartholomew, 152, 408–09, 411, 417–19
Hobhouse, Emily, 39–40
Hofmeyr, Jan, 53
Houphouet-Boigny, Felix, 167
Howe, Sir Geoffrey, 218
Huddleston, Trevor, 32
Hurley, Denis, 301–2

Irvine, Reed, 191

Jackson, Jesse, 213–14
Johnson, Lyndon B., 167

Kadalie, Clements, 355
Kalangula, Peter, 292, 306, 367
Kapuuo, Chief Clemens, 292, 404
Kaunda, Kenneth, 237, 240–42, 275, 286, 294, 298–99, 314–15
Kave, Nokonono Delphine, 408, 424–40
Kennedy, Senator Edward, 204, 298

Index

Kerina, Mburumba, 299
Keyes, Alan, 158, 203
Kissinger, Henry, 167, 247, 277
Koornhof, Piet, 81–82
Kozonguizi, Jariretundu, 232, 235, 295–96, 445–46
Kruger, Paul, 35

Lenin, 350
Lipton, Merle, 211–12
Ludi, Gerard, 354, 412–15, 419–22
Luthuli, Chief Albert, 421–22

Mabhida, Moses, 87
Machel, Samora Moises, 307, 315, 317, 328, 338
Macmillan, W.M., 19, 24
Maharaj, Mac, 89
Makatini, Johnny, 78, 187
Malan, Magnus, 109, 136, 231
Mandela, Nelson, 78, 153
Mandela, Winnie, 65–66, 194
Mangope, Chief Lucas, 49
Matessangaisse, Andre, 316
Mathias, Senator Charles, 204
Mbeki, Govan, 141
Merriman, J.X., 32, 37, 42–43
Merwe, Stoffel van der, 134, 145
Milner, Lord Alfred, 40–41
Mokoena, Bishop Isaac, 140
Mtolo, Bruno: 149, 353, 375, 384–85, 393, 398;
   his testimony, 409–11, 416–17, 423–24
Mudge, Dirk, 292
Mugabe, Robert: 276, 278–86, 299, 320;
   conspiracy against Malawi, 342–45;
   in Mozambique, 338–39;
   and violence, 251–2
Mulder, Cornelius, 104
Muzorewa, Bishop Abel, 277
Mvubelo, Lucy, 65–66, 103
Mxenge, Victoria, 98

Neto, Agostinho, 257, 274
Nickel, Herman, 182–3, 185
Nkomo, Joshua, 251, 276, 284–5
Norman, Dennis, 341
Nujoma, Sam, 290–91, 294, 305, 366
Nyerere, Julius, 232–3, 286, 315
Nzo, Alfred, 78–79, 193

O'Brien, Conor Cruise, 168
Orr, Wendy, 70

Paton, Alan, 13, 17, 55–56, 231, 238–9
Pepper, Claude, 180
Philip, John, 15, 22–25, 28–32

Ramaphosa, Cyril, 131
Ramphal, Shridath, 190
Raspberry, William, 235
Reagan, Ronald, 158, 164–65, 358

Rees, John 173, 178
Retief, Piet, 25
Robinson, Randall, 174–76

Sabelo, Winnington, 99
Sandys, Duncan, 252
Santos, Jose dos, 308
Savimbi, Jonas: 267–269, 307–320;
   1988 Angolan negotiations, 367, 358–64, 370–71;
   character of, 259;
   effects of Portuguese abandonment on, 258;
   military success in 1983, 335–36;
   on South Africa's history, 225;
   and the West, 213, 334, 357;
   on the West's complicity, 357
Sebe, Lennox, 83, 105
Selborne, Lord William, 45–49, 52
Seme, Pixley, 95, 110
Shaganovitch, Konstantin, 336
Shevardnadze, Eduard, 358
Shevchenko, Arkady, 179, 254, 351
Shipanga, Andreas, 296, 377, 436–37
Sisulu, Albertina, 87
Sisulu, Walter, 87
Sisulu, Zwelakhe, 144
Sithole, Reverend Ndabaningi, 276
Slabbert, Frederik van Zyl, 84
Slovo, Joe, 193, 229
Smith, Ian 238, 241, 247–48, 250–53, 275–77
Smuts, Jan, 14, 15, 25–27, 33, 37–38, 40, 42–44, 54–55
Soares, Mario, 271
Sobukwe, Robert, 93
Sonn, Franklin, 56–57, 128
Spinola, General Antonio de, 237, 246, 256, 259–70, 274
Stacy, Roy, 331
Stalin, 350
Sullivan, Reverend Leon, 217
Suzman, Helen, 54, 71, 73, 76, 83, 127
Symms, Senator Steve, 157–158, 168–69, 181–82

Tambo, Oliver, 76–77, 235
Thatcher, Margaret, 217, 277
Toivo, Toivo Ya 296, 367
Tutu, Archbishop Desmond, 77, 93, 119, 142, 145–46, 302

Venter, Al J., 58, 243, 257
Verwoerd, Hendrik, 32, 238–39
Viljoen, Gerrit, 94, 105
Vlok, Adriaan, 119–120
Vorster, B.J., 236–41, 247–8, 254, 289–90

Walls, Peter, 356
Walters, Vernon, 337
Wells, Melissa, 327
Wilson, Harold, 248–51
Wolpe, Howard, 185–86
Worthington, Peter, 267